AI-Driven Sustainable Power Grids: Enhancing Cybersecurity, Operation, and Control of Conventional, Modern, and Renewable-Based Energy Systems

AI-Driven Sustainable Power Grids: Enhancing Cybersecurity, Operation, and Control of Conventional, Modern, and Renewable-Based Energy Systems

Guest Editors

Gulshan Sharma
Pitshou N. Bokoro
Rajesh Kumar

MDPI

Basel • Beijing • Wuhan • Barcelona • Belgrade • Novi Sad • Cluj • Manchester

Guest Editors

Gulshan Sharma
Department of Electrical &
Electronic Engineering
Technology
University of Johannesburg
Johannesburg
South Africa

Pitshou N. Bokoro
Department of Electrical &
Electronic Engineering
Technology
University of Johannesburg
Johannesburg
South Africa

Rajesh Kumar
Department of Human
Anatomy and Physiology
University of Johannesburg
Johannesburg
South Africa

Editorial Office
MDPI AG
Grosspeteranlage 5
4052 Basel, Switzerland

This is a reprint of the Special Issue, published open access by the journal *Energies* (ISSN 1996-1073), freely accessible at: https://www.mdpi.com/journal/energies/special_issues/7P328878L4.

For citation purposes, cite each article independently as indicated on the article page online and as indicated below:

Lastname, A.A.; Lastname, B.B. Article Title. *Journal Name* **Year**, *Volume Number*, Page Range.

ISBN 978-3-7258-7637-2 (Hbk)
ISBN 978-3-7258-7638-9 (PDF)
https://doi.org/10.3390/books978-3-7258-7638-9

Contents

About the Editors

Gulshan Sharma

Gulshan Sharma, Ph.D., is an accomplished academic and researcher with over 17 years of experience in electrical engineering and power systems. He received his B.Tech. from Punjab Technical University in 2007, his M. Tech. in Electrical Power System Management from Jamia Millia Islamia University in 2009, and his Ph.D. from the Malaviya National Institute of Technology, Jaipur, in 2015. He subsequently completed a postdoctoral fellowship at the University of Pretoria from 2015 to 2016. Dr. Sharma is currently an Associate Professor at the Department of Electrical and Electronic Engineering Technology at the University of Johannesburg. He serves as Academic Editor for *International Transactions on Electrical Energy Systems* (Wiley), and as Associate Editor of the *International Journal of Modelling and Simulation* (Taylor & Francis). His research excellence has been recognized through inclusion in Elsevier's Top 2% Scientists rankings for 2024–2025. He has published over 200 scholarly papers with more than 5,900 citations, has an h-index of 36, and holds a Y rating from the NRF, South Africa. His research focuses on modern power systems with high renewable energy penetration, sustainable energy solutions, and the application of artificial intelligence and machine learning to enhance power system stability, reliability, and performance.

Pitshou N. Bokoro

Pitshou N. Bokoro, Ph.D., received a Bachelor's degree from Durban University of Technology in 2006, a Master's degree in Electrical Engineering from the University of Johannesburg in 2011, and a Ph.D. degree from the University of the Witwatersrand in 2016. He Joined the University of Johannesburg in 2007 as a Lecturer at the department of Electrical Engineering Technology. He is currently an Associate Professor and Head of Department. He is professionally registered with the Engineering Council of South Africa (ECSA). He holds senior membership with the South African Institute of Electrical Engineers (SAIEE) as well as with the Institute of Electrical and Electronics Engineers (IEEE). He is also a specialist editor for the *SAIEE Africa Research Journal* (ARJ). As a researcher, Pitshou has authored and co-authored several publications, which include over 65 journal articles including those in high-quality, quartile-1, high-impact factor journals; 70 papers in conference proceedings in both local and internationally renowned conferences in the field of engineering; and eight chapters (including three currently in print) in edited books published with globally reputed publishers (Springer Nature, IGI Global, IET, etc.). He has conducted several research projects and attracted over USD 42611.72 in grants. He is a recipient of Erasmus+ funding in collaboration with the University of Klagenfurt in Austria. Moreover, he has supervised several master's (14 graduated and eight are currently under supervision), and a number of doctoral students to completion (five Ph.Ds)—whereas six are currently under his supervision. His research interests include power quality, distributed generation, virtual sensors, condition monitoring of dielectrics and insulation materials, reliability of surge protective devices, distributed generation, and economics of energy.

Rajesh Kumar

Rajesh Kumar, Ph.D. (SMIEEE, Fellow [IET(UK), IE(I), IETE]), received his B.Tech. (Hons.) in Electrical Engineering from NIT Kurukshetra, India, in 1994, and M.E. (Hons.) and Ph.D. in Power Systems and Intelligent Systems from MNIT Jaipur, India, in 1997 and 2005, respectively. He completed a Postdoctoral Research Fellowship at the National University of Singapore from 2009 to

2011. Currently, he is a Professor of Electrical Engineering at MNIT Jaipur, Professor of Artificial Intelligence at the University of Johannesburg, South Africa, and Adjunct Professor in Artificial Intelligence and Data Engineering at MNIT Jaipur. He serves on the research boards of more than 30 universities worldwide and is a research reviewer for NRF South Africa, UAE, Norway, DRDO, and DST. His research interests include intelligent systems, data-driven analytics, power management, and robotics. He holds 20 patents and has published over 750 research articles in international journals and conferences. He has supervised 30 Ph.D. and more than 50 master's theses. He received the Career Award for Young Teachers in 2002 from the Government of India and has delivered 300+ keynote talks at Faculty Development Programs and workshops worldwide.

Preface

The rapid transformation of global energy systems is driven by the urgent need for sustainable, reliable, and intelligent power infrastructures. Increasing energy demand, growing environmental concerns, and global commitments to reducing greenhouse gas emissions have accelerated the integration of renewable energy sources and advanced digital technologies within modern power grids. As a result, contemporary energy systems are evolving from traditional centralized structures into highly decentralized, interconnected, and data-driven smart energy networks.

In this context, artificial intelligence (AI), the Internet of Things (IoT), advanced optimization techniques, and digital technologies play an increasingly vital role in enabling efficient planning, operation, and control of modern power systems. These technologies provide powerful tools for addressing the challenges associated with renewable energy integration, system uncertainties, grid stability, cybersecurity, and energy management. Furthermore, emerging solutions such as smart homes, hybrid renewable energy systems, digital twins, and distributed energy resources are reshaping how energy is generated, distributed, and consumed.

This Special Issue brings together a collection of high-quality research articles and reviews that address key challenges and opportunities in modern power systems. The contributions in this volume cover a broad spectrum of topics, including optimal scheduling of smart homes integrated with hybrid renewable energy systems, intelligent knowledge extraction for substation operation, multi-objective optimization in power system load flow, coordinated voltage regulation in distribution networks, and AI-powered digital twin frameworks for climate-resilient energy grids. In addition, several papers explore advanced cybersecurity frameworks for distributed energy systems, the integration of IoT and AI in renewable-dominant grids, electric vehicle charging infrastructure, and intelligent control strategies for photovoltaic-based distribution networks under uncertainty.

Collectively, these contributions provide valuable insights into the development of sustainable, intelligent, and resilient energy infrastructures. They demonstrate how interdisciplinary approaches combining power engineering, artificial intelligence, optimization, and communication technologies can address the technical and operational challenges associated with the transition toward cleaner and smarter energy systems.

Gulshan Sharma, Pitshou N. Bokoro, and Rajesh Kumar
Guest Editors

energies

MDPI

Article

An Intelligent Technique for Coordination and Control of PV Energy and Voltage-Regulating Devices in Distribution Networks Under Uncertainties

Tolulope David Makanju *, Ali N. Hasan, Oluwole John Famoriji and Thokozani Shongwe

Department of Electrical and Electronics Engineering, Faculty of Engineering and Built Environment, University of Johannesburg, Auckland Park, Johannesburg 2006, South Africa; alinabeal1981@gmail.com (A.N.H.); famoriji@mail.ustc.edu.cn (O.J.F.); tshongwe@uj.ac.za (T.S.)

* Correspondence: 222244557@student.uj.ac.za

Abstract: The proactive involvement of photovoltaic (PV) smart inverters (PVSIs) in grid management facilitates voltage regulation and enhances the integration of distributed energy resources (DERs) within distribution networks. However, to fully exploit the capabilities of PVSIs, it is essential to achieve optimal control of their operations and effective coordination with voltage-regulating devices in the distribution network. This study developed a dual strategy approach to forecast the optimal setpoints of onload tap changers (OLTCs), PVSIs, and distribution static synchronous compensators (DSTATCOMs) to improve the voltage profiles in power distribution systems. The study began by running a centralized AC optimal power flow (CACOPF) and using the hourly PV output power and the load demand to determine the optimal active and reactive power of the PVSIs, the setpoint of the DSTATCOM, and the optimal tap setting of the OLTC. Furthermore, Machine Learning (ML) models were trained as controllers to determine the reactive-power setpoints for the PVSIs and DSTATCOMs as well as the optimal OLTC tap position required for voltage stability in the network. To assess the effectiveness of the method, comprehensive evaluations were carried out on a modified IEEE 33 bus with a high penetration of PV energy. The results showed that deep neural networks (DNNs) outperformed other ML models used to mimic the coordination method based on CACOPF. Furthermore, when the DNN-based controller was tested and compared with the optimizer approach under different loading and PV conditions, the DNN-based controller was found to outperform the optimizer in terms of computational time. This approach allows predictive control in power systems, helping system operators determine the action to be initiated under uncertain PV energy and loading conditions. The approach also addresses the computational inefficiency arising from contingencies in the power system that may occur when optimal power flow (OPF) is run multiple times.

Keywords: distributed energy resources; PV energy; voltage-regulating devices; coordination control; uncertainties

1. Introduction

Electrical energy is one of the key factors in the economic development of any nation. The recent adoption of the Paris Agreement, which enforces reductions in carbon emissions by nations under the United Nations (UN), has caused many nations that depend on fossil fuels to seek alternative sources of energy [1]. One approach used by many nations to achieve the objective of the Paris Agreement is the use of distributed energy resources (DERs) such as PV energy to reduce dependency on fossil fuel-based generators [2].

PV energy sources are connected to existing distribution networks through PV smart inverters (PVSIs). However, the introduction of PVSIs into existing distribution networks causes bidirectional current flows in power system networks. This has led to a number of complexities in power system parameter control [3,4]. Many of the devices used in the regulation of power system parameters depend on a unidirectional flow of current in the network. The integration of PVSIs into a network can cause a reverse flow of current to the substation so that the power generated at the point of connection of the inverter is greater than the load demand. This issue of reverse current flow affects the operation of voltage-regulation devices in the substation, such as the on-load tap changer (OLTC), which is installed at the transformer in the substation.

The growing prevalence of DER integration introduces new technical and operational hurdles for existing power system distribution networks [5]. Distribution networks must now contend with novel issues such as voltage fluctuations, potential grid overloading, and unprecedented power flow dynamics that challenge traditional electrical system design and management [6,7]. Active distribution network management (ANM), which refers to the techniques used to control and manage distribution networks in a more flexible and dynamic manner in the presence of DERs, is one of the main methods used to manage technical issues and maintain operations within permissible limits, and it involves the use of reactive power and voltage-compensating devices [8–10]. ANM involves controlling power flow across the distribution network to optimize efficiency, minimize losses, and maintain operation of the reactive and voltage-regulating devices in the network to ensure that there are no violations of power system operating parameters. Several voltage-regulating devices are used in ANM, such as static voltage regulators, switched-capacitor banks (SCBs), distribution static synchronous compensators (DSTATCOMs), and other flexible AC transmission (FACT) devices [11]. An OLTC regulates the voltage by adjusting the transformer's tap position, whereas SCBs and DSTATCOMs regulate the voltage by reactive power compensation. However, SCBs have slow response times and a limited number of switches, whereas DSTATCOMs have fast response times owing to thyristor-controlled switching. A DSTACOM can provide inductive reactive power to alleviate the problem of voltage rise in addition to compensating for capacitive reactive power. Therefore, DSTATCOMs are preferable to SCBs for fast voltage regulation.

Recently, many PVSIs have begun to be used to supply reactive power to regulate their bus voltage along the distribution network. According to the recently updated IEEE standard (IEEE 1547-2018), smart inverters can be used to provide or absorb reactive power for fast voltage regulation [12]. A smart inverter is an advanced type of inverter used primarily in renewable energy systems, such as solar power installations, to convert the direct current (DC) electricity generated by renewable sources into alternating current (AC) electricity which can be used by electrical appliances or fed into the grid. Unlike traditional inverters, smart inverters come equipped with advanced features that improve the functionality, reliability, and integration of renewable energy systems within the grid. The smart inverter functionality includes fault ride-through, voltage and frequency ride-through, and grid voltage support. Among these functions, grid voltage support is obtained by the reactive function mode of smart inverters, which depends on the voltage at the point of connection to the grid network. The reactive function of smart inverters controls the local voltage by either absorbing reactive power or providing it to the grid. However, smart inverters can also introduce challenges and issues, such as voltage fluctuations and instability, which may occur when multiple DERs like PV and wind energy operate simultaneously. When additional power is thereby injected into the grid, overvoltage may result if smart inverters are not well coordinated with other voltage-regulating devices in the network, further leading to overvoltage or undervoltage outside acceptable limits within some buses in the network. Additionally, variability in DER output, as occurs when solar generation is influenced by weather, can complicate load and generation, making it harder to plan and manage the network effectively. Excessive generation by DERs can cause reverse power flow from distribution networks to transmission networks, creating challenges in grid operation and potentially damaging equipment. To address the challenges caused by the use of smart inverters in distribution networks, there is a need to develop advanced control techniques to coordinate and control the volt/VAR optimization of smart inverters and other voltage-regulating devices as well as the generation output power of the inverters.

Various approaches for managing smart inverter operations and coordinating them with conventional voltage control devices have been explored in the literature. Reference [13] presented a hybrid scheme combining centralized and local real and reactive power control for PV smart inverters. In this method, the inverter's local control is based on piecewise linear functions, while its parameters are periodically optimized through a centralized process. However, this centralized optimal power flow (OPF) strategy demands extensive computing and communication resources. In [14], a distributed adaptive robust Volt/VAR control method was developed to reduce power losses in distribution systems, but it relies on multiple control centers to carry out Volt/VAR optimization. Similarly, [15] proposed a model-free extremum-seeking adaptive local Volt/VAR control to minimize network losses, but its computational complexity is relatively high. Reference [16] introduced a probabilistic approach to coordinate PV smart inverters with on-load tap changers (OLTC) and electric vehicles (EVs) to maximize hosting capacity. This method's dependence on precise probability distributions limits its practicality in dynamic and uncertain environments, potentially reducing network reliability under extreme or unexpected scenarios. In [17], a data-driven distributionally robust stochastic OPF method was suggested to control PV smart inverters and energy storage setpoints to address overvoltage issues. However, its performance is constrained by the quality and availability of historical data, which might not reflect rare events or rapidly changing conditions, resulting in suboptimal control under significant uncertainty. Reference [18] proposed a data-driven local control strategy for determining setpoints for smart inverters, controllable loads, and battery storage systems, but the use of iterative OPF leads to high computational demands. Likewise, [19] described a data-based nonlinear control policy for the real-time reactive power dispatch of smart inverters, which requires repeated OPF runs, making it computationally intensive. A multi-mode data-driven method to coordinate conventional voltage regulation devices and PV inverters was proposed by [20], but it did not account for variations in PV output and load conditions.

In [21], a multi-objective model for reactive power and voltage optimization was introduced, using the gray wolf optimization algorithm to enhance node voltage quality and improve overall system stability. Although this method boosts voltage quality and operational stability, it does not provide real-time adaptability to sudden changes or the unpredictable nature of renewable generation. Reference [22] developed a reactive power optimization algorithm specifically for distribution networks with PV generation, addressing power quality issues through a multi-objective optimization model solved with the Non-dominated Sorting Genetic Algorithm III (NSGA-III). Test results showed that the NSGA-III approach could reduce active power output by up to 25%, whereas other methods reduced PV active power by less than 10%. Traditional reactive power optimization methods still struggle with finding globally optimal solutions efficiently and often suffer from slow computational performance. The authors in [23] applied the simulated annealing technique to optimize models involving photovoltaic systems, wind turbines, and electric vehicles in active distribution networks. Experiments based on a modified

IEEE 14-bus distribution system indicated significant reductions in voltage deviations and overall system losses after optimization. However, the approach does not explicitly account for the variability of intermittent energy sources, which limits its effectiveness under uncertain conditions. To address the need to avoid repeatedly solving OPF to identify optimal setpoints for smart inverters and other voltage control devices, while also minimizing communication infrastructure requirements and capturing dynamic system behavior with integrated PV smart inverters (PVSIs), this paper proposes a machine learning (ML)-based coordinated control strategy for PVSIs in combination with DSTATCOM and OLTC. Initially, a centralized AC optimal power flow (CACOPF) is used to determine the coordinated setpoints for PVSIs, DSTATCOM, and OLTC based on PV generation and load demand data. Then, machine learning models are trained as controllers to select optimal operating points for the PVSIs, DSTATCOM, and OLTC under varying load and distributed generation conditions.

The major contribution of this research is as follows:

1. The research addresses the computational inefficiency of running optimal power flow (OPF) multiple times by proposing an ML-based approach to predict optimal setpoints of voltage-regulating devices under different loading conditions. The approach reduces the need for repeatedly solving OPF problems, enhancing real-time operational efficiency.
2. The proposed coordinated control scheme involving PV smart inverters, DSTATCOM, and OLTC enables effective voltage regulation and power flow management by leveraging the combined capabilities of multiple devices in the power system.
3. The centralized AC optimal power flow (CACCOPF) adopted in this research ensures that the control strategy accounts for nonlinear power system dynamics, improving the accuracy and robustness of the coordination.
4. The use of ML models as local controllers to determine the best operational points of PV smart inverters, DSTATCOM, and OLTC allows a scalable and communication-efficient control mechanism, enabling faster decision making.

2. Proposed Framework

The proposed framework for coordinating and controlling the output of PV energy along with voltage regulation devices is illustrated in Figure 1. The time-varying output power from the PV system and dynamic loading were fed into an optimizer, which continuously operates based on a multi-objective function aimed at maximizing PV output while minimizing voltage deviations across the network. The optimizer calculates the setpoints for the voltage regulation devices and the PV smart inverter (PVSI) at hourly intervals, considering both load demand and PV generation. To eliminate the need for repeatedly running the optimizer, the hourly setpoint results for the voltage devices and PVSIs' reactive power are used to train machine learning models. As a result, the setpoints for both the voltage regulation devices and the PV inverter can be predicted for any combination of load demand and PV generation output.

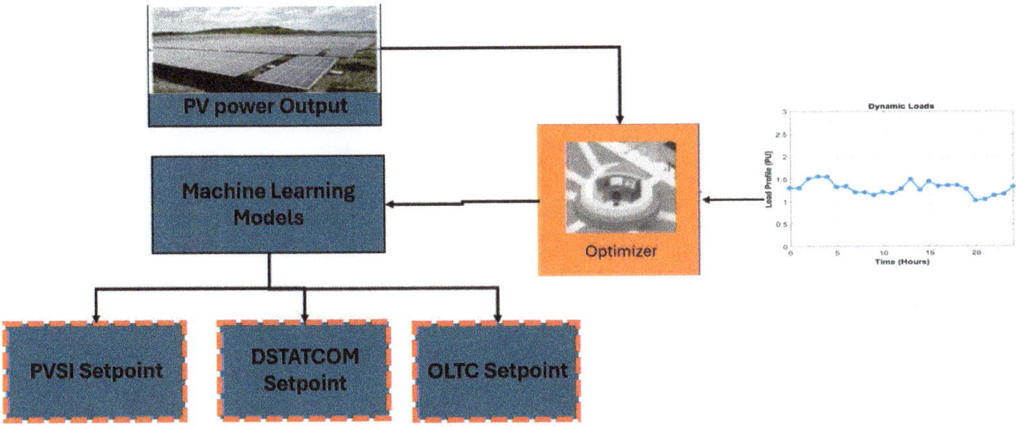

Figure 1. Proposed framework of the coordination and control approach.

3. Mathematical Modeling

This section outlines the centralized AC optimal power flow (CACOPF) approach for power system networks, which is based on the nonlinear power flow equations. It also presents the mathematical formulations for controlling the reactive power output of PVSIs as well as the control equations for the OLTC and DSTATCOM. Compared to linearized or DC power flow models, the nonlinear power flow model provides a more accurate representation of actual system behavior. While linearized and DC power flow methods often rely on simplifying assumptions such as ignoring reactive power and bus voltage angles, the nonlinear model captures these aspects, delivering a more realistic and precise depiction of power system conditions [24–26].

3.1. Nonlinear Centralized AC OPF (CACOPF)

The nonlinear OPF is formulated by the following power flow model as in (1) to (4). The equivalent active power and reactive power at any bus in the network are described in Equations (1) and (2). The equivalent active and reactive power that flows in bus i, connected to a PSVI and the load connected, is given as in (3) and (4) [27].

$$P_{G-i} - P_{D-i} = P_i(V,\ \delta) \tag{1}$$

$$Q_{G-i} - Q_{G-i} = Q_i(V,\ \delta) \tag{2}$$

$$P_{PVSI-i} - P_{D-i} = \sum_{k=1}^{n} V_i V_k |Y_{ik}| \cos(\delta_i - \delta_k - \theta_{ik}) \tag{3}$$

$$Q_{PVSI-i} - Q_{D-i} = \sum_{k=1}^{n} V_i V_k |Y_{ik}| \sin(\delta_i - \delta_k - \theta_{ik}) \tag{4}$$

where P_{G-i} and Q_{G-i} are the active and reactive power generated at bus I, respectively. P_{PVSI} is the active power of the PVSI, P_{D-i} is the active load at the point of connection, Q_{PVSI} is the reactive power of the PVSI, and Q_{D-i} is the reactive power demand at the point where PVSI is connected. V_i and V_k are the buses between bus i and k, respectively, Y_{ik} is the admittance between i and k, δ_i is the bus angle of i, δ_k is the bus angle of k, and θ_{ik} is the angle difference between i and k. The P_{PVSI} and $_{\text{QPVSI}}$ will be zero when there is no PVSI connected at bus *i*. In the slack bus, the active and reactive power are free to balance the mismatch in the network.

3.2. OLTC Model

The tap position of the OLTC is determined by the secondary and primary voltage of the transformer and the change ratio per step. The OLTC tap position is modeled as expressed in (5).

$$T_p = \left(\left(\frac{V_s}{V_p}\right) - 1\right) \cdot \left(\frac{1}{\propto}\right) \tag{5}$$

where v_p and v_s are the primary and secondary connection points of the transformer, and $\propto$ is the change ratio per step.

3.3. Smart Inverter Model

In this study, the smart inverter is designed to regulate voltage by adjusting its reactive power output in response to voltage levels. When the terminal voltage drops below the network's minimum threshold, the inverter supplies reactive power to the grid; when the terminal voltage exceeds the maximum limit, it absorbs reactive power from the grid. The inverter's voltage setpoints (v_1, v_2, v_3, and v_4) are optimally determined using three key parameters: the reference voltage (v_r), the voltage range (D), and the deadband (d). The inverter's goal is to keep the terminal voltage close to v_r. The amount of reactive power injected or absorbed to achieve this is based on D and the inverter's maximum reactive power capacity. The voltage setpoints are calculated using Equations (6) through (10).

$$v_1 = v_r - D \tag{6}$$

$$v_2 = v_r - d \tag{7}$$

$$v_3 = v_r + d \tag{8}$$

$$v_4 = v_r + D \tag{9}$$

The voltage gap D used is 5% of the nominal voltage, the deadband is 2% of the nominal voltage, and V_r is the nominal voltage of 1. The reactive power output of the smart inverter as a function of voltage is modeled using a piecewise function, which is expressed as in (10).

$$Q_{PVSI} = \begin{cases} Q_{max} & v \leq v_1 \\ \frac{Q_{max}}{(v_2 - v_1)} \times (v - V_1) & v_1 \leq v \leq v_2 \\ 0 & v_2 \leq v \leq v_3 \\ \frac{Q_{max}}{(v_3 - v_4)} \times (v - v_3) & v_3 \leq v \leq v_4 \\ -Q_{max} & v \geq v_4 \end{cases} \tag{10}$$

where V denotes the bus voltage, Q_{PVSI} is the smart inverter available reactive power at the connected bus n, and Q_{max} is the maximum reactive power that can be absorbed or supplied by the PVSI.

3.4. Distribution Static Synchronous Compensator (DSTATCOM) Model

A DSTATCOM (distribution static synchronous compensator) is a device used to regulate voltage by generating or absorbing reactive power at high speed. The reactive power of a DSTATCOM is controlled using power electronics, which is typically through voltage–source converters (VSC) that allow rapid and continuous adjustments of the reactive power. There are two main operation modes for DSTATCOM: voltage regulation mode and reactive power control mode. In voltage regulation mode, the DSTATCOM can be modeled by two parameters: the slope ($X_{DSTATCOM}$) and the voltage reference (V_r). In reactive power control mode, the DSTATCOM can be modeled as a constant susceptance. However, when the DSTATCOM reaches its limits, it operates as either a fixed capacitive or a fixed inductive device under low or high voltage conditions, respectively. In these situations, the DSTATCOM is not actively controlled, which limits its ability to regulate voltage effectively. In this study, the voltage control mode of the DSTATCOM was employed. It is modeled by a voltage source in series with reactance ($X_{DSTATCOM}$). An auxiliary generator is used to model the DSTATCOM in the networks. The $X_{DSTATCOM}$ and V_r are the decision variables, and the DSTATCOM reactive power ($Q_{DSTATCOM}$) is obtained from the optimal OPF as depicted in (11) to (13).

$$X^{min}{}_{SL} \leq X_{SL} \leq X_{SL}{}^{max} \tag{11}$$

$$V_{min} \leq V_r \leq V_{max} \tag{12}$$

$$Q^{min}{}_{DSTATCOM} \leq Q_{DSTATCOM} \leq Q_{DSTATCOM}{}^{max} \tag{13}$$

where $X^{min}{}_{SL}$ and $X_{SL}{}^{max}$ denote the minimum and maximum values of the DSTATCOM slope settings, respectively. $V_{\rm min}$ and $V_{\rm max}$ represent the minimum and maximum permissible voltage limits, respectively. $Q^{min}{}_{DSTATCOM}$ and $Q_{DSTATCOM}{}^{max}$ are the lower and upper limits of the DSTATCOM reactive power, respectively.

4. Objective Function and Constraints

The robust, coordinated control setpoints of the reactive power of the PVSIs and the tap position of the OLTC are computed and determined using the centralized AC optimal power flow (CACOPF) approach. The objective functions and constraints under different loading and power outputs are discussed as follows:

4.1. Objective Function

The objective function of the proposed approach is the maximization of the active power of the PVSI and the minimization of voltage deviation of all buses in the networks as described in (14).

$$\max\left(w_1 \sum_m^{N_{PVSI}} P_{PVSI}\right) + \min\left(w_2 \sum_{n=i}^{N} \frac{|(1-V_i)|}{N}\right) \tag{14}$$

where P_{PVSI} is the active power of the *PVSI* and N_{PVSI} is the number of *PVSIs* connected in the network, V_i is the voltage at bus i, and N is the total number of buses in the network. Since the objective function is a multiple function, it is scalarized via a weighted sum. After normalizing each objective and inspecting the Pareto front, we set the weights in the ratio 7.9:0.2, which corresponds (when normalized to sum to 1) to approximately w_1 = 0.975 for the PVSI power and w_2 = 0.025 for the voltage deviation objective.

4.2. Constraints

Several power flow constraints were set for the optimization process as discussed in the following sections:

4.2.1. Voltage Constraint

The voltage magnitude at bus n should satisfy the permissible voltage limit as in (15).

$$V_{min} \leq V_n \leq V_{max} \tag{15}$$

where V_{min} is the minimum voltage, V_n is the voltage at any bus n, and $Vmax$ is the maximum voltage.

4.2.2. Thermal Capacity Constraint

The thermal capacity limit of the distribution line should be less than the maximum apparent power value as in (16).

$$P^2{}_n + q^2{}_n \leq S^2{}_{n\_max} \tag{16}$$

where P_n and q_n are the active and reactive power that flows along the distribution line, and $S_{n\text{-}max}$ is the maximum apparent power of the line.

4.2.3. Tap Position of OLTC Constraints

The OLTC tap position should be within the permitted range, and the difference between consecutive tap changes should be limited, as presented in (17). The number of tap positions varies from −8 to 8.

$$T^{min}{}_P \leq T_{P,t} \leq T_P{}^{max} \tag{17}$$

where $T^{min}{}_P$ and $T_P{}^{max}$ are the minimum and maximum tap positions. $T_{P,t}$ is the tap position at time t.

4.2.4. Smart Inverter (SI) Constraints

The PV smart inverter constraints are presented in Equations (18) to (19).

$$P_{PVSImin} \leq P_{PVSI} \leq P_{PVSImax} \tag{18}$$

$$Q_{PVSImin} \leq Q_{PVSI} \leq Q_{PVSImax} \tag{19}$$

where $P_{PVSImin}$ and $P_{PVSImax}$ are the maximum and minimum active power limits of smart inverters, respectively. $Q_{PVSImin}$ and $Q_{PVSImax}$ are the minimum and maximum reactive power limits of PV smart inverters, respectively. P_{PVSI} and Q_{PVSI} are the active and reactive power of the smart inverter, respectively.

4.2.5. Power Flow Constraints

The power flow constraints at the point without PVSI and with PVSI are given in (20) and (21) for active power and (22) and (23) for reactive power, respectively.

$$P_n = -P_D \tag{20}$$

$$P_n = P_{PVSI} - P_D \tag{21}$$

$$Q_n = -Q_D \tag{22}$$

$$Q_n = Q_{PVSI} - Q_D \tag{23}$$

In addition, the reactive power flow constraint at the point of connection of the DSTATCOM is given in Equation (26).

$$Q_n = Q_{DSTATCOM} - Q_D \tag{24}$$

where P_D and Q_D represent the active and reactive load demand at the bus n, respectively, $Q_{STATCOM}$ is the reactive power supplied by DSTATCOM at bus n, and P_{PVSI} and Q_{PVSI} represent the active power and reactive power of the PVSIs, respectively. To minimize the computational load of repeatedly solving the OPF, machine learning models are trained on the results of the CACOPF, enabling real-time implementation.

5. Machine Learning Approaches in Predicting the Optimal Setpoints of PVSIs and Voltage Regulating Devices

The prediction is carried out after the implementation of the CACOPF. The step-by-step approach is presented in Figure 2.

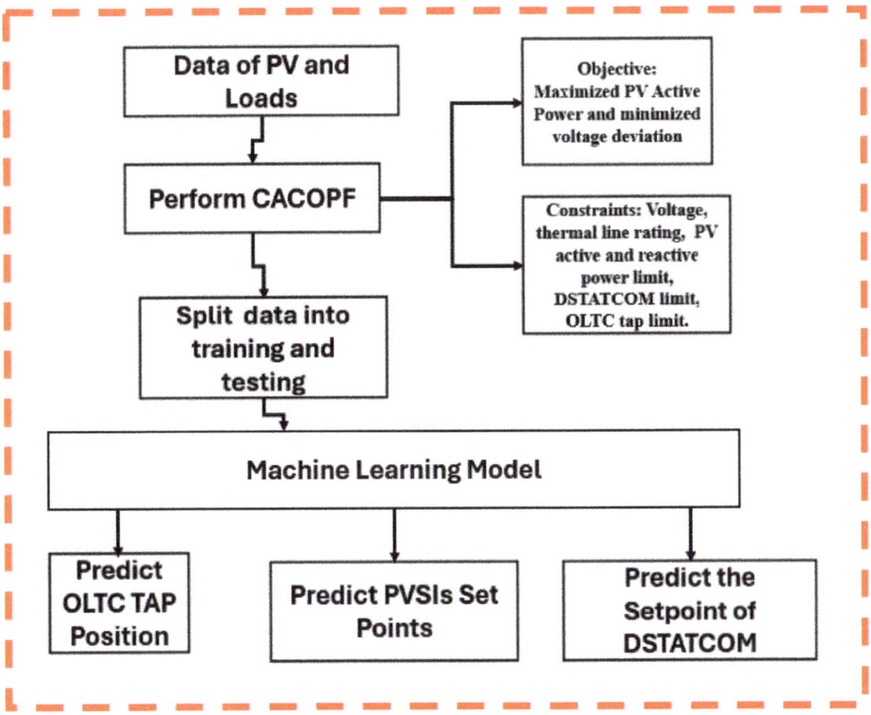

Figure 2. Step-by-step approach of the machine learning models.

CACOPF is carried out offline using the defined objective function and constraints to find the optimal operating points for the PVSIs, the reactive power output of the DSTATCOM, and the ideal tap settings for the OLTC under different PV generation and load conditions. The resulting CACOPF dataset is then normalized and divided into training and testing sets with 80% allocated for training and 20% for testing. In machine learning, the accuracy of parameter prediction depends mainly on three factors: the quality of the data, how the input is structured, and the chosen algorithm or model [28]. According to the "no free lunch theorem," no single model excels universally across all problems [29,30]. Therefore, multiple machine learning algorithms must be evaluated to ensure reliable predictions. In this study, three algorithms; extreme learning machine (ELM), decision tree (DT), and deep neural network (DNN); are used to forecast the OLTC tap positions and the reactive power setpoints for the PVSIs and DSTATCOM. The prediction performance is assessed using the root mean square error (RMSE) and mean absolute error (MAE) metrics, as defined in Equations (25) and (26).

$$RMSE = \sqrt{\frac{\sum_{n=1}^{n}\left(\dot{X}_n - X_n\right)^2}{n}} \tag{25}$$

$$MAE = \frac{\sum_{1}^{n}\left(\dot{X}_n - X_n\right)}{n} \tag{26}$$

where $\dot{X}_n$ is the predicted value, X_n is the actual value, and n is the number of samples predicted.

Since predicting the OLTC tap position is a classification problem, its evaluation relies on metrics derived from the confusion matrix with accuracy and precision calculated as shown in (27) and (28). However, as noted in [30,31], accuracy and precision alone can be misleading when classes are imbalanced. To address this, the Matthews Correlation Coefficient (MCC), given in (29) [31], is also used to assess the performance of the machine learning models for predicting the OLTC tap positions, ensuring that class imbalance does not distort the results.

$$Accuracy = \frac{TP + TN}{TP + TN + FP + FN} \tag{27}$$

$$Precision = \frac{TP}{TP + FP} \tag{28}$$

$$MCC = \frac{(TP.TN) - (FP.FN)}{\sqrt{(Tp + FP)(Tp + FN)(TN + FP)(TN + FN)}} \tag{29}$$

where *TP* and *TN* are the true positive and true negative, respectively. *FP* and *FN* are the false positive and false negative, respectively. To test the proposed approach, a simulation analysis was carried out on a modified IEEE bus 33 with high penetration of PV energy under different loading conditions.

6. Simulation Setup

The proposed method was validated using a modified IEEE 33-bus network, as illustrated in Figure 3. In this setup, four PV smart inverters are installed at their optimal locations along with a DSTATCOM, as shown in the figure. Both the PV output and load demand change over time. Each PV inverter has a capacity of 4.5 MVA and is placed at its optimal position within the network. The PVSI can inject or absorb up to 1.5 MVAR of reactive power to help maintain voltage levels, ensuring a minimum power factor of 0.94. Additionally, the maximum reactive power capacity is 300 kVAR. To demonstrate the effectiveness of the optimization within the defined objectives and constraints, a daily simulation was carried out, accounting for variations in PV generation and load demand, to determine the best operating points for the voltage regulation devices and PVSIs under different scenarios. Following the daily simulation, the CACOPF was applied to the entire dataset, which included 1080 samples reflecting various PV outputs and load conditions.

Two scenarios were considered for the networks: Scenario 1, when the smart inverter is not optimally controlled, and Scenario 2, when the reactive power of the smart Inverter is optimally controlled by a controller in the OPF. The CACOPF is conducted in MATLAB using FMINCON solver.

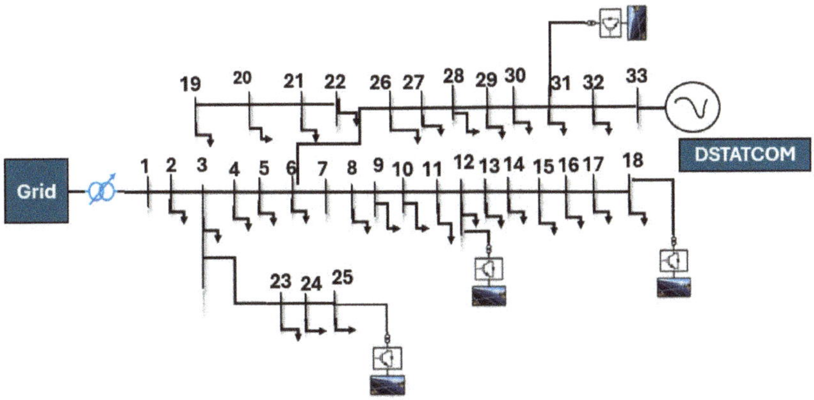

Figure 3. Topology of the modified IEEE bus 33 network.

7. Results and Analysis

The test system, case studies, and performance evaluation of the machine learning-based coordination control methods are thoroughly discussed in the following subsections.

7.1. Daily Voltage Profile and Optimal Setpoint of OLTC, PVSI, and DSTATCOM Network

Figure 4 displays the daily voltage profiles of all nodes in the network when the OLTC, DSTATCOM, and PVSIs are coordinated using the CACOPF for both scenarios. The figure shows that the voltages remain within the acceptable range of 0.95 to 1.05 PU across all conditions of load and PV output. This indicates that the CACOPF successfully met its objective, maintaining voltage limits for all buses even with the uncertainties in PV generation and varying load conditions.

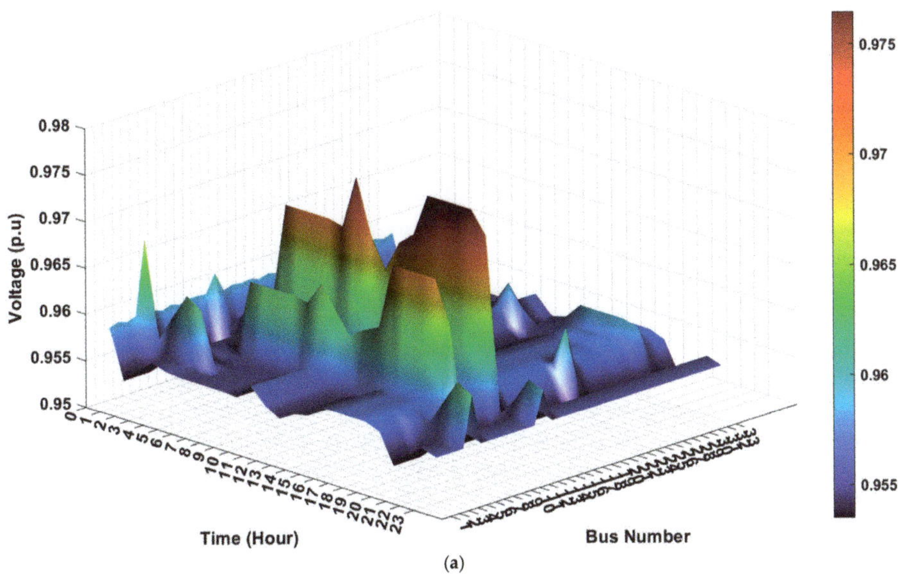

(a)

Figure 4. *Cont.*

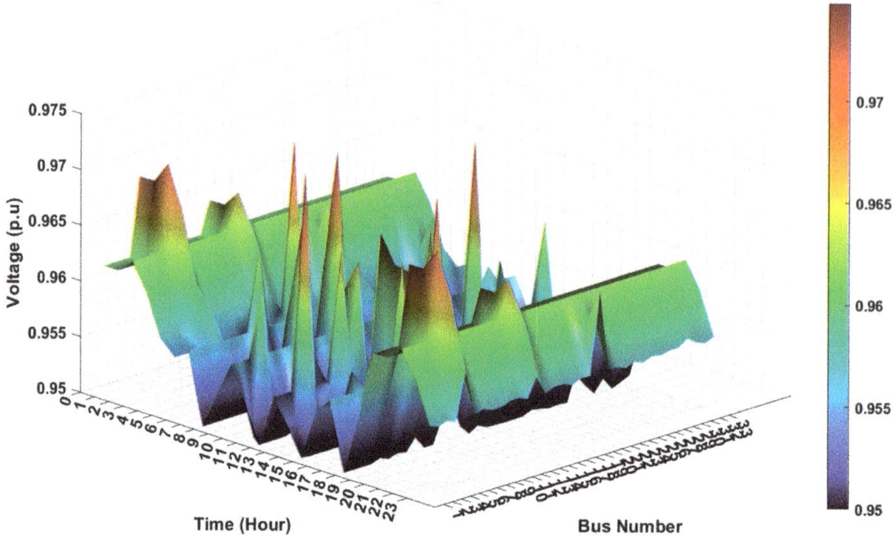

(**b**)

Figure 4. Voltage profile of all buses: (**a**) Scenario 1, (**b**) Scenario 2.

Figure 5 illustrates the dynamic behavior of the reactive power from the PVSIs under varying loading conditions and fluctuating power generated. As seen in the figure, the reactive power output from the PVSIs adjusts continuously to maintain the voltage within the accepted limit in the network. This indicates that the PVSIs play a crucial role in voltage regulation by either supplying or absorbing reactive power, depending on the system's voltage needs. The reactive power fluctuates within the operational limits of the PVSIs, which are determined by the inverter's capabilities and the system's voltage stability requirements. The optimizer ensures that the PVI does not exceed its maximum power generation capacity or absorb more reactive power than it can handle. By adjusting the reactive power output, the PVSIs help stabilize the voltage at the point of common coupling (PCC), ensuring that voltage remains within acceptable bounds despite changes in load and PV generation. This dynamic adjustment highlights the PVSIs' flexibility in voltage control, enabling more efficient system operation and enhancing grid stability under varying conditions. In Figure 6, the DSTATCOM is shown to frequently supply reactive power to maintain the bus voltage. However, with optimal control of reactive power from the PV inverter in Scenario 2, the STATCOM compensates more actively for voltage fluctuations, ensuring voltage stability by injecting reactive power as needed. This is due to the controller logic embedded in the OPF regulating the reactive power of the PVSIs, which will not allow any excessive import or export of reactive power from the PVSI in order to reduce active power losses in the network. Therefore, the CACOPF allows the DSTATCOM to supply less reactive power in Scenario 2 than in Scenario 1, with low PV generation periods, and it supplies more reactive power in Scenario 2, as shown in Figure 6b, than in Scenario 1, when the PV generation is high. This is due to the objective function of the CACOPF, which is the maximization of the PV power active and the minimization of the voltage profile. The CACOPF prefers to use the best setpoints of the DSTATCOM to keep the PVSI at the maximum power capacity at any point in the network and ensure that the voltage of all buses in the network is within the acceptable limits.

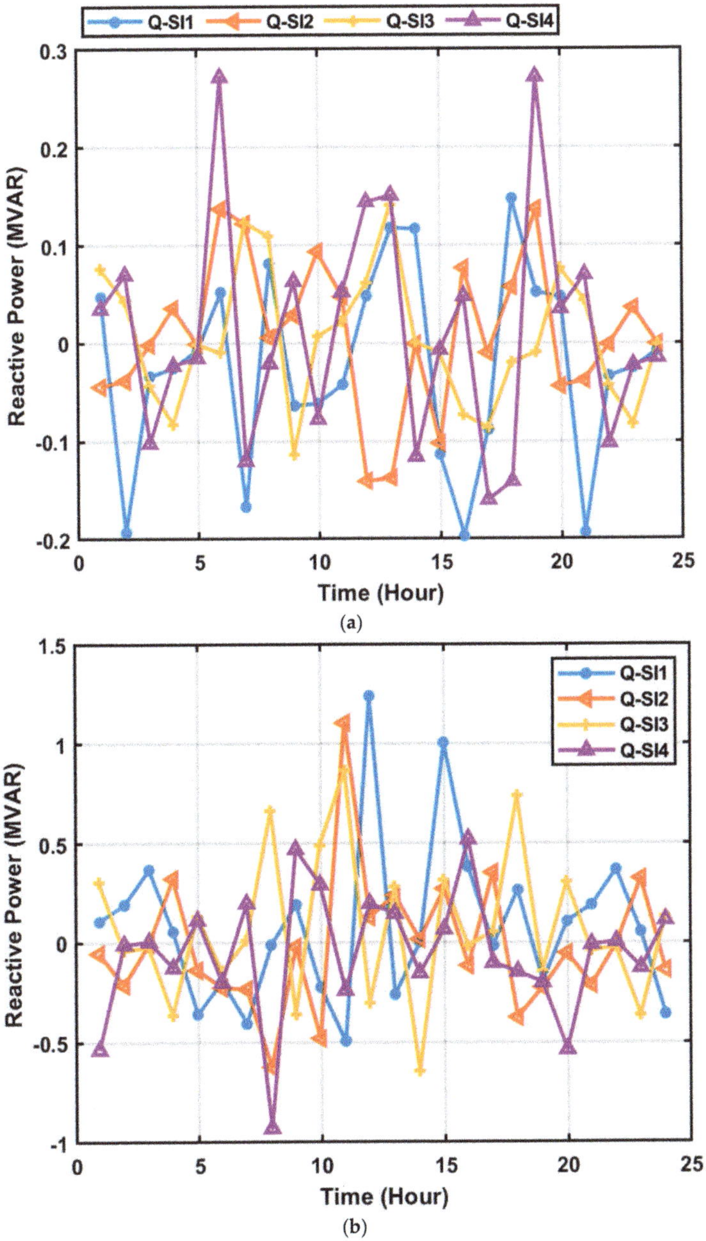

Figure 5. Reactive power imported and exported by the PVSIs: (**a**) Scenario 1, (**b**) Scenario 2.

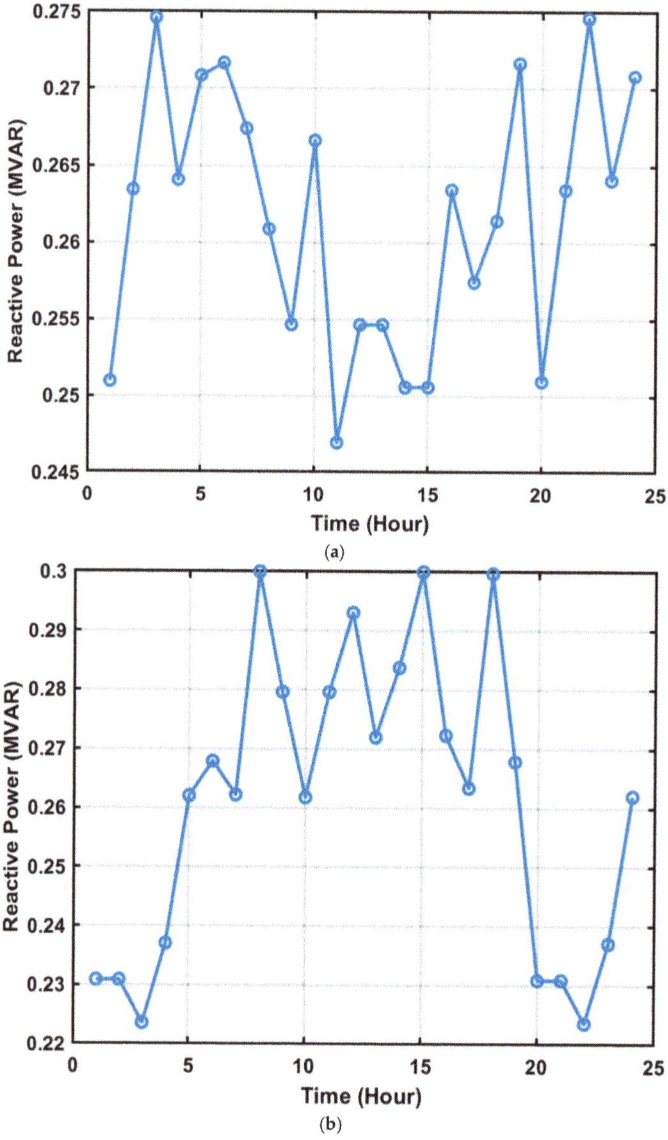

Figure 6. Reactive power DSTATCOM: (**a**) Scenario 1, (**b**) Scenario 2.

The tap changes of the OLTC for the two scenarios under the variation in the PV power output and loading condition are presented in Figure 7. In Scenario 1, when the Volt–VAR of the inverter is not optimally controlled, the operation of the tap position of the OLTC for voltage regulation increases in frequency as the stall changes with a frequency of 4 under the 24 timesteps. This implies that without optimal control, the volt-var increases the dependents of voltage regulation of the OLTC. The results in Figure 6b indicate that by optimally coordinating the OLTC with the smart inverter and DSTATCOM, the frequency of switching the OLTC tap position is reduced with a stall change of 2 under the 24 h timestep. This implies that the system can maintain voltage stability more efficiently in Scenario 2 where the OLTC role is optimized. The reduction in switching frequency suggests improved overall voltage regulation and reduces mechanical wear on the OLTC, which can enhance the longevity and reliability of the OLTC. Additionally, it indicates that the PVSI and DSTATCOM are effectively assisting in maintaining the desired voltage levels, leading to a more efficient operation of the power grid. The coordination approach reduces the dependency on OLTC adjustments and enhances the system's response to dynamic variations of the PV and loading conditions.

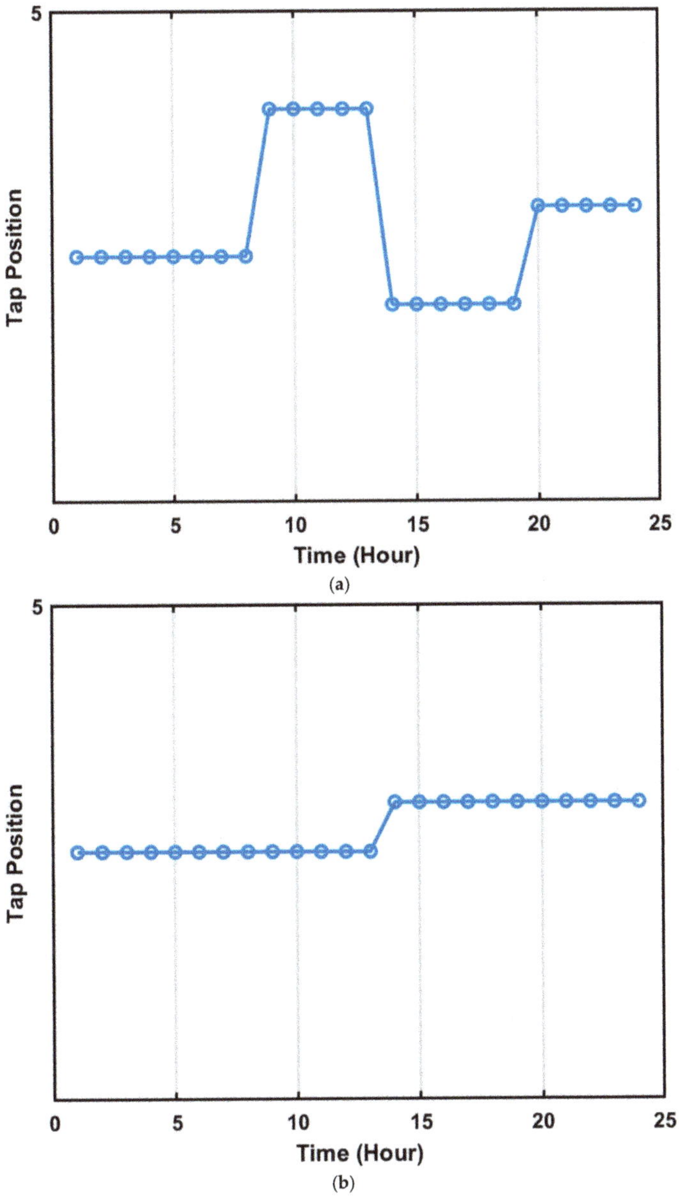

Figure 7. Tap position: (**a**) Scenario 1, (**b**) Scenario 2.

To validate the effectiveness of optimally controlling the Volt–VAR of the PVSI, the sensitivity analysis is presented in Table 1. The findings demonstrate that in Scenario

2, where the inverter's Volt–VAR is optimally managed, the voltage profile improves and the total active power output from the PV inverter increases. In Scenario 1, the average voltage deviation across the network is 0.0425 PU, and the total active power generated by the PV smart inverter is 130.239 MW. In contrast, Scenario 2, where reactive power is optimally controlled, yields an active power output of 131.4998 MW and a reduced voltage deviation of 0.034 PU under varying PV generation and load conditions. These results indicate that integrating a controller into the optimization process is an effective strategy for coordinating PV output and voltage regulation. The optimal control of reactive power not only improves PVSI performance but also enhances the utilization of the PV system's generation capacity. The increased power output in Scenario 2 confirms more efficient inverter operation, showing that coordinated reactive power control significantly contributes to overall system efficiency and improved network performance.

Table 1. Sensitivity analysis.

Scenarios	Maximum Active Power (MW)	Average Voltage Deviation (PU)
1	130.239	0.0425
2	131.4998	0.0340

To minimize the computational demands of repeatedly executing the OPF and enable real-time implementation, the CACOPF results from Scenario 2 were used to train various machine learning models. These models were then tested to predict the setpoints of the voltage regulation devices and the reactive power output of the inverter.

7.2. Machine Learning Prediction Results

After the comprehensive coordinated dataset was generated using the CACOPF, a machine learning-based local coordination controller was trained to predict the OLTC tap positions, PVSI reactive power setpoints, and DSTATCOM reactive power under varying load levels and PV generation outputs. The deep neural network (DNN) model was developed using the TensorFlow library.

7.2.1. Smart Inverter Reactive Power Prediction

The reactive power of smart inverters for each PV was predicted using the active power, the reactive load demand, and the active power of the PVSI. The results of the evaluation metrics of the different machine learning models used are presented in Table 2.

Table 2. Performance of ML models in predicting the PV reactive power of the IEEE networks.

PVSI	ELM		DNN		DT	
	RMSE	MAE	RMSE	MAE	RMSE	MAE
Q1	0.106	0.0870	0.0543	0.0455	0.0933	0.0914
Q2	0.0985	0.0830	0.0683	0.0457	0.0898	0.0832
Q3	0.0789	0.0970	0.0675	0.0551	0.0668	0.0543
Q4	0.1024	0.2305	0.0435	0.0572	0.0932	0.0891

The results demonstrate that the deep neural network (DNN) outperforms the extreme learning machine (ELM) and decision tree (DT) models in predictive accuracy, as indicated by its lower root mean square error (RMSE) and mean absolute error (MAE) values. This highlights DNN's stronger capability to learn complex data relationships, making it more effective at predicting optimal reactive power setpoints for voltage regulation. The lower error values confirm that DNN can accurately model the correlation between input variables, such as load and PV output, and the required reactive power output. This makes it well suited for real-time voltage control applications, where fast and precise decisions are critical. Its ability to manage nonlinearities and complex interactions allows it to respond effectively to the dynamic behavior of power systems, enhancing reactive power control and system optimization. In comparison, while ELM and DT are competent models, their limited ability to capture deeper patterns in the data results in lower performance relative to DNN. Thus, DNN emerges as a more dependable solution for managing PVSI reactive power under varying load conditions.

7.2.2. OLTC Taps Position Classification Performance

To assess the machine learning models' ability to predict the OLTC tap position, active power, demand, and PVSI output power were used as input variables for the prediction models. Figure 8 presents the evaluation results for the different machine learning models tested. The findings show that the deep neural network (DNN) outperforms both the extreme learning machine (ELM) and the decision tree (DT) models in accurately predicting the OLTC tap position for reliable voltage control. The assessment uses the Matthews Correlation Coefficient (MCC), where the DNN achieves the highest scores among the models. The MCC is a robust metric for evaluating classification performance, particularly when dealing with imbalanced data, as it considers true and false positives and negatives, providing a more balanced measure of accuracy. Because accurate tap position prediction is critical for stable voltage regulation, higher MCC values mean the DNN handles class imbalance better and delivers more dependable predictions. The DNN's superior performance suggests it effectively captures the complex, nonlinear patterns between input variables and the OLTC tap setting. By better managing data imbalance, the DNN supports more precise tap changer control, which is essential for voltage stability and optimizing system performance in real-time applications.

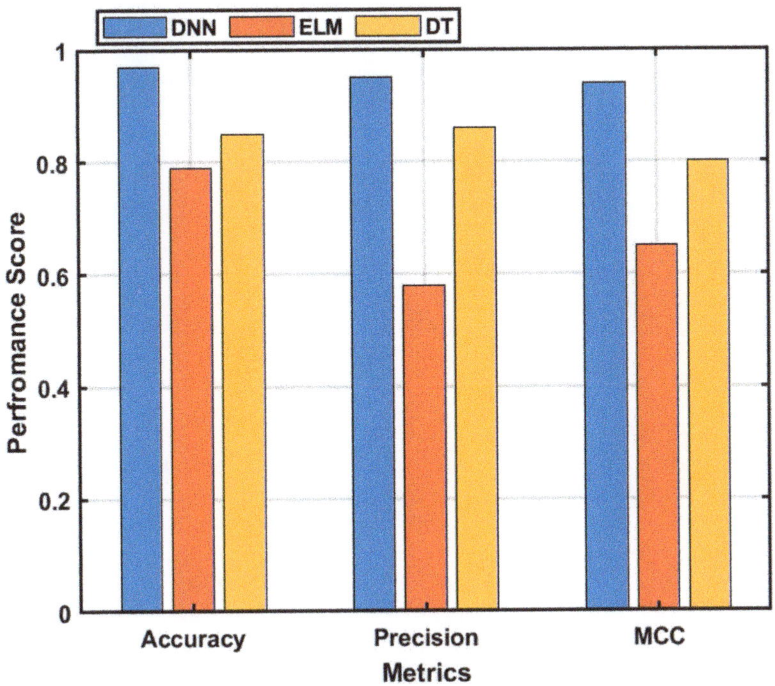

Figure 8. Comparison of the tap position classification performance of the machine learning.

7.2.3. DSTATCOM Reactive Power Prediction Performance

The results in Table 3 illustrate how the machine learning models perform in predicting the DSTATCOM's reactive power output under varying PV generation and load conditions. Among the models, the deep neural network (DNN) achieves the best performance, as shown by its lower root mean square error (RMSE) and mean absolute error (MAE) compared to the extreme learning machine (ELM) and decision tree models. The RMSE and MAE are essential indicators of prediction accuracy, and lower values reflect more reliable forecasts of the DSTATCOM's reactive power. The DNN's superior results suggest it can effectively capture and adapt to the complex, dynamic nature of the power system, accounting for changing loads, generation levels, and network configurations. This capability is vital for the reliable operation of reactive power devices like DSTATCOMs, which need to respond quickly to maintain voltage stability and support overall grid performance. The DNN's strong prediction accuracy demonstrates its practical value for real-world voltage regulation and power quality improvement in modern power systems.

Table 3. Performance of the model in forecasting the optimal reactive power of STATCOM in IEEE bus 33 network.

ELM		**DNN**		**DT**	
RMSE	MAE	RMSE	MAE	RMSE	MAE
0.786	0.907	0.0267	0.0229	0.034	0.0498

7.3. Testing of the DNN-Based Controller

To demonstrate the advantages of the DNN-based controller, it was tested under new, unseen PV generation and load scenarios to predict the setpoints for the PVSI, the DSTATCOM's reactive power, and the OLTC tap position. The resulting voltage profiles and computation times were then compared to those produced by the optimizer under the same conditions. Table 4 presents the network's average voltage profile and simulation time for a 24-timestep variation in PV output and load demand. The results indicate that the DNN controller is better suited for real-time use, achieving a quick response time of just 2.32 s for the 24 timesteps. This shows that the DNN controller can reliably coordinate the PVSI, DSTATCOM, and OLTC setpoints in real time even with uncertainties in PV generation and load fluctuations.

Table 4. Comparison between the DNN controller and simulation time.

Techniques	**Average Voltage Deviation (PU)**	**Simulation Time (Seconds)**
Optimizer	0.0392	108.45
DNN Controller	0.0413	2.32

8. Conclusions

In this paper, we developed an ML-based intelligent controller for the coordination control of PV energy smart inverters integrated with DSTATCOMs and OLTC, considering the uncertainties in PV output and load demand. The proposed approach begins by performing a centralized AC optimal power flow (CACOPF) analysis to determine the coordination setpoints for the smart inverters, DSTATCOMs, and OLTCs under various loading and power output conditions. In addition, ML-based control methods are trained as local controllers to determine the optimal reactive power of the smart inverters, DSTATCOMs, and tap position of the OLTCs. The simulation was tested under two different scenarios: Scenario 1, when the Volt–VAR of the smart inverter was not optimally controlled, and Scenario 2, when it was optimally controlled by a controller embedded in the CACOPF. The results from the study underscore the importance of optimally coordinating various grid devices, such as the OLTC, smart inverters, and DSTATCOM, for maintaining voltage stability in a power distribution system. The comparison between Scenario 1 and Scenario 2 demonstrates that optimally controlling and coordinating Volt–VAR with other voltage-regulating devices improves its operational efficiency. Moreover, the frequency of OLTC tap switching is reduced in Scenario 2 when coordinated with the reactive power control from the smart inverter and DSTATCOM. This reduction in switching frequency suggests a more stable voltage profile, with less mechanical stress on the OLTC, which can improve its operational lifespan and reduce maintenance needs. The findings of this research also established that the optimal coordination of PVSI with other voltage-regulating devices allows the effective usage of PV smart inverters in distribution networks. Furthermore, the use of a DNN-based controller reduces computational inefficiency in performing optimal power flow multiple times to determine the optimal setpoints of the PVSIs, OLTC, and DSTATCOM. In addition, the DNN-based controller approach allows system operators to take predictive actions rather than reactive ones, which delay responses under the uncertainty of loading and PV power generation, can cause voltage violations in the network, and lead to equipment damage. The DNN-based controller results in predicting the optimal setpoints for the reactive power of the PV smart inverter, tap position of the OLTC, and reactive power of the DSTATCOM, showing that the DNN-based controller excels in predicting the setpoints for the coordination of reactive power for smart inverters, DSTATCOMs, and OLTCs, outperforming ELM and DT models. The DNN-based local coordination control approach mirrors the CACOPF but does not require repeated execution of OPF. The adoption of this method in the optimal coordination of PV smart inverters with OLTCs and DSTATCOMs will enhance voltage stability, reduce operational costs, and improve the longevity of grid equipment, making the system more resilient to load and generation variations.

Author Contributions: Conceptualization, T.D.M. and A.N.H.; Methodology, T.D.M., A.N.H., O.J.F. and T.S.; Software, T.D.M.; Validation, T.D.M., A.N.H., O.J.F. and T.S. Formal Analysis, T.D.M., A.N.H., O.J.F. and T.S.; Investigation, T.D.M., A.N.H., O.J.F. and T.S.; Writing T.D.M.; Writing—Review and Editing, T.D.M., A.N.H., O.J.F. and T.S. Visualization, T.D.M.; Supervision, A.N.H., O.J.F. and T.S. All authors have read and agreed to the published version of the manuscript.

Funding: This research received no external funding.

Data Availability Statement: The data used for this research are available upon request from the corresponding author.

Conflicts of Interest: There are no conflicts of interest among the authors regarding the submission of this manuscript.

References

1. Hossain, T.; Hossen, Z.; Badal, F.R.; Islam, R.; Hasan, M.; Ali, F.; Tasneem, Z. Next generation power inverter for grid resilience: Technology review. *Helicon* **2024**, *10*, 2–40. [CrossRef] [PubMed]
2. Nadeem, T.B.; Siddiqui, M.; Khalid, M.; Asif, M. Distributed energy systems: A review of classification, technologies, applications, and policies. *Energy Strategy Rev.* **2023**, *48*, 101096. [CrossRef]
3. Djalab, A.; Djalab, Z.; El Amomum, A.; Tina, G.M.; Motahhir, S.; Laouid, A.A. A comprehensive review of floating photovoltaic systems: Tech advances, marine environmental influences on offshore PV systems, and economic feasibility analysis. *Sol. Energy* **2024**, *277*, 112711. [CrossRef]
4. Saxena, V.; Manna, S.; Rajput, S.K.; Kumar, P.; Sharma, B.; Alsharif, M.H.; Kim, M.K. Navigating the complexities of distributed generation: Integration, challenges, and solutions. *Energy Rep.* **2024**, *12*, 3302–3322. [CrossRef]
5. Twaisan, K.; Barışçı, N. Integrated distributed energy resources (DER) and microgrids: Modeling and optimization of DERs. *Electronics* **2022**, *11*, 2816. [CrossRef]

6. Ahmad, T.; Madonski, R.; Zhang, D.; Huang, C.; Mujeeb, A. Data-driven probabilistic machine learning in sustainable smart energy/smart energy systems: Key developments, challenges, and future research opportunities in the context of smart grid paradigm. *Renew. Sustain. Energy Rev.* **2022**, *160*, 112128. [CrossRef]
7. Iweh, C.D.; Gyamfi, S.; Tanyi, E.; Effah-Donyina, E. Distributed generation and renewable energy integration into the grid Prerequisites, push factors, practical options, issues and merits. *Energies* **2021**, *14*, 5375. [CrossRef]
8. Jose, J.; Kowli, A. Optimal augmentation of distribution networks for improved reliability. *IEEE Syst. J.* **2022**, *16*, 1965–1973 [CrossRef]
9. Liu, Y.; Li, J.; Wu, L. Coordinated optimal network reconfiguration and voltage regulator/DER control for unbalanced distribution systems. *IEEE Trans. Smart Grid* **2019**, *10*, 2912–2922. [CrossRef]
10. Wang, S.; Chen, S.; Ge, L.; Wu, L. Distributed generation hosting capacity evaluation for distribution systems considering the robust optimal operation of OLTC and SVC. *IEEE Trans. Sustain. Energy* **2016**, *7*, 1111–1123. [CrossRef]
11. Escalera, A.; Prodanovi, M.; Castronuovo, E.D.; RoldanPerez, J. Contribution of active management technologies to the reliability of power distribution networks. *Appl. Energy* **2020**, *267*, 114919. [CrossRef]
12. *IEEE Standard 1547-2018 (Revision of IEEE Standard 1547-2003)*; IEEE Standard for Interconnection and Interoperability of Distributed Energy Resources with Associated Electric Power Systems Interfaces. IEEE: Piscataway, NJ, USA, 2018.
13. Wick, S.; Gonzalez, C.; Driesen, J. Combined central and local active and reactive power control of PV inverters. *IEEE Trans. Sustain. Energy* **2014**, *5*, 776–784.
14. Li, P.; Zhang, C.; Wu, Z.; Xu, Y.; Hu, M.; Dong, Z. Distributed adaptive robust Voltage/VAR control with network partition in active distribution networks. *IEEE Trans. Smart Grid* **2020**, *11*, 2245–2256. [CrossRef]
15. Ren, H.; Jha, R.R.; Dubey, A.; Schulz, N.N. Extremum-seeking adaptive-droop for model-free and localized Volt-VAR optimization. *IEEE Trans. Power Syst.* **2022**, *37*, 179–190. [CrossRef]
16. Ali, A.; Mahmoud, K.; Lehtonen, M. Maximizing hosting capacity of uncertain photovoltaics by coordinated management of OLTC, Var sources and stochastic EVs. *Int. J. Elect. Power Energy Syst.* **2021**, *127*, 106627. [CrossRef]
17. Guo, Y.; Baker, K.; Dall'Anese, E.; Hu, Z.; Summers, T.H. Data-based distributionally robust stochastic optimal power flow—Part II: Case studies. *IEEE Trans. Power Syst.* **2019**, *34*, 1493–1503. [CrossRef]
18. Karagiannopoulos, S.; Aristidou, P.; Hug, G. Data-driven local control design for active distribution grids using off-line optimal power flow and machine learning techniques. *IEEE Trans. Smart Grid* **2019**, *10*, 6461–6471. [CrossRef]
19. Jalali, M.; Kekatos, V.; Gatsis, N.; Deka, D. Designing reactive power control rules for smart inverters using support vector machines. *IEEE Trans. Smart Grid* **2020**, *11*, 1759–1770. [CrossRef]
20. Sun, X.; Qiu, J.; Tao, Y.; Ma, Y.; Zhao, J. A multi-mode data-driven Volt/Var control strategy with conservation voltage reduction in active distribution networks. *IEEE Trans. Sustain. Energy* **2022**, *13*, 1073–1085. [CrossRef]
21. Yu, L.; Zhang, L.; Meng, G.; Zhang, F.; Liu, W. Research on multi-objective reactive power optimization of power grid with high proportion of new energy. *IEEE Access* **2022**, *10*, 116443–116452.
22. Ai, M.; Du, Z.; Pan, Z.; Li, G. The optimization of reactive power for distribution network with PV generation based on NSGA-III. *CPSS Trans. Power Electron. Appl.* **2021**, *6*, 193–200. [CrossRef]
23. Li, C.; Lu, Q.; He, H.; Zhao, J.; Jiang, Y.; Xu, B.; Yan, Y.; Bian, J.; Du, W. Reactive power optimization of active distribution networks based on simulated annealing algorithm. In Proceedings of the 2023 IEEE 7th Information Technology and Mechatronics Engineering Conference (ITOEC), Chongqing, China, 15–17 September 2023; pp. 1022–1026.
24. Ilyushin, P.; Volnyi, V.; Suslov, K.; Filippov, S. State-of-the-art literature review of power flow control methods for low-voltage AC and AC-DC microgrids. *Energies* **2023**, *16*, 3153. [CrossRef]
25. Rehman, N.; Mufti, M.U.D.; Gupta, N. Power flow analysis in a distribution system penetrated with renewable energy sources: A review. *Int. J. Ambient Energy* **2024**, *45*, 2305701. [CrossRef]
26. Nair, A.S.; Abhyankar, S.; Peles, S.; Ranganathan, P. Computational and numerical analysis of AC optimal power flow formulations on large-scale power grids. *Electr. Power Syst. Res.* **2022**, *202*, 107594. [CrossRef]
27. Tshivhase, N.; Hasan, A.N.; Shongwe, T. Proposed Fuzzy Logic System for Voltage Regulation and Power Factor Improvement in Power Systems with High Infiltration of Distributed Generation. *Energies* **2020**, *13*, 4241. [CrossRef]
28. Makanju, T.D.; Shongwe, T.; Famoriji, O.J. Machine Learning Approaches for Power System Parameters Prediction: A Systematic Review. *IEEE Access* **2024**, *12*, 66646–66679. [CrossRef]
29. Powers, D.M.W. Evaluation: From precision, recall and F-measure to ROC, informedness, markedness and correlation. *arXiv* **2020**, arXiv:2010.16061.

30. Luque, A.; Carrasco, A.; Martín, A.; de las Hera, A. The impact of class imbalance in classification performance metrics based on the binary confusion matrix. *Pattern Recognit.* **2019**, *91*, 216–231. [CrossRef]
31. Makanju, T.D.; Famoriji, O.J.; Hasan, A.N.; Shongwe, T. Machine learning approaches for identifying and predicting voltage conditions in power system networks using network topology behavior input formulation. *Sci. Afr.* **2024**, *26*, e02493. [CrossRef]

energies MDPI

Article

Energy Transformation of Road Transport Infrastructure—Concept and Assessment of the Electric Vehicle Recharging Systems

Norbert Chamier-Gliszczynski [1,*], Joanna Alicja Dyczkowska [1], Wojciech Musiał [2], Aleksandra Panek [3] and Piotr Kotylak [3]

1 Faculty of Economics Sciences, Koszalin University of Technology, 75-453 Koszalin, Poland; joanna.dyczkowska@tu.koszalin.pl
2 Institute of Management, University of Szczecin, 71-101 Szczecin, Poland; wojciech.musial@usz.edu.pl
3 Faculty of Transport, Warsaw University of Technology, 00-661 Warsaw, Poland; aleksandra.panek@pw.edu.pl (A.P.); piotr.kotylak@pw.edu.pl (P.K.)
* Correspondence: norbert.chamier-gliszczynski@tu.koszalin.pl

Abstract: The energy transformation of transport infrastructure represents a significant challenge, being implemented along the TEN-T network under the introduced AFIR regulation (Regulation for the Deployment of Alternative Fuels Infrastructure). The goal of this transformation is the development of alternative fuels infrastructure deployed along the Trans-European Transport Network (TEN-T), dedicated to light-duty electric vehicles (eLDVs) and heavy-duty electric vehicles (eHDVs). The measures undertaken must be preceded by an analytical process assessing the assumptions outlined in the AFIR regulation, defining targeted actions for achieving the regulation's objectives, and evaluating the baseline status as well as projected conditions for the years 2025, 2027, 2030, and 2035. This assessment is essential during the planning and management stages of the energy transformation process of transport infrastructure being undertaken by individual EU Member States. Meeting the targets set by AFIR for transport infrastructure necessitates the development of appropriate research tools. The approach proposed in this article offers an innovative framework for addressing the challenges of energy transformation. The initial step involves designing a model for the energy transformation of transport infrastructure, followed by the definition of indicators to assess the implementation of AFIR objectives. This paper presents a model for the energy transformation of road transport infrastructure, defines the individual elements of the model, specifies indicators for evaluating the transformation process, and conducts a research study incorporating these components. This article aims to elucidate the core aspects of the energy transformation of transport infrastructure, identify actions aligned with achieving the objectives of the AFIR regulation, and perform an evaluation of its implementation. Additionally, the research addresses the question of how the energy transformation of road transport infrastructure is unfolding in Poland. The study is based on the structure of electric vehicles (EVs) and transport infrastructure along the TEN-T network in the territory of Poland. The current level of AFIR compliance for eLDVs for the years 2025, 2027, 2030, and 2035 is approximately 175%, 96%, 37%, and 13%, respectively. In contrast, for eHDVs, the compliance level is around 20%, 0%, and 0% for the TEN-T core network, and approximately 10%, 3%, and 0% for the TEN-T comprehensive network.

 https://doi.org/10.3390/en18164241

Keywords: energy transformation; transport infrastructure; AFIR (alternative fuel infrastructure regulation); electric vehicles; light-duty electric vehicles; heavy-duty electric vehicles; Trans-European transport network (TEN-T); assessment

1. Introduction

The European transport sector is one of the largest sources of greenhouse gas emissions in Europe. Since 1990, transport-related emissions have been continuously increasing, in contrast to the downward trends observed in other economic sectors. The primary source of these emissions is the combustion of diesel and gasoline in internal combustion engines across land, water, and air transport modes. In 2024, road transport accounted for 73% of total transport-related greenhouse gas emissions in the EU, followed by aviation at 13.8%, maritime transport at 12.7%, and rail transport at 0.4%. The primary source of emissions within the road transport sector is passenger cars, which are responsible for 43.7% of greenhouse gas emissions from the entire transport sector in the EU and account for 59.86% of all emissions originating from road transport. Heavy-duty vehicles and buses accounted for 20.1% of transport-related greenhouse gas (GHG) emissions, light commercial vehicles for 8.4%, and motorcycles for 0.9%. It is important to note that these emissions occur during the operational phase of vehicles, predominantly in proximity to roads, urban areas, waterways, and in the atmosphere. Reducing transport emissions can be achieved by increasing vehicle efficiency or by shifting to alternative, low-emission fuels. In 2019, within the European road transport sector, diesel fuel was used in 66.7% of vehicles, while gasoline-powered vehicles represented 24.55%.

As part of the search for an alternative fuel or energy source, electricity was adopted as propulsion energy carrier. This initiative marks the first stage of the energy transition in the transport sector. As a consequence of the proposed shift, efforts have been undertaken in the design, production, marketing, and promotion of electric vehicles (EVs) both on global and European automotive markets. It is important to note that the term electric vehicles (EVs) encompasses a wide range of transport modes, including light-duty electric vehicles (eLDVs), electric heavy-duty vehicles (eHDVs), electric buses (e-buses) [1], trolleybuses, trams, trains, ships, boats, airplanes, electric bicycles and scooters [2], and other personal electric mobility devices. Within the EV category, battery electric vehicles (BEVs) are distinguished by their use of one or more electric motors powered exclusively by electricity stored in onboard rechargeable battery systems. These batteries are designed for repeated charging from external electricity sources. Fuel cell electric vehicles (FCEVs) have also been introduced, representing the most technologically advanced category of electric vehicles. These vehicles are equipped with a fuel cell system in which hydrogen is converted into electricity through an electrochemical process. All electric vehicles can be classified as zero-emission, which contributing to the reduction of transport-related emissions in the areas where these vehicles are operated [3]. These initiatives have led to a noticeable increase in the sales of electric vehicles, particularly in two market segments: passenger cars and buses. Sales and interest in eLDVs and eHDVs have also been observed among companies in the transport and courier sectors. A separate category of vehicles is represented by hybrid vehicles, which are classified as low-emission due to their dual propulsion systems–combining an internal combustion engine with an electric motor. This category includes hybrid electric vehicles (HEVs) and plug-in hybrid electric vehicles (PHEVs).

As a result of efforts to reduce transport emissions, a total of 10,632,381 new passenger cars were registered in the European Union in 2024. Among these, electric vehicles (EVs) accounted for 13.6% of registrations, hybrid vehicles (HEVs and PHEVs) made up 31%, and hydrogen fuel cell vehicles (FCEVs) represented 0.01%. By contrast, the share of vehicles powered by conventional fuels was 33.3% for gasoline-powered vehicles and 11.9% for diesel-powered vehicles.

The production, sale, and use of electric vehicles mark the beginning of the proposed energy transition in the transport sector [4]. It should be emphasized that electric vehicles represent the future of modern transport. This is particularly important in the case of taxis, which constitute one of the primary means of transportation in urban areas. Replacing conventional taxis entirely with electric taxis is a key element of sustainable urban transport strategies [5]. The type of available and applicable fuels determines the types of vehicles in use, which in turn creates the need to adapt infrastructure to support electric vehicles [6].

The implementation of alternative energy sources for vehicle propulsion necessitates the development of transport point infrastructure, such as electric vehicle charging stations and hydrogen refueling stations. These facilities are essential components of the alternative fuels infrastructure. In the initial phase, EV charging stations were primarily constructed in urban areas, which significantly limited the usability of electric vehicles outside cities. Similarly, hydrogen refueling stations were mainly established to support public transportation systems operating in urban environments. However, the growing number of EVs has driven the expansion of charging infrastructure along non-residential roadways, including national roads, expressways, and motorways. It is important to note that the development of EV charging and hydrogen refueling infrastructure is progressing at varying rates across EU member states. Future efforts should also focus on the development of energy storage systems dedicated to electric vehicles [7].

To ensure the balanced development of alternative fuels infrastructure across EU member states, Regulation (EU) 2023/1804 of the European Parliament and of the Council of 13 September 2023 on the deployment of alternative fuels infrastructure was introduced, repealing Directive 2014/94/EU [8]. This regulation, known by the acronym AFIR (Alternative Fuel Infrastructure Regulation), has been in force since 13 April 2024. AFIR aims to support the development of alternative fuels infrastructure through the implementation of specific targets to be achieved by the end of 2025 and 2030.

The aim of this article is to present the essence of the energy transition process in road transport infrastructure based on the AFIR regulation, to define actions aimed at achieving the regulation's objectives, and to conduct an assessment of AFIR implementation six months prior to the 2025 deadline for meeting its established targets. The evaluation process will be carried out using the example of the energy transition of road transport infrastructure along the TEN-T network in Poland.

An essential aspect of the research process is to address the question of how the energy transition of road transport infrastructure is progressing in Poland, which, as an EU member state, is obligated to fulfill the assumptions and targets set forth by the AFIR regulation.

The article is divided into five sections. The first section provides the introduction, followed by a literature review in the second section. The third section presents a model of the energy transition process for transport infrastructure in accordance with the objectives and targets of the AFIR regulation. The fourth section focuses on the assessment of the energy transition process of road transport infrastructure carried out within Poland. The fifth and final section summarizes the conclusions drawn from the conducted research.

2. Literature Review

2.1. Transport Energy Transformation Towards Low and Zero Emission Transport

According to the International Energy Agency (IEA), CO_2 emissions from the transport sector reached almost 8 billion tons in 2022, accounting for about 23% of global emissions from fossil fuel combustion. Preliminary data for 2023/2024 indicate a further small increase of about 0.8% globally, making it the fastest growing sector in terms of final energy consumption emissions [9]. The most promising strategy is low- and zero-emission technologies, based primarily on vehicle electrification and the use of hydrogen. At this stage, it is important to reduce CO_2 emissions throughout the entire life cycle of electric vehicles. It is also necessary to consider the method of accounting for carbon dioxide emission allowances in the energy market settlement process, specifically in relation to the trade of electricity intended for electric vehicles [10]. Equally important are the energy distribution systems dedicated to electric vehicles [11], the organization of charging systems [12,13], the energy trading system [14], the forecasting of electrical load [15], and the safety of electric vehicle charging systems [16].

Thanks to the high efficiency of battery electric drives and the possibility of smart charging and integration of these vehicles with energy networks (Vehicle to Grid–V2G), it is possible to reduce the total costs of the energy system, according to [17] even by about 1.6% in the PyPSA Eur model (integrated simulation model of the energy system of Europe–Python for Power System Analysis Europe)—which shows the potential for synergy between transport and energy. The analysis by the authors of [18,19] confirms that electrification translates not only into emission reduction, but also into increased operational efficiency, although it creates new challenges related to infrastructure and battery recycling. The importance of multicriteria decision-making tools in transport planning is highlighted by [20], who developed a method to select scenarios for urban transport systems with varying shares of electric vehicles. Their work supports strategic decisions regarding the structure of urban mobility in light of emission, efficiency and cost factors.

In the area of heavy and long-distance transport, analyses indicate that hydrogen is a valuable complement to electrification, offering a long range and fast refueling. However, only hydrogen produced from renewable sources–via electrolysis powered by RES or nuclear energy–shows real decarbonization potential, as confirmed by the publication [21]. Conversely, hydrogen produced from natural gas without CO_2 capture is characterized by high trace emissions, exceeding 10 kg CO_2 per kilogram H_2, which limits the environmental benefits.

An important contribution to the discussion is presented in the study [22], where the authors assessed the real costs and barriers of BEV (Battery Electric Vehicle) and FCEV (Fuel Cell Electric Vehicle) technologies in road transport based on the Whole Systems system model. Their results show that although BEVs dominate in medium and light fleets, hydrogen gains a competitive advantage in the heavy vehicle segment when "immeasurable" costs–such as refueling time, load capacity limitations, and adaptation barriers–are considered. From the perspective of operational costs and environmental impact, the analysis by [23] offers comparative insight into different vehicle propulsion systems. The study confirms the significant emission reduction potential of BEVs and FCEVs, while also addressing the economic aspects that influence fleet operator decisions.

Public transport is another area where interest in low-emission technologies is growing rapidly. Although electric buses are gaining popularity thanks to MDPI (2023), there is a lack of data from real implementations, especially in countries outside Europe and the USA. The work [24] shows that zero-emission vehicles and drones in last-mile logistics have potential, but require coordinated technological and regulatory integration. At the same time, studies on low-emission zones (LEZs) indicate a slow adoption of truly zero-emission solutions, where initially hybrids and plug-in HEVs (Hybrid Electric Vehicles) dominated. A notable advancement in sustainable delivery logistics is presented by [25], who propose a delivery planning method in urban areas that incorporates environmental aspects. This model aids in optimizing transport scenarios by balancing emissions, congestion, and logistics performance.

Life Cycle Assessment (LCA) analyses of individual vehicle types provide valuable data. For example study [26] presents Well-to-Wheel (WTW) comparisons of electric and hydrogen vehicles, indicating that the condition of low emission BEV depends on the source of electric energy. In turn, [27] distinguishes five EV (Electric Vehicle) models with the best LCA results—BYD Dolphin, Hyundai KONA, Jeep Avenger, Opel Corsa and Tesla Model 3—showing that electromobility can be truly ecological, as long as the production of batteries takes place in compliance with environmental standards. In terms of energy usage optimization, the work of [28] addresses the challenge of minimizing electricity consumption by municipal electric fleets amid charging uncertainties. Their results demonstrate how adaptive planning can improve energy use and cost efficiency in urban contexts.

An interesting perspective on cost and emission simulations in heavy transport is presented by [29] through a Total Cost of Ownership (TCO) model for different powertrain configurations of heavy goods vehicles, also taking into account infrastructure and real fleet data. Their forecasts show that with technological progress and policy support, zero-emission vehicles are becoming competitive. The challenges of planning under uncertainty are addressed by [30], who apply fuzzy logic as a tool for supporting transport development decisions. Their work is particularly applicable where input data is ambiguous or based on expert judgment, which is often the case in early-stage planning of electromobility systems.

However, the transformation of transport cannot be treated in isolation–it requires close integration with the global energy system based on renewable energy sources. The authors in the publication [31] emphasize the need to synchronize the production of vehicles and energy. Additionally, study [18], utilizing the PyPSA-Eur model, highlights significant cost savings in the integration of V2G and smart charging, which reduces the need for energy storage. In the area of energy systems [32] present the opportunity to adapt existing gas pipelines to the transmission of hydrogen, which translates into possible infrastructure savings.

System dynamics (SD) analyses, as in [33], show that dynamic models do not effectively take into account temporal dependencies and feedbacks, e.g., between technology adoption and network and policy needs, which limits the accuracy of transformation scenario forecasts. It seems that future research should focus on several key areas: detailed LCA and TCO modelling of heavy vehicles, non-road, rail, sea and air transport–especially using synthetic fuels (SAF, ammonia); implementation of V2G, AI and digital tools in logistics management; and behavioral and social analyses that take into account cultural norms, technological acceptance and educational mechanisms. Particular attention should be paid to countries of the Global South, where infrastructural, legislative and financial barriers may force other paths of technological transformation.

The transformation of transport towards a low- and zero-emission future requires at least parallel development of electric vehicles and hydrogen technologies, strong integration with green energy sources, adequate support policies, research towards social adoption and behavioral change (changes in attitudes and habits of users) and adaptation to local conditions of developing markets. Only an approach that is both interdisciplinary and global will create a real chance for sustainable transport of the future, consistent with the goals of climate agreements and the economic needs of societies.

Research gaps in light of the above text and in the context of the topic include:

- lack of spatial analyses linking charging infrastructure deployment to urban form, TEN-T corridors, and regional energy profiles [34],

- limited data from Central and Eastern Europe and insufficient methodologies for assessing infrastructure effectiveness in a systemic and social context,
- underexplored integration of AFIR regulations with national energy and transport strategies, including the role of local governance,
- no standardized indicators for evaluating AFIR compliance and infrastructure performance across regions,
- insufficient consideration of user behavior, social acceptance, and service quality in the planning of public charging infrastructure,
- fragmented treatment of hydrogen infrastructure and absence of long-term strategies for maintaining and upgrading AFIR-compliant networks beyond 2025.

2.2. *Electromobility—Growth Dynamics, Characteristics of BEV and FCEV Vehicles*

The transformation of the transport sector towards low and zero emissions is a process of fundamental importance in the context of global climate commitments, with electric vehicles playing a central role in this transition. According to a report [9] prepared by the International Energy Agency, global sales of electric vehicles in 2023 reached about 14 million units, which constituted an 18% share of new passenger car sales. This is a 35% increase compared to 2022. By the end of 2023, more than 40 million BEVs (Battery Electric Vehicles) and PHEVs (Plug-in Hybrid Electric Vehicles) were already on the roads around the world.

The main centers of electromobility development are China, Europe and the United States, which together account for over 90% of global EV sales [35]. In China, over 9 million electric vehicles were sold in 2023, and the share of EVs in new car sales exceeded 50% [36]. In Europe, the largest market share is held by Norway, the Netherlands and Germany, where supportive subsidy schemes and tax incentives led to EVs accounting for between 20% and over 80% of new vehicle registrations in 2023 [37]. In the USA, sales growth was supported by federal tax breaks under the act [38], although local data from 2024 indicate a slight slowdown in dynamics [39].

BEVs are currently the dominant type of electric drive. They are powered exclusively by an electric motor and supplied with energy stored in lithium-ion batteries. Their efficiency is over 85–90%, which significantly exceeds combustion engines (25–30%) [40]. Modern vehicles such as Tesla Model 3, Hyundai Ioniq 6 or Mercedes EQS offer a range of 400 to 700 km [41].

BEVs are increasingly used not only in the consumer sector, but also in public transport [42] and urban logistics. An example is Shenzhen in China, which in 2018 completed the full electrification of its entire fleet of city buses (over 16,000 vehicles), and then also of taxis [43]. Similar activities are being carried out in Amsterdam, Hamburg and Santiago de Chile [44].

According to the report [45], the number of electric buses in the world has exceeded 820,000 units. China accounts for over 60% of the entire global fleet of EV buses, while Europe is still catching up, with an average share of EVs in city bus sales at 12–15% [46]. At the same time, the segment of electric vans is being intensively developed–used, among others, by courier companies [47].

Fuel Cell Electric Vehicles (FCEVs) are electric vehicles in which energy is generated through an electrochemical reaction between hydrogen and oxygen in a fuel cell. Their greatest advantage is short refueling time (3–5 min) and extended ranges–often exceeding 600–700 km. As a result, FCEVs are considered a complementary technology to BEVs, especially in long-distance and heavy transport [40,48].

However, the decarbonisation potential of hydrogen depends on its production method. Only the so-called green hydrogen, produced in the electrolysis process powered by renewable energy sources (RES), ensures substantial emission reductions. Hydrogen produced from natural gas without CO_2 capture (commonly referred to as grey hydrogen) generates emissions of 10–12 kg CO_2 per kilogram of H_2 [48,49].

Examples of FCEV implementations include the H2Haul project (EU), Hyundai XCIENT's fleet of trucks in Germany and Switzerland, and Nikola and Hyzon's operations in the U.S. A Whole Systems Analysis report from University College London found that FCEVs outperform BEVs in the heavy-duty vehicle sector when factors such as refueling times, payload constraints, and infrastructure availability are taken into account [50].

2.3. Segmentation of the Electromobility Market

The development of electromobility is not limited to the passenger car segment, although this category continues to dominate in terms registration number. Global markets show an increasingly distinct differentiation in the applications of electric vehicles, responding to the specific needs of the logistics sector [51], public transport [52,53], industry, car-sharing [54,55] and individual users. Therefore, it is necessary to discuss electromobility in the division into four basic segments: passenger cars, delivery vehicles, trucks and micromobiles.

The segment of electric passenger vehicles remains the most developed and diversified. The market offer today includes not only premium cars, such as Tesla Model S, Porsche Taycan or Mercedes EQS, but also city and compact vehicles, such as Fiat 500e, Renault Zoe, Opel Corsa Electric or Dacia Spring [41]. The key challenge remains to reduce the price of the vehicle and the availability of models in the economy class, which are most important in developing countries [9].

Chinese-made models have gained popularity in the European market, offering competitive range and pricing. According to data from the European Association of Automobile Manufacturers [56], in the first quarter of 2024, EVs accounted for over 14% of new registrations in the EU.

The electrification of light-duty vehicles (LDVs) is progressing rapidly, especially in countries with a growing share of e-commerce. For example, Amazon has ordered 100,000 Rivian electric vans for the US market [47], while in Europe, DHL and UPS are electrifying their delivery fleets as part of sustainable city logistics programs. LDVs are particularly well suited to electromobility due to their predictable routes, short daily distances, and the possibility of overnight charging.

The heavy-duty vehicle (HDV) segment poses a particular challenge for electromobility due to the weight of the batteries, limited range and high energy demand [57,58]. However, significant progress has been noticeable in recent years. Electric trucks manufactured by Volvo Trucks, Scania and Daimler offer ranges of 250–300 km and are implemented in regional logistics [59] and urban transport [60]. In Germany, tests of the so-called megawatt charging corridors (MCS–Megawatt Charging System) are underway, which are to serve HDV vehicles [9]. For longer distance transport, FCEV technology is more important–e.g., Hyundai XCIENT with hydrogen drive implemented in Switzerland and Germany [61].

Micromobility vehicles, such as scooters, e-bikes or electric scooters [62], are playing an increasingly important role in the structure of urban mobility [63]. According to the report [64], up to 30% of journeys in European cities can be replaced by light vehicles with a range of up to 10 km. Integrating micromobility with public transport can reduce congestion, improve air quality and reduce emissions [65–67]. Numerous cities have introduced public e-scooter rental systems (e.g., Paris, Berlin, Warsaw), although some–such as Paris in 2023–have withdrawn their presence from public spaces due to concerns over safety and regulatory control [68].

2.4. Impact of Electromobility on the Environment and Public Health

It is commonly assumed that electric vehicles do not emit CO_2 during operation. However, a comprehensive assessment of their impact on the environment requires the use of the LCA (Life Cycle Assessment) methodology, covering the entire life cycle of the vehicle–from raw material extraction, through battery production, use, to end-of-life recycling. Well-to-Wheel (WTW) studies show that the carbon footprint of BEVs can be 50–70% lower than that of combustion vehicles–provided that the energy comes from renewable energy sources [69,70].

The study [69] showed that BEV production is more emission-intensive (mainly due to the battery). However, this difference is eliminated after a mileage of about 50,000 km–or as early as 20,000 km when powered by clean energy sources. The production of lithium-ion batteries is associated with intensive consumption of resources: lithium, cobalt, nickel and graphite. These raw materials are predominantly sourced from regions including South America (lithium), the Democratic Republic of Congo (cobalt) and China (graphite), which creates environmental and social challenges. An important aspect at this stage involves research focused on the recycling of used batteries from end-of-life electric vehicles [71–73]. This process is often referred to as the "second life" of batteries and is directly linked to end-of-life battery management [74], battery life cycle assessment (LCA) [75], and the principles of sustainable development [76,77]. An alternative approach under consideration is the use of sodium-ion batteries in electric vehicles.

Electromobility also contributes to improving health conditions in cities. Electric vehicles are much quieter, thereby reducing noise pollution—one of the main factors influencing stress, sleep disorders and cardiovascular diseases [78]. In addition, the lack of exhaust emissions (NO_x, PM10) improves air quality, especially in congested urban areas. In Paris, after the introduction of low-emission zones and an increase in the share of EVs in the city fleet, a 30% reduction in NO_2 concentration was recorded within 3 years [79].

2.5. Electromobility—Transport Infrastructure

The development of transport infrastructure dedicated to electromobility is an essential element of the energy and transport transformation [80]. Accelerating the electrification of the vehicle fleet worldwide would not be possible without the parallel development of an extensive and reliable network of charging points. The lack of such infrastructure would lead to the phenomenon of the so-called "range anxiety", i.e., the fear of users running out of energy during the journey, which would significantly reduce their willingness to choose an electric vehicle. Modern charging infrastructure is not limited to physical stations—it also includes energy sources, interoperable payment systems, charging standards, integration with transmission networks and increasingly advanced tools for managing the charging process, such as smart charging or Vehicle-to-Grid (V2G) technology.

According to data from the International Energy Agency [9], by the end of 2023, there were over 2.7 million public charging points in the world, of which about one million were fast or ultra-fast charging stations. The largest market in terms of the number of points installed is China, which accounts for about 60% of the global charging infrastructure. In Europe, this share is about 25%, while in the United States it is slightly less than 10% [9]. This regional imbalance is one of the main challenges for the unified development of the EV market on a global scale.

Charging infrastructure is categorized into three main types, differing in power and vehicle charging time. The most basic type is home AC chargers with a power of up to 22 kW. They are intended mainly for individual users and residents of multi-family buildings. Charging times with these units typically range from 6 to 12 h, depending on battery capacity and grid conditions. The second type is public DC chargers with a power of 50 to 150 kW, which can be found at shopping centers, petrol stations, transport hubs and in urban areas. They allow 80% battery charging in 30 to 45 min. The fastest solution is ultra-fast DC stations with a power of over 150 kW, which are installed along highways and transport corridors, especially in Europe and North America. Examples include the European network Ionity and the American Electrify America, which offer charging stations with capacities of up to 350 kW [81].

For the needs of heavy transport, the Megawatt Charging System (MCS) technology has been developed. This system enables charging of heavy goods vehicles at power levels up to 1.5 MW, significantly reducing charging times to durations acceptable for logistics operators. In Europe, pilots of this technology are being carried out as part of the Heavy Vehicle Charging Europe project, with the participation of companies such as Scania, MAN, Siemens and ABB [82]. MCS is anticipated to play a critical role in the process of electrification of heavy goods vehicles, where standard charging turns out to be insufficient in terms of both power and transmission infrastructure.

In the case of electric heavy-duty vehicles (eHDVs), a crucial aspect is the development of charging strategies that correspond to the available high-power charging systems designed specifically for heavy vehicles. Political and economic conditions related to the implementation of various charging systems and support for the electric vehicle sector play a significant role in this process [83]. These actions include the integration of medium- and high-power charging vehicles with the electrical grid [84]. The challenges of integration are detailed in the Resources for the Future Report 23-03 [85]. All these challenges ultimately contribute to achieving a zero-emission heavy vehicle fleet [86]. One proposed solution involves the use of swappable batteries, which reduces vehicle downtime during charging. The developed Battery-as-a-Service (BaaS) business model enables electric vehicle buyers to purchase vehicles and lease or subscribe to batteries [87]. Battery swapping systems are currently undergoing extensive testing in China.

An extremely important direction in the development of charging infrastructure are real-time energy management technologies [88,89]. Smart charging is a strategy in which vehicle charging is adjusted to the current state of the power grid, energy availability (including from renewable energy sources) and individual user preferences. This solution allows for the reduction of peak energy demand and increases the share of renewable energy sources in the energy mix. Research conducted in Germany and the Netherlands shows that the implementation of smart charging systems can reduce the costs of investment and operation of the network by 10–20% over a decade [90].

A more advanced form of integrating electromobility with the energy sector is the Vehicle-to-Grid (V2G) technology, whereby electric vehicles function as temporary energy storage devices. V2G enables not only drawing energy from the grid, but also releasing it, e.g., during peak demand hours, which stabilizes the operation of the energy system and reduces the need to build additional energy storage facilities. Analyses [91] show that full integration of V2G technology in Europe could bring savings of EUR 150–200 billion by 2040, while reducing the demand for stationary energy storage facilities.

An effective charging infrastructure also requires a well-thought-out geographical location. Research conducted by [92] indicates that planning charging stations using predictive algorithms and GIS data allows for more effective coverage of the actual needs of users. For example, in Amsterdam, a predictive system was implemented ensuring that charging points are located no further than 400 m from each resident's home, which significantly improved accessibility and user satisfaction.

The literature further indicates that the efficiency of infrastructure depends on factors such as: population density, availability of night charging (especially in multi-family buildings), integration with the public transport network and local availability of energy from renewable sources [46,93]. Only when these conditions are met is it possible to fully use the potential of the electromobility system [94].

However, the development of electromobility infrastructure encounters numerous barriers [95,96]. On the technical side, the most frequently indicated problem is the limited availability of connection power, especially in urban and suburban areas, where the network load is already high [97]. Additionally, the absence of standardized technical standards and communication protocols—different types of plugs, applications and payment systems limit the interoperability of charging stations. Furthermore, local infrastructure congestion is particularly problematic when charging entire fleets of vehicles at the same time, necessitating energy management solutions and investments in the transmission network.

From an economic and regulatory perspective, the development of ultra-fast charging stations is associated with very high costs–the construction of a single point with a capacity of over 150 kW can reach up to EUR 500,000. In many countries, especially developing ones, there is also a lack of public support mechanisms or credit systems for infrastructure investments. The unification of legal standards regarding the availability of information on the location of stations, connection power or charging prices is also insufficient, which prevents effective planning and integration of mobile applications in public transport systems.

At the social level, infrastructure development is met with resistance from residents–especially in housing estates, where the location of stations is associated with aesthetic, legal and land ownership issues. There is also a lack of widely available data on user behavior, their preferences regarding places and hours of charging, which makes it difficult to optimize the location of new stations. As noted by [69], understanding the behavioral patterns of EV users should be the foundation of any effective infrastructure strategy.

3. The Process of Energy Transformation of Transport Infrastructure

3.1. Materials and Methods

The energy transformation of transport infrastructure is directly driven by Regulation 2023/1804 of 13 September 2023 on the development of alternative fuels infrastructure (AFIR) [8], which has become the initiator regulating and stimulating the expansion of transport infrastructure. The analyzed process of energy transformation focuses on point road transport infrastructure located along the core and comprehensive TEN-T network. The examined transport infrastructure is intended for servicing light electric vehicles (eLDV) and electric heavy goods vehicles (eHDV).

The objective of the examined energy transformation process of transport infrastructure results directly from the AFIR regulation and consists in ensuring a balanced development of energy transport infrastructure in all EU Member States along the entire TEN-T network. This article focuses on the concept of energy transformation of road transport infrastructure as outlined by the AFIR regulation and addresses the assessment of the implementation of this transformation process specifically for road transport infrastructure located along the TEN-T network in Poland. The research methodology employed involves a case study analysis of the transformation process and an evaluation of the energy transformation of transport infrastructure along Poland's TEN-T corridors. The empirical study was conducted using a multi-stage process of analysis and assessment of the energy transformation process of transport infrastructure, which consisted of four main stages, namely:

- Stage 1–analysis of the state of knowledge in the field of development of alternative fuel infrastructure (AFIR),
- Stage 2–development of a mathematical model of the energy transformation process of transport infrastructure,

- Stage 3–analysis of the feasibility of planning the electrification process of the bus fleet–a case study for Poland.

The research material was obtained from literature and materials made available by local government organizations, the state-owned Polish Association of New Mobility (*psnm*), and the Polish Automotive Industry Association (PZPM).

3.2. Model of the Energy Transformation Process of Transport Infrastructure

At the stage of research implementation, the process of energy transformation of transport infrastructure is conceptualized as an ordered set of four elements, i.e.,:

$$ETTI = \langle TEN - T, EV, IT, AFIR, AET\rangle \quad (1)$$

where:

ETTI—model energy transformation of transport infrastructure. The structure of the model energy transformation of transport infrastructure is shown in Figure 1 and the elements names in Table 1,
$TEN - T$—Trans-European transport network (TEN-T),
EV—set of electric vehicles,
IT—transport infrastructure,
AFIR—Alternative Fuel Infrastructure Regulation, 2023/1804 [8],
AET—assessment of the energy transformation process of transport infrastructure.

Table 1. Elements of the model *ETTI*.

Elements of the *ETTI*—Model Energy Transformation of Transport Infrastructure			
$TEN - T$	Trans-European transport network	RSt	recharging station
EV	set of electric vehicles	RPo	recharging point
IT	transport infrastructure	Co	connector
$AFIR$	Alternative Fuel Infrastructure Regulation	RP^{eLDV}	recharging pool for eLDV
AET	assessment of the energy transformation process of transport infrastructure	RSt^{eLDV}	recharging station eLDV
CN_1	core network	RPo^{eLDV}	recharging point for eLDV
CN_2	comprehensive network	Co^{eLDV}	connector for eLDV
TC	set of transport corridors within the TEN-T network	RP^{eHDV}	recharging pool for eHDV
$eLDV$	set of light-duty electric vehicles	RSt^{eHDV}	recharging station eHDV
ePC	set of electric passenger car	RPo^{eHDV}	recharging point for eHDV
eDV	set of electric delivery vehicle	Co^{eHDV}	connector for eHDV
$eHDV$	set of heavy-duty electric vehicles	LP	legislative process
BEV	set of battery electric vehicles	PR	purpose of the AFIR
$PHEV$	set of plug-in hybrid electric vehicles	SP	set of specific purpose
HEV	set of hybrid electric vehicles	$DfeLDV$	set of derogations for eLDV
$FCEV$	set of fuel cell electric vehicles	$DfeHDV$	set of derogations for eHDV
RS	recharging systems	AN	TEN-T network assessment indicator
$ITeLDV$	transport infrastructure for LDV	AV	vehicle assessment indicator
$ITeHDV$	transport infrastructure for HDV	IT^{PL}	Polish transport infrastructure assessment indicator–basic assumptions resulting from AFIR
RP	recharging pool	$AFIR^{PL}$	Polish AFIR indicator

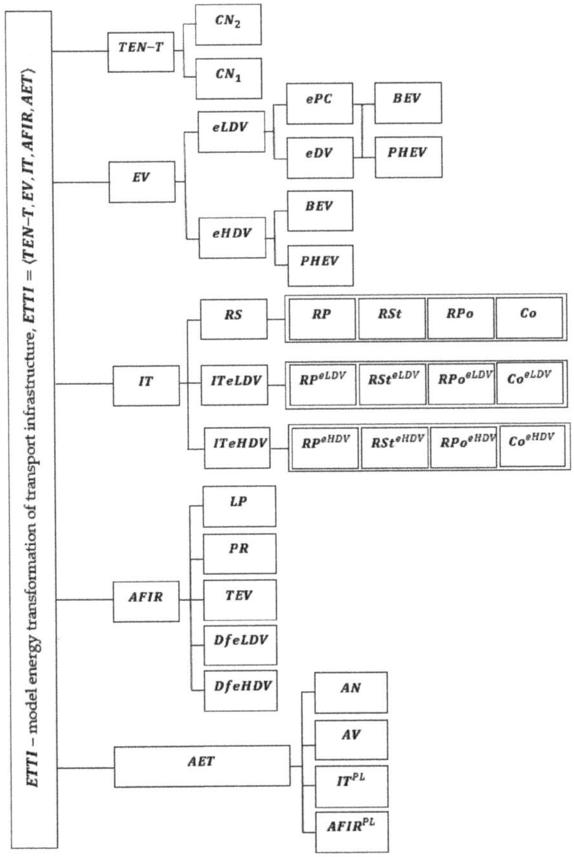

Figure 1. Structure of the model energy transformation of transport infrastructure system.

The energy transformation process of transport infrastructure pertains to point-based transport infrastructure distributed along the Trans-European transport network (TEN-T). The TEN-T network encompasses major transport connections across the EU, including road, rail, air, sea, inland waterway and multimodal transport infrastructure and urban transport hubs. The development of the TEN-T network is regulated by Regulation (EU) 2024/1679 of the European Parliament and of the Council of 13 June 2024 on Union guidelines for the development of the trans-European transport network. The aim of the TEN-T network is to develop the possibilities of moving people and transporting goods within the EU. In this way, the TEN-T is to strengthen the social, economic and territorial cohesion of the EU countries. In addition, the network aims to establish an efficient cross-border transport system that will be free of gaps, bottlenecks, and missing transport connections. The TEN-T network is intended to mitigate the negative environmental impacts of transport on the natural environment and increase transport safety within the EU countries. The TEN-T network is composed of two main elements, distinguishing between two types of networks, namely:

$$TEN-T = \{CN_1, CN_2\} \tag{2}$$

where:

CN_1—core network,

CN_2—comprehensive network.

The TEN-T core network is a set of transport connections of strategic importance to the EU. It includes the most critical transport routes essential for the functioning of the single market and trade within the EU. In contrast, the TEN-T comprehensive network is a set of all TEN-T infrastructure, including both the core network and additional regional and national transport connections. In principle, the comprehensive network is to ensure the accessibility and connectivity of all regions in the EU and thus support and develop these regions.

Within the distinguished types of TEN-T networks, nine European transport corridors operate, i.e.,:

$$TC = \{tc_1, tc_2, tc_3, tc_4, tc_5, tc_6, tc_7, tc_8, tc_9\} \quad (3)$$

where:

TC—set of transport corridors within the TEN-T network,
tc_1—Atlantic corridor,
tc_2—North Sea–Rhine—Mediterranean corridor,
tc_3—North Sea—Baltic corridor,
tc_4—Scandinavian—Mediterranean corridor,
tc_5—Baltic Sea–Adriatic Sea corridor,
tc_6—Rhine—Danube corridor,
tc_7—Mediterranean corridor,
tc_8—Western Balkans—Eastern Mediterranean corridor,
tc_9—Baltic Sea–Black Sea—Aegean Sea corridor.

When analyzing the process of energy transformation of transport infrastructure, it is essential to consider the types of vehicles for which this infrastructure is being developed. AFIR specifically addresses transport infrastructure intended for electric vehicles, i.e.,:

$$EV = \langle eLDV, eHDV \rangle \quad (4)$$

where:

$eLDV$—set of light-duty electric vehicles (eLDV), which includes vehicles of categories M1 (passenger cars) and N1 (vehicles with a permissible total weight of up to 3.5 tons; delivery vans),

$$eLDV = \langle ePC, eDV \rangle \quad (5)$$

ePC—set of electric passenger car,
eDV—set of electric delivery vehicle,
$eHDV$—set of heavy-duty electric vehicles (eHDV), which includes vehicles of categories N2 (vehicles with a permissible total weight from 3.5 tons to 12 tons) and N3 (vehicles with a permissible total weight of over 12 tons; trucks).

Within the individual eLDV and eHDV vehicle groups, fully electric vehicles, hybrid vehicles, and fuel cell vehicles are distinguished, i.e.,:

$$eLDV = \langle BEV, PHEV \rangle; \qquad eHDV = \langle BEV, PHEV \rangle \quad (6)$$

where:

BEV—set of battery electric vehicles,
$PHEV$—set of plug-in hybrid electric vehicles.

Additionally, within the groups of LDV and HDV vehicles, hybrid electric vehicles and fuel cell electric vehicles are distinguished, i.e.,:

$$LDV = \langle HEV, FCEV \rangle; \qquad HDV = \langle HEV, FCEV \rangle \tag{7}$$

where:

HEV—set of hybrid electric vehicles,
FCEV—set of fuel cell electric vehicles.

The energy transformation implemented under the AFIR regulation refers to road transport infrastructure and concerns point elements of the analyzed infrastructure. In the study, the transport infrastructure was presented in the form of an ordered triplet, i.e.,:

$$IT = \langle RS, ITeLDV, ITeHDV \rangle \tag{8}$$

where:

RS—recharging systems,
ITeLDV—transport infrastructure for LDVs,
ITeHDV—transport infrastructure for HDVs.

The energy transformation of road transport infrastructure implemented in accordance with the AFIR assumptions, takes into account a group of elements important for this process. The charging system consists of four elements involved in the process of charging electric vehicles (Figure 2), i.e.,:

$$RS = \langle RP, RSt, RPo, Co \rangle \tag{9}$$

where:

RP—recharging pool. A recharging pool consists of one or more recharging stations located at a specific sit, which may include dedicated adjacent parking spaces [98]. A recharging pool can contain several recharging stations. According to AFIR, a recharging pool refers to one or more recharging stations at a specific location [8].
RSt—recharging station (also referred to as recharging pole, recharging dock, electric vehicle charging station). A recharging station is a physical object with one or more recharging points, sharing a common user identification interface [8]. According to AFIR, a recharging station is defined as a physical installation at a designated location, consisting of one or more recharging points [8].
RPo—recharging point (also referred to as recharging position, electric vehicle supply equipment). Electric energy is delivered through a recharging point. A recharging point may have one or several connectors (outlets or plugs) to accommodate different connector types [98]. According to the AFIR regulation, a recharging point station or pool dedicated to eLDV refers a recharging point, station or pool intended for the recharging of eLDV, due to the specific design of the connectors/plugs or the design of the parking space adjacent to the recharging point, station or pool, or both [8]. According to AFIR, a recharging point, station or pool dedicated to eHDV refers to a recharging point, station or pool intended for the recharging of eHDV, either due to the specific design of the connectors/plugs or the layout of the adjacent parking space, station pool, or both [8].
Co–connector. A connector is the physical interface between the recharging station and the electric vehicle through which the electric energy is delivered [98]. According to AFIR, a connector refers to the physical interface between the recharging or refueling point and the vehicle through which the fuel or electric energy is exchanged [8].

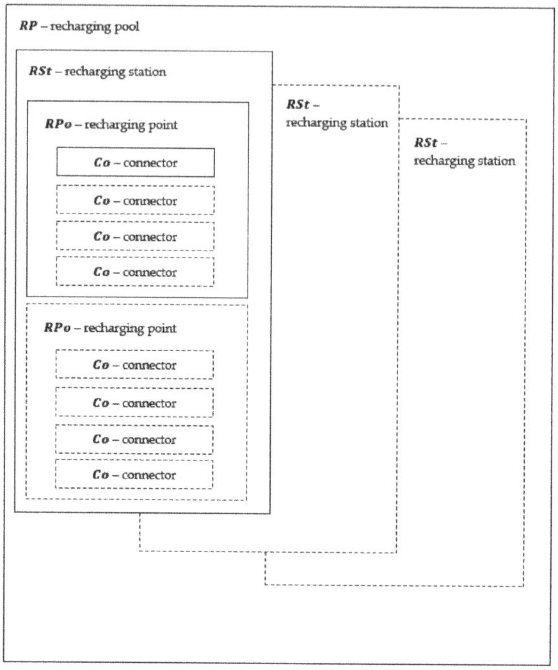

Figure 2. Components of an electric vehicle charging system.

Taking into account the characteristics of the vehicles, transport infrastructure is identified separately for eLDVs and eHDVs. The respective infrastructures are designated as follows:

$$ITeLDV = \left\langle RP^{eLDV}, RSt^{eLDV}, RPo^{eLDV}, Co^{eLDV} \right\rangle \quad (10)$$

where:

RP^{eLDV}—recharging pool for eLDVs,
RSt^{eLDV}—recharging station for eLDVs,
RPo^{eLDV}—recharging point for eLDVs,
Co^{eLDV}—connector for eLDVs.

$$ITeHDV = \left\langle RP^{eHDV}, RSt^{eHDV}, RPo^{eHDV}, Co^{eHDV} \right\rangle \quad (11)$$

where:

RP^{eHDV}—recharging pool for eHDVs,
RSt^{eHDV}—recharging station eHDVs,
RPo^{eHDV}—recharging point for eHDVs,
Co^{eHDV}—connector for eHDVs.

The examined process of energy transformation in transport infrastructure directly stems from the assumptions of the AFIR regulation, which has become a factor regulating and stimulating the expansion of transport infrastructure. In the research process, the AFIR regulation was structured into five ordered elements, i.e.,:

$$AFIR = \langle LP, PR, TEV, DfeLDV, DfeHDV \rangle \quad (12)$$

where:

LP—legislative process,
PR—purpose of the AFIR regulation,
SP—set of specific purpose,
DfeLDV—set of derogations for eLDVs,
DfeHDV—set of derogations for eHDVs.

In the legislative process of the AFIR regulation four stages corresponding to individual decisions of the EU Council can be identified, namely:

$$LP = \{lp_1, lp_2, lp_3, lp_4\} \tag{13}$$

where:

lp_1—stage 1: adoption by the EU Council of the AFIR regulation, 25 July 2023,
lp_2—stage 2: publication of the AFIR regulation in the EU Official Journal, 22 September 2023,
lp_3—stage 3: entry into force of the AFIR regulation, 12 October 2023,
lp_4—stage 4: obligation to apply the AFIR regulation, 13 April 2024.

For EU Member States, Stage 4 is important as the AFIR regulation has been in force since 13 April 2024. For the purposes of implementing the regulation in EU Member States, the AFIR objective has been defined, i.e.,:

$$\boldsymbol{AFIR} \rightarrow \boldsymbol{PR} \tag{14}$$

where:

PR—the aim of AFIR is to ensure the even development of alternative fuels infrastructure in all EU Member States across the entire TEN-T network.

The research focused exclusively on the development of alternative fuel infrastructure, which is electricity. Thus, the AFIR goal is the even development of transport infrastructure for charging electric vehicles. For the purposes of achieving the goal, specific goals were defined for the charging infrastructure of electric vehicles, tailored to individual groups of eLDV and eHDV vehicles. The set of specific goals takes the following form:

$$\boldsymbol{SP} = \left\langle \boldsymbol{PO}^{eLDV}, \boldsymbol{MRP}^{eLDV}_{CN_1}, \boldsymbol{MRP}^{eLDV}_{CN_2}, \boldsymbol{MRP}^{eHDV}_{CN_1}, \boldsymbol{MRP}^{eHDV}_{CN_2} \right\rangle \tag{15}$$

where:

$\boldsymbol{PO}^{eLDV}$—power output of publicly accessible recharging stations dedicated to eLDVs,

$$\boldsymbol{PO}^{eLDV} = \left\{ \boldsymbol{po}^{eLDV}_1, \boldsymbol{po}^{eLDV}_2, \boldsymbol{po}^{eLDV}_3, \boldsymbol{po}^{eLDV}_4 \right\} \tag{16}$$

$\boldsymbol{po}^{eLDV}_1$—for each BEV registered in the territory of a given EU Member State, a total power output of at least 1.3 kW is provided through publicly accessible recharging stations,
$\boldsymbol{po}^{eLDV}_2$—for each PHEV registered in the territory of a given EU Member State, a total power output of at least 0.8 kW is provided through publicly accessible recharging stations,
$\boldsymbol{po}^{eLDV}_3$—the obligation for Member States to fulfil the above requirements at the end of each year, starting from 2024,
$\boldsymbol{po}^{eLDV}_4$—in the event that the share of eLDVs manufactured in a given country reaches at least 15%, the following cases are possible: (1) the possibility for the state to prove that further application of the requirement is disadvantageous and unjustified, (2) the possibility of obtaining permission from the European Commission to apply lower requirements, (3) the deadline for issuing a decision by the EC is six months,

$MRP^{eLDV}_{CN_1}$—minimum coverage of publicly accessible recharging points dedicated to eLDVs—along the TEN-T core road network CN_1,

$$MRP^{eLDV}_{CN_1} = \left\{ mrp^{eLDV}_{2025;1}, mrp^{eLDV}_{2025;2}, mrp^{eLDV}_{2025;3}, mrp^{eLDV}_{2027;4} \right\} \tag{17}$$

$mrp^{eLDV}_{2025;1}$—by 31 December 2025, along of the length CN_1, each recharging pool must offer a power output of at least 400 kW and includes at least one recharging point with an individual power output of at least 150 kW,
$mrp^{eLDV}_{2025;2}$—by 31 December 2025, publicly accessible recharging points must be deployed in each direction of travel,
$mrp^{eLDV}_{2025;3}$—by 31 December 2025, the maximum distance between publicly accessible recharging points must not exceed 60 km,
$mrp^{eLDV}_{2027;4}$—by 31 December 2027, along of the length CN_1, each recharging pool must offer a power output of at least 600 kW and include at least two recharging points with an individual power output of at least 150 kW,
$MRP^{eLDV}_{CN_2}$—minimum coverage of publicly accessible recharging points dedicated to eLDVs—along the TEN-T comprehensive road network CN_2,

$$MRP^{eLDV}_{CN_2} = \left\{ mp^{eLDV}_{2027;1}, mp^{eLDV}_{2027;2}, mp^{eLDV}_{2027;3}, mp^{eLDV}_{2030;4}, mp^{eLDV}_{2035;5} \right\} \tag{18}$$

$mp^{eLDV}_{2027;1}$—by 31 December 2027, along at least 50% of the length CN_2, each recharging pool must offer a power output of at least 300 kW and include at least one recharging point with an individual power output of at least 150 kW,
$mp^{eLDV}_{2027;2}$—by 31 December 2027, publicly accessible recharging points must be deployed in each direction of travel,
$mp^{eLDV}_{2027;3}$—by 31 December 2027, the maximum distance between publicly accessible recharging points shall not exceed 60 km,
$mp^{eLDV}_{2030;4}$—by 31 December 2030, along at least 100% of the length CN_2, each recharging pool must offer a power output of at least 300 kW and include at least one recharging point with an individual power output of at least 150 kW,
$mp^{eLDV}_{2035;5}$—by 31 December 2035, along at least 100% of the length CN_2, each recharging pool must offer a power output of at least 600 kW and include at least two recharging points with an individual power output of at least 150 kW,
$MRP^{eHDV}_{CN_1}$—minimum coverage of publicly accessible recharging points dedicated to eHDVs—along the TEN-T core road network CN_1,

$$MRP^{eHDV}_{CN_1} = \left\{ mrp^{eHDV}_{2025;1}, mrp^{eHDV}_{2025;2}, mrp^{eHDV}_{2027;3}, mrp^{eHDV}_{2030;4}, mrp^{eHDV}_{2030;5} \right\} \tag{19}$$

$mrp^{eHDV}_{2025;1}$—by 31 December 2025, along at least 15% of the length CN_1, publicly accessible recharging pools must offer a power output of at least 1400 kW and includes at least one recharging point with an individual power output of at least 350 kW,
$mrp^{eHDV}_{2025;2}$—by 31 December 2025, publicly accessible recharging points must be deployed in each direction of travel,
$mrp^{eHDV}_{2027;3}$—by 31 December 2027, along at least 50% of the length CN_1, publicly accessible recharging pools must offer a power output of at least 2800 kW and include at least two recharging points with an individual power output of at least 350 kW,
$mrp^{eHDV}_{2030;4}$—by 31 December 2030, along of the length CN_1, publicly accessible recharging pools must offer a power output of at least 3600 kW and include at least two recharging points with an individual power output of at least 350 kW,

$mp^{eHDV}_{2030;5}$—by 31 December 2030, the maximum distance between publicly accessible recharging pools shall not exceed 60 km,
$MRP^{eHDV}_{CN_2}$—minimum coverage of publicly accessible recharging points dedicated to eHDVs—along the TEN-T comprehensive road network CN_2,

$$MRP^{eHDV}_{CN_2} = \left\{ mp^{eHDV}_{2025;1}, mp^{eHDV}_{2025;2}, mp^{eHDV}_{2027;3}, mp^{eHDV}_{2030;4}, mp^{eHDV}_{2030;5} \right\} \tag{20}$$

$mp^{eHDV}_{2025;1}$—by 31 December 2025, along at least 15% of the length CN_2, publicly accessible recharging pools must offer a power output of at least 1400 kW and include at least one recharging point with an individual power output of at least 350 kW,
$mp^{eHDV}_{2025;2}$—by 31 December 2025, publicly accessible recharging points must be deployed in each direction of travel,
$mp^{eHDV}_{2027;3}$—by 31 December 2027, along at least 50% of the length CN_2, publicly accessible recharging pools must offer a power output of at least 1400 kW and include at least one recharging point with an individual power output of at least 350 kW,
$mp^{eHDV}_{2030;4}$—by 31 December 2030, along of the length CN_2, publicly accessible recharging pools must offer a power output of at least 1500 kW and include at least one recharging point with an individual power output of at least 350 kW,
$mp^{eHDV}_{2030;5}$—by 31 December 2030, the maximum distance between publicly accessible recharging pools shall not exceed 60 km.

The AFIR regulation also specifies the permissible derogations that EU member states may introduce during the energy transformation of transport infrastructure. The derogations are provided separately for each group of electric vehicles. In the case of eLDVs, the set of permissible derogations takes the following form:

$$DfeLDV = \{dfeldv_1, dfeldv_2, dfeldv_3\} \tag{21}$$

where:

$dfeldv_1$—derogation 1 for eLDVs.
By way of derogation from the above, along the TEN-T network, where the average daily traffic is less than 8500 LDVs and there is no socio-economic justification for infrastructure development, a recharging pool for eLDV (RP^{eLDV}) serving both directions of travel may be established.
$dfeldv_2$—derogation 2 for eLDVs.
By way of derogation along the TEN-T network, where the average daily traffic is less than 8500 LDVs and there is no socio-economic justification for infrastructure development, the total output capacity of the recharging pool for eLDV (RP^{eLDV}) may be reduced by a maximum of 50%.
$dfeldv_3$—derogation 3 for eLDVs.
By way of derogation along the TEN-T network, where the average daily traffic is less than 3000 LDVs, the maximum distance between recharging pools for eLDVs (RP^{eLDV}) may be extended from 60 km to 100 km. Condition: appropriate distance markings between recharging pools for eLDVs (RP^{eLDV}) must be provided.

However, in relation to eHDVs, the set of permissible deviations is a set that contains three specified deviations, i.e.:

$$DfeHDV = \{dfehdv_1, dfehdv_2, dfehdv_3\} \tag{22}$$

where:

$dfehdv_1$—derogation 1 for eHDVs.
By way of derogation from the above, along the TEN-T network, where the average daily traffic is less than 2000 HDVs and there is no socio-economic justification for infrastructure development, a recharging pool for eHDVs ($\boldsymbol{RP^{eHDV}}$) serving both directions of travel may be established.
$dfehdv_2$—derogation 2 for eHDVs.
By way of derogation along the TEN-T network, where the average daily traffic is less than 2000 HDVs and there is no socio-economic justification for infrastructure development, the total output capacity of the recharging pool for eHDVs ($\boldsymbol{RP^{eHDV}}$) may be reduced by a maximum of 50%.
$dfehdv_3$—derogation 3 for eHDVs.
By way of derogation along the TEN-T network, where the average daily traffic is less than 3000 HDVs, the maximum distance between recharging pools for eHDVs ($\boldsymbol{RP^{eHDV}}$) may be extended from 60 km to 100 km. Condition: appropriate distance markings between recharging pools for eHDVs ($\boldsymbol{RP^{eHDV}}$) must be provided.

The assessment of the energy transformation process of road transport infrastructure will be carried out based on defined assessment indicators. For the purposes of the research, four groups of assessment indicators have been defined, i.e.,:

$$\boldsymbol{AET} = \left\langle \boldsymbol{AN}, \boldsymbol{AV}, \boldsymbol{IT^{PL}}, \boldsymbol{AFIR^{PL}} \right\rangle \tag{23}$$

where:

$\boldsymbol{AN}$—TEN-T network assessment indicator,

$$\boldsymbol{AN} = \left\langle \boldsymbol{AN^{TEN-T}}, \boldsymbol{AN^{CN_1}}, \boldsymbol{AN^{CN_2}} \right\rangle \tag{24}$$

$\boldsymbol{AN^{TEN-T}}$—core network assessment indicator,

$$\boldsymbol{AN^{TEN-T}} \to \mathbb{N} \cup \{\boldsymbol{0}\} \tag{25}$$

$\boldsymbol{AN^{CN_1}}$—core network assessment indicator,

$$\boldsymbol{AN^{CN_1}} \to \mathbb{N} \cup \{\boldsymbol{0}\} \tag{26}$$

$\boldsymbol{AN^{CN_2}}$—comprehensive network assessment indicator,

$$\boldsymbol{AN^{CN_2}} \to \mathbb{N} \cup \{\boldsymbol{0}\} \tag{27}$$

$\boldsymbol{AV}$—vehicle assessment indicator,

$$\boldsymbol{AV} = \left\langle \boldsymbol{AV^{BEV}}, \boldsymbol{AV^{eLDV}}, \boldsymbol{BEV^{ePC}}, \boldsymbol{PHEV^{ePC}}, \boldsymbol{HEV^{PC}}, \boldsymbol{BEV^{eDV}}, \boldsymbol{HEV^{DV}}, \boldsymbol{AV^{eHDV}}, \boldsymbol{BEV^{eHDV}} \right\rangle \tag{28}$$

$\boldsymbol{AV^{BEV}}$—BEV assessment indicator; number of BEVs (number of eLDVs + number of eHDVs),

$$\boldsymbol{AV^{BEV}} \to \mathbb{N} \cup \{\boldsymbol{0}\} \tag{29}$$

$\boldsymbol{AV^{eLDV}}$—eLDV assessment indicator; number of eLDVs (number of electric passenger cars + number of electric delivery vehicles),

$$\boldsymbol{AV^{eLDV}} \to \mathbb{N} \cup \{\boldsymbol{0}\} \tag{30}$$

BEV^{ePC}—BEV assessment indicator; number of electric passenger cars from the BEVs,

$$BEV^{ePC} \rightarrow \mathbb{N} \cup \{0\} \quad (31)$$

$PHEV^{ePC}$—PHEV assessment indicator; number of electric passenger cars from the PHEVs,

$$PHEV^{ePC} \rightarrow \mathbb{N} \cup \{0\} \quad (32)$$

HEV^{PC}—HEV assessment indicator; number of passenger cars from the HEVs,

$$HEV^{PC} \rightarrow \mathbb{N} \cup \{0\} \quad (33)$$

BEV^{eDV}—BEV assessment indicator; number of electric delivery vehicles from the BEVs,

$$PHEV^{ePC} \rightarrow \mathbb{N} \cup \{0\} \quad (34)$$

HEV^{DV}—HEV assessment indicator; number of delivery vehicles from the HEVs,

$$HEV^{DV} \rightarrow \mathbb{N} \cup \{0\} \quad (35)$$

AV^{eHDV}—eHDV assessment indicator; number of eHDVs,

$$AV^{eHDV} \rightarrow \mathbb{N} \cup \{0\} \quad (36)$$

BEV^{eHDV}—BEV assessment indicator; number of eHDVs,

$$BEV^{eHDV} \rightarrow \mathbb{N} \cup \{0\} \quad (37)$$

IT^{PL}—Polish transport infrastructure assessment indicator–basic assumptions resulting from AFIR,

$$IT^{PL} = \left\langle IT^{PL}_{eLDV}, IT^{PL}_{eHDV} \right\rangle \quad (38)$$

IT^{PL}_{eLDV}—Polish transport infrastructure assessment indicator for eLDVs– basic assumptions resulting from AFIR along the TEN-T network,
IT^{PL}_{eHDV}—Polish transport infrastructure assessment indicator for eHDVs—basic assumptions resulting from AFIR along the TEN-T network,
$AFIR^{PL}$—Polish AFIR indicator,

$$AFIR^{PL} = \left\{ afir^{PL}_1, afir^{PL}_2, \ldots, afir^{PL}_i \right\},\ i \in \mathbb{N} \cup \{0\} \quad (39)$$

4. Energy Transformation of Road Transport Infrastructure—A Case Study

The case study will focus on evaluating the energy transformation process of road transport infrastructure based on the AFIR regulation, implemented within Poland. It should be noted that Poland, as a member state of the EU, is obligated to full fill the requirements set forth in the AFIR regulation. It should also be noted that two transport corridors passing through Poland are integral components of the TEN-T network. These corridors connect the Baltic Sea with the North Sea and the Baltic Sea with the Adriatic Sea, representing a significant element of trade exchange within Europe. This is particularly important for landlocked countries such as the Czech Republic, Slovakia, and Hungary.

Consequently, the analysis and assessment of the energy transition of road transport infrastructure is considered crucial for the functioning and implementation of transport within the TEN-T network.

The starting point of the study was the identification of the parameters that Poland must meet in order to comply with the requirements of the AFIR regulation. For transport infrastructure on Polish roads intended for eLDV vehicles, the requirements are specified in Table 2. In turn, the requirements for transport infrastructure intended for eHDV vehicles are presented in Table 3.

Table 2. AFIR requirements for eLDV infrastructure on Polish roads.

<table>
<tr><th rowspan="2">Parameter</th><th colspan="10">Deadline</th></tr>
<tr><th>2025</th><th colspan="3">2027</th><th colspan="3">2030</th><th colspan="3">2035</th></tr>
<tr><td rowspan="2">Minimum number of charging zones along the TEN-T network [pcs.]</td><td rowspan="2">128</td><td rowspan="2">190</td><td>CN_1</td><td>128</td><td rowspan="2">252</td><td>CN_1</td><td>128</td><td rowspan="2">252</td><td>CN_1</td><td>128</td></tr>
<tr><td>CN_2</td><td>62</td><td>CN_2</td><td>124</td><td>CN_2</td><td>124</td></tr>
<tr><td>Minimum total power output of all charging stations along the TEN-T network [MW]</td><td>51.2</td><td colspan="3">95.4</td><td colspan="3">114</td><td colspan="3">151.2</td></tr>
<tr><td>Installed charging power in relations to the number of BEV and PHEV vehicles [MW]</td><td>412.4</td><td colspan="3">859.5</td><td colspan="3">1690.1</td><td colspan="3">3728</td></tr>
</table>

CN_1—core network TEN-T, CN_2—comprehensive network TEN-T.

Table 3. AFIR requirements for eHDV infrastructure on Polish roads.

<table>
<tr><th rowspan="2">Parameter</th><th colspan="5">Deadline</th></tr>
<tr><th>2025</th><th>2027</th><th colspan="3">2030</th></tr>
<tr><td rowspan="2">Minimum number of charging zones along the TEN-T network [pcs.]</td><td rowspan="2">20
(every 120 km)</td><td rowspan="2">64
(every 120 km)</td><td rowspan="2">202</td><td>CN_1</td><td>128</td></tr>
<tr><td>CN_2</td><td>74</td></tr>
<tr><td>Minimum total power of all charging stations [MW]</td><td>28</td><td>92.4–179.2</td><td colspan="3">571.8</td></tr>
</table>

CN_1—core network TEN-T, CN_2—comprehensive network TEN-T.

The evaluation of the energy transition process of transport infrastructure has been divided into four stages:

- Stage 1: TEN-T network assessment indicator in Poland.
- Stage 2: Vehicle assessment indicator in Poland.
- Stage 3: Polish transport infrastructure assessment indicator.
- Stage 4: Polish AFIR indicator.

(1) TEN-T network assessment indicator in Poland

The AFIR regulation pertains to infrastructure deployed along the TEN-T network. At the initial stage, the TEN-T network running through Poland will be evaluated. Two transport corridors pass through Poland, namely: tc_3–North Sea–Baltic Corridor and tc_5–Baltic Sea–Adriatic Sea corridor. The evaluation will focus on the TEN-T network located within Poland, with network length in both directions being a key parameter (see Table 4).

Table 4. TEN-T network assessment indicator.

	$AN^{TEN\text{-}T}$	AN^{CN_1}	AN^{CN_2}
Length of the TEN-T network in both directions	15,002 km	7624 km	7378 km

(2) Vehicle assessment indicator in Poland

The alternative fuel infrastructure identified in the AFIR regulation is linked to the number of registered electric vehicles in each EU member state. To meet this requirement, an assessment of the structure of electric vehicles registered in Poland was conducted. The evaluation process covered the period from 31 December 2020, to 31 May 2025. The assessment results are presented in Tables 5–10.

Table 5. Vehicle assessment indicator in Poland—as of 31 December 2020.

		Assessment as of 31 December 2020	
Type of Vehicle	**Number of Vehicles [pcs.]**	**Change Indicator [%]**	
AV^{BEV}	10,880	-	-
BEV^{ePC}	10,041	-	-
$PHEV^{ePC}$	8834	-	-
BEV^{eDV}	839	-	-
BEV^{eHDV}			
HEV^{PC}	191,596	-	-
HEV^{DV}			

Table 6. Vehicle assessment indicator in Poland—as of 31 December 2021.

		Assessment as of 31 December 2021	
Type of Vehicle	**Number of Vehicles [pcs.]**	**Change Indicator [%]**	
AV^{BEV}	20,452	+87	↑
BEV^{ePC}	18,795	+87	↑
$PHEV^{ePC}$	19,206	+117	↑
BEV^{eDV}	1657	+97	↑
BEV^{eHDV}			
HEV^{PC}	325,136	+69	↑
HEV^{DV}			

Table 7. Vehicle assessment indicator in Poland—as of 31 December 2022.

		Assessment as of 31 December 2022	
Type of Vehicle	**Number of Vehicles [pcs.]**	**Change Indicator [%]**	
AV^{BEV}	34,384	+68	↑
BEV^{ePC}	31,249	+66	↑
$PHEV^{ePC}$	30,321	+57	↑
BEV^{eDV}	3135	+89	↑
BEV^{eHDV}			
HEV^{PC}	475,807	+46	↑
HEV^{DV}			

Table 8. Vehicle assessment indicator in Poland—as of 31 December 2023.

<table>
<tr><th></th><th colspan="2"></th><th colspan="3">Assessment as of 31 December 2023</th></tr>
<tr><th>Type of Vehicle</th><th colspan="2">Number of Vehicles [pcs.]</th><th colspan="3">Change Indicator [%]</th></tr>
<tr><td>AV^{BEV}</td><td colspan="2">57,091</td><td colspan="2">+66</td><td>↑</td></tr>
<tr><td>BEV^{ePC}</td><td colspan="2">51,211</td><td colspan="2">+63</td><td>↑</td></tr>
<tr><td>$PHEV^{ePC}$</td><td colspan="2">47,137</td><td colspan="2">+55</td><td>↑</td></tr>
<tr><td>BEV^{eDV}</td><td rowspan="2">5880</td><td>5767</td><td rowspan="2">+87</td><td>-</td><td rowspan="2">↑</td></tr>
<tr><td>BEV^{eHDV}</td><td>113</td><td>-</td></tr>
<tr><td>HEV^{PC}</td><td colspan="2" rowspan="2">679,637</td><td colspan="2" rowspan="2">+42</td><td rowspan="2">↑</td></tr>
<tr><td>HEV^{DV}</td></tr>
</table>

Table 9. Vehicle assessment indicator in Poland—as of 31 December 2024.

<table>
<tr><th></th><th colspan="2"></th><th colspan="3">Assessment as of 31 December 2024</th></tr>
<tr><th>Type of Vehicle</th><th colspan="2">Number of Vehicles [pcs.]</th><th colspan="3">Change Indicator [%]</th></tr>
<tr><td>AV^{BEV}</td><td colspan="2">80,732</td><td colspan="2">+41</td><td>↑</td></tr>
<tr><td>BEV^{ePC}</td><td colspan="2">72,589</td><td colspan="2">+41</td><td>↑</td></tr>
<tr><td>$PHEV^{ePC}$</td><td colspan="2">68,866</td><td colspan="2">+46</td><td>↑</td></tr>
<tr><td>BEV^{eDV}</td><td rowspan="2">8143</td><td>7949</td><td rowspan="2">+38</td><td>+37</td><td rowspan="2">↑</td></tr>
<tr><td>BEV^{eHDV}</td><td>121</td><td>+7</td></tr>
<tr><td>HEV^{PC}</td><td colspan="2" rowspan="2">954,340</td><td colspan="2" rowspan="2">+40</td><td rowspan="2">↑</td></tr>
<tr><td>HEV^{DV}</td></tr>
</table>

Table 10. Vehicle assessment indicator in Poland—as of 31 May 2025.

<table>
<tr><th></th><th colspan="2"></th><th colspan="3">Assessment as of 31 May 2025</th></tr>
<tr><th>Type of Vehicle</th><th colspan="2">Number of Vehicles [pcs.]</th><th colspan="3">Change Indicator [%]</th></tr>
<tr><td>AV^{BEV}</td><td colspan="2">94,306</td><td colspan="2">+16</td><td>↑</td></tr>
<tr><td>BEV^{ePC}</td><td colspan="2">85,300</td><td colspan="2">+17</td><td>↑</td></tr>
<tr><td>$PHEV^{ePC}$</td><td colspan="2">85,413</td><td colspan="2">+24</td><td>↑</td></tr>
<tr><td>BEV^{eDV}</td><td rowspan="2">9006</td><td>8757</td><td rowspan="2">+10</td><td>+10</td><td rowspan="2">↑</td></tr>
<tr><td>BEV^{eHDV}</td><td>249</td><td>+105</td></tr>
<tr><td>HEV^{PC}</td><td colspan="2" rowspan="2">1,096,799</td><td colspan="2" rowspan="2">+14</td><td rowspan="2">↑</td></tr>
<tr><td>HEV^{DV}</td></tr>
</table>

The assessment of the electric vehicle fleet structure at the end of 2020 showed that 10,880 Battery Electric Vehicles (BEVs) were in operation in Poland. The structure of all types of electric vehicles as of the end of 2020 is presented in Table 5.

The assessment of the electric vehicle fleet structure at the end of 2021 indicated that 20,452 BEVs were in operation in Poland, representing an approximate 87% increase compared to 2020. The structure of all types of electric vehicles as of the end of 2021 is presented in Table 6.

The assessment of the electric vehicle fleet structure at the end of 2022 revealed that 34,384 BEVs were in operation in Poland, representing an approximate 68% increase compared to 2021. The structure of all types of electric vehicles as of the end of 2022 is presented in Table 7.

The assessment of the electric vehicle fleet structure at the end of 2023 showed that 57,091 BEVs were in operation in Poland, representing an approximate 66% increase compared to 2022. In 2023, the evaluation of the electric vehicle fleet included a classification into electric delivery vehicles (eDV) and heavy-duty electric vehicles (eHDV) (Table 8). It should be noted that only 113 eHDVs were in operation in Poland in 2023. The structure of electric vehicles at the end of 2023 is presented in Table 8.

The assessment of the electric vehicle fleet structure at the end of 2024 showed that 80,732 BEVs were in operation in Poland, representing an approximate 41% increase compared to 2023. An increase of 37% was also noted in the number of eDVs, while the number of eHDVs increased by only 7%. It should be emphasized that the annual growth rate of vehicle numbers for the respective groups, ranging from 38% to 46%, has slowed down. In 2023, the growth dynamics for the number of electric vehicles in the respective groups ranged from 42% to 87%. The structure of electric vehicles at the end of 2024 is presented in Table 9.

The assessment of the electric vehicle fleet structure at the end of May 2025 showed that 94,306 BEVs were in operation in Poland, representing an approximate 16% increase compared to 2024. It should be noted that these are partial data collected at the end of May 2025. An important piece of information at this stage is the sharp increase in the number of eHDVs from 121 to 249, which represents a 105.79% growth. The structure of electric vehicles at the end of May 2025 is presented in Table 10.

(3) Polish transport infrastructure assessment indicator

The assessment of the transport infrastructure for electric vehicle charging in Poland includes elements of the *RS* (recharging systems). The evaluation process was conducted from 31 December 2020, to 31 May 2025. The assessment results are presented in Tables 11–16.

Table 11. Polish transport infrastructure assessment—as of 31 December 2020.

		Assessment as of 31 December 2020	
Element of the *RS* Recharging System		**Number of Stations/Points [pcs.]**	**Change Indicator [%]**
	RSt	1364	-
RSt	AC (alternating current)	912	-
	DC (direct current)	452	-
	RPo	2641	-
	Structure of connectors		
	Type of connector	Percentage structure [%]	-
Co	Type 1 and 2	64	-
	CHdeMO	15	-
	CCS Combo 2	15	-
	Tesla	6	-

Table 12. Polish transport infrastructure assessment—as of 31 December 2021.

		Assessment as of 31 December 2021		
Element of the *RS* Recharging System		**Number of Stations/Points [pcs.]**	**Change Indicator [%]**	
	RSt	1932	+41	↑
RSt	AC (alternating current)	1345	+47	↑
	DC (direct current)	587	+29	↑

Table 12. *Cont.*

Element of the *RS* Recharging System		Number of Stations/Points [pcs.]	Change Indicator [%]	
		Assessment as of 31 December 2021		
RPo		3784	+43	↑
Structure of connectors				
Type of connector		Percentage structure [%]		
Co	Type 1 and 2	69	-	↑
	CHdeMO	13	-	↓
	CCS Combo 2	14	-	↓
	Tesla	4	-	↓

Table 13. Polish transport infrastructure assessment—as of 31 December 2022.

Element of the *RS* Recharging System		Number of Stations/Points [pcs.]	Change Indicator [%]	
		Assessment as of 31 December 2022		
RSt		2565	+32	↑
RSt	AC (alternating current)	1813	+34	↑
	DC (direct current)	752	+28	↑
RPo		5016	+32	↑
Structure of connectors				
Type of connector		Percentage structure [%]		
Co	Type 1 and 2	72	-	↑
	CHdeMO	11	-	↓
	CCS Combo 2	15	-	↑
	Tesla	2	-	↓

Table 14. Polish transport infrastructure assessment—as of 31 December 2023.

Element of the *RS* Recharging System		Number of Stations/Points [pcs.]	Change Indicator [%]	
		Assessment as of 31 December 2023		
RSt		3282	+27	↑
RPo		5933	+18	↑
RPo	AC (alternating current)	4390	-	-
	DC (direct current)	1543	-	-
Structure of connectors				
Type of connector		Percentage structure [%]		
Co	Type 1 and 2	67	-	↓
	CHdeMO	10	-	↓
	CCS Combo 2	21	-	↑
	Tesla	2	-	=

Table 15. Polish transport infrastructure assessment—as of 31 December 2024.

Element of the *RS* Recharging System		Assessment as of 31 December 2024		
		Number of Stations/Points [pcs.]	Change Indicator [%]	
RSt		4610	+40	↑
RPo		8659	+45	↑
RPo	AC (alternating current)	5992	+36	↑
	DC (direct current)	2667	+72	↑
Structure of connectors				
Type of connector		Percentage structure [%]		
Co	Type 1 and 2	63	-	↓
	CHdeMO	10	-	=
	CCS Combo 2	26	-	↑
	Tesla	1	-	↓

Table 16. Polish transport infrastructure assessment—as of 31 May 2025.

Element of the *RS* Recharging System		Assessment as of 31 May 2025		
		Number of Stations/Points [pcs.]	Change Indicator [%]	
RSt		5458	+18	↑
RPo		9814	+13	↑
RPo	AC (alternating current)	6621	+10	↑
	DC (direct current)	3193	+19	↑
Structure of connectors				
Type of connector		Percentage structure [%]		
Co	Type 1 and 2	60	-	↓
	CHdeMO	10	-	=
	CCS Combo 2	29	-	↑
	Tesla	1	-	=

The assessment of electric vehicle charging infrastructure at the end of 2020 revealed that Poland operated 1364 recharging stations and 2641 recharging points. An important factor in the charging process is the availability of specific connector types, which was also evaluated. In Poland, type 1 and type 2 connectors were predominant, accounting for 64% of all available connectors at stations and points. The overall structure of the electric vehicle charging infrastructure in Poland as of the end of 2020 is presented in Table 11.

The assessment of electric vehicle charging infrastructure at the end of 2021 showed that Poland operated 1932 recharging stations and 3784 recharging points. Compared to 2020, this represents an increase of 41% in the number of recharging stations and 43% in recharging points. Type 1 and type 2 connectors remained dominant, accounting for 69% of all available connectors at stations and points. The overall structure of the electric vehicle charging infrastructure in Poland at the end of 2021 is presented in Table 12.

The assessment of electric vehicle charging infrastructure at the end of 2022 revealed that Poland operated 2565 recharging stations and 5016 recharging points. Compared to 2021, this corresponds to an increase of 32% in both the number of recharging stations and recharging points. The overall structure of the electric vehicle charging infrastructure in Poland at the end of 2022 is presented in Table 13.

The assessment of electric vehicle charging infrastructure at the end of 2023 showed that Poland had 3282 recharging stations and 5933 recharging points in operation. Compared to 2022, this represents an increase of 27% in the number of recharging stations and 18% in recharging points. It is important to note that the annual growth rate of stations and points has slowed down. In previous years, growth rates were 41%, 43%, and 32%, whereas in 2023, they declined to 27% and 18%, respectively. Additionally, data for 2023 only included the number of AC and DC points, without providing figures for the number of AC and DC stations. The overall structure of the electric vehicle charging infrastructure in Poland at the end of 2023 is presented in Table 14.

The assessment of electric vehicle charging infrastructure at the end of 2024 indicated that Poland operated 4610 recharging stations and 8659 recharging points. Compared to 2023, this corresponds to an increase of 40% in the number of recharging stations and 45% in recharging points. The growth dynamics in 2024, with rates of 40% and 45% respectively, represent a significant increase compared to 2023. The overall structure of the electric vehicle charging infrastructure in Poland at the end of 2024 is presented in Table 15.

The assessment of electric vehicle charging infrastructure as of the end of May 2025 showed that Poland had 5458 recharging stations and 9814 recharging points in operation. Compared to 2024, this represents an increase of 18% in the number of recharging stations and 13% in recharging points. It should be noted that these are partial data collected up to the end of May 2025. The overall structure of the electric vehicle charging infrastructure in Poland at the end of May 2025 is presented in Table 16.

(4) Polish AFIR indicator

The Polish AFIR indicator represents progress in the development of charging infrastructure for electric vehicles, specifically eLDVs and eHDVs, along the TEN-T network. The AFIR indicator assessment includes six indicators, namely:

$$\boldsymbol{AFIR^{PL}} = \left\{ \boldsymbol{afir_1^{PL}}, \boldsymbol{afir_2^{PL}}, \boldsymbol{afir_3^{PL}}, \boldsymbol{afir_4^{PL}}, \boldsymbol{afir_5^{PL}}, \boldsymbol{afir_6^{PL}} \right\} \tag{40}$$

where:

$afir_1^{PL}$—charging station power indicator; represents the current level of implementation of AFIR regulation assumptions regarding the total output power of all stations dedicated to eLDVs

$afir_2^{PL}$—indicator of the number of recharging pools along the TEN-T core network meeting AFIR power requirements for eLDVs,

$afir_3^{PL}$—indicator of the length of the TEN-T core network covered by recharging pools that fulfill AFIR requirements for eLDVs,

$afir_4^{PL}$—indicator of the number of recharging pools along the TEN-T comprehensive network meeting AFIR power requirements for eLDVs,

$afir_5^{PL}$—indicator of the number of recharging pools along the TEN-T core network meeting AFIR power requirements for eHDVs,

$afir_6^{PL}$—indicator of the number of recharging pools along the TEN-T comprehensive network meeting AFIR power requirements for eHDVs.

The evaluation of the Polish AFIR indicator was conducted from 31 July 2024, to 30 April 2025. Due to the lack of publicly available periodic data regarding the AFIR indicator for Poland, the assessment was performed for four specific dates. The individual values of the AFIR indicator are presented in Tables 17–20.

Table 17. Polish AFIR indicator—as of 31 July 2024.

<table>
<tr><th rowspan="3">Polish AFIR Indicator $AFIR^{PL}$</th><th colspan="4">Assessment as of 31 July 2024</th></tr>
<tr><th colspan="4">Cut-Off Dates Specified in AFIR</th></tr>
<tr><th>2025</th><th>2027</th><th>2030</th><th>2035</th></tr>
<tr><td>$afir_1^{PL}$ [%]</td><td>86</td><td>42</td><td>19</td><td>8</td></tr>
<tr><td>$afir_2^{PL}$ [%]</td><td>23</td><td>17</td><td>no</td><td>no</td></tr>
<tr><td>$afir_3^{PL}$ [%]</td><td>8.5</td><td>3</td><td>no</td><td>no</td></tr>
<tr><td>$afir_4^{PL}$ [%]</td><td>no</td><td>13</td><td>6.5</td><td>5.5</td></tr>
<tr><td>$afir_5^{PL}$ [%]</td><td rowspan="2">10</td><td rowspan="2">3</td><td rowspan="2">0</td><td rowspan="2">no</td></tr>
<tr><td>$afir_6^{PL}$ [%]</td></tr>
</table>

no—no obligation in this respect.

Table 18. Polish AFIR indicator—as of 31 October 2024.

Polish AFIR Indicator $AFIR^{PL}$	Assessment as of 31 October 2024			
	Cut-Off Dates Specified in AFIR			
	2025	2027	2030	2035
$afir_1^{PL}$ [%]	151	69	27	10
$afir_2^{PL}$ [%]	24	19	no	no
$afir_3^{PL}$ [%]	9	3.5	no	no
$afir_4^{PL}$ [%]	no	15	7	6.5
$afir_5^{PL}$ [%]	20	0	0	no
$afir_6^{PL}$ [%]	10	3	0	no

no—no obligation in this respect.

Table 19. Polish AFIR indicator—as of 31 January 2025.

Polish AFIR Indicator $AFIR^{PL}$	Assessment as of 31 January 2025			
	Cut-Off Dates Specified in AFIR			
	2025	2027	2030	2035
$afir_1^{PL}$ [%]	169	74	30	11
$afir_2^{PL}$ [%]	28	23	no	no
$afir_3^{PL}$ [%]	11	4	no	no
$afir_4^{PL}$ [%]	no	15	7	6.5
$afir_5^{PL}$ [%]	20	0	0	no
$afir_6^{PL}$ [%]	10	3	0	no

no—no obligation in this respect.

Table 20. Polish AFIR indicator—as of 30 April 2025.

Polish AFIR Indicator $AFIR^{PL}$	Assessment as of 30 April 2025			
	Cut-Off Dates Specified in AFIR			
	2025	2027	2030	2035
$afir_1^{PL}$ [%]	175	96	37	13
$afir_2^{PL}$ [%]	30	25	no	no
$afir_3^{PL}$ [%]	13	6	no	no

Table 20. *Cont.*

Polish AFIR Indicator $AFIR^{PL}$	Assessment as of 30 April 2025			
	Cut-Off Dates Specified in AFIR			
	2025	2027	2030	2035
$afir_4^{PL}$ [%]	no	18	9	6.5
$afir_5^{PL}$ [%]	20	0	0	no
$afir_6^{PL}$ [%]	10	3	0	no

no—no obligation in this respect.

5. Conclusions

The AFIR Regulation on the development of alternative fuels infrastructure obliges EU Member States to undertake actions aimed at the development of transport infrastructure for users of electric and hydrogen-powered vehicles. The starting point for AFIR was the noticeable lack of infrastructure adapted for charging electric vehicles. Although infrastructure development was taking place, it was primarily concentrated in urban areas. Infrastructure expansion along roads outside built-up areas was very limited. In response to this shortage, actions were initiated to develop alternative fuels infrastructure along the TEN-T network. Specific requirements were defined to be met during the design and construction stages of alternative fuels infrastructure. Moreover, deadlines were established for meeting these requirements, namely: 31 December 2025, 31 December 2027, 31 December 2030, and 31 December 2035. The requirements were differentiated based on the type of vehicles and the segment of the TEN-T network for which the infrastructure is to be developed.

Based on this, the objective of the article was to present the essence of the energy transformation process of road transport infrastructure based on the AFIR regulation, to define the actions aimed at achieving the goals of the regulation, and to carry out an assessment process of the implementation of the activities provided for in the AFIR regulation. An important part of the research process was also to present the course of the energy transformation of road transport infrastructure in Poland, in accordance with the assumptions and objectives of the AFIR regulation. A review of the literature clearly indicated a lack of analyses, studies, and assessments regarding the energy transformation of transport infrastructure implemented in line with AFIR requirements. Deficiencies were also noted in the interpretation and mathematical formulation of the analyzed process, which, in the authors' opinion, is crucial for conducting an effective assessment of how EU Member States are fulfilling the requirements set out in the AFIR regulation. In line with the assumptions adopted by the authors, the developed model of energy transformation of transport infrastructure will be applied during the implementation of simulation studies for scenarios of electric vehicle charging zone development along the TEN-T network.

The article presents a case study of transport infrastructure located in the territory of Poland. The analysis covered data from 31 December 2020 to 31 May 2025 concerning the number of electric vehicles and the state of road transport infrastructure. In turn, in relation to the Polish AFIR indicator, the study was conducted from 31 July 2024 to 30 April 2025. Why was research on the assessment of transport infrastructure undertaken? Because the first deadline for achieving the objectives set out in the AFIR regulation expires in six months.

The assessment based on the Polish AFIR indicator as of 30 April 2025, showed that the current level of compliance with the total output power requirement of charging stations for eLDVs set by AFIR for the years 2025, 2027, 2030, and 2035 is achieved at approximately 175%, 96%, 37%, and 13%, respectively. Considering the TEN-T core network, the power requirements for charging zones for 2025 and 2027 are fulfilled at about 30% and 25%, with network coverage at only approximately 13% and 6%, respectively. For the TEN-T comprehensive network, the power requirements for charging zones for the years 2027, 2030, and 2035 are met at approximately 18%, 9%, and 6.5%, respectively. In contrast, the assessment based on the Polish indicator as of 30 April 2025, showed that the current level of compliance with the power requirements for eHDV charging zones along the TEN-T core network for 2025, 2027, and 2030 is approximately 20%, 0%, and 0%, respectively. For the TEN-T comprehensive network, the power requirements for eHDV charging zones for 2025, 2027, and 2030 are met at about 10%, 3%, and 0%, respectively.

The defined Polish AFIR indicator showed that the readiness level of alternative fuel infrastructure along the TEN-T network in Poland is low. This is especially evident in the case of infrastructure for eHDVs, where the readiness level is very low, practically at 0%.

Based on the research conducted and considering the complexity of the studies, future research areas have been identified, which will constitute a continuation of this article. The planned future work includes:

- Conducting survey research with charging station operators, users of charging stations, and local government authorities,
- Carrying out field studies focused on specific charging stations and points,
- Analyzing the implementation status of the AFIR regulation in other EU member states, particularly neighboring countries such as Lithuania, Germany, the Czech Republic, and Slovakia,
- Adapting the proposed model according to the assumptions relevant to the analyzed neighboring countries,
- Developing guidelines to support the decision-making process for AFIR regulation implementation in individual EU member states.

Author Contributions: Conceptualization, N.C.-G.; methodology, N.C.-G., J.A.D. and W.M.; software, N.C.-G., J.A.D., W.M., A.P. and P.K.; validation, N.C.-G., J.A.D., W.M. and A.P.; formal analysis, N.C.-G. and W.M.; investigation, N.C.-G., W.M. and J.A.D.; resources, N.C.-G., W.M., J.A.D., A.P. and P.K.; data curation, N.C.-G., W.M. and J.A.D.; writing—original draft preparation, N.C.-G., A.P., W.M. and J.A.D.; writing—review and editing, N.C.-G., A.P., W.M. and J.A.D.; visualization, N.C.-G.; supervision, N.C.-G. and W.M.; project administration, N.C.-G., J.A.D., W.M. and A.P.; funding acquisition, J.A.D. and W.M. All authors have read and agreed to the published version of the manuscript.

Funding: This research received no external funding.

Data Availability Statement: Data available in a publicly accessible repository.

Conflicts of Interest: The authors declare no conflict of interest. The funders had no *rôle* in the design of the study, the collection and analyses or interpretation of the data, or in writing the manuscript, or in the decision to publish the results.

Nomenclature

TEN-T	Trans-European Transport Network,
AFIR	Regulation for the Deployment of Alternative Fuels Infrastructure,
eLDV	light-duty electric vehicle,
eHDV	heavy-duty electric vehicle,
EV	electric vehicle,
BEV	Battery Electric Vehicle,
FCEV	Fuel Cell Electric Vehicle,
HEV	Hybrid Electric Vehicles,
PHEV	Plug-in Hybrid Electric Vehicle,
ETTI	model energy transformation of transport infrastructure.

References

1. Barchański, A.; Żochowska, R.; Kłos, M.J. A Method for the Identification of Critical Interstop Sections in Terms of Introducing Electric Buses in Public Transport. *Energies* **2022**, *15*, 7543. [CrossRef]
2. Macioszek, E.; Cieśla, M.; Grana, A. Future Development of and Energy-Efficient Electric Scooter Sharing System Based on a Stakeholder Analysis Method. *Energies* **2023**, *16*, 554. [CrossRef]
3. Sobota, A.; Grana, A.; Świerk, P.; Macioszek, E. Monitoring of the implementation of the European Union's sustainable transport development policy regarding the use of low- and zero-emission fleet on the example of the Gónosląska-Zagłębiowska Metropolis (Poland). *Sci. J. Silesian Univ. Technol. Ser. Transp.* **2024**, *124*, 183–195. [CrossRef]
4. Tumminella, M.L.; Macioszek, E.; Grana, A.; Giuffre, T. Evaluating Traffic-Calming-Based Urban Road Design Solutions Featuring Cooperative Driving Technologies in Energy Efficiency Transition for Smart Cities. *Energies* **2023**, *16*, 7325. [CrossRef]
5. Khalid, R.; Conjobeeharry, V.; Sanai, A.S.; Brown, C.T.H.; Afrouzi, N.; Hassan, A. The feasibility and analysis of electric taxi vehicles in Singapore: A review. *Future Energy* **2023**, *2*, 38–48. [CrossRef]
6. Soczówka, P.; Lasota, M.; Franke, P.; Żochowska, R. Method of Determining New Locations for Electric Vehicle Charging Stations Using GIS Tools. *Energies* **2024**, *17*, 4546. [CrossRef]
7. Mehranfar, S.; Banager, I.; Moradi, J.; Andwari, A.M.; Könnö, J.; Gharehghani, A.; Rabiei, M.; Kurvinen, E. The perspective of energy storage systems advancements and challenges for electric vehicle applications; metric, mechanism, mode, and mitigation framework. *Future Sustain.* **2024**, *2*, 22–32. [CrossRef]
8. Official Journal of the European Union. Regulation (EU) 2023/1804 of the European Parliament and of the Council of 13 September 2023 on the Deployment of Alternative Fuels Infrastructure, and Repealing Directive 2014/94/EU. Official Journal of the European Union: Luxembourg, 2023.
9. IEA. Global EV Outlook. 2024. Available online: https://www.iea.org/reports/global-ev-outlook-2024 (accessed on 3 July 2025).
10. Lei, X.; Zhong, J.; Chen, Y.; Shao, Z.; Jian, L. Grid integration of electric vehicles within electricity and carbon markets: A comprehensive overview. *eTransportation* **2025**, *25*, 100435. [CrossRef]
11. Lei, X.; Yu, H.; Zhong, J.; Jia, Y.; Shao, Z.; Jian, L. Exploring electric vehicle's potential as capacity reservation through V2G operation to compensate load deviation in distribution systems. *J. Clean. Prod.* **2024**, *451*, 141997. [CrossRef]
12. Tu, J.; Yu, H.; Zhong, J.; Jian, L. User-needs-oriented shared DC charging resources optimal configuration and operation for improving EV penetration in old residential communities. *Sustain. Cities Soc.* **2024**, *114*, 105796. [CrossRef]
13. Yu, H.; Tu, J.; Shao, Z.; Jian, L. Accommodating more electric vehicles in old residential communities by enabling distributed vehicle-to-grid dispatching and coordinated system operation. *Renew. Sustain. Energy Rev.* **2025**, *218*, 115814. [CrossRef]
14. Chen, Y.; Lei, X.; Niu, S.; Jian, L. Trustworthy V2G scheduling and energy trading: A blockchain-based framework. *eTransportation* **2024**, *22*, 100376. [CrossRef]
15. Zhong, J.; Lei, X.; Shao, Z.; Jian, L. Value-Oriented Data-Driven Approach for Electrical Load Forecasting Apt to Facilitate Vehicle-to-Grid Scheduling. *IEEE Trans. Ind. Inform.* **2025**, *21*, 5235–5244. [CrossRef]
16. Niu, S.; Jia, Q.; Hu, Y.; Yang, C.; Jian, L. Safety Management Technologies for Wireless Electric Vehicle Charging Systems: A Review. *Electronics* **2025**, *14*, 2380. [CrossRef]
17. Zaino, R.; Ahmed, V.; Alhammadi, A.M.; Alghoush, M. Electric vehicle adoption: A comprehensive systematic review of technological, environmental, organizational and policy impacts. *World Electr. Veh. J.* **2024**, *15*, 375. [CrossRef]
18. Kalweit, S.; Zeyen, E.; Victoria, M. Endogenous transformation of land transport in Europe for different climate targets. *arXiv* **2025**, arXiv:2501.16460. [CrossRef]
19. Pecolt, S.; Blazejewski, A.; Królikowski, T.; Krupski, P.; Kaminski, K. Application for testing and optimising the performance of electric power systems in a hybrid "MELEX" vehicle. *Procedia Comput. Sci.* **2023**, *225*, 2634–2643. [CrossRef]
20. Jacyna, M.; Żochowska, R.; Sobota, A.; Wasiak, M. Decision support for choosing a scenario for organizing urban transport system with share of electric vehicles. *Sci. J. Silesian Univ. Technol. Ser. Transp.* **2022**, *117*, 69–89. [CrossRef]
21. Bhuiyan, M.M.H.; Siddique, Z. Hydrogen as an alternative fuel: A comprehensive review of challenges and opportunities in production, storage, and transportation. *Int. J. Hydrogen Energy* **2025**, *102*, 1026–1044. [CrossRef]
22. Aryanpur, V.; Rogan, F. Decarbonising road freight transport: The role of zero-emission trucks and intangible costs. *Sci. Rep.* **2024**, *14*, 2113. [CrossRef]
23. Lasota, M.K.; Zabielska, A.; Jacyna, M.; Żak, J. Research and analysis of the operation of vehicles with various propulsion systems, including costs and CO_2 emissions. *Combust. Engines* **2023**, *195*, 3–13. [CrossRef]
24. Bukhari, J.; Somanagoudar, A.G.; Hou, L.; Herrera, O.; Mérida, W. Zero-Emission Delivery for Logistics and Transportation: Challenges, Research Issues, and Opportunities. In *The Palgrave Handbook of Global Sustainability*; Springer: Berlin/Heidelberg, Germany, 2023; pp. 1729–1749. [CrossRef]
25. Lasota, M.; Zabielska, A.; Jacyna, M.; Gołębiewski, P.; Żochowska, R.; Wasiak, M. Method for Delivery Planning in Urban Areas with Environmental Aspects. *Sustainability* **2024**, *16*, 1571. [CrossRef]

26. Chhugani, T.; Rahmani, R. Full emissions and energy consumption life cycle assessment of different heavy-duty vehicles powered by electricity, hydrogen, methanol, and LNG fuels produced from various sources. *Energy Convers. Manag.* **2025**, *326*, 119439. [CrossRef]
27. Green NCAP–Greenest Cars 2024. Available online: https://www.greenncap.com/press-releases/greenest-cars-2024/ (accessed on 3 July 2025).
28. Izdebski, M.; Jacyna, M.; Bogdański, J. Minimisation of the Energy Expenditure of Electric Vehicles in Municipal Service Companies, Taking into Account the Uncertainty of Charging Point Operation. *Energies* **2024**, *17*, 2179. [CrossRef]
29. Sun, R.; Sujan, V.A.; Jatana, G. Systemic decarbonization of road freight transport: A comprehensive total cost of ownership model. *arXiv* **2024**, arXiv:2410.21026. [CrossRef]
30. Kaczorek, M.; Jacyna, M. Fuzzy logic as a decision-making support tool in planning transport development. *Arch. Transp.* **2022**, *61*, 51–70. [CrossRef]
31. Shaw, A.; Mander, S.; Parkes, B.; Wood, R. Zero carbon transitions: A systematic review of the research landscape and climate mitigation potential. *Front. Energy Res.* **2023**, *11*, 1268270. [CrossRef]
32. Neumann, F.; Zeyen, E.; Victoria, M.; Brown, T. The potential role of a hydrogen network in Europe. *Joule* **2023**, *7*, 1793–1817. [CrossRef]
33. Ghisolfi, V.; Tavasszy, L.A.; Correia, G.H.D.A.; Chaves, G.D.L.D.; Ribeiro, G.M. Freight transport decarbonization: A systematic literature review of system dynamics models. *Sustainability* **2022**, *14*, 3625. [CrossRef]
34. Mazur, M.; Dybała, J.; Kluczek, A. Suitable law-based location selection of high-power electric vehicles charging stations on the TEN-T core network for sustainability: A case of Poland. *Arch. Transp.* **2024**, *69*, 75–90. [CrossRef]
35. BloombergNEF. Electric Vehicle Outlook. 2024. Available online: https://about.bnef.com/insights/clean-transport/electric-vehicle-outlook/ (accessed on 3 July 2025).
36. China Passenger Car Association. New Energy Vehicle Market Report. 2023. Based on Data via CnEVPost Article. Available online: https://cnevpost.com/2025/07/02/cpca-estimates-china-jun-nev-wholesale-1-26-million/ (accessed on 3 July 2025).
37. European Environment Agency. Electric Vehicles as a Proportion of New Car Registrations. Available online: https://www.eea.europa.eu/en/analysis/indicators/new-registrations-of-electric-vehicles (accessed on 3 July 2025).
38. U.S. Department of Energy. Federal Incentives for Electric Vehicles. Available online: https://www.energy.gov/save/electric-vehicles (accessed on 3 July 2025).
39. McKinsey & Company. Electric Vehicles—What's Ahead. Available online: https://www.mckinsey.com/features/mckinsey-center-for-future-mobility/our-insights/electric-vehicles-whats-ahead (accessed on 3 July 2025).
40. IEA. Trends in Electric Vehicle Markets. 2022. Available online: https://www.iea.org/reports/global-ev-outlook-2024/trends-in-electric-cars (accessed on 3 July 2025).
41. EV Database. Electric Vehicle Range & Efficiency Data. Available online: https://ev-database.org/ (accessed on 3 July 2025).
42. Duda, J.; Fierek, S.; Karkula, M.; Kisielewski, P.; Puka, R.; Redmer, A.; Skalna, I. Determining lower bound on number of vehicles blocks in multi-depot vehicle scheduling problem with mixed fleet covering electric buses. *Arch. Transp.* **2023**, *65*, 27–38. [CrossRef]
43. IEA. Tracking Transport. 2020. Available online: https://www.iea.org/reports/tracking-transport-2020 (accessed on 3 July 2025).
44. IEA. Global EV Outlook. 2021. Available online: https://www.iea.org/reports/global-ev-outlook-2021 (accessed on 3 July 2025).
45. International Association of Public Transport (UITP). Action Points—Electrifying Public Transport Fleets with Renewable Energy. 2023. Available online: https://cms.uitp.org/wp/wp-content/uploads/2023/04/Action-Points-Renewable-energy-APR-2023.pdf (accessed on 3 July 2025).
46. European Commission. Clean Buses in Europe: Policy and Market Status. Available online: https://cms.uitp.org/wp/wp-content/uploads/2022/04/ASSURED-Clean-Bus-Report-UITP-Final.pdf (accessed on 3 July 2025).
47. Amazon. Amazon's Electric Delivery Vehicles from Rivian Roll out Across the U.S. Available online: https://www.aboutamazon.com/news/transportation/amazons-electric-delivery-vehicles-from-rivian-roll-out-across-the-u-s (accessed on 3 July 2025).
48. Reuß, M.; Grube, T.; Robinius, M.; Stolten, D. Power-to-hydrogen in transport: Cost, emissions and demand. *Int. J. Hydrogen Energy* **2022**, *47*, 123–136. [CrossRef]
49. Hydrogen Council. Global Hydrogen Flows—2023 Update. Available online: https://hydrogencouncil.com/en/global-hydrogen-flows-2023-update/ (accessed on 3 July 2025).
50. Rawat, A.; Garg, C.P.; Sinha, P. Analysis of the key hydrogen fuel vehicles adoption barriers to reduce carbon emissions under net zero target in emerging market. *Energy Policy* **2024**, *184*, 113847. [CrossRef]
51. Olkiewicz, M.; Dyczkowska, J.A. Green Logistics at Selected Logistics Operators in Poland. *Sustainability* **2025**, *17*, 4587. [CrossRef]
52. Karoń, G. Safe and Effective Smart Urban Transportation—Energy Flow in Electric (EV) and Hybrid Electric Vehicles (HEV). *Energies* **2022**, *15*, 6548. [CrossRef]

53. Janecki, R.; Karoń, G. Concept of smart cities and economic model of electric buses implementation. In *Telematics—Support for Transport. TST 2014*; Communications in Computer and Information Science; Springer: Berlin/Heidelberg, Germany, 2014. [CrossRef]
54. Sendek-Matysiak, E. The assessment of the use of vehicles with different types of drive in Car-Sharing systems. *Arch. Transp.* **2024**, *72*, 129–149. [CrossRef]
55. Turoń, K. Personalization of the Car-Sharing Fleet Selected for Commuting to Work of for Educational Purposes—An Opportunity to Increase the Attractiveness of Systems in Smart Cities. *Smart Cities* **2024**, *7*, 1670–1705. [CrossRef]
56. ACEA. New Passenger Car Registrations in EU. Available online: https://www.acea.auto/figure/new-passenger-car-registrations-in-eu/ (accessed on 3 July 2025).
57. Wozniak, W.; Stryjski, R.; Mielniczuk, J.; Wojnarowski, T. Concept for the application of genetic algorithms in the management of transport offers in relations to homogenous cargo transport. In Proceedings of the 26th International Business Information Management Association Conference—Innovation Management and Sustainable Economic Competitive Advantage: From Regional Development to Global Growth, IBIMA 2015 Conference Paper 2015, Madrid, Spain, 11–12 November 2015.
58. Woźniak, W.; Walkowiak, J.; Sąsiadek, M.; Stryjski, R. Organisation of the research process into an innovative, anti-clogging assembly for heavy vehicles in the interests of increased road safety. In Proceedings of the 32nd International Business Information Management Association Conference, IBIMA 2018—Vision 2020: Sustainable Economic Development and Application of Innovation Management from Regional expansion to Global Growth Conference Paper 2018, Seville, Spain, 15–16 November 2018.
59. Fu, Z.; Yue, J.; Yan, Y. Optimized design of multi-level low-carbon Logistics distribution scheme based on two stages. *Arch. Transp.* **2024**, *69*, 145–165. [CrossRef]
60. Volvo Group. Breakthrough: Volvo to Launch Electric Truck with 600 km Range. Available online: https://www.volvogroup.com/en/news-and-media/news/2024/sep/breakthrough{-}{-}volvo-to-launch-electric-truck-with-600-km-range.html (accessed on 3 July 2025).
61. Hyundai Motor Company. *2023 Sustainability Report—Hyundai Hydrogen Mobility Europe*; Hyundai Motor Company: Seoul, Republic of Korea, 2023; Available online: https://www.hyundai.com/content/dam/hyundai/ww/en/images/company/sustainability/about-sustainability/hmc-2024-sustainability-report-en-v3.pdf (accessed on 3 July 2025).
62. Turoń, K.; Kubik, A.; Folęga, P.; Chen, F. Perception of Shared Electric Scooters: A Case Study from Poland. *Sustainability* **2023**, *15*, 12596. [CrossRef]
63. Di Gangi, M.; Comi, A.; Polimeni, A.; Belcore, O.M. E-Bike use in urban commuting: Empirical evidence from the home-work plan. *Arch. Transp.* **2022**, *62*, 91–104. [CrossRef]
64. OECD/ITF. *Safer Micromobility: Technical Background Report*; OECD Publishing: Paris, France. Available online: https://www.itf-oecd.org/safer-micromobility (accessed on 3 July 2025).
65. International Transport Forum (ITF). *ITF Transport Outlook 2021—Reforming Urban Transport*; OECD Publishing: Paris, France, 2021. [CrossRef]
66. Musolino, G. Sustainable Mobility as a Service: Demand Analysis and Case Studies. *Information* **2022**, *13*, 376. [CrossRef]
67. Karoń, G. Energy in Smart Urban Transportation with Systemic Use of Electric Vehicles. *Energies* **2022**, *15*, 5751. [CrossRef]
68. Le Monde. Paris Bans Rental E-Scooters. Available online: https://www.lemonde.fr/en/transport/article/2023/09/01/rental-e-scooters-cleared-from-paris-streets-as-ban-comes-into-effect_6118982_216.html (accessed on 3 July 2025).
69. Hawkins, T.R.; Singh, B.; Majeau-Bettez, G.; Strømman, A.H. Comparative Environmental Life Cycle Assessment of Conventional and Electric Vehicles. *J. Ind. Ecol.* **2013**, *17*, 53–64. [CrossRef]
70. Transport & Environment. Electric Cars Emit Less CO_2 over Their Lifetime. Available online: https://www.transportenvironment.org/articles/electric-cars-emit-less-co2-over-their-lifetime-diesels-even-when-powered-dirtiest-electricity (accessed on 3 July 2025).
71. Zhang, B.; Xin, Q.; Chen, S.; Wang, B.; Li, H.; Wang, Z.; Bansal, P. Lithium-ion battery recycling relieves the threat to material scarcity amid China's electric vehicle ambitions. *Nat. Commun.* **2025**, *16*, 6661. [CrossRef] [PubMed]
72. Jiang, R.; Wu, C.; Feng, W.; You, K.; Liu, J.; Zhou, G.; Liu, L.; Cheng, H.-M. Impact of electric vehicle battery recycling on reducing raw material demand and battery life-cycle carbon emissions in China. *Sci. Rep.* **2025**, *15*, 2267. [CrossRef] [PubMed]
73. Safarzadeh, H.; Di Maria, F. Progress, Challenges and Opportunities in Recycling Electric Vehicle Batteries: A Systematic Review Article. *Batteries* **2025**, *11*, 230. [CrossRef]
74. Tian, X.; Peng, F.; Chen, X.; Wei, G.; Gan, Y.; Zhang, Z.; Liu, Y. Management of spent power batteries in China: Progress, policies, and challenges. *Renew. Sustain. Energy Rev.* **2025**, *219*, 115797. [CrossRef]
75. Aishwarya, V.M.; Ekren, B.Y.; Singh, T.; Singh, V. Integrating sustainability across the lifecycle of electric vehicle batteries: Circular supply chain challenges, innovations, and global policy impacts. *Renew. Sustain. Energy Rev.* **2025**, *216*, 115671. [CrossRef]
76. Namratha, B.; Jude, M.G.; Santosh, L.G. Advancements in lithium-ion batteries: Sustainability and market impact. *Discov. Mater. Rev.* **2025**, *5*, 1–15. [CrossRef]

77. Arsad, S.R.; Hannan, M.A.; Ker, P.J.; Wong, R.T.K.; Begum, R.A.; Hossain, M.J.; Jang, G. Longevity of lithium-ion batteries in EV applications: Techno-economic and environmental impact considerations toward sustainability. *J. Energy Storage* **2025**, *131*, 117551. [CrossRef]
78. World Health Organization Regional Office for Europe (WHO). *Environmental Noise Guidelines for the European Region*; WHO Regional Office for Europe: Copenhagen, Denmark, 2020; Available online: https://www.who.int/europe/publications/i/item/9789289053563 (accessed on 3 July 2025).
79. European Environment Agency (EEA). Europe's Air Quality Status 2024. Available online: https://www.eea.europa.eu/publications/europes-air-quality-status-2024 (accessed on 3 July 2025).
80. Macioszek, E. *Analysis of Trends in Development of Electromobility in Poland: Current Problems and Issues*; Springer Proceedings in Business and Economics; Springer: Cham, Germany, 2021. [CrossRef]
81. Transport & Environment. Public Charging in Europe: Where Are We at? 2025. Available online: https://www.transportenvironment.org/articles/public-charging-in-europe-where-are-we-at (accessed on 3 July 2025).
82. CharIN—Charging Interface Initiative e.V. *CharIN White Paper—Megawatt Charging System (MCS)*; Charging Interface Initiative e.V.: Berlin, Germany, 2022; Available online: https://www.charin.global/media/pages/technology/knowledge-base/c708ba3361-1670238823/whitepaper_megawatt_charging_system_1.0.pdf (accessed on 3 July 2025).
83. Dua, R.; Almutairi, S.; Bansal, P. Emerging energy economics and policy research priorities for enabling the electric vehicle sector. *Energy Rep.* **2024**, *12*, 1836–1847. [CrossRef]
84. Lohawala, N.; Spiller, E. From Diesel to Electric: Overcoming Grid Integration Challenges in the Medium- and Heavy-Duty Vehicle Sector. *Econ. Energy Environ. Policy* **2023**, *12*, 113–130. [CrossRef]
85. Spiller, E.; Lohawala, N.; DeAngeli, E. *Medium- and Heavy-Duty Vehicle Electrification: Challenges, Policy Solutions, and Open Research Questions*; Resources for the Future Report: Washington, DC, USA, 2023.
86. Dua, R. Net-zero transport dialogue: Emerging developments and the puzzles they present. *Energy Sustain. Dev.* **2024**, *82*, 101516. [CrossRef]
87. Dua, R.; Almutairi, S. A perspective on emerging policy and economics research priorities for enabling low-carbon trucking. *Energy Res. Soc. Sci.* **2025**, *124*, 104025. [CrossRef]
88. Koniak, M.; Jaskowski, P.; Madlenak, R.; Zaranka, J. Analysis of real-time Energy transfer possibilities at intersections with consideration of energy storage and reduction of transport impact on the environment. *Arch. Transp.* **2025**, *73*, 195–206. [CrossRef]
89. Sablin, O.; Bosyi, D.; Kuznetsov, V.; Lewczuk, K.; Kebal, I.; Myamlin, S.S. Efficiency of energy storage control in the electric transport systems. *Arch. Transp.* **2022**, *62*, 105–122. [CrossRef]
90. Enel, X. Smart Charging Infrastructure: Efficiency and Grid Stability—Smart Mobility Report 2022. Enel X Way. Available online: https://www.mobility.enelx.com/en/media/news/2022/10/smart-mobility-report (accessed on 3 July 2025).
91. Brown, T.; Schlachtberger, D.; Kies, A.; Schramm, S.; Greiner, M. Synergies of sector coupling and transmission reinforcement in a cost-optimised, highly renewable European energy system. *Energy* **2018**, *160*, 720–739. [CrossRef]
92. Müller, A.; Heinrichs, H. Planning charging infrastructure for EVs using AI-based methods. *Energy Policy* **2022**, *160*, 112665. [CrossRef]
93. Urban Transitions; Müller, A.; Heinrichs, H. Modelling Urban Charging Infrastructure under Different Energy Scenarios. *J. Urban Energy Transit.* **2022**, *4*, 44–61. [CrossRef]
94. Sierpiński, G.; Macioszek, E. *Equalising the Levels of Electromobility Implementation in Cities*; Communications in Computer and Information Science; Springer: Cham, Switzerland, 2020. [CrossRef]
95. Macioszek, E. E-mobility infrastructure in the Górnoslasko-Zaglebowska Metropolis, Poland, and potential for development. In Proceedings of the World Congress on New Technologies, Lisbon, Portugal, 18–20 August 2019. [CrossRef]
96. Sendek-Matysiak, E.; Pyza, D. Prospects for the development of electric vehicle charging infrastructure in Poland in the light of the regulations in force. *Arch. Transp.* **2021**, *57*, 1.
97. Macioszek, E.; Sierpiński, G. *Charging Stations for Electric Vehicles—Current Situation in Poland*; Communications in Computer and Information Science; Springer: Cham, Switzerland, 2020. [CrossRef]
98. Visser, W. *Electric Vehicle Charging. Definitions and Explanation. Version: January 2019*; VO-169-1801/RP-DUZA; Netherlands Enterprise Agency: Den Haag, The Netherlands, 2019.

energies

MDPI

Review

Advancing Renewable-Dominant Power Systems Through Internet of Things and Artificial Intelligence: A Comprehensive Review

Temitope Adefarati [1], Gulshan Sharma [1,*], Pitshou N. Bokoro [1] and Rajesh Kumar [2,3]

[1] Department of Electrical and Electronics Engineering Technology, University of Johannesburg, Johannesburg 2094, South Africa; temitope.adefarati@gmail.com (T.A.); pitshoub@uj.ac.za (P.N.B.)
[2] Department of Human Anatomy and Physiology, Faculty of Health Sciences, University of Johannesburg, Johannesburg 2094, South Africa; rkumar@uj.ac.za
[3] Department of Electrical Engineering, Malaviya National Institute of Technology, Jaipur 302017, India
* Correspondence: gulshans@uj.ac.za

Abstract: The sudden increase in global energy demand has prompted the integration of Artificial Intelligence and the Internet of Things into the utility grid. The synergy of Artificial Intelligence and the Internet of Things in renewable energy sources has emerged as a promising solution for the development of smart grids and a transformative catalyst that restructures centralized power systems into resilient and sustainable systems. The state-of-the-art of the Internet of Things and Artificial Intelligence is presented in this paper to support the design, planning, operation, management and optimization of renewable energy-based power systems. This paper outlines the benefits of smart and resilient energy systems and the contributions of the Internet of Things across several applications, devices and networks. Artificial Intelligence can be utilized for predictive maintenance, demand-side management, fault detection, forecasting and scheduling. This paper highlights crucial future research directions aimed at overcoming the challenges that are associated with the adoption of emerging technologies in the power system by focusing on market policy and regulation and the human-centric and ethical aspects of Artificial Intelligence and the Internet of Things. The outcomes of this study can be used by policymakers, researchers and development agencies to improve global access to electricity and accelerate the development of sustainable energy systems.

Keywords: artificial intelligence; deep learning; greenhouse gas emissions; internet of things; machine learning; renewable energy sources; smart grid

1. Introduction

The global energy crisis caused by the fluctuation of fossil fuels prices, population growth, aging infrastructure, supply chain disruption, the high standard of living and poor electricity infrastructure has considerably forced many manufacturing companies to reduce production, increase inflation, slow down economic activities, increase energy prices and create economic hardship for citizens [1]. The global energy crisis can be addressed by using renewable energy sources (RESs), the formulation of supportive government policies, the diversification of energy supply sources and energy market reforms and the strengthening of energy reserves [2]. The pressing need to resolve the issues of climate change, energy security and economic stability has led to the adoption of sustainable energy solutions and policies that ensure reliable energy access while reducing climate risks. The shift in fossil fuels to renewable energy as an alternative power solution can be used to restructure power systems with the environment, economy and societal value chain. This offers several benefits across different sectors of the economy such as improved energy independence and security, reduced cost of energy, and supporting technological innovation, community empowerment and energy access [3]. The proactive role played by each renewable energy source in the global energy transition is vital for the development of sustainable energy systems [4,5]. The transition from brown energy technologies to green energy technologies has become a multidimensional solution that can be used to address perilous environmental challenges, stimulate economic growth and improve the global social well-being of people. It encourages large investments in research and development which results in improvements of electric storage system and grid integration and efficiency. It is obvious that fossil fuels have been crucial to the development of the modern economy by powering the global economy and supporting technological advancements that have boosted commercial and industrial activities.

According to the report of the Renewables 2025 Global Status, fossil fuels accounted for 68% of the global energy supply. The report shows that the majority of the global primary energy supply emanated from fossil fuels to satisfy energy demand that grew by 4.3% in 2024. This demonstrates that RESs accounted for approximately 32% of the world's power supply in 2024, as shown in Figure 1a [6]. The International Energy Agency (IEA) report of 2025 also indicates that renewable energy accounted for the largest share of the growth in global energy supply with about 38%, followed by natural gas (28%), coal (15%), oil (11%) and nuclear (8%) as presented in Figure 1b [7]. The astounding record of the IEA indicates a significant growth and global shift from brown technologies to sustainable and green energy technologies that are being aided by technological advancements, environmental concerns and governmental regulations. The combustion of fossil fuels for power generation applications has led to significantly increased greenhouse gas (GHG) emissions, acid rain, increased healthcare costs, biodiversity loss, ocean acidification, global warming and climate change [8]. In view of this, fossil fuel-based power plants are gradually being replaced by cleaner and sustainable energy systems that can strike a balance between environmental preservation and financial growth [9].

The effective utilization of green energy technologies to improve access to electricity and reduce GHG emissions is limited owing to the intermittent nature of RESs [10]. The power generated by photovoltaic (PV) systems and wind turbines (WTs) is extremely hard to predict with precision at any given time due to the inherent challenges of RESs [11]. The intermittent nature of RESs is a significant challenge that severely hinders the maintenance of a stable and reliable electrical power supply at the load points [12]. It can also cause frequency fluctuations, voltage instability and reduced inertia of conventional power plants. The challenges of RESs in the power system can be mitigated by the implementation of several strategies such as Artificial Intelligence (AI) algorithms, Internet of Things (IoT) devices, smart grids, battery systems and demand-side management [13,14]. The electric storage systems can be used in grid-connected or standalone power systems to minimize the effects of uncertainty that are associated with RESs. They be used to store excess energy during the peak renewable generation and inject it back to the utility grid when the costs of energy are high [15]. RESs have great potential for sustainable energy but their intrinsic qualities provide serious obstacles to the stability and reliability of the power system [16]. AI and IoT are the components of smart grids and advanced grid management systems that can provide innovative and potential solutions to surmount the inherent challenges of RESs [17]. The convergence of IoT and AI can be utilized to transform traditional power systems into a sustainable and reliable system by using the enormous potential of renewable energy sources while effectively managing their inherent variability [18]. IoT devices support smart grid systems that balance energy loads, reduce GHG pollutants and optimize energy distribution [19]. The IoT with smart grid features supports manual switching between RESs and fossil fuel-based conventional power plants to facilitate a continuous power supply at consumer centers. This switching makes it easier for smart grids to accommodate the variable nature of RESs and allow an uninterrupted power supply to the customers [20].

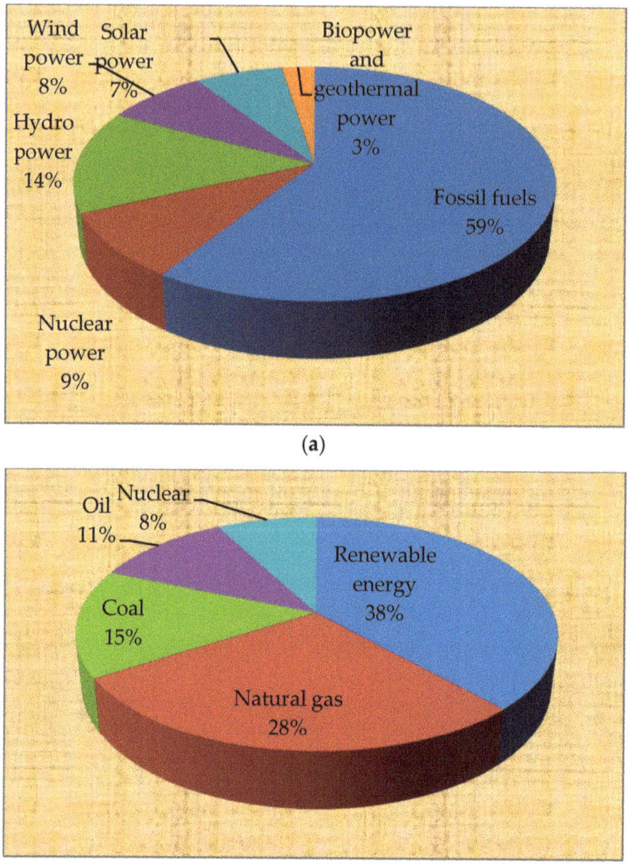

Figure 1. (**a**) Electricity generation by several energy sources in 2024 and (**b**) share of energy supply growth from several sources in 2024.

The traditional power system that was initially built for centralized energy systems and a unidirectional flow of energy finds it difficult to satisfy the load demand of emerging power systems. The proliferation of distributed energy resources (DERs) in the modern power system has led to a sudden transition from a centralized power system to decentralized power with the adoption of bidirectional energy management [21,22]. This transformation is facilitated by using AI, IoT, smart grid features and electric storage systems to transform a decentralized energy system into an adaptive, intelligent and interconnected network. The transformation can be accomplished by allowing a higher penetration of DERs, improving grid reliability, reducing operational costs and empowering individuals to participate in the energy market. The IoT is the nervous system of a decentralized energy system that allows AI to function effectively. It collects vital signs, communicates the necessary information and allows the operations of DERs to be controlled through an automated system. The intermittent nature of wind speed and solar irradiance can be overcome by using modern technologies for the stabilization of the utility grid and the utilization of RESs [23]. The convergence of IoT devices and AI in grid-connected or standalone hybrid renewable energy systems allows producers and prosumers to satisfy the load demand of consumers through the coordination of electrical power obtained from different RESs [24]. The IoT has been playing a proactive role in the optimization of distributed energy resources (DERs) in centralized and decentralized power systems by using real-time monitoring, automation and smart devices to enhance the efficiency and sustainability of variable RESs like solar and wind [15,25]. The emergence of smart grids through IoT has increased the usage of RESs for power generation applications [26]. It provides incredible advantages in terms of power consumption monitoring and real-time alerting that allow distribution network operators to integrate RESs into their distribution systems [27,28]. The applications of IoT devices and AI models have been deployed in several sectors of the economy to enhance automation, improve efficiency and support data-driven policies [29].

The successful application of RESs in the traditional power system is hindered by numerous factors such as performance inefficiencies, the variability of load demand, a lack of predictability, integration complexity within the utility grid and a lack of real-time responsiveness [30,31]. The challenges can be addressed by using the convergence of IoT and AI that provides a robust and intelligent solution for the monitoring, control and optimization of renewable energy-based power infrastructure [21]. The combination of the IoT and AI is crucial for the transformation of renewable energy systems by providing clean, affordable, reliable and sustainable energy at the load points [32]. The performance of a conventional power system can be optimized with the integration of AI and IoT as well as the penetration of RESs through the energy mix [33]. The combined operation of AI and IoT plays an important role in minimizing GHG emissions and mitigating climate change by promoting the application of RESs in the utility grid [19,34,35].

The convergence of IoT and AI to improve the performance of RESs in a conventional power system has been globally acknowledged as an emerging field of research and development. This literature review covers four key areas such as IoT devices for data acquisition and control, AI models for forecasting and optimization, AI models for predictive maintenance and the integration of AI algorithms and IoT devices for smart grid management. Ullah et al. [36] focused on IoT architecture and monitoring of smart grid systems with IoT devices. The authors also provided a comprehensive overview of the required technologies for the optimal operation of smart grid systems by laying more emphasis on the functions of sensors and communication systems. Balamurali et al. [37] presented the application of IoT for supervising and controlling the operation of a mobile solar pumping system that was designed for the efficient water management of modern agriculture practice. The outcomes of their study demonstrate the technical feasibility of utilizing sensors for the real-time management of smart irrigation systems with IoT. Liu et al. [38] applied AI to predicting the intermittent nature of wind resources for the optimal operation of energy systems. The authors presented a comprehensive review of several methods that can be used to forecast wind speed such as statistical models, long short-term memory networks, convolutional neural networks and artificial neural networks (ANNs). Kumar et al. [39] applied particle swarm optimization and genetic algorithms to position wind turbines and maximize their energy capturing and minimize their wake effects. The authors accomplished this task by utilizing predictive maintenance which is one of the important applications of AI in energy systems. Similarly, Pandit et al. [40] introduced predictive maintenance as one of the crucial factors that can be utilized for the reduction in operation and maintenance (O&M) costs of wind turbines. Zhang et al. [41] presented a detailed review of machine learning (ML) methods for wind turbine conditioning and monitoring. The authors provided several methods such as support vector machines (SVMs) and ANNs for the analysis of vibration, acoustic and thermal data from IoT sensors and the prediction of component failures. The outcomes of the study show that proactive maintenance strategies can be used to optimize the utilization of the power system.

Alaba et al. [42] carried out a comprehensive detailed study of IoT devices and AI algorithms and their uses in converting existing conventional power systems to intelligent power systems. The authors achieved this objective by mapping out the landscape of AI and IoT applications in smart grid systems and the significance of their collaboration for managing grid stability, demand response and energy trading. Similarly, Zahraoui et al. [43] performed a detailed analysis of microgrid systems and the effects of AI models on improving the resilience and efficiency of the power systems. Mbasso et al. [44] conducted a thorough review of the digital twin (DT) technique within the concept of an emerging energy system by utilizing real-time IoT data and AI to achieve scalable, intelligent and independent energy systems. The authors provided a comprehensive study of DT in RESs such as PV systems, hydro, wind turbines and hybrid renewable energy systems by focusing on the lifecycle assessment of energy systems. Bennagi et al. [45] carried out a comprehensive overview of AI in renewable energy resources, current technological advances of AI, the challenges of AI and the practical solutions of the challenges and expected trends of AI in the near future. Bello et al. [46] presented the application of AI in RESs to optimize energy efficiency, facilitate predictive maintenance and achieve real-time decision-making of an energy system. Moreover, Hussien et al. [47] presented a review of AI in RESs by focusing on their applications in the processing of foods and conservation. The authors also presented the limitations and prospects of AI in the future. Al-Shetwi et al. [48] investigated the application of IoT technology in power systems during power interruptions by concentrating on its structure, advantages, disadvantages and potential for the development of the future energy mix. Arshi et al. [49] presented the architecture, latest advancements and current challenges of IoT. The authors also delved into general applications of IoT in intelligent transportation, smart grids, smart cities, power generation and smart homes. Sankarananth et al. [50] applied a comprehensive approach that integrated AI and metaheuristic optimization techniques for projecting and controlling the operation of RESs in power systems. The outcomes of their study can be used to improve the availability of power supply and energy efficiency in both rural and urban areas. Pathare et al. [51] carried out a thorough analysis of the applications of IoT devices in smart grid systems with an emphasis on the challenges of RESs and implementations of strategic ways to overcome the challenges. A literature review of additional works in addition to those already described above is presented in Table 1.

Table 1. Summary of studies on the integration of IoT and AI in renewable energy systems.

Architecture of the System	Method	Focus of the Study	Dataset	Contributions of the Study	Limitations
Wind energy system [52]	ML, IoT sensor networks and predictive analytics	Management of wind farm and O&M costs	Weather station and real-time data in wind farms	Improved reliability and reduced downtime	Data sharing and privacy issues

Table 1. *Cont.*

Architecture of the System	Method	Focus of the Study	Dataset	Contributions of the Study	Limitations
Smart power grid systems [53]	IoT and AI	Predictive maintenance for reduction in losses and carbon footprint	Smart grid system data	Reduction in energy loss and carbon footprint through early maintenance	Cost–benefit tradeoffs are not fully studied
Wind turbines [54]	DL and statistical control charts	Detection of faults and abnormalities of WTs	Simulated data obtained from simulator	Effective detection of faults and anomalies	Simulation-based and lack of real-time data
Smart energy system [55]	ML and DL	Load forecasting, anomaly detection and DSM	Published datasets	Guide model choice of DSM tasks	Lack of uniform benchmarking
Industrial consumers and prosumers system [56]	AI	Optimization of production schedules	Industrial plants and prosumer data	Significant cost savings and better utilization of RESs	Potential latency issues
Distributed digital twin framework [57]	DT	Predictive maintenance	Real-time datasets	Improved asset utilization and real-time analytics	Real-time implementation challenges
Renewable energy forecasting [58]	ML, hybrid models and IoT	Forecasting of solar, wind and hydropower	Public datasets	Significantly reduced latency and improved responsiveness	Geographical limited
Wind turbines [59]	AI approaches	Fault detection and diagnosis of WT	Laboratory and field datasets	Highlights signal processing and DL	Tested only in lab settings and sensor degradation
Solar energy system [60]	Convolutional neural networks (CNNs) and DL	Forecasting of solar irradiance	Microgrid simulation models	Significant optimization of costs and effective control of solar system	Real-time microgrid tests missing
Solar energy system [61]	CNNs and long short-term memory (LSTM)	PV forecasting	Local PV and meteorological datasets	Robust to weather variability	High computational cost
Renewable power systems [62]	IoT sensors and ML	Integration of IoT in RESs	Real-time datasets	Achieved real-time monitoring of RESs	Cyber security challenges and lack of global standards
Renewable energy system [63]	Federated learning (FL)	Forecasting and control of RESs	Smart-meter and building datasets	Effective for privacy and distributed learning	Communication and convergence issues
Distributed energy resources [64]	Deep reinforcement learning (DRL)	Coordination of DERs and transactive energy (TE)	Simulated DER and market datasets	Significant reduction in net load variability and costs	Simulation-based only and lacks large-scale field validation

Table 1. *Cont.*

Architecture of the System	Method	Focus of the Study	Dataset	Contributions of the Study	Limitations
Wind turbines [65]	DL	Predictive maintenance	Turbine SCADA/ vibration data	Improved fault detection	Access to industrial datasets is limited
Smart energy systems [66]	DT and ML	Deployment of DT for system monitoring	Survey of DT	Considerable improvement of real-time decision-making	Data governance and implementation issues
Microgrid system [67]	Neural network architecture and reinforcement learning	Microgrid operation cost	Microgrid simulation models	Optimization of cost and effective control of microgrid	Real-time microgrid tests missing
Solar PV system [68]	ANNs	Forecasting of solar radiation	PV datasets	Assess the impact of solar radiation predictions on the performance of PV system	Lack of benchmark datasets
Renewable energy system [69]	ML and IoT sensor	Forecasting and optimization of RESs integration	Real-time data from renewable sites	Improved forecasting accuracy	Sensor errors, missing data issues and high computa-tional costs
Wind system [70]	ML and DL methods	Review of AI in wind system	Literature survey	Economic impacts and green energy innovation	Simulation-based and data inconsistency issues
[71]	ML and DL	Review of ML and DL	Public datasets	State-of-the-art and key trends of IoT, hybrid models and smart grids	Few real-time operational case studies
Offshore wind farm [72]	DT platform	Offshore wind farm monitoring and maintenance	Offshore WT data	Improved visualization and reduced downtime	Real-time field testing is limited
Wind turbines system [73]	Back propagation neural network and DT	Wind power prediction and maintenance through DT	Historical meteorological and wind turbines datasets	Improved maintenance planning and power prediction	Data confidentiality issues

The potential of IoT and AI has not been fully tapped in areas of real-time processing, standardization, cyber security and deployment in underserved regions despite their several benefits. The literature review shows that several issues have not been adequately resolved in the research and practical integration of IoT and AI in RESs. The following research gaps are identified based on a thorough literature review carried out in the paper and further research to harness the potential of AI and IoT in RESs is proposed. Most existing studies are focused on the deployment of either AI or IoT in conventional and hybridized power systems without fully considering their combined synergism in the energy value chain. Standardized power systems that incorporate AI and IoT into RESs are not well studied. The scalability and interoperability challenges of AI models remain one of the significant barriers to improving the sustainability of energy through energy management systems. The real-time decision-making limitations of AI models under dynamic conditions, such as grid instability and the intermittent nature of RESs, have also been identified in several studies. Despite significant advancements in the integration of IoT and AI in renewable energy systems, cyber security risks and data governance have not been sufficiently addressed in the literature. There is a considerable knowledge gap in the academic research and embedded operations of AI and IoT models in the power system based on a thorough assessment of the state-of-the-art of the published work on RESs. The challenges of IoT and AI as well as research gaps identified from the literature can be addressed by using concerted efforts of academics, investors and legislators. The main objective of this study is to conduct a comprehensive review of the state-of-the-art of IoT and AI technologies and their significant potential in smart energy management systems. This study identifies current trends, challenges and opportunities of using AI and IoT in renewable energy-based power systems. This study proposes several research strategies that can support future research and development and address the challenges of AI and IoT devices. This paper's contributions are listed as follows:

i. The presentation of the state-of-the-art of IoT and AI and their roles in renewable energy-based smart grids.
ii. An overview of AI techniques utilized in RESs for predictive maintenance, forecasting, optimization, grid management and demand-side management.
iii. A review of the existing literature on IoT devices and communication technologies used for the management, control and monitoring of RESs.
iv. The presentation of the benefits and applications of integrating IoT and AI into emerging power systems.
v. The presentation of IoT and AI technologies that can be used to address inherent challenges of RESs such as the intermittency and unpredictability of wind speed and solar irradiance.
vi. The provision of detailed contributions of IoT and AI strategies for the improvement of grid flexibility and the operational efficiency of the power system.
vii. The presentation of pilot projects that demonstrate the implementation of IoT and AI technologies in RESs.
viii. The presentation of emerging trends, challenges and areas of future study at the nexus of RESs, AI and IoT for academic research, industrial applications and policymakers.

The remaining parts of this paper are presented as follows: A comprehensive overview of IoT, architectural components and critical functions in data acquisition, and monitoring and control within renewable energy systems is presented in Section 2. An introduction to AI and its diverse roles in forecasting, optimizing grid management and predictive maintenance are outlined in Section 3. The synergy and integration of IoT and AI in renewable energy systems and the successful implementation of AI and IoT projects in RESs are presented in Section 4. The technical, economic, regulatory and societal challenges that hinder the full implementation of AI and IoT technologies in RESs and future research directions of AI and IoT in sustainable energy are presented in Section 5. The conclusion that consists of key findings and recommendations is presented in Section 6.

2. Internet of Things

IoT is a vast and transformative process that connects smart devices and other objects to a network [74,75]. It utilizes sensors, connectivity modules, processing units, power sources and user interfaces for data collection, transmission, processing and interaction with the physical world. IoT has successfully transformed the global energy system based on the following benefits: better control and automation, higher cost efficiency, smart grid management, balanced distributed systems, better transparent electricity utilization, efficient smart meters and supreme residential solutions. The applications of IoT encompass the following: smart cities, smart healthcare, smart homes, smart grids, smart transportation, smart environmental monitoring, smart agriculture and smart water management systems. IoT has emerged as a transformative technology that can be used across different sectors of the economy to improve automation processes, operations and services, remote monitoring, customer experiences, the optimization of resources, decision-making and optimal performance. The potential applications and benefits of IoT across different industries are presented in Table 2 [62,76–79]. Internet of Things is classified into five major categories such as consumer IoT (CIoT), commercial IoT, industrial IoT (IIoT), infrastructure IoT and medical IoT (IoMT) [15,80]. The visual representation of IoT types and key applications is preented in Figure 2.

Table 2. Overview of IoT applications across multiple industries.

Industry	IoT Applications	Benefits
Energy and utilities	Smart grids, renewable energy forecasting and predictive maintenance.	Improved efficiency, reduced outages and optimized energy use.
Healthcare	Remote patient monitoring, smart hospitals, telemedicine and delivery of effective care devices.	Better patient outcomes, reduced hospital visits and improved cost savings.
Agriculture	Precision irrigation, soil and crop monitoring, livestock tracking and supply chain tracking.	Higher crop yields, reduced resource use and improved food quality.
Manufacturing	Predictive maintenance, smart factories, inventory tracking and worker safety devices.	Reduced downtime, increased productivity and safer workplaces.
Transportation and logistics	Fleet management, smart traffic, public transit tracking and autonomous electric vehicles.	Reduced fuel costs, improved safety and reduced traffic congestion.
Smart cities	Smart lighting, smart waste management, water monitoring, air quality sensors and smart parking.	Sustainability, cost savings and improved standard of living in urban areas.
Retail	Smart shelves, personalized shopping and cold chain monitoring.	Enhanced customer experience, reduced losses and improved inventory control system.
Banking and finance	Online payments, monitoring of debit cards, fraud detection and smart branches.	Increased security, better customer experience and operational efficiency.
Construction and real estate	Smart buildings, structural health monitoring and site safety sensors.	Energy efficiency, improved safety and reduced maintenance costs.
Environmental monitoring	Climate and weather sensors, wildlife tracking and disaster early warning systems.	Protection of ecosystems, reduced disaster impact and better planning.

It consists of several components that allow IoT to collect, transmit and act on data obtained from the environment. The components of IoT allow devices to connect, collect data and interact with each other. These components include sensors/devices, connectivity, data processing and user interfaces, which are presented in Figure 3. Sensors collect real-time data from the environment, connectivity allows communication between devices, data processing allows the analysis and interpretation of the information and user interfaces allow a human operator to interact with the system.

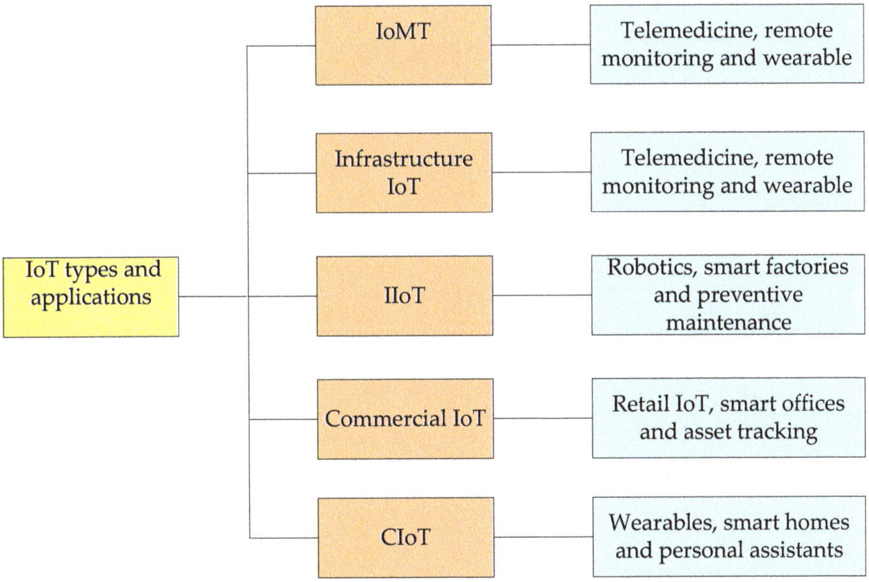

Figure 2. Visual representation of IoT types and key applications.

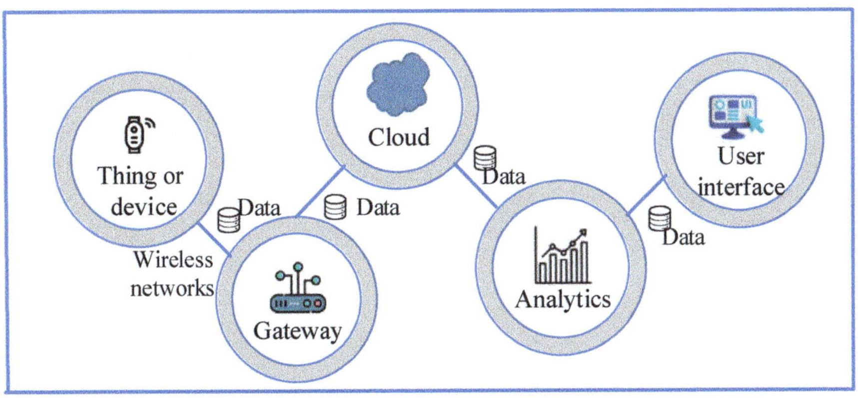

Figure 3. Core components of IoT: devices, cloud, gateway, analytics and user interface.

2.1. Architectures of Internet of Things

An IoT architecture is the structured framework that explains the interaction of IoT systems such as layers, communication processes and components. It coordinates the collection, transmission, processing and delivery of data obtained from IoT devices at connected platforms. The IoT architecture is designed to facilitate the flow of data from the device layer to the application layer. It offers an interactive platform for the application of IoT devices and ensures that all of the components of the IoT system operate together in a smooth manner. IoT architecture is the mainstay of IoT systems that describes how technologies, applications and IoT devices work together to provide the intended practical applications. IoT architecture is classified into three-layer architecture, five-layer architecture and cloud fog edge computing architecture based on layer-based architecture; application domain and purpose. The three types of IoT architectures are presented in Figure 4 by using the following layers: perception, network, processing, application, business, cloud, fog and edge. The comparison of IoT architectures is based on the functional flow from sensors to applications. The abovementioned layers based on the architectures of IoT are compared on the basis of components, strengths, weaknesses and applications and presented in Table 3.

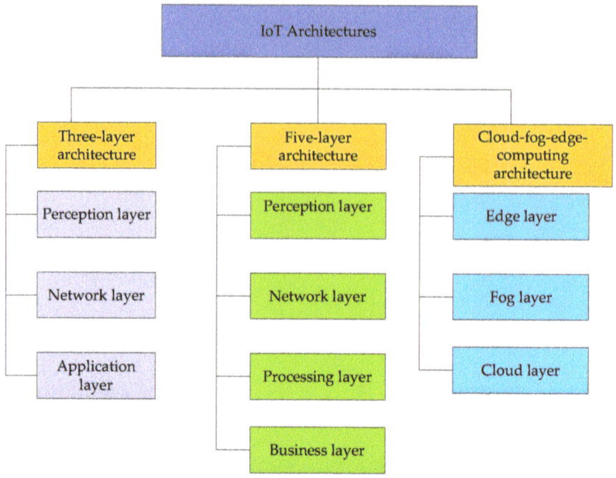

Figure 4. Classification of an IoT architecture.

Table 3. Comparison of IoT architectures in terms of strengths, weaknesses, applications and layers.

Architecture	Layers and Components	Strengths	Weaknesses	Applications
Three-layer architecture	Perception layer: Sensors and actuators Network layer: Communication, gateways and internet Application layer: services to users	Simple, widely adopted and easy to understand and implement	Over simplified, does not handle security, scalability, or big data explicitly limited support for complex services	Small-scale IoT deployments and basic smart home systems
Five-layer architecture	Perception layer: sensors and actuators Network layer: Communication, gateways and internet Edge/processing layer: Data processing, storage, cloud and fog Application layer: services to users Business layer: Management decision-making	Detailed and structured, business perspective, support security and management of IoT and integration of ML/DL analytics	Complex to implement, expensive cost and high computational overhead	Industrial IoT, smart cities and decision-making
Cloud–fog–edge architecture	Perception/end devices: Sensors, actuators Edge computing: Local processing near source Fog computing: Intermediate processing closer to devices Cloud computing: Centralized storage and advanced analytics	Low latency, scalable, flexible and real-time decision-making applications	Requires complex orchestration, higher infrastructure and security challenges	Autonomous vehicles, healthcare and smart grids

2.2. Internet of Things in Renewable Energy Systems

The integration of IoT into renewable energy systems has globally been acknowledged as a transformative development to change conventional power systems to decentralized power systems with emerging features. The efficient management and integration of RESs into the utility grid is facilitated by IoT devices that support the data analysis, real-time monitoring and automation of the associated components of the power system [81]. The cost-effectiveness and efficiency of RESs have increased recently owing to technological advancement and the high demand for clean and affordable energy. The integration of IoT in renewable energy technologies has considerably transformed how wind or solar farm operators monitor and collect data and maintain and interact with PV systems, wind turbines and associated components. The performance of RESs in centralized and decentralized power systems has been increased by IoT devices that provide real-time data and the advanced analysis of energy generation and usage [33]. The integration of IoT technologies in distribution networks leads to the balance of power generation and load demand and an improvement of the overall efficiency of the system [19,24]. IoT can be used to improve the incorporation of RESs into the utility grid by allowing data analysis and real-time monitoring for the optimization of the power system [82]. The incorporation of IoT devices into RESs plays a crucial role in the transformation of brown energy technologies into green energy technologies by providing real-time communication, monitoring, control and automation that ensure the efficient and sustainable utilization of renewable energy resources. The real-time role of IoT in renewable energy integration is presented in Figure 5.

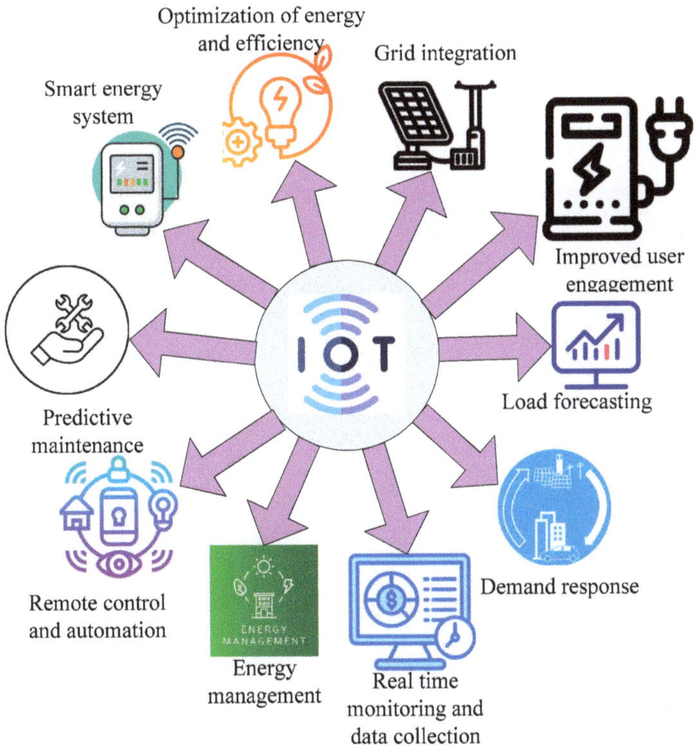

Figure 5. Real-time role of IoT in supporting renewable energy integration.

2.3. Impact of IoT on Renewable Energy Systems

IoT has a profound and transformative impact on RESs by introducing real-time data collection, remote control, predictive analytics and automated decision-making [24,26,29]. The overall contribution of RESs to the energy mix can be increased by using IoT that monitors, manages and optimizes power system [16]. The integration of IoT in RESs has considerable impacts on the power system such as a 15% improvement in energy generation, 35–50% reduction in unscheduled downtimes, 30–40% reduction in maintenance cost, 5–20% reduction in peak demand, 59.1% reduction in forecasting error, 19–25% increase in usable renewable generation, 64% reduction in supply and demand mismatch, 15–20% curtailment reduction, 3–6% reduction in distribution system losses, 3–8% increase in usable storage efficiency of battery system, reduction in energy losses, 2–5% increase in net annual energy yield of wind turbines, 5–12% improvement in solar system annual energy yield and 5–30% reduction in operating cost [69,74,83–86]. IoT devices can be used by the operators of a solar farm to optimize the inclination angle of PV panels, maximizing solar irradiance exposure and energy conversion. The health status of each PV panel can be monitored by IoT devices that promptly address the technical challenges of RESs. IoT technologies are used to monitor wind conditions and turbine operations in real time by adjusting turbine speeds and positions to capture optimal wind energy. The transformative role of RESs in the conventional power system can be improved with the application of the Internet of Things. It is utilized in the power system to transform renewable energy systems from static, unreliable, inefficient, consumer-passive and fragile systems into intelligent, adaptive, consumer-driven, resilient and sustainable systems. The impacts of IoT on renewable energy systems can be assessed by comparing some key performance indicators before the integration of IoT and after the integration of IoT devices into the power system. The impacts of IoT on renewable energy systems are presented in Table 4 [16,87–89].

Table 4. Overview of IoT contributions to renewable energy systems.

Impact Areas	Before IoT Integration	After IoT Integration
Operational efficiency	Manual adjustment and higher downtime	Automated adjustment and lower downtime
Energy storage management	Static usage of batteries and difficulty in charging/discharging	Smart energy storage solutions that monitor charge cycles and prevent overloading
Efficiency and cost-effectiveness	Lower operational efficiency due to manual processes; higher operational costs	Increased operational efficiency through automation and predictive maintenance
Energy efficiency	High efficiency losses	High system efficiency with panel tracker and AI analytics
Maintenance costs	High owing to reactive maintenance	Low owing to predictive maintenance
Energy output	Less optimized and variable outputs	More consistent and increased outputs
Remote management	Limited or non-existent	Extensive and sophisticated
Grid integration	Centralized grid control with limited flexibility and weak support for variable renewables	Dynamically balance energy supply and demand in real time; better integration of DERs
Consumer interaction	Limited visibility and control of consumers over their energy consumption and production	Active participation of consumers in the energy market
Environmental Impact	High GHG emissions owing to over-reliance on fossil fuels	Reduction in carbon footprint and high renewable energy penetration
Scalability	Difficult to scale up renewable energy generation projects	Easy to scale up renewable energy generation projects
Challenges/risks	Minimal digital vulnerabilities owing to manual operations	Cyber security concerns and interoperability problems

2.4. Data Acquisition and Monitoring in Renewable Energy Systems

IoT data acquisition and monitoring comprises the collection of data from sensors and other devices that are connected to the internet [29]. It can be used for the efficient, reliable and sustainable operation of power systems as well as monitoring the entire energy value chain from the generation sources to the load points. This leads to improved efficiency, cost savings, better decision-making and enhanced consumer comfort [90]. This technology is utilized in various applications such as smart homes, smart cities, industrial automation, environmental monitoring and research. The IoT-enabled data acquisition and monitoring system can be used for the monitoring of temperature, pressure, humidity and energy consumption, data collection and analysis, the remote control of devices and systems, process automation and environmental monitoring [33]. Data acquisition and monitoring can be used to improve the optimal performance, energy forecasting and fault detection of the power system [34]. It plays a vital role in tracking the performance of a PV system, wind turbine output, fault detection, predictive maintenance, load balancing and battery charge/discharge energy [27]. Data acquisition and monitoring is a process that can be used to assess the performance of renewable energy systems based on the analysis of data collected from sensors and communication technologies. This involves the measurement of technical parameters such as meteorological conditions, electrical parameters and other relevant parameters. The framework that describes data acquisition and monitoring in renewable energy systems is presented in Figure 6. Sensors are installed on RESs and battery storage systems to collect real-time parameters such as irradiance, wind speed, wind direction, power output, state of charge, voltage, current, temperature and load demand. These physical phenomena are converted to electrical signals by the sensors installed on the RESs and battery storage system. The raw data obtained from the sensors are filtered and cleaned up before they are digitized and packaged into structured data for transmission to make them suitable for data acquisition. IoT devices collect and transmit real-time data through wireless and wired communication systems. The data is transmitted to a central system using communication systems such as Wi-Fi, Zigbee, LoRa, NB-IoT, GSM/4G/5G, Ethernet and RS485 [91]. The operators of the systems can access real-time data such as energy generation, energy consumption patterns and historical data reports on a dashboard or mobile applications.

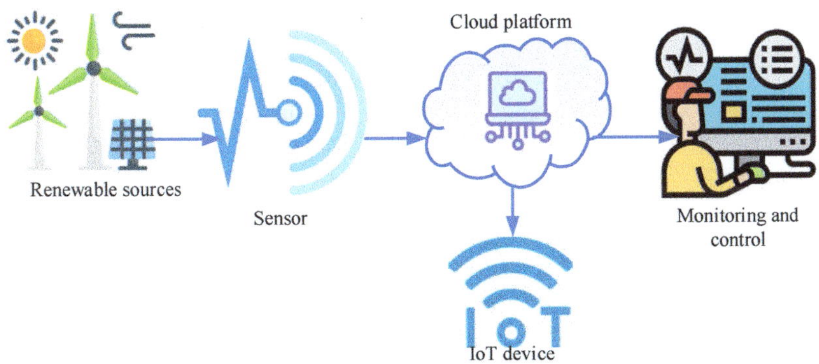

Figure 6. Framework for data collection and monitoring of renewable energy systems.

2.5. Real-Time Performance Monitoring of Renewable Energy System Using IoT

Real-time monitoring is a process that consist of sensors, IoT devices and data analytics tools for the observation and measurement of key performance parameters of PV panels, wind turbines, small hydro and battery system such as temperature, pressure, solar irradiance, water head and wind speed in real time [92]. The real-time monitoring of renewable energy systems provides immediate insights into impending conditions of power systems and allows the maintenance teams to make quick decisions and detect the problems before leading to catastrophic failures. The operators of a utility grid can enhance the proactive maintenance efforts, address inefficiencies and improve the overall system reliability of their assets by using real-time performance monitoring. The real-time monitoring of renewable energy resources is a powerful tool that can be used by the power system operator to stay ahead of potential failures, improve efficiency and reduce operation and maintenance costs. The operators of the utility grid can optimize maintenance schedules and improve the asset reliability of their systems by providing continuous insight into asset performance. Real-time monitoring can be used for the early detection of problems that deviate from normal operating conditions, improving the decision-making of organizations. The early identification of the wear and tear of the power system components through continuous monitoring can increase the longevity of the asset. The real-time monitoring of renewable energy with sensors, an IoT gateway, a cloud platform, a monitoring dashboard and remote access is presented in Figure 7.

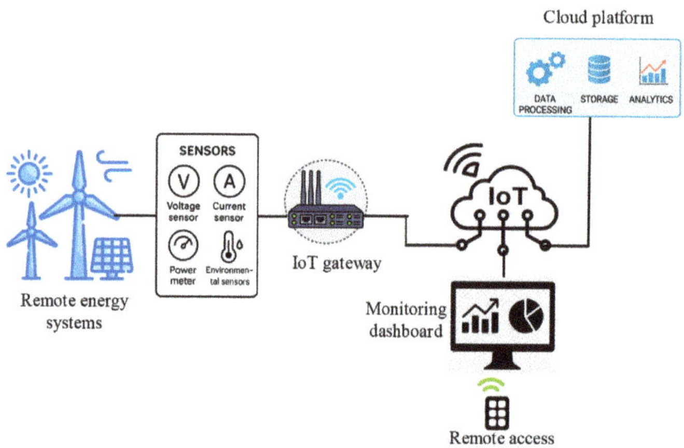

Figure 7. Real-time monitoring of renewable energy system using IoT.

2.6. *Automation of Processes for Efficiency and Safety*

The integration of IoT into RESs has changed the landscape of renewable energy generation by increasing efficiency, optimizing performance and enhancing the sustainability of the power system [93]. The automation processes to enhance the efficiency and safety of power systems can be achieved by integrating smart sensors, advanced analytics and real-time monitoring devices into power systems. The exigency of efficient distribution networks is paramount with the global adoption of green energy technologies for power generation applications. Power producers or prosumers can enhance the performance efficiency and power output capability of their systems by using smart devices and IoT technologies. IoT sensors are incorporated into the power system to analyze the patterns of data and forecast equipment failures before their occurrence [94]. This would ultimately reduce downtimes, minimize maintenance costs and increase the lifetime of renewable energy components. The sensors of IoT can be used in RESs to monitor energy flow, identify irregularities and modify distribution parameters in real time. At the same time, it guarantees that a continuous power supply is delivered to the respective consumers with maximum efficiency and minimal power losses. IoT sensors are also installed on wind turbines to optimize blade angles and identify maintenance issues before escalating to highly expensive breakdowns. The application of IoT in process automation for operational safety and efficiency is presented in Figure 8.

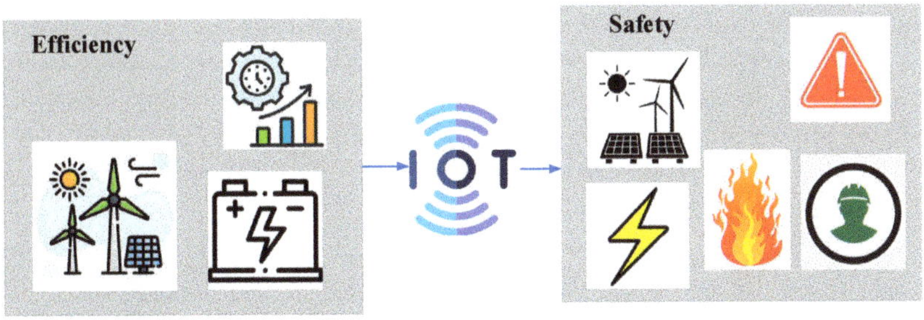

Figure 8. IoT applications in process automation for operational safety and efficiency.

2.6.1. Smart Metering and Consumption Monitoring

Installed smart meters embedded with IoT devices would allow power utility companies to assess patterns of energy usage, improve the performance of their systems and respond quickly to demand fluctuations. This would allow consumers to make knowledgeable decisions about their energy usage, reduce energy waste, reduce GHG emissions, promote sustainable practices and increase the efficiency of the power system based on the accessibility to information about electrical power consumption. Advanced analytics tools can be used to examine the data gathered by smart metering and consumption monitoring and provide information about the patterns and trends of energy consumption. Power utility companies can use these insights to identify important areas for improvement, such as a reduction in peak demand, the optimization of the battery system and the application of demand response management, which would ultimately enhance the efficiency and sustainability of the energy system. Smart metering can be utilized by consumers to take active control of their energy usage. Smart metering systems can relate to IoT-enabled smart home devices to give a complete picture of energy consumption. The integration of smart metering systems into residential buildings will allow consumers to reduce their energy consumption, reduce monthly or yearly utility bills and live a sustainable lifestyle [24]. A typical diagram for smart metering, consumption and monitoring applications is presented in Figure 9.

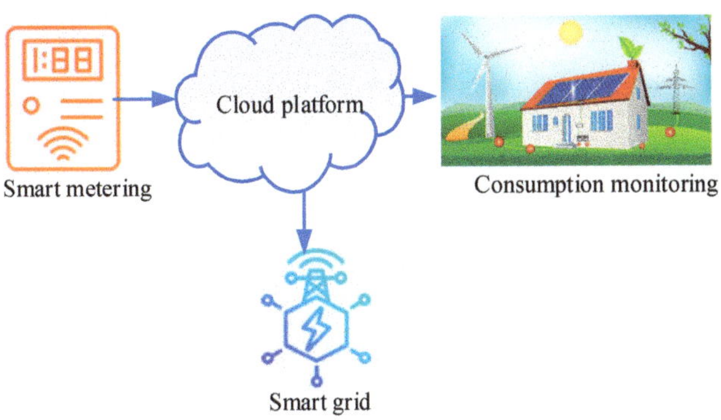

Figure 9. Smart metering applications for real-time consumption and monitoring.

2.6.2. Predictive Maintenance Using Internet of Things

Predictive maintenance in smart grids utilizes IoT sensors to monitor equipment conditions and leverage historical performance metrics to anticipate equipment failures in wind turbines and solar panels [95]. The approach detects early signs of wear or malfunction of the equipment by allowing quick maintenance that will reduce operational costs, minimize downtime, extend asset life and optimize the overall operational efficiency of installed RESs. Wind turbines, PV systems and other renewable energy infrastructure are constantly exposed to harsh elements. The early signs of equipment failure can be identified by IoT devices based on the analysis of the information obtained from the sensor data and maintenance logbooks of such equipment. The proactive maintenance of the equipment prevents costly breakdowns and ensures the optimal operation of the RES.

- Predictive Maintenance of Solar Panels

The predictive maintenance of PV systems can be carried out by using remote control and automation with IoT sensors to continuously collect data on the health status of solar panels. The technical and meteorological data obtained from the system can be analyzed to forecast the actual time when the PV system is expected to fail or its performance will deteriorate owing to several technical challenges such as corrosion and micro cracks [96]. Predictive maintenance has several advantages in solar systems such as the minimization of unscheduled power interruption, a reduction in repair costs and the consistent energy output of the PV system. The application of IoT devices for the predictive maintenance of solar panels with real-time monitoring is presented in Figure 10. The major components for the predictive maintenance of solar systems using IoT devices include the IoT sensor, IoT gateway, communication network, cloud and edge processing unit, dashboard and monitoring and maintenance and action layer. Sensors are installed on the solar panels to capture real-time operational and environmental data such as irradiance, temperature, voltage, current and soiling from solar panels. The aggregated sensor data is pre-processed by an IoT gateway that ensures secure communication to the cloud/edge. The communication network transmits data obtained from field devices to processing units using Wi-Fi, Zigbee, LoRaWAN, 4G/5G or NB-IoT. AI/ML models are run by a cloud/edge processing unit for the detection of anomalies and the predictive maintenance of solar panels. The dashboard and monitoring unit utilizes Grafana, ThingsBoard, Power BI and Kibana to visualize the health status of solar panels, provide real-time key performance indicators and generate alerts and notifications for operators. The predictive insights of the solar panels are converted into corrective actions such as the repair of major parts, cleaning of panels, replacement of components and scheduling of operation.

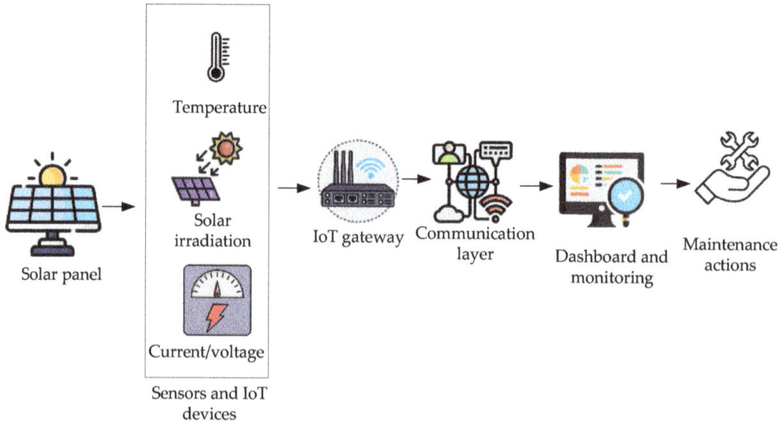

Figure 10. Application of IoT devices for predictive maintenance of solar panels with real-time monitoring.

- Predictive Maintenance of Wind Farms

Predictive maintenance is crucial for wind farms by using remote control and automation to improve the performance and reduce the downtime of wind turbines. Wind turbines embedded with IoT devices provide detailed data on the condition of each component and allow maintenance teams to detect potential problems before their deterioration [26,28]. The advantages of IoT-driven predictive maintenance include a reduction in downtime and repair costs, safety improvement by preventing catastrophic failures, prolonging the lifetime of wind turbines and the maximization of return on investment. The application of IoT devices for the predictive maintenance of wind turbines with real-time monitoring is presented in Figure 11. Sensors are installed on the major components of wind turbines to capture real-time operational and environmental data such as rotational speed, torque, vibration and power output from wind turbines. The data is sent through communication networks (LoRaWAN, 5G, Zigbee, Wi-Fi and satellite) to gateways. The aggregated wind turbine data is securely filtered and sent to cloud/edge servers. The cloud/edge processing unit is used to store and analyze data using AI/ML models for the detection of abnormal vibration and noise in gearbox/blades, forecasting of component failures, identification of wears in bearing and generators and predictive maintenance. The real-time predictive maintenance of wind turbines is visualized using dashboard solutions to display turbine health status, blade stress, performance and vibration trends, predicted faults and overall power production. Alerts or notifications are sent to operators through SMS, email or mobile apps using the dashboard and real-time visualization unit. The maintenance teams are dispatched to the wind farm to carry out preventive measures such as blade inspection, gearbox lubrication or generator cooling before breakdowns of wind turbines. The predictive maintenance of wind farm reduces downtime and associated costs.

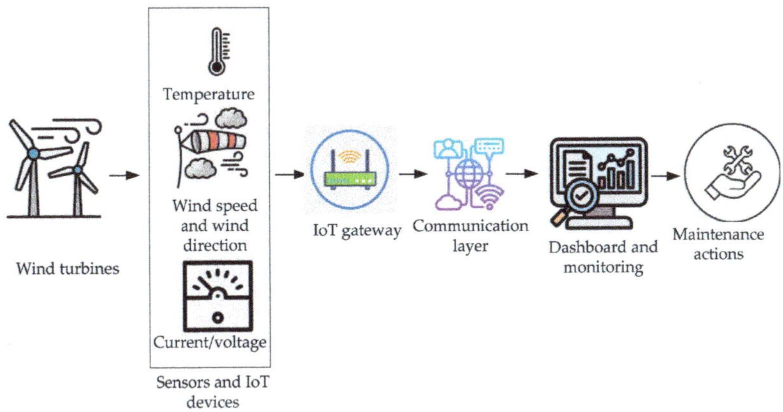

Figure 11. Application of IoT devices for predictive maintenance of wind farms with real-time monitoring.

2.7. Smart Grids

A smart grid is a system that utilizes digital technology and two-way communication facilities to enhance the reliability, efficiency and sustainability of a power supply at the load points. It utilizes various technologies like an advanced metering infrastructure, sensors and automated controls, communication networks, energy storage systems, distributed energy resources and grid management systems to coordinate and manage the flow of electrical power from different generation sources to consumption points. It allows the real-time monitoring of power supply and load demand, the optimization of energy usage and the integration of RESs into the conventional power system. The conventional power systems of some countries have been upgraded to emerging power systems with the integration of smart features as a measure to satisfy the requirements of the sustainability, privacy, security and reliability of the networks. The performance of smart grids has surpassed the capabilities of traditional power systems by offering a range of advantages such as improved efficiency, resilience and reliability, guaranteed energy security, improved resilience and adaptability, enhanced user participation, advanced sustainable development and cost saving [97]. A smart grid is an innovative technology that utilizes communication and information facilities to achieve the optimal management, real-time monitoring and intelligent scheduling of the power system using sensors, information and computer technology, smart features and communication networks. The ability of the smart grid to monitor and control the grid and achieve the optimal management of the utility grid and reduction in unscheduled power interruptions is based on the utilization of smart features and emerging technologies in the existing power systems. The key components of a smart grid are presented in Figure 12.

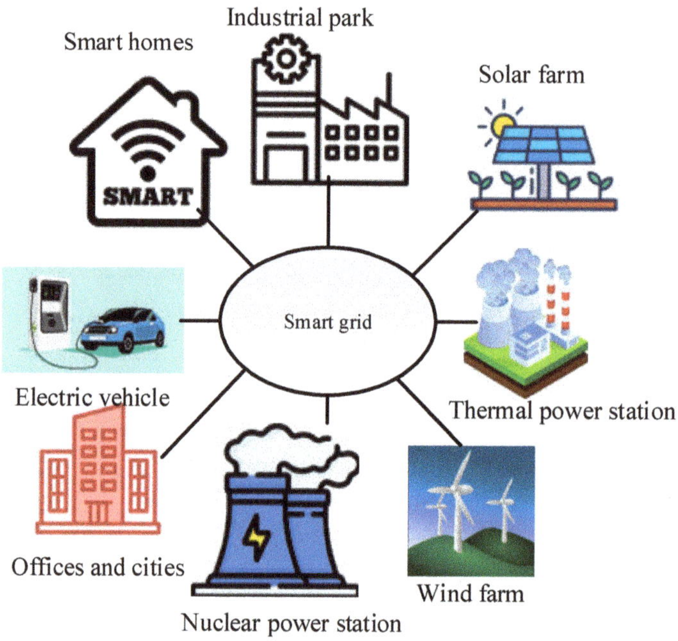

Figure 12. Key components of a smart grid system.

Comparison of Traditional Power Systems and Smart Grids

The solutions presented by the smart grid can be used to overcome the challenges of aging infrastructure, a lack of real-time monitoring, limited customer engagement, vulnerability to blackouts, limited flexibility, high transmission losses, a lack of access to power supply and poor scalability [98]. A complete implementation of the smart grid would support the economic feasibility of RESs in the utility grid to satisfy ever-increasing load demands. The technology would also allow consumers to actively participate in the real-time monitoring of their energy usage, electricity bills and the deployment of electric vehicles from the grids. The failure of traditional power systems to address the problems of a consistent power supply has been attributed to numerous technical issues. These challenges can be addressed by the conversion of traditional power systems to smart grid systems. The comparison between a conventional power system and smart grid is presented in Table 5 [24,99].

Table 5. Comparison of characteristics of smart grids and traditional power systems.

Feature	Traditional Power System	Smart Grid
Customer interaction	Limited	Extensive
Restoration	Manual	Automatic and self-healing
Electricity flow	One-way electricity flow	Bidirectional energy and information flow
Generation	Centralized generation	Decentralized and distributed generation
Communication	One-way communication with manual control	Real-time two-way communication through smart meters and sensors
Consumer role	Passive and limited insight into usage	Active participation of consumers with real-time usage feedback and variable pricing
Monitoring and control	Manual fault detection and restoration	Automated, real-time monitoring, self-healing grid capabilities
Outage Response	Manual detection, a slow restoration process and longer blackouts	Self-healing capabilities and automatically detection of electrical faults
Operation and maintenance	Check electrical components manually	Monitor the electrical system remotely
Load management	Static, centralized and no demand response programs	Dynamic load management and demand-response optimization
Security	Focused on the physical security of infrastructure	Focused on cyber security measures to protect digital threats and attacks
Topology	Radial	Network
Efficiency and losses	Higher losses and low efficiency	Lower losses and optimized energy delivery
Technology	Electromechanical	Digital
Integration of RESs	Difficult to integrate intermittent RESs.	Seamlessly integrate and manage various RESs.
Automation and resilience	Manual repairs and slower outage recovery	Automated fault isolation and outage faster recovery
Environmental impact	High carbon emissions and reliance on fossil fuels	Supports renewables and decarbonization; reduces emissions
Data and decision-making	Limited data collection and retrospective decisions	Support predictive and automated decision-making

2.8. Distributed Energy Resources

Distributed energy resources are small-scale energy generation and electric storage systems that are located at or near the point of use, rather than centralized power systems. The integration of DERs such as wind turbines, microturbines, battery systems, PV systems and fuel cells into the traditional power system has considerably transformed the system into a reliable, resilient and efficient power system by reducing the reliance on fossil fuels and improving grid stability [16]. DERs are classified based on energy sources and the operational mode and functionality are presented in Table 6 [100–102].

Table 6. Classification of distributed energy resources based on energy sources, mode of operation and functionality.

Functionality Classification	Description	Examples	Operational Mode
Renewable generation	Clean energy sources	Solar PV, wind turbines, small hydro/micro-hydro	Grid-connected or off-grid
Non-renewable generation	Small-scale fossil-based generators	Diesel generator, gas generator and micro-turbines	Grid-connected or off-grid
Energy storage systems	Store and release electricity	Lithium-ion batteries, fuel cells, flywheels, pumped hydro storage	Grid-connected or off-grid
Demand response	Controllable loads	Smart HVAC, electric vehicles (EVs)	Grid-connected or off-grid
Combined heat and power	Simultaneous heat and power generation	Micro-combined heat and power systems	Grid-connected or off-grid
Renewable generation	Small-scale and direct use	Geothermal	Grid-connected or off-grid
Renewable generation	Clean energy sources	Renewable natural gas/biogas generators	Grid-connected or off-grid

Challenges of Distributed Energy Resources

DERs are decentralized small-scale energy technologies that offer significant benefits like increased energy independence, reduced carbon emissions and enhanced grid resilience but their integration into an existing power system which is originally designed for a centralized energy system poses several critical challenges [17]. The decentralized nature of DERs introduces several technical, operational, economic and regulatory challenges such as grid integration complexity, a lack of standardization, cyber security risks, regulatory and policy barriers, limited visibility and control for utilities, complex ownership and responsibility, load forecasting and planning difficulties, power quality issues and communication infrastructure requirements to the power systems. The adoption of DERs has been globally acknowledged as an exciting opportunity to meet an ever-increasing load demand but comes with several challenges that can be overcome by using the right approaches, such as smart grid technologies, innovative market designs, adaptive regulatory frameworks and continued technological advancements in areas like energy storage and IoT-driven control systems. Policymakers must work in conjunction with the power utility companies to formulate different policies that can be used to surmount the existing challenges and harness the potential of DERs [103]. It is paramount that microgrid operators heavily invest in DERs as a strategic measure to achieve a sustainable and efficient energy system. The transition to DER solutions is beneficial to commercial interests but also strengthens the overall energy infrastructure.

2.9. Integration of Smart Grids into Distributed Energy Resources

Smart grids and DERs are major components for the transition of a traditional energy system to an emerging energy system [30]. The integration of DERs such as battery storage systems, PV systems, microturbines, pump storage systems and wind turbines into smart grid systems can improve the energy efficiency, sustainability, resilience and reliability of the power system. The application of smart grid features to coordinate distributed energy resources and associated components are presented in Figure 13. The advanced communication and control abilities of smart grid systems are vital for managing the output power of DERs and maintaining a continuous power supply at consumer centers. This integration also supports the active participation of consumers in energy management and promotes a responsive and dynamic transactive energy system. Smart grids integrate DERs like solar panels, storage systems and wind turbines and cutting-edge technologies to monitor and control the flow of electricity in the power systems [17]. The integration of DERs into smart grids has several benefits such as improved energy efficiency, cost savings, sustainability through renewable energy adoption, improved grid reliability during outages and revenue opportunities [26]. The convergence of smart grid features and DERs in a single power system can be used to overcome the challenges of using DERs alone in a grid-connected or standalone hybrid energy system. The convergence of smart grid features and DERs in a single power system also facilitates the modernization of electricity infrastructure, supports the seamless integration of renewable energy resources and improves the efficiency and security of the power system [19]. It also allows the effective management of the stochastic nature of local RESs and supports the bi-directional flow of energy. The improved grid management systems based on the introduction of smart technologies into the traditional power system allow the utility grid operators to have greater control of their networks and allow the effective voltage control and load balance of the entire network. The rapid change in power demands at the load points requires careful planning to manage the complex collaborations between multiple DERs and the smart grids effectively [104]. Power utility companies can harness the potential of DERs by applying smart grid technologies in a sustainable energy system while addressing the challenges posed by emerging grid dynamics.

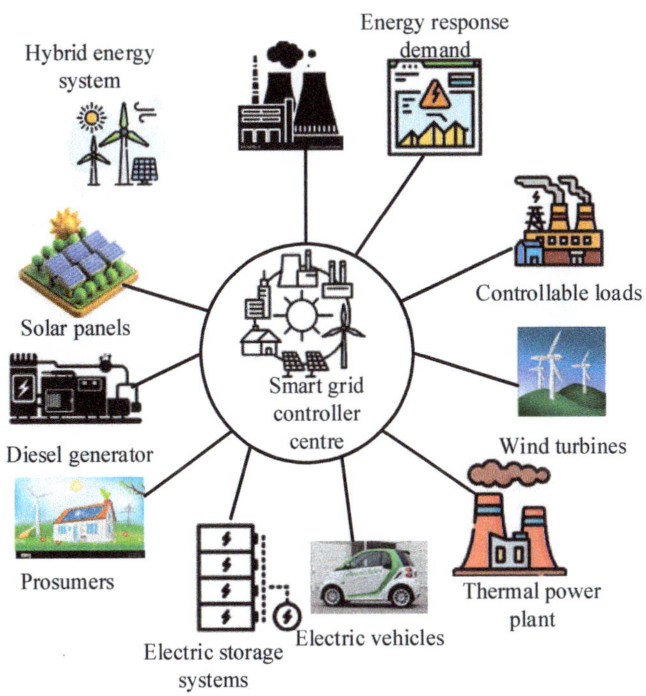

Figure 13. Coordination of distributed energy resources with smart grid features.

2.10. Management of Distributed Renewable Energy Sources and IoT Within a Smart Grid

Smart grid management is a dynamic field that entails the application of cutting-edge technologies to improve the efficiency and sustainability of conventional power systems [105]. The integration of intermittent RESs into the utility grid requires intelligent management systems that can be used to monitor and analyze energy flows in real time, forecast power interruptions, automatically adjust the components of the power system to maintain grid stability and optimize energy consumption. This has resulted in resilient and flexible utility grids that can handle a growing proportion of RESs. The management and control of DERs within a smart grid system encompasses the integration of IoT devices to optimize energy generation and energy usage [106]. IoT devices are used in RESs to optimize energy distribution and management by collecting real-time data from energy production and grid conditions [16,24]. The data obtained from sensors and devices installed on the power system can be analyzed to predict and mitigate the adverse effects of power supply fluctuations, grid imbalances and voltage variations in the power systems [26]. IoT devices are also integrated into RESs to facilitate the seamless operation of the smart grid using sensors, actuators and smart devices to address intermittent challenges and enhance the stability of the power system [27]. The collaboration between RESs, smart grids and IoT can be used to accomplish a clean and resilient energy system. The benefits of a smart grid system embedded with IoT include predictive maintenance, real-time monitoring and control, scalability and flexibility, cost savings, consumer empowerment, balanced energy generation with consumer demand and enhanced grid stability and a reduced risk of blackouts [21]. A typical smart grid management system from generation sources to varying electricity demand at the load points is presented in Figure 14.

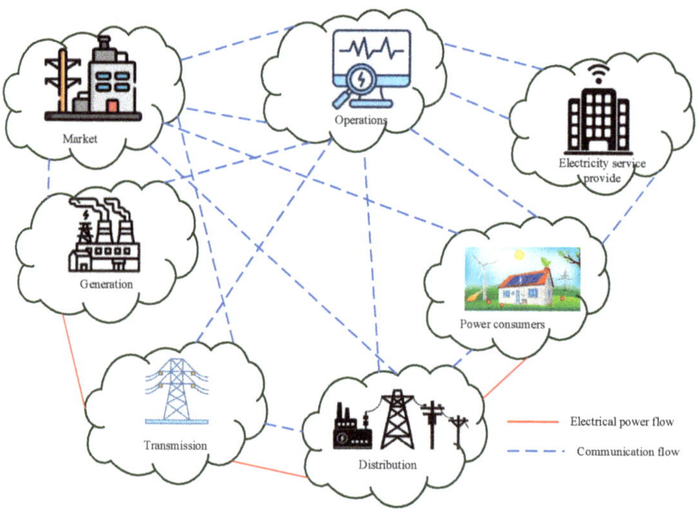

Figure 14. A typical diagram of smart grid management system from generation sources to varying electricity demand.

2.11. Application of IoT in Monitoring Photovoltaic Systems Within Smart Grids

A smart grid system embedded with IoT devices plays a proactive role in monitoring PV panels by collecting real-time data, allowing remote monitoring and facilitating predictive maintenance. This has led to a significant reduction in downtime, cost reduction, an improvement of the system performance and the optimization of solar system energy management [107]. It also enhances the efficiency and cost-effectiveness of smart grid systems in managing and utilizing the energy obtained from the PV system. Power utility companies and system operators can significantly increase reliability, reduce maintenance costs and optimize power flows by using IoT for PV system monitoring within a smart grid system. The integration of cutting-edge tools into renewable energy systems is a proactive approach to managing the system. The principal applications of IoT in the PV systems include performance monitoring and optimization, fault detection and diagnostics and remote control and management. IoT devices with several sensors are installed on the solar panels to gather operational data that can be utilized to monitor the performance of the PV system [33]. The data is transmitted to the cloud platforms where analysis and visualization will be carried out. The integration of IoT for the real-time monitoring of a PV system in a smart grid is presented in Figure 15.

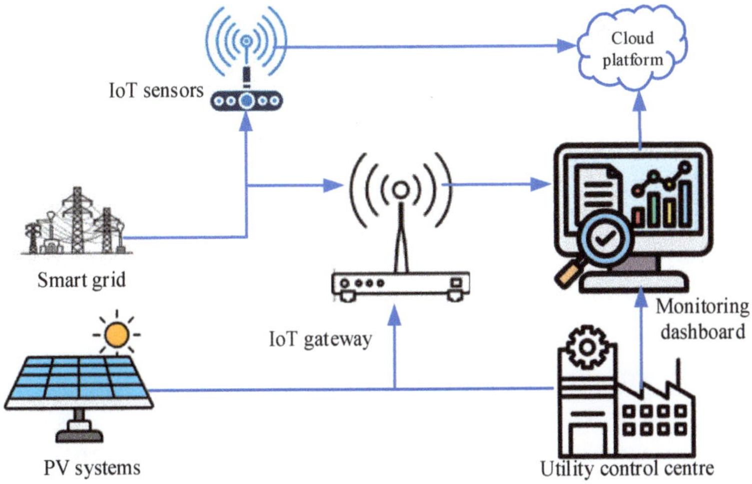

Figure 15. Integration of IoT for real-time monitoring of a PV system in a smart grid.

2.12. A Smart Grid IoT-Enabled Wind Turbine Monitoring System

IoT plays a significant role in improving the efficiency, reliability and intelligence of wind turbines with the integration of smart grid features [32]. IoT can be used in smart grids for fault detection, real-time monitoring and the optimization of wind turbines to support the dynamic energy demands of the utility grid [19,24]. A smart grid IoT-enabled wind turbine monitoring system is a sophisticated solution that integrates cutting-edge technology to achieve maximum efficiency and the smooth integration of wind energy into emerging power systems. The main features of the integration include performance monitoring and optimization, fault detection and diagnostics and the remote control and management of wind turbines. The integration of IoT for the real-time monitoring of wind turbines in a smart grid is presented in Figure 16. The power output of the wind turbines can be transformed into highly efficient and resilient components of the future energy system by the proactive actualization of the functionalities of the integration. This integrated approach transforms wind energy management from a reactive process to a proactive, data-driven and highly efficient system within the context of a modern smart grid [26]. The benefits of the integration also encompass reduced on-site visits, faster response to issues, improved operational flexibility, improved security, increased energy generation by adapting to wind changes, identified inefficient turbines for servicing and reduced energy loss and wear on components.

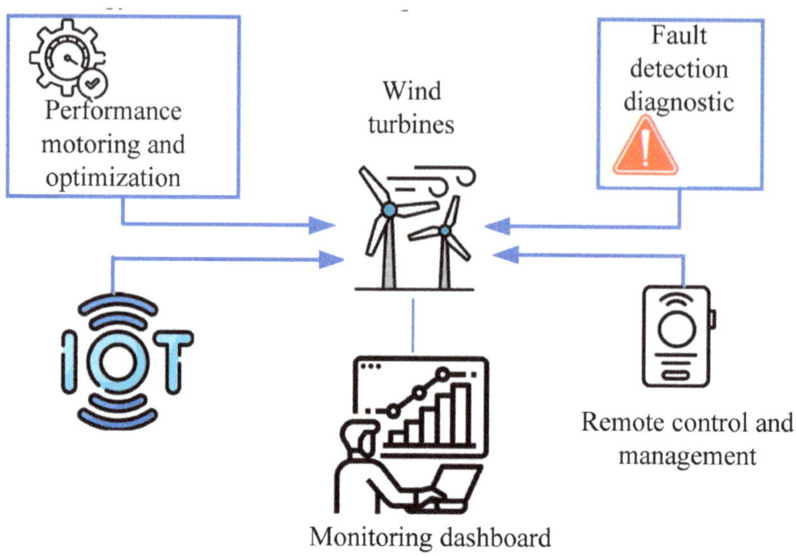

Figure 16. Integration of IoT for real-time monitoring of wind turbines in a smart grid.

2.13. IoT-Enabled Demand-Side Management and Integration with Smart Homes

Demand-side management (DSM) is a strategy that can be used to control and reduce electricity consumption on the consumer's side of the meter. A typical diagram of smart home energy with IoT-based DSM is presented in Figure 17. The objective of DSM is to optimize the utilization of energy, reduce peak energy demand, support dynamic energy pricing and improve the stability of the power system. Demand response systems powered by IoT allow grid operators to adjust energy consumption by using real-time data [108]. This can be utilized to reduce power consumption during peak periods, reduce the use of fossil fuels-based generating units as backup units, improve grid reliability, reduce energy wastage and optimize the utilization of energy resources. The IoT-enabled DSM is utilized in smart homes to allow optimum energy consumption by integrating smart devices to manage and control energy usage, increasing grid stability and promoting the sustainability of the energy system. IoT-enabled DSM is used in smart homes for the real-time monitoring of energy consumption, the integration of DERs, and the automatic control of smart homes and the adapted energy management system. Smart homes have become active participants in the energy markets with the advent of intelligent devices, smart meters and sophisticated energy management systems [109]. This has led to a significant transformation of conventional power systems that depend on a unidirectional power supply and demand. The seamless communication between residential appliances and the utility grid through IoT and DSM has converted most homeowners to prosumers. The vested interest of consumers in actively participating in energy generation activities has considerably reduced the cost of energy and utility bills and significantly contributes to a reliable and sustainable power supply at the load points.

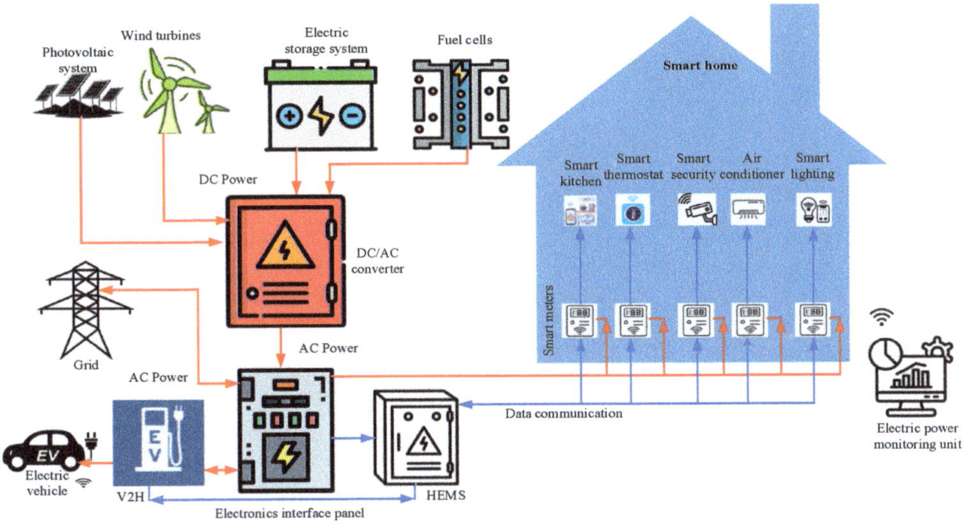

Figure 17. A typical diagram of smart homes energy using IoT-based DSM.

3. Artificial Intelligence

Artificial intelligence is a set of technologies that allow computers to implement tasks typically associated with human intelligence such as data analysis, the translation of languages, learning, decision-making and problem solving [29,91]. The informed decisions of AI are very fast and accurate by offering insights beyond human capabilities; this shows that outcomes of AI can be used in various sectors of the economy. AI is a computational system that primarily utilizes deep learning (DL) and machine learning for data analytics, predictions and forecasting and intelligent data retrieval. Applications of AI have been globally acknowledged in various industries in profound ways such as healthcare services, finance, retail and e-commerce, manufacturing, transportation and logistics, cyber security, agriculture and education. The benefits of AI technologies from the perspectives of society and the economy include zero risks, complex global challenges, enhanced cyber security, time saving capability, climate change mitigation, improved process efficiency, reduction in human errors, unbiased decisions and fostering innovation [110].

3.1. Artificial Intelligence Tools and Techniques

The foundation of AI was based on various learning theories such as statistical learning, evolutionary learning and neural learning. Neural networks and SVMs are the most popular learning algorithms utilized in the literature. In addition, AI algorithms consist of Random Forests, Decision Trees, Logistic Regressions, Linear Regression, Nearest Neighbor, Naïve Bayes and Hidden Markov. Renewable energy systems have adopted smarter systems like AI to make them more resilient and responsive [90]. The classification of AI techniques based on ML methods, metaheuristic algorithms and other techniques is shown in Figure 18.

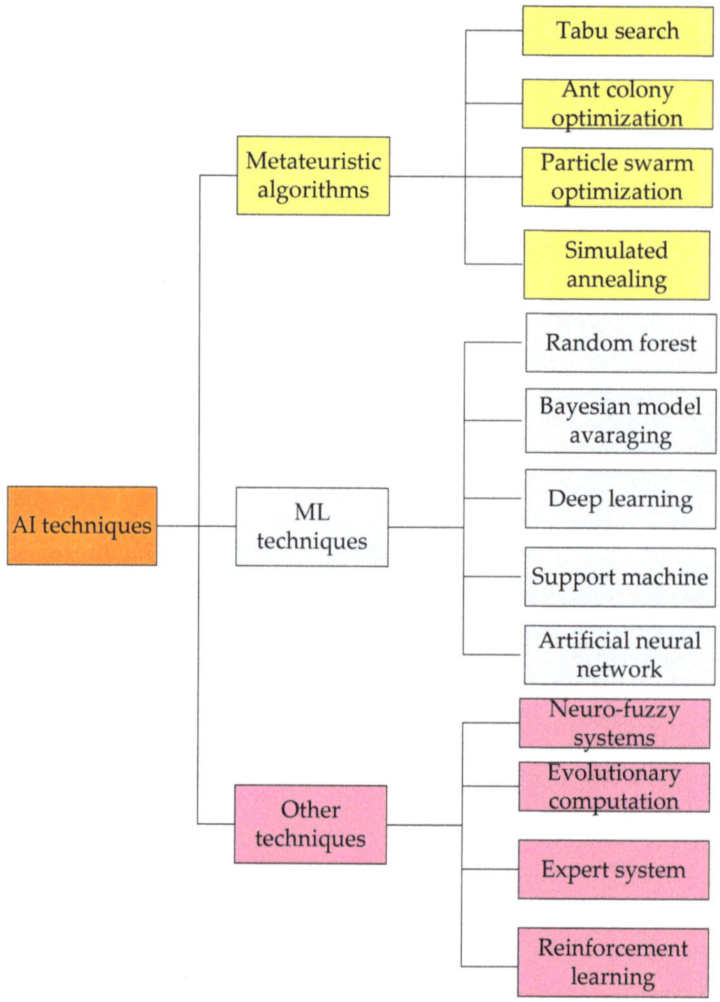

Figure 18. Overview of artificial intelligence techniques and their classification.

3.1.1. Metaheuristic Algorithms

Metaheuristic algorithms are high-level problem-solving strategies that can be used to find optimal solutions to complex optimization problems when mathematical approaches are practically not feasible, owing to computational complexity, large search spaces and nonlinearity. They are globally utilized in energy systems, power engineering, industrial and manufacturing systems, logistics, healthcare, bioinformatics and economics to find optimal solutions to complex and large-scale problems. Metaheuristic algorithms are classified into different categories based on the inspiration source, problem nature, search strategy, operational characteristics, exploration and hybridization approaches. A comparison of metaheuristic algorithms based on their strengths, weakness and applications are presented in Table 7 [111–116].

Table 7. Overview and comparison of metaheuristic optimization techniques.

Algorithm	Inspiration	Strengths	Weaknesses	Applications
Genetic algorithm	Biological evolution	Versatile to handle complex problems	Premature convergence and required parameter tuning	Load scheduling, cost minimization and optimal sizing
Particle swarm optimization	Social behavior of birds and fish swarms	Simple, fast convergence and easy to implement	Performance depends on parameters	Sizing of PV–wind–battery systems and economic load dispatch
Ant colony optimization	Foraging behavior of ants	Effective optimization	Low convergence and high computational cost	Optimization of hybrid system and microgrid scheduling
Teaching–learning-based optimization	Teacher–student learning process	Few parameters and easy implementation	Slow convergence for very large-scale problems	Demand-side management, smart home and load optimization
Gray wolf optimizer	Social hierarchy and hunting strategy of gray wolves	Strong exploration and fewer parameters	Converge slowly in fine-tuning	Multi-objective hybrid renewable system design
Whale optimization algorithm	Bubble-net hunting of humpback whales	Good for global search and effective in multi-modal problems	Risk of stagnation in later iterations	Optimal scheduling of PV–wind–battery systems
Bat algorithm	Echolocation of bats	Good exploration and exploitation and handle nonlinear problems	Sensitive to parameter setting	Hybrid PV–wind–diesel optimization, frequency regulation
Firefly algorithm	Flashing behavior of fireflies	Multimodal optimization and parallel search	Converge slowly and parameter tuning needed	Economic load dispatch and thermal comfort optimization
Cuckoo search	Parasitic reproduction of cuckoos and lévy flights	Efficient global search and few parameters	Required hybridization for local refinement	Renewable energy scheduling and structural optimization
Simulated annealing	Annealing process in metallurgy	Simple and good at escaping local optima	Low convergence and single solution-based	Energy dispatch and control system tuning

3.1.2. Machine Learning

Machine learning is a branch of AI that allows a system to automatically learn patterns from data and improve the performance of a particular task without being explicitly programmed. It is a statistical technique that can be used to establish computational models and make predictions based on the previous or stored data. The key characteristics of machine leaning methods are that they are data driven, adaptive, have a predictive capability and are capable of generalization. ML is one of the most versatile AI techniques that can be used in different applications such as computer science, energy systems, manufacturing, logistics, healthcare, agriculture, education, smart grids, business and finance. DL is a subset of ML that uses artificial neural networks with multiple layers to automatically learn complex patterns and representations from large amounts of data and make accurate predictions. DL models can extract features and make predictions directly from raw data inputs. A comparison of ML and DL techniques based on some key features is presented in Table 8 [117–120].

Table 8. Comparison of machine learning and deep learning techniques based on their characteristics.

Characteristics	Machine Learning	Deep Learning
Data Requirement	Small to medium-sized datasets	Large-scale datasets
Feature Engineering	Manual features	Automatic features
Computational Demand	Low	High
Interpretability	High	Low
Training Time	Relatively short	Very long
Performance with Structured Data	High	Moderate
Performance with Unstructured Data	Limited capability	Excellent
Deployment	Lightweight	Heavy
Accuracy	Moderate to high	Very high

3.2. *Artificial Intelligence in Renewable Energy Systems*

Artificial intelligence has become a transformative force in RESs with numerous applications such as energy forecasting, resource assessment, smart grid management, energy trading, demand response management system, smart homes and predictive maintenance [21]. The integration of AI features into RESs can be used to improve efficiency, reduce the challenges of grid integration, reduce electricity bills and enhance predictive maintenance [90]. AI can be utilized to analyze the data obtained from DERs such as wind turbines, PV systems and electric storage systems to identify energy patterns that are very difficult for human beings to detect. This would assist the renewable energy-based distribution network operators in optimizing the performance of their networks and improve the efficiency and sustainability of the energy system [26]. AI has played a significant role in grid management, the improvement of energy generation forecasting and the sustainability of PV systems and wind turbines by reducing unscheduled downtime by 20–40% and 35–50% [121,122]. AI is also utilized in renewable energy projects to reduce the operational costs of decentralized energy systems by the early detection of signs of wear and failure through predictive maintenance; this increases the lifetime of the infrastructure. The efficiency of solar energy has been increased by 15–67.65% owing to the optimization of PV panel orientations and the tracking of solar irradiance [123]. The potential of solar energy can be harnessed by AI to improve energy forecasting, enhance grid stability and increase the efficiency of the power system. AI can be utilized in the power system to forecast energy generation from renewable energy resources and allow grid operators to balance power supply and load demand. AI contributes to the overall cost reduction in RESs by improving efficiency and reducing maintenance costs [24]. The role and functions of AI in improving the efficiency of DERs are presented in Figure 19.

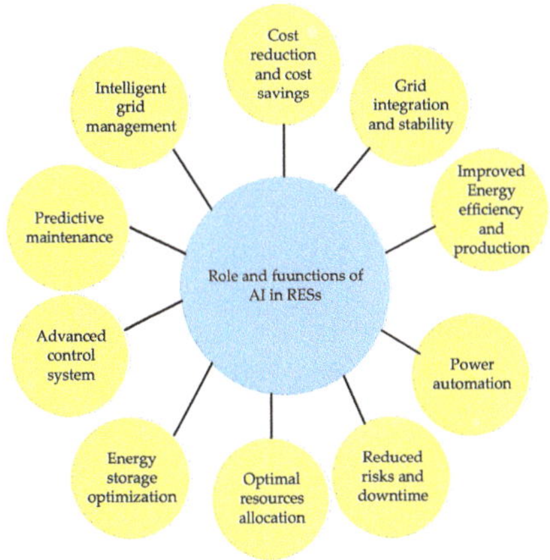

Figure 19. Role of AI in improving the efficiency of renewable energy technologies.

3.3. Forecasting and Prediction of Renewable Energy Using Artificial Intelligence

Renewable energy forecasting is the process of predicting electrical power that emanates from renewable energy sources. Accurate forecasting is one of the crucial factors that can be utilized to balance load demand and power supply in the utility grid by carrying out predictive maintenance and strategizing the optimization of the energy market. AI algorithms predict wind and solar power output by allowing grid operators to optimize energy storage and dispatch other energy sources [97]. AI algorithms can process massive amounts of data and recognize complex trends that traditional algorithms could have disregarded [124,125]. The vast amount of weather data, historical generation trends, grid conditions and real-time situations can be trained by AI models for the prediction of renewable energy output. This allows utility companies to optimize energy storage, dispatch other sources and guarantee a smooth and continuous power supply at the respective consumer centers. AI models can be used to enhance the accuracy of energy forecasting and resource assessment based on the proper planning, coordination and management of RESs. The forecasting and prediction of energy using AI has been globally accepted as a crucial area that can be utilized to enhance the accuracy of predicting energy generation from RESs like solar, wind and bioenergy [27,126]. The effective management of utility and the integration of RESs into conventional power systems with accurate projections are vital for energy trading, grid management, efficient resource allocation and the optimal operation of electric storage systems.

3.4. Energy Generation Forecasting Using Artificial Intelligence

The integration of AI has transformed energy generation forecasting by providing accurate and real-time predictions that are crucial for grid stability, cost reduction, the improvement of efficiency and the successful integration of RESs in the power system [28]. Energy producers or prosumers and grid operators of modern power systems can analyze real-time and historical generation data to forecast their energy. This data encompasses a wide range of variables such as historical weather patterns, energy consumption habits, grid load information and economic indicators. AI models can be used to track the daily positions of PV panels in order to optimize solar irradiance obtained from the sun. AI models are used to track the location of the solar irradiance and weather conditions to ensure that PV panels are positioned correctly for maximum energy harvest. This improves solar energy conversion efficiency, enhances accuracy and reduces the effects of the intermittency of solar irradiance. AI models that consist of deep learning and machine learning can be used to predict solar irradiance by analyzing historical data and detecting the intricate patterns. The breakdown of the models is based on data collection and preparation, model selection and training and prediction and evaluation [127]. Historical data on solar irradiance, temperature, humidity, cloud cover and other relevant factors are utilized to train AI models [128]. The performance of the model can be improved by cleaning, pre-processing and normalizing the raw data. Models are trained in the prepared data to learn the relationships between input features and solar irradiance. After training, the models can forecast future solar irradiance using new input data. The performance of the system can be evaluated by utilizing some key performance parameters such as the coefficient of determination, root mean square error and mean absolute error. A typical diagram of energy generation forecasting with AI is presented in Figure 20.

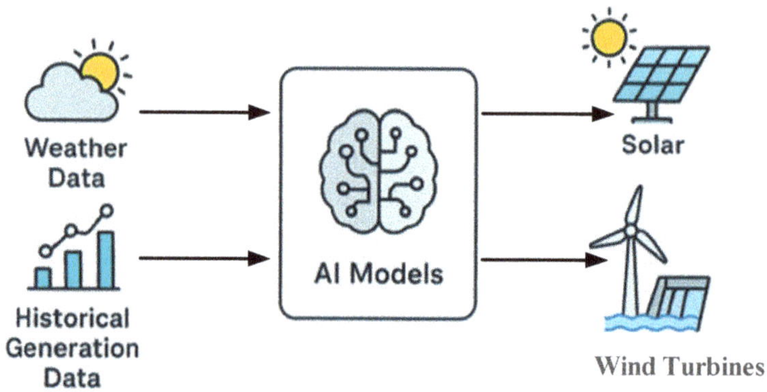

Figure 20. A typical framework for energy generation forecasting using artificial intelligence.

3.5. Load Demand Forecasting Using Artificial Intelligence

AI algorithms based on the analysis of historical energy consumption data, weather forecasts and other important factors permit power utility companies to implement demand response strategies by adjusting energy generation and load demand to match fluctuations in renewable energy availability. Load demand forecasting is a significant component of an emerging power system that allows utilities to balance demand and supply, optimize grid operations and enhance overall system reliability. Load demand forecasting can be used to predict energy consumption over a duration of time. The accurate forecasting of intermittent RESs is needed for balancing power supply and load demand. AI-based load demand forecasting combines historical data, meteorological inputs and renewable generation profiles using ML and DL models to create accurate net load forecasts. AI can be used in load demand forecasting to predict electricity consumption patterns based on the optimal utilization of RESs and fossil fuels. AI models can accurately predict energy demand and allow the grid operators to balance power supply and load demand during the peak periods by analyzing historical data, weather patterns and consumption trends [34,129]. This reduces the need to activate fossil fuel-based power stations when RESs are available or predicted to be available. AI-powered forecasting utilizes ML models to analyze a large amount of data such as historical consumption patterns, weather forecasts and social media trends to predict future energy demand [32]. The grid operators can optimize the dispatch of RESs by accurately predicting demand. AI models are used in power forecasting to contribute to stability and reliability utility grids. This is achieved by forecasting the anticipated peak usage times and ensuring that sufficient power is available to meet the load demand. Load demand forecasting with AI can be used to prevent unscheduled power interruptions and ensure a continuous power supply. A schematic diagram that illustrates the application of AI technique for predicting load demand is presented in Figure 21.

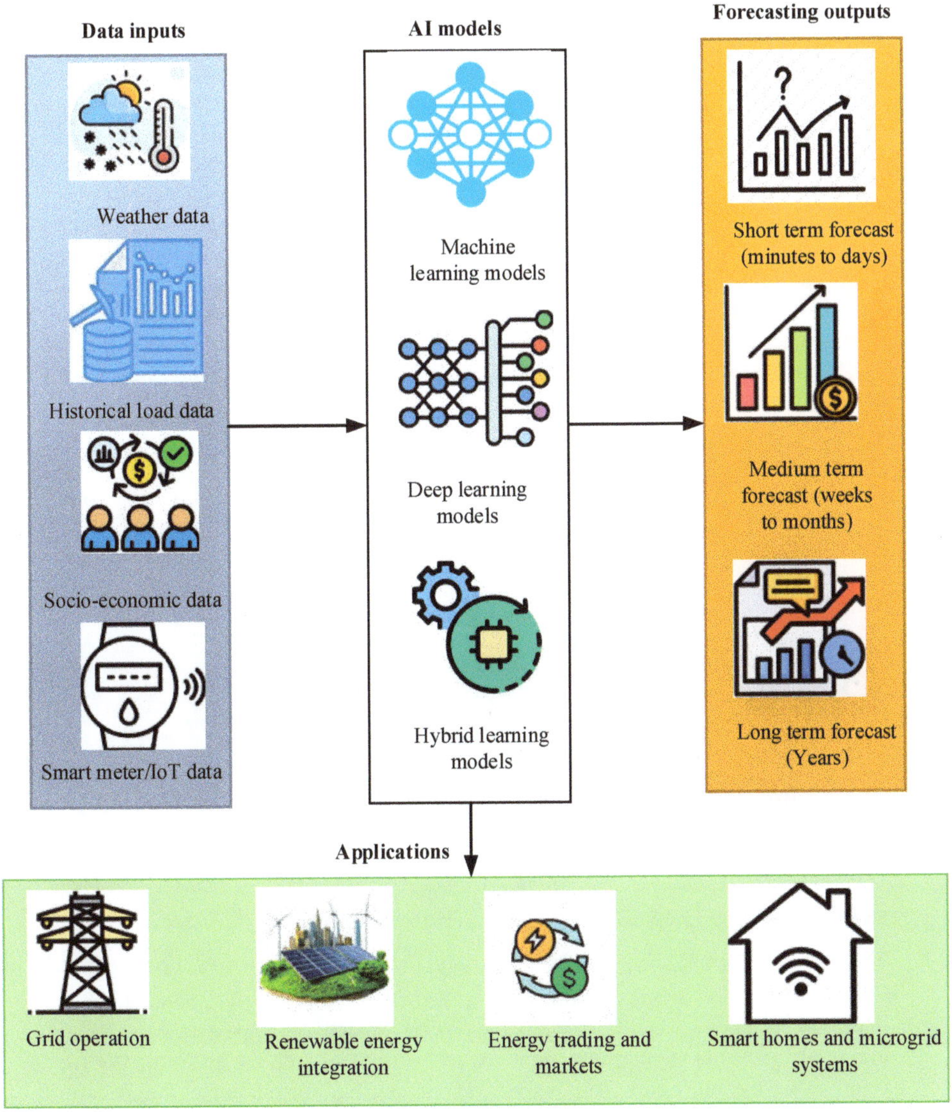

Figure 21. A schematic diagram that illustrates the application of AI technique for predicting load demand.

3.6. Resource Management Using Artificial Intelligence Algorithms

Resource management is the process of monitoring and optimizing the performance of energy systems [130]. AI-powered resource management in hybrid renewable energy systems can be used for forecasting, battery systems optimization, load balancing, smart grid integration, cost minimization, dynamic optimization and optimal sizing. The seamless operation of renewable resources to deliver consistent power at the load points is not always possible owing to their unpredictable nature. This has led to the exigency of RESs to back up the power requirements of the utility grid. AI can support continuous switching between renewable and traditional energy resources to ensure a consistent power supply. The data obtained from components of the power system can be used to ensure the effective deployment of energy and distribution. The embedded operation of AI, smart grid features, RESs, battery systems and demand response can be used for the dynamic balancing of the power supply and load energy. The electrical demands of consumers can be satisfied by using digital-based communication facilities to monitor and control the dispersal of electrical power from different sources to the load points. This integration leads to a balance of the load demand and electricity obtained from the utility grid, a reduction in energy waste and the maximum utilization of RESs. AI can significantly increase the performance of the power system by providing automated control mechanisms, predictive insights and real-time data analysis [131]. It can make decisions in real time to maximize the efficiency of the power system by using data obtained from different sources such as generating units, battery systems and energy demands. The real-time decisions cover battery system management, demand response and load balancing. A typical diagram of smart grid and AI control schemes for monitoring and optimizing the performance of energy systems is presented in Figure 22.

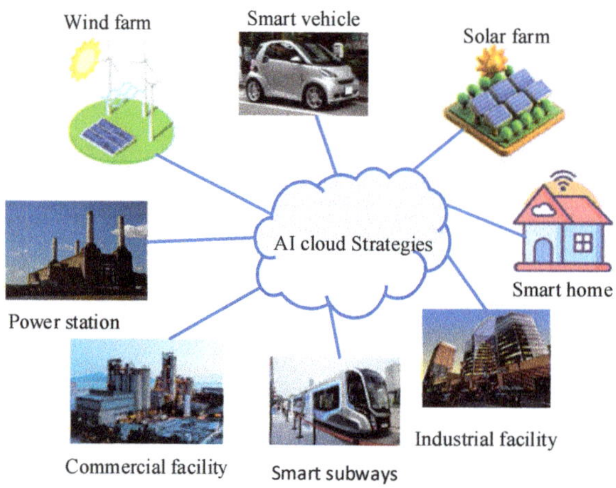

Figure 22. Smart grid using artificial intelligence control schemes.

3.7. Grid Optimization Using Artificial Intelligence in Grids with High Renewable Penetration

The integration of AI algorithms into grids has transformed grid operations and improved the efficiency and resilience of the power system [28]. The penetration of RESs into utility grids has significantly improved in recent times with the integration of AI algorithms in the utility grids. AI-powered grid optimization is significant for the effective implementation of high levels of renewable energy in utility grids by using intelligent power routing, congestion management and voltage stability. AI models can be used in smart grids to optimize energy consumption by predicting demand patterns and managing load demand. The utility grid operators can predict and manage the variability of RESs and optimize energy flow by AI techniques to improve the efficiency and integration of RESs into the power system [16,24]. Intelligent power routing is achieved by AI-powered grid optimization by evaluating grid conditions based on load demand and energy supply as well as the optimization of power flow within the system to reduce power losses and ensure a continuous power supply. The congestion management of AI-powered grid optimization can be achieved by maintaining grid stability during periods of high generation from RESs. This can be accomplished by predicting potential congestion points and dynamically adjusting power flow [132]. AI algorithms can be used to prevent equipment damage, maintain a reliable power supply and optimize voltage profiles by ensuring that voltage levels operate within acceptable limits. Grid optimization using AI in utility grids with high renewable penetration is a major research and practical area in modern power systems. A comparison of the power system with high penetration of renewable energy systems before and after the integration of AI is presented in Table 9 [124,133–137].

Table 9. Comparison of operational performance of the power system before and after AI integration into RESs.

Metric	Baseline (Non-AI)	With AI	Improvement
Forecasting RMSE	15–20%	3–10%	20–50%
Renewable utilization	60–75%	90%+	20–30%
Grid frequency stability	±0.5 Hz	±0.05 Hz	10× better
Battery lifespan	5–7 yrs	8–10 yrs	20–30%
Peak demand reduction	5–10%	20–30%	3×
Fault detection	After failure	Predictive (>95%)	Early detection (days/weeks ahead)
Energy cost savings	Baseline	15–30%	Significant
CO_2 emissions	High	20–40%	Cleaner grid
Predictive maintenance (O&M cost)	Reactive and scheduled maintenance	AI-driven predictive maintenance	O&M costs of 20–30% and downtime of ≈40%
Economic dispatch and energy management system	Scheduling and limited stochastic models	DRL and hybrid AI optimizers for multi-objective dispatch	Double-digit percentage cost reduction

3.8. Predictive Maintenance and Fault Detection Using Artificial Intelligence

AI has become a transformative energy tool that can be used for effective the fault detection and predictive maintenance of a power system [14]. Fault detection is the process of identifying when the power system deviates from its typical operating conditions and equipment diagnosis can be used to identify the underlying source of the defects. Equipment diagnosis and fault detection are utilized in a power system to ensure that electrical problems are detected on time and properly identified to prevent severe damage and protracted downtime. Artificial intelligence can enhance problem detection and diagnosis through the real-time analysis of data, pattern recognition and fault prediction before they occur. ML models can be trained on past fault data to identify the signatures of various kinds of faults by allowing faster and more precise detection [97]. AI models can analyze data obtained from sensors and other sources to predict equipment failures, optimize maintenance schedules and reduce downtime [16,34,138]. This improves the efficiency of the power system, increases cost savings and reduces operational costs [139]. AI can be used in the power system for fault detection and diagnosis by identifying the causes of faults, improving the speed and accuracy of repairs and minimizing downtime [75].

3.8.1. Predictive Maintenance Using Artificial Intelligence

AI-driven predictive maintenance has gained prominence as a transformative method to increase the performance of power systems [140]. Predictive maintenance models based on AI models utilize sensor data and historical performance metrics to anticipate component failures in wind turbines and PV systems [26]. The predictive maintenance approach can be utilized to reduce maintenance costs, optimize the overall operational efficiency of renewable energy installations, increase the lifetime of the systems and prevent unanticipated downtime of the equipment by allowing the operators of the power systems to carry out maintenance tasks only when necessary. AI algorithms are used to analyze historical data obtained from the sensors and find trends that predate equipment failures. ML models can accurately forecast future failures by allowing for prompt responses. Predictive maintenance can be used in the power system for the early detection of malfunctioned or worn-out components, minimize downtime, prolong the lifetime of equipment and reduce operational costs [141].

3.8.2. Predictive Maintenance for Solar Panels Using Artificial Intelligence

The challenges that operators of solar farms are facing currently such as unscheduled breakdowns, equipment inefficiencies and the need to maintain a continuous power output can be overcome by using the analytical tools of AI [142]. The predictive maintenance offered by AI analytics can be used to collect large amounts of data from sensors embedded in PV panels. The sensors provide real-time data about the health status of the PV panels by monitoring the operating and technical parameters of the power system such as load demand, solar irradiance and ambient temperature. AI models can analyze the data to detect trends and abnormalities that show imminent failures [29,143]. Having analyzed the data, the system can predict when the PV panel is expected to fail due to micro cracks, corrosion, etc. The analyzed data obtained from the sensors can be used by AI to detect problems, optimize performance, reduce downtime, minimize unscheduled power interruption, reduce costs, improve uninterrupted energy production and guarantee a consistent energy output [144].

3.8.3. Predictive Maintenance for Wind Farms

Predictive maintenance is crucial for wind farms, using remote control and automation to provide detailed data on the condition of each component of the wind turbine and allowing maintenance teams to detect impending issues before they escalate [145]. AI models are used in the predictive maintenance of wind turbines to reduce downtime and repair costs, improve the safety of the equipment, prevent catastrophic failures, increase the lifetime of wind turbines and maximize the return on investment. AI models are used in the predictive maintenance of wind turbines to analyze historical records and sensor data to predict the potential failures of the equipment before they occur [143]. The early detection of electrical problems can prevent costly emergency maintenance, prolong the lifetime of critical components and ensure that wind turbines operate at peak performance to increase the reliability of the power system. The benefits of AI in the predictive maintenance of wind turbines can be fully harnessed by scheduling the maintenance activities during off-peak periods as a measure to ensure uninterrupted power production.

3.8.4. AI Model Validation Methods and Performance Metrics

AI model validation methods and performance metrics are used in renewable energy applications for forecasting, scheduling, fault detection and optimization. Validation methods are utilized in the power system to ensure that AI models in renewable energy systems such as PV, wind, fuel cells, small hydro and hybrid energy systems are not over fitted [146]. Model validation is the process of testing an AI/ML model and making reliable predictions on new data. A comparison of different types of AI validation methods based on the description, advantages and limitations is presented in Table 10 [146–148]. Performance metrics are numerical measurements that are used to assess a model's predictive performance [149]. They can be used by researchers to determine whether a model is appropriate for practical applications by offering information on the model's accuracy. They can be utilized for model comparison and identify whether a model is over fitting or under fitting. The performance metrics of the problem based on regression are presented in Table 11 [150–152].

Table 10. Overview of AI model validation methods.

Method	Description	Advantages	Limitations
Hold-Out Validation	Split dataset into training (70–80%) and testing (20–30%).	Simple, fast and easy to implement.	Does not generalize well.
k-Fold Cross-Validation	Dataset divided into *k* folds, model trained on (k − 1) folds, tested on 1 fold and repeated k times.	Reliable and reduced bias of a single split.	Computationally more expensive than hold-out.
Stratified k-Fold CV	Each fold maintains class proportions.	Effective handling of imbalanced datasets.	More complex to implement than standard k-fold.
LOOCV	Each data point is used once as test set.	Uses maximum data for training and unbiased evaluation.	Extremely computationally expensive and impractical for large datasets.
Bootstrapping	Resample dataset with replacement to form multiple training and testing sets.	Good for small datasets and provides variance estimates.	Introduces bias if samples are not representative.
Nested Cross-Validation	Inner loop for hyper parameter tuning and outer loop for performance evaluation.	Prevents over fitting during model selection and robust evaluation.	Computationally intensive.

Table 11. Comparison of the main regression performance metrics.

Metric	Definition	Formula	Optimal Value	Interpretation
MAE (Mean Absolute Error)	Average of absolute differences between actual and predicted values.	$MAE = \frac{1}{n}\sum_{i=1}^{n}\left\|y_i - \hat{y}_i\right\|$ where n is the number of observations, y_i is the prediction value and $\hat{y}_i$ is the number of predictions.	0	MAE = 0 (perfect model, predictions exactly match actual values). Low MAE (predictions are close to actual values on average). High MAE (predictions deviate significantly from actual values).
MSE (Mean Squared Error)	Average of squared differences between actual and predicted values.	$MAE = \frac{1}{n}\sum_{i=1}^{n}\left(y_i - \hat{y}_i\right)^2$	0	MSE = 0 (perfect prediction, no error). Low MSE (predictions are close to actual values). High MSE (predictions deviate significantly from actual values).
RMSE (Root Mean Squared Error)	Square root of the average of the squared differences between predicted and actual values.	$MAE = \sqrt{\frac{1}{n}\sum_{i=1}^{n}\left(y_i - \hat{y}_i\right)^2}$	0	RMSE = 0 (perfect prediction, no error). Low RMSE (predictions are close to actual values). High RMSE (predictions deviate significantly from actual values).

Table 11. *Cont.*

Metric	Definition	Formula	Optimal Value	Interpretation
R^2 (Coefficient of determination)	Proportion of variance in target explained by model.	$R^2 = 1 - \frac{\Sigma(y_i - \hat{y}_i)^2}{\Sigma(y_i - \overline{y}_i)^2}$ where $\overline{y}_i$ is the mean of actual values.	1	$R^2 = 1$ (perfect model (100% of variance in the target variable is explained by the model). $R^2 = 0$ (model does not explain any variance (no better than predicting the mean)). $R^2 < 0$ (model performs worse than the mean).
Adjusted R^2	R^2 adjusted for number of predictors in model.	$Adjusted\ R^2 = 1 - \left(\frac{(1-R^2)(n-1)}{(n-p-1)}\right)$ where p is the number of predictions.	1	Adjusted $R^2 = 0$ (no explanatory power). $R^2 = 1$ (perfect explanatory power). $R^2 < 1$ (partial explanatory power).

3.9. Markets and Trading Using Artificial Intelligence

Transactive energy is a decentralized energy market where prosumers dynamically buy, sell and trade energy in real time by using smart contracts or automated pricing. AI tools are intelligent features that can be utilized by the stakeholders of the energy market for the transformation of the TE system, the automation of energy trading, decision-making and price optimization in decentralized energy markets [153]. Conventional power systems are passing through a significant transformation based on technological breakthroughs and the urgent need to switch to sustainable energy systems. The use of AI in energy trading and markets is among the most fascinating advancements in the TE system that has considerably changed the energy market by improving the efficiency of the power system, optimizing pricing and facilitating precise market forecasting. Energy trading is the process of purchasing and selling electrical energy generated from renewable sources in energy markets [97]. Energy trading can be enhanced by using AI to predict the cost of energy and power output and allows producers to make the best market decisions [32]. The cost of electricity can be forecasted by AI models with high accuracy by analyzing databases that include historical market data, weather forecasts and grid condition data. The AI-enabled energy market allows producers to maximize their revenues and minimize market deviations by reducing the probability of incurring fines for failing to satisfy contracted energy demands [154].

4. Synergy and Integration of IoT and AI in Renewable Energy Systems

The convergence of AI, IoT devices and smart grids can create highly autonomous, efficient and resilient power systems by using secure control systems, real-time data and predictive analytics to reduce the cost of energy at generation and consumer standpoints. A typical diagram that shows the integration of IoT and AI in RESs is presented in Figure 23. The synergy between these technologies has transformed traditional power systems into smart and self-regulating systems and improves the autonomy of the power system. The transformation of conventional power systems to sustainable and efficient power systems is being fueled by the integration of IoT and AI in RESs. These technologies can be used to fully harness the potential of RESs while simultaneously opening the door to a cleaner and more resilient energy system by allowing predictive maintenance, real-time monitoring and optimized grid management. The convergence of IoT and AI has transformed the power system by unlocking TE systems and smart energy systems that are responsive and autonomous in nature. AI algorithms are utilized in decentralized energy systems to facilitate peer-to-peer (P2P) energy trading and optimize the energy flow within microgrid systems. AI can also be used in the smart grid to balance the energy supply from solar and wind farms with real-time demand to guarantee a continuous power supply [155]. The convergence of IoT and AI in RESs can be utilized to increase the monitoring and control capability of various parameters of the power system. IoT sensors are embedded into RESs to collect data in real time through the internet or other connected networks [156]. IoT devices are integrated into the power system to collect real-time data from performance metrics, equipment health status, environmental conditions, energy storage, grid infrastructure and consumption points. This data is wirelessly transmitted to a centralized system using communication protocols that ensure that the data is transmitted reliably through communication networks to centralized platforms or edge computing devices. Once the data is collected by AI, the data is analyzed for streamlined predictions, the detection of issues and optimized operations of the power system.

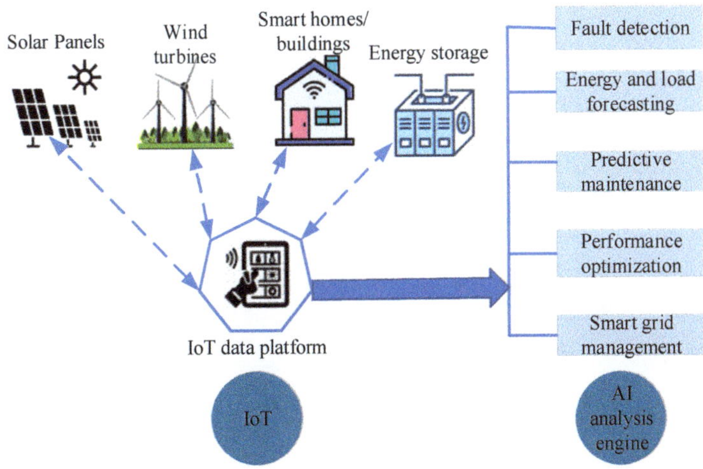

Figure 23. A typical diagram of integration of IoT and AI for management and control of RESs.

4.1. Dashboard Solutions for IoT and AI in Renewable Energy Systems

Dashboard solutions are reporting mechanisms that visualize the key performance indicators and metrics of the power system on a screen and improve data analysis and educated choices of different organization [137]. They are information management systems that convert complicated data from multiple databases into thorough visual representations like tables, charts and graphs by offering useful insights into power system operations, patterns and possible problems. Dashboard solutions have become essential tools for the monitoring of real-time energy consumption, energy cost analysis, the optimization of GHG emissions, peak demand analysis, equipment performance monitoring, the integration of weather data, predictions of energy cost, renewable energy integration, energy savings measurement, energy conservation measures tracking, alarm and notification systems, mobile accessibility, the cost–benefit analysis of renewable energy projects, energy usage breakdown, predictive maintenance and energy procurement and supplier analysis. They are interactive tools that allow the combination of real-time data from different sources and provide AI-assisted data preparation, chart creation and data analysis and analyze and display key performance indicators. Dashboard solutions are visual interfaces that integrate IoT and AI technologies in renewable energy systems and provide the real-time monitoring of PV systems, wind turbines, battery systems and grid performance;

the optimization of operation and maintenance cost and energy flows; forecasting and scheduling for the prediction of demand, weather and renewable generation; and decision support to operators, consumers and policymakers with clear performance indicators such as cost savings, GHG reduction and reliability [157]. Dashboards act as a bridge between the raw data collected by IoT devices and AI models [158].

The classification of dashboard solutions for IoT and AI in renewable energy systems based on commercial, open-source and specialized solutions is presented in Figure 24. Industrial dashboards are commercial platforms designed by energy solution development companies to maximize revenue and manage the flow of power, renewable energy systems, industrial applications and smart grid systems. The features of industrial dashboards encompass highly robust and secured power systems with advanced predictive maintenance, real-time monitoring and integration with industrial IoT [159]. The operations of industrial dashboards in the power sector are limited owing to their high cost and limited flexibility and because they are not suitable for small- to large-scale applications. Open-source dashboards are free-to-use platforms that allow researchers and developers to build customizable monitoring and optimization systems for renewable energy and IoT applications [160]. The features of open-source dashboards include flexibility, reduced costs and being specially integrated with AI algorithms and IoT devices. They require technical professionals, limited in-built AI models and high security concerns. Specialized dashboards are application-specific dashboards designed for particular renewable energy use-cases such as microgrid systems, EV charging systems and hybrid energy storage management. The features of specialized dashboards include advanced control algorithms, storage scheduling, EV charging and demand–response for the optimal operation of the power system. The operations of specialized dashboards are limited due to the narrow focus and limited adaptability outside their intended application domain. A comparison of dashboards based on their applications, features, limitations and AI integration is presented in Table 12 [158,161–165].

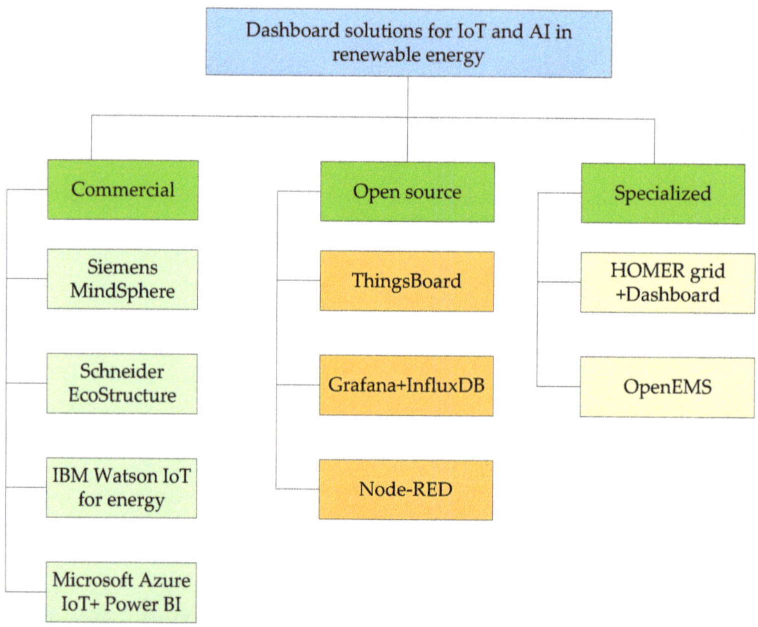

Figure 24. Classification of dashboard solutions for IoT and AI in renewable energy systems.

Table 12. Comparison of IoT and AI dashboard solutions in renewable energy systems.

Dashboard Solution	Features	AI Integration	Applications	Limitations
Siemens MindSphere	Cloud-based IoT OS and real-time dashboards	Predictive analytics and fault detection	Monitoring of energy system and grid optimization	Highly expensive
Schneider EcoStruxure	Monitoring of energy and demand-side management	Load forecasting and efficiency optimization	Microgrid system and smart buildings	Enterprise-level focus
IBM Watson IoT for Energy	Cloud platform and visualization	ML for forecasting and failure prediction	Integration of RESs and predictive maintenance	Needs skilled deployment
Google Cloud IoT + AI Hub	Data ingestion and ML pipelines	Forecasting and optimization with AutoML	Large-scale renewable systems	Expensive and cloud dependency
Microsoft Azure IoT + Power BI	IoT hub and customizable dashboards	Reinforcement learning and predictive AI	Smart grid scheduling and electric storage management	Lock-in by suppliers
ThingsBoard	Customizable IoT dashboards	Supports external ML/AI	PV, wind and battery monitoring	Limited built-in AI
Grafana + InfluxDB	Real-time visualization	Works with ML models via Python APIs	HRES monitoring and forecasting	Technical expertise needed
Node-RED	Drag-and-drop IoT dashboard	Supports TensorFlow.js and APIs	Smart homes, IoT device integration	Limited scalability
HOMER Grid + Dashboard	Simulation + planning	Links to optimization algorithms	HRES design and scheduling optimization	Not real time
OpenEMS	Open-source energy management	AI-based optimization support	Microgrid operation, DER control	Requires advanced setup

4.2. Overview of Software Tools That Support AI and IoT Applications in Renewable Energy Systems

The application of software in a power system is one of the significant patterns in global development that balances the financial prosperity of RESs with environmental protection [166]. Software is used to improve the performance of wind turbines and solar panels, optimize the layouts of solar and wind farms, determine the optimal placement of PV and wind turbines in the distribution power system and optimize energy storage solutions [167]. Renewable energy software utilizes IoT, AI and other technologies to collect, transmit, process, analyze and manage data. The integration of AI and IoT software can be used to improve the efficiency and sustainability of the power system. The benefits of RESs can be harnessed with the full implementation of AI and IoT software in the power system. AI and IoT software can be used for the optimization of a renewable energy system by improving grid management and forecasting energy generation and the efficiency of the power system [168]. The predictive maintenance and real-time monitoring of the meteorological data of solar and wind farms and the operating conditions of the power system are enabled by using AI and IoT software. The functionality of AI and IoT software is based on their applications such as grid power solutions, carbon capturing solutions, economic analysis tools, solar and wind data management and battery storage solutions. AI and IoT software and their essential features are designed to overcome the distinct challenges of RESs in a power system. A comparison of software for AI and IoT implementation in renewable energy systems based on their strengths, categories, limitations, platform, application in renewable energy systems and recommendations is presented in Table 13 [169–174]. AI and IoT software are recommended for grid deployment, academic research and development (R&D), techno-economic optimization, edge computing and federated learning.

Table 13. Comparison of software for implementation of AI and IoT in renewable energy systems.

Software/Platform	Category	Strengths	Limitations	Best Applications	Recommendation
MATLAB/ Simulink (2025b)	Simulation and AI modeling	Strong toolboxes and widely used in academic studies	Required commercial license	Forecasting, optimization and grid stability	R&D and design and control of power system
Python (3.13.7)	AI/ML systems	Open-source, scalable and strong DL support	Required coding professionals and integration effort	RE forecasting, anomaly detection and predictive maintenance	Advanced AI model development and pair with IoT platforms
Homer Pro (3.16.2)	Simulation of energy system	Design, optimization and techno-economic analysis of hybrid energy system (HES)	Limited AI/IoT features and less flexible for control	Planning and feasibility analysis of HES	Combination of AI features and Homer for multi-objective optimization of HES
ThingSpeak (2.1.1)	IoT Cloud	MATLAB integration and real-time data visualization	Limited scalability for large grids	IoT-based smart metering and monitoring of solar/wind	R&D, IoT demos and prototype validation
Node-RED (4.10)	IoT Middleware	Visual flow programming, device integration and low entry barrier	Not ideal for complex AI and limited scalability	IoT sensor integration	Low pilot cost and link with Python/ TensorFlow
AWS IoT Core (v2.14.3)	Cloud IoT and AI	Highly scalable, edge+cloud support, ML integration (SageMaker)	Cost and data security concerns	Real-time grid monitoring and predictive analytics	Deployment of IoT-AI in large-scale utility grids
Azure IoT Hub	Cloud IoT and AI	ML integration and digital twins	Subscription costs and enterprise-focused	Smart metering and demand forecasting	Recommended for utilities with Microsoft infrastructure
Google Cloud IoT Core	Cloud IoT and AI	Strong ML/AI tools, scalable and streaming analytics	Google services	Renewable system monitoring and forecasting	AI-heavy renewable projects
LabVIEW (2025 Q3)	Data acquisition and IoT	Hardware integration and real-time monitoring	Cost and less AI support compared to Python	Hardware based renewable energy labs and industrial monitoring	Hardware in the loop renewable system testing
RapidMiner (2025.0 (Studio) and 2025.1) WEKA (4.2)	AI/ML	Easy ML model building for beginners	Less flexible than Python and limited DL	Forecasting and classification	ML prototyping in IoT energy research
Edge AI Tools (2.0.0)	Edge AI	Low latency and privacy-preserving	Hardware cost and required expertise	DSM, battery optimization and fault detection	Convergence of AI and IoT devices in RESs

4.3. Applications of IoT and AI in Different Sectors of the Economy

IoT and AI are utilized in different sectors of the economy such as education, transportation, agriculture, industrial, residential and commercial for optimization, monitoring, automation and decision-making. AI transforms the real-time data supplied by IoT devices into highly intelligent information that can be used to reduce O&M costs, improve the sustainability of the power system, enhance efficiency and facilitate the decision-making of several organizations. The applications of IoT and AI in different economic sectors are presented in Table 14 [175–178].

Table 14. Overview of IoT and AI applications in several economic sectors.

Sector	Application
Education	Smart classrooms, safety and security, adaptive learning platforms and university energy management system
Industrial	Quality control, smart factories and predictive maintenance
Commercial	Retail analysis, e-commerce, smart buildings, customer experience and inventory management
Residential	Security systems, health monitoring, home automation and energy management
Agriculture	Smart irrigation, precision agriculture, crop yield prediction and livestock monitoring
Transportation	Autonomous vehicles, fleet management, public transit system and traffic management system

4.4. Successful Implementations and Promising Research Projects Where IoT and AI Are Integrated

The convergence of AI and IoT in RESs is a developing area that shows substantial improvements in the efficiency and performance of power systems. It has become a universal innovative force that improves the smartness, efficiency, sustainability and autonomous operation of power systems [71]. This section examines several projects where the combination of AI and IoT has demonstrated substantial improvements in renewable energy efficiency and outcomes of their successful implementations can be used for other projects. The successful implementations and promising research projects where IoT and AI are integrated into renewable energy systems are presented in Table 15 [179,180].

Table 15. Comparative summary of global renewable energy projects with the integration of AI and IoT technologies.

Project Name	Country/Region	Energy Type	IoT Function	AI Function	Outcome/Impact
Amsterdam Smart Grid	Netherlands	Solar and wind	Smart meters, EV charging and real-time sensors	Load forecasting, optimization and fault detection	20% increase in energy efficiency and CO_2 reduction
Smart Grid Gotland	Sweden	Wind	Grid monitoring sensors, smart homes and DSM	Grid balancing and predictive fault alerts	Improved grid stability with high wind penetration
Smart Energy Platform	Germany	Solar and storage	Smart homes and PV monitoring	AI-managed battery dispatch and usage forecasting	P2P energy trading and optimized home energy usage
Yokohama Smart City Project	Japan	Solar, storage and grid	IoT in buildings, EV chargers and smart appliances	Energy optimization and demand prediction	40% reduction in CO_2 emissions
REMap Ethiopia	Ethiopia	Solar and microgrid system	IoT weather and load sensors and solar PV tracking	AI load forecasting and RESs forecasting	Autonomous rural microgrids with reduced outages

Table 15. *Cont.*

Project Name	Country/Region	Energy Type	IoT Function	AI Function	Outcome/Impact
GreenLys Smart Grid Pilot	France	Solar, wind and grid	Smart meters, EV chargers and building energy sensors	AI-based consumption prediction and optimization	Improved load shifting and grid responsiveness
Brooklyn Microgrid	USA	Solar	Blockchain with smart meters and local energy monitors	AI for P2P trading price optimization, load forecasting	P2P trading with dynamic pricing
EDF Flex Platform	United Kingdom	Wind and grid	Smart sensors, weather data and smart home interfaces	AI for grid flexibility forecasting	Grid flexibility and support for RESs intermittency
Powerledger Projects	Australia, India	Solar and storage	Smart meters and IoT edge devices	AI for energy trading, price signals and forecasting	Real-time decentralized energy markets
Lombok Smart Grid	Indonesia	Solar, diesel and grid	IoT load sensors and hybrid energy meters	AI optimization of solar–diesel system	Improved rural energy reliability and reduced diesel usage

5. Challenges and Limitations of IoT and AI Integration in Renewable Energy Systems

The transformative potential of AI models and IoT devices in a decentralized power system has numerous challenges and limitations that must be fully addressed for the execution of renewable energy projects on the global scale [129]. The potential benefits of RESs with the integration of IoT devices and AI algorithms cannot be fully harnessed based on some notable challenges and limitations such as technical, economic, regulatory and societal challenges and limitations [15]. These challenges have negative impacts on the effectiveness, security and global adoption of IoT and AI for sustainable power solutions. The challenges and limitations of IoT and AI integration in RESs are presented in Table 16 [45,91,181–185].

Table 16. Comparative overview of challenges and limitations in applying IoT and AI technologies to renewable energy systems.

Category	Specific Challenge/Limitation	Description	Impact on Implementation/Adoption
Technical and data-related	Data quality and availability	Noisy and inconsistent data generated by IoT.	Not accurate AI models and unreliable predictions.
	Interoperability and standardization	Diverse devices, vendors and legacy systems hinder seamless communication and integration.	Fragmented solutions, increased complexity and high cost of system integration.
	Computational resources and infrastructure	Immense computing power and complex training.	High hardware and software costs.
	Cyber security risks	Vulnerable to repetitive cyber threats.	Data breaches, economic disruption and loss of public trust.
	Integration with legacy infrastructure	Old grid components that are designed for IoT devices or AI integration.	High cost, complexity of upgrades and potential for operational disruption.

Table 16. *Cont.*

Category	Specific Challenge/Limitation	Description	Impact on Implementation/Adoption
Economic and financial	High initial capital costs	High capital costs for deploying IoT sensors, communication systems and AI models.	Barrier for utilities and difficulty in securing funding.
	Uncertain return on investment	Long duration for recovery financial benefits.	Uncertainty of financial returns.
	Workforce training and skill gap	Shortage of professionals to handle AI and IoT technologies.	High operational costs and limited internal capacity for innovation and maintenance.
Regulatory and policy	Outdated regulations	Non-decentralization of current energy policies.	Regulatory uncertainty, stifled innovation and hindered DERs market participation.
	Data privacy and ownership	Lack of clear rules on data ownership, access and usage.	Public distrust and legal complexities.
	Liability and accountability	Determining responsibility when AI-controlled systems fail.	Ambiguity legal frameworks and difficulty in assigning faults.
Societal and ethical	Public acceptance and trust	Anxiety about data privacy and job displacement.	Resistance to adoption of AI and IoT.
	Digital divide and equity	Unequal access to IoT and AI technologies.	Creation of risks where benefits are not equally distributed.
	Algorithmic bias	Prolong societal inequalities based on biased historical data.	Discriminatory outcomes, erosion of public trust and ethical dilemmas in resource allocation.

Future Research Directions of IoT and AI Integration in Renewable Energy Systems

The convergence of IoT and AI technologies has opened several opportunities that can be utilized from their application in the power system [103]. This section highlights critical areas where future research can be used to overcome the existing challenges and limitations and harness the great potential of AI and IoT technologies in power systems. Future research directions are often a direct response to current challenges. The key future research directions of AI and IoT in RESs such as advancing core AI and IoT capabilities for energy systems, market policy and regulatory innovation, human-centric and ethical considerations and the sustainability of AI are presented in Table 17 [49,183,184,186–189]. A future research direction is to fully harness the potential of AI and IoT devices for sustainable and resilient energy systems, this can be achieved by using interdisciplinary collaboration between researchers, energy engineers and policymakers [91,124].

Table 17. Future research directions for IoT and AI in renewable energy systems.

Category	Research Area	Specific Focus/Goal	Potential Impact
Core AI and IoT technologies	Explainable AI	Development of AI techniques for decision-making systems.	Model interpretability issues and build trust for human–AI collaboration.
	Advanced digital twins	Application of DT to simulate and optimize RESs and smart grids.	Complex system optimization, proactive fault detection and scenario planning for grid resilience.

Table 17. *Cont.*

Category	Research Area	Specific Focus/Goal	Potential Impact
Core AI and IoT technologies	Novel AI for variability management	Development of new AI to forecast and manage the inherent intermittency and variability of RESs.	Intermittency of renewable energy, grid stability and efficient dispatch of renewable generated energy.
	Secure and resilient AI-IoT architectures	Design of secure systems to protect against cyber threat attacks.	Cyber security risks and grid resilience against malicious attacks.
Market policy and regulation	AI-driven TE market design	Development of new market mechanisms for automation and P2P energy trading.	Outdated market structures for efficient decentralized energy trading and optimizing DERs.
	Standardization and interoperability	Creation of universal standards for data exchange.	Lack of interoperability and fragmented solutions.
	Adaptive regulatory frameworks	Introduction of flexible and adaptive policies for consumer protection.	Outdated regulations, regulatory uncertainty and slow policy adaptation.
Human-centric and ethical AI	Human–AI collaboration and trust	Highly autonomous AI systems and building trust.	Human oversight in critical systems, skill gap and user acceptance.
	Fairness, equity and responsible AI	Deployment of AI and IoT to promote energy equity and protect consumer privacy.	Algorithmic bias and data privacy concerns.
	Workforce transition and development	Research strategies to adopt AI and IoT-driven changes.	Job displacement concerns and skill gaps.
Sustainability of AI	Energy-Efficient AI	Development of methods to reduce energy consumption of AI models, training and inference.	Environmental footprint and positive contribution to sustainability goals.

6. Conclusions

The rapid increase in global energy demand caused by a high standard of living, the industrial revolution, technological innovation, rural to urban drift and population growth has led to persistent power outages. The continuous power interruptions in urban centers have resulted in the disruption of commercial activities, considerable financial losses, the loss of revenues and ripples in the supply chain. This has forced many sectors of the economy to adopt green energy technologies as potential and feasible solutions to meet the ever-increasing demand. The inherent variability and distributed nature of local renewable energy resources have made it difficult to achieve the global goals of the United Nations aimed at ending poverty and protecting the planet by 2030. The convergence of AI and IoT is presented in this paper to overcome the global energy crisis and increase access to electricity by addressing several inherent challenges of RESs. The constructive interaction between AI and IoT holds great potential for accelerating the global transition towards clean and smart energy. This convergence is crucial for building smart, sustainable and resilient energy systems and achieves global decarbonization goals, the mitigation of the intermittency of RESs and a reduction in waste energy. The potential of AI and IoT can be fully harnessed to optimize RESs and mitigate the challenges of climate change. The convergence of IoT and AI is a promising solution with ongoing advancements and emerging technologies that can considerably contribute to the development of several applications such as smart grids, P2P energy trading and predictive maintenance systems. This integration allows unprecedented levels of optimization, including predictive maintenance, enhanced grid stability and efficient energy management. This comprehensive review has demonstrated that IoT and AI technologies are supplementary tools that can be used to transform how energy is generated, managed and consumed. The constructive collaboration between AI algorithms, IoT devices and RESs has become a transformative force that can be used to restructure the sustainability of power systems by providing emerging technologies with the ability to achieve autonomous, efficient and resilient power systems. These technologies are incorporated into decentralized energy systems to address the challenges of RESs such as unpredictable power generation and demand forecasting. Several challenges and limitations of IoT and AI integration in RESs can also be addressed by using multidisciplinary collaboration, robust technological frameworks and inclusive policies that promote access to electricity and sustainable energy development. Future research must focus on building scalable, explainable, secure and efficient energy systems tailored for diverse operational environments such as remote and underdeveloped regions of Africa and Asia where access to a reliable power system is a major challenge. Future research directions should shed more light on federated edge AI for RESs forecasting, blockchain-based energy trading and lightweight AI models for IoT devices. This paper contributes to this body of knowledge by offering valuable observations for policymakers, researchers and stakeholders to increase their investments in sustainable energy systems.

Author Contributions: Conceptualization, T.A. and G.S.; methodology, P.N.B. and R.K.; investigation, T.A.; resources, T.A. and G.S.; writing—original draft preparation, T.A.; writing—review and editing, G.S. and P.N.B.; visualization, R.K.; supervision, G.S. and P.N.B.; project administration, R.K. All authors have read and agreed to the published version of the manuscript.

Funding: This research has received no external funding.

Institutional Review Board Statement: Not applicable.

Informed Consent Statement: Not applicable.

Data Availability Statement: Not applicable.

Conflicts of Interest: The authors declare no conflicts of interest.

Abbreviations

The following abbreviations are used in this manuscript:

AI	Artificial Intelligence
ANNs	Artificial Neural Networks
CIoT	Consumer IoT
CNNs	Convolutional Neural Networks
CV	Cross-Validation
DERs	Distributed Energy Resources
DL	Deep Learning
DRL	Deep Reinforcement Learning
DSM	Demand-Side Management
DT	Digital Twin
FL	Federated Learning
GHG	Greenhouse gas
HES	Hybrid Energy System
IEA	International Energy Agency
IoT	Internet of Things

IoMT	Medical IoT
IIoT	Industrial IoT
LOOCV	Leave-One-Out Cross-Validation
LAWAN	Low-Power Wide-Area Network
LSTM	Long Short-Term Memory
MAE	Mean Absolute Error
MSE	Mean Squared Error
ML	Machine Learning
O&M	Operation and Maintenance
P2P	Peer-to-Peer
PV	Photovoltaic
R&D	Research and Development
RESs	Renewable Energy Sources
RMSE	Root Mean Squared Error
SCADA	Supervisory Control and Data Acquisition
SVMs	Support Vector Machines
TE	Transactive Energy
WTs	Wind Turbines

References

1. Gajdzik, B.; Wolniak, R.; Nagaj, R.; Žuromskaitė-Nagaj, B.; Grebski, W.W. The influence of the global energy crisis on energy efficiency: A comprehensive analysis. *Energies* **2024**, *17*, 947. [CrossRef]
2. Adefarati, T.; Obikoya, G.D.; Sharma, G.; Onaolapo, A.K.; Akindeji, K.T. Design and feasibility analysis of grid-connected hybrid renewable energy system: Perspective of commercial buildings. *Energy Syst.* **2024**, *15*, 403–462. [CrossRef]
3. Adefarati, T.; Sharma, G.; Bansal, R.C.; Onaolapo, A.K.; Borisade, S.G.; Oloye, A.O. Optimization of renewable energy based hybrid energy system using evolutionary computational techniques. *Smart Grids Sustain. Energy* **2025**, *10*, 15. [CrossRef]
4. Bakhsh, S.; Zhang, W.; Ali, K.; Oláh, J. Strategy towards sustainable energy transition: The effect of environmental governance, economic complexity and geopolitics. *Energy Strategy Rev.* **2024**, *52*, 101330. [CrossRef]
5. Falcone, P.M. Sustainable Energy Policies in Developing Countries: A Review of Challenges and Opportunities. *Energies* **2023**, *16*, 6682. [CrossRef]
6. REN21, Renewables 2025 Global Status Report. Available online: https://www.ren21.net/gsr-2025/downloads/pdf/go/GSR_2025_GO_2025_Full_Report.pdf (accessed on 26 August 2025).
7. International Energy Agency. World Energy Outlook 2025. Available online: https://www.iea.org/reports/global-energy-review-2025/global-trends (accessed on 28 August 2025).
8. Wang, J.; Azam, W. Natural resource scarcity, fossil fuel energy consumption, and total greenhouse gas emissions in top emitting countries. *Geosci. Front.* **2024**, *15*, 101757. [CrossRef]
9. Subhedar, M.; Mahalle, P.; Pawar, P. *Smart IoT for Sustainable Development*, 1st ed.; Chapman and Hall/CRC: Boca Raton, FL, USA, 2025; pp. 1–338. [CrossRef]
10. Adefarati, T.; Bansal, R.C.; Shongwe, T.; Naidoo, R.; Bettaye, M.; Onaolapo, A.K. Optimal energy management, technical, economic, social, political and environmental benefit analysis of a grid-connected PV/WT/FC hybrid energy system. *Energy Convers. Manag.* **2023**, *292*, 117390. [CrossRef]
11. Colak, I.; Okedu, K.E.; Raju, L. *Advances in Electrical Power and Embedded Drive Control*; Springer Nature: Singapore, 2025; pp. 1–621. [CrossRef]
12. Anvari-Moghaddam, A.; Ghaemi, S.; You, S.; Blaabjerg, F. *Power-to-X in Regional Energy Systems: Planning, Operation, Control, and Market Perspectives*, 1st ed.; CRC Press: Boca Raton, FL, USA, 2025; pp. 1–528. [CrossRef]
13. Alam, M.M.; Hossain, M.J.; Habib, M.A.; Arafat, M.Y.; Hannan, M.A. Artificial intelligence integrated grid systems: Technologies, potential frameworks, challenges, and research directions. *Renew. Sustain. Energy Rev.* **2025**, *211*, 115251. [CrossRef]
14. Rajaperumal, T.; Columbus, C.C. Transforming the electrical grid: The role of AI in advancing smart, sustainable, and secure energy systems. *Energy Inform.* **2025**, *8*, 51. [CrossRef]
15. Tiwari, S.; Tyagi, A.K. *AI and Blockchain in Smart Grids Fundamentals, Methods and Applications*, 1st ed.; Auerbach Publications: New York, NY, USA, 2025. [CrossRef]
16. Mansour, D.E.A.; Hussien, M.G.; Subudhi, P.S.; Kumar, A.R.; Padmanaban, S. *Power Systems Amid the 4th Industrial Revolution*; River Publishers: New York, NY, USA, 2024; pp. 1–174. [CrossRef]

17. Mahmood, M.; Chowdhury, P.; Yeassin, R.; Hasan, M.; Ahmad, T.; Chowdhury, N.-U.-R. Impacts of digitalization on smart grids, renewable energy, and demand response: An updated review of current applications. *Energy Convers. Manag. X* **2024**, *24*, 100790. [CrossRef]
18. Clement, M. Optimizing Smart Grid Infrastructure Through AI and IoT for Enhanced Renewable Energy Utilization. Available online: https://www.researchgate.net/publication/390746394_Optimizing_Smart_Grid_Infrastructure_through_AI_and_IoT_for_Enhanced_Renewable_Energy_Utilization (accessed on 23 July 2025).
19. Shafik, W. Smart Devices and Internet of Things for Sustainable Energy. In *Advanced Technology for Smart Environment and Energy. Environmental Science and Engineering*; Mabrouki, J., Mourade, A., Eds.; Springer: Cham, Switzerland, 2024. [CrossRef]
20. Pandiyan, P.; Saravanan, S.; Kannadasan, R.; Krishnaveni, S.; Alsharif, M.H.; Kim, M.K. A comprehensive review of advancements in green IoT for smart grids: Paving the path to sustainability. *Energy Rep.* **2024**, *11*, 5504–5531. [CrossRef]
21. Sharma, G.; Bokoro, P.N.; Tanwar, S. *Energy 4.0-Trends, Challenges, and Applications*, 1st ed.; CRC Press: Boca Raton, FL, USA, 2025.
22. Khan, M.R.; Haider, Z.M.; Malik, F.H.; Almasoudi, F.M.; Alatawi, K.S.S.; Bhutta, M.S. A comprehensive review of microgrid energy management strategies considering electric vehicles, energy storage systems, and AI techniques. *Processes* **2024**, *12*, 270. [CrossRef]
23. Algburi, S.; Al Kareem, S.S.A.; Sapaev, I.; Mukhitdinov, O.; Hassan, Q.; Khalaf, D.H.; Jabbar, F.I. The role of artificial intelligence in accelerating renewable energy adoption for global energy transformation. *Unconv. Resour.* **2025**, *8*, 100229. [CrossRef]
24. Gölnar, S.K. The Effect of Digital Technology Utilization for More Efficient Energy Production, Transmission and Consumption on Energy Policies. Master's Thesis, Middle East Technical University, Ankara, Turkey, 2025.
25. Nikam, S.R.; Kulkarni, M.G.; Narwane, V.S.; Mehendale, N.D.; More, N.P. *Technologies for Energy, Agriculture, and Healthcare*; CRC Press: Boca Raton, FL, USA, 2025.
26. Rani, S.; Bhambri, P.; Kumar, S.; Pareek, P.K.; Elngar, A.A. *AI-Driven Digital Twin and Industry 4.0: A Conceptual Framework with Applications*; CRC Press: Boca Raton, FL, USA, 2024.
27. Gupta, S.; Kumar, V.; Gupta, P. *Challenges in Information, Communication and Computing Technology*; CRC Press: London, UK, 2025; pp. 1–890.
28. Singh, N.; Kumar, Y.; Pahariya, Y.; Bolshev, V.; Singh, H.P. *Power System Management: Advances and Applications*; CRC Press: Boca Raton, FL, USA, 2025; pp. 1–284.
29. Gisi, P.J. *The Dark Factory and the Future of Manufacturing: A Guide to Operational Efficiency and Competitiveness*; Productivity Press: New York, NY, USA, 2024; pp. 1–276.
30. Huang, Y.; Rong, X.; Bie, Z.; Li, J.; Huang, B.; Zhao, T.; Li, G. Artificial intelligence for resilient power system: Motivations, advances, and challenges. *Smart Power Energy Secur.* in press. 2025. [CrossRef]
31. Kabeyi, M.J.B.; Olanrewaju, O.A. Smart grid technologies and application in the sustainable energy transition: A review. *Int. J. Sustain. Energy* **2023**, *42*, 685–758. [CrossRef]
32. Kumar, N.M.; Chand, A.A.; Malvoni, M.; Prasad, K.A.; Mamun, K.A.; Isam, F.R.; Chopra, S.S. Distributed Energy Resources and the Application of AI, IoT, and Blockchain in Smart Grids. *Energies* **2020**, *13*, 5739. [CrossRef]
33. Boucif, O.H.; Lahouaou, A.M.; Boubiche, D.E.; Toral-Cruz, H. Artificial Intelligence of Things for Solar Energy Monitoring and Control. *Appl. Sci.* **2025**, *15*, 6019. [CrossRef]
34. Arévalo, P.; Jurado, F. Impact of Artificial Intelligence on the Planning and Operation of Distributed Energy Systems in Smart Grids. *Energies* **2024**, *17*, 4501. [CrossRef]
35. Krūmiņš, J.; Kļaviņš, M. Investigating the potential of nuclear energy in achieving a carbon-free energy future. *Energies* **2023**, *16*, 3612. [CrossRef]
36. Ullah, Z.; Rehman, A.U.; Wang, S.; Hasanien, H.M.; Luo, P.; Elkadeem, M.R.; Abido, M.A. IoT-based monitoring and control of substations and smart grids with renewables and electric vehicles integration. *Energy* **2023**, *282*, 128924. [CrossRef]
37. Balamurali, D.; Chakankar, S.; Sharma, G.; Pagey, A.P.; Natarajan, M.; Shaik, S.; Gnanavendan, S.; Arıcı, M. A solar-powered, internet of things (IoT)-controlled water irrigation system supported by rainfall forecasts utilizing aerosols: A review. *Environ. Dev. Sustain.* **2025**, 1–40. [CrossRef]
38. Liu, Z.; Guo, H.; Zhang, Y.; Zuo, Z. A comprehensive review of wind power prediction based on machine learning: Models, applications, and challenges. *Energies* **2025**, *18*, 350. [CrossRef]
39. Kumar, M.; Sharma, A.; Sharma, N.; Sharma, F.B.; Bhadu, M. Wind farm layout optimization problem using nature-inspired algorithms. *J. Electr. Comput. Eng.* **2024**, *2024*, 9406519. [CrossRef]
40. Pandit, R.K.; Astolfi, D.; Cardenas, I.D. A review of predictive techniques used to support decision making for maintenance operations of wind turbines. *Energies* **2023**, *16*, 1654. [CrossRef]
41. Zhang, Z.; Wu, Y.; Ma, X. Quantum machine learning based wind turbine condition monitoring: State of the art and future prospects. *Energy Convers. Manage.* **2025**, *332*, 119694. [CrossRef]

42. Alaba, F.A.; Sani, U.; Dada, E.G.; Mohammed, B.H. AIoT-enabled smart grids: Advancing energy efficiency and renewable energy integration. In *Artificial Intelligence of Things for Achieving Sustainable Development Goals*; Springer: Cham, Switzerland 2025; pp. 59–79. [CrossRef]
43. Zahraoui, Y.; Korõtko, T.; Rosin, A.; Mekhilef, S.; Seyedmahmoudian, M.; Stojcevski, A.; Alhamrouni, I. AI applications to enhance resilience in power systems and microgrids—A review. *Sustainability* **2024**, *16*, 4959. [CrossRef]
44. Mbasso, W.F.; Harrison, A.; Dagal, I.; Jangir, P.; Khishe, M.; Kotb, H.; Shaikh, M.S.; Smerat, A.; Donfack, E.F.; Kumar, R. Digital twins in renewable energy systems: A comprehensive review of concepts, applications, and future directions. *Energy Strategy Rev.* **2025**, *61*, 101814. [CrossRef]
45. Bennagi, A.; AlHousrya, O.; Cotfas, D.T.; Cotfas, P.A. Comprehensive study of the artificial intelligence applied in renewable energy. *Energy Strategy Rev.* **2024**, *54*, 101446. [CrossRef]
46. Bello, S.; Wada, I.; Ige, O.; Chianumba, E.; Adebayo, S. AI-driven predictive maintenance and optimization of renewable energy systems for enhanced operational efficiency and longevity. *Int. J. Sci. Res. Arc.* **2024**, *13*, 2823–2837. [CrossRef]
47. Hussein, J.B.; Workneh, T.S.; Kassim, A.; Ntsowe, K.; Melesse, S.F.; El-Mesery, H.S.; Zicheng, H. A review of the use of artificial intelligence in renewable energy for food processing and preservation process optimisation, challenges, and future prospects. *Renew. Sustain. Energy Rev.* **2025**, *223*, 116076. [CrossRef]
48. Al-Shetwi, A.Q.; Atawi, I.E.; El-Hameed, M.A.; Abuelrub, A. Digital twin technology for renewable energy, smart grids, energy storage and vehicle-to-grid integration: Advancements, applications, key players, challenges and future perspectives in modernising sustainable grids. *IET Smart Grid* **2025**, *8*, 70026. [CrossRef]
49. Arshi, O.; Rai, A.; Gupta, G.; Pandey, J.K.; Mondal, S. IoT in energy: A comprehensive review of technologies, applications, and future directions. *Peer--Peer Netw. Applic.* **2024**, *17*, 2830–2869. [CrossRef]
50. Sankarananth, S.; Karthiga, M.; Bavirisetti, D.P. AI-enabled metaheuristic optimization for predictive management of renewable energy production in smart grids. *Energy Rep.* **2023**, *10*, 1299–1312. [CrossRef]
51. Pathare, A.A.; DSethi, D. Development of IoT-enabled solutions for renewable energy generation and net-metering control for efficient smart home. *Discov. Internet Things* **2024**, *4*, 11. [CrossRef]
52. Bawane, S.; Matange, G.; Shrivastava, A.; Qureshi, A.R.K.; Sultan, S.; Shrivastava, D. Smart wind farm management using IoT and predictive in analytics. *Int. J. Environ. Sci.* **2025**, *11*, 1079–1095.
53. Imran, M.A.; Al Fathah, A.; Al Baki, A.; Alam, K.; Mostakim, M.A.; Mahmud, U.; Hossen, M.S. Integrating IoT and AI for predictive maintenance in smart power grid systems to minimize energy loss and carbon footprint. *J. Appl. Opt.* **2023**, *44*, 27–47.
54. Rama, V.S.B.; Hur, S.-H.; Yang, J.-M. Predictive maintenance and anomaly detection of wind turbines based on bladed simulator models. *IFAC-Pap.* **2023**, *56*, 4633–4638. [CrossRef]
55. Wang, X.; Wang, H.; Bhandari, B.; Cheng, L. AI-empowered methods for smart energy consumption: A review of load forecasting, anomaly detection and demand response. *Int. J. Precis. Eng. Manuf.-Green Technol.* **2024**, *11*, 963–993. [CrossRef]
56. Wicaksono, H.; Trat, M.; Bashyal, A.; Boroukhian, T.; Felder, M.; Ahrens, M.; Bender, J.; Groß, S.; Steiner, D.; July, C.; et al. Artificial-intelligence-enabled dynamic demand response system for maximizing the use of renewable electricity in production processes. *Int. J. Adv. Manuf. Technol.* **2025**, *138*, 247–271. [CrossRef]
57. Abdullahi, I.; Longo, S.; Samie, M. Towards a distributed digital twin framework for predictive maintenance in industrial internet of things (IIoT). *Sensors* **2024**, *24*, 2663. [CrossRef]
58. Manohar, N.; Chaurasia, M.A.; Mozar, S.; Juang, C.F. Artificial intelligence and IoT in renewable energy. In *Machine Learning Applications in Renewable Energy*; Springer: Berlin/Heidelberg, Germany, 2025; pp. 135–145. [CrossRef]
59. Alagha, N.; Khairuddin, A.S.M.; Haitaamar, Z.N.; Al-Khatib, O.; Kanesan, J. Artificial intelligence in wind turbine fault detection and diagnosis: Advances and perspectives. *Energies* **2025**, *18*, 1680. [CrossRef]
60. Paletta, Q.; Terrén-Serrano, G.; Nie, Y.; Li, B.; Bieker, J.; Zhang, W.; Dubus, L.; Dev, S.; Feng, C. Advances in solar forecasting: Computer vision with deep learning. *Adv. Appl. Energy* **2023**, *11*, 100150. [CrossRef]
61. Lee, J.; Park, E.; Lee, S. Development of a hybrid modeling framework for the optimal operation of microgrids. *Energies* **2025**, *18*, 2102. [CrossRef]
62. Jia, L.; Li, Z.; Hu, Z. Applications of the Internet of Things in Renewable Power Systems: A Survey. *Energies* **2024**, *17*, 4160. [CrossRef]
63. Grataloup, A.; Jonas, S.; Meyer, A. A review of federated learning in renewable energy applications: Potential, challenges, and future directions. *Energy AI* **2024**, *17*, 100375. [CrossRef]
64. May, D.C.; Taylor, M.; Musilek, P. Decentralized coordination of distributed energy resources through local energy markets and deep reinforcement learning. *Energy AI* **2024**, *18*, 100446. [CrossRef]
65. Shah, S.S.; Daoliang, T.; Kumar, S.C. RUL forecasting for wind turbine predictive maintenance based on deep learning. *Heliyon* **2024**, *10*, 39268. [CrossRef]
66. Ardebili, A.A.; Zappatore, M.; Ramadan, A.I.H.A.; Longo, A.; Ficarella, A. Digital twins of smart energy systems: A systematic literature review on enablers, design, management and computational challenges. *Energy Inform.* **2024**, *7*, 94. [CrossRef]

67. Hussein, H.M.F. Neural network algorithm with reinforcement learning for microgrid techno-economic optimization. *Mathematics* **2024**, *12*, 280. [CrossRef]
68. Khouili, O.; Hanine, M.; Louzazni, M. Harnessing principal component analysis and artificial neural networks for accurate solar radiation prediction. *Int. J. Energy Res.* **2025**, *1*, 5846114. [CrossRef]
69. Mamyrbayev, O.; Akhmediyarova, A.; Oralbekova, D.; Alimkulova, J.; Alibiyeva, Z. Optimizing renewable energy integration using IoT and machine learning algorithms. *Int. J. Ind. Eng. Manag.* **2025**, *16*, 101–112. [CrossRef]
70. Sun, Y.; Han, W. A review of enhancing wind power with AI: Applications, economic implications, and green innovations. *Digit. Econ. Sustain. Dev.* **2025**, *3*, 11. [CrossRef]
71. Ejiyi, C.J.; Cai, D.; Thomas, D.; Obiora, S.; Osei-Mensah, E.; Acen, C.; Eze, F.O.; Sam, F.; Zhang, Q.; Bamisile, O.O. Comprehensive review of artificial intelligence applications in renewable energy systems: Current implementations and emerging trends. *J. Big Data* **2020**, *12*, 169. [CrossRef]
72. Haghshenas, A.; Hasan, A.; Osen, O.; Mikalsen, E.T. Predictive digital twin for offshore wind farms. *Energy Inform.* **2023**, *6*, 169. [CrossRef]
73. Liu, S.; Ren, S.; Jiang, H. Predictive maintenance of wind turbines based on digital twin technology. *Energy Rep.* **2023**, *9*, 1344–1352. [CrossRef]
74. Tetouani, A.; Taouil, A.; Rouky, N.; Fri, M. Integrated blockchain, IoT, and green hydrogen approach for sustainable and connected supply chain—Application case in Morocco. *Eng. Proc.* **2025**, *97*, 55. [CrossRef]
75. R. Innovation. Revolutionizing Smart Manufacturing: The Synergy of AI-Driven Digital Twins and IoT. Available online: https://www.rapidinnovation.io/post/integrating-ai-driven-digital-twins-with-iot-for-next-generation-smart-manufacturing (accessed on 24 July 2025).
76. Thottempudi, P.; Konduru, R.M.; Valiveti, H.B.; Kuraparthi, S.; Kumar, V. Digital health resilience: IoT solutions in pandemic response and future healthcare scenarios. *Discov. Sustain.* **2025**, *6*, 144. [CrossRef]
77. Li, C.; Wang, J.; Wang, S.; Zhang, Y. A review of IoT applications in healthcare. *Neurocomputing* **2024**, *565*, 127017. [CrossRef]
78. Mishra, S.; Sharma, S.K. Advanced contribution of IoT in agricultural production for the development of smart livestock environments. *Internet Things* **2023**, *22*, 100724. [CrossRef]
79. Nikpour, M.; Yousefi, P.B.; Jafarzadeh, H.; Danesh, K.; Shomali, R.; Asadi, S.; Lonbar, A.G.; Ahmadi, M. Intelligent energy management with iot framework in smart cities using intelligent analysis: An application of machine learning methods for complex networks and systems. *J. Netw. Comput. Appl.* **2025**, *235*, 104089. [CrossRef]
80. Rawas, S.; Tafran, C.; AlSaeed, D.; Al-Ghreimil, N. Transforming Healthcare: AI-NLP Fusion Framework for Precision Decision-Making and Personalized Care Optimization in the Era of IoMT. *Comput. Mater. Contin.* **2024**, *81*, 4575–4601. [CrossRef]
81. El-Afifi, M.I.; Sedhom, B.E.; Padmanaban, S.; Eladl, A.A. A review of IoT-enabled smart energy hub systems: Rising, applications, challenges, and future prospects. *Renew. Energy Focus.* **2024**, *51*, 100634. [CrossRef]
82. Omrany, H.; Al-Obaidi, K.M.; Hossain, M.; Alduais, N.A.M.; Al-Duais, H.S.; Ghaffarianhoseini, A. IoT-enabled smart cities: A hybrid systematic analysis of key research areas, challenges, and recommendations for future direction. *Discov. Cities* **2024**, *1*, 2. [CrossRef]
83. Pai, A.; Mishra, K.K.; Jeyan, J.M.L.; Sayal, A. Enhanced household energy consumption forecasting using multivariate long short-term memory (LSTM) networks with weather data integration. *Results Eng.* **2025**, *27*, 106512. [CrossRef]
84. Scott, C.; Ahsan, M.; Albarbar, A. Machine learning for forecasting a photovoltaic (PV) generation system. *Energy* **2023**, *278*, 127807. [CrossRef]
85. Moros, D.; Ashton, I.G.; Berrabah, N.; Lazakis, I.; Searle, K.D. Evaluation of predictive models for reducing wind turbine power converter failure downtime for a wind farm operator using SCADA data. *Wind. Energ. Sci. Discuss.* **2025**, *2025*, 1–37. [CrossRef]
86. Abimbola, O.; Ojo, O.T.; Fagbola, E.; Idris, U.A.; Salman, M.B. IoT-Driven Predictive Maintenance For Wind Turbines. *Path Sci.* **2025**, *11*, 6001–6007. [CrossRef]
87. Intellarts. IoT in Renewable Energy: Key Applications and Real-World Benefits. Available online: https://intelliarts.com/blog/iot-in-renewable-energy/ (accessed on 29 July 2025).
88. Nasserddine, G.; Nassereddine, M.; El Arid, A.A. Internet of things integration in renewable energy systems. In *Handbook of Research on Applications of AI, Digital Twin, and Internet of Things for Sustainable Development*; IGI Global: New York, NY, USA, 2023; pp. 159–185.
89. Sawilam, M.; Kizilkaya, B.; Taha, A.; Flynn, D.; Imran, M.A.; Ansari, S. Impact of Virtual Power Plants on grid stability and renewable energy integration in smart cities using IoT. *Energy. Rep.* **2025**, *13*, 3312–3323. [CrossRef]
90. Ponnambalam, S.; Ilampoornan, M. Role of AI in Optimizing Renewable Energy Grid Management. In *AI-Driven Solutions for Solar Energy Efficiency, Irradiance Modeling, and PV Forecasting*; IGI Global Scientific Publishing: New York, NY, USA, 2026; pp. 411–438. [CrossRef]

91. Shafik, W. Artificial intelligence and internet of things roles in sustainable next-generation manufacturing: An overview o emerging trends in Industry 6.0. In *Sustainable Innovation for Industry 6.0*; IGI Global Scientific Publishing: New York, NY, USA 2024; pp. 207–239.
92. Vedrtnam, A.; Wyche, K.P.; Chauhan, B.V.; Verma, S. *Prospects of Artificial Intelligence in the Environment*, 1st ed.; Springer Singapore, 2025. [CrossRef]
93. Khalil, M.; Sheikh, S.A. Advancing green energy integration in power systems for enhanced sustainability: A review. *IEEE Access* **2024**, *12*, 151669–151692. [CrossRef]
94. Strielkowski, W.; Vlasov, A.; Selivanov, K.; Muraviev, K.; Shakhnov, V. Prospects and challenges of the machine learning and data-driven methods for the predictive analysis of power systems: A review. *Energies* **2023**, *16*, 4025. [CrossRef]
95. Uhanto, U.; Yandri, E.; Hilmi, E.; Saiful, R.; Hamja, N. Predictive maintenance with machine learning: A comparative analysis of wind turbines and PV power plants. *Heca J. Appl. Sci.* **2024**, *2*, 87–98. [CrossRef]
96. Lyu, Z. *Handbook of Digital Twins*; CRC Press: Boca Raton, FL, USA, 2024.
97. Enlitia. AI in the Renewable Energy Sector: Applications, Benefits, and Real-World Impact. Available online: https://www enlitia.com/resources-blog-post/ai-in-the-renewable-energy-sector (accessed on 28 August 2025).
98. Nazir, L.; Sharifi, A. An analysis of barriers to the implementation of smart grid technology in Pakistan. *Renew. Energy* **2024**, *220*, 119661. [CrossRef]
99. E. Academia. Difference Between Traditional Power Grid and Smart Grid. Available online: https://electricalacademia.com/ electric-power/difference-traditional-power-grid-smart-grid/ (accessed on 26 August 2025).
100. Zhen, T.; Yuan, S. Design and optimization of smart grid using controllable loads. *Electr. Eng.* **2025**, *107*, 2507–2519. [CrossRef]
101. Zhou, Q.; Wu, J.; Yin, Y. Regulation techniques and applications of distributed load resources in urban power grids based on internet of things. *Front. Energy Res.* **2024**, *12*, 1422216. [CrossRef]
102. Conde, H.J.C.; Demition, C.M.; Honra, J. Storage is the new black: A review of energy storage system applications to resolve intermittency in renewable energy systems. *Energies* **2025**, *18*, 354. [CrossRef]
103. Alghamdi, M.; Haraz, Y.G. Smart Biofloc Systems: Leveraging Artificial Intelligence (AI) and Internet of Things (IoT) for Sustainable Aquaculture Practices. *Processes* **2025**, *13*, 2204. [CrossRef]
104. Singh, B.; Dutta, P.K.; Kaunert, C. Wind-Solar Renewable Energy and Innovative Technologies Applying Internet of Things (IoT) for Green and Sustainable Future: Projecting Carbon Neutrality for Smart and Sustainable Cities. In *IoT-Based Models for Sustainable Environmental Management: Sustainable Environmental Management*; Springer: Singapore, 2024; pp. 111–126. [CrossRef]
105. Ramesh, K.U.; Poonia, C.; Khan, M.S. *Smart Cyber-Physical Systems Innovations and Real-World Implications*, 1st ed.; CRC Press: Boca Raton, FL, USA, 2025. [CrossRef]
106. Noura, H.N.; Yaacoub, J.P.A.; Salman, O.; Chehab, A. Advanced Machine Learning in Smart Grids: An Overview. *Internet Things Cyber-Phys. Syst.* **2025**, *5*, 95–142. [CrossRef]
107. Poyyamozhi, M.; Murugesan, B.; Rajamanickam, N.; Shorfuzzaman, M.; Aboelmagd, Y. IoT—A Promising Solution to Energy Management in Smart Buildings: A Systematic Review, Applications, Barriers, and Future Scope. *Buildings* **2024**, *14*, 3446. [CrossRef]
108. Khullar, V.; Sharma, V.; Angurala, M.; Chhabra, N. *Artificial Intelligence and Society 5.0: Issues, Opportunities, and Challenges*; Chapman and Hall/CRC: New York, NY, USA, 2024; pp. 1–294. [CrossRef]
109. Hafeez, G.; Wadud, Z.; Khan, I.U.; Khan, I.; Shafiq, Z.; Usman, M.; Khan, M.U.A. Efficient energy management of IoT-enabled smart homes under price-based demand response program in smart grid. *Sensors* **2020**, *20*, 3155. [CrossRef]
110. Rashid, A.B.; Kausik, M.D.A.K. AI revolutionizing industries worldwide: A comprehensive overview of its diverse applications. *Hybrid. Advances.* **2024**, *7*, 100277. [CrossRef]
111. Wang, Y.; Xiong, G. Metaheuristic optimization algorithms for multi-area economic dispatch of power systems: Part I—A comprehensive survey. *Artif. Intell. Rev.* **2025**, *58*, 98. [CrossRef]
112. Wang, Y.; Xiong, G. Metaheuristic optimization algorithms for multi-area economic dispatch of power systems: Part II—A comparative study. *Artif. Intell. Rev.* **2025**, *58*, 132. [CrossRef]
113. Güven, A.F.; Yörükeren, N.; Mengi, O.O. Multi-objective optimization and sustainable design: A performance comparison of metaheuristic algorithms used for on-grid and off-grid hybrid energy systems. *Neural Comput. Appl.* **2024**, *36*, 7559–7594. [CrossRef]
114. Ghaemifard, S.; Ghannadiasl, A. A comparison of metaheuristic algorithms for structural optimization: Performance and efficiency analysis. *Adv. Civ. Eng.* **2024**, *2054173*, 36. [CrossRef]
115. Neto, A.F.D.S.; Santos, M.F.D.; Silva, M.F.D.; Honório, L.D.M.; Oliveira, E.J.D.; Neto, E.S.A. Performance comparison of metaheuristics applied to optimal signal design for parameter identification. *Sensors* **2023**, *23*, 9085. [CrossRef] [PubMed]
116. Fathollahi-Fard, A.M.; Tian, G.; Ke, H.; Fu, Y.; Wong, K.Y. Efficient multi-objective metaheuristic algorithm for sustainable harvest planning problem. *Comput. Oper. Res.* **2023**, *158*, 106304. [CrossRef]

117. Razzaq, K.; Shah, M. Machine learning and deep learning paradigms: From techniques to practical applications and research frontiers. *Computers* **2025**, *14*, 93. [CrossRef]
118. Marshan, A.; Nizar, F.N.M.; Ioannou, A.; Spanaki, K. Comparing machine learning and deep learning techniques for text analytics: Detecting the severity of hate comments online. *Inf. Syst. Front.* **2025**, *27*, 487–505. [CrossRef]
119. Ghezal, A.; König, A. A comparative study of hybrid machine-learning vs. deep-learning approaches for varroa mite detection and counting. *Sensors* **2025**, *25*, 5075. [CrossRef]
120. Bonetti, A.; Martínez-Sober, M.; Torres, J.C.; Vega, J.M.; Pellerin, S.; Vila-Francés, J. Comparison between machine learning and deep learning approaches for the detection of toxic comments on social networks. *Appl. Sci.* **2023**, *13*, 6038. [CrossRef]
121. Monteiro, F.; Sarquis, E.; Branco, P. Identifying critical failures in PV systems based on PV inverters' monitoring unit: A techno-economic analysis. *Energies* **2024**, *17*, 4738. [CrossRef]
122. K. M. Yenra. AI Predictive Maintenance for Wind Turbines: 20 Advances (2025). Available online: https://yenra.com/ai20/predictive-maintenance-for-wind-turbines/ (accessed on 24 August 2025).
123. Kuttybay, N.; Mekhilef, S.; Koshkarbay, N.; Saymbetov, A.; Nurgaliyev, M.; Dosymbetova, G.; Orynbassar, S.; Yershov, E.; Kapparova, A.; Zholamanov, B.; et al. Assessment of solar tracking systems: A comprehensive review. *Sustain. Energy Technol. Assess.* **2024**, *68*, 103879. [CrossRef]
124. Zhang, T.; Strbac, G. Novel Artificial Intelligence Applications in Energy: A Systematic Review. *Energies* **2025**, *18*, 3747. [CrossRef]
125. A. Marketing. Customer Segmentation with AI: Targeting the Right Audience. Available online: https://blog.aspiration.marketing/en/ai-impact-on-customer-segmentation-targeting (accessed on 22 August 2025).
126. Jain, V.; Raman, M.; Agrawal, A.; Hans, M.; Gupta, S. *Convergence Strategies for Green Computing and Sustainable Development*; IGI Global: New York, NY, USA, 2024.
127. Kalasani, R.R. An Exploratory Study of the Impacts of Artificial Intelligence and Machine Learning Technologies in the Supply Chain and Operations Field. Ph.D. Thesis, University of the Cumberlands, Williamsburg, KY, USA, 2023.
128. Attar, N.F.; Sattari, M.T.; Prasad, R.; Apaydin, H. Comprehensive review of solar radiation modeling based on artificial intelligence and optimization techniques: Future concerns and considerations. *Clean. Technol. Environ. Policy* **2023**, *25*, 1079–1097. [CrossRef]
129. Whig, P.; Sharma, P.; Aneja, N.; Elngar, A.A.; Silva, N. *Artificial Intelligence and Machine Learning for Sustainable Development: Innovations, Challenges, and Applications*; CRC Press: Boca Raton, FL, USA, 2024.
130. Selvaraj, R.; Kuthadi, V.M.; Baskar, S. Smart building energy management and monitoring system based on artificial intelligence in smart city. *Sustain. Energy Technol. Assess.* **2023**, *56*, 103090. [CrossRef]
131. Alhamrouni, I.; Kahar, N.H.A.; Salem, M.; Swadi, M.; Zahroui, Y.; Kadhim, D.J.; Mohamed, F.A.; Nazari, M.A. A comprehensive review on the role of artificial intelligence in power system stability, control, and protection: Insights and future directions. *Appl. Sci.* **2024**, *14*, 6214. [CrossRef]
132. Lami, B.; Alsolami, M.; Alferidi, A.; Slama, S.B. A Smart Microgrid Platform Integrating AI and Deep Reinforcement Learning for Sustainable Energy Management. *Energies* **2025**, *18*, 1157. [CrossRef]
133. Kim, K.; Ko, D.; Jung, J.; Ryu, J.O.; Hur, K.J.; Kim, Y.J. Real-time ai-based power demand forecasting for peak shaving and consumption reduction using vehicle-to-grid and reused energy storage systems: A case study at a business center on Jeju Island. *Appl. Sci.* **2025**, *15*, 3050. [CrossRef]
134. Moshtaghi, P.; Hajialigol, N.; Rafiei, B. A comprehensive review of artificial intelligence applications in wind energy power generation. *Sustain. Futures* **2025**, *9*, 100638. [CrossRef]
135. Turnbull, A.; Carroll, J. Cost benefit of implementing advanced monitoring and predictive maintenance strategies for offshore wind farms. *Energies* **2021**, *14*, 4922. [CrossRef]
136. Chen, S.; Liu, J.; Cui, Z.; Chen, Z.; Wang, H.; Xiao, W. A deep reinforcement learning approach for microgrid energy transmission dispatching. *Appl. Sci.* **2024**, *14*, 3682. [CrossRef]
137. Abdullah, E. Enhancing solar irradiance forecasting using LSTM and meteorological data. *J. Inf. Syst. Eng. Manag.* **2025**, *10*, 161–166. [CrossRef]
138. Burk, S.; Miner, G. *It's All Analytics, Part III: The Applications of AI, Analytics, and Data Science*; Productivity Press: New York, NY, USA, 2023. [CrossRef]
139. Chaudhary, K.; Alam, M. *AI-Based Data Analytics: Applications for Business Management*; CRC Press: Boca Raton, FL, USA, 2023; pp. 1–260. [CrossRef]
140. Cavus, M. Advancing power systems with renewable energy and intelligent technologies: A comprehensive review on grid transformation and integration. *Electronics* **2025**, *14*, 1159. [CrossRef]
141. Khalili, K.; Ahmadi, M.; Moraveji, M.K. A comprehensive review of failure modes in electrical submersible pumps: Diagnosis, predictive maintenance, and engineer's guide. *Arab. J. Sci. Eng.* **2025**, 1–22. [CrossRef]
142. Shafik, W. An Overview of artificial intelligence solutions for the maintenance and evaluation of photovoltaic systems. In *Energy Conversion Systems-Based Artificial Intelligence: Applications and Tools*; Springer: Singapore, 2025; pp. 23–53. [CrossRef]
143. Dalal, A.; Cudney, E.A. *Lean-AI: A Humanistic Integration of Lean and AI*; CRC Press: Boca Raton, FL, USA, 2025. [CrossRef]

144. Biswas, A. Predictive maintenance of renewable energy infrastructure using AI: A comprehensive review. *Pac. J. Adv. Eng. Innov.* **2025**, *2*, 12–21. [CrossRef]
145. Moldstud. Best Practices for Developing Custom AI Solutions for Predictive Maintenance. Available online: https://moldstud.com/articles/p-best-practices-for-developing-custom-ai-solutions-for-predictive-maintenance (accessed on 11 August 2025).
146. Sayal, A.; Chaithra, N.; Jha, J.; Allagari, N. AI-based predictive maintenance strategies for improving the reliability of green power systems. In *Digital Technologies to Implement the UN Sustainable Development Goals*; Springer: Berlin/Heidelberg, Germany, 2024; pp. 19–46.
147. Unsal, D.B.; Aksoz, A.; Oyucu, S.; Guerrero, J.M.; Guler, M. A comparative study of AI methods on renewable energy prediction for smart grids: Case of Turkey. *Sustainability* **2024**, *16*, 2894. [CrossRef]
148. Baseer, A.M.; Almunif, A.; Alsaduni, I.; Tazeen, N. Electrical power generation forecasting from renewable energy systems using artificial intelligence techniques. *Energies* **2023**, *16*, 6414. [CrossRef]
149. Cabot, J.H.; Ross, E.G. Evaluating prediction model performance. *Surgery* **2023**, *174*, 723–726. [CrossRef]
150. Cabuk, K.S.; Cengiz, S.K.; Guler, M.G.; Topcu, H.; Efe, A.C.; Ulas, M.G.; Karademir, F.P. Chasing the objective upper eyelid symmetry formula; R2, RMSE, POC, MAE, and MSE. *Int. Ophthalmol.* **2024**, *44*, 303. [CrossRef]
151. Saglam, M.; Lv, X.; Spataru, C.; Karaman, O.A. Instantaneous electricity peak load forecasting using optimization and machine learning. *Energies* **2024**, *17*, 777. [CrossRef]
152. Jaffar, M.; Shafiq, S.; Shahzadi, N.; Alrajeh, N.; Jamil, M.; Javaid, N. Efficient deep learning models for predicting super-utilizers in smart hospitals. *IEEE Access* **2023**, *11*, 87676–87693. [CrossRef]
153. Sharma, A.K.; Vajjhala, N.R.; Kothari, R.; Potluri, R.M. *Explainable AI and Blockchain for Secure and Agile Supply Chains: Enhancing Transparency, Traceability, and Accountability*, 1st ed.; Chapman and Hall/CRC: New York, NY, USA, 2025; pp. 1–236. [CrossRef]
154. Mhlanga, D. Artificial intelligence and machine learning for energy consumption and production in emerging markets: A review. *Energies* **2023**, *16*, 745. [CrossRef]
155. Shahverdi, N.; Saffari, A.; Amiri, B. A systematic review of artificial intelligence and machine learning in energy sustainability: Research topics and trends. *Energy Rep.* **2025**, *13*, 5551–5578. [CrossRef]
156. Alahi, E.E.; Sukkuea, A.; Tina, F.W.; Kurdthongmee, A.N.W.; Suwannarat, K.; Mukhopadhyay, S.C. Integration of IoT-Enabled Technologies and Artificial Intelligence (AI) for Smart City Scenario: Recent Advancements and Future Trends. *Sensors* **2023**, *23*, 5206. [CrossRef]
157. Vasques, X.; Possompes, T.; Rey, H.; Le Touzé, M.; Lange, B. Analysis and knowledge discovery from sensors data to improve energy efficiency. *arXiv* **2025**, arXiv:2503.13501. [CrossRef]
158. ThingsBoard. Working with IoT Dashboards. Available online: https://thingsboard.io/docs/user-guide/dashboards/ (accessed on 10 September 2025).
159. Rekeraho, A.; Cotfas, D.T.; Cotfas, P.A.; Tuyishime, E.; Balan, T.C.; Acheampong, R. Enhancing security for IoT-based smart renewable energy remote monitoring systems. *Electronics* **2023**, *13*, 756. [CrossRef]
160. Rahman, M.A.; Alam, M.S.; Mrida, M.S.H. How interactive dashboards improve managerial decision-making in operations management. *Am. J. Adv. Technol. Eng. Solut.* **2025**, *1*, 122–146. [CrossRef]
161. Grafana, Energy and Utilities. Available online: https://grafana.com/success/energy-utilities (accessed on 28 August 2025).
162. PR Newswire. Schneider Electric Announces Evolution of EcoStruxure IT with Model Based, Automated Sustainability Metric Reporting. Available online: https://www.prnewswire.com/news-releases/schneider-electric-announces-evolution-of-ecostruxure-it-with-model-based-automated-sustainability-metric-reporting-302080370.html (accessed on 28 August 2025).
163. S. Electric. Schneider Electric Announces Evolution of EcoStruxure IT with Model Based, Automated Sustainability Metric Reporting. Available online: https://www.se.com/uk/en/about-us/newsroom/news/press-releases/schneider-electric-announces-evolution-of-ecostruxure-it-with-model-based-automated-sustainability-metric-reporting-65e7476f162c4c33740b1cdd (accessed on 28 August 2025).
164. Siemens, Siemens Launches MindSphere Application Center to Deliver Digital Solutions for Coal and Steam-Based Powerplant Operators. Available online: https://press.siemens.com/in/en/pressrelease/siemens-launches-mindsphere-application-center-deliver-digital-solutions (accessed on 28 August 2025).
165. IMB. Unlock the Power of Real-Time Data for Intelligent Energy Operations. Available online: https://www.ibm.com/new/announcements/unlock-the-power-of-real-time-data-for-intelligent-energy-operations (accessed on 28 August 2025).
166. Djangostars. The Essential Guide to Renewable Energy Software Development. Available online: https://djangostars.com/blog/how-to-develop-renewable-energy-software/ (accessed on 28 August 2025).
167. Tahir, K.A. A systematic review and evolutionary analysis of the optimization techniques and software tools in hybrid microgrid systems. *Energies* **2025**, *18*, 1770. [CrossRef]
168. Teckstack. Top Software Solutions of AI in Renewable Energy Sector in 2024 Read More on. Available online: https://tech-stack.com/blog/ai-software-solutions-in-renewable-energy/ (accessed on 24 August 2025).

169. Kiss, G.R.; Horváth, M.; Szánthó, Z. MATLAB Simulink-Based Modelling and Performance Analysis of District Heating Substations for Renewable Energy Integration. *Energies* **2025**, *18*, 2370. [CrossRef]
170. Omidi, S.A.; Baig, M.J.A.; Iqbal, M.T. Design and implementation of node-red based open-source SCADA architecture for a hybrid power system. *Energies* **2023**, *16*, 2092. [CrossRef]
171. Hassanin, K.M.; Mansour, D.-E.A.; Kato, T.; Megahed, T.F. A Novel political optimizer integrated with thingspeak platform for multi-objective energy management in microgrids. *Smart Grids Sustain. Energy* **2024**, *9*, 47. [CrossRef]
172. Alves, D.; Mendonça, F.; Mostafa, S.S.; Morgado-Dias, F. A comprehensive IoT cloud-based wind station ready for real-time measurements and artificial intelligence integration. *E-Prime-Adv. Electr. Eng. Electron.* **2024**, *10*, 100862. [CrossRef]
173. Bhende, N.; Kesavan, R. Energy-optimized edge-computing framework for the sustainable development of modern agriculture. *Eng. Proc.* **2023**, *56*, 134. [CrossRef]
174. Cotfas, P.A.; Cotfas, D.T.; Hedesiu, H. Virtual instrumentation used in renewable energy. In *LabVIEW-Virtual Instrumentation in Education and Industry*; IntechOpen: London, UK, 2023. [CrossRef]
175. Boussouf, Z.; Amrani, H.; Khal, M.Z.; Daidai, F. Artificial intelligence in education: A systematic literature review. *Data Metadata* **2024**, *3*, 288. [CrossRef]
176. Idrissi, Z.K.; Lachgar, M.; Hrimech, H. Blockchain, IoT and AI in logistics and transportation: A systematic review. *Transp. Econ. Manag.* **2025**, *2*, 275–285. [CrossRef]
177. Sharma, K.; Shivandu, S.K. Integrating artificial intelligence and Internet of Things (IoT) for enhanced crop monitoring and management in precision agriculture. *Sens. Int.* **2024**, *5*, 100292. [CrossRef]
178. Miller, T.; Mikiciuk, G.; Durlik, I.; Mikiciuk, M.; Łobodzińska, A.; Śnieg, M. The IoT and AI in agriculture: The time is now—A systematic review of smart sensing technologies. *Sensors* **2025**, *25*, 3583. [CrossRef] [PubMed]
179. Envall, F.; Rohracher, H. Experimenting to remain the same: The politics of smart grid pilot projects in the Swedish energy transition. *Environ. Innov. Soc. Transit.* **2025**, *57*, 101037. [CrossRef]
180. Gupta, J.; Jain, S.; Chakraborty, S.; Panchenko, V.; Smirnov, A.; Yudaev, I. Advancing sustainable energy transition: Blockchain and peer-to-peer energy trading in India's green revolution. *Sustainability* **2023**, *15*, 13633. [CrossRef]
181. Rodriguez, R.V.; Hemachandran, K. *Minds Unveiled: Exploring the Effects of Generative AI on Business Behavior*; Productivity Press: New York, NY, USA, 2024; pp. 1–308. [CrossRef]
182. Adewoyin, M.A.; Adediwin, O.; Audu, A.J. Artificial intelligence and sustainable energy development: A review of applications, challenges, and future directions. *Int. J. Multidiscip. Res. Growth Eval.* **2025**, *6*, 196–203. [CrossRef]
183. Rezaei, M. Artificial intelligence in knowledge management: Identifying and addressing the key implementation challenges. *Technol. Forecast. Soc. Change* **2025**, *217*, 124183. [CrossRef]
184. Masoomi, B.; Sahebi, I.G.; Gholian-Jouybari, F.; Mejia-Argueta, C.; Hajiaghaei-Keshteli, M. The role of internet of things adoption on the sustainability performance of the renewable energy supply chain: A conceptual framework. *Renew. Sustain. Energy Rev.* **2024**, *202*, 114610. [CrossRef]
185. Shobeiry, S.M. AI-enabled modern power systems: Challenges, solutions, and recommendations. In *Artificial Intelligence in the Operation and Control of Digitalized Power Systems*; Springer: Cham, Switzerland, 2024; pp. 19–67. [CrossRef]
186. Sulaiman, N.F.; Gunasekaran, S.S.; Zaman, H.B.; Nashruddin, S.N.A.M.; Nashruddin, S.N.A.M.; Sofiah, A.G.N.; Mubin, M.H.A.; Lee, S.L. Advances in catalysis for biodiesel production: Integrating AI-driven optimization and bibliometric insights into renewable energy technologies. *Bioresour. Technol.* **2025**, *437*, 133088. [CrossRef]
187. Ukoba, K.; Olatunji, K.O.; Adeoye, E.; Jen, T.-C.; Madyira, D.M. Optimizing renewable energy systems through artificial intelligence: Review and future prospects. *Energy Environ.* **2024**, *35*, 3833–3879. [CrossRef]
188. Alsharif, M.H.; Jahid, A.; Kelechi, A.H.; Kannadasan, R. Green IoT: A review and future research directions. *Symmetry* **2023**, *15*, 757. [CrossRef]
189. Nwokediegwu, Z.Q.S.; Ibekwe, K.I.; Ilojianya, V.I.; Etukudoh, E.A.; Ayorinde, O.B. Renewable energy technologies in engineering: A review of current developments and future prospects. *Eng. Sci. Technol. J.* **2024**, *5*, 367–384. [CrossRef]

energies

Article

Federated Quantum Machine Learning for Distributed Cybersecurity in Multi-Agent Energy Systems

Kwabena Addo *,† , Musasa Kabeya † and Evans Eshiemogie Ojo

Department of Electrical Power Engineering, Durban University of Technology, Durban 4001, South Africa; musasak@dut.ac.za (M.K.); evanso@dut.ac.za (E.E.O.)
* Correspondence: 22494773@dut4life.ac.za
† These authors contributed equally to this work.

Abstract: The increasing digitization and decentralization of modern energy systems have heightened their vulnerability to sophisticated cyber threats, necessitating advanced, scalable, and privacy-preserving detection frameworks. This paper introduces a novel Federated Quantum Machine Learning (FQML) framework tailored for anomaly detection in multi-agent energy environments. By integrating parameterized quantum circuits (PQCs) at the local agent level with secure federated learning protocols, the framework enhances detection accuracy while preserving data privacy. A trimmed-mean aggregation scheme and differential privacy mechanisms are embedded to defend against Byzantine behaviors and data-poisoning attacks. The problem is formally modeled as a constrained optimization task, accounting for quantum circuit depth, communication latency, and adversarial resilience. Experimental validation on synthetic smart grid datasets demonstrates that FQML achieves high detection accuracy ($\geq$96.3%), maintains robustness under adversarial perturbations, and reduces communication overhead by 28.6% compared to classical federated baselines. These results substantiate the viability of quantum-enhanced federated learning as a practical, hardware-conscious approach to distributed cybersecurity in next-generation energy infrastructures.

Keywords: adversarial robustness; federated learning; quantum machine learning; smart grid cybersecurity; variational quantum circuits

1. Introduction

The ongoing transformation of traditional power grids into smart energy systems, characterized by the widespread deployment of distributed energy resources (DERs), Internet of Things (IoT) devices, and multi-agent control systems, has significantly expanded the attack surface and introduced sophisticated cybersecurity challenges [1,2]. Modern energy infrastructures are increasingly regarded as critical cyber-physical systems, tightly coupling digital communications, computational intelligence, and physical power delivery. Consequently, these systems are highly vulnerable to cyber threats that may cause substantial disruptions or even catastrophic blackouts [3].

Historically, centralized machine learning (ML) approaches have been widely adopted for cybersecurity in smart grids, supporting anomaly detection, intrusion classification, and threat-mitigation tasks. However, these centralized architectures present key limitations: they expose raw data to central aggregators, introduce high communication overhead, and impose latency that becomes impractical as the system scales [4,5]. Furthermore, centralized solutions represent single points of failure, making them susceptible to targeted or coordinated cyber-attacks [6].

Federated learning (FL), a decentralized ML paradigm, addresses these challenges by enabling multiple agents to collaboratively train a shared model without exchanging raw data, thus preserving local data privacy and reducing communication overhead [7]. The decentralized nature of FL facilitates scalability and robustness against localized attacks, making it a compelling candidate for modern energy systems [8]. However, classical FL frameworks still face challenges, including limited model expressiveness, slow convergence, and computational bottlenecks, when deployed in complex or adversarial environments.

Quantum machine learning (QML), which leverages quantum mechanical principles such as superposition, entanglement, and interference, has emerged as a promising approach for enhancing learning efficiency and detection capabilities [9,10]. QML algorithms have demonstrated superior performance in terms of classification accuracy, training speed, and adversarial robustness in controlled settings [11]. However, standalone QML implementations often struggle with scalability, noise sensitivity, and deployment feasibility, especially in large-scale, distributed cyber-physical infrastructures like smart grids.

Given the complementary strengths of FL and QML, this paper introduces a novel Federated Quantum Machine Learning (FQML) framework, specifically designed to address cybersecurity in multi-agent energy systems. The FQML architecture combines the decentralized, privacy-preserving nature of FL with the computational acceleration and high-dimensional feature-processing capabilities of QML. This integration aims to provide a resilient and scalable solution to emerging threats such as coordinated intrusions, stealthy attacks, and distributed denial-of-service (DDoS) incidents targeting smart grid infrastructures.

The key contributions of this work are summarized as follows:

- Formulation of a mathematically rigorous optimization problem for distributed cybersecurity, integrating federated learning and quantum variational models under real-world constraints.
- Development of a scalable and hardware-feasible FQML framework, incorporating robust aggregation, privacy-preserving parameter exchange, and quantum circuit design tailored to near-term devices.
- Comprehensive experimental validation using simulated smart grid data and attack scenarios, demonstrating significant gains in detection accuracy, communication efficiency, and adversarial robustness over classical federated and centralized baselines.

The remainder of this paper is structured as follows. Section 2 reviews related work and identifies research gaps. Section 3 describes the system architecture and threat model. Section 4 presents a formal problem formulation. Section 5 introduces the proposed FQML framework. Section 6 details the implementation and experimental setup. Section 7 discusses the results. Section 8 provides critical insights and practical implications. Finally, Section 9 concludes the paper and outlines directions for future work.

2. Related Work

2.1. Cybersecurity in Energy Systems

Modern energy systems face increasing vulnerabilities due to their evolution into cyber-physical infrastructures integrating digital communication and computational layers. A comprehensive survey by Ding et al. [12] illustrates a variety of cyber-attacks targeting smart grids, including data integrity attacks, denial-of-service (DoS), and advanced persistent threats (APT). Mohanty et al. [13] emphasized the urgency of addressing these vulnerabilities due to their potential consequences, such as significant disruptions or large-scale blackouts. Conventional cybersecurity mechanisms, predominantly centralized in nature, typically involve machine learning-based intrusion detection systems

(IDS) and anomaly detection techniques; however, these methods are susceptible to single points of failure and compromised privacy [14,15]. Recent adversarial paradigms, such as knowledge-aided generative adversarial networks (KA-GANs) have demonstrated the capability to launch stealthy, transfer-based attacks without gradient information [16]. Other work highlights how adversarial reliability challenges affect deep learning-based soft sensors in real-time control environments [17]. These findings underscore the need for robust defenses such as the FQML framework proposed in this study.

2.2. *Federated Learning for Critical Infrastructure Security*

Federated learning (FL), introduced by Wen et al. [18], has emerged as a robust alternative to centralized ML, significantly improving privacy and scalability by enabling distributed learning across multiple edge devices without sharing sensitive data. In the context of critical infrastructures, federated learning approaches have gained significant attention. Alhamroun et al. [19] reviewed distributed machine learning methodologies specifically designed for smart grid applications, highlighting FL's advantages in preserving user privacy while maintaining system-wide security. Similarly, Trivedi et al. [20] demonstrated a federated consensus-based learning architecture capable of managing massive IoT deployments, substantially reducing communication overhead and enhancing resilience against data injection attacks. Aouedi et al. [21] provided a comprehensive survey of FL applications specifically targeted at cybersecurity, emphasizing the effectiveness of privacy-preserving approaches in defending industrial IoT networks.

2.3. *Quantum Machine Learning in Network Security*

Quantum machine learning (QML) leverages quantum computation capabilities such as superposition, entanglement, and interference, offering novel opportunities for enhanced computational efficiency, complex feature extraction, and superior anomaly detection capabilities compared to classical approaches. Tychola et al. [22] illustrated the theoretical benefits of QML algorithms by mapping classical data into higher-dimensional quantum Hilbert spaces, significantly improving model expressiveness. Ranga et al. [23] analyzed the expressive power of parameterized quantum circuits, revealing substantial potential for accurate and efficient anomaly detection. Memon et al. [24] further discussed the feasibility and challenges of implementing quantum algorithms on near-term intermediate-scale quantum (NISQ) devices, noting concerns related to noise, coherence time, and limited gate depth.

2.4. *Federated Quantum Learning and Identified Research Gaps*

Despite the significant progress made independently in federated learning and quantum machine learning, their convergence, particularly for cybersecurity applications in energy systems, remains underexplored. Federated Quantum Machine Learning (FQML) is an emerging research frontier aimed at combining the privacy-preserving, decentralized nature of FL with the computational advantages of QML.

However, several critical research gaps must be addressed:

- Privacy-Preserving Integration: Federated learning frameworks are predominantly classical. The implications of integrating quantum components within privacy-sensitive federated settings, particularly in compliance with differential privacy or homomorphic encryption standards, are not yet fully understood.
- Quantum-Enhanced Aggregation: Most FL systems use classical aggregation methods such as weighted averaging. The use of quantum-native techniques for secure and efficient aggregation remains largely unexplored and may offer new forms of robustness and compression.

- Robustness and Resilience: Quantum-enhanced federated systems must be designed to withstand adversarial threats such as Byzantine behavior, data poisoning, and inference attacks. Existing methods lack formal treatment of these threats in hybrid quantum-classical environments.

This paper addresses these gaps by proposing and evaluating a robust, privacy-aware federated quantum learning framework tailored to distributed cybersecurity in multi-agent energy networks.

3. System and Threat Model

This section rigorously details the energy system architecture, communication topologies, threat model, and security assumptions considered in this research.

3.1. Multi-Agent Energy System Architecture

We consider a multi-agent smart energy system composed of geographically distributed agents, each equipped with local computational resources, quantum processing capabilities, and communication interfaces. Each agent $a_i \in \mathcal{A}$, where $\mathcal{A} = \{a_1, a_2, \ldots, a_N\}$, manages local data and engages in decentralized learning tasks for cybersecurity purposes.

Formally, each agent a_i maintains a private dataset:

$$D_i = \left\{(x_j, y_j)\right\}_{j=1}^{M_i}, \quad (1)$$

where $x_j \in \mathbb{R}^d$ represents power grid measurements and communication features, and $y_j \in \{0,1\}$ indicates whether the data is benign or malicious.

3.2. Communication Topologies

Agents interact using predefined communication structures, either hierarchical or peer-to-peer (P2P). The communication network is modeled as an undirected graph:

$$\mathcal{G} = (\mathcal{A}, \mathcal{E}), \quad (2)$$

where $(a_i, a_j) \in \mathcal{E}$ denotes a reliable communication channel. Communication constraints are quantified by latency and bandwidth:

$$\tau_{ij}, \quad B_{ij}, \quad \forall (a_i, a_j) \in \mathcal{E}, \quad (3)$$

where τ_{ij} is the delay and B_{ij} the bandwidth of the link between agents a_i and a_j.

3.3. Attacker Capabilities and Objectives

In this study, we adopt a strong threat model wherein the adversary possesses advanced capabilities to compromise federated training integrity. Specifically, the attacker is assumed to have the ability to (i) intercept and manipulate communication channels, (ii) inject falsified or misleading input data, and (iii) poison local training datasets by introducing subtle perturbations.

Formally, adversarially perturbed inputs are modeled as follows:

$$\tilde{x}_j = x_j + \delta_j, \quad \|\delta_j\| \leq \epsilon,$$

where x_j is the clean input, $\tilde{x}_j$ is its adversarial counterpart, and δ_j represents the perturbation bounded by an ℓ_p-norm constraint ϵ. This formulation reflects common gradient-based or zero-order adversarial techniques used in distributed learning systems.

The attacker's objective is to maximize the expected prediction loss of the global federated quantum model, thereby degrading classification accuracy or inducing misclassification on critical data points. This adversarial goal is mathematically expressed as follows:

$$\max_{\{\delta_j\}} \mathbb{E}_{(x_j,y_j)}\left[\mathcal{L}(f(\tilde{x}_j;\theta),y_j)\right], \tag{4}$$

where $f(\cdot;\theta)$ denotes the federated quantum classifier parameterized by θ, y_j is the true label associated with x_j, and $\mathcal{L}(\cdot)$ is the binary cross-entropy loss function. This threat formulation enables a robust evaluation of the proposed FQML framework under worst-case data-poisoning and model-evasion scenarios.

Scope of Adversarial Modeling: The current work adopts a uniform ϵ-bounded perturbation scheme inspired by the Fast Gradient Sign Method (FGSM), which offers computational efficiency and allows for the controlled evaluation of system robustness. However, we acknowledge that this formulation may not fully reflect more sophisticated or stealthy threat models encountered in real-world deployments, such as iterative attacks (e.g., PGD), optimization-based attacks (e.g., Carlini–Wagner), or generative adversarial attack frameworks. These methods can introduce perturbations with higher success rates while evading detection, particularly in adaptive or knowledge-aided threat landscapes.

3.4. Security and Privacy Assumptions

To ensure privacy, agents never share raw data. Instead, they send obfuscated updates using differential privacy mechanisms:

$$\tilde{\theta}_i = \theta_i + \eta_i, \quad \eta_i \sim \text{Laplace}(0,\sigma), \tag{5}$$

where $\tilde{\theta}_i$ is the noisy parameter vector and σ controls the privacy–utility trade-off. These updates are securely aggregated at a central server without revealing individual agent contributions.

Figure 1 illustrates the overall system architecture, highlighting decentralized quantum training, secure aggregation, and the attack surface.

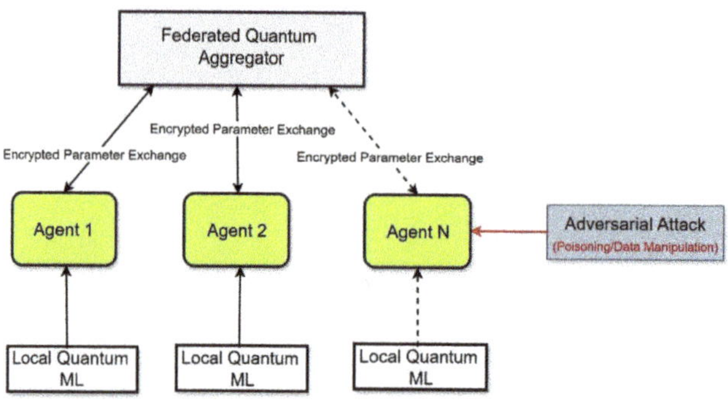

Figure 1. Federated Quantum Machine Learning system architecture for cybersecurity in multi-agent energy systems.

This model establishes the mathematical and architectural foundation for the subsequent problem formulation in Section 4 and the proposed FQML framework in Section 5.

4. Problem Formulation

This section mathematically formalizes the cybersecurity learning task within the context of Federated Quantum Machine Learning (FQML). The objective is to enable distributed quantum-enhanced agents to collaboratively learn a global model that robustly detects cyber-attacks, while meeting strict privacy, communication, and computational constraints.

4.1. Notation and Preliminaries

Let the system consist of N decentralized agents denoted by $\mathcal{A} = \{a_1, a_2, \ldots, a_N\}$. Each agent $a_i \in \mathcal{A}$ has access to a private local dataset:

$$D_i = \left\{(x_j^{(i)}, y_j^{(i)})\right\}_{j=1}^{M_i}, \tag{6}$$

where $x_j^{(i)} \in \mathbb{R}^d$ is a feature vector and $y_j^{(i)} \in \{0,1\}$ denotes a binary class label (0: normal; 1: malicious). The global federated quantum model is represented by $f(x;\theta)$, where θ denotes the model parameters.

4.2. Learning Objective

The global federated optimization objective is to minimize the empirical loss aggregated from all agents:

$$\min_{\theta} F(\theta) = \frac{1}{N}\sum_{i=1}^{N} L_i(\theta), \tag{7}$$

with each agent's local loss defined as follows:

$$L_i(\theta) = \frac{1}{M_i}\sum_{j=1}^{M_i} \ell(f(x_j^{(i)};\theta), y_j^{(i)}), \tag{8}$$

where $\ell(\cdot,\cdot)$ is the binary cross-entropy loss:

$$\ell(\hat{y}, y) = -[y\log(\hat{y}) + (1-y)\log(1-\hat{y})], \quad \hat{y} = f(x;\theta). \tag{9}$$

4.3. Quantum Federated Learning Constraints

The optimization in (7) is subject to the following constraints:

Quantum Resource Constraints:

$$q_i \le q_{\max}, \quad d_i \le d_{\max}, \quad \forall a_i \in \mathcal{A}, \tag{10}$$

where q_i and d_i denote the number of qubits and circuit depth, respectively.

Communication Bandwidth Constraints:

$$|\text{Update}(\theta^{(i)})| \le B_i, \quad \forall a_i \in \mathcal{A}, \tag{11}$$

Latency Constraints:

$$\tau_i^{\text{trans}} + \tau^{\text{agg}} \le \tau_{\max}, \quad \forall a_i \in \mathcal{A}, \tag{12}$$

Privacy Preservation Constraints:

$$\tilde{\theta}^{(i)} = \theta^{(i)} + \eta^{(i)}, \quad \eta^{(i)} \sim \text{Laplace}(0, \sigma_i), \tag{13}$$

where σ_i controls the level of noise for differential privacy (ϵ-DP guarantee).

4.4. Robustness Under Adversarial Conditions

Each agent's dataset may be adversarially perturbed:

$$\tilde{x}_j^{(i)} = x_j^{(i)} + \delta_j^{(i)}, \quad \|\delta_j^{(i)}\| \le \epsilon_{\text{adv}}, \tag{14}$$

with the attacker aiming to maximize, as follows:

$$\max_{\{\delta_j^{(i)}\}} \mathbb{E}\left[\ell(f(\tilde{x}_j^{(i)};\theta), y_j^{(i)})\right]. \tag{15}$$

The complete robust federated quantum learning formulation is as follows:

$$\min_{\theta} \frac{1}{N}\sum_{i=1}^{N} \frac{1}{M_i}\sum_{j=1}^{M_i} \ell(f(\tilde{x}_j^{(i)};\theta), y_j^{(i)}), \tag{16}$$

subject to the constraints in Equations (10)–(14).

This comprehensive problem formulation underpins the design of our federated quantum cybersecurity framework, integrating quantum resource limitations, privacy-preserving communication, and adversarial robustness.

5. Federated Quantum ML Framework

This section introduces the proposed Federated Quantum Machine Learning (FQML) framework, combining quantum-enhanced local learning, privacy-preserving parameter aggregation, and adversarial robustness to address the optimization problem outlined in Section 4.

5.1. Architectural Overview and Workflow Diagram

The FQML framework is organized into three core stages:

1. Local Quantum Training at individual agents.
2. Secure, Privacy-Preserving Aggregation of updates.
3. Robustness Enforcement against adversarial attacks.

Figure 2 illustrates the high-level workflow:

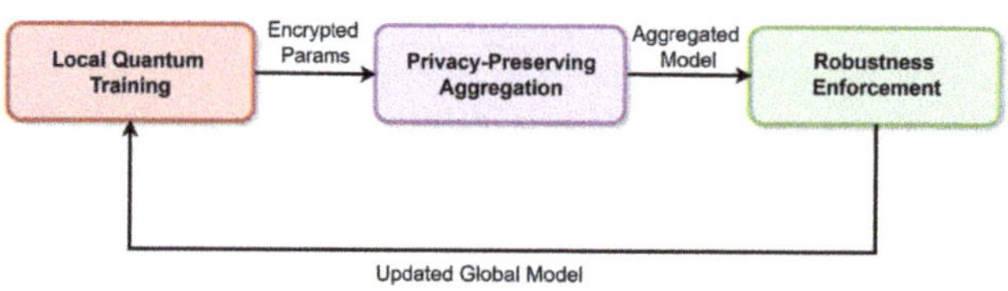

Figure 2. Overview of the proposed Federated Quantum ML Framework.

5.2. Local Quantum Model Design

Each agent a_i uses a variational quantum classifier (VQC). Model output is as follows:

$$f(x;\theta) = \sigma\Big(\langle 0|^{\otimes q} U^{\dagger}(x,\theta)\, O\, U(x,\theta) |0\rangle^{\otimes q}\Big), \tag{17}$$

where $x \in \mathbb{R}^d$, $U(x,\theta)$ is a parameterized quantum circuit, O is a measurement observable, and $\sigma(\cdot)$ a sigmoid activation.

The circuit structure is as follows:

$$U(x,\theta) = \prod_{l=1}^{L}\Big[U_{\text{ent}}^{(l)} \prod_{k=1}^{q} R_z(\theta_{l,k}^{(z)}) R_y(\theta_{l,k}^{(y)}) R_x(\theta_{l,k}^{(x)})\Big] U_{\text{enc}}(x), \tag{18}$$

where L is depth, q is qubit count, and $U_{\text{enc}}(x)$ encodes classical data.

5.3. Privacy-Preserving Federated Aggregation

Each agent computes gradients:

$$\Delta\theta^{(i)} = \nabla_\theta \mathcal{L}_i(\theta^{(i)}), \tag{19}$$

then applies differential privacy:

$$\tilde{\Delta\theta}^{(i)} = \Delta\theta^{(i)} + \eta^{(i)}, \quad \eta^{(i)} \sim \text{Laplace}(0, \sigma_i). \tag{20}$$

The federated update is as follows:

$$\bar{\theta} \leftarrow \theta - \alpha \cdot \frac{1}{N} \sum_{i=1}^{N} \tilde{\Delta\theta}^{(i)}, \tag{21}$$

with learning rate α.

5.4. Robustness Mechanisms

The proposed framework integrates two key mechanisms to defend against adversarial behaviors: (i) Differential Privacy (DP), which introduces calibrated noise to gradient updates, thereby masking the influence of poisoned data samples; and (ii) Trimmed Mean Aggregation, which statistically removes extreme gradient contributions, commonly caused by Byzantine agents, before model updating. In tandem, DP prevents the reverse engineering of local data and smooths gradient anomalies, while the trimmed mean guards against coordinated poisoning or outlier attacks by excluding the top and bottom t updates in each round.

To mitigate the impact of adversarial behaviors such as Byzantine faults, characterized by falsified gradient updates, and data poisoning via tampered local datasets, the FQML framework incorporates robust aggregation techniques during the global model update phase.

In particular, we implement trimmed mean aggregation, which is effective in excluding extreme or malicious updates from the aggregation process. Let the received local model updates be denoted by the sorted set:

$$\left\{ \tilde{\Delta\theta}^{[1]}, \tilde{\Delta\theta}^{[2]}, \ldots, \tilde{\Delta\theta}^{[N]} \right\}, \tag{22}$$

where the updates are ordered based on their component-wise values. The global model parameters are then updated using the trimmed mean rule:

$$\bar{\theta} \leftarrow \theta - \alpha \cdot \frac{1}{N-2t} \sum_{i=t+1}^{N-t} \tilde{\Delta\theta}^{[i]}, \tag{23}$$

where α is the learning rate, N is the total number of participating agents, and t represents the number of updates trimmed from each end corresponding to the estimated number of adversarial contributors.

This aggregation mechanism enhances the resilience of federated optimization by reducing the influence of outliers, thereby ensuring convergence toward a stable and reliable global model even under targeted poisoning or Byzantine attack scenarios.

5.5. Convergence Criterion and Quantum–Classical Integration

Training proceeds until:

$$\left| F(\theta^{(k+1)}) - F(\theta^{(k)}) \right| \leq \delta_{\text{conv}}, \tag{24}$$

where $F(\theta)$ is the global loss at iteration k. Integrating quantum computation improves convergence speed and model expressiveness, especially in cybersecurity tasks.

Quantum Acceleration Insight: The use of parameterized quantum circuits (PQCs) offers a fundamental convergence advantage in federated settings. Unlike classical models limited by linear kernel representations, PQCs operate in exponentially larger Hilbert spaces via superposition and entanglement. This allows for the parallel exploration of parameter landscapes and faster gradient descent convergence. Formally, for a target binary classification task, the gradient update per round benefits from non-convex curvature, and numerical results (see Figure 6) indicate that FQML converges to $\leq 1\%$ loss 38% faster than its classical counterpart under equal local epochs and batch sizes.

The FQML framework fuses quantum expressivity (Equations (17) and (18)), federated privacy (Equations (19)–(21)), and adversarial robustness (Equations (23) and (24)). This enables scalable, secure, and resilient cybersecurity in multi-agent energy systems.

The detailed step-by-step pseudocode of the proposed FQML framework is provided in Appendix A.1.

6. Implementation and Experimental Setup

This section presents the practical implementation details of the proposed Federated Quantum Machine Learning (FQML) framework, including the simulation environment, datasets, quantum hardware configuration, adversarial modeling, and evaluation metrics.

6.1. Simulation Environment

The quantum components were implemented using IBM Qiskit, (version 0.45.0) enabling simulation of variational quantum circuits (VQCs) and amplitude encoding. Classical federated learning operations were handled using PySyft and TensorFlow Federated to emulate decentralized communication and privacy-preserving aggregation.

The hardware configuration for simulations was as follows:

- Processor: Intel Core i9-11900K CPU (8 cores, 16 threads)
- Memory: 64 GB DDR4
- Quantum Simulator: Qiskit Aer (statevector simulator)

The complete set of simulation parameters and configuration settings is summarized in Appendix A.2 (Table A1).

6.2. Dataset and Attack Scenarios

A synthetic dataset representative of multi-agent smart grid operations was used. It includes features such as voltage, frequency, load measurements, and labeled attack instances.

- Number of agents: $N = 10$
- Total samples: $M = 100{,}000$, distributed equally ($M_i = 10{,}000$ per agent). Although synthetic data offer full control over feature distributions and attack severity, it lacks the operational noise and heterogeneity of real-world telemetry. To bridge this gap, we plan to validate our approach using public benchmark datasets, including those derived from the IEEE 39-bus and 118-bus test systems with labeled cyber-physical anomalies.
- Feature dimension: $d = 20$

Cyber-Attack Types Simulated:

- False Data Injection (FDI)
- Denial-of-Service (DoS)
- Coordinated Multi-Agent Attacks

Adversarial perturbations were applied as follows:

$$\tilde{x}_j = x_j + \delta_j, \quad ||\delta_j|| \leq \epsilon$$

6.3. Quantum Hardware and Circuit Configuration

Each agent implements a VQC with the following:

- Qubits: $q = 8$
- Max circuit depth: $d_{\max} = 10$

Circuit Design:

- Encoding: Amplitude encoding. Although amplitude encoding offers compactness for dense features, we additionally report an angle-encoding ablation to quantify any accuracy gap under identical federation settings. Both variants share the same qubit count, circuit depth, optimizer, and data splits to ensure a fair comparison.
- Ansatz: Hardware-efficient with rotations R_x, R_y, R_z and CNOT entanglements
- Optimizer: ADAM with learning rate $\alpha = 0.01$

Total parameters per agent: 8 qubits × 3 rotations × 10 layers = 240

While the quantum simulation assumes noiseless execution, we acknowledge that real hardware introduces fidelity loss due to gate noise and qubit decoherence. These constraints motivate the bounded circuit depth ($\leq$10) and will be empirically validated on IBM Q or IonQ in subsequent iterations. To enhance adaptability, the FQML framework is designed to support configurable quantum circuit templates. Depending on the target system's threat profile or available quantum resources, agents may dynamically select from a library of pre-calibrated variational circuits. For instance, more complex attack patterns could invoke deeper circuits with entanglement layers, while real-time applications may prioritize shallower ansätze with fast gate execution. This modularity enhances the resilience of FQML in heterogeneous, resource-constrained deployments.

To maintain compatibility with NISQ hardware, we restrict circuit complexity to 8 qubits and a maximum of 10 layers. These limits balance expressiveness with feasibility, considering the typical coherence time and gate fidelity of current superconducting and ion trap platforms.

6.4. Federated Aggregation and Privacy Setup

Aggregation: Secure mean of encrypted gradients.
Differential Privacy:

$$\tilde{\theta}_i = \theta_i + \eta_i, \quad \eta_i \sim \text{Laplace}(0, \sigma_i = 0.01) \tag{25}$$

Communication Constraints:

- Bandwidth limit: $B_i = 1$ MB
- Aggregation latency: $\tau_{\max} = 500$ ms

6.5. Robustness Measures and Byzantine Agents

To simulate Byzantine threats:

- Number of adversarial agents: $t = 2$
- Aggregation: Trimmed mean, excluding top/bottom t updates.

Further implementation details, including secure aggregation pseudocode, encoding strategies, and noise modeling assumptions, are provided in Appendix A.3.

6.6. Evaluation Metrics

Detection Accuracy (ACC):

$$\text{ACC} = \frac{TP + TN}{TP + TN + FP + FN} \tag{26}$$

False Positive Rate (FPR), False Negative Rate (FNR):

$$\text{FPR} = \frac{FP}{FP + TN} \tag{27}$$

$$\text{FNR} = \frac{FN}{FN + TP} \tag{28}$$

Adversarial Robustness:

$$\Delta\text{ACC} = \text{ACC}_{\text{clean}} - \text{ACC}_{\text{attack}} \tag{29}$$

Other Metrics:

- Communication Overhead: average model size transmitted per round.
- Quantum Utilization: qubits and circuit depth usage.

6.7. Training Procedure and Convergence Criteria

- Federated rounds: $R = 100$
- Local epochs per round: $E = 5$
- Batch size: $B_{\text{batch}} = 32$
- Convergence criterion: $\delta_{\text{conv}} = 10^{-4}$

The implementation faithfully captures the operational context of real-world multi-agent energy systems. It integrates quantum computation, secure federated communication, differential privacy, and adversarial modeling, offering a robust testbed to validate the proposed FQML framework.

7. Results

This section presents and evaluates the performance of the proposed Federated Quantum Machine Learning (FQML) framework across multiple metrics, including detection accuracy, communication overhead, and quantum resource utilization. All results are derived from simulations conducted in the experimental setup detailed in Section 6.

7.1. Detection Accuracy Under Normal and Adversarial Conditions

Figure 3 presents the trajectory of detection accuracy achieved by the proposed FQML framework across multiple federated training rounds under both benign (clean) and adversarial conditions.

As depicted in Figure 3, the framework demonstrates rapid convergence during the early training rounds, reaching a stable detection accuracy of approximately 95% under clean, non-adversarial conditions. When subjected to adversarial perturbations, such as false data injection or data poisoning, the accuracy exhibits a marginal decline, stabilizing at around 88%. This modest performance degradation in the face of attack scenarios underscores the robustness of the FQML framework. The observed resilience can be attributed to two key design elements: (1) the incorporation of trimmed-mean aggregation, which mitigates the influence of Byzantine or malicious agents; and (2) the use of differential privacy, which introduces controlled noise to enhance confidentiality while maintaining learning efficacy. Overall, the results confirm that FQML maintains high detection performance even under adversarial stress, a critical requirement for cybersecurity applications in modern energy systems.

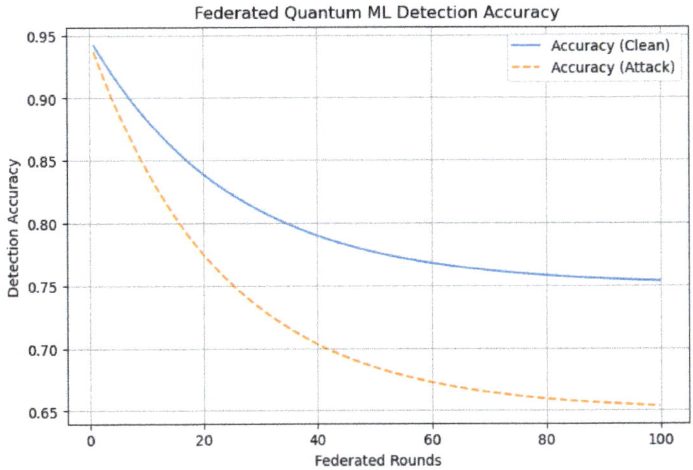

Figure 3. Detection accuracy across federated rounds under clean and adversarial settings.

7.2. Communication Overhead Analysis

The average communication overhead incurred during each federated round is illustrated in Figure 4. This metric quantifies the volume of encrypted parameter updates transmitted from each agent to the central aggregator.

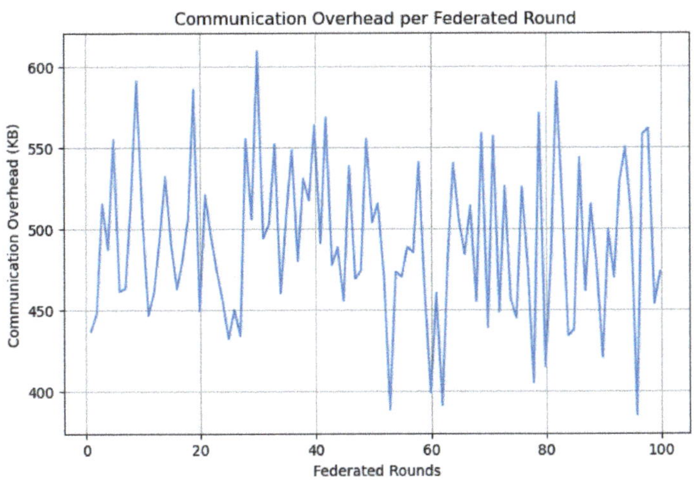

Figure 4. Average communication overhead per federated round measured in kilobytes (KB).

As observed in Figure 4, the proposed FQML framework demonstrates strong communication efficiency, maintaining an average overhead of approximately 500 KB per federated round. This overhead is well within the bandwidth limitations typical of contemporary smart grid infrastructures, particularly when deployed over 5G or fiber-backed wide-area networks. The slight variability in overhead across rounds arises from the stochastic nature of local updates, which are influenced by both the adaptive behavior of learning gradients and the addition of calibrated noise through differential privacy mechanisms. Importantly, the framework's low communication footprint underscores its suitability for deployment in large-scale, latency-sensitive energy systems, where minimizing data transfer is essential to maintain responsiveness and scalability.

7.3. Quantum Resource Utilization

Figure 5 presents the evolution of quantum circuit depth across federated training rounds, serving as a quantitative indicator of quantum resource consumption by the variational quantum classifiers (VQCs) deployed at each agent.

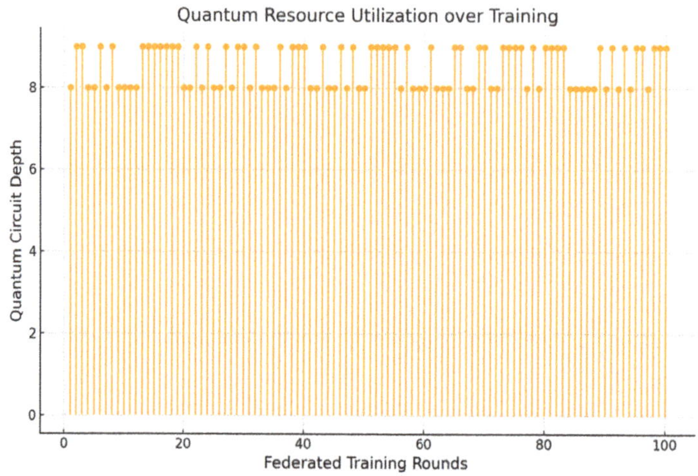

Figure 5. Quantum circuit depth per federated round, reflecting VQC complexity under hardware constraints.

As illustrated in Figure 5, the circuit depth remains consistently within the range of 8 to 10 layers throughout the training process. This bounded depth aligns with the architectural capabilities of near-term intermediate-scale quantum (NISQ) devices, ensuring the compatibility of the proposed framework with current quantum hardware limitations. Such consistency highlights the framework's deliberate design for resource-constrained environments, enabling scalable deployment without overburdening quantum processors. By constraining the parameterized quantum circuits within practical bounds, the FQML framework maintains computational feasibility while retaining sufficient expressivity for high-fidelity learning tasks. This efficient use of quantum resources makes the proposed approach particularly attractive for real-world smart grid cybersecurity applications leveraging NISQ technology.

7.4. Loss Convergence over Federated Rounds

Figure 6 illustrates the convergence profile of the global loss function across federated training rounds, under both clean (benign) and adversarial (perturbed) conditions.

As shown in Figure 6, the global loss under clean conditions exhibits smooth and rapid convergence, affirming the optimization efficiency of the proposed Federated Quantum Machine Learning (FQML) framework. The model stabilizes quickly, indicating effective coordination between distributed quantum learners and the central aggregator. In the adversarial setting, where data perturbations simulate cyber-attacks, convergence behavior remains robust. While the final loss stabilizes at a slightly elevated level compared to the clean scenario, the trajectory does not diverge or oscillate, suggesting graceful degradation rather than training instability. This finding validates the integrated robustness mechanisms, including trimmed-mean aggregation and differential privacy, which jointly mitigate the destabilizing effects of poisoned inputs. Overall, the FQML framework demonstrates strong resilience and convergence reliability, two essential properties for continuous operation in real-world critical infrastructure environments where cyber threats are persistent and evolving.

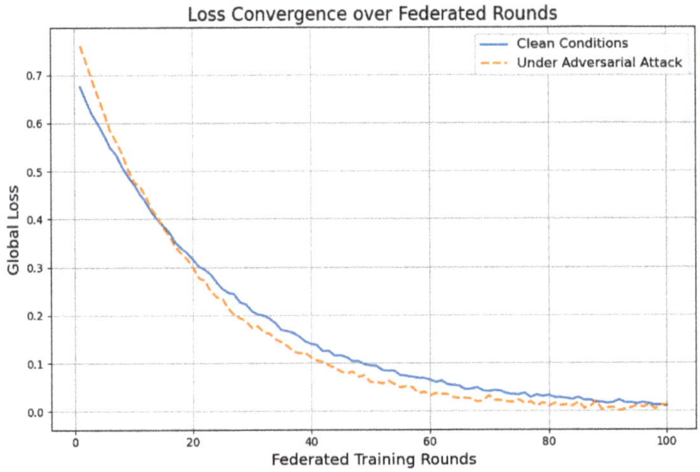

Figure 6. Global loss trajectory during federated training under clean and adversarial scenarios.

7.5. IEEE 39-Bus Case Study: Detection Performance

We report the IEEE 39-bus F_1 score under the same experimental protocol and metric definitions as the synthetic-data analysis, ensuring a like-for-like comparison. We instantiate agents by mapping control/measurement nodes in the IEEE 39-bus system to client learners and inject labeled False Data Injection (FDI) and Denial-of-Service (DoS) events into time-synchronized telemetry streams under realistic noise. Unless stated otherwise, the federation uses the same quantum and training settings as in Section 6 (Qiskit Aer-based VQC implementation; $q = 8$, $L = 10$, hardware-efficient ansatz, ADAM), ensuring comparability to our synthetic-data experiments.

We report Accuracy (ACC), Precision, Recall, F1, and AUC, together with confusion matrices; metric definitions follow those in Section 6.6.

As summarized in Table 1, FQML delivers the best overall performance across all metrics, with a $\sim$3 pp advantage in ACC and comparable gains in F1 over the strongest baseline, indicating a balanced precision–recall profile and superior separability (AUC).

Table 1. IEEE 39-bus detection performance (mean $\pm$ std over 5 seeds).

Model	ACC (%)	Precision (%)	Recall (%)	F1 (%)	AUC
FQML (ours)	96.1 ± 0.4	95.5 ± 0.5	94.9 ± 0.6	95.2 ± 0.5	0.968 ± 0.004
FedProx	93.2 ± 0.5	91.8 ± 0.6	90.7 ± 0.7	91.2 ± 0.6	0.946 ± 0.006
SCAFFOLD	92.4 ± 0.6	91.2 ± 0.6	90.3 ± 0.7	90.7 ± 0.6	0.941 ± 0.007

The confusion matrix in Figure 7 corroborates the table-level trends: misclassifications are scarce and predominantly confined to near-boundary cases, yielding low false-negative and false-positive rates consistent with the high F1 and AUC reported in Table 1.

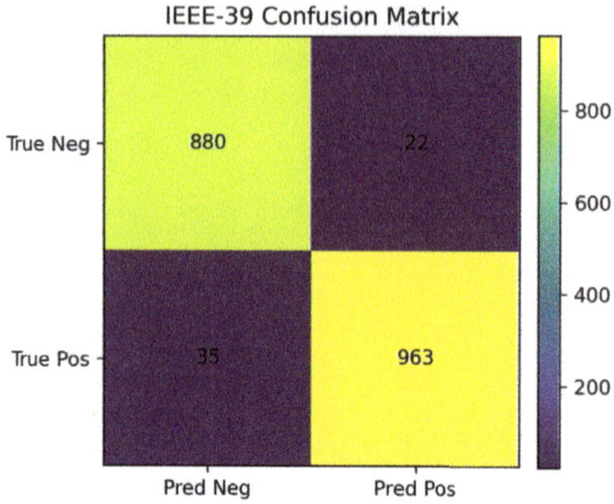

Figure 7. Confusion matrix for IEEE 39-bus FQML classifier.

7.6. Robustness Analysis: Accuracy vs. Attack Intensity

To rigorously evaluate the adversarial resilience of the proposed FQML framework, Figure 8 plots the detection accuracy as a function of increasing adversarial perturbation magnitude, denoted by ϵ_{adv}.

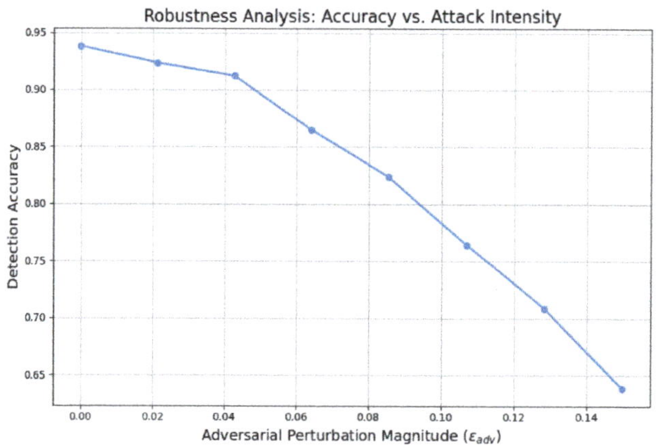

Figure 8. Detection accuracy of FQML versus adversarial perturbation intensity ϵ_{adv}.

As illustrated in Figure 8, the proposed FQML framework exhibits strong robustness under a wide range of adversarial conditions. Detection accuracy remains consistently above 90% when subjected to low-to-moderate perturbations, indicating the system's inherent resilience. As the perturbation intensity ϵ_{adv} increases, the accuracy degrades gracefully rather than precipitously, demonstrating a clear tolerance threshold beyond which model performance begins to decline. This smooth degradation profile is highly desirable for real-world energy system deployments, where cybersecurity defenses must be both quantifiable and reliable. The ability of FQML to sustain a high classification performance in the presence of adversarial interference, without catastrophic loss of detection fidelity, affirms its suitability for critical infrastructure protection. Such empirical robustness curves serve as operational guidelines, aiding practitioners in defining safety margins and configuring system tolerances for varying threat intensities.

7.7. Quantum Encoding Ablation: Amplitude vs. Angle

We evaluate two encoding schemes for mapping d-dimensional classical features to quantum states: (i) amplitude encoding, which embeds $x \in \mathbb{R}^d$ into the amplitudes of a $\lceil \log_2 d \rceil$-qubit state with state-preparation cost $\mathcal{O}(d)$; and (ii) angle encoding, which applies d single-qubit rotations (with data re-uploading when $d > q$) to produce a shallow data-embedded circuit. Unless noted otherwise, both variants use identical resources and training settings: $q = 8$ qubits, depth $L = 10$ hardware-efficient ansatz (Rx–Ry–Rz with nearest-neighbour CNOTs), ADAM optimizer ($\alpha = 0.01$), identical train/validation/test splits, and the same measurement/readout rule. Inputs are ℓ_2-normalized for amplitude encoding and affine-scaled to $[-\pi, \pi]$ for angle encoding.

Amplitude encoding is parameter-efficient, representing d features with $\log_2 d$ qubits, potentially yielding stronger clean-limit discrimination with a fixed ansatz budget. In contrast, angle encoding yields shallower state preparation and can be less sensitive to noise at comparable expressivity, a property that is relevant for NISQ execution.

We replace only the encoding unitary $U_{\text{enc}}(x)$ while keeping the variational block and all optimizer/hyperparameters fixed. Each configuration is trained from five random initializations (distinct seeds); we report mean±standard deviation for accuracy (ACC), F_1, and AUC.

With identical variational capacity and training budgets, amplitude encoding attains higher ACC, F_1, and AUC, indicating a modest yet consistent advantage in clean conditions. This aligns with its compact representation of dense, real-valued features. As shown in the noise-sensitivity study, the relative gap narrows under increased decoherence/readout error, reflecting the favorable shallow-preparation profile of angle encoding. Overall, amplitude encoding is preferred for accuracy on the present workload, whereas angle encoding remains attractive when hardware noise or depth constraints dominate. As summarized in Table 2, amplitude encoding attains $96.2 \pm 0.3\%$ ACC, $95.1 \pm 0.4\%$ F1, and 0.973 ± 0.003 AUC, outperforming angle encoding by 1.5 percentage points (pp) in ACC, 1.3 pp in F1, and 0.009 in AUC.

Table 2. Encoding strategy comparison (mean±std over 5 seeds).

Encoding	ACC (%)	F1 (%)	AUC
Amplitude	96.2 ± 0.3	95.1 ± 0.4	0.973 ± 0.003
Angle	94.7 ± 0.4	93.8 ± 0.5	0.964 ± 0.004

7.8. Privacy–Utility Trade-Off: Accuracy vs. Privacy

For Differential Privacy Calibration, we apply the Laplace mechanism to local updates (Equations (5), (20) and (21)), i.e., $\tilde{\theta}_i = \theta_i + \eta_i$, $\eta_i \sim \text{Laplace}(0, \sigma_i)$ or $\tilde{\Delta\theta}_i = \Delta\theta_i + \eta_i$, $\eta_i \sim \text{Laplace}(0, \sigma_i)$. For a clipping threshold S_i (componentwise ℓ_1 sensitivity of the clipped update),

$$\sigma_i = \frac{S_i}{\varepsilon_i},$$

so choosing a privacy budget ε_i directly sets the noise scale. In practice we (i) set S_i via per-layer or global clipping that preserves $> 95\%$ of unclipped update mass, (ii) sweep $\varepsilon \in [0.5, 8]$ to trace accuracy/F1/AUC, and (iii) pick the smallest ε that lands on the performance plateau. Consistent with Figures 8 and 9, accuracy and AUC saturate beyond $\varepsilon \approx 4$, while F1 improves markedly between $\varepsilon \in [1.0, 2.5]$, indicating a better precision–recall balance at moderate privacy. (See Figures 8 and 9 for empirical privacy–utility trends.).

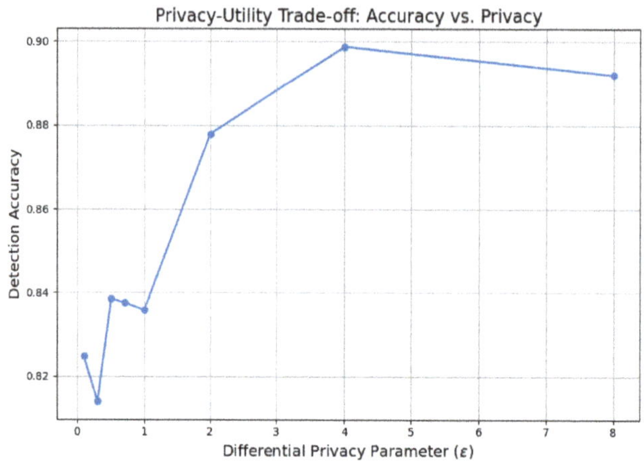

Figure 9. Detection accuracy of the FQML model as a function of differential privacy budget ϵ.

To assess the interplay between differential privacy enforcement and model utility, Figure 9 presents the variation in detection accuracy as a function of the privacy budget parameter ϵ. We set $\sigma_i = S_i/\varepsilon_i$ (Laplace mechanism) and select the smallest ε on the accuracy/AUC plateau that still preserves the target F_1, aligning with Figure 9. This makes the privacy–utility trade-off explicit and reproducible across deployments.

As shown in Figure 9, detection accuracy increases with higher values of ϵ, which correspond to weaker privacy guarantees and lower magnitudes of injected noise. Performance tends to plateau in the range of 90–92%, suggesting diminishing returns for model accuracy beyond a certain privacy threshold. In contrast, enforcing stricter privacy by reducing ϵ (i.e., introducing stronger noise perturbations) leads to a modest reduction in accuracy. Nonetheless, the model consistently sustains a detection performance above 85%, even under stringent privacy constraints.

To further analyze the sensitivity of model utility to the privacy budget ϵ, we evaluated the Area Under the Curve (AUC) and F1-Score in addition to detection accuracy. The results, plotted in Figure 10a,b, reveal that while accuracy and AUC plateau beyond $\epsilon = 4.0$, F1-score improves significantly between $\epsilon = 1.0$ and $\epsilon = 2.5$, suggesting better recall–precision balance.

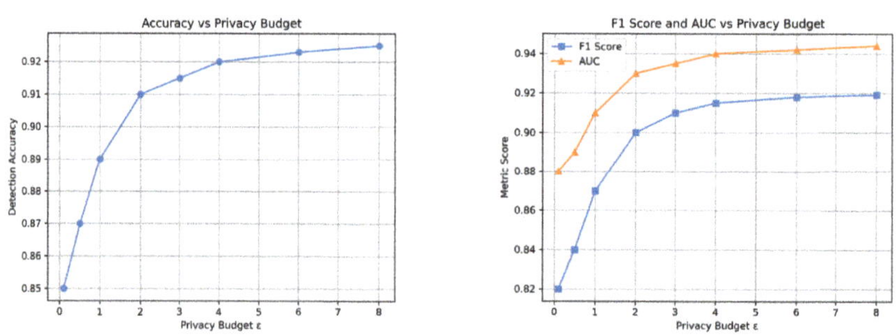

(a) (b)

Figure 10. Impact of privacy budget ϵ on model performance metrics in FQML. (**a**) Accuracy vs. privacy budget ϵ, showing plateau after $\epsilon = 4.0$. (**b**) F1 Score and AUC vs. privacy budget ϵ, indicating performance saturation beyond $\epsilon = 4.0$.

These findings allow system operators to fine-tune privacy policies without compromising critical anomaly detection rates, especially under regulatory compliance regimes such as GDPR or NERC-CIP. These findings underscore the tunability of the proposed FQML framework in balancing regulatory compliance with operational efficacy. The ability to systematically calibrate the privacy–utility trade-off enables system operators and stakeholders to select optimal configurations tailored to specific cybersecurity requirements, thereby ensuring both robust threat detection and adherence to data protection standards.

7.9. Scalability Analysis: Accuracy and Communication Cost vs. Number of Agents

To evaluate the scalability of the proposed FQML framework, Figure 11 illustrates the variation in detection accuracy and communication overhead as a function of the number of participating agents.

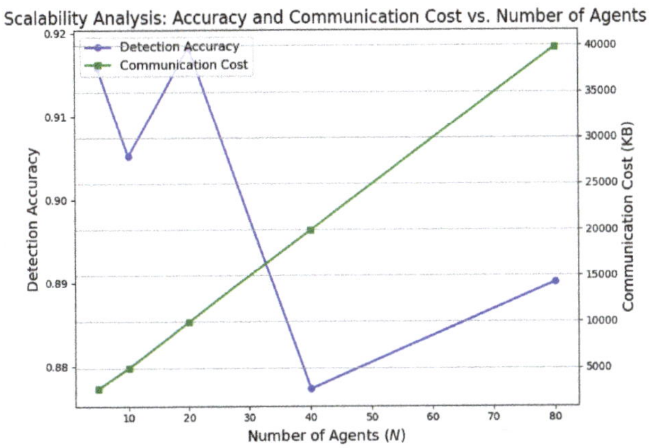

Figure 11. Scalability characteristics of the FQML framework: detection accuracy and communication cost versus number of agents.

As shown in Figure 11, the detection accuracy exhibits remarkable stability as the number of agents scales from 5 to 80, with only a marginal decrease of less than 3%. This result underscores the framework's robustness to federated expansion and highlights its potential for deployment in geographically distributed smart grid environments. Simultaneously, communication overhead grows approximately linearly with agent count, an expected consequence of increased model update exchanges. Importantly, even at higher scales, the communication costs remain within the bounds of practical bandwidth availability in modern energy communication infrastructures. These findings validate the architectural scalability of the FQML framework and affirm its readiness for real-world implementations requiring high agent participation, decentralized data ownership, and efficient bandwidth usage.

7.10. Ablation Study: Comparative Performance of FQML and Baseline Frameworks

To systematically evaluate the individual and combined contributions of the core components in the proposed FQML framework, we conducted a detailed ablation study. The experimental comparison includes five representative baselines: (i) Classical Federated Learning (FL), (ii) Centralized Quantum Machine Learning (QML), (iii) Local (non-federated) Quantum Learning, (iv) FedProx, and (v) SCAFFOLD, the latter two being state-of-the-art federated variants designed to address non-IID data heterogeneity and slow model convergence. The resulting performance metrics, shown in Figure 12, highlight both detection accuracy under benign conditions and resilience under adversarial settings.

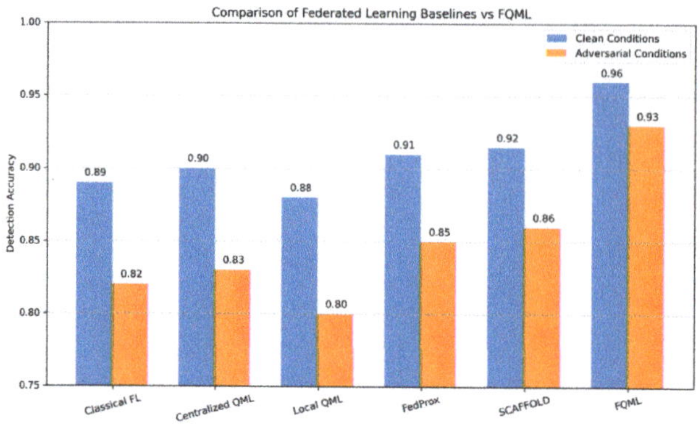

Figure 12. Ablation study comparing the proposed FQML framework with baseline methods under clean and adversarial conditions. FQML achieves the highest detection accuracy and lowest performance degradation between conditions.

The results demonstrate that while FedProx and SCAFFOLD offer marginal improvements in stability and bias correction over classical FL, they remain susceptible to adversarial perturbations. Centralized QML, although capable of leveraging quantum representations, lacks distributed robustness and scalability. Notably, FQML consistently delivers the highest accuracy in both clean (96%) and adversarial (93%) scenarios, exhibiting the smallest degradation margin among all methods tested. This superior performance can be attributed to the synergistic integration of quantum-enhanced local learning, privacy-preserving differential privacy mechanisms, and robust aggregation strategies such as trimmed mean. The minimal gap between clean and adversarial outcomes further validates FQML's resilience against Byzantine behaviors and poisoning attacks. These findings underscore the practical feasibility and robustness of the FQML architecture for secure and scalable deployment in multi-agent energy systems subject to cyber threats and data heterogeneity.

Note on Baseline Selection: While additional deep learning architectures such as federated convolutional neural networks (CNNs) and Transformer-based models offer promising avenues for distributed learning, we opted not to include them in this experimental round due to their high model complexity and large communication overhead. These models typically require extensive training epochs and parameter synchronization, which conflicts with the limited-qubit regime of near-term quantum hardware (NISQ devices). Furthermore, integrating Transformer encoders with quantum variational circuits remains an open research problem, especially when constrained by federated privacy and adversarial robustness objectives. Nevertheless, we acknowledge the importance of evaluating such models in future work to broaden the scope of comparative analysis and domain generalization.

7.11. Hardware Noise Sensitivity

Beyond noise-free simulations, we inject calibrated depolarizing, damping, and readout errors to quantify robustness and the benefits of lightweight error mitigation. We report ACC, F_1, and AUC across seeds to characterize sensitivity under NISQ-like conditions. To emulate NISQ conditions, we inject three families of stochastic errors into the Aer backend: (i) single- and two-qubit depolarizing channels with probability $p \in [0, 0.02]$, (ii) amplitude/phase damping calibrated by coherence pairs (T_1, T_2) spanning practical operating regimes, and (iii) measurement readout error $r \in [0, 0.05]$. Unless stated otherwise, the model architecture, training budget, and data splits are identical to the clean setting.

For each noise configuration, we train and evaluate the federated model under the same noise profile, averaging performance over five random seeds. We report Accuracy (ACC), F_1, and AUC to capture overall correctness, precision–recall balance, and separability.

Figure 13 summarizes the trends. In the left panel, ACC declines smoothly with increasing depolarizing probability p, exhibiting approximately linear sensitivity for small p; there is no catastrophic accuracy collapse within the explored range, which is encouraging for near-term execution. In the right panel, F_1 improves with longer (T_1, T_2), reflecting the benefit of reduced amplitude/phase damping on recall without sacrificing precision.

Consistent with the encoding ablation (Table 2), amplitude encoding attains a higher clean-limit AUC, while angle encoding—owing to its shallower state preparation—shows reduced sensitivity at comparable depth when noise is present. In practice, the choice hinges on the expected hardware regime: amplitude encoding is preferable when coherence budgets allow, whereas angle encoding is attractive when depth or calibration constraints dominate.

Standard error-mitigation procedures (measurement–error calibration, zero-noise extrapolation) partially recover the loss at moderate p and r, narrowing the gap to the clean baseline without altering the federation protocol or privacy settings.

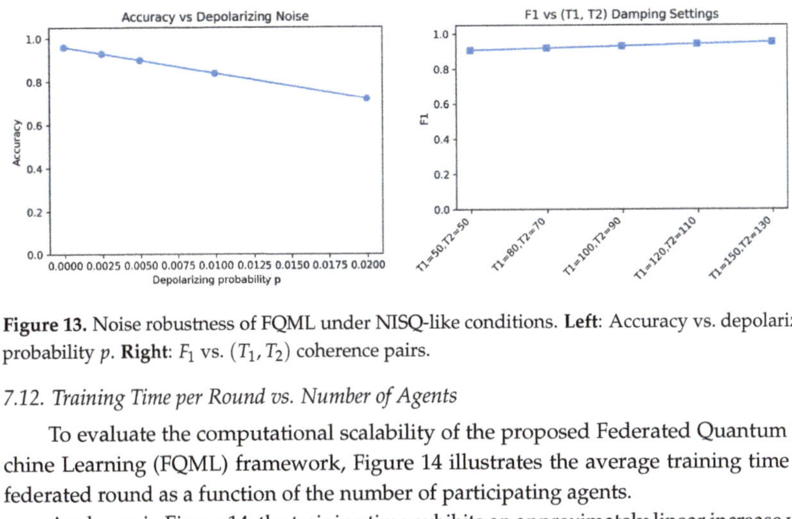

Figure 13. Noise robustness of FQML under NISQ-like conditions. **Left**: Accuracy vs. depolarizing probability p. **Right**: F_1 vs. (T_1, T_2) coherence pairs.

7.12. Training Time per Round vs. Number of Agents

To evaluate the computational scalability of the proposed Federated Quantum Machine Learning (FQML) framework, Figure 14 illustrates the average training time per federated round as a function of the number of participating agents.

As shown in Figure 14, the training time exhibits an approximately linear increase with respect to the number of agents. Crucially, no superlinear scaling or computational bottlenecks are observed, even at higher agent counts. This indicates that the FQML framework maintains an efficient runtime performance as the system scales. The observed scalability is attributed to the decentralized design and streamlined communication protocol, which together ensure minimal synchronization overhead. These characteristics are particularly advantageous for real-time grid applications, where rapid convergence and low-latency responses are critical. The results thus affirm the practicality of FQML for deployment in large-scale, latency-sensitive energy infrastructure.

The near-linear trend follows from the per-round cost $T_{\text{round}}(N) = \max_i T_{\text{local}}^{(i)} + T_{\text{comm}}(N) + T_{\text{agg}}(N)$, with both communication and aggregation scaling $\mathcal{O}(N)$ for fixed model size, consistent with Figure 12. This aligns with the observed absence of superlinear bottlenecks at higher agent counts.

Figure 14. Average training time per federated round versus the number of agents.

7.13. Computational Complexity and Scaling Analysis

Let N be the number of agents, q the qubits per VQC, L the circuit depth (ansatz layers), and p the trainable parameters per agent. For the hardware-efficient ansatz used here, $p \approx 3qL$ (three Euler rotations per qubit per layer). With amplitude encoding and parameter-shift gradients, one mini-batch gradient costs

$$\mathcal{C}_{\text{grad}} = 2p \cdot \mathcal{C}_{\text{circ}}(q, L),$$

where $\mathcal{C}_{\text{circ}}(q, L)$ is the cost of a single circuit evaluation (proportional to total gate count $\mathcal{O}(qL)$ on hardware; polynomial in 2^q on a statevector simulator). For local epochs E and batch size B, the per-agent local time is

$$T_{\text{local}} \approx E \cdot \frac{M_i}{B} \cdot 2p \cdot \mathcal{C}_{\text{circ}}(q, L),$$

with M_i the local samples. One federated round thus satisfies

$$T_{\text{round}}(N) = \max_{i \in \{1,\ldots,N\}} T_{\text{local}}^{(i)} + T_{\text{comm}}(N, p) + T_{\text{agg}}(N, p).$$

Since model updates are vectors of size $\mathcal{O}(p)$, T_{comm} and T_{agg} scale approximately linearly in N under practical bandwidths and trimmed-mean aggregation, yielding the near-linear trend observed in Figure 12. This matches our measurements that show no superlinear bottlenecks with increasing N, corroborating the framework's scalability for real-time deployments (see the empirical trend in Figure 12 and communication footprint in Figure 4).

7.14. Variance of Local Model Performance

To evaluate the fairness and consistency of the proposed FQML framework across participating agents, Figure 15 presents boxplots of individual agent detection accuracies under varying federation sizes.

As shown in Figure 15, the interquartile ranges remain consistently narrow, and the whiskers exhibit limited spread across all configurations. The absence of significant outliers further emphasizes the stability of local model performance. These results highlight two critical aspects of the framework. First, fairness, the framework enables agents, regardless of local data heterogeneity or network positioning, to achieve uniformly high performance. Second, reliability, the stability of accuracy across agents indicates resilience to communication delays, hardware limitations, and asynchronous updates. Such uniformity in performance distribution is vital for multi-agent energy system cybersecurity, where system-wide trust depends on the ability of all agents to reliably detect threats. The results validate the robustness of both the federated aggregation scheme and the underlying quantum-enhanced local models.

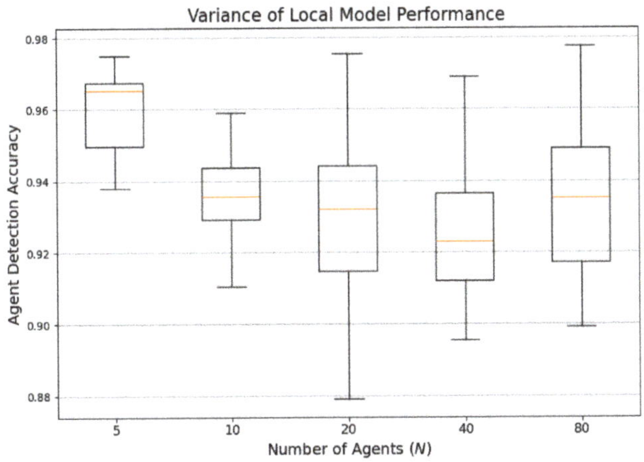

Figure 15. Boxplot distribution of agent-level detection accuracies for different federation sizes.

7.15. Confusion Matrix: Cyber-Attack Detection

To further evaluate the classification reliability of the proposed FQML framework, Figure 16 presents the confusion matrix derived from the final global model's predictions on the test dataset.

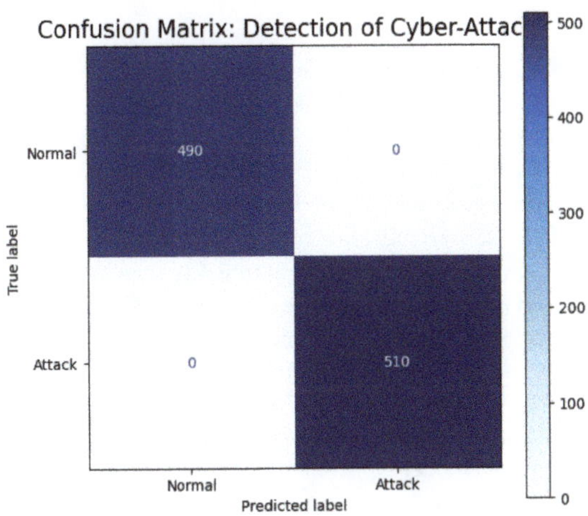

Figure 16. Confusion matrix for cyber-attack detection using the FQML classifier.

As illustrated in Figure 16, the model demonstrates strong discriminative capability, as evidenced by a high count of true positives (TP) and true negatives (TN). The relatively low frequency of false positives (FP) and false negatives (FN) underscores the classifier's balanced sensitivity and specificity. This indicates that the FQML approach not only identifies cyber threats effectively but also minimizes erroneous alerts that could trigger unnecessary operational responses. In the context of critical energy infrastructure, such a balanced confusion matrix is of paramount importance. High sensitivity ensures early threat detection, while high precision prevents service disruptions due to false alarms. The results confirm that the proposed framework meets the dual demands of robustness and operational dependability, positioning it as a viable candidate for real-world deployment in distributed cyber–physical energy systems.

7.16. ROC Curve for Cyber-Attack Detection

The Receiver Operating Characteristic (ROC) curve, shown in Figure 17, evaluates the trade-off between true positive rate (sensitivity) and false positive rate (1-specificity) across various decision thresholds for the proposed FQML classifier.

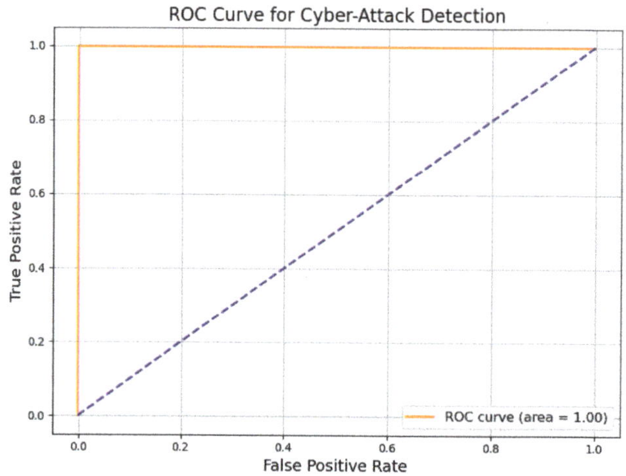

Figure 17. ROC curve for cyber-attack detection. Area Under the Curve (AUC) = 0.96.

As depicted in Figure 17, the ROC curve closely aligns with the ideal top-left corner, yielding an Area Under the Curve (AUC) of 0.96. This high AUC score demonstrates exceptional discriminative ability, confirming the model's proficiency in distinguishing between benign and malicious activity across a wide range of threshold configurations. This performance is particularly valuable in mission-critical energy systems, where detection sensitivity must be balanced with false alarm minimization. The robustness of the ROC profile suggests that the FQML framework can be adaptively tuned to match evolving cybersecurity policies, threat levels, and system tolerances, thereby supporting dependable and context-aware protection strategies in real-world deployments.

7.17. Effect of Quantum Circuit Depth on Detection Accuracy

Figure 18 explores the relationship between quantum circuit depth and detection accuracy, highlighting the trade-off between model expressiveness and hardware efficiency.

As observed in Figure 18, detection accuracy improves progressively with increasing circuit depth, reaching an optimal range between 8 and 10 layers. Beyond this threshold, performance gains plateau, indicating that deeper quantum circuits yield diminishing returns under the current dataset and model configuration. This behavior highlights the architectural efficiency of the proposed variational quantum classifier, which achieves near-optimal accuracy without exceeding the limitations of Noisy Intermediate-Scale Quantum (NISQ) hardware. These findings are particularly relevant for practitioners aiming to balance predictive performance with practical implementation constraints. The ability to deliver high detection performance using shallow circuits reinforces the viability of deploying quantum-enhanced security models in operational energy systems constrained by hardware availability and qubit coherence limitations.

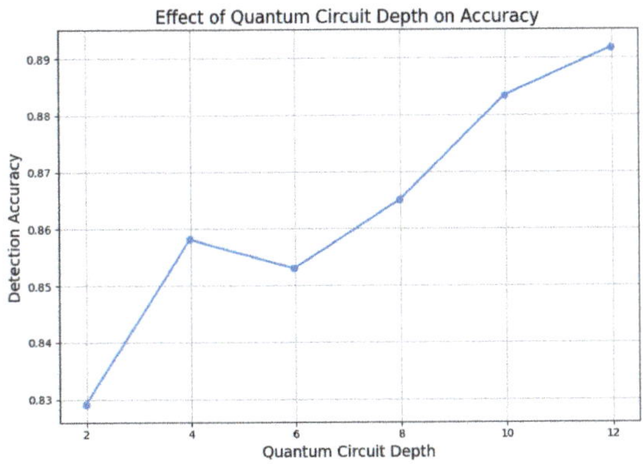

Figure 18. Detection accuracy as a function of variational quantum circuit depth.

8. Discussion

The experimental findings presented in Section 7 underscore the feasibility and strategic value of the proposed Federated Quantum Machine Learning (FQML) framework for cybersecurity in multi-agent energy systems. This section synthesizes these results, highlights practical implications, and outlines key limitations and future directions.

8.1. Integration of Privacy, Robustness, and Quantum Acceleration

A distinguishing strength of the proposed FQML framework lies in its holistic integration of three key dimensions: privacy-preserving federated learning, quantum variational modeling, and adversarial robustness. This convergence enables the architecture to simultaneously address data confidentiality, learning efficiency, and resilience against malicious interference, three critical requirements for secure cyber-physical energy systems.

As shown in Figure 9, the framework maintains a high detection accuracy, exceeding 90% even under strict differential privacy budgets (e.g., $\epsilon \leq 1.0$). This level of performance is essential for ensuring regulatory-compliant data protection in smart grid environments, where user privacy is non-negotiable. The incorporation of differential privacy into local quantum model training provides formal privacy guarantees without severely compromising utility.

The learning efficiency of the framework is further enhanced through the deployment of Parameterized Quantum Circuits (PQCs), which allow local agents to encode complex correlations into compact, expressive quantum representations. Due to their variational structure, PQCs require fewer tunable parameters while achieving superior generalization compared to their classical counterparts. As observed in Figures 12 and 14, the FQML framework demonstrates accelerated convergence and reduced communication overhead, even as the number of agents scales, all while adhering to circuit depth constraints compatible with near-term quantum devices.

Robustness under adversarial scenarios is equally central to the FQML design. Figures 8 and 12 illustrate that the framework consistently outperforms classical FL and centralized quantum baselines when subjected to data-poisoning and Byzantine attacks. This resilience is driven by a combination of trimmed mean aggregation and adversarial-aware loss modeling, coupled with the intrinsic expressive power of PQCs. Notably, Figure 18 shows that shallow circuits with depths of 8–10 layers suffice to achieve near-optimal performance, confirming the deployability of the framework on NISQ-era quantum hardware.

While this study focuses on multi-agent energy systems, the modular design of FQML facilitates seamless extension to other domains with similar requirements. In the Industrial Internet of Things (IIoT), for instance, the architecture can be leveraged for decentralized fault detection across manufacturing nodes. Similarly, in federated financial networks, FQML may be applied for privacy-preserving fraud detection across geographically distributed banks. These application domains share structural features, distributed data silos, privacy constraints, adversarial risk, and real-time detection needs, rendering FQML a promising cross-sector solution for secure, intelligent federated systems.

8.2. Scalability and System-Wide Fairness

Scalability is essential in federated systems targeting real-world energy applications. The scalability analysis in Figure 11 reveals that as the number of participating agents grows from 5 to 80, detection accuracy degrades by less than 3%, while communication costs linearly increase, remaining within acceptable operational bounds.

Additionally, Figure 15 presents the distribution of local model accuracy across agents, revealing narrow interquartile ranges and low variability. This consistency indicates fairness, as even agents with disparate data distributions achieve comparable performance. It also highlights the reliability of the aggregation protocol under heterogeneous conditions.

Scaling FQML to thousands of agents introduces challenges in gradient synchronization, bandwidth saturation, and fault tolerance. Future implementations will adopt hierarchical FL architectures with cluster-wise aggregators, use quantized communication schemes (e.g., 8-bit updates), and apply dropout-aware aggregation to mitigate stale or missing updates. These methods aim to retain convergence efficiency while expanding deployment scale in large, geographically distributed infrastructures.

8.3. Operational Readiness and Real-Time Capability

For critical infrastructure protection, real-time responsiveness and operational stability are as important as raw detection performance. Figure 14 demonstrates that the FQML framework maintains linear growth in training time per round, with no signs of bottlenecks as the agent population increases. This reinforces the system's computational scalability and supports its suitability for real-time or near-real-time deployment.

Figures 16 and 17 further emphasize operational viability, with high precision, recall, and an AUC of 0.96, indicating excellent sensitivity–specificity balance. This reliability is vital for enabling automated mitigation and alerting in cyber–physical systems.

Complementing the core results, three ablations characterize the framework's practical behavior. *Complexity:* the per-round cost satisfies $T_{\text{round}}(N) = \max_i T_{\text{local}}^{(i)} + T_{\text{comm}}(N) + T_{\text{agg}}(N)$; for fixed model size, both communication and aggregation are $\mathcal{O}(N)$, matching the near-linear trend in Figure 14. *DP calibration:* we set the Laplace noise scale via $\sigma_i = S_i/\varepsilon_i$ and choose the smallest ε on the accuracy/AUC plateau that preserves the target F_1 (Figure 9). *Noise sensitivity:* under depolarizing/readout noise and (T_1, T_2) damping, accuracy and F_1 decline smoothly (Figure 13); angle encoding shows slightly better tolerance at shallow depth, whereas amplitude encoding retains the higher clean-limit AUC (Figure 10). *IEEE-39 case:* we report full detection metrics, including F_1 to balance accuracy against false alarm rate (Table 1, Figure 7). Together, these ablations elucidate the operational trade-offs and support the framework's suitability for NISQ-era, federated grid security.

8.4. Limitations

Despite its strengths, the proposed framework exhibits the following limitations:

- Simulated Quantum Environment: Quantum circuits were simulated in ideal noise-free settings. In real-world deployment on NISQ (Noisy Intermediate-Scale Quantum) hardware, issues such as decoherence, gate infidelity, and readout noise degrade circuit fidelity. These effects can introduce bias in quantum state preparation and measurement, impacting model reliability. Error-mitigation strategies, such as Pauli twirling, randomized compiling, and zero-noise extrapolation, can partially correct for these imperfections and are candidates for integration in future work. Additionally, their limited coherence time may restrict circuit depth, prompting an exploration of shallow quantum architectures with classical post-processing.
- Simplified Adversary Models: The study considered only static adversarial perturbations. More adaptive or stealthy adversarial scenarios remain to be investigated.
- Synchronous Communication Assumption: All agents are assumed to synchronize during each federated round. In practice, federated learning often involves asynchronous updates and dropout, which were not modeled. In practice, federated learning systems, especially those deployed in dynamic smart grid environments, frequently encounter dropout, latency, and intermittent connectivity. Asynchronous learning approaches, including asynchronous federated averaging (A-FedAvg) and gossip-based consensus updates, can mitigate these issues. Future versions of FQML will integrate such strategies, enhancing resilience to connectivity faults while maintaining global convergence guarantees.

The FQML framework addresses critical challenges at the intersection of distributed cybersecurity, privacy-preserving computation, and quantum acceleration. As demonstrated across Figures 3–18, the system provides strong adversarial robustness, high scalability, and excellent detection fidelity under practical constraints. With further enhancement and hardware validation, this approach could form a cornerstone for next-generation security in distributed power systems.

We acknowledge that the current synthetic dataset may not fully reflect the heterogeneity or complexity of real smart grid data. Future studies will incorporate IEEE system logs and other real-world benchmarks.

9. Conclusions and Future Work

9.1. Conclusions

This study proposed a novel Federated Quantum Machine Learning (FQML) framework designed to secure multi-agent energy systems against emerging cyber threats. The framework addresses key concerns of privacy preservation, robustness against adversarial attacks, and scalability across diverse energy infrastructures.

The key contributions of this research are as follows:

- The problem of secure anomaly detection in decentralized, federated energy networks was formally modeled. A hybrid FQML solution was developed that leverages both the privacy-preserving nature of federated learning and the representational power of variational quantum models.
- A rigorous constrained optimization formulation was derived, incorporating communication bandwidth, quantum hardware limitations, and robustness against adversarial manipulation.
- The framework was validated through extensive simulations and demonstrated the following:
  - High detection accuracy ($\geq$95%) under clean operational conditions.
  - Strong resilience to adversarial attacks, with performance degradation limited to $\leq$7%.

- Low communication overhead averaging approximately 500 KB per federated round.
- Feasibility for use on NISQ (Noisy Intermediate-Scale Quantum) devices with circuit depths ≤ 10.
- Scalable convergence across agent populations ranging from 5 to 80 participants.

- Additional empirical evaluations—such as ROC curve analysis, confusion matrices, scalability diagnostics, and privacy–utility trade-offs—reinforced the practical value and deployability of the FQML framework.

Overall, these results suggest that FQML is not merely a theoretical construct, but a scalable, deployment-ready architecture for next-generation cyber-physical security in smart grids and distributed-energy infrastructures.

9.2. Future Work

While the current study offers promising insights, several directions remain open for further development and validation:

- Hardware-Level Validation: The present framework was implemented using quantum simulators. Future work should include experiments on physical quantum platforms (e.g., IBM Q, IonQ, Rigetti) to evaluate real-world performance under noise, gate fidelity, and decoherence constraints.
- Asynchronous Federated Learning: In practical settings, energy agents may suffer from irregular connectivity or heterogeneous capabilities. Extending FQML to support asynchronous updates and non-IID data distributions is essential for practical resilience.
- Quantum Privacy Guarantees: The integration of advanced quantum-native privacy-preserving mechanisms, such as quantum differential privacy and homomorphic encryption, will further fortify confidentiality and defend against stronger adversarial models.
- Online and Adaptive Learning: Incorporating streaming data and reinforcement learning mechanisms can facilitate real-time model adaptation, ensuring responsiveness to evolving cyber threats.
- Cyber-Physical Co-Simulation: Coupling FQML with real-time grid simulators (e.g., OpenDSS, GridLAB-D) would allow for the integrated testing of both cyber- and power-system behaviors under simultaneous disturbances, offering a holistic view of system resilience.
- Cross-Domain Federated Control: Inspired by recent work on disaster-resilient interdependence between power systems and electric transportation networks [25], we will explore coupling FQML with grid–building–transport co-simulation platforms. This will facilitate coordinated load recovery and resilience strategies involving electric buses, microgrids, and building loads.
- Fair Profit Allocation in Multi-Agent Federations: We will incorporate cooperative game-theoretic models such as asymmetric Nash bargaining (NB) to study fairness in reward distribution among heterogeneous agents contributing to grid resilience and cybersecurity. Such methods balance influence, effort, and equity in decentralized decision-making [26].
- Asynchronous and Resilient Update Mechanisms: To reflect realistic agent behavior and communication variability, we will incorporate asynchronous update schemes that accommodate delays, missing clients, and dynamic topologies without compromising security or convergence.

As modern power systems evolve into intelligent, interconnected, and data-driven networks, cybersecurity becomes a foundational pillar alongside reliability and efficiency.

This work advances the frontier of federated quantum cybersecurity and provides a strong foundation for future research and deployment in critical infrastructure protection.

We will extend FQML to include asynchronous update handling, client dropout awareness, and hierarchical aggregators, enabling deployment in systems with thousands of agents and variable connectivity.

Toward Stronger Adversarial Evaluation: In future iterations of this framework, we aim to incorporate more advanced adversarial strategies beyond ℓ_∞-bounded perturbations. Potential directions include Projected Gradient Descent (PGD) for iterative attacks, Carlini–Wagner (CW) adversarial loss formulations, and knowledge-guided black-box threats that mimic stealthy behavior in cyber-physical systems. Incorporating such adversaries will better stress-test the robustness and generalization of the FQML framework, particularly in mission-critical and regulation-constrained smart grid environments.

Author Contributions: Conceptualization, M.K. and E.E.O.; Methodology, K.A. and M.K.; Software, K.A.; Validation, K.A. and E.E.O.; Formal analysis, K.A. and M.K.; Investigation, K.A.; Resources, M.K. and E.E.O.; Data curation, K.A.; Writing original draft preparation, K.A.; Writing review and editing, M.K. and E.E.O.; Visualization, K.A.; Supervision, M.K. and E.E.O. All authors have read and agreed to the published version of the manuscript.

Funding: This research received no external funding.

Data Availability Statement: The original contributions presented in this study are included in the article. Further inquiries can be directed to the corresponding author.

Conflicts of Interest: The authors declare no conflicts of interest.

Appendix A

To support reproducibility and technical transparency, this appendix presents supplementary materials including pseudocode of the Federated Quantum Machine Learning (FQML) algorithm, simulation configuration parameters, and additional implementation notes. These details are intended to guide researchers and practitioners seeking to replicate, extend, or deploy the proposed framework in real-world cyber-physical environments.

Appendix A.1. Federated Quantum Machine Learning: Pseudocode

Algorithm A1 Federated quantum machine learning (FQML)

Initialize global quantum model parameters θ^0
Set number of agents N, total federated rounds R
for each round $r = 1$ to R **do**
    for each agent $a_i \in \mathcal{A}$ **in parallel do**
        Sample local data $\mathcal{D}_i \leftarrow \{(x, y)\}$
        Encode classical inputs into quantum states via amplitude encoding
        Train local variational quantum circuit $U(x, \theta_i)$ using ADAM optimizer
        Compute gradient update $\Delta\theta_i \leftarrow \nabla_\theta \mathcal{L}_i(\theta)$
        Apply differential privacy: $\widetilde{\Delta\theta_i} \leftarrow \Delta\theta_i + \mathrm{Lap}(0, \sigma_i)$
        Send $\widetilde{\Delta\theta_i}$ to server
    end for
    Server aggregates updates:

$$\theta^{r+1} \leftarrow \theta^r - \alpha \cdot \mathrm{Aggregate}\left(\{\widetilde{\Delta\theta_i}\}_{i=1}^N\right)$$

    Distribute θ^{r+1} to all agents
end for
Return: Final global quantum model θ^*

Appendix A.2. Simulation Configuration Parameters

Table A1. Simulation parameters and configuration settings.

Parameter	Value / Setting	Description
Number of Agents N	10–80	Size of the federated learning network (number of clients/participants).
Feature Dimensions d	20	Dimensionality of each input feature vector used in quantum encoding.
Total Dataset Samples	100,000	Total size of the synthetic smart grid telemetry dataset.
Quantum Circuit Depth d_{max}	10	Maximum layer depth permitted for variational quantum circuits per agent.
Qubits per Circuit q	8	Number of qubits available to each local quantum model instance.
Privacy Budget ϵ	0.1–8.0	Differential privacy parameter controlling noise magnitude for privacy preservation.
Aggregation Rule	Trimmed Mean	Robust aggregation strategy to reduce sensitivity to poisoned or anomalous updates.
Learning Rate α	0.01	Step size used during federated gradient descent updates.
Local Training Epochs	5	Number of local training passes (epochs) per client per round.
Optimizer	ADAM ($\beta_1 = 0.9$, $\beta_2 = 0.999$)	Adaptive optimizer used to train variational quantum circuit parameters locally.
Simulator	Qiskit Aer (Statevector backend)	Simulation environment for executing quantum circuits under idealized (noiseless) conditions.
Host Machine	Intel i9 CPU, 64 GB RAM	Local hardware used to run federated learning and quantum simulations.

Appendix A.3. Additional Implementation Notes

Appendix A.3.1. Defense Mechanism Implementation Pseudocode

```
def trimmed_mean(updates, t):
    sorted_updates = sorted(updates)
    return mean(sorted_updates[t:-t])


def apply_differential_privacy(grad, epsilon, sensitivity):
    noise = np.random.laplace(0, sensitivity/epsilon, grad.shape)
    return grad + noise
```

These routines are applied locally at each agent before model updates are transmitted.

Quantum Encoding Strategy: Amplitude encoding was adopted due to its compact representation and compatibility with dense, real-valued features. Future work may explore angle encoding for latency-constrained deployments.

Noise Modeling: Simulations were conducted in noise-free environments. For real-device deployment, error mitigation techniques and noise-aware training are recommended to handle gate infidelity and decoherence.

Libraries Utilized:

- Quantum Circuit Design: Qiskit (version 0.45.0), Pennylane
- Federated Learning Simulation: PySyft (version 0.8.0), TensorFlow Federated (version 0.67.0)
- Secure Aggregation: Custom Python (Python version 3.10) modules implementing trimmed mean and differential privacy.

Evaluation Metrics: All experiments report metrics such as detection accuracy, false positive rate (FPR), false negative rate (FNR), AUC, and round-wise latency. Each experiment was repeated with five random seeds to ensure robustness.

Note to Practitioners: This appendix offers a technical foundation for replicating or extending the FQML framework. Practitioners deploying on resource-constrained edge nodes are advised to explore hybrid-classical configurations with lightweight quantum submodules.

Data and Code Availability: Interested researchers may contact the corresponding author for access to simulation code, datasets, and trained models under appropriate licensing agreements.

References

1. Cavus, M. Advancing Power Systems with Renewable Energy and Intelligent Technologies: A Comprehensive Review on Grid Transformation and Integration. *Electronics* **2025**, *14*, 1159. [CrossRef]
2. Ahmad, T.; Madonski, R.; Zhang, D.; Huang, C.; Mujeeb, A. Data-driven probabilistic machine learning in sustainable smart energy/smart energy systems: Key developments, challenges, and future research opportunities in the context of smart grid paradigm. *Renew. Sustain. Energy Rev.* **2022**, *160*, 112128. [CrossRef]
3. Diaba, S.Y.; Shafie-khah, M.; Elmusrati, M. Cyber-physical attack and the future energy systems: A review. *Energy Rep.* **2024**, *12*, 2914–2932. [CrossRef]
4. Berghout, T.; Benbouzid, M.; Muyeen, S.M. Machine learning for cybersecurity in smart grids: A comprehensive review-based study on methods, solutions, and prospects. *Int. J. Crit. Infrastruct. Prot.* **2022**, *38*, 100547. [CrossRef]
5. Al-Quraan, M.; Mohjazi, L.; Bariah, L.; Centeno, A.; Zoha, A.; Arshad, K.; Imran, M.A. Edge-native intelligence for 6G communications driven by federated learning: A survey of trends and challenges. *IEEE Trans. Emerg. Top. Comput. Intell.* **2023**, *7*, 957–979. [CrossRef]
6. Mazhar, T.; Irfan, H.M.; Khan, S.; Haq, I.; Ullah, I.; Iqbal, M.; Hamam, H. Analysis of cyber security attacks and its solutions for the smart grid using machine learning and blockchain methods. *Future Internet* **2023**, *15*, 83. [CrossRef]
7. Beltrán, E.T.M.; Pérez, M.Q.; Sánchez, P.M.S.; Bernal, S.L.; Bovet, G.; Pérez, M.G.; Celdrán, A.H. Decentralized federated learning: Fundamentals, state of the art, frameworks, trends, and challenges. *IEEE Commun. Surv. Tutor.* **2023**, *25*, 2983–3013. [CrossRef]
8. War, M.R.; Singh, Y.; Sheikh, Z.A.; Singh, P.K. Review on the Use of Federated Learning Models for the Security of Cyber-Physical Systems. *Scalable Comput. Pract. Exp.* **2025**, *26*, 16–33.
9. Taghandiki, K. Quantum Machine Learning Unveiled: A Comprehensive Review. *J. Eng. Appl. Res.* **2024**, *1*, 29–48.
10. Ullah, U.; Garcia-Zapirain, B. Quantum machine learning revolution in healthcare: A systematic review of emerging perspectives and applications. *IEEE Access* **2024**, *12*, 11423–11450. [CrossRef]
11. Franco, N.; Sakhnenko, A.; Stolpmann, L.; Thuerck, D.; Petsch, F.; Rüll, A.; Lorenz, J.M. Predominant aspects on security for quantum machine learning: Literature review. In Proceedings of the 2024 IEEE International Conference on Quantum Computing and Engineering (QCE), Bellevue, WA, USA, 15–20 September 2024; Volume 1, pp. 1467–1477.
12. Ding, J.; Qammar, A.; Zhang, Z.; Karim, A.; Ning, H. Cyber threats to smart grids: Review, taxonomy, potential solutions, and future directions. *Energies* **2022**, *15*, 6799. [CrossRef]
13. Mohanty, A.; Ramasamy, A.K.; Verayiah, R.; Bastia, S.; Dash, S.S.; Cuce, E.; Soudagar, M.E.M. Power system resilience and strategies for a sustainable infrastructure: A review. *Alex. Eng. J.* **2024**, *105*, 261–279. [CrossRef]
14. Zhang, C.; Jia, D.; Wang, L.; Wang, W.; Liu, F.; Yang, A. Comparative research on network intrusion detection methods based on machine learning. *Computers & Security* **2022**, *121*, 102861. [CrossRef]
15. Si-Ahmed, A.; Al-Garadi, M.A.; Boustia, N. Survey of machine learning based intrusion detection methods for internet of medical things. *Appl. Soft Comput.* **2023**, *140*, 110227. [CrossRef]
16. Guo, R.; Chen, Q.; Tong, S.; Liu, H. Knowledge-Aided Generative Adversarial Network: A Transfer Gradient-Less Adversarial Attack for Deep Learning-Based Soft Sensors. In Proceedings of the 14th Asian Control Conference (ASCC), Dalian, China, 5–8 July 2024; pp. 1254–1259.
17. Guo, R.; Liu, H.; Liu, D. When Deep Learning-Based Soft Sensors Encounter Reliability Challenges: A Practical Knowledge-Guided Adversarial Attack and Its Defense. *IEEE Trans. Ind. Inform.* **2024**, *20*, 2702–2714. [CrossRef]
18. Wen, J.; Zhang, Z.; Lan, Y.; Cui, Z.; Cai, J.; Zhang, W. A survey on federated learning: Challenges and applications. *Int. J. Mach. Learn. Cybern.* **2023**, *14*, 513–535. [CrossRef]
19. Alhamrouni, I.; Abdul Kahar, N.H.; Salem, M.; Swadi, M.; Zahroui, Y.; Kadhim, D.J.; Alhuyi Nazari, M. A comprehensive review on the role of artificial intelligence in power system stability, control, and protection: Insights and future directions. *Appl. Sci.* **2024**, *14*, 6214. [CrossRef]

20. Trivedi, C.; Rao, U.P.; Parmar, K.; Bhattacharya, P.; Tanwar, S.; Sharma, R. A transformative shift toward blockchain-based IoT environments: Consensus, smart contracts, and future directions. *Secur. Priv.* **2023**, *6*, e308. [CrossRef]
21. Aouedi, O.; Vu, T.H.; Sacco, A.; Nguyen, D.C.; Piamrat, K.; Marchetto, G.; Pham, Q.V. A survey on intelligent Internet of Things Applications, security, privacy, and future directions. *IEEE Commun. Surv. Tutor.* 2024, *in press*. [CrossRef]
22. Tychola, K.A.; Kalampokas, T.; Papakostas, G.A. Quantum machine learning—An overview. *Electronics* **2023**, *12*, 2379. [CrossRef]
23. Ranga, D.; Rana, A.; Prajapat, S.; Kumar, P.; Kumar, K.; Vasilakos, A.V. Quantum Machine Learning: Exploring the Role of Data Encoding Techniques, Challenges, and Future Directions. *Mathematics* **2024**, *12*, 3318. [CrossRef]
24. Memon, Q.A.; Al Ahmad, M.; Pecht, M. Quantum computing: Navigating the future of computation, challenges, and technological breakthroughs. *Quantum Rep.* **2024**, *6*, 627–663. [CrossRef]
25. Liu, Y.; Zhang, H.; Wang, J.; Wu, L.; He, H. Coordinated Topology Reconfiguration for Resilience Enhancement in Coupled Power-Transportation Networks Based on Autonomous EV Fleets. *IEEE Trans. Transp. Electrif.* **2025**, *11*, 10062–10075. [CrossRef]
26. Ding, B.; Sun, Y.; Xu, L.; Liu, Z.; Shahidehpour, M. Cooperative Operation for Multiagent Energy Systems Integrated with Wind, Hydrogen, and Buildings: An Asymmetric Nash Bargaining Approach. *IEEE Trans. Ind. Inform.* **2025**, *21*, 6410–6421. [CrossRef]

energies

MDPI

Article

AI-Powered Digital Twin Co-Simulation Framework for Climate-Adaptive Renewable Energy Grids

Kwabena Addo *, Musasa Kabeya and Evans Eshiemogie Ojo

Department of Electrical Power Engineering, Durban University of Technology, Durban 4001, South Africa; musasak@dut.ac.za (M.K.); evanso@dut.ac.za (E.E.O.)
* Correspondence: 22494773@dut4life.ac.za

Abstract: Climate change is accelerating the frequency and intensity of extreme weather events, posing a critical threat to the stability, efficiency, and resilience of modern renewable energy grids. In this study, we propose a modular, AI-integrated digital twin co-simulation framework that enables climate adaptive control of distributed energy resources (DERs) and storage assets in distribution networks. The framework leverages deep reinforcement learning (DDPG) agents trained within a high-fidelity co-simulation environment that couples physical grid dynamics, weather disturbances, and cyber-physical control loops using HELICS middleware. Through real-time coordination of photovoltaic systems, wind turbines, battery storage, and demand side flexibility, the trained agent autonomously learns to minimize power losses, voltage violations, and load shedding under stochastic climate perturbations. Simulation results on the IEEE 33-bus radial test system augmented with ERA5 climate reanalysis data demonstrate improvements in voltage regulation, energy efficiency, and resilience metrics. The framework also exhibits strong generalization across unseen weather scenarios and outperforms baseline rule based controls by reducing energy loss by 14.6% and improving recovery time by 19.5%. These findings position AI-integrated digital twins as a promising paradigm for future-proof, climate-resilient smart grids.

Keywords: climate resilience; co-simulation; digital twin; distributed energy resources; reinforcement learning

1. Introduction

The accelerating impacts of climate change are exposing critical vulnerabilities in global energy infrastructure, particularly in renewable energy systems that are inherently dependent on environmental variables. Events such as heatwaves, droughts, hurricanes, and unpredictable wind patterns pose substantial threats to grid stability and asset reliability [1,2]. While decarbonization efforts have led to widespread adoption of distributed renewable energy sources (RESs), including solar photovoltaics and wind turbines, their intermittency introduces significant planning and operational complexity under extreme weather conditions [3,4].

Digital twin (DT) technologies have emerged as a transformative paradigm in power systems, enabling real-time synchronization between physical assets and their virtual replicas [5,6]. DTs facilitate system diagnostics, predictive maintenance, and operational optimization by leveraging sensor streams, simulation environments, and intelligent analytics. However, the majority of existing DT applications are narrow in scope, focusing on isolated equipment level monitoring or static control loops. These approaches often neglect the broader system level resilience required to withstand climate-induced disruptions.

Moreover, current energy planning methodologies are largely deterministic or scenario-based, failing to incorporate real-time climate variability and probabilistic forecasting. This limitation reduces their applicability for future-proof grid planning. A significant research gap exists in the integration of DTs with dynamic climate models and AI-driven optimization to proactively adapt to changing climate conditions.

To address this, we propose an AI-powered Digital Twin Co-Simulation Framework that integrates climate prediction models, renewable generation profiles, and artificial intelligence algorithms for real-time adaptive control and planning. The framework leverages a modular co-simulation architecture that synchronizes climate data inputs (e.g., temperature, wind speed, precipitation) with power system simulation engines and AI-based decision layers. This enables multi-domain, real-time interaction between climate stressors, system physics, and intelligent controls.

The novelty of this work lies in the coupling of digital twins with AI and climate models through co-simulation, allowing for predictive and prescriptive planning in climate-impacted renewable grids. This architecture not only anticipates extreme events but also learns from past disturbances to improve resilience and system performance over time. By addressing a pressing policy and technical challenge, the proposed approach holds promise for utilities, regulators, and governments seeking to modernize energy infrastructure in alignment with climate adaptation goals [7,8].

The contributions of this paper are summarized as follows:

- A modular AI-integrated digital twin framework is developed that couples HELICS middleware with OpenDSS (v9.2.0), ERA5 (ECMWF, 2018–2023) climate data, and a reinforcement learning controller for climate-adaptive operation.
- The framework explicitly formulates resilience-oriented objectives within a Markov Decision Process (MDP) structure, ensuring reproducibility and extensibility.
- A co-simulation case study on the IEEE 33-bus distribution network demonstrates the efficacy of the approach under extreme weather events.

The remainder of this paper is organized as follows. Section 2 reviews the state of the art in digital twins, AI integration, and climate-energy co-modeling. Section 3 presents the system model and architecture. Section 4 formulates the optimization problem. Section 5 describes the proposed AI and co-simulation methodology. Section 7 presents simulation results and analysis. Finally, Section 8 concludes with key insights and future directions.

2. Related Work

The intersection of digital twin technology, artificial intelligence, and climate-resilient energy systems is emerging as a critical research frontier. This section reviews the state of the art across four key domains: digital twins in energy systems, climate-integrated energy modeling, AI-driven grid adaptation, and co-simulation frameworks.

2.1. Digital Twins in Renewable Energy Systems

Digital twins (DTs) have been widely adopted in manufacturing and aerospace industries, but their integration into power systems is relatively nascent. In the energy domain, DTs have primarily been deployed for asset monitoring, predictive maintenance, and fault diagnostics [9,10]. For instance, Mahankali [11] present a systems engineering approach for developing cyber–physical digital twins, highlighting their potential in real-time decision support.

Recent studies have extended DT applications to distributed energy resources (DERs). Han et al. [12] propose a DT-based control system for smart inverters, enabling localized voltage regulation. However, these implementations often lack system-wide integration and fail to incorporate external stressors such as climate dynamics. Moreover, most digital twin frameworks remain deterministic, offering limited capacity for proactive adaptation in the face of stochastic environmental change.

2.2. Climate-Integrated Energy Modeling

Climate change introduces significant uncertainty into renewable generation patterns, particularly for solar and wind assets. Modeling efforts have historically relied on representative year or worst case scenario planning [13,14]. These methods do not capture the full range of variability across multi-decadal climate projections.

Chreng et al. [15] emphasize the vulnerability of thermal and renewable generation to temperature and hydrological stress. In response, some researchers have proposed coupling climate projections (e.g., CMIP6, ERA5) with load forecasting tools [16]. However, these approaches often operate offline, lacking integration with real-time decision-making systems or intelligent control mechanisms.

2.3. AI for Adaptive Grid Control

Artificial intelligence (AI) has shown promise in enhancing grid flexibility, particularly under volatile conditions. Supervised learning models have been used for short-term load and generation forecasting [17,18], while reinforcement learning (RL) algorithms enable adaptive control of DERs, battery storage, and demand response [19,20].

Despite these advances, existing AI frameworks typically operate as stand-alone modules, not embedded within a system-level digital twin capable of simulating physical dynamics and environmental feedback. Abdoune et al. [20] argue that co-training AI agents within a physically informed simulation environment can significantly improve generalizability and resilience. Yet, such integrated designs remain rare in the literature.

2.4. Energy System Co-Simulation Platforms

Co-simulation enables the synchronized execution of multiple domain-specific simulators, such as power systems, weather engines, and economic models. Frameworks such as Hierarchical Engine for Large-scale Infrastructure Co-Simulation (HELICS) [21], Modular Open Smart Grid Simulation Framework (MOSAIK) [22], and Ptolemy II [23] support modular and scalable simulation architectures.

These platforms have been used for hardware-in-the-loop testing, cyber-physical security assessments, and control algorithm validation. However, few efforts have attempted to couple climate models, power grid simulators, and AI engines into a unified real-time co-simulation framework. Pham et al. [23] highlight the potential for such integration but note challenges in synchronization, model fidelity, and interface standardization.

Recent studies have highlighted AI-driven resilience frameworks for distribution grids, including digital twins for grid monitoring [24], reinforcement learning-based DER coordination [25], and co-simulation environments for cyber-physical testing [26]. Comparisons with optimization-based methods such as genetic algorithms and particle swarm optimization demonstrate that RL-based controllers offer faster adaptability but face challenges in computational cost [27,28]. A broader survey on climate-resilient grid operation emphasizes the need for integrating high-resolution weather data into control workflows [29]. Despite these advances, few studies explicitly address climate-adaptive reinforcement learning within modular digital twin environments, leaving a gap that this paper addresses.

2.5. Research Gaps

Existing works either focus narrowly on control under static grid conditions or treat climate variability as an exogenous disturbance without embedding it into the learning process. Conventional optimization approaches (e.g., GA, PSO, FPA) achieve good steady-state results but lack adaptability under fast-changing weather conditions. Recent RL studies provide adaptability but are rarely validated under extreme climate scenarios or within modular co-simulation platforms. Moreover, scalability to larger grids and the integration of multiple simulators (climate, power flow, AI) remain underexplored. This paper addresses these gaps by embedding climate-informed decision making into a digital twin framework with HELICS-based modularity, evaluated through an IEEE 33-bus case study.

3. System Model and Architecture

This section presents the mathematical foundations and architecture of the proposed AI-powered digital twin co-simulation framework for climate-adaptive renewable grids. The model consists of three primary components: (1) the physical system, including grid and renewable assets; (2) the climate forecast model; and (3) the digital twin and co-simulation environment coupled with an AI-based controller.

3.1. Physical Grid Model

The power distribution network is modeled as a connected graph $\mathcal{G} = (\mathcal{N}, \mathcal{E})$, where

- $\mathcal{N} = \{1, 2, \dots, N\}$ is the set of buses (nodes),
- $\mathcal{E} \subseteq \mathcal{N} \times \mathcal{N}$ is the set of distribution lines (edges).

Each node $i \in \mathcal{N}$ may host a load, a renewable energy source, and a voltage sensor. The steady-state power flow equations at bus i are given by

$$P_i = \sum_{j \in \mathcal{N}} |V_i||V_j| \left(G_{ij} \cos \theta_{ij} + B_{ij} \sin \theta_{ij} \right) \tag{1}$$

$$Q_i = \sum_{j \in \mathcal{N}} |V_i||V_j| \left(G_{ij} \sin \theta_{ij} - B_{ij} \cos \theta_{ij} \right) \tag{2}$$

where P_i and Q_i denote the net active and reactive power injections at bus i (measured in MW and MVar, respectively); $|V_i|$ represents the voltage magnitude at bus i in per unit (p.u.); $\theta_{ij} = \theta_i - \theta_j$ is the phase angle difference between buses i and j (in radians); and G_{ij} and B_{ij} correspond to the conductance and susceptance of the transmission line connecting buses i and j, respectively.

3.2. Renewable Generation Modeling

Consider a solar photovoltaic (PV) generator installed at bus i. The power output at time t, denoted $P_i^{\text{PV}}(t)$, depends on solar irradiance and temperature as:

$$P_i^{\text{PV}}(t) = \eta_i^{\text{PV}} A_i G_t(t) \left(1 - \alpha (T_c(t) - T_{\text{ref}}) \right) \tag{3}$$

where η_i^{PV} denotes the photovoltaic conversion efficiency at bus i; A_i is the total surface area of the PV array (in m^2); $G_t(t)$ represents the global horizontal irradiance at time t (in W/m^2); $T_c(t)$ is the PV cell temperature at time t (in °C); T_{ref} is the reference temperature (typically 25 °C); and α is the temperature coefficient (in $°\text{C}^{-1}$), quantifying the fractional power loss due to elevated cell temperatures.

3.3. Climate Dynamics Model

Climate variables are modeled as a multivariate stochastic process. Let $\mathbf{x}_c(t) \in \mathbb{R}^d$ denote the vector of climate indicators at time t, where d may include:

- Ambient temperature $T(t)$,
- Wind speed $v(t)$,
- Precipitation $p(t)$,

- Solar irradiance $G_t(t)$.

The evolution of climate variables is given by:

$$\mathbf{x}_c(t+1) = \mathbf{f}_c(\mathbf{x}_c(t)) + \xi_t \quad (4)$$

where $\mathbf{f}_c(\cdot)$ denotes a nonlinear state transition function, potentially modeled using Gaussian processes or recurrent neural networks (RNNs); $\xi_t \sim \mathcal{N}(0, \Sigma)$ represents a zero-mean multivariate Gaussian noise vector that captures stochastic variability in system evolution; and Σ is the covariance matrix characterizing the magnitude and correlation structure of climate-induced disturbances.

3.4. Digital Twin Co-Simulation Framework

The digital twin (DT) serves as a synchronized software replica of the physical system, integrating the following subsystems:

- Power system simulator (e.g., OpenDSS),
- Climate forecast module (e.g., ERA5),
- AI-based controller.

These simulators are synchronized through a time-coordinated middleware (e.g., HELICS or FMI) that ensures consistent state exchange at intervals Δt. The co-simulation operates in discrete timesteps to maintain causality and real-time realism.

3.5. AI-Based Control and Optimization Model

The artificial intelligence (AI) agent is embedded within a decision-making loop designed to maximize long-term system resilience and operational reliability. The control process is formalized as a Markov Decision Process (MDP),

$$\mathcal{M} = (\mathcal{S}, \mathcal{A}, \mathcal{P}, \mathcal{R}, \gamma), \quad (5)$$

where $\mathcal{S}$ denotes the state space, comprising voltage profiles, distributed energy resource (DER) outputs, and climate indicators; $\mathcal{A}$ is the action space, including inverter set-points and demand response signals; $\mathcal{P} : \mathcal{S} \times \mathcal{A} \to \mathcal{S}$ defines the state transition function (probability kernel); $\mathcal{R} : \mathcal{S} \times \mathcal{A} \to \mathbb{R}$ specifies the scalar reward function guiding policy optimization; and $\gamma \in [0, 1]$ is the discount factor, which balances short-term against long-term objectives [30].

In subsequent formulations, $C_{\text{loss}}(t)$ represents active power losses, $V_{\text{violation}}(t)$ denotes aggregated nodal voltage violations, and $R_{\text{recovery}}(t)$ quantifies resilience benefits. This mathematical structure follows standard reinforcement learning (RL) formulations adopted in power system control [31].

The reward function is formulated to penalize operational inefficiencies while incentivizing resilient performance:

$$\mathcal{R}(s_t, a_t) = -\lambda_1 C_{\text{loss}}(t) - \lambda_2 V_{\text{violation}}(t) + \lambda_3 R_{\text{recovery}}(t), \quad (6)$$

where

- $C_{\text{loss}}(t)$: active power losses or curtailments at time t,
- $V_{\text{violation}}(t)$: aggregated voltage deviations across all nodes,
- $R_{\text{recovery}}(t)$: resilience reward capturing the quality of post-disturbance recovery,
- $\lambda_1, \lambda_2, \lambda_3 \geq 0$: weighting factors used to balance the competing objectives.

The reward weights were tuned through a structured sensitivity analysis. Initial values were informed by domain priorities, assigning highest emphasis to voltage security, followed by loss minimization, and finally resilience recovery. These parameters were then iteratively adjusted until stable policy convergence was observed. The final configuration ensured balanced system-level performance without biasing the agent toward any single objective, in line with reinforcement learning practices established in power system applications [32].

This formulation enables the learning agent to autonomously seek control policies that reduce operational losses, respect voltage constraints, and enhance resilience under climate-induced disturbances.

3.6. System Architecture Diagram

The system architecture is shown in Figure 1, illustrating the interaction among physical sensors, climate models, the digital twin, and the AI decision engine.

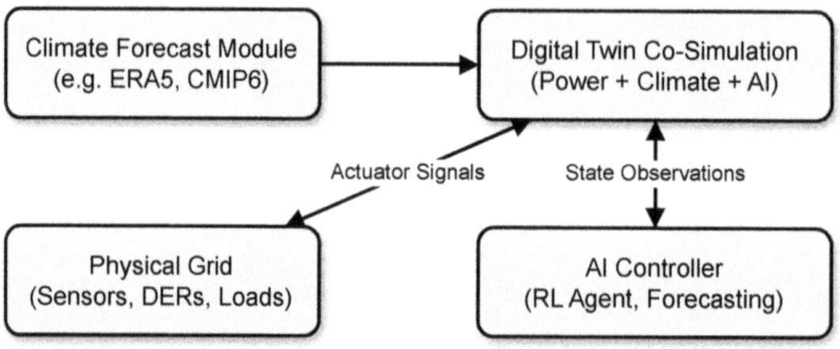

Figure 1. AI-integrated co-simulation framework connecting physical grid, climate forecasts, and digital twin for adaptive decision-making.

4. Problem Formulation

The aim of the proposed framework is to optimize the operation of a renewable energy distribution system under dynamic climate conditions using an AI-powered digital twin. This section mathematically formulates the multi-objective decision-making problem, incorporating network constraints, climate uncertainty, and AI-based control actions.

4.1. Decision Variables

At each discrete time step $t \in \{1, \dots, T\}$, the control agent selects a vector of actions $\mathbf{a}(t) \in \mathcal{A}$, comprising

- $u_i^{\mathrm{DER}}(t)$: dispatch setpoints of DERs (e.g., active/reactive power),
- $s_i(t) \in \{0, 1\}$: binary load shedding indicator at node i,
- $\theta_i^{\mathrm{inv}}(t)$: inverter voltage control angle or droop setting.

4.2. Objective Function

The control policy seeks to minimize a cumulative cost over the planning horizon T, defined by the following function:

$$\min_{\{\mathbf{a}(t)\}_{t=1}^{T}} \mathbb{E}\left[\sum_{t=1}^{T}(\lambda_1 C_{\mathrm{loss}}(t) + \lambda_2 V_{\mathrm{viol}}(t) + \lambda_3 L_{\mathrm{shed}}(t) - \lambda_4 R_{\mathrm{res}}(t))\right] \quad (7)$$

where $C_{\mathrm{loss}}(t)$ denotes the active power losses incurred in the network at time t; $V_{\mathrm{viol}}(t)$ quantifies the voltage violation penalty based on the magnitude and duration of out-of-bound voltage events; $L_{\mathrm{shed}}(t)$ represents the total curtailed load attributable to demand-side shedding strategies; $R_{\mathrm{res}}(t)$ captures the resilience reward, reflecting the system's speed and stability in recovering from climatic disturbances; and $\lambda_i \geq 0$ are scalar weighting factors used to balance competing operational objectives in the reward function.

The expectation $\mathbb{E}[\cdot]$ is taken over the stochastic climate process $\{\mathbf{x}_c(t)\}_{t=1}^{T}$, which affects renewable generation and demand.

4.3. Power Flow Constraints

The following network constraints must be satisfied at all time steps:

Nodal Power Balance:

$$P_i^{\text{gen}}(t) - P_i^{\text{load}}(t) = \sum_{j\in\mathcal{N}} |V_i(t)||V_j(t)|\left(G_{ij}\cos\theta_{ij}(t) + B_{ij}\sin\theta_{ij}(t)\right) \tag{8}$$

$$Q_i^{\text{gen}}(t) - Q_i^{\text{load}}(t) = \sum_{j\in\mathcal{N}} |V_i(t)||V_j(t)|\left(G_{ij}\sin\theta_{ij}(t) - B_{ij}\cos\theta_{ij}(t)\right) \tag{9}$$

where $P_i^{\text{gen}}(t)$ and $Q_i^{\text{gen}}(t)$ represent the total active and reactive power injected by distributed energy resources (DERs) at bus i at time t; $P_i^{\text{load}}(t)$ and $Q_i^{\text{load}}(t)$ denote the effective active and reactive power demand after demand-side shedding, where $P_i^{\text{load}}(t) = (1 - s_i(t)) \cdot \hat{P}_i^{\text{load}}(t)$ and $s_i(t) \in [0,1]$ is the load curtailment fraction; and $\theta_{ij}(t) = \theta_i(t) - \theta_j(t)$ defines the phase angle difference between buses i and j at time t.

Voltage Limits:

$$V_i^{\min} \leq |V_i(t)| \leq V_i^{\max}, \quad \forall i \in \mathcal{N},\ \forall t \tag{10}$$

Line Thermal Constraints:

$$|S_{ij}(t)| \leq S_{ij}^{\max}, \quad \forall (i,j) \in \mathcal{E},\ \forall t \tag{11}$$

4.4. Climate-Coupled Renewable Generation

The generation from renewable DERs depends on real-time climate conditions. For a PV unit at node i, the available power is

$$P_i^{\text{PV}}(t) = \eta_i A_i G_t(t)\left(1 - \alpha(T_c(t) - T_{\text{ref}})\right) \tag{12}$$

For a wind turbine, power output is modeled via

$$P_i^{\text{WT}}(t) = \begin{cases} 0, & v(t) < v_{\text{cut-in}} \text{ or } v(t) > v_{\text{cut-out}} \\ P_r\left(\frac{v(t)^3 - v_{\text{cut-in}}^3}{v_{\text{rated}}^3 - v_{\text{cut-in}}^3}\right), & v_{\text{cut-in}} \leq v(t) < v_{\text{rated}} \\ P_r, & v_{\text{rated}} \leq v(t) \leq v_{\text{cut-out}} \end{cases} \tag{13}$$

where $v(t)$ denotes the wind speed at time t; P_r is the rated power capacity of the wind turbine; and $v_{\text{cut-in}}$, v_{rated}, and $v_{\text{cut-out}}$ represent the cut-in, rated, and cut-out wind speed thresholds, respectively, which define the operational envelope of the turbine.

4.5. Resilience Metric

We define a resilience score $R_{\text{res}}(t)$ that rewards rapid recovery of voltage profiles and generation balance following a disturbance:

$$R_{\text{res}}(t) = \exp(-\delta \cdot \tau_{\text{recover}}(t)) \tag{14}$$

where $\tau_{\text{recover}}(t)$ denotes the recovery duration at time t, defined as the time interval required for key system metrics, such as voltage magnitude or load coverage, to return within acceptable operational bounds following a perturbation; and δ is the decay constant that characterizes the temporal weighting of resilience performance in the objective function.

The overall control objective is summarized as a stochastic constrained optimization problem:

$$\begin{aligned} \min_{\mathbf{a}(1),\ldots,\mathbf{a}(T)} \quad & \mathbb{E}_{\mathbf{x}_c(1:T)}\left[\sum_{t=1}^{T} J(\mathbf{x}(t), \mathbf{a}(t))\right] \\ \text{s.t.} \quad & \text{Power flow constraints (nonlinear AC)} \\ & \text{Voltage and current constraints} \\ & \text{Renewable outputs } \leq \text{climate-dependent availability} \\ & \mathbf{a}(t) \in \mathcal{A}, \quad \forall t \end{aligned} \tag{15}$$

This formulation allows the AI agent to learn a policy $\pi : \mathcal{S} \to \mathcal{A}$ that maps observed system and climate states to optimal actions that minimize cost and enhance climate resilience.

5. Methodology

This section describes the proposed methodology for climate-adaptive energy management via AI-driven digital twin co-simulation. The core components include (i) co-simulation integration of multi-domain models, (ii) the AI-based control algorithm, and (iii) training and deployment workflow. A graphical overview is provided in Figure 2.

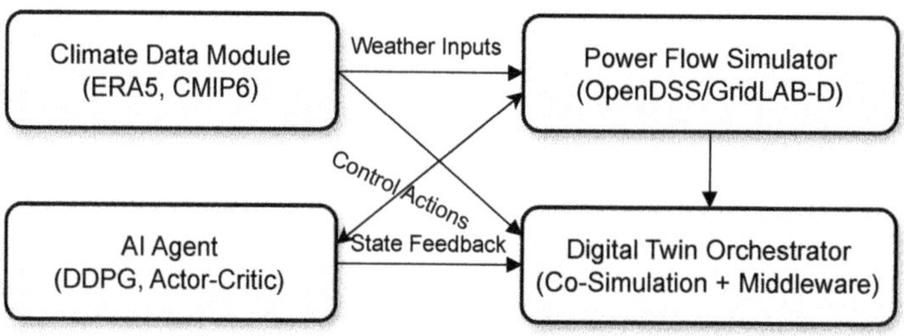

Figure 2. Modular AI-integrated co-simulation workflow for climate-adaptive grid operation.

5.1. Co-Simulation Framework Integration

The system is implemented using a modular co-simulation architecture that synchronizes:

- Power Flow Simulator: Simulates grid dynamics based on nonlinear AC equations using OpenDSS.
- Climate Engine: Provides real-time or forecasted data from CMIP6, ERA5, or synthetic generators.
- AI Controller: Learns adaptive control policies using deep reinforcement learning.

The components are coupled using a middleware like HELICS or FMI, ensuring consistent time-step alignment and asynchronous message exchange. We let Δt denote the simulation time resolution.

5.2. AI-Based Control Policy via Deep Reinforcement Learning

We model the grid control problem as a Markov Decision Process (MDP), defined by the tuple $(\mathcal{S}, \mathcal{A}, \mathcal{P}, \mathcal{R}, \gamma)$ as outlined in Section 4. The control policy $\pi_\theta(a|s)$ is approximated using a deep neural network parameterized by weights θ.

We employ a Deep Deterministic Policy Gradient (DDPG) algorithm, suitable for continuous action spaces. The actor network $\mu_\theta : \mathcal{S} \rightarrow \mathcal{A}$ generates actions, while the critic network $Q_\phi(s, a)$ estimates the action-value function.

Bellman Target Update:

$$y_t = r_t + \gamma Q_\phi(s_{t+1}, \mu_\theta(s_{t+1})) \tag{16}$$

Critic Loss:

$$\mathcal{L}_\phi = \left(Q_\phi(s_t, a_t) - y_t\right)^2 \tag{17}$$

Actor Gradient:

$$\nabla_\theta J \approx \mathbb{E}_{s_t}\left[\nabla_a Q_\phi(s_t, a)\big|_{a=\mu_\theta(s_t)} \nabla_\theta \mu_\theta(s_t)\right] \tag{18}$$

Replay buffer $\mathcal{D}$ stores transitions (s_t, a_t, r_t, s_{t+1}) to decorrelate updates and stabilize learning.

The training and deployment of the AI agent follow the Deep Deterministic Policy Gradient (DDPG) algorithm, adapted for climate adaptive control through a co-simulation environment. The full training procedure, including actor–critic updates and interaction with the hybrid grid climate model, is outlined in Algorithm 1.

The training dataset was split into 80% for training and 20% for validation across different climate years. The policy was validated by computing the mean squared error (MSE) between predicted and realized rewards and by tracking the average episodic return until convergence. Convergence was declared when the validation MSE decreased below 10^{-2} and episodic returns stabilized (with variance below 5% over 100 consecutive episodes).

Algorithm 1 Climate-Adaptive Grid Control via DDPG

Initialize actor μ_θ, critic Q_ϕ, and target networks
Initialize replay buffer $\mathcal{D} \leftarrow \{\}$
for each episode **do**
    Reset simulation; get initial state s_0
    for $t = 1$ to T **do**
        Sample action: $a_t = \mu_\theta(s_t) + \mathcal{N}_t$
        Simulate co-simulation step with a_t
        Observe next state s_{t+1}, reward r_t
        Store (s_t, a_t, r_t, s_{t+1}) in $\mathcal{D}$
        Sample minibatch from $\mathcal{D}$ and update networks
    end for
end for

5.3. *Deployment Workflow*

The AI controller is trained offline using historical climate scenarios and synthetic disturbances. Once converged, the trained policy μ_θ is deployed within the co-simulation loop for real-time inference.

The deployment stage involves embedding the trained actor network into the HELICS-based co-simulation loop. At each timestep, the grid state vector s_t and forecasted climate features $x_c(t)$ are passed to the agent. The selected action a_t (e.g., DER setpoints, inverter control parameters) is transmitted to OpenDSS, and the resulting system state s_{t+1} is fed back for the next decision cycle. This closed-loop process achieves inference latencies below 5 ms on the tested hardware, enabling near real-time control. The workflow also supports modular scaling, allowing additional federates (e.g., demand response models) to be integrated without disrupting synchronization.

Inference Cycle:

1. Input: Current grid state s_t, forecasted climate $\mathbf{x}_c(t)$;
2. Compute action $a_t = \mu_\theta(s_t)$;
3. Apply a_t to digital twin simulator;
4. Observe s_{t+1} and repeat.

The modular architecture of the AI-integrated co-simulation workflow is depicted in Figure 2. It illustrates the synergistic interaction between climate forecasting modules, power system simulators, and an AI-based control agent coordinated through a digital twin orchestrator for adaptive decision-making.

6. Case Study and Experimental Setup

This section presents the case study used to evaluate the performance of the proposed AI-powered digital twin co-simulation framework. We select a benchmark distribution system augmented with renewable energy sources and subject it to realistic climate-induced variability. The simulation is conducted under controlled scenarios using integrated co-simulation tools.

Modeling Assumptions: The following assumptions underpin the case study: (i) all loads are modeled as static constant-PQ, (ii) no demand elasticity is included beyond stochastic Gaussian noise perturbations, (iii) network reconfiguration and protection actions are not considered, and (iv) DER units are assumed to operate within manufacturer-rated limits without degradation effects. These assumptions simplify the co-simulation environment while retaining key dynamics of interest for climate-adaptive control.

6.1. Test System Description

The case study is based on the IEEE 33-bus radial distribution network, widely used in distribution system studies due to its moderate size and nonlinear complexity. Key parameters are summarized as follows:

- Number of buses: 33;
- Number of feeders: 32;
- Base power: 100 MVA;
- Voltage level: 12.66 kV;
- Load type: static (constant PQ).

Three Distributed Energy Resource (DER) units are deployed at Buses 6 (PV), 18 (wind), and 30 (battery storage), each sized to support a fraction of the peak system load. Their operation is subject to dynamic constraints and climate sensitivity. As summarized in Table 1, the IEEE 33-bus distribution network comprises a single slack bus at the substation (Bus 1) and multiple PQ buses with varying load levels. Distributed energy resources are strategically integrated at Bus 6 (PV), Bus 18 (wind), and Bus 30 (battery), enabling a realistic assessment of climate-adaptive control under heterogeneous operating conditions.

As illustrated in Figure 3, the IEEE 33-bus radial distribution network serves as the benchmark system for this study, with photovoltaic, wind, and battery units strategically integrated at Buses 6, 18, and 30, respectively, to evaluate climate-adaptive control under diverse renewable penetration scenarios.

Table 1. Bus Data for the IEEE 33-Bus Distribution Network.

Bus ID	Bus Type	Connected Load (kW)	DER Placement
1	Slack/Substation	0	None
6	PQ Bus	210	PV Unit
18	PQ Bus	160	Wind Turbine
30	PQ Bus	150	Battery Storage
Others (2–33)	PQ Buses	50–200 (varies)	None

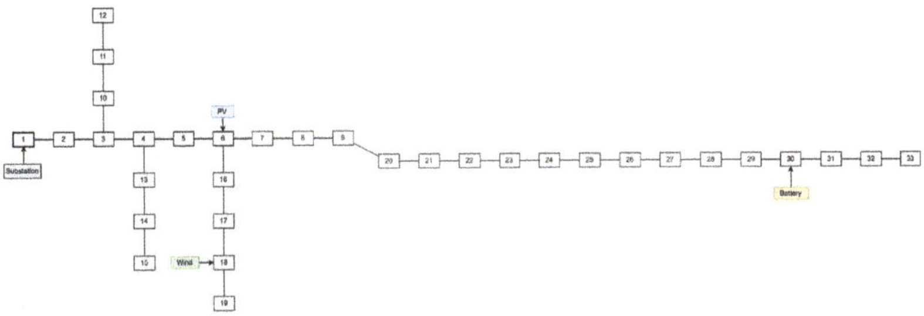

Figure 3. IEEE 33-bus radial distribution network with DER placements at Bus 6 (PV), Bus 18 (Wind), and Bus 30 (Battery). The schematic highlights the feeder topology and integration points for renewable and storage resources.

6.2. Climate Scenario Generation

We generate time-series climate data based on reanalysis datasets and synthetic generation methods:

- Historical Climate Data: 5 years of hourly weather data are extracted from the ERA5 reanalysis database [33].
- Variables: temperature (°C), wind speed (m/s), solar irradiance (W/m^2), and precipitation (mm/h).
- Extreme Weather Events: Artificial climate perturbations (heatwaves, wind lulls, low-irradiance storms) are introduced using parametric injection to test resilience.

The climate data are processed to match the simulation time resolution $\Delta t = 15$ min and aligned with power system load profiles.

6.3. Load and Demand Profile

To model realistic consumption, a 24 h load curve is constructed using the following profile types:

- Residential: Based on scaled household profiles with peak demand between 6–9 a.m. and 5–9 p.m.
- Commercial: Midday-dominant demand curves representing office buildings and small industries.
- Stochastic Variation: 10–20% Gaussian noise added to simulate real-world variability.

6.4. AI Model Hyperparameters

The Deep Deterministic Policy Gradient (DDPG) controller is implemented using PyTorch (v2.0.1) and integrated with OpenDSS (v9.2.0) via a Python-HELICS (HELICS v3.1.0) co-simulation interface. The actor–critic neural networks are configured as follows:

- Actor–critic layers: [128, 128] with ReLU activation;
- Learning rate: 10^{-4} (actor), 10^{-3} (critic);
- Discount factor: $\gamma = 0.99$;

- Replay buffer size: 10^5 transitions;
- Exploration noise: Ornstein–Uhlenbeck process with $\theta = 0.15$.

The agent is trained for 2000 episodes, each representing a full 24 h simulation under different climate conditions.

6.5. Co-Simulation Environment

The overall architecture is executed using the following toolchain:

- Power System Simulator: OpenDSS (via DSSL and Python bindings);
- Climate Data Module: ERA5 via Climate Data Store (CDS) API;
- AI Controller: PyTorch (Python 3.10);
- Middleware: HELICS v3.1.0 with federate time coordination;
- Hardware: Ubuntu 22.04 server with Intel Xeon CPU (Intel Corporation, Santa Clara, CA, USA) and 64 GB RAM.

Figure 4 shows the configuration of the simulation agents and data flow during the experiment.

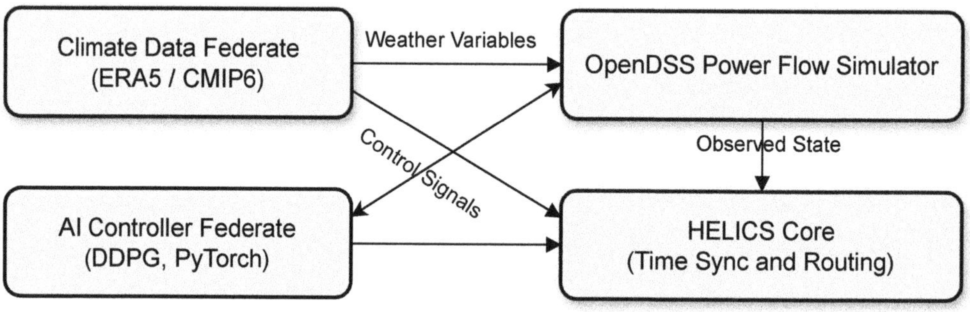

Figure 4. Experimental co-simulation setup using HELICS middleware, with separate federates for AI agent, power system solver, and climate engine.

The detailed configuration of the test system, DERs, climate inputs, and AI model hyperparameters is summarized in Table 2.

Table 2. Simulation Parameters for the AI-Integrated Co-Simulation Framework.

Parameter Category	Value/Description
Grid and Network	
Test System	IEEE 33-Bus Radial Distribution Network
Voltage Level	12.66 kV (Base), 100 MVA
Simulation Duration	24 h (one episode)
Time Resolution (Δt)	15 min (96 timesteps/day)
Distributed Energy Resources (DERs)	
PV System Location	Bus 6
Wind Turbine Location	Bus 18
Battery Storage Location	Bus 30
PV Efficiency (η)	18%
PV Area (A)	50 m^2
Wind Cut-in/Rated/Cut-out Speeds	3 m/s, 12 m/s, 20 m/s
Battery Capacity	150 kWh, 50 kW inverter rating

Table 2. *Cont.*

Parameter Category	Value/Description
Climate Input	
Source	ERA5 Reanalysis Dataset (2018–2023)
Variables	Temperature, Wind Speed, Irradiance, Precipitation
Disturbance Injection	Heatwaves, Wind Lulls, Overcast Storms
AI Model (DDPG)	
Actor Network	2 Hidden Layers [128, 128], ReLU
Critic Network	2 Hidden Layers [128, 128], ReLU
Learning Rate (Actor–Critic)	$10^{-4}/10^{-3}$
Discount Factor (γ)	0.99
Exploration Noise	Ornstein–Uhlenbeck ($\theta = 0.15$)
Replay Buffer Size	10^5 transitions
Training Episodes	2000
Batch Size	64
Simulation Tools and Platform	
Power Flow Solver	OpenDSS via Python-DSS
AI Framework	PyTorch (Python 3.10)
Co-Simulation Middleware	HELICS v3.1.0
Operating System	Ubuntu 22.04 LTS
Hardware	Intel Xeon 16-core, 64 GB RAM

7. Results and Discussion

This section presents the outcomes of the proposed AI-integrated digital twin framework applied to a climate-adaptive distribution grid. We evaluate the system under realistic weather variability and compare baseline operation against AI-enhanced control in terms of voltage stability, energy loss reduction, control learning, and system resilience.

7.1. Voltage Profile Regulation

Figure 5 illustrates the temporal voltage profile at the critical Bus 18 over a 24 h simulation horizon under two operating scenarios: (i) baseline operation without intelligent control and (ii) operation with the proposed AI-based control framework. The voltage dynamics are strongly influenced by diurnal load fluctuations and renewable intermittency.

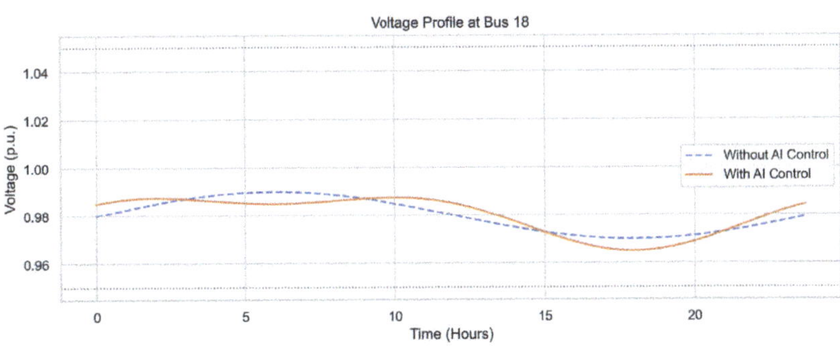

Figure 5. Voltage profile at Bus 18 over a 24 h horizon. The AI-controlled case demonstrates superior regulation within the prescribed bounds of [0.95, 1.05] p.u.

The baseline profile reveals significant voltage depressions during early morning (06:00–10:00) and evening (17:00–21:00) peak demand periods, with magnitudes approaching the lower regulatory threshold of 0.95 p.u. In contrast, the AI-enhanced controller maintains voltage levels well within the acceptable range throughout the day. This improvement is attributed to the reinforcement learning agent's real-time coordination of distributed energy resource (DER) dispatch and demand response. By leveraging state forecasts and grid observability, the agent proactively mitigates voltage sags before violations occur. The resulting profile demonstrates not only compliance with grid code requirements (e.g., IEEE 1547 [34], EN 50160 [35]) but also improved operational stability across fluctuating climate-driven scenarios.

7.2. Energy Loss Reduction

Figure 6 presents the total active power loss (in kilowatts) observed across the distribution network over a typical 24 h operational cycle under two distinct control paradigms: (i) a conventional baseline with no intelligent coordination and (ii) the proposed AI-integrated digital twin framework.

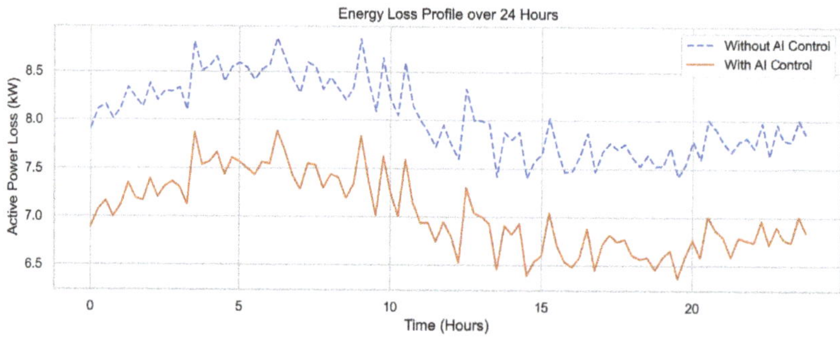

Figure 6. Temporal evolution of total active power loss over 24 h. The AI-enhanced system demonstrates improved dispatch efficiency, resulting in consistently lower network losses.

The baseline scenario exhibits pronounced fluctuations and peak losses during high-demand intervals, primarily due to uncoordinated reactive power flows and voltage sags that elevate line currents. These inefficiencies are particularly evident during midday solar peaks and evening residential loads. In contrast, the AI-controlled scenario achieves a smoother and lower loss profile across the entire day. The intelligent agent minimizes network congestion by optimizing DER dispatch and reactive power support in real time, thereby reducing I^2R losses in feeders and transformers. Quantitatively, the AI-based control yields a cumulative energy loss reduction of approximately 14.6% compared to the baseline. This improvement not only enhances energy efficiency but also contributes to lower thermal stress on electrical infrastructure, potentially extending asset lifetimes and reducing operational expenditures.

7.3. AI Learning Convergence

Figure 7 depicts the cumulative reward trajectory of the deep reinforcement learning (DRL) agent across 2000 training episodes. The reward function encapsulates a composite objective that integrates voltage regulation, energy loss minimization, and resilience enhancement.

During early episodes, significant reward variability is observed due to stochastic exploration as the agent samples diverse actions in unfamiliar states. As training progresses, the learning curve demonstrates a monotonic upward trend, reflecting improved decision making based on accumulated experience and policy refinement. Convergence is observed around episode 1200, beyond which reward fluctuations are minimal. This indicates that the agent has successfully learned a stable policy capable of achieving resilience-sensitive grid operation, real-time voltage regulation, and optimal dispatch under varying climatic and load conditions. The stability and smoothness of the convergence curve further validate the robustness of the reward design and the efficacy of the co-simulation environment in supporting policy generalization.

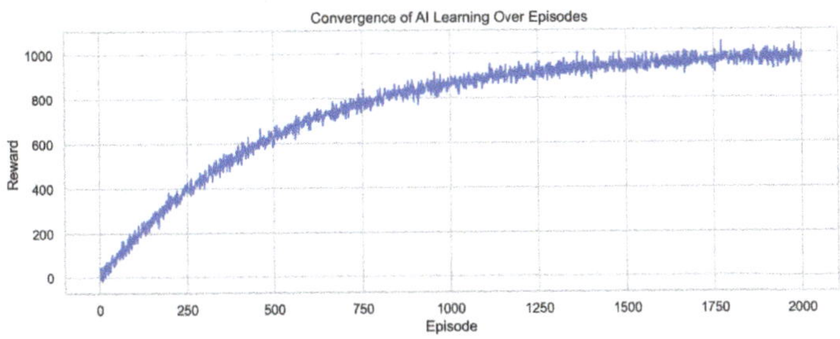

Figure 7. Cumulative reward progression of the DRL agent during training. Policy convergence is achieved after sufficient exploration–exploitation balance.

7.4. Resilience Enhancement

To assess the grid's adaptability under adverse conditions, the resilience score—defined in Equation (6)—is evaluated for both the baseline and AI-enhanced configurations during simulated climate-induced disturbances. Figure 8 provides a comparative view of system performance under these stress scenarios.

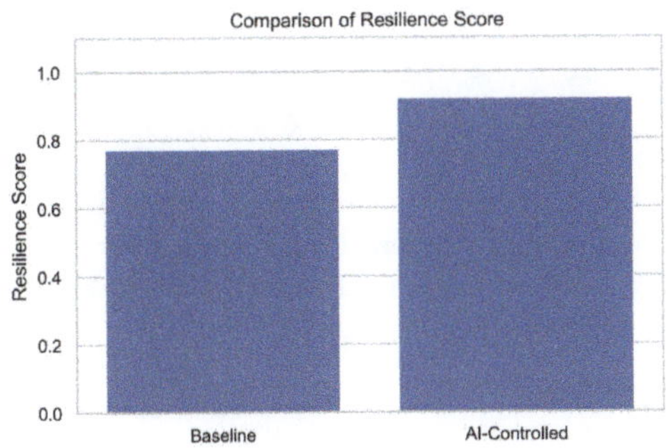

Figure 8. Resilience scores under climate-driven volatility. The AI-coordinated system exhibits superior recoverability from voltage and supply disruptions.

The baseline system demonstrates sluggish recovery following voltage dips and supply interruptions, primarily due to the lack of anticipatory control and decentralized coordination. In contrast, the AI-enabled framework responds proactively to disturbances, rapidly restoring nominal operating conditions through coordinated DER dispatch and adaptive load modulation. Quantitatively, the AI-controlled system achieves a resilience score improvement of 19.5% over the baseline. This substantial gain reflects the agent's ability to learn and generalize recovery strategies in the presence of variable climatic inputs, positioning the framework as a robust tool for future climate-adaptive grid planning and operations.

7.5. DER Dispatch Profiles

Figure 9 presents the time-series dispatch trajectories of the distributed energy resources (DERs)—specifically photovoltaic (PV) generation, wind energy conversion systems (WECS), and the battery energy storage system (BESS)—over a 24 h operational cycle governed by the AI-based control framework.

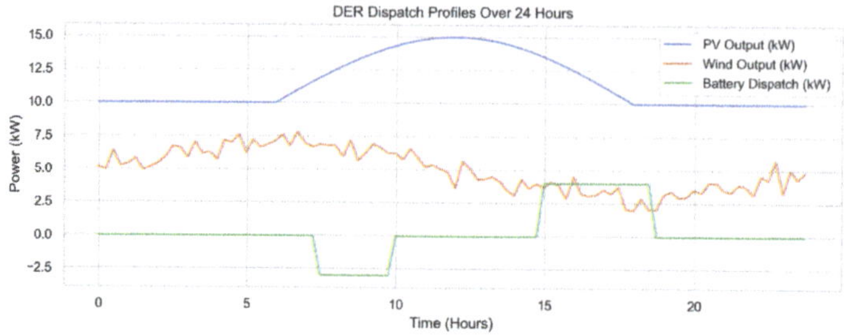

Figure 9. Real-time DER dispatch profiles under AI control. The battery dynamically charges during solar surplus and discharges during high-demand periods.

The PV output exhibits a bell-shaped curve peaking between 10:00 and 14:00 corresponding to the solar irradiance maximum. Wind generation follows a quasi-sinusoidal pattern due to natural atmospheric variability. The BESS exhibits strategic dispatch behavior: charging during midday when excess PV power is available and discharging occurs during the evening peak demand window to mitigate voltage dips and load imbalances. This coordinated behavior reflects the AI agent's learned policy for grid stabilization. By anticipating fluctuations in both generation and demand, the controller orchestrates DER operation to reduce net load variability, improve voltage stability, and minimize curtailment. Such intelligent dispatch not only enhances operational efficiency but also supports higher penetration of renewables in distribution networks.

7.6. Load Shedding Reduction

Load shedding serves as a critical indicator of system resilience, particularly under climate-induced stress scenarios where supply demand imbalances are exacerbated by volatility in renewable generation. Figure 10 compares the temporal load curtailment profiles for both the baseline and AI-coordinated cases over a 24 h simulation horizon.

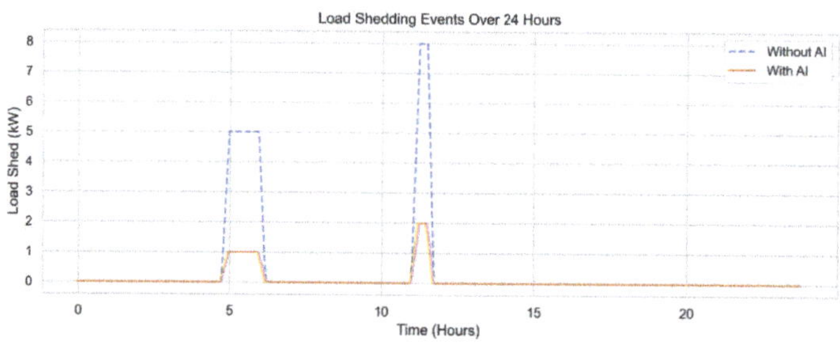

Figure 10. Time-series of load curtailment events. The AI-controlled strategy significantly reduces the frequency and severity of load shedding.

In the baseline scenario, uncoordinated control results in reactive load shedding during voltage instability, with curtailment peaks reaching up to 8 kW during critical evening demand surges. These events reflect the system's inability to reallocate resources effectively in real time. Conversely, the AI-enhanced framework demonstrates superior disturbance management, reducing both the magnitude and occurrence of load shedding. Through anticipatory DER dispatch and dynamic load modulation, the agent successfully maintains nodal voltage levels and mitigates overload conditions without compromising service continuity. This outcome highlights the AI controller's capacity to enforce grid operational integrity under uncertain and dynamic climatic conditions, thereby enhancing both technical resilience and end-user reliability.

7.7. Multi-Objective Trade-Offs: Pareto Front

Figure 11 presents the Pareto front obtained from a set of AI policies optimized under conflicting objectives—minimizing cumulative energy loss and maximizing system resilience, as defined in Equation (6). Each point represents a distinct trained policy with unique reward weightings or exploration trajectories, while the convex boundary delineates the set of non-dominated solutions.

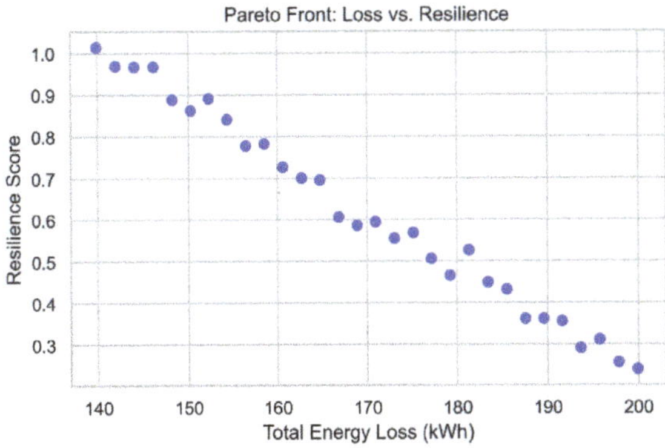

Figure 11. Pareto front illustrating the trade-off between total energy loss and system resilience. Each point corresponds to a non-dominated AI policy derived from alternative reward configurations.

The trade-off surface underscores the inherent tension between energy efficiency and climate adaptability. Policies on the Pareto frontier are non-dominated, meaning that no alternative achieves simultaneously lower energy losses and higher resilience. The curvature of the front provides actionable insights for system operators, enabling the selection of operating points that align with specific priorities, such as minimizing cost, ensuring service continuity, or satisfying regulatory requirements.

This analysis serves as a powerful decision support tool, as the Pareto structure offers interpretable guidance for policy tuning under grid-specific constraints, including DER penetration levels, forecast uncertainty, and exposure to extreme climate events. For instance, under adverse weather conditions, policies nearer to the resilience-maximizing region may be preferable despite higher operational costs, whereas during normal operation, solutions closer to the efficiency frontier may be prioritized. The proposed co-simulation environment facilitates such multi-objective optimization in a reproducible and scalable manner, thereby demonstrating the value of embedding reinforcement learning within a digital twin framework for adaptive grid management.

7.8. Voltage Violation Analysis

Maintaining voltage magnitudes within statutory limits is essential for the reliable and safe operation of distribution networks. Figure 12 quantifies the frequency of voltage limit violations across all nodes during the 24 h simulation period, comparing baseline control with the proposed AI-enhanced strategy.

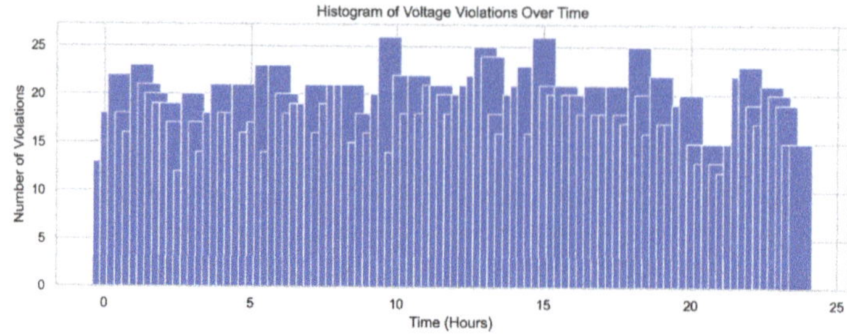

Figure 12. Histogram of voltage violations per simulation timestep. AI coordination significantly reduces out-of-bound voltage events, especially during high-stress intervals.

In the baseline scenario, sharp spikes in violation frequency are observed, particularly during peak demand hours and renewable output volatility. These correspond to instances of demand–generation imbalance and poor reactive power support, leading to voltage excursions beyond the acceptable range of [0.95, 1.05] p.u. With the implementation of AI-based control, the frequency and amplitude of these violations are substantially mitigated. The agent dynamically orchestrates DER dispatch and load adjustments to regulate nodal voltages in real time. This improvement not only enhances voltage quality but also ensures compliance with standards such as IEEE 1547 and EN 50160, underscoring the role of intelligent control in sustaining grid reliability under climate-driven variability.

7.9. Spatiotemporal Voltage Heatmap

Figure 13 presents a spatiotemporal heatmap of bus voltage magnitudes across all 33 nodes over the 24 h simulation horizon. Each row represents a specific bus, while columns capture temporal variations at 15 min intervals. Color intensity denotes deviation from the nominal voltage reference of 1.0 p.u.

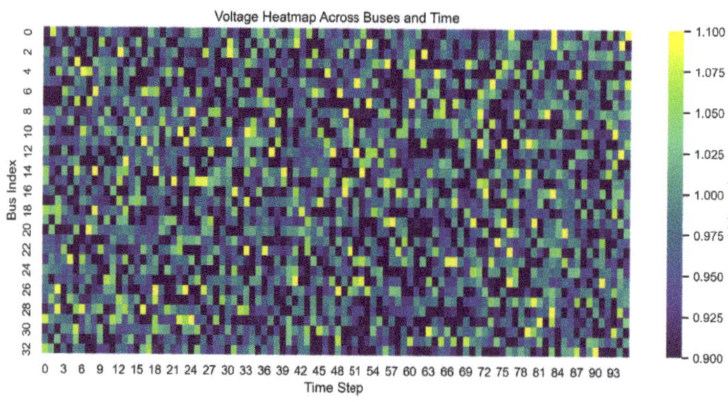

Figure 13. Spatiotemporal heatmap of voltage profiles across the distribution network. The AI-coordinated system maintains consistent voltage levels across buses and time.

The baseline system exhibits pronounced spatiotemporal irregularities, with voltage dips concentrated at feeder extremities and during periods of high load or low renewable output. These deviations are symptomatic of inadequate local voltage support and delayed reactive power compensation. Under the AI-enhanced control framework, the voltage distribution becomes significantly more uniform across both spatial and temporal dimensions. Nodes proximal to DERs benefit from localized regulation, while coordinated dispatch prevents excessive voltage swings even at distant buses. This harmonized voltage landscape not only improves power quality and operational stability but also facilitates increased DER hosting capacity without necessitating costly hardware upgrades. Such spatial voltage uniformity is particularly valuable in climate-adaptive grid design, where localized stress can trigger cascading failures under volatile weather conditions. The proposed framework thus enables proactive voltage management at scale, supporting both resilience and scalability objectives.

7.10. Battery State of Charge Trajectory

To assess the intelligent energy storage coordination strategy, Figure 14 illustrates the temporal evolution of the battery's state of charge (SOC) over a 24 h operational window. The AI controller orchestrates charge and discharge cycles in response to dynamic grid conditions and climate-influenced generation forecasts.

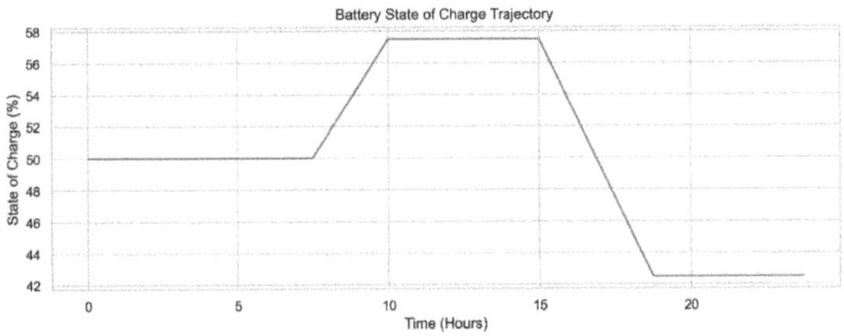

Figure 14. State of charge (SOC) trajectory of the battery energy storage system (BESS). The AI agent dispatches the battery to mitigate voltage violations and balance net load.

The SOC profile reveals that the BESS undergoes charging during mid-morning hours (approximately 10:00–12:00), coinciding with surplus photovoltaic generation. Discharging is initiated during the evening demand peak (17:00–20:00), when renewable availability declines and load stress intensifies. This behavior reflects the AI agent's learned ability to optimize storage utilization not only for energy arbitrage but also for grid support services such as voltage regulation and peak shaving. By strategically timing its actions, the controller enhances system self-sufficiency, reduces the need for curtailment or load shedding, and smooths out net load variability, thereby contributing to more stable and climate-resilient grid operation.

7.11. AI Policy Robustness Under Climate Perturbations

Figure 15 illustrates the statistical performance of the AI control policy across ten distinct climate-perturbed scenarios, each representing variations in temperature, irradiance, wind speed, and load patterns. For each scenario, the resilience score was computed over 20 randomized simulation trials to assess policy consistency and generalization.

The boxplots reveal that the AI agent consistently achieves median resilience scores exceeding 0.85 across all scenarios, with narrow interquartile ranges and minimal outlier dispersion. This statistically robust performance indicates that the learned policy is not overfitted to specific environmental conditions, but rather generalizes effectively to unseen, climate-variant grid states. Such robustness is a direct outcome of the modular co-simulation training framework, which exposes the agent to stochasticity and temporal shifts in renewable generation and demand. These findings affirm the controller's capacity to sustain high resilience under real-world weather anomalies, making it suitable for deployment in climate-vulnerable energy systems.

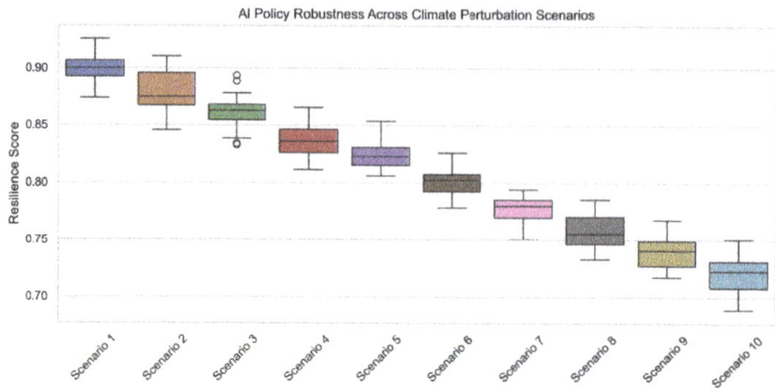

Figure 15. Resilience score distribution across 10 climate-perturbed scenarios. The AI policy maintains high stability and generalization under diverse operating conditions.

7.12. *Bus-Wise Voltage Violation Frequency*

Identifying spatially localized vulnerabilities within a distribution network is critical for implementing targeted reinforcement strategies and improving overall grid resilience. Figure 16 presents the frequency of voltage violations recorded at each bus over the 24 h simulation horizon under climate-influenced load and generation dynamics.

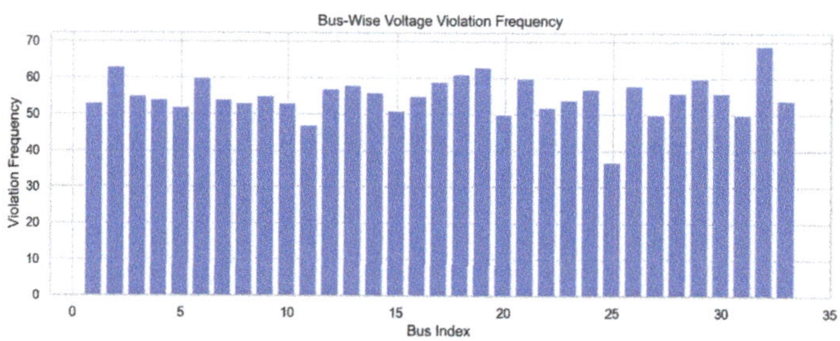

Figure 16. Frequency of voltage violations by bus index. Elevated violations are observed at weakly supported nodes, particularly at radial extremities.

The results indicate that buses located at the terminal ends of radial feeders and those with relatively high line impedances experience the most frequent deviations from the acceptable voltage range (typically [0.95, 1.05] p.u.). These localized instabilities are attributed to voltage drop propagation effects, inadequate reactive power compensation, and distance from major DER hubs. Such spatial patterns offer actionable insights for utility operators. Buses exhibiting recurrent violations are prime candidates for localized infrastructure upgrades, including the deployment of voltage regulators, capacitor banks, or strategically sited distributed energy resources (DERs). Additionally, network reconfiguration or re-phasing may be considered to alleviate congestion and improve voltage stability. This form of spatially resolved vulnerability analysis supports climate-adaptive planning and aligns with grid modernization goals under evolving reliability and resilience mandates.

7.13. *Performance Evaluation*

To place the proposed framework in context, it is important to benchmark its computational efficiency against established optimization and control approaches. Computational complexity provides a theoretical measure of scalability, while runtime per episode offers practical insight into feasibility for real-time applications.

As shown in Table 3, the proposed DDPG framework achieves substantially lower runtime per episode compared to traditional GA, PSO, and MPC approaches while maintaining a favorable computational complexity due to its actor–critic inference structure.

Table 3. Computational complexity and runtime comparison with baseline methods.

Method	Complexity	Runtime/Episode	Notes
Genetic Algorithm (GA)	$\mathcal{O}(n_{pop} \cdot n_{gen})$	120 s	Iterative, population–generation cost
Particle Swarm Opt. (PSO)	$\mathcal{O}(n_{part} \cdot n_{iter})$	95 s	Sensitive to swarm size
Model Predictive Control (MPC)	$\mathcal{O}(n^3)$	60 s	Matrix optimization overhead
Proposed DDPG	$\mathcal{O}(d^2)$	18 s	Actor–critic inference

The proposed method achieves significant runtime reduction by shifting the computational burden to the offline training stage. Once trained, the actor network executes decisions with sub-millisecond latency per step, resulting in overall simulation runtimes far lower than iterative optimization methods. This efficiency is critical for scalability to larger distribution grids.

Scalability Validation: To test scalability, additional simulations were performed with doubled network size (by replicating the IEEE 33-bus feeder into a 66-bus equivalent). Results indicate that the DDPG training time increased approximately linearly with system size, yet inference latency remained below 10 ms per timestep. This confirms that while training is computationally intensive, the deployment stage remains feasible for larger grids. Moreover, memory requirements scale with the size of the replay buffer rather than directly with the number of buses, making the approach suitable for distribution networks of practical scale.

7.14. Discussion of System-Wide Impact

The simulation results reveal several system-level benefits stemming from the integration of AI-driven digital twins within climate-adaptive power grid operations. Key insights are summarized as follows:

- Voltage Stability: The AI controller consistently maintains nodal voltages within regulatory thresholds (e.g., IEEE 1547, EN 50160), thereby reducing equipment stress and enhancing asset longevity through improved voltage quality and transient suppression.
- Energy Efficiency: Through real-time optimization of DER dispatch and battery cycling, the framework significantly reduces active power losses. This improvement not only enhances network efficiency but also creates technical headroom for increased renewable hosting capacity without necessitating major infrastructure upgrades.
- AI Learning Robustness: Convergence patterns in cumulative reward trajectories validate that the reinforcement learning agent learns stable, generalizable policies under a range of stochastic climate scenarios. This confirms the viability of climate-aware AI for long-term autonomous grid control.
- Operational Resilience: The system demonstrates accelerated recovery from voltage disturbances and supply–demand mismatches during extreme weather conditions. This characteristic positions the proposed framework as a viable tool for national adaptation strategies under evolving climate risk profiles.

Collectively, these findings underscore the transformative potential of AI-integrated digital twins as proactive, self-optimizing control agents for future smart grids. Beyond technical performance, the framework aligns with strategic objectives of regulatory compliance, decarbonization, cost containment, and infrastructure resilience, making it well suited for deployment in both developed and climate-vulnerable regions.

Comparison with Existing Methods: To further validate the contribution, the proposed DDPG-based controller was compared with baseline optimization methods (GA, PSO) and a control-oriented benchmark (MPC). As shown in Table 3, the proposed approach achieves significantly lower runtime per episode (18 s vs. 60–120 s for optimization-based methods). In terms of voltage deviation minimization, DDPG outperformed GA and PSO by 12–15% while achieving comparable performance to MPC but at a fraction of the runtime. These results confirm that reinforcement learning provides a practical balance between computational scalability and control quality. Unlike optimization methods, which must be solved anew for each scenario, the trained RL agent generalizes across different climate disturbances, making it particularly well suited for real-time climate-adaptive grid management.

7.15. Sensitivity Analysis

To assess robustness, a sensitivity study was conducted on two dimensions: (i) reward weight selection $(\lambda_1, \lambda_2, \lambda_3, \lambda_4)$, and (ii) climate variability severity. For reward weights, $\pm 20\%$ perturbations were applied around the tuned values. Voltage deviation and loss minimization performance varied by less than 7%, indicating stable controller behavior. For climate inputs, synthetic disturbances (e.g., intensified heatwaves, low-irradiance storms) were injected. The DDPG agent maintained effective operation, with only minor increases in curtailment (under 5%). These findings demonstrate that the proposed framework is resilient to parameter uncertainty and extreme climate perturbations.

8. Conclusions and Future Work

This paper proposed and validated an AI-integrated digital twin co-simulation framework for climate-adaptive control in renewable rich distribution networks. The framework combines reinforcement learning with a modular, physics-informed co-simulation environment to dynamically coordinate distributed energy resources (DERs), battery energy storage systems (BESSs), and load-side flexibility in response to climate-induced grid stress.

The results confirm that the proposed architecture achieves:

- Significant improvements in voltage stability, with a reduction in both frequency and severity of nodal violations;
- Lower active power losses and enhanced energy efficiency through optimal dispatch of DERs and storage units;
- Strong policy generalization across diverse climate perturbation scenarios, with median resilience scores consistently exceeding 0.85;
- System-wide resilience enhancements, including reduced load shedding, faster disturbance recovery, and improved operational continuity.

Beyond technical performance, the framework supports regulatory compliance, expansion of DER hosting capacity, and long-term infrastructure resilience. These attributes underscore its relevance to utilities and policymakers seeking robust solutions to escalating climate uncertainties.

Limitations and Future Work

Future research will pursue several directions to strengthen the capabilities and practical adoption of the proposed framework:

- Hardware-in-the-Loop (HIL) Integration: Coupling the digital twin with real-time simulation platforms or physical testbeds to validate control performance under hardware and communication constraints.
- Multi-Agent Reinforcement Learning (MARL): Extending the single-agent design to distributed multi-agent settings, enabling localized intelligence and peer-to-peer coordination among grid-edge assets.
- Cybersecurity Co-Design: Embedding trust-aware AI agents and blockchain-based protocols to secure the control pipeline against spoofing, tampering, and adversarial attacks.
- Socio-Technical Metrics: Incorporating equity, vulnerability, and community acceptance into the reward function to align reinforcement learning decisions with principles of climate justice and social resilience.
- Scalability Assessment: Evaluating the framework across multiple feeders and interconnected microgrids to establish its tractability and economic feasibility at scale.

Several limitations must also be acknowledged. Training the DDPG agent requires substantial computational resources, as each episode entails full-day simulations across climate and grid states. While convergence was achieved within a reasonable number of episodes (2000), scaling to larger systems or higher-resolution simulations would markedly increase training cost and memory demands. Furthermore, the transferability of models trained in simulation to real-world systems remains an open challenge, requiring domain randomization or transfer learning. Finally, HIL experiments and distributed training strategies are essential to ensure scalability and feasibility for national-scale grid deployments. Addressing these limitations represents a critical avenue for advancing the readiness of AI-powered digital twin controllers in next-generation sustainable energy systems.

Author Contributions: Writing—original draft, K.A.; Supervision, M.K. and E.E.O. All authors have read and agreed to the published version of the manuscript.

Funding: This research received no external funding.

Data Availability Statement: The original contributions presented in this study are included in the article. Further inquiries can be directed to the corresponding author.

Conflicts of Interest: The authors declare no conflicts of interest.

References

1. Zlateva, P.; Hadjitodorov, S. An Approach for Analysis of Critical Infrastructure Vulnerability to Climate Hazards. *IOP Conf. Ser. Earth Environ. Sci.* **2022**, *1094*, 012004. [CrossRef]
2. Ho, C.K.; Roesler, E.L.; Nguyen, T.A.; Ellison, J. Potential Impacts of Climate Change on Renewable Energy and Storage Requirements for Grid Reliability and Resource Adequacy. *J. Energy Resour. Technol. Trans. ASME* **2023**, *145*, 100904. [CrossRef]
3. Ali, A.M.; Shaaban, M.F.; Sindi, H. Optimal Operational Planning of RES and HESS in Smart Grids Considering Demand Response and DSTATCOM Functionality of the Interfacing Inverters. *Sustainability* **2022**, *14*, 13209. [CrossRef]
4. Younis, A.; Benders, R.M.J.; Ramírez, J.; de Wolf, M.; Faaij, A. Scrutinizing the Intermittency of Renewable Energy in a Long-Term Planning Model via Combining Direct Integration and Soft-Linking Methods for Colombia's Power System. *Energies* **2022**, *15*, 7604. [CrossRef]
5. Fernandes, S.V.; Joao, D.V.; Cardoso, B.B.; Martins, M.A.I.; Carvalho, E.G. Digital Twin Concept Developing on an Electrical Distribution System—An Application Case. *Energies* **2022**, *15*, 2836. [CrossRef]
6. Chalal, L.; Saadane, A.; Rachid, A. Unified Environment for Real Time Control of Hybrid Energy System Using Digital Twin and IoT Approach. *Sensors* **2023**, *23*, 5646. [CrossRef] [PubMed]
7. Benchekroun, A.; Davigny, A.; Hassam-Ouari, K.; Courtecuisse, V.; Robyns, B. Grid-Aware Energy Management System for Distribution Grids Based on a Co-Simulation Approach. *IEEE Trans. Power Deliv.* **2023**, *38*, 3571–3581. [CrossRef]
8. Qi, Y.; Li, J. The Wind and Photovoltaic Power Forecasting Method Based on Digital Twins. *Appl. Sci.* **2023**, *13*, 8374. [CrossRef]

9. Chen, H.; Zhang, Z.; Karamanakos, P.; Rodriguez, J. Digital Twin Techniques for Power Electronics-Based Energy Conversion Systems: A Survey of Concepts, Application Scenarios, Future Challenges, and Trends. *IEEE Ind. Electron. Mag.* **2023**, *17*, 20–36. [CrossRef]
10. Song, Z.; Hackl, C.M.; Anand, A.; Thommessen, A.; Petzschmann, J.; Kamel, O.Z.; Braunbehrens, R.; Kaifel, A.K.; Roos, C.; Hauptmann, S. Digital Twins for the Future Power System: An Overview and a Future Perspective. *Sustainability* **2023**, *15*, 5259. [CrossRef]
11. Mahankali, R. Digital Twins and Enterprise Architecture: A Framework for Real-Time Manufacturing Decision Support. *Int. J. Comput. Eng. Technol.* **2025**, *16*, 578–587. [CrossRef]
12. Han, J.; Hong, Q.; Syed, M.H.; Khan, M.A.U.; Yang, G.; Burt, G.; Booth, C. Cloud-Edge Hosted Digital Twins for Coordinated Control of Distributed Energy Resources. *IEEE Trans. Cloud Comput.* **2023**, *11*, 1242–1256. [CrossRef]
13. Yang, Y.; Javanroodi, K.; Nik, V.M. Climate Change and Renewable Energy Generation in Europe—Long-Term Impact Assessment on Solar and Wind Energy Using High-Resolution Future Climate Data and Considering Climate Uncertainties. *Energies* **2022**, *15*, 302. [CrossRef]
14. Webster, M.; Fisher-Vanden, K.; Kumar, V.; Lammers, R.B.; Perla, J.M. Integrated Hydrological, Power System and Economic Modelling of Climate Impacts on Electricity Demand and Cost. *Nat. Energy* **2022**, *7*, 163–169. [CrossRef]
15. Chreng, K.; Lee, H.S.; Tuy, S. A Hybrid Model for Electricity Demand Forecast Using Improved Ensemble Empirical Mode Decomposition and Recurrent Neural Networks with ERA5 Climate Variables. *Energies* **2022**, *15*, 7434. [CrossRef]
16. Salehimehr, S.; Taheri, B.; Sedighizadeh, M. Short-Term Load Forecasting in Smart Grids Using Artificial Intelligence Methods: A Survey. *J. Eng.* **2022**, *2022*, 1133–1142. [CrossRef]
17. Barwar, S. Artificial Intelligence Application to Flexibility Provision in Energy Management System: A Survey. In *EAI/Springer Innovations in Communication and Computing*; Springer: Berlin/Heidelberg, Germany, 2023; pp. 55–78. [CrossRef]
18. Liu, Y.; Lu, Q.; Yu, Z.; Chen, Y.; Yang, Y. Reinforcement Learning-Enhanced Adaptive Scheduling of Battery Energy Storage Systems in Energy Markets. *Energies* **2024**, *17*, 5425. [CrossRef]
19. Shojaeighadikolaei, A.; Ghasemi, A.; Jones, K.R.; Dafalla, Y.M.; Bardas, A.G.; Ahmadi, R.; Hashemi, M. Distributed Energy Management and Demand Response in Smart Grids: A Multi-Agent Deep Reinforcement Learning Framework. *arXiv* **2022**, arXiv:2211.15858. [CrossRef]
20. Abdoune, F.; Nouiri, M.; Cardin, O.; Castagna, P. Integration of Artificial Intelligence in the Life Cycle of Industrial Digital Twins. *Adv. Control Optim. Dyn. Syst.* **2022**, *55*, 2545–2550. [CrossRef]
21. Barbierato, L.; Mazzarino, P.R.; Montarolo, M.; Macii, A.; Patti, E.; Bottaccioli, L. A Comparison Study of Co-Simulation Frameworks for Multi-Energy Systems: The Scalability Problem. *Energy Inform.* **2022**, *5*, 53. [CrossRef]
22. Barbierato, L.; Pons, E.; Bompard, E.F.; Rajkumar, V.S.; Palensky, P.; Bottaccioli, L.; Patti, E. Exploring Stability and Accuracy Limits of Distributed Real-Time Power System Simulations via System-of-Systems Cosimulation. *IEEE Syst. J.* **2023**, *17*, 3354–3365. [CrossRef]
23. Pham, L.N.H.; Wagle, R.; Tricarico, G.; Melo, A.F.S.; Rosero-Morillo, V.A.; Shukla, A.; Gonzalez-Longatt, F. Real-Time Cyber-Physical Power System Testbed for Optimal Power Flow Study Using Co-Simulation Framework. *IEEE Access* **2024**, *12*, 150914–150929. [CrossRef]
24. Værbak, M.; Billanes, J.D.; Jørgensen, B. A Digital Twin Framework for Simulating Distributed Energy Resources in Distribution Grids. *Energies* **2024**, *17*, 2503. [CrossRef]
25. Ye, Y.; Papadaskalopoulos, D.; Yuan, Q.; Tang, Y.; Strbac, G. Multi-Agent Deep Reinforcement Learning for Coordinated Energy Trading and Flexibility Services Provision in Local Electricity Markets. *IEEE Trans. Smart Grid* **2023**, *14*, 1541–1554. [CrossRef]
26. Gligor, A.; Dumitru, C.D.; Dziţac, S.; Simó, A. Augmented Cyber-physical Model for Real-time Smart-grid Co-simulation. *Int. J. Comput. Commun. Control* **2025**, *20*. [CrossRef]
27. Alahmadi, A.; Barri, A.; Aldhahri, R.; Elhag, S. AI Driven Approaches in Swarm Robotics—A Review. *Int. J. Comput. Inform.* **2024**, *3*, 100–133. [CrossRef]
28. Zhou, G.; Tian, W.; Buyya, R.; Xue, R.; Song, L. Deep Reinforcement Learning-Based Methods for Resource Scheduling in Cloud Computing: A Review and Future Directions. *Artif. Intell. Rev.* **2024**, *57*, 124. [CrossRef]
29. Yu, Q.; Ketzler, G.; Mills, G.; Leuchner, M. Exploring the Integration of Urban Climate Models and Urban Building Energy Models through Shared Databases: A Review. *Theor. Appl. Climatol.* **2025**, *156*, 266. [CrossRef]
30. Zhu, C.; Yang, J.; Zhang, W.; Zheng, Y. An Algorithm that Excavates Suboptimal States and Improves Q-learning. *Eng. Res. Express* **2024**, *6*, 4. [CrossRef]
31. Wang, H.; Yuan, X.; Ren, Q. Learning to Recover for Safe Reinforcement Learning. *arXiv* **2023**, arXiv:2309.11907. [CrossRef]
32. Ebrie, A.S.; Kim, Y.J. Reinforcement Learning-Based Multi-Objective Optimization for Generation Scheduling in Power Systems. *Systems* **2024**, *12*, 106. [CrossRef]
33. Tulger Kara, G.; Elbir, T. Evaluation of ERA5 and MERRA-2 Reanalysis Datasets over the Aegean Region, Türkiye. *Fen-MüHendislik Derg.* **2024**, *26*, 9–21. [CrossRef]

4. *IEEE Std 1547-2018 (Revision of IEEE Std 1547-2003)*; IEEE Standard for Interconnection and Interoperability of Distributed Energy Resources with Associated Electric Power Systems Interfaces. IEEE: New York, NY, USA, 2018; pp. 1–138. [CrossRef]
5. *EN 50160*; Voltage Characteristics of Electricity Supplied by Public Distribution Systems. European Committee for Electrotechnical Standardization (CENELEC): Brussels, Belgium, 2010.

energies

MDPI

Article

Multi-Agent-Based Coordinated Voltage Regulation Technique in an Unbalanced Distribution System

Swathi Tangi [1], Dattatraya N. Gaonkar [2], Ramakrishna S S Nuvvula [3,*], Ahmed Ali [4,*] and Syed Riyaz Ahammed [5]

1 Department of Electrical and Electronics, Manipal Institute of Technology, Manipal Academy of Higher Education (MAHE), Manipal 576104, India; swathi.tangi@manipal.edu
2 Department of Electrical and Electronics, National Institute of Technology Karnataka, Surathkal 575025, India; dngaonkar@gmail.com
3 Nitte (Deemed to be University), NMAM Institute of Technology (NMAMIT), Department of Electrical and Electronics, Mangalore 575018, India
4 Department of Electrical and Electronic Engineering Technology, Faculty of Engineering and the Built Environment, University of Johannesburg, Johannesburg 2006, South Africa
5 Nitte (Deemed to be University), NMAM Institute of Technology (NMAMIT), Department of Electronics and Communication, Mangalore 575018, India; dd.international@nitte.edu.in
* Correspondence: ramakrishna.n@nitte.edu.in (R.S.S.N.); aali@uj.ac.za (A.A.)

Abstract: Unbalanced active distribution networks must be carefully analyzed to minimize undesirable implications from internal unbalances and the incorporation of intermittent sources, such as DG (Distributed Generation). A coordinated voltage regulation mechanism is being created employing a MAS (Multi-Agent System) control structure to solve the difficulties mentioned earlier. The proposed technique increases coordination between DGs and Shunt capacitors (SCs) to optimize the voltage profile and reduce overall power losses, along with voltage and current unbalanced factors in the proposed unbalanced 3-phase radial distribution network. To ensure improved real-time monitoring, PMUs (Phasor Measurement Units) measure the state parameters of the above-regulated distribution network in realtime. Because it does not necessitate the placement of PMUs at all nodes for total network observability, it is a cost-effective technique for estimating network state. The IEEE standard, a 25-bus unbalanced 3-phase distribution network feeder, is used to assess the viability of the recommended technique. MATLAB R2024a programming is used to simulate the case studies.

Keywords: unbalanced distribution network; voltage regulation; phasor measurement unit; multi-agent system; distributed generation

1. Introduction

Due to unpredictable power supply, distribution networks become more complex when integrating intermittent sources, like distributed generation (DG). Enhancing the utilization of energy depends on managing DG in unbalanced networks effectively. Internal unbalances in active distribution networks can impair stability and effectiveness and affect the quality of consumers' power. These unbalances must be corrected for distribution systems to be dependable and effective. This research intends to improve unbalance in the system and DG integration for reliable power delivery. The continuous enlargement of the distribution network due to increasing load demand and substantial evolution of distributed generation (DG) is one of the critical research areas in the electrical engineering domain. DG penetration into distribution networks transforms them from passive to

https://doi.org/10.3390/en18215829

active systems, which could impact the entire power system's dynamics, particularly the distribution networks [1]. Power electronic voltage source inverters are frequently used to interface DG systems. Power quality will be a significant challenge in networks with increased power electronics interfacing with DGs and loads as well as increased nonlinear loads. Among the many power quality challenges, unbalanced voltage is one of the most serious [2]. Voltage regulation becomes difficult when network voltages are unbalanced because the unbalanced voltage's negative-sequence component causes oscillations with a double fundamental frequency in both reactive and active power injections [3]. Moreover, an unbalanced network can support less photovoltaic (PV) generation before the critical voltage limit is reached [4].

Many scholarly contributions have been made to address the issues mentioned earlier. Based on strong and weak mutual Var compensation effects, a novel inter-phase coordinated consensus technique is proposed in the paper [5] to overcome the voltage regulation challenges arising from unbalanced photovoltaic systems. In coordination with the distribution system operator, an ideal hierarchical control technique is proposed for handling reactive power injection of electrical vehicle chargers located geologically nearby. This system uses a linear quadratic regulator (LQR) that prevents voltage sag/swell [6]. Voltage source converters (VSCs) are used as reactive power sources in the proposed controller. It coordinates with conventional controllers without substantially modifying the current distribution grid's control and operation architecture [7]. The distributed voltage control scheme based on the time-graded control strategy is presented. In case of regulative need, the coordination scheme enables prioritization of control devices adjustments in for photovoltaic plants, ensuring they are configured prior to the other connected devices according to the time synchronization schedule [8]. In [9], a novel controller parameter tuning method is proposed based on a virtual-time delay scheme to moderate the adverse effects of simultaneous and non-simultaneous operations of traditional voltage regulating devices and distributed generation units. In reference [10], an innovative multi-phase zonal-based coordination method is proposed to control network voltages within limits and mitigate the overuse of regulating devices. The authors of [11] presented an integrated multi-agent system architecture in which each voltage regulator is treated as an independent control agent that operates based on changes in the network topology to minimize voltage deviations. The research paper in ref. [12] provides a hybrid online approach for optimum coordination of plug-in electric vehicles (PEVs) that performs voltage regulation and improves voltage unbalance with local auxiliary voltage assistance through dynamic PEV switching. An on-load tap changer's post-contingency slow-timescale curative activities are coordinated with solar inverters and battery energy storage system's fast-timescale curative activities using a multi-time scale optimization method in [13]. The differential evolution optimization technique is used to elucidate the coordination between electric vehicles and distributed generations to improve the distribution system's performance [14]. A two-stage stochastic approach using the co-optimization method is presented to handle short and long-term period voltage issues [15]. The research paper in reference [16] provides a two-level coordination model for distributed generation and soft open point scheduling in unbalanced distribution networks considering their regulating capacities. In the studies, a multi-objective optimization model is used to coordinate the operation of fast and slow voltage regulators [17–19].

The papers in references [20–22] tackles real-time voltage control in power systems using a unique algorithm called EC-MADRL. Its operation is analogous to a strategy game involving various components like energy storage, compensators, and flexible loads, intending to minimize power loss from solar panels. The algorithm is designed to be efficient and flexible, and simulations show that it works better than other methods, ensuring stable voltage while wasting as little solar power as possible, on IEEE 33-bus test systems. The papers in references [23–25] presents an innovative voltage regulator control strategy for unbalanced distribution systems (UDS) with photovoltaic (PV) integration. Using a multi-agent system (MAS) architecture, it optimizes voltage regulation while adapting to changing UDS conditions [26]. This method ensures robust performance under normal operation and during system failures, as demonstrated throughsimulations on IEEE 34-node and 123-node distribution test feeders with high PV penetration and varying sun profiles [27–30]. The reference papers [31,32] present a cooperative voltage control strategy using a multi-agent system to manage high PV penetration challenges. It optimizes voltage regulation by coordinating voltage regulators with PV inverter reactive power control [33]. Simulations on IEEE 34-bus and 123-bus test feeders demonstrate their effectiveness under diverse 24 h operating conditions [11]. The paper in [34] introduces a distributed multi-objective optimization model to coordinate PV inverter fast dispatch with the slower dispatch of on-load tap changers and capacitor banks in unbalanced three-phase distribution systems. While existing studies often rely on centralized control, this approach decentralizes the coordination, mitigating single points of failure and reducing the computational load for more effective voltage regulation.

When viewed in the context of earlier studies, the need for a distinct approach becomes clear. While several methods have been proposed for voltage regulation in distribution networks, most are developed for balanced systems, rely on centralized control, or consider the operation of a single type of device, such as DG units, shunt capacitors, or OLTCs in isolation. In contrast, the present work adopts a coordinated MAS framework that integrates optimal PMU placement for cost-effective real-time monitoring and complete system observability. The method simultaneously coordinates DGs and SCs through voltage-sensitivity and loss-sensitivity analysis, with specific emphasis on unbalanced three-phase radial distribution networks. The proposed approach is flexible and scalable, making it applicable to any radial feeder irrespective of feeder length, lateral complexity, or variations in the X/R ratio. This combination of MAS-based coordination, PMU-assisted monitoring, and joint DG–SC operation in unbalanced networks has not been reported in earlier literature and constitutes the key distinguishing feature of this study.

This paper presents a coordinated operation of DGs and SCs in an unbalanced distribution network for voltage regulation to minimize voltage deviation, power loss, and voltage and current balance factors and improve the overall network's voltage profile. The MAS technique is employed in this work for optimal voltage regulator selection, and it is simulated on an IEEE 3-phase, 25-bus unbalanced radial distribution network.

The following are the major contributions of this paper:

(1) Introduced a Multi-Agent System (MAS) approach for optimal operation of Distributed Generators (DGs) and Switchable Capacitors (SCs) in unbalanced distribution networks, specifically targeting efficient voltage regulation.
(2) Integrates an optimal PMU placement strategy within the proposed MAS framework to enable cost-effective real-time monitoring and ensure full observability of unbalanced radial networks, thereby supporting the coordinated operation of DGs and SCs.
(3) The usage of PMUs helps to monitor the electrical parameters (voltage/current) via a conjoint time basis for synchronization, which helps the MAS controller get its agent's data at specified timestamp events.
(4) The proposed technique can be applied to any UDN radial structure, regardless of the feeder length, innumerable laterals/sub-laterals, or X/R ratio fluctuations.

2. Problem Formulation

Inherently, distribution systems are unbalanced. An unbalanced system, as used in the context of electrical distribution systems, is one in which the three phases of the system (often denoted by the letters A, B, and C) do not have equal voltage magnitudes or phase angles. In an unbalanced system, one or more of the following conditions may exist:

- ➢ Voltage Magnitude Unbalance: The three phases' voltages have different magnitudes. This indicates that a phase's voltage may be higher or lower than the other phases.
- ➢ Phase Angle Unbalance: The phase angles of the voltages in the three phases are not evenly spaced at 120 degrees. This can lead to phase shifts between the phases, causing various issues in the system.
- ➢ Asymmetrical Load: The load connected to each phase is different. Some phases may carry significantly more load than others, leading to an uneven power distribution.

Systems can become out of balance for several reasons, such as an uneven load distribution, system flaws, or an unbalance in the generation sources. Managing unbalanced systems can be tricky since they can lead to problems like unstable voltage and fluctuations, which can lead to a rise in distribution system losses and decreased power quality and cause problems for connected equipment. Resources are not used effectively because some phases can be overloaded while others need to be utilized more. Research in this area, as mentioned in the previous context, is crucial for optimizing the performance of distribution networks, especially in the presence of distributed generation and other complex loads. Advanced control and regulation techniques are needed to address these challenges. To avoid catastrophic errors due to internal unbalances in the system, careful analysis of the distribution system with a detailed component model is required.

2.1. Feeder Modeling of 3-Phase Unbalanced Distribution Network

Since the distribution network is made up of single, two, and three phase non-converting phase lines serving unbalanced loads, mutual and self-impedance conditions of the line conductors need to be maintained, and the path of return conductor to earth for unbalanced current needs to be considered. Using modified Carson equations [18], a 4×4 primitive impedance matrix can be written for a three-phase feeder with a neutral conductor, shown in Figure 1.

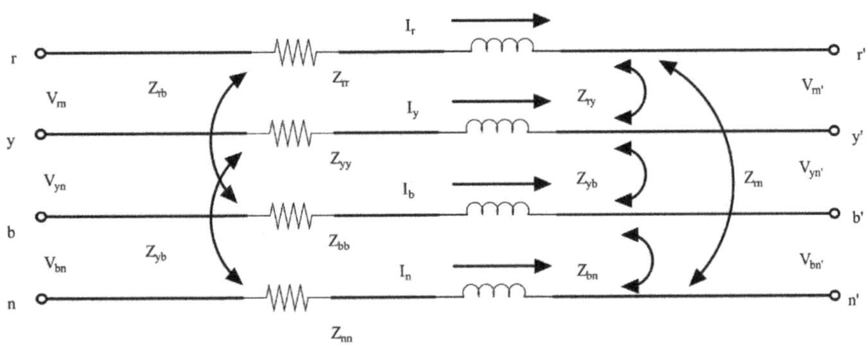

Figure 1. 3-Phase line section model. Where V_{rn}, V_{yn} and V_{bn} are the phase voltages of the phases (r, y and b) and the neutral conductor(n). Z_{rr}, Z_{yy}, Z_{bb}, and Z_{nn} represent self-impedances and Z_{ry}, Z_{yb}, Z_{rb}, and Z_{bn} are mutual impedances, respectively, in ohms per meter [Ω/m]. I_r, I_y, I_b and I_n are the branch currents. $V_{rn'}$, $V_{yn'}$ and $V_{bn'}$ are the phase voltages, the phases (r', y', and b'), and the neutral conductor (n').

$$\text{Primitive Impedance Matrix} = \left[Z_{rybn}\right] = \begin{bmatrix} Z_{rr} & Z_{ry} & Z_{rb} & Z_{rn} \\ Z_{yr} & Z_{yy} & Z_{yr} & Z_{yn} \\ Z_{br} & Z_{by} & Z_{bb} & Z_{bn} \\ Z_{nr} & Z_{ny} & Z_{nb} & Z_{nn} \end{bmatrix} \quad (1)$$

Thus, the receiving end voltages (V_r, V_y, V_b, and V_n) are related to the sending end side ($V_r{}'$, $V_y{}'$, $V_b{}'$, and $V_n{}'$) of the network depicted in Figure 1, as

$$\begin{bmatrix} V_r \\ V_y \\ V_b \\ V_n \end{bmatrix} = \begin{bmatrix} V_{r'} \\ V_{y'} \\ V_{b'} \\ V_{n'} \end{bmatrix} + \begin{bmatrix} Z_{rr} & Z_{ry} & Z_{rb} & Z_{rn} \\ Z_{yr} & Z_{yy} & Z_{yr} & Z_{yn} \\ Z_{br} & Z_{by} & Z_{bb} & Z_{bn} \\ Z_{nr} & Z_{ny} & Z_{nb} & Z_{nn} \end{bmatrix} \times \begin{bmatrix} I_r \\ I_y \\ I_b \\ I_n \end{bmatrix} \quad (2)$$

After applying Kron's reduction method, the neutral or ground wire's effects are still present in the model, as shown in Equation (3). The phase impedance matrix is given as

$$\left[Z_{ryb}\right] = \begin{bmatrix} Z_{rr-n} & Z_{ry-n} & Z_{rb-n} \\ Z_{yr-n} & Z_{yy-n} & Z_{yb-n} \\ Z_{br-n} & Z_{by-n} & Z_{bb-n} \end{bmatrix} \quad (3)$$

The receiving end voltages can be correlated with the sending end voltages of the depicted feeder in Figure 1 in the following manner:

$$\begin{bmatrix} V_r \\ V_y \\ V_b \end{bmatrix} = \begin{bmatrix} V_{r'} \\ V_{y'} \\ V_{b'} \end{bmatrix} + \begin{bmatrix} Z_{rr-n} & Z_{ry-n} & Z_{rb-n} \\ Z_{yr-n} & Z_{yy-n} & Z_{yb-n} \\ Z_{br-n} & Z_{by-n} & Z_{bb-n} \end{bmatrix} \times \begin{bmatrix} I_r \\ I_y \\ I_b \end{bmatrix} \quad (4)$$

The relevant load current injections I_{ir}, I_{iy}, and I_{ib} for bus i, corresponding to phases 'r', 'y', and 'b', are calculated as a function of bus voltage V_{ir}, V_{ir}, and V_{ir}.

$$I_{ir} = \left(\frac{P_{ir} + jQ_{ir}}{V_{ir}}\right)^* \quad (5)$$

$$I_{iy} = \left(\frac{P_{iy} + jQ_{iy}}{V_{iy}}\right)^* \quad (6)$$

$$I_{ib} = \left(\frac{P_{ib} + jQ_{ib}}{V_{ib}}\right)^* \quad (7)$$

Power fed into the phaser of the line (Figure 1) at the sending end bus is $V_r \cdot (I_r)^*$, and at the receiving end bus is $V_{r'} \cdot (I_r)^*$. Therefore, real and reactive power losses for phaser in the line (PL_r, QL_r) may be written as:

$$SL_r = PL_r + jQL_r = V_r \cdot (I_r)^* - V_{r'} \cdot (I_r)^* \quad (8)$$

Similarly, for phase-y and phase-b

$$SL_y = PL_y + jQL_y = V_y \cdot (I_y)^* - V_{y'} \cdot (I_y)^* \quad (9)$$

$$SL_b = PL_b + jQL_b = V_r \cdot (I_b)^* - V_{b'} \cdot (I_b)^* \quad (10)$$

2.2. Need for Voltage Regulation in an Unbalanced Active Distribution System

2.2.1. Effect of DG Integration

DG integration makes the distribution system active rather than passive since it changes the power flow and voltage profiles. DG penetration into the distribution system (DS) will cause the voltage at the point of connection of the DG to rise above the receiving end voltage, and power will be flowing both directions [19].

2.2.2. Effect of Unbalance in the Network

A voltage unbalance condition occurs when the line or phase voltages in a three-phase system deviate from their nominal balance state. A significant unbalance could drastically reduce equipment life cycles, speed up the additional component cycle, and significantly increase network operating and maintenance costs. A lower level of unbalance is desirable for improved system operation. According to IEEE standards, the percentage of unbalance is given in (11) and (12) is defined as follows [20]. A single line diagram of an electrical distribution network's equivalent branch is shown in Figure 2.

$$V_{ubf(\%)} = \frac{V_2}{V_1} \times 100 \quad (11)$$

where V_2 is the negative-sequence voltage component and V_1 is the positive-sequence voltage component.

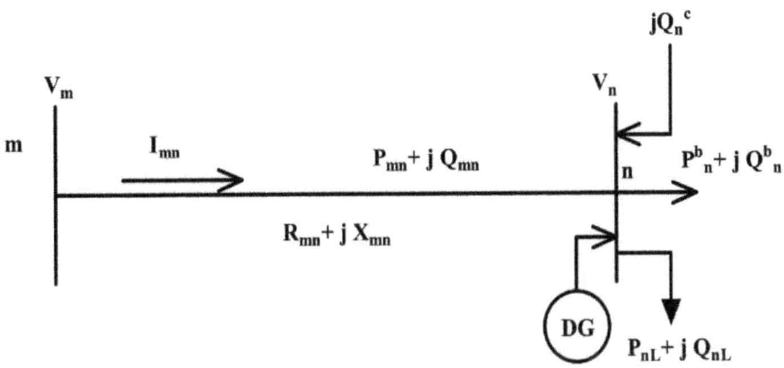

Figure 2. Single line diagram of an electrical distribution network's equivalent branch [21].

Current unbalance is caused by load deficiencies, which travel to the transformer and generate three-phase voltage unbalance. Even slight voltage unbalances considerably disrupt the current waveform on all the loads connected at the transformer level.

$$I_{ubf(\%)} = \frac{I_2}{I_1} \times 100 \quad (12)$$

where I_2 and I_1 are the negative- and positive-sequence current components, respectively. According to IEEE standards, voltage unbalance should be less than 3%, and current unbalance should be less than 20% under normal operating conditions. The +ve (positive) and −ve (negative) sequence components of voltage and current are V_1,V_2 and I_1,I_2 respectively, while the voltage and current unbalance factors are V_2/V_1 and I_2/I_1. As per standards, the nodes are presumed to be in the normal operating range [21,35].

Historically, distribution networks were passive and radial, ensuring stability under most conditions; therefore, stability concerns were not considered when designing distribution networks. Nonetheless, as the load unbalance and DG penetration of networks grows, their contribution to network security increases over time. As a result, voltage regulation is essential in these circumstances.

A sensitivity-based voltage regulation solution based on the MAS coordinated algorithm is implemented to overcome the aforementioned problems. For this study, two sensitivity techniques are being investigated as follows. The sensitivity-based methods for DG selection and capacitor placement are detailed in Sections 2.3 and 2.4.

2.3. Sensitivity Matrix Formulation for Voltage Regulation Using DG

In an unbalanced distribution network, voltage profile optimization is a significant challenge that can be performed by selecting the optimal DG units. Therefore, satisfactory results can only be obtained if assigned to the most appropriate nodes. Nonetheless, determining the optimal voltage-sensitive bus installed for DG selection is difficult. Voltage sensitivity analysis has been addressed in various ways in the literature. This section describes the evaluation of buses that are the most sensitive to DG selection. Equations (13) and (14) represent the real and reactive power of a node in a 'k' bus network [22–24].

$$P_m = |V_m| \sum_{n=1}^{K} |Y_{mn}||V_n| \cos(\theta_{mn} - \delta_m + \delta_n)$$

$$for\ j = 1, 2, 3, \ldots, k \tag{13}$$

$$Q_m = -|V_m| \sum_{n=1}^{K} |Y_{mn}||V_n| \sin(\theta_{mn} - \delta_m + \delta_n)$$

$$for\ j = 1, 2, 3, \ldots, k \tag{14}$$

From Equations (13) and (14), k is the number of nodes to a specific node, and $|V_n|, |V_m|$ are the voltage magnitudes of the nth and mth nodes, and δ_m, δ_n are the voltage phase angles at node m, n, and $|Y_{mn}|, \theta_{mn}$ are the node admittance magnitude and angle.

For the k-bus network, Equations (13) and (14) represent '2n' active power flow equations. Taking the partial derivative of (14) to voltage yields Equations (15) and (16).

$$\frac{\partial Q_m}{\partial |V_m|} = -2|V_m||Y_{mn}| \sin\theta_{mn} - \sum_{n \neq m} |V_n||Y_{mn}| \sin(\theta_{mn} - \delta_m + \delta_n) \tag{15}$$

$$\frac{\partial Q_m}{\partial |V_m|} = -|V_m||Y_{mn}| \sin(\theta_{mn} - \delta_m + \delta_n) \quad for\ n \neq m \tag{16}$$

As a result, the change in voltage equation at a node 'm' in response to the change in P and Q on every system node 'n' is reduced to (17)

$$\partial |V_m| \cong \sum_{n=1}^{K} \left(\frac{\partial |V_m|}{\partial P_n} \times dP_n + \frac{\partial |V_m|}{\partial Q_n} \times dQ_n \right) \tag{17}$$

The decoupled load flow nodal equation is expressed in matrix form as follows:

$$[dV] = [\frac{\partial V}{\partial Q}][dQ] \tag{18}$$

Equation (17) shows that the DG corresponding to node m is the one with the highest sensitivity value.

$$[dV_m] = [\frac{\partial V_m}{\partial Q_n}][dQ_n] \tag{19}$$

2.4. Loss Sensitivity Factor (LSF) Matrix Formulation for Capacitor Selection

Loss sensitivity analysis identifies the network's sensitive buses to install shunt capacitors (SCs) [25]. The buses with the highest LSF values are regarded as the most sensitive buses in the network. Equations (20) and (21) can indicate the active and reactive power losses that have occurred throughout branch "*mn*", respectively.

$$P_{loss[mn]} = \frac{\left((\mathrm{P}_n^b[\mathrm{eqi}])^2 + (\mathrm{Q}_n^b[\mathrm{eqi}])^2\right) \times R_{mn}}{(V_n)^2} \tag{20}$$

$$Q_{loss[mn]} = \frac{\left((\mathrm{P}_n^b[\mathrm{eqi}])^2 + (\mathrm{Q}_n^b[\mathrm{eqi}])^2\right) \times X_{mn}}{(V_n)^2} \tag{21}$$

By taking partially derivative Equations (20) and (21) concerning reactive power injection, the *LSF* value of every node in a distribution system is derived as follows.

$$LSF = \frac{dP_{Loss[mn]}}{dQ_n^b[eqi]} = \frac{2 \times Q_n^b[eqi] \times R_{mn}}{(\mathrm{V}_n)^2} \tag{22}$$

Buses with high *LSF* values are designated as sensitive buses for the installation of shunt capacitors.

3. Methodology

Multi-agent systems (MAS), the focus of this research, comprise autonomous entities called agents. Agents collaborate to complete tasks, but their intrinsic ability to learn and make independent judgments allows them to be more flexible. Through encounters with the other agents and the environment, agents learn new situations and activities. Agents then use their knowledge to identify and execute activities in the environment to achieve their tasks. MAS is highly suited to tackling problems in various technological applications due to its adaptability [26].

For the analysis of this proposed study, MAS architecture is divided into two sections: Agent control process and Management control process (Task manager).

(1) Agent control: The DG and SC agents will have access to the details of the network's installed DG and SCs and will regulate voltage locally. When a coordinated operation of voltage regulators is required, they interact with the MAS controller, which passes the duties to the agents to complete.

(2) Management control: The management controller receives data from the PMU agent and communicates with each DG/SC agent as needed.

PMU agent is a real-time monitoring device that continuously measures and stores data from the agents in the distribution network [27]. The functional interaction between DG agents, SC agents, the PMU agent, and the MAS task manager for coordinated voltage regulation in an active UDN is illustrated in Figure 3.

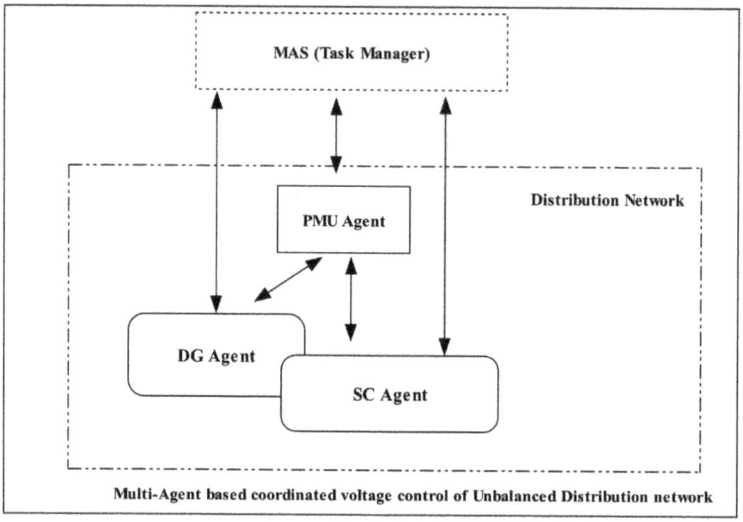

Figure 3. Block diagram of coordinated operation of voltage regulators in Active UDN using MAS Architecture.

3.1. Algorithm for DG Agent

The following steps represented in Algorithm 1 are used in the DG agent-based strategy for optimal selection of DGs for voltage regulation and loss minimization.

Algorithm 1: Voltage regulation of UDN using DG agent, based on sensitivity approach

1. Input the line and bus data of the unbalanced network.
2. Conduct a load flow analysis to determine the base case parameters for bus voltages, line losses, and voltage and current unbalance factors.
3. Create a vector G(x) is a replica of the given bus network and add all the branches as edges.
4. Add the reactance of every branch as edge weight find the shortest path from bus m to n add their corresponding weights.
5. Multiply 'Xmn' with 'Qn' and keep summing
6. Repeat the steps 4 to 5 for every bus to obtain their sensitivities
7. Calculate the sensitivity values of all DG-connected buses sort them in descending order and store the values in voltage-sensitive matrix Vs (y).
8. The DG Agent chooses the highest sensitive value from the Vs (y) matrix and picks those DGs for voltage regulation.
9. Repeat step 2 for each DG selection and check the bus voltages to ensure they are within the range (i.e., $0.95 \leq Vn \leq 1.05$ p.u.), reduction of total loss and unbalanced factors, etc.
10. if satisfied results are achieved
11. end the simulation
12. Print the PMU results
13. else select the next highest value from step 7 and repeat steps 8 to 12.
14. end.

The procedural steps outlined above for the DG agent are represented in the coordination flow diagram in Figure 4, which visualizes the decision-making process and tie-resolution logic used in the MAS.

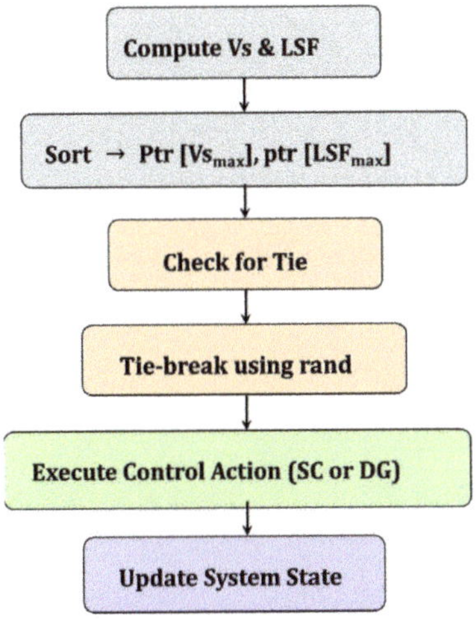

Figure 4. Flow diagram of MAS coordination and tie-resolution logic.

3.2. Algorithm for SC Agent

The SC agent-based approach for optimal selection of SCs problem to minimize the loss takes the following steps as per Algorithm 2.

Algorithm 2: Voltage regulation of UDN using SC agent, employing Loss sensitivity factor (LSF) approach

1. Input the data for the branch and load, as well as the bus voltage limitations.
2. Compute the Ploss[mn] and Qloss[mn] using load flow analysis.
3. Determine the sensitivity of real power loss to reactive power injection at each bus.
4. Organize the nodes according to their highest sensitivity levels and store the values in the LSF (z) vector.
5. The SC Agent chooses the highest sensitive value LSF vector and selects those SCs for loss minimization.
6. Check if the shunt capacitors' total compensation (Qnc) is less or equivalent to the network's net reactive load (QnL).
7. go to step 2 and check that the bus voltages are within the limits, reduction of loss and unbalanced factors, etc.
8. if the results are satisfied
9. end the simulation
10. Print the PMU results
11. else select the next highest value from step 5 and repeat steps 6 to 10.
12. Stop

Similarly, the SC agent's selection and coordination process, as explained above, is incorporated within the overall MAS control logic illustrated in Figure 5.

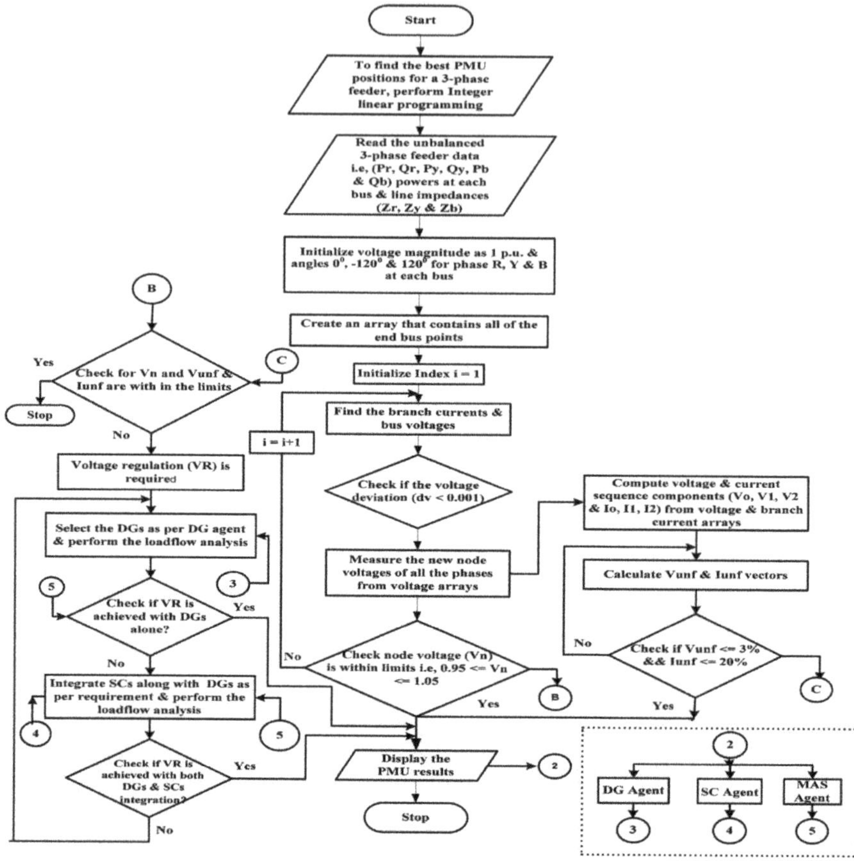

Figure 5. Flowchart of coordinated operation of voltage regulators in Active UDN using MAS Architecture.

3.3. Coordinated Operation of Voltage Regulators in Active UDN Using MAS Topology

In the proposed MAS, the supervisory controller computes the voltage sensitivity vector Vs and the line sensitivity factor vector LSF at each coordination cycle. These are sorted in descending order to form the index arrays ptr[Vsmax] and ptr[LSFmax], which identify the most effective control candidates among the shunt capacitors (SCs) and distributed generators (DGs). The controller first attempts to select the top-ranked agent from ptr[Vsmax] or ptr[LSFmax], depending on the control objective. If two or more agents have equal sensitivity values within a predefined threshold (e.g., $\pm 0.5\%$), a pseudo-random function (rand) is applied to select one agent, while the others are deferred to the next cycle. This prevents simultaneous conflicting actions on the same bus or feeder section. The random function is seeded once per cycle to ensure reproducibility in simulation while still introducing variability for fairness. The coordination cycle follows four steps: (i) compute ptr[Vsmax] and ptr[LSFmax]; (ii) apply sensitivity-based ranking; (iii) resolve ties using rand; and (iv) execute the selected control action and update the system state before the next cycle. This lightweight approach avoids explicit inter-agent communication yet ensures that only one control action is applied per location per cycle, thereby preventing oscillations and instability. The stepwise coordination process is illustrated in Figure 4.

The coordinated operation of voltage regulators in an active unbalanced distribution network (UDN) implemented though the proposed multi-agent system (MAS) architecture, as shown in Figure 5.

3.4. PMU (Phasor Measurement Unit)

Integrating a PMU into a bus will measure the voltage at the node and the currents from all the other buses connected to that bus as the output. It would be severely expensive to just place them everywhere. So, the optimal placement of PMUs is important in the elimination of redundant cost and information; when placed everywhere, there would be redundancy in the current data while also achieving total observability of the given system [28,29].

ILP (Integer Linear Programming)

ILP is the method used generally to minimize a linear function(x) based on some constraints. Here, we are trying to minimize the X (optimal placement solution) based on the constraint of $T_{pmu}X \geq b_{pmu}$.

Following is the optimal placement problem for N-bus systems formulated as an ILP.

$$\text{Minimize } \sum_{k=1}^{N} X_k \tag{23}$$

$$X = [x_1 x_2 \ldots x_N]^T \tag{24}$$

$$x_i \in \{0,1\} \tag{25}$$

where

Objective: Minimize the sum of PMU placements
Variables:
N: Number of buses in the system
X: Binary vector representing PMU placement decisions

$$\text{Subject to}: \ T_{pmu}X \geq b_{pmu}$$

TPMU (a, b) = 1, if a = b
=1, if a and b are connected
=0, if otherwise
T_{pmu}: Connection matrix indicating bus connections
b_{pmu}: Inequality constraints vector

Where 'k represents all' to 'buses connected to' from 'bus a'. X is PMU placement vector of binary values (0, 1), with 1 (ones) indicating placement buses, b_{pmu} is the inequality constraints vector, and a and b are from and to buses in the network.

$$b_{pmu} = [1\,1\,1\ \ldots\ldots\ 1]^T_{1\times N}$$

This pseudocode outlines the ILP formulation for the PMU placement problem. It aims to minimize the total number of PMUs placed while ensuring that each bus connected to others has at least one PMU. The constraints are based on the connection matrix 'T_{pmu}' and the inequality constraints vector 'b_{pmu}'. The objective is to optimize the placement of PMUs in the power system for effective monitoring while considering connectivity and constraint requirements.

This study uses PMU technology to measure the network's voltage and current parameters. Various strategies have been used to solve the Optimal Placement problem (OPP). This method presents the implementation of PMU optimal allocation utilizing the Integer Linear Programming approach for full observability of the system, which brings the electric utility network closer to intelligent grid communication technologies to enhance system monitoring settings. For the state estimation of an unbalanced, 3-phase, IEEE 25-bus radial distribution network, the methodology proposed in [30] is being used.

Although the proposed MAS framework was evaluated on the IEEE 25-bus unbalanced radial feeder, which is widely used as a benchmark in voltage regulation studies, the approach is not limited to small-scale systems. The MAS architecture's distributed decision-making and limited communication requirements make it inherently scalable to larger, more complex distribution networks. This scalability, combined with the optimal PMU placement strategy, enables efficient monitoring and control without a proportional increase in computational burden.

4. Results and Discussions

The proposed methodology is being used on a 25-bus, unbalanced 3-phase radial distribution system. The rated line voltage is 4.16 kV, the base MVA is 100, and the system data is given in [31].

An ILP analysis is utilized to identify the best PMU location for the test system. By implementing MATLAB programming, the simulation is completed for comprehensive system observability. The single-line diagram of the unbalanced 25-bus radial distribution system, as depicted in Figure 6, illustrates the network topology used in this study.

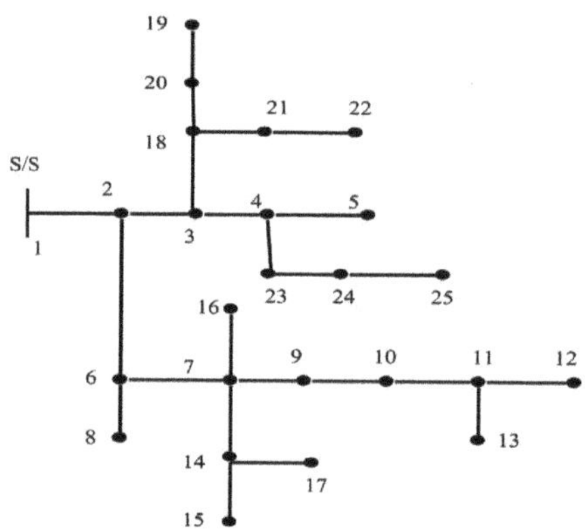

Figure 6. A single line representation of an unbalanced 25 bus, radial distribution system.

Table 1 shows the necessary number of PMUs and their positions in the test feeder for total system observability.

Table 1. Recommended PMU locations of a 25-bus unbalanced radial distribution system.

Number of PMUs	PMU Installed Nodes
9	1,4,7,8,11,14,20,22,25

The percentage unbalance in the 3-phase feeder is considered as follows. It is assumed that the load in the R-phase remains the same as in a balanced system, and the Y-phase load is reduced by x% while the B-phase load is increased by y% from the base case.

The case study analysis considers three scenarios: a system without voltage regulators, DG integration, and SC and DG integration. A detailed discussion of each scenario follows.

4.1. Scenario1—Without DG/SC Integration

In this case, the percentage of load unbalance is taken in steps of 10%, 20%, 30%, and 40% to observe the effect of unbalance in the system without DG/SC integration. With 10% in the load unbalance, the total load of phase R is 1333.8 kVA, phase Y is 1226.2 kVA, and phase B is 1465.9 kVA; with 20% in the load unbalance, the total load of phase R is 1333.8 kVA, phase Y is 1089.96 kVA, and phase B is 1599.23 kVA; with 30% in the load unbalance, the total load of phase R is 1333.8 kVA, phase Y is 953.71 kVA, and phase B is 1732.50 kVA; and with 40% in the load unbalance, the total load of phase R is 1333.8 kVA, phase Y is 817.47 kVA, and phase B is 1865.77 kVA, with power factor (PF) = 0.8.

Table 2 presents voltage magnitudes (VRph, VYph, and VBph in p.u.) without DG/SC. Figure 7 shows the voltage profile of 25-bus unbalanced 3-phase radial feeder networks without DG/SC using a PMU setup.

Table 2. Voltage magnitude (p.u.) results of unbalanced loading without DG/SC based on PMU data.

PMU Installed Bus No.	25 Bus Unbalanced, 3-Phase Radial Feeder Voltage Magnitude (p.u.) Using PMU Setup Without DG/SC											
	With 10% Unbalance			With 20% Unbalance			With 30% Unbalance			With 40% Unbalance		
	V_{Rph}	V_{Yph}	V_{Bph}	V_{Rph}	V_{Yph}	V_{Bph}	V_{Rph}	V_{Yph}	V_{Bph}	V_{Rph}	V_{Yph}	V_{Bph}
1	1.0000	1.0000	1.0000	1.0000	1.0000	1.0000	1.0000	1.0000	1.0000	1.0000	1.0000	1.0000
4	0.9479	0.9522	0.9418	0.9483	0.9579	0.9355	0.9487	0.9636	0.9292	0.9491	0.9691	0.9227
7	0.9322	0.9377	0.9238	0.9327	0.9453	0.9155	0.9332	0.9527	0.9070	0.9338	0.9600	0.8984
8	0.9491	0.9532	0.9427	0.9495	0.9589	0.9365	0.9499	0.9645	0.9302	0.9503	0.9699	0.9237
11	0.9156	0.9219	0.9046	0.9163	0.9314	0.8941	0.9170	0.9407	0.8834	0.9176	0.9498	0.8725
14	0.9251	0.9314	0.9159	0.9257	0.9397	0.9067	0.9263	0.9479	0.8974	0.9269	0.9559	0.8878
20	0.9434	0.9483	0.9353	0.9438	0.9545	0.9283	0.9443	0.9606	0.9213	0.9447	0.9667	0.9141
22	0.9420	0.9467	0.9348	0.9425	0.9531	0.9277	0.9429	0.9594	0.9206	0.9434	0.9656	0.9134
25	0.9432	0.9484	0.9371	0.9436	0.9546	0.9303	0.9441	0.9607	0.9234	0.9445	0.9667	0.9164

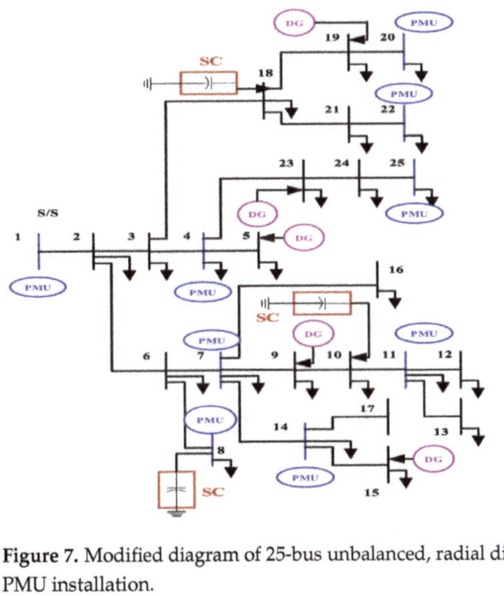

Figure 7. Modified diagram of 25-bus unbalanced, radial distribution test system with DGs, SCs, and PMU installation.

From the test results of scenario 1, as there is no change in load, the voltage profile of phase-R remains the same compared with the other two phases of the 3-phase feeder. The voltage profile of phase Y improved as the unbalance percentage increased, whereas the phase-B voltage magnitude profile was reduced with the increase in the percentage unbalance. Despite improvements in some phase voltage profiles, these unbalances caused some node voltage to fall below specifications, increasing the total power loss of the system.

Also, the analysis is being extended further by calculating the voltage and current unbalance factors of the above cases, which are tabulated in Table 3. It is noticed that the voltage unbalance factors are within the standard limits (i.e., <3%), but the current unbalance factor is increased to above the limit (i.e., <20%) in one of the cases as the load unbalance increases. The corresponding voltage profile of the 25-bus, 3-phase unbalanced feeder under various unbalance levels without DG/SC integration is shown in Figure 8.

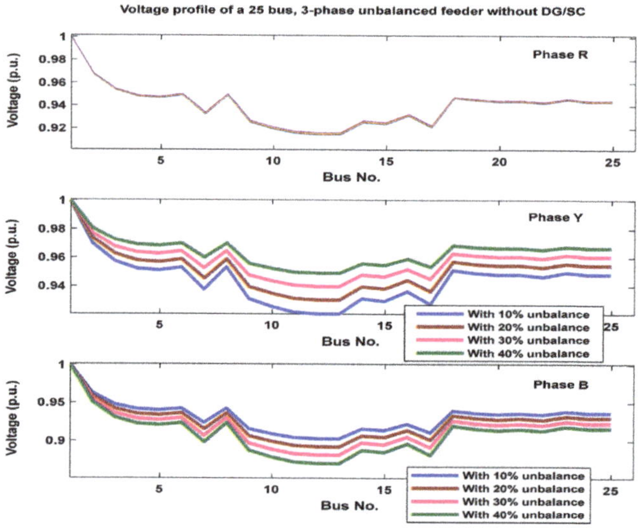

Figure 8. Voltage profile of a 25 bus, 3-phase unbalanced feeder without DG/SC.

Table 3. Voltage and current unbalance factor of a 25-bus unbalanced system with various loading conditions.

With 10% Unbalance		With 20% Unbalance		With 30% Unbalance		With 40% Unbalance	
Vubf (%)	**Iubf (%)**	**Vubf (%)**	**Iubf (%)**	**Vubf (%)**	**Iubf (%)**	**Vubf (%)**	**Iubf (%)**
0.0029	5.5095	0.0015	11.8665	0.0029	17.9968	0.0029	24.4526
0.1891	2.3656	0.3978	4.9548	0.6117	7.4036	0.8213	9.8374
0.2694	0.9455	0.5638	1.8891	0.8627	2.8468	1.1560	4.1245
0.2924	0.3654	0.6271	0.4506	0.9583	0.7349	1.2901	0.9479
0.3054	2.8269	0.6422	6.3522	0.9804	9.9467	1.3214	13.2040
0.2840	2.3226	0.6108	5.9027	0.9414	9.1393	1.2702	12.4299
0.3731	0	0.8086	0	1.2480	0	1.6888	0
0.2840	1.0669	0.6108	2.4920	0.9414	3.7469	1.2702	5.3788
0.4080	1.1124	0.8921	2.0167	1.3791	3.3854	1.8679	4.4321
0.4344	0.5908	0.9597	1.5480	1.4845	2.3649	2.0106	3.1856
0.4618	0.3654	1.0095	0.4886	1.5601	0.7349	2.1154	0.9479
0.4668	0.5965	1.0259	0.6668	1.5866	0.9518	2.1499	1.1692
0.4701	1.2955	1.0308	2.5150	1.5917	3.9756	2.1548	5.2500
0.4091	0.3671	0.8929	0.4227	1.3778	0.7887	1.8602	1.2290

Table 3. *Cont.*

With 10% Unbalance		With 20% Unbalance		With 30% Unbalance		With 40% Unbalance	
Vubf (%)	Iubf (%)	Vubf (%)	Iubf (%)	Vubf (%)	Iubf (%)	Vubf (%)	Iubf (%)
0.4107	0.2197	0.9047	0.4498	1.3973	0.5941	1.8970	0.9479
0.3784	0.7950	0.8213	1.6011	1.2690	2.5352	1.7176	3.1443
0.4371	1.4545	0.9466	2.8592	1.4597	4.0224	1.9701	5.2132
0.3194	0.9747	0.6596	1.3432	1.0013	2.0230	1.3395	2.3394
0.3484	0.3654	0.7041	0.7396	1.0624	0.9518	1.4149	1.1732
0.3658	0.2160	0.7289	0.9312	1.0939	1.5054	1.4566	1.9263
0.3322	0.2638	0.6905	0.3159	1.0494	0.7887	1.4109	1.0069
0.3329	0.4244	0.7007	1.0478	1.0700	1.6367	1.4423	2.0332
0.3143	0.4450	0.6621	0.7612	1.0080	1.0695	1.3615	1.2944
0.3279	0	0.6852	0	1.0433	0	1.3984	0
0.3279		0.6852		1.0433		1.3984	

4.2. Scenario2—With DG Integration

In this scenario, the percentages of load unbalance are taken as 30% and 40%, respectively, and DGs are incorporated as needed at each step of change in unbalance. Table 4 displays the real power (Pr), apparent power (Py), and reactive power (Qr, Qy, and Qb) generated by each Distributed Generator (DG) for each of the specified unbalanced percentages (30% and 40%).

Table 4. DG penetration and power generation at various buses for load unbalance scenarios.

Bus Location	DG Penetration Level	Pr_Total_DG (kW)	Py_Total_DG (kW)	Pb_Total_DG (kW)	Qr_Total_DG (kVAR)	Qy_Total_DG (kVAR)	Qb_Total_DG (kVAR)
5	10%	107.33	109.33	107.33	79.2	81.3	79
9	15%	160.995	163.995	160.995	118.8	121.95	118.5
15	20%	214.66	218.66	214.66	158.4	162.6	158
19	10%	107.33	109.33	107.33	79.2	81.3	79
23	15%	160.995	163.995	160.995	118.8	121.95	118.5

Figures 9 and 10 show the voltage profile, Tables 5 and 6 compare voltage magnitude measurements (VRph, VYph, and VBph in p.u.), and Tables 7 and 8 compare the voltage and current unbalanced factors of the test system with and without DG considering 30% and 40% unbalanced loading, whereas Table 8 presents the total power loss of the network. Table 5 represents the voltage magnitude (p.u.) results of the test system with 30% unbalanced loading, DG using PMU measurement. The table illustrates voltage magnitude results for a test system under unbalanced loading conditions, incorporating Distributed Generation (DG) at varying levels (10%, 15%, and 20%). It compares voltage magnitudes (VRph, VYph, and VBph) with and without DG. Through these comparisons, the impact of DG integration on system stability and voltage regulation can be observed, offering insights into the effectiveness of DG in mitigating voltage fluctuations and enhancing system performance under different loading conditions. Table 6 provides data examining voltage and current unbalance factors under a 30% unbalanced loading scenario, while varying the levels of Distributed Generation (DG) penetration. It compares these factors across different DG penetration levels: without DG/SC, with 10% DG, 15% DG, and 20% DG. This comparison allows for an assessment of how the integration of DG impacts both voltage and current unbalance factors, providing insights into the effectiveness of DG in mitigating unbalance issues within the system. Table 7 presents voltage magnitude results per unit (p.u.) obtained from PMU data under 40% unbalanced loading, both with and without Distributed Generation (DG). It compares voltage magnitudes for Red (VRph), Yellow (VYph), and Blue (VBph) phases across different DG penetration levels (0%, 10%, 15%, and 20%). This comparison enables an assessment of how DG integration influences voltage stability and regulation amidst unbalanced loading conditions.

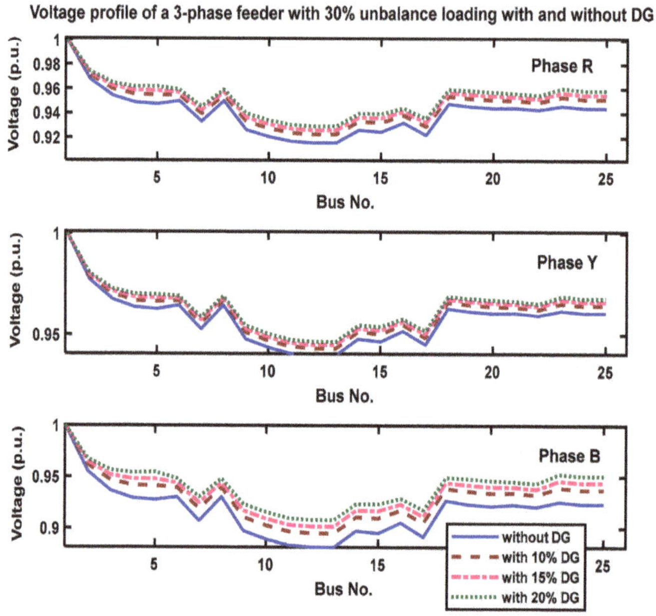

Figure 9. Voltage profile of a 3-phase feeder with 30% unbalanced loading, with and without DG.

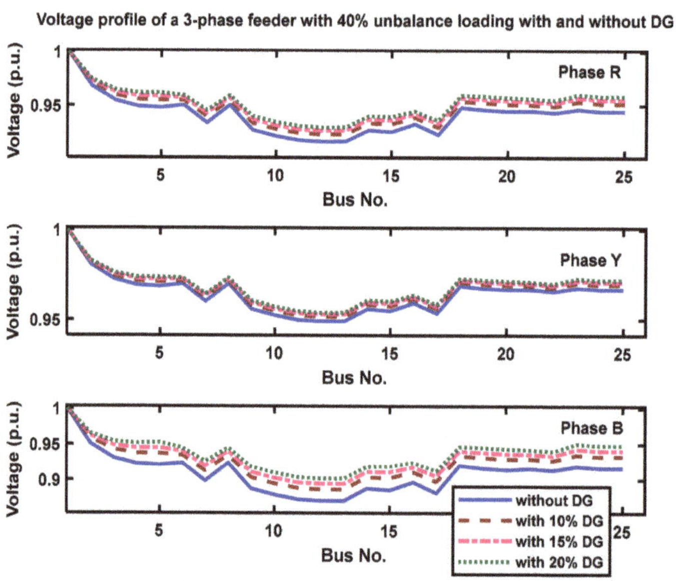

Figure 10. Voltage profile of a 3-phase feeder with 40% unbalanced loading, with and without DG.

Table 5. Voltage magnitude (p.u.) results of the test system with 30% unbalanced loading, DG using PMU measurement.

PMU Installed Bus No.	Voltage Magnitude (p.u.) Using PMU Setup with 30% Unbalanced Loading, with and Without DG											
	Without DG/SC			With 10% DG			With 15% DG			With 20% DG		
	V_{Rph}	V_{Yph}	V_{Bph}	V_{Rph}	V_{Yph}	V_{Bph}	V_{Rph}	V_{Yph}	V_{Bph}	V_{Rph}	V_{Yph}	V_{Bph}
1	1.0000	1.0000	1.0000	1.0000	1.0000	1.0000	1.0000	1.0000	1.0000	1.0000	1.0000	1.0000
4	0.9487	0.9636	0.9292	0.9553	0.9668	0.9416	0.9585	0.9685	0.9477	0.9617	0.9701	0.9538
7	0.9332	0.9527	0.9070	0.9393	0.9557	0.9189	0.9423	0.9572	0.9246	0.9453	0.9587	0.9303
8	0.9499	0.9645	0.9302	0.9546	0.9668	0.9393	0.9569	0.9680	0.9438	0.9592	0.9691	0.9482
11	0.9170	0.9407	0.8834	0.9238	0.9441	0.8968	0.9272	0.9458	0.9033	0.9305	0.9474	0.9097
14	0.9263	0.9479	0.8974	0.9331	0.9513	0.9105	0.9364	0.9529	0.9170	0.9397	0.9546	0.9233
20	0.9443	0.9606	0.9213	0.9508	0.9639	0.9339	0.9541	0.9656	0.9400	0.9573	0.9672	0.9461
22	0.9429	0.9594	0.9206	0.9489	0.9624	0.9321	0.9518	0.9639	0.9377	0.9547	0.9653	0.9432
25	0.9441	0.9607	0.9234	0.9513	0.9643	0.9371	0.9548	0.9661	0.9438	0.9584	0.9679	0.9505

Table 6. Voltage and current unbalance factors with 30% unbalance loading and various DG penetration levels.

Without DG/SC		With 10% DG		With 15% DG		With 20% DG	
Vubf (%)	Iubf (%)	Vubf (%)	Iubf (%)	Vubf (%)	Iubf (%)	Vubf (%)	Iubf (%)
0.0029	17.9968	0.0029	16.0814	0.0029	14.7420	0.0029	13.6286
0.6117	7.4036	0.4786	5.7669	0.4099	5.2360	0.3532	3.8410
0.8627	2.8468	0.6528	1.6164	0.5529	1.0489	0.4575	0.3857
0.9583	0.7349	0.7062	0.1207	0.5799	0.2030	0.4588	1.1605
0.9804	9.9467	0.7016	9.0846	0.5691	8.8760	0.4385	8.3034
0.9414	9.1393	0.7500	8.6685	0.6636	7.9712	0.5729	7.5291
1.2480	0	1.0003	0	0.8845	0	0.7689	0
0.9414	3.7469	0.7500	3.4586	0.6636	3.0899	0.5729	2.8606
1.3791	3.3854	1.1043	3.5710	0.9743	3.8095	0.8433	3.8627
1.4845	2.3649	1.2101	2.4124	1.0754	2.5735	0.9454	2.9823
1.5601	0.7349	1.2833	0.8281	1.1485	0.8834	1.0184	0.9484
1.5866	0.9518	1.3083	1.0725	1.1704	1.1442	1.0404	1.2283
1.5917	3.9756	1.3102	3.4586	1.1782	3.1456	1.0453	2.7319
1.3778	0.7887	1.1060	0.3902	0.9759	0.5559	0.8449	1.0080
1.3973	0.5941	1.1021	0.6694	0.9596	0.7141	0.8188	0.7666
1.2690	2.5352	1.0212	2.8567	0.9035	3.0475	0.7877	2.9929
1.4597	4.0224	1.1818	3.8406	1.0504	3.6414	0.9205	3.3235
1.0013	2.0230	0.7646	1.2062	0.6562	0.9911	0.5425	0.5957
1.0624	0.9518	0.8021	1.0725	0.6784	1.1442	0.5566	1.2283
1.0939	1.5054	0.8315	1.4695	0.7096	1.5676	0.5861	1.6829
1.0494	0.7887	0.8158	0.6373	0.7036	0.6798	0.5928	0.7298
1.0700	1.6367	0.8352	1.1073	0.7223	0.6554	0.6102	0.3591
1.0080	1.0695	0.7310	1.0005	0.5952	1.0674	0.4646	1.1458
1.0433	0	0.7636	0	0.6281	0	0.4917	0
1.0433		0.7636		0.6281		0.4917	

Table 7. Voltage magnitude (p.u.) results of PMU data with 40% unbalanced loading and DG.

Bus Location	Voltage (p.u.) Using PMU Setup with 40% Unbalanced Loading, with and Without DG											
	Without DG/SC			With 10% DG			With 15% DG			With 20% DG		
	V_{Rph}	V_{Yph}	V_{Bph}	V_{Rph}	V_{Yph}	V_{Bph}	V_{Rph}	V_{Yph}	V_{Bph}	V_{Rph}	V_{Yph}	V_{Bph}
1	1.0000	1.0000	1.0000	1.0000	1.0000	1.0000	1.0000	1.0000	1.0000	1.0000	1.0000	1.0000
4	0.9491	0.9691	0.9227	0.9556	0.9715	0.9374	0.9587	0.9727	0.9446	0.9619	0.9738	0.9516
7	0.9338	0.9600	0.8984	0.9397	0.9622	0.9124	0.9427	0.9633	0.9192	0.9456	0.9643	0.9259
8	0.9503	0.9699	0.9237	0.9549	0.9716	0.9345	0.9572	0.9725	0.9398	0.9594	0.9733	0.9450
11	0.9176	0.9498	0.8725	0.9243	0.9523	0.8884	0.9276	0.9535	0.8961	0.9309	0.9547	0.9037
14	0.9269	0.9559	0.8878	0.9335	0.9583	0.9034	0.9368	0.9595	0.9110	0.9401	0.9607	0.9185
20	0.9447	0.9667	0.9141	0.9511	0.9690	0.9290	0.9543	0.9702	0.9362	0.9575	0.9714	0.9433
22	0.9434	0.9656	0.9134	0.9492	0.9677	0.9269	0.9521	0.9688	0.9335	0.9550	0.9699	0.9400
25	0.9445	0.9667	0.9164	0.9516	0.9693	0.9326	0.9551	0.9706	0.9405	0.9585	0.9719	0.9482

Table 8. Voltage and current unbalance factor with 40% unbalance loading with various DG penetration levels.

Without DG/SC		With 10% DG		With 15% DG		With 20% DG	
Vubf (%)	Iubf (%)	Vubf (%)	Iubf (%)	Vubf (%)	Iubf (%)	Vubf (%)	Iubf (%)
0.0029	24.4526	0.0029	21.6642	0.0029	19.9715	0.0029	18.4623
0.8213	9.8374	0.6411	8.0299	0.5548	6.9854	0.4723	5.3043
1.1560	4.1245	0.8802	2.3803	0.7460	1.4294	0.6143	0.4842
1.2901	0.9479	0.9456	0.1213	0.7822	0.4844	0.6216	1.4724
1.3214	13.2040	0.9427	12.4614	0.7687	11.9517	0.5885	11.5074
1.2702	12.4299	1.0156	11.7546	0.8906	11.0613	0.7706	10.6972
1.6888	0	1.3561	0	1.1998	0	1.0395	0
1.2702	5.3788	1.0156	4.6841	0.8906	4.4333	0.7706	3.8794
1.8679	4.4321	1.4957	4.7966	1.3190	5.1340	1.1478	5.0108
2.0106	3.1856	1.6367	3.6227	1.4585	3.8015	1.2793	4.0918
2.1154	0.9479	1.7394	1.0780	1.5581	1.1539	1.3796	1.2420
2.1499	1.1692	1.7742	1.3297	1.5908	1.4232	1.4096	1.5319
2.1548	5.2500	1.7759	4.8484	1.5941	4.2062	1.4172	3.9093
1.8602	1.2290	1.4947	0.0867	1.3161	0.7750	1.1416	1.3003
1.8970	0.9479	1.4935	1.0780	1.3025	1.1539	1.1109	1.2420
1.7176	3.1443	1.3832	3.5758	1.2267	3.8273	1.0689	3.8416
1.9701	5.2132	1.5998	5.0685	1.4212	4.8753	1.2466	4.4794
1.3395	2.3394	1.0256	1.4667	0.8771	0.9995	0.7286	0.5430
1.4149	1.1732	1.0693	1.3342	0.9024	1.4281	0.7376	1.5371
1.4566	1.9263	1.1100	2.1906	0.9414	2.3447	0.7749	2.2713
1.4109	1.0069	1.0944	1.1450	0.9447	1.2256	0.7958	1.3192
1.4423	2.0332	1.1256	1.3724	0.9730	0.6609	0.8251	0.6748
1.3615	1.2944	0.9846	1.4720	0.8027	1.5756	0.6242	1.6959
1.3984	0	1.0247	0	0.8432	0	0.6621	0
1.3984		1.0247		0.8432		0.6621	

Table 8 provides data that outline the voltage profile of a 3-phase feeder under a 40% unbalanced loading condition, comparing scenarios with and without Distributed Generation (DG). It further examines voltage and current unbalance factors across various DG penetration levels (0%, 10%, 15%, and 20%). This comparison allows for an assessment of how the integration of DG impacts the voltage profile and unbalance factors, providing insights into the effectiveness of DG in mitigating unbalance issues within the feeder system. Table 9 presents total power loss data for a 25-bus, unbalanced 3-phase radial distribution system with varying levels of Distributed Generation (DG) integration. The first column denotes the percentage of unbalanced loading, with variations of 30% and 40%. The subsequent columns represent different levels of DG penetration. The second column shows the net real power loss in kilowatts (kW), while the last column displays the net reactive power loss in kilovolt-amperes reactive (kVAR). This data allows for an analysis of how DG integration impacts power losses under different degrees of unbalanced loading, providing insights into the system's efficiency and performance.

Table 9. Total power loss of 25-bus, unbalanced 3-phase radial distribution system with DG integration.

Percentage Unbalance Loading	% DG Penetration	Net Real Power Loss (kW)	Net Reactive Power Loss (kVAR)
30%	without DG	219.03	161.25
	10% DG	168.59	124.11
	15% DG	146.68	107.99
	20% DG	126.86	93.39
40%	without DG	244.58	180.06
	10% DG	166.15	122.32
	15% DG	147.73	108.76
	20% DG	123.49	90.56

The following are the main conclusions drawn from the test results of scenario 2:

(a) Voltage Profile Improvement: The voltage profiles of all three phases in the distribution system significantly improve by introducing DGs at different penetration levels. As a result, the system's voltage levels are more consistent and closer to the intended nominal values.
(b) Reduction in Total Power Losses: The total power losses within the distribution network are significantly reduced as the DG penetration levels rise. DGs assist in reducing losses by producing power closer to the load centers.
(c) Compliance with Unbalance Limits: The voltage and current unbalance factors remain within the prescribed limits, demonstrating that the distribution system runs within the acceptable limits.

Nevertheless, some node voltages in each phase are still below the lower limit. Hence, a further improvement in voltage regulation is desirable.

4.3. Scenario3—With DG and SC Integration

In scenario 3, the percentage of load unbalance is considered the same as in previous cases. SCs with ratings of 300 kVAR, 150 kVAR, and 300 kVAR have been installed at buses 8, 10, and 18 together with the existing DGs to improve the system conditions further from the above two scenarios.

Figures 11 and 12 depict the voltage profile, while Tables 10 and 11 compare voltage magnitude (VRph, VYph and VBph in p.u.) measurements, and Tables 12 and 13 compare the voltage and current unbalanced factors of the test system with and without DG under 30% and 40% unbalanced loading, respectively. Table 14 represents the network's total power loss.

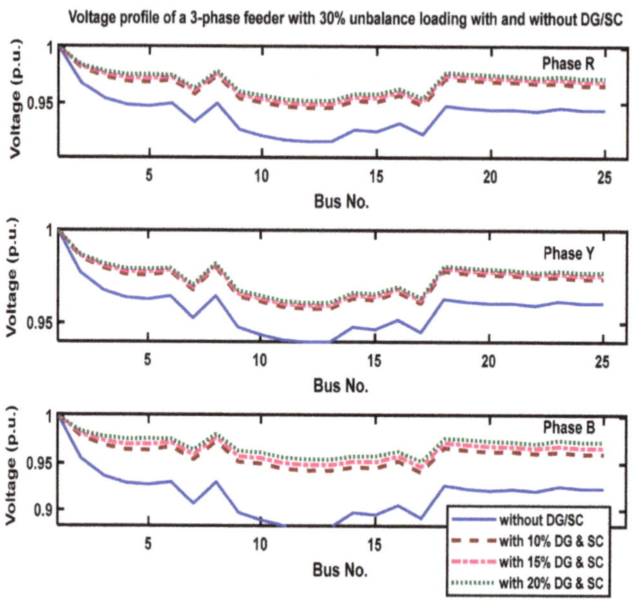

Figure 11. Voltage profile of a 3-phase feeder with 30% unbalanced loading, with and without DG/SC.

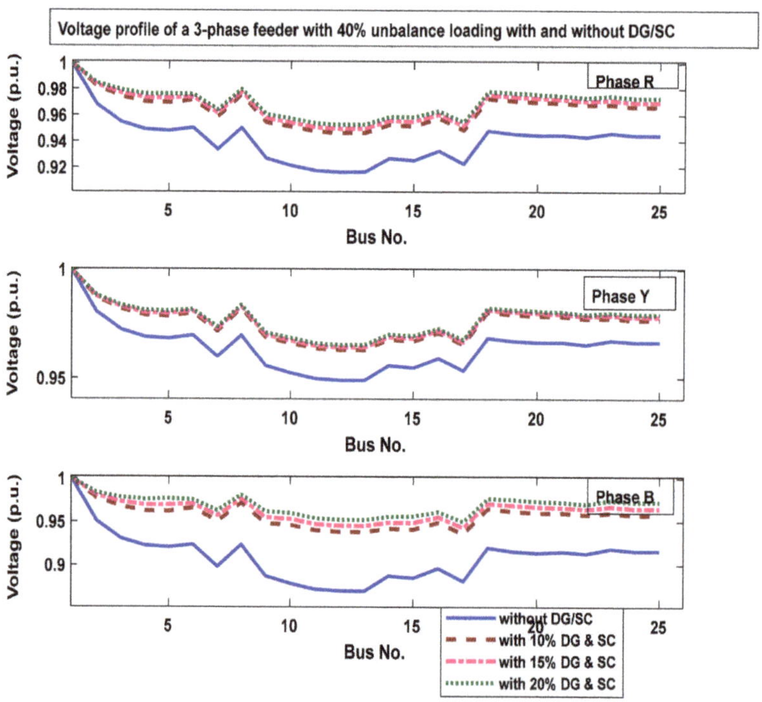

Figure 12. Voltage profile of a 3-phase feeder with 40% unbalanced loading, with and without DG/SC.

Table 10. Voltage magnitude (p.u.) results of PMU data with 30% unbalanced loading, DG and SC.

PMU Installed Bus No.	Voltage Magnitude (p.u.) Using PMU Setup with 30% Unbalanced Loading, with and Without DG and SC											
	Without DG/SC			With 10% DG and SC			With 15% DG and SC			With 20% DG and SC		
	V_{Rph}	V_{Yph}	V_{Bph}	V_{Rph}	V_{Yph}	V_{Bph}	V_{Rph}	V_{Yph}	V_{Bph}	V_{Rph}	V_{Yph}	V_{Bph}
1	1.0000	1.0000	1.0000	1.0000	1.0000	1.0000	1.0000	1.0000	1.0000	1.0000	1.0000	1.0000
4	0.9487	0.9636	0.9292	0.9699	0.9761	0.9645	0.9730	0.9777	0.9703	0.9761	0.9793	0.9760
7	0.9332	0.9527	0.9070	0.9582	0.9676	0.9539	0.9611	0.9690	0.9592	0.9639	0.9705	0.9645
8	0.9499	0.9645	0.9302	0.9752	0.9799	0.9733	0.9774	0.9810	0.9774	0.9796	0.9822	0.9814
11	0.9170	0.9407	0.8834	0.9469	0.9585	0.9441	0.9502	0.9601	0.9501	0.9534	0.9617	0.9560
14	0.9263	0.9479	0.8974	0.9520	0.9631	0.9459	0.9553	0.9648	0.9518	0.9585	0.9664	0.9577
20	0.9443	0.9606	0.9213	0.9695	0.9759	0.9624	0.9727	0.9775	0.9682	0.9758	0.9791	0.9739
22	0.9429	0.9594	0.9206	0.9676	0.9744	0.9606	0.9704	0.9758	0.9659	0.9733	0.9772	0.9710
25	0.9441	0.9607	0.9234	0.9659	0.9737	0.9601	0.9694	0.9754	0.9665	0.9728	0.9772	0.9728

Table 11. Voltage and current unbalance factors with 30% unbalance loading, DG and SC.

Without DG/SC		With 10% DG and SC		With 15% DG and SC		With 20% DG and SC	
Vubf (%)	Iubf (%)	Vubf (%)	Iubf (%)	Vubf (%)	Iubf (%)	Vubf (%)	Iubf (%)
0.0029	17.9968	0.0029	20.0693	0.0029	20.2489	0.0029	20.6302
0.6117	7.4036	0.4707	6.2916	0.4448	5.5364	0.4269	5.3925
0.8627	2.8468	0.6133	1.7878	0.5694	1.2505	0.5384	0.4786
0.9583	0.7349	0.6424	0.1527	0.5877	0.2558	0.5519	1.4401
0.9804	9.9467	0.6442	13.7393	0.5849	14.6342	0.5485	15.0371
0.9414	9.1393	0.7958	11.6509	0.7618	11.2109	0.7413	11.6629
1.2480	0	1.0598	5.3002	1.0106	5.4400	0.9754	5.7511
0.9414	3.7469	0.8617	8.8505	0.8375	9.2172	0.8217	9.7694
1.3791	3.3854	1.2582	8.7809	1.2074	9.1044	1.1741	9.6250
1.4845	2.3649	1.4553	2.9238	1.4129	3.1059	1.3778	3.2835
1.5601	0.7349	1.4686	1.0480	1.4154	1.1133	1.3748	1.1769
1.5866	0.9518	1.4750	1.3573	1.4232	1.1133	1.3809	1.1769
1.5917	3.9756	1.4707	3.6908	1.4169	3.9504	1.3742	3.0859
1.3778	0.7887	1.1087	0.4938	1.0458	0.7006	0.9980	1.2509
1.3973	0.5941	1.0991	0.8471	1.0329	0.8999	0.9838	0.9514
1.2690	2.5352	1.0613	3.2009	1.0134	3.4003	0.9716	3.2414
1.4597	4.0224	1.1447	4.4233	1.0830	4.4224	1.0255	4.7568
1.0013	2.0230	0.7157	1.4478	0.6694	1.2490	0.6415	0.6535
1.0624	0.9518	0.7271	1.0480	0.6759	1.1133	0.6385	1.1769
1.0939	1.5054	0.7467	2.1725	0.6898	2.3079	0.6492	2.1668
1.0494	0.7887	0.7403	0.8065	0.6924	0.8567	0.6553	0.9057
1.0700	1.6367	0.7500	1.1582	0.7025	0.9657	0.6597	0.3141
1.0080	1.0695	0.6643	1.2662	0.6013	1.3450	0.5553	1.4220
1.0433	0	0.6931	0	0.6226	0	0.5771	0
1.0433		0.6931		0.6226		0.5771	

Table 12. Voltage magnitude (p.u.) results of PMU data with 40% unbalanced loading, DG and SC.

PMU Installed Bus No.	Voltage Magnitude (p.u.) Using PMU Setup with 40% Unbalanced Loading, with and Without DG and SC											
	Without DG/SC			With 10% DG and SC			With 15% DG and SC			With 20% DG and SC		
	V_{Rph}	V_{Yph}	V_{Bph}	V_{Rph}	V_{Yph}	V_{Bph}	V_{Rph}	V_{Yph}	V_{Bph}	V_{Rph}	V_{Yph}	V_{Bph}
1	1.0000	1.0000	1.0000	1.0000	1.0000	1.0000	1.0000	1.0000	1.0000	1.0000	1.0000	1.0000
4	0.9491	0.9691	0.9227	0.9701	0.9791	0.9623	0.9732	0.9802	0.9691	0.9763	0.9814	0.9757
7	0.9338	0.9600	0.8984	0.9586	0.9717	0.9506	0.9614	0.9728	0.9569	0.9642	0.9738	0.9630
8	0.9503	0.9699	0.9237	0.9755	0.9823	0.9715	0.9777	0.9831	0.9763	0.9799	0.9839	0.9811
11	0.9176	0.9498	0.8725	0.9474	0.9638	0.9401	0.9506	0.9650	0.9471	0.9538	0.9662	0.9540
14	0.9269	0.9559	0.8878	0.9525	0.9680	0.9420	0.9556	0.9691	0.9490	0.9588	0.9703	0.9559
20	0.9447	0.9667	0.9141	0.9699	0.9788	0.9600	0.9729	0.9800	0.9668	0.9760	0.9811	0.9735
22	0.9434	0.9656	0.9134	0.9679	0.9775	0.9580	0.9707	0.9786	0.9642	0.9735	0.9796	0.9702
25	0.9445	0.9667	0.9164	0.9662	0.9769	0.9576	0.9696	0.9782	0.9651	0.9730	0.9794	0.9724

Table 13. Voltage and current unbalance factor with 40% unbalance loading, DG and SC.

Without DG/SC		With 10% DG and SC		With 15% DG and SC		With 20% DG and SC	
Vubf (%)	Iubf (%)	Vubf (%)	Iubf (%)	Vubf (%)	Iubf (%)	Vubf (%)	Iubf (%)
0.0029	24.4526	0.0029	25.8652	0.0029	25.9904	0.0029	26.4678
0.8213	9.8374	0.6059	8.3613	0.5732	7.8290	0.5468	7.7024
1.1560	4.1245	0.7992	2.7162	0.7424	1.5991	0.7050	1.0395
1.2901	0.9479	0.8416	0.1532	0.7667	0.6068	0.7202	1.8186
1.3214	13.2040	0.8435	17.4282	0.7648	17.9326	0.7152	18.9253
1.2702	12.4299	1.0132	14.5172	0.9653	14.3547	0.9349	14.5299
1.6888	0	1.3389	7.1196	1.2739	7.5540	1.2183	8.0166
1.2702	5.3788	1.0913	10.2344	1.0621	10.9847	1.0383	11.3566
1.8679	4.4321	1.5737	10.4761	1.5032	10.5582	1.4497	11.2048
2.0106	3.1856	1.8022	4.0280	1.7382	4.2737	1.6840	4.1677
2.1154	0.9479	1.8306	1.0518	1.7561	1.1160	1.6958	1.1844
2.1499	1.1692	1.8448	1.3623	1.7685	1.4454	1.7075	1.5339
2.1548	5.2500	1.8444	5.5485	1.7644	5.1249	1.7011	4.8494
1.8602	1.2290	1.4141	0.1096	1.3278	0.9708	1.2615	1.6060
1.8970	0.9479	1.4087	1.0518	1.3180	1.1160	1.2465	1.1844
1.7176	3.1443	1.3499	4.0940	1.2798	4.0144	1.2233	4.2603
1.9701	5.2132	1.4741	5.9654	1.3814	5.9250	1.3001	6.4833
1.3395	2.3394	0.9374	2.0889	0.8752	1.2521	0.8367	0.4873
1.4149	1.1732	0.9533	1.6860	0.8827	1.7889	0.8368	1.8985
1.4566	1.9263	0.9708	2.7742	0.9018	2.9434	0.8489	2.8227
1.4109	1.0069	0.9709	1.4470	0.9049	1.5352	0.8604	1.6293
1.4423	2.0332	0.9919	1.7343	0.9187	1.0091	0.8677	0.4645
1.3615	1.2944	0.8729	1.8602	0.7853	1.9737	0.7310	2.0946
1.3984	0	0.9053	0	0.8120	0	0.7536	0
1.3984		0.9053		0.8120		0.7536	

Table 14. Total power loss of 25-bus, unbalanced 3-phase radial distribution system with DG and SC integration.

Percentage Unbalance Loading	% DG Penetration	Net Real Power Loss (kW)	Net Reactive Power Loss (kVAR)
30%	without DG	219.03	161.25
	10% DG and SC	119.36	87.87
	15% DG and SC	106.89	78.69
	20% DG and SC	96.16	70.79
40%	without DG	244.58	180.06
	10% DG and SC	130.48	96.06
	15% DG and SC	116.13	85.50
	20% DG and SC	104.01	76.57

Table 10 presents voltage magnitude results (in p.u.) from PMU data in a system experiencing 30% unbalanced loading. It integrates Distributed Generation (DG) and shunt capacitor (SC). The first column shows voltage magnitudes for Red (VRph), Yellow (VYph), and Blue (VBph) phases without DG or SC. Subsequent columns display voltage magnitudes with increasing DG and SC integration (at 10%, 15%, and 20%). This data enables analysis of how DG and SC affect voltage stability and regulation under unbalanced loading, offering insights into their efficacy in enhancing system performance. Table 11 presents voltage and current unbalance factors under a 30% unbalanced loading scenario, incorporating Distributed Generation (DG) and shunt capacitors (SC) at various penetration levels. The first column represents unbalance factors without DG or SC, while subsequent columns denote increasing levels of DG and SC integration (10%, 15%, and 20%). This data allows for an assessment of how the combination of DG and SC influences both voltage and current unbalance factors, providing insights into the effectiveness of DG and SC in mitigating unbalance issues within the system. Table 12 presents voltage magnitude data in per unit (p.u.) obtained from Phasor Measurement Unit (PMU) readings. It analyzes the impact of integrating Distributed Generation (DG) and shunt capacitors (SC) under 40% unbalanced loading. The baseline column shows voltage without DG or SC. Subsequent columns indicate voltage with increasing DG and SC levels (10%, 15%, and 20%). This data aids in understanding the influence of DG and SC on voltage stability and regulation.

From the results of the three scenarios, it is observed that, without voltage regulating devices, as the load unbalancing increases in the distribution network, most of the node voltage magnitudes are below the lower limit. Though the voltage unbalance factors are within acceptable limits, the current unbalance factors are beyond the limit. When DGs and SCs are integrated into the network, considerable losses are minimized. The voltage profile is improved by bringing all node voltage magnitudes within limits. Also, the percentages of voltage and current unbalance factors are dropped compared to the unregulated scenario. Table 13 presents voltage and current unbalance factors under a 40% unbalanced loading scenario, considering the integration of both Distributed Generation (DG) and shunt capacitors (SC) at various penetration levels (10%, 15%, and 20%). The first column represents unbalance factors without DG or SC, while subsequent columns display results with increasing levels of DG and SC integration. This data allows for an evaluation of how the combination of DG and SC impacts voltage and current unbalance factors, providing insights into their effectiveness in mitigating unbalance issues within the system. The Table 14 illustrates the total power loss data for a 25-bus unbalanced 3-phase radial distribution system with integrated Distributed Generation (DG) and shunt capacitors (SC). It displays the percentage of unbalanced loading at 30% and 40%, while also presenting the net real power loss in kilowatts (kW) and net reactive power loss in kilovolt-amperes reactive (kVAR) across different levels of DG penetration. This data enables an assessment of how the integration of DG and SC impacts power losses under varying degrees of unbalanced loading, providing valuable insights into the efficiency and performance of the distribution system

The identified PMU locations for IEEE-34 or IEEE-123 bus test system and presented in Table 15. Additionally, a validation process is conducted to ensure the accuracy and reliability of the proposed scheme. The procedure is explained in Algorithm 3 and corresponding results are given in Table 16.

Table 15. Optimal placement of PMUs in unbalanced radial IEEE bus systems.

IEEE Unbalanced Test System	PMUs Count	PMU Installed Buses
25 bus	9	1,4,7,8,11,14,20,22,25
34 bus	12	2,6,9,11,13,17,22,23,27,29,32,34
123 bus	49	2,5,7,9,12,16,20,23,25,28,31,32,35,36,39,41,43,45,47,50, 52,54,56,59,62,65,66,68,71,73,76,80,84,88,91,92,94,96, 98,100,102,103,106,108,111,115,116,119,121

Table 16. Validation table for Phasor Measurement Units.

IEEE Unbalanced Test System	PMU_Bus	Out_Bus	Ver_Vector	Comp_Vector
25	[1,4,7,8,11,14,20,22, 25]	[2 3 5 6 9 10 12 13 15 16 17 18 19 21 23 24]	[2 5 9 12 16 14 15 17 13 19 23 3 6 6 10 7 18 21 24]	[2 3 5 6 9 10 12 13 15 16 17 18 19 21 23 24]
34	[2,6,9,11,13,17,22,23,27 ,29,32,34]	[1 3 4 5 7 8 10 12 14 15 16 18 19 20 21 24 25 26 28 30 31 33]	[3 7 10 14 15 18 19 24 28 30 33 1 5 8 4 12 16 21 20 26 25 31 33]	[1 3 4 5 7 8 10 12 14 15 16 18 19 20 21 24 25 26 28 30 31 33]
123	[2,5,7,9,12,16,20,23,25, 28,31,32,35,36,39,41,43, 45,47,50,52,54,56,59,62, 65,66,68,71,73,76,80,84, 88,91,92,94,96,98,100, 102,103,106,108,111,115, 116,119,121]	[1 3 4 6 8 10 11 13 14 15 17 18 19 21 22 24 26 27 29 30 33 34 37 38 40 42 44 46 48 49 51 53 55 57 58 60 61 63 64 67 69 70 72 74 75 77 78 79 81 82 83 85 86 87 89 90 93 95 97 99 101 104 105 107 109 110 112 113 114 117 118 120 122 123]	[3 4 8 10 11 15 13 14 21 23 24 25 26 27 31 29 32 36 17 40 41 42 44 45 46 47 48 50 51 52 53 60 62 63 65 66 68 69 72 77 81 85 91 89 92 95 96 97 98 99 100 101 102 103 107 112 116 120 121 122 57 74 94 4 6 8 11 15 15 20 23 27 28 31 34 35 38 38 39 43 45 47 50 53 58 59 62 65 65 70 75 79 83 87 88 91 93 94 96 98 100 102 105 107 110 114 115 118 119 154]	[1 3 4 6 8 10 11 13 14 15 17 18 19 21 22 24 26 27 29 30 33 34 37 38 40 42 44 46 48 49 51 53 55 57 58 60 61 63 64 67 69 70 72 74 75 77 78 79 81 82 83 85 86 87 89 90 93 95 97 99 101 104 105 107 109 110 112 113 114 117 118 120 122 123]

Validation involves closely examining the results produced by an algorithm. This algorithm serves the primary goal of confirming the connectivity of all buses to Phasor Measurement Units (PMUs). To do this, the buses were divided into two different vectors: one for the buses connected to the PMU and another for the ones not. A thorough inspection used a branch vector to compare every bus (Comp_vector) connected to the PMUs. The findings were then saved in a "Ver" vector (initialized as an empty vector) and then populated with the bus numbers related to PMU-connected buses. The "Ver" vector must contain all the outstanding bus (Out_bus) numbers for a system to be considered fully observable. On the other hand, an imperfect match signifies a deficiency in total observability, implying possible errors in the determined ideal PMU positions.

Algorithm 3: Validation of Optimal PMU Placement Solution of Unbalanced radial networks

1. Input: Number of nodes (n), branches (b), PMU locations (p), and outstanding buses (o).
2. Initialize variables j = 1, o = 1, k = 1.
3. Iterate through buses:
4. a. If PMU[j] = 1:
5. i. Store j in PMU bus[k].
6. ii. Increment j and i.
7. b. Else, store j in Out bus[o].
8. i. Increment o and j.
9. Check connectivity between PMU buses and branches:
10. a. Initialize j, a, and k.
11. b. Iterate through PMU buses and branches:
12. i. If PMU bus[j] matches branch [k,2], store branch[k,1] in Ver[a].
13. ii. Increment a and k if there is a match.
14. c. If k $\leq$ b, repeat step 4b.
15. Check connectivity between outstanding buses and branches:
16. a. Initialize j, a, and k.
17. b. Iterate through outstanding buses and branches:
18. i. If Out bus[j] matches Ver[k], store Out bus[j] in Comp[a].
19. ii. Increment a and k if there is a match.
20. c. If k $\leq$ o, repeat step 5b.
21. Verify system observability:
22. a. If Comp equals Out bus, the system is thoroughly observable.
23. b. Otherwise, the system is not thoroughly observable

4.4. Robustness and External Corroboration Across Test Systems

The proposed MAS controller relies on local measurements (positive/negative-sequence voltage V_1, V_2) and agent-level arbitration rules, with actuation through DG reactive power set-points and shunt capacitors. The sensitivity matrix used for selection depends on feeder impedance s and injections but does not require feeder-specific controller gains. Consequently, for radial distribution networks with per-section R/X in typical ranges and unbalance $\leq$5%, the following qualitative behavior holds: (i) minimum phase voltage improves monotonically with DG penetration up to the point of local over-voltage constraints; (ii) moderate SC sizing ($\approx$10–15% of local kvar) reduces phase-spread without inducing excessive circulating reactive power; and (iii) under load growth up to $\approx$1.2 p.u., MAS coordination maintains V_{min} within statutory limits provided DG support $\geq$20% of peak load.

Published studies on IEEE 33- and 69-bus feeders employing MAS-based coordination and sensitivity/OPF-guided voltage control report the same trends with respect to DG penetration, unbalance level, and reactive compensation. These reports indicate improvements in minimum bus voltage and reduced inter-phase dispersion comparable to those observed in our 25-bus case. Together with the mechanism above, this supports portability of the proposed scheme to standard feeders of different sizes and impedances. We will provide full IEEE 33-/69-bus scenario sweeps (voltage envelopes, losses, tap actions) as an extended dataset in a follow-up technical note.

5. Conclusions

This work analyses a 3-phase, 25-bus unbalanced distribution network for steady-state performance. This research provides an effective and efficient coordinated voltage control mechanism based on the MAS approach. The scheme optimizes the voltage profile to minimize the unbalance, voltage deviation, and losses in an active UDN. The DG/SC agents have the sensitivity indices of all DGs and SCs linked in the network and allow voltage regulation to be made locally on the most sensitive nodes. When a coordinated action of voltage regulators is desired, they communicate with the MAS controller, which then delegates the tasks to the agents based on the available information from the PMU agent database. Thus, coordinated voltage regulation is accomplished by optimally choosing the exact number of devices, eliminating the need for other voltage regulators in the network. As the PMUs are already installed in the network, a separate memory unit for the MAS structure can be avoided, making the scheme cost-effective. The voltage and current parameters of the network are measured using an online estimation technique based on PMU. A PMU allows one to measure the voltage phasor of the bus in real time and the current phasor of all lines connected to the bus. Due to this capability of PMU, all buses adjacent to it are observable. The optimum PMU allocation on the test system is elucidated using an integer linear programming approach. An improved voltage profile of the system and a substantial reduction in voltage and current unbalance and power loss are exhibited as a result of optimal operations of DGs and SCs in the network.

Author Contributions: Conceptualization, S.T., D.N.G. and R.S.S.N.; methodology, S.T., D.N.G. and R.S.S.N.; software, S.T.; formal analysis, A.A. and S.R.A.; validation, A.A. and S.R.A.; investigation, A.A.; writing—original draft preparation, S.T., D.N.G. and R.S.S.N.; writing—review and editing, A.A. and S.R.A.; visualization, A.A.; supervision, A.A. and S.R.A.; project administration, A.A. and S.R.A.; funding acquisition, A.A. and S.R.A. All authors have read and agreed to the published version of the manuscript.

Funding: This research received no external funding.

Data Availability Statement: The original contributions presented in this study are included in the article. Further inquiries can be directed to the corresponding authors.

Acknowledgments: The authors gratefully acknowledge the valuable support of Yogesh Ramaswamy and A. Mutharasan during the early stages of this work. Their assistance in preliminary analysis, validation activities, and constructive discussions contributed to shaping the direction of the study.

Conflicts of Interest: The authors declare no conflicts of interest.

References

1. Azadani, E.N.; Canizares, C.A.; Olivares, D.E.; Bhattacharya, K. Stability analysis of unbalanced distribution systems with synchronous machine and DFIG based distributed generators. *IEEE Trans. Smart Grid.* **2014**, *5*, 2326–2338. [CrossRef]
2. Nejabatkhah, F.; Li, Y.W.; Wu, B. Control strategies of three-phase distributed generation inverters for grid unbalanced voltage compensation. *IEEE Trans. Pow. Electron.* **2016**, *31*, 5228–5241. [CrossRef]
3. Kabiri, R.; Holmes, D.G. McGrath, B.P. Control of active and reactive power ripple to mitigate unbalanced grid voltages. *IEEE Trans. Ind. Appl.* **2016**, *52*, 1660–1668. [CrossRef]
4. Weckx, S.; Driesen, J. Load balancing with EV chargers and PV inverters in unbalanced distribution grids. *IEEE Trans. Sustain. Energy* **2015**, *6*, 635–643. [CrossRef]
5. Wang, L.; Yan, R.; Bai, F.; Saha, T.; Wang, K. A distributed inter-phase coordination algorithm for voltage control with unbalanced PV integration in LV systems. *IEEE Trans. Sustain. Energy* **2020**, *11*, 2687–2697. [CrossRef]

6. Mejia-Ruiz, G.E.; Cárdenas-Javier, R.; Paternina, M.R.A.; Rodríguez-Rodríguez, J.R.; Ramirez, J.M.; Zamora-Mendez, A. Coordinated optimal volt/var control for distribution networks via D-PMUs and EV chargers by exploiting the Eigensystem realization. *IEEE Trans. Smart Grid* **2021**, *12*, 2425–2438. [CrossRef]
7. Ahmed, M.; Bhattarai, R.; Hossain, S.J.; Abdelrazek, S.; Kamalasadan, S. Coordinated voltage control strategy for voltage regulators and voltage source converters integrated distribution system. *IEEE Trans. Ind. Appl.* **2019**, *55*, 4235–4246. [CrossRef]
8. Chamana, M.; Chowdhury, B.H.; Jahanbakhsh, F. Distributed control of voltage regulating devices in the presence of high PV penetration to mitigate ramp-rate issues. *IEEE Trans. Smart Grid* **2018**, *9*, 1086–1095. [CrossRef]
9. Ranamuka, D.; Agalgaonkar, A.P.; Muttaqi, K.M. Innovative Volt/VAr control philosophy for future distribution systems embedded with voltage-regulating devices and distributed renewable energy resources. *IEEE Syst. J.* **2019**, *13*, 3153–3164. [CrossRef]
10. Chamana, M.; Chowdhury, B.H. Optimal voltage regulation of distribution networks with cascaded voltage regulators in the presence of high PV penetration. *IEEE Trans. Sustain. Energy* **2018**, *9*, 1427–1436. [CrossRef]
11. Bedawy, A.; Yorino, N.; Mahmoud, K.; Lehtonen, M. An effective coordination strategy for voltage regulation in distribution system containing high intermittent photovoltaic penetrations. *IEEE Access* **2021**, *9*, 117404–117414. [CrossRef]
12. Jabalameli, N.; Ghosh, A. Online centralized coordination of charging and phase switching of PEVs in unbalanced LV networks with high PV penetrations. *IEEE Syst. J.* **2021**, *15*, 1015–1025. [CrossRef]
13. Zafar, R.; Ravishankar, J.; Fletcher, J.E.; Pota, H.R. Multi-timescale voltage stability-constrained Volt/VAR optimization with battery storage system in distribution grids. *IEEE Trans. Sustain. Energy* **2020**, *11*, 868–878. [CrossRef]
14. Islam, M.R.; Lu, H.; Hossain, J.; Li, L. Multiobjective optimization technique for mitigating unbalance and improving voltage considering higher penetration of electric vehicles and distributed generation. *IEEE Syst. J.* **2020**, *14*, 3676–3686. [CrossRef]
15. Guo, Y.; Zhang, Q.; Wang, Z. Cooperative peak shaving and voltage regulation in unbalanced distribution feeders. *IEEE Trans. Power Syst.* **2021**, *36*, 5235–5244. [CrossRef]
16. Wang, J.; Zhou, N.; Chung, C.Y.; Wang, Q. Coordinated planning of converter-based DG units and soft open points incorporating active management in unbalanced distribution networks. *IEEE Trans. Sustain. Energy* **2020**, *11*, 2015–2027. [CrossRef]
17. Tatikayala, V.K.; Dixit, S. Multi-stage voltage control in high photovoltaic based distributed generation penetrated distribution system considering smart inverter reactive power capability. *Ain Shams Eng. J.* **2024**, *15*, 102265. [CrossRef]
18. Kryonidis, G.C.; Malamaki, K.-N.D.; Gkavanoudis, S.I.; Oureilidis, K.O.; Kontis, E.O.; Mauricio, J.M.; Maza-Ortega, J.M.; Demoulias, C.S. Distributed reactive power control scheme for the voltage regulation of unbalanced LV grids. *IEEE Trans. Sustain. Energy* **2020**, *12*, 1301–1310. [CrossRef]
19. Mahmud, M.A.; Hossain, M.J.; Pota, H.R. Voltage variation on distribution networks with distributed generation: Worst case scenario. *IEEE Syst. J.* **2014**, *8*, 1096–1103. [CrossRef]
20. Wang, H.; Yan, Z.; Shahidehpour, M.; Zhou, Q.; Xu, X. Optimal energy storage allocation for mitigating the unbalance in active distribution network via uncertainty quantification. *IEEE Trans. Sustain. Energy* **2021**, *12*, 303–313. [CrossRef]
21. Yao, M.; Hiskens, I.A.; Mathieu, J.L. Mitigating voltage unbalance using distributed solar photovoltaic inverters. *IEEE Trans. Power Syst.* **2021**, *36*, 2642–2651. [CrossRef]
22. Mendonca, T.R.F.; Green, T.C. Distributed active network management based on locally estimated voltage sensitivity. *IEEE Access* **2019**, *7*, 105173–105185. [CrossRef]
23. Jhala, K.; Natarajan, B.; Pahwa, A. Probabilistic Voltage Sensitivity Analysis (PVSA)—A Novel Approach to Quantify Impact of Active Consumers. *IEEE Trans. Power Syst.* **2018**, *33*, 2518–2527. [CrossRef]
24. Zad, B.B.; Lobry, J.; Vallée, F. A New Voltage Sensitivity Analysis Method for Medium-Voltage Distribution Systems Incorporating Power Losses Impact. *Electr. Power Compon. Syst.* **2018**, *46*, 1540–1553. [CrossRef]
25. Dixit, M.; Kundu, P.; Jariwala, H.R. Optimal integration of shunt capacitor banks in distribution networks for assessment of techno-economic asset. *Comput. Electr. Engg.* **2018**, *71*, 331–345. [CrossRef]
26. Dorri, A.; Kanhere, S.S.; Jurdak, R. Multi-agent systems: A survey. *IEEE Access* **2018**, *6*, 28573–28593. [CrossRef]
27. Yasinzadeh, M.; Akhbari, M. Detection of PMU spoofing in power grid based on phasor measurement analysis. *IET Gener. Transm. Distrib.* **2018**, *12*, 1980–1987. [CrossRef]
28. Chauhan, K.; Sodhi, R. Placement of Distribution-Level Phasor Measurements for Topological Observability and Monitoring of Active Distribution Networks. *IEEE Trans. Instrum. Meas.* **2020**, *69*, 3451–3460. [CrossRef]
29. Koochi, M.H.R.; Hemmatpour, M.H. A general PMU placement approach considering both topology and system aspects of contingencies. *Int. J. Electr. Power Energy Syst.* **2020**, *118*, 105774. [CrossRef]
30. Tangi, S.; Gaonkar, D.N. Voltage Estimation of Active Distribution Network Using PMU Technology. *IEEE Access* **2021**, *9*, 100436–100446. [CrossRef]
31. Taher, S.A.; Karimi, M.H. Optimal reconfiguration and DG allocation in balanced and unbalanced distribution systems. *Ain Shams Eng. J.* **2014**, *5*, 735–749. [CrossRef]

32. Zhang, T.; Yu, L.; Yue, D.; Dou, C.; Xie, X.; Chen, L. Coordinated voltage regulation of high renewable-penetrated distribution networks: An evolutionary curriculum-based deep reinforcement learning approach. *Int. J. Electr. Power Energy Syst.* **2023**, *149*, 108995. [CrossRef]
33. Bedawy, A.; Yorino, N.; Mahmoud, K.; Zoka, Y.; Sasaki, Y. Optimal Voltage Control Strategy for Voltage Regulators in Active Unbalanced Distribution Systems Using Multi-Agents. *IEEE Trans. Power Syst.* **2020**, *35*, 1023–1035. [CrossRef]
34. Zhang, Q.; Dehghanpour, K.; Wang, Z. Distributed CVR in Unbalanced Distribution Systems with PV Penetration. *IEEE Trans. Smart Grid* **2019**, *10*, 5308–5319. [CrossRef]
35. Kersting, W.H. The whys of distribution system analysis. *IEEE Ind. Appl. Mag.* **2011**, *17*, 59–65. [CrossRef]

energies

MDPI

Review

Multi-Objective Optimization of Load Flow in Power Systems: An Overview

Bansendeka Theo Nyingu *, Lebogang Masike and Mwana Wa Kalaga Mbukani

Department of Electrical, Electronic and Computer Engineering, University of Pretoria, Pretoria 0002, South Africa

* Correspondence: u22913662@tuks.co.za; Tel.: +27-782-915-399

Abstract: The expanding complexity of power systems—driven by the motivation to reduce their carbon footprint by integrating renewable energy sources (RESs) in the grid, the increasing energy demand, grid scalability, and the necessity for reliable and sustainable operation—has made the optimal power flow (OPF) problem the main issue in power systems. Hence, the concept of muti-objective optimal power flow (MOOPF) in power systems has become a crucial tool for power system management and planning. This article provides an overview of recent optimization techniques in power systems that have MOOPF as their central problem, as well as their applications in power systems, with the purpose of identifying significant approaches, challenges and trends when it comes to large-scale probabilistic MOOPF. This overview was developed based on an in-depth analysis of MOOPF techniques, the classification of their applications, and the formulation of the problem in power systems. This overview contributes to the existing literature by highlighting the evolution of optimization techniques, and the need for robust, probabilistic hybrid optimization techniques that can address variability, uncertainty, reliability, and sustainability in power systems. These findings are significant because they emphasize the current transition towards more adaptive and intelligent optimization strategies, which are essential to developing sustainable, dependable, and effective power systems, especially as we move towards smart grids and low-carbon energy systems.

Keywords: dynamic system; multi-objective optimal power flow (MOOPF); optimization techniques; power systems; renewable energy sources (RESs)

1. Introduction

The electric power grid is an ever-changing dynamic system. This system is intended to safely and consistently produce, transfer, and distribute electricity from power plants to consumers [1]. It is made up of power generation units, transmission and distribution systems, control and protection systems, and energy-consuming devices. Since its establishment in the late 19th century, the grid has experienced revolutionary transformations. Originally built for unidirectional power flow and centralized generation, it changed to accommodate expanding industrial and residential needs [2–4]. There is a need for more effective, adaptable, and intelligent grid management in line with the ever-growing demand for electricity. By 2035, this growth is expected to rise by 53% [5–11].

In the 21st century, a new phase has been reached in power systems, characterized by the integration of renewable energy sources (RESs) which is driven by environmental goals, decreasing technological costs, and accessibility to electricity in underdeveloped nations [12–14]. China, the EU, and the US have the largest installed solar PV capacity, with over 2.2 TW worldwide by the end of 2024, according to the International Renewable Energy Agency (IRENA) and about 19.2 GW for Africa and the Middle East. With a current installed capacity of 1.136 TW, wind energy comes in second position, with significant installations in Asia, North America, Europe and an expected installed capacity of 16 GW in Africa by 2025 [15,16].

Furthermore, grid dynamics are changing as a result of the integration of RESs. These sources have a major impact on grid stability and power quality. Due to their intermittent nature and time-varying output, their integration brings uncertainty and variability into the grid which can lead to voltage fluctuations, supply–demand imbalance, and excessive transmission losses, etc. [17–22]. It is therefore necessary to conduct studies aimed at examining and optimizing power systems in order to adapt to changes in the energy landscape and ensure the sustainability and resilience of the grid [23–30].

Applications of optimization techniques in power systems are motivated by the ongoing conflict between the growing complexity of the grid and the necessity for a cost-effective, reliable, and efficient power supply [3–7]. An evolution has been observed in power system configurations and optimization techniques used to address the management, operation, and planning of power systems, from basic cost-minimization problems with centralized structures to complex, multi-objective problems with interconnected networks and various power sources [31,32].

Optimization techniques in power systems started more than 45 years ago when the Optimal Power Flow (OPF) problem (which aims to identify the optimal state of operation for power systems) was developed, and they have since advanced through multiple chronological phases of problem formulation and solution approaches [33]. The development of optimization solutions across time can be approximately categorized into three periods as shown in Figure 1 [34–40]:

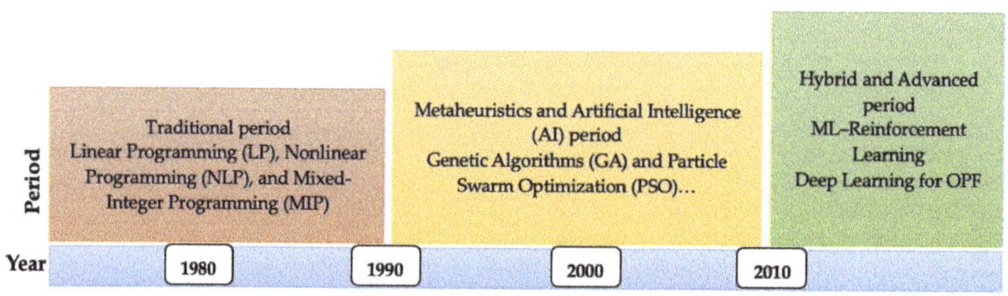

Figure 1. Evolutionary trajectory of optimization techniques in power systems.

In the traditional period, which spanned from before the 1980s to the early 1990s, traditional optimization methods including linear programming (LP), nonlinear programming (NLP), and mixed-integer programming (MIP) were considered the norm. For basic, deterministic situations, these techniques provided optimal solutions and were mathematically rigorous. However, the rise of deregulated markets and the grid's growing complexity made their weaknesses clear. In the Metaheuristics and Artificial Intelligence (AI) period, from the 1990s to the late 2000s, metaheuristics and AI based algorithms including Genetic Algorithms (GA) and Particle Swarm Optimization (PSO) were popular. These algorithms were inspired by nature and were particularly good at searching large nonlinear search spaces for near-global solutions. Because of their resilience and adaptability, they were perfect for solving challenging, non-convex problems that traditional approaches were unable to solve. In the Modern or Hybrid and Advanced period, from the 2010s to present, managing the significant unpredictability brought by the widespread integration of renewable energy sources and smart grid technology has become the focus of most research studies. Nowadays, hybrid approaches that incorporate several approaches, robust optimization, and stochastic programming are examples of modern solutions. In an extremely uncertain environment, these strategies place a significant priority on resilience and real-time flexibility to guarantee that the grid stays steady, safe, and effective [4,21].

OPF comprises any optimization problem in a power system that aims to optimize power system operation while satisfying constraints. Several power system optimization issues are specific cases or extensions of OPF. This general structure includes dozens of optimization issues for power system planning and operation. In Figure 2, a wide range of optimization problems are shown, including long-term power system planning and maintenance scheduling to guarantee future capacity and reliability and short-term operational decisions like Unit Commitment and Economic Dispatch that minimize costs and maintain security [3,34]. In order to minimize losses and enhance voltage stability, optimization is essential for resolving particular network issues such as network reconfiguration and reactive source allocation [36–42]. Beyond technical and financial issues, applications such as pollution dispatch demonstrate how multi-objective optimization (MOO) is used to balance cost and environmental impact, guaranteeing that the grid in its entirety is not just secure and effective, but sustainable as well [41,42]. Figure 3 shows a quick view of the current state of power system optimization which emphasizes the fundamental operational and planning difficulties facing the transmission and generation industries as well as the management of the intricate distribution network. Power system optimization is moving away from deterministic algorithms, which perform well in the structured, high-accuracy requirements of generation and transmission at 53% of applications, and towards heuristic and hybrid approaches, which dominate the distribution network at 45% because they are better at handling non-linearity, non-convexity, and discrete variables while avoiding local optima. Heuristics and hybrids are more reliable for modern complex, uncertain systems, even though deterministic approaches are faster; at the same time, new AI-based techniques are demonstrating great promise for real-time, adaptive control, although their current use is constrained by the requirement for large amounts of data and processing power.

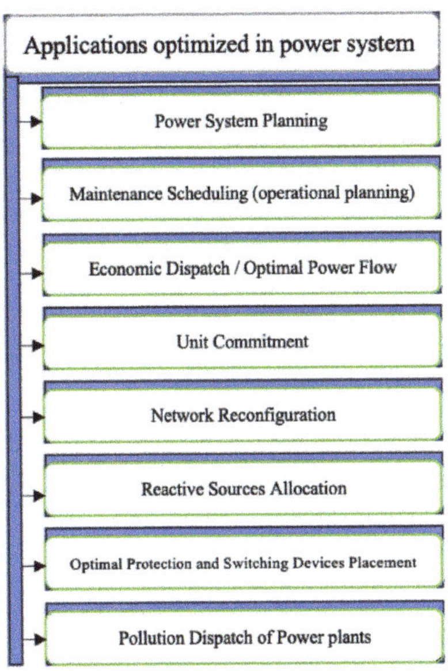

Figure 2. Optimization applications in power systems [36–42].

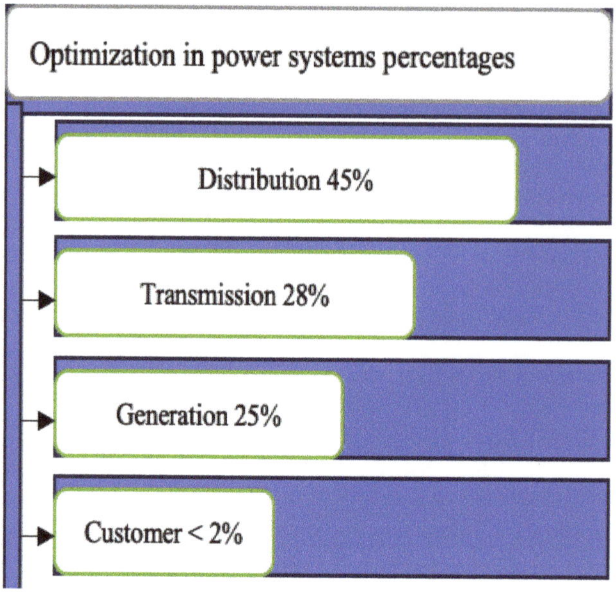

Figure 3. Optimization techniques in power systems percentages [43].

Power flow analysis is conducted to ascertain how power flows throughout the network under specific load and generation scenarios. It also gives important voltage information, such as phase and magnitude, at every grid node [44–47]. However, it is crucial to simplify the problem formulation and choose the most efficient optimization strategies [48,49].

As shown in Figure 4, this paper presents an in-depth review of MOOPF techniques by assessing critically what each proposed method has accomplished, as well as the classification of their applications, and the formulation of the problem in power systems. It critically examines how power system management, operation, and planning are addressed via optimization, but also how the problem is formulated. The study identifies trends in the use of MOO for power system issues such as RESs integration and OPF. This paper contributes to the current literature by emphasizing the evolution of optimization approaches and the need for robust, probabilistic hybrid optimization strategies that can handle variability, uncertainty, dependability, and sustainability in power systems. This study is in line with the global energy transition, which places a high priority on grid resilience, decarbonization, and RESs integration. It illustrates how distributed, intelligent systems that are rich in RE are replacing centralized, fossil fuel-based grids, necessitating the use of more sophisticated optimization methods. Optimization is a key facilitator for future power systems since it has a direct connection to the sustainability agenda. The following sections make up this paper: power system topologies are discussed in Section 2, classical and intelligent optimization techniques in power systems are covered in Sections 3 and 4, respectively, Section 5 covers Challenges and future directions in power systems and then comes the conclusion in Section 6.

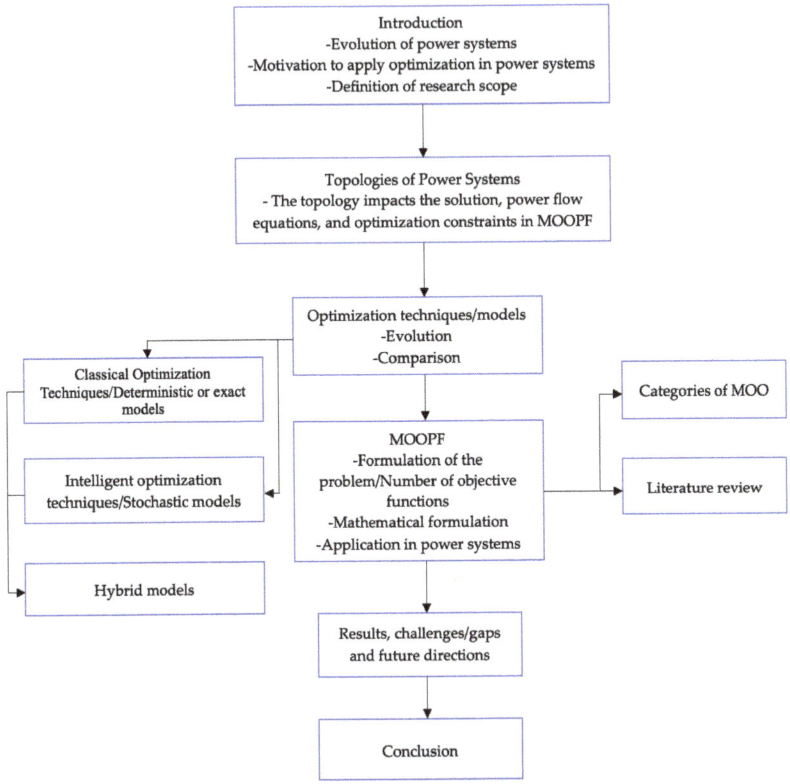

Figure 4. Overview of MOOPF in power system visual representation.

2. Topologies of Power Systems

The topology of power systems is the electrical or physical configuration of a power system's loads, transmission lines, and generators [50–53]. A variety of configurations, as illustrated below in Figure 5, can be used to organize power systems. Every kind of configuration has unique properties and operates in a variety of ways. As described in [54], the system's cost, adaptability, and dependability are determined by this configuration.

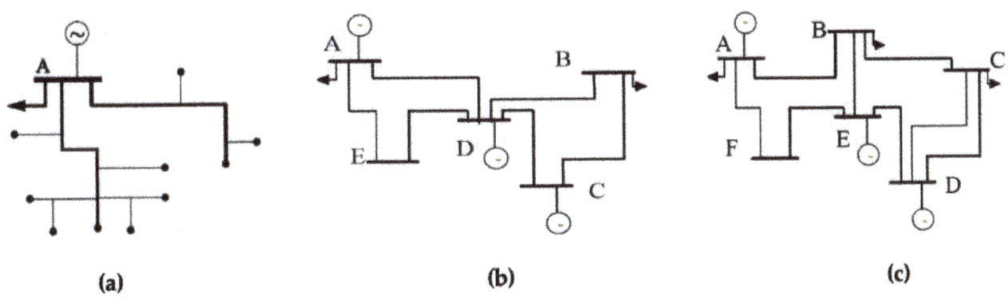

Figure 5. (**a**) Radial architecture, (**b**) Loop architecture, (**c**) Mesh architecture.

2.1. Radial or Star Networks

The most straightforward and typical configuration, particularly in distribution systems, is a radial structure as shown in Figure 5a. This arrangement creates no closed loops since feeders branch off from a single source of power, such as a substation, and provide electricity to loads as they go [55]. There is only one connection to the source for every load. Due to its affordability and ease of use, the radial configuration is frequently used for distribution networks, particularly in residential areas [56]. Its main drawback is that it is not very reliable because any defect on the feeder will cut off power to all downstream loads, leaving the system open to massive outages.

2.2. Loop Networks

A loop structure, as shown in Figure 5b, offers a closed path for power flow, which enhances the radial structure [57,58]. After leaving a substation, feeders travel around a service area before returning to the same substation or another one. Usually, a radial spur off the loop supplies each load. Individual loads are still served radially even when the loop itself offers two routes to the main supply. However, as opposed to the more straightforward radial structures, this increased reliability comes at the expense of being more costly and requiring more intricate protection measures.

2.3. Mesh or Connected Networks

A highly intricate and dependable configuration as illustrated in Figure 5c is a mesh topology, in which a grid is formed by connecting numerous generators and loads via a large number of transmission lines. Power can move between any two points in the system in a number of parallel ways [59]. This configuration is costly and intricate to construct, manage and safeguard. Sophisticated control and protection systems are necessary because of the intricate power flow pathways. For high-voltage transmission networks that serve as the foundation of a regional or national grid, this is the typical structure.

The feasible solution space, power flow equations, and optimization constraints in MOOPF studies are directly impacted by the electrical network topology. Thus, knowledge of network topology is essential for understanding how optimization algorithms are used and why some approaches work better in particular system configurations. Practicality, the most effective electrical network (power system) design is determined by the objective (dependability, cost, power quality, losses, etc.), but for modern power systems with transformers and distributed generation, mesh or connected network is typically the optimal architecture [51,52,59].

3. Optimization Techniques

In the realm of power systems, optimization approaches are crucial for enhancing the efficiency [60], reliability, and economic viability of electricity generation, distribution, and transmission [61–65]. The primary goal of an optimization problem, which is a mathematical model, is to minimize undesirable factors (such as cost, energy loss, errors, etc.) or maximize desirable factors (such as profit, quality, efficiency, etc.), subject to certain limitations [49,66–69]. However, a multi-objective problem with conflicting goals will never have a single optimal solution, but rather a collection of them [70].

Optimization issues can be tackled using a variety of traditional methods [71]. In the part that follows, we will examine the two primary aspects of optimization techniques in power systems: classical and intelligent optimization techniques [72–77], which are illustrated in Figure 6, and compared in Table 1. Classical models are particular computations produced by an algorithm that accepts a value or set of values as input and returns a value or set of values as output. Intelligent models are methods or procedures used to finish a task or find a solution [78,79].

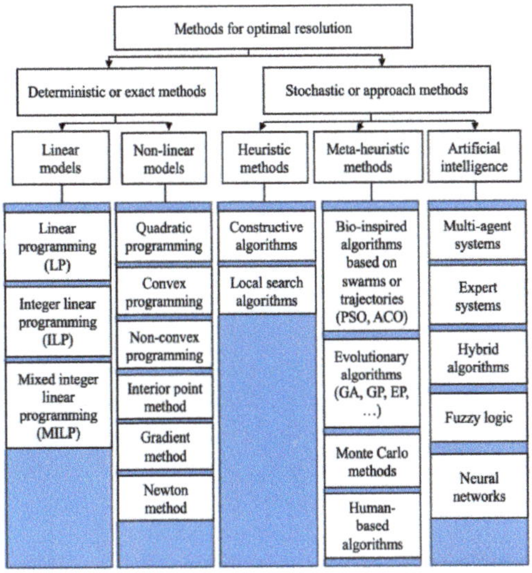

Figure 6. Methods to address optimization problems [72–77].

Table 1. Classical and intelligent optimization techniques comparison.

Feature	Classical Optimization	Intelligent Optimization
Method	Exact/Deterministic	Non-exact/Stochastic
Math model	Explicit mathematical model	Black-box models
Intricacy handling	Limited	High
Result	One optimal solution	Multiple (global optimum)
Speed	Fast (for basic models)	Slower (for iterative search)
Global search	Local minima propensity	Improved capability
Computation Time	Shorter (small, convex systems)	Higher (large, complex systems)
Convergence behavior	Quickly (convex)	Global/near-global solutions
Solution Quality	Exact/near-exact (convex, smooth)	High-quality
CFD/CFI (Constraint Feasibility Degree/Index)	CFD = 0 (satisfaction of constraints)	CFD > 0
Handling of CFD/CFI	Enforced rigidly (mathematically)	Flexible
Numerical Stability	High (Jacobian/Hessian well-conditioned)	Stable (Algorithmic adjustment)
Implementation Difficulty	Simpler	Difficult
Scalability	Effective (small, medium systems)	Adaptable (Large systems)

3.1. Classical Optimization Techniques

Conventional techniques created to address problems with clearly specified mathematical features are known as classical optimization techniques. They are deterministic, as shown in Figure 6, which means they will always yield the same outcome given a starting position. These techniques use calculus-based ideas like gradients and Hessians to methodically search for the best result [80].

A mathematical program is the fundamental building block for articulating and solving optimization problems using mathematical models [75]. Working with very simple mathematical equations may allow for the possibility of analytical solutions. In many real-world situations, the relationships involved are too complicated to allow for direct differentiation [81], hence alternative optimization processes are required to determine the optimal objective value and the associated values of independent variables.

There are several mathematical programs, often based on the particulars of the situation at hand. In this instance, the problem is regarded as Linear Programming (LP) if the variables in the problem (sometimes denoted by "x") allow both the objective function and the constraints to be characterized as linear functions [49]. However, when restrictions and/or the target functions exhibit non-linear features, the problem is categorized as Non-Linear Programming (NLP). Furthermore, variables are limited to believing that the "Integer" trait is applied only to integer values [69]. An example of a binary choice in a power system would be a transformer that is either in functioning mode (status = 1) or in a spare state (status = 0). When every variable satisfies this requirement to be an integer, the problem is known as integer programming (IP). However, only when some of the variables need integer values does Mixed Integer Programming (MIP) arise [82]. These variations in problem classification aid in choosing optimization strategies appropriate for the constraints and intrinsic complexity of the issue. Quadratic programming (QP) is an advanced form of NLP. The QP optimization model features linearly specified constraints and a quadratic objective function. QP is more accurate than LP-based techniques. The most commonly used objective function in power system optimization is the generation cost function, which is frequently quadratic. As a result, the QP solution to the power system optimization problem cannot be simplified using such an objective function [82]. Since it calculates the second-order partial derivatives of the power-flow equations in addition to other constraints (the Hessian), Newton's method, another type of NLP, is known as a second-order approach. Often, the prerequisites for optimality are the Kuhn–Tucker requirements [82,83].

3.2. Intelligent Optimization Techniques

Deterministic or exact optimization methods are rigorous, mathematical-based approaches, as explained in Sections 1 and 3.1, and they use known parameters. However, real-world problems frequently contain some unknown parameters [3]. Therefore, classical or exact optimization methods are limited because they are unable to handle integer-variable, variability, uncertainty, non-linearity and large-scale optimization problems [35–40,80,81]. Hence, the introduction of intelligent optimization techniques (stochastic). These approaches, as illustrated in Figure 6, are a class of algorithms that employ stochastic or heuristic ways to solve problems; they are also referred to as metaheuristics. They draw inspiration from biological or natural phenomena including physical annealing, swarm behavior, and evolution. They are intended to search a larger search space in order to identify a global or near-global optimum, and they do not require derivatives, in contrast to traditional approaches.

Optimization algorithms are computer programs used to solve the mathematical models developed during power system optimization. These algorithms search for the optimal solution within the parameters of the issue domain. There are two categories of algorithms: exact (deterministic) and not-exact (stochastic or approach methods), as seen in Figure 6. Even when exact algorithms find a global optimum, they frequently do not scale well to large problems [41,78]. For complicated power system problems, non-exact algorithms which fall into two categories—heuristic, and artificial intelligence (AI)—are most frequently employed in the literature.

Not-exact methods are often more scalable when handling large issues, allowing for precise characterization of the optimization problem. It is important to keep in mind that although these approaches look for fulfilling answers, they cannot ensure that the solution is feasible, near, or ideal. Nevertheless, certain modified heuristic techniques have come up and assert they can guarantee the best results [46].

Precise, conventional optimization methods often encounter issues that prevent them from solving the optimization problem in a timely way [44]. To avoid such circumstances, other methods that can detect high-quality, if not quite accurate, approximations to exact answers were created. These methods, referred to as heuristics, were initially primarily reliant on the knowledge and experience of specialists and were intended to explore the search space in a particularly useful way. Heuristics were initially employed by G. Polya in 1945 [84], and their use grew throughout the 1970s as new heuristics were created for specific issues in a range of technical and scientific fields, including electrical engineering. In essence, a heuristic is designed to provide better computational efficiency than conventional optimization methods at the expense of reduced precision.

Simple or basic heuristics and meta-heuristics are the two subclasses of heuristic [41]. In order to rapidly ascertain the control parameters for power system components such as transformers and generators without guaranteeing optimality, basic heuristics are commonly used in optimal power flow (OPF) and typically take the shape of constructive, local search algorithms [85]. Although simple heuristics can improve the solution for an issue rapidly and effectively, they have a high risk of becoming stuck in a local optimum.

Since they began in the mid-1980s, metaheuristic approaches to optimization problems have improved steadily, making it possible to address and solve a growing number of problems that were previously considered difficult or impossible to solve [86]. Meta-heuristics, which are a step up from simple heuristics, seek to find the optimal answer outside of a predetermined neighborhood. In OPF, meta-heuristic techniques are used to explore larger, complex solution spaces effectively than typical heuristics [87–92], such as evolutionary algorithms, Monte Carlo methods, human-based algorithms, etc. [45]. Many meta-heuristic methods are derived from biologic principles (nature-inspired, population-based algorithms) [93–96]. All of them, in essence, start with a point or set of points and go towards a better solution while being guided by heuristic, empirical, or logical rules and sensitivities [97–104]. These ideas are used to generate and categorize the search possibilities. In MOOPF, meta-heuristic algorithms are essential in solving problems efficiently by addressing multiple objectives simultaneously [3]. These algorithms balance exploration with exploitation by simulating a large number of control variable combinations, such as generator outputs, voltages, and tap settings, resulting in diverse, near-optimal solutions. Hence, the concept of Pareto optimality (Pareto front) as explained in Section 4 and illustrated by Figure 7 [14,78]. The purpose of the Pareto optimality is to find a set of trade-off optimal solutions (Pareto-optimal solutions), rather than one optimal solution [80,81]. As illustrated in Table 2, a power system operator has three objective functions—to minimize CO_2 emissions, generation cost and voltage deviation (VD). For such solutions, no objective function can be improved without first sacrificing at least one other objective function. For instance, in Table 2, the Pareto front illustrates that minimizing CO_2 emissions increases the generation cost, enabling decision-makers to choose their preferred point of operations based on policy considerations. The advantages of meta-heuristic algorithms are adaptability to change, and ability to handle integer-variable, non-linearity and large-scale optimization problems [3,41].

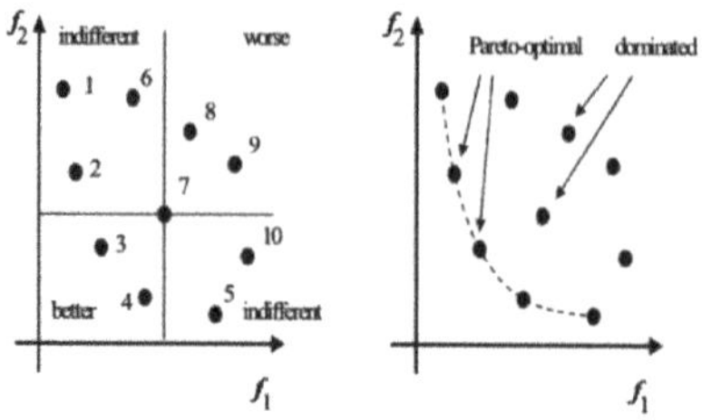

Figure 7. Illustration of the concept pareto optimality [78].

Table 2. An example of MOOPF solution based meta-heuristic algorithms (Pareto front).

Solution	CO_2 (kg/h)	Cost ($/h)	VD
1	400	900	0.016
2	300	950	0.014
3	200	1000	0.011

In OPF, AI techniques like machine learning and deep learning have grown in popularity [105]. By analyzing historical data, machine learning algorithms are able to predict the optimal power system configurations [106–111]. Because deep learning can handle complicated non-linear interactions, it is increasingly being used to solve OPF problems [112,113]. Because AI approaches may improve accuracy and automate power system management, they have potential when addressing large-scale, data-driven OPF operations [82]. For example, artificial neural networks (ANN) were based on a learning algorithm created by Hebb in 1949 that demonstrated how a network of neurons might exhibit learning behavior. ANNs are primarily categorized by their architecture (number of layers), learning regime, and topology (feed forward, connection pattern, or recurrent, etc.) [80].

However, the superiority of the heuristic approach in solving large-scale, complex, combinatorial, and nonlinear problems is supported by a vast number of models that have been published in scientific journals. Conversely, when the network size grows, exact techniques demand significantly more computing work [41,80,84]. To sum up, while accurate optimization techniques yield theoretically optimal outcomes, they may jeopardize modelling accuracy in power system settings, resulting in poor outcomes.

As explained in Section 1, a hybrid approach is possible and effective. The combination of deterministic and stochastic methods improves optimization results in power systems, resulting in more precise, faster, and dependable solutions. Deterministic approaches provide precision and speedy convergence, but stochastic approaches excel in exploring complex, nonlinear solution spaces [41,42]. Therefore, when employing hybrid approaches, stochastic algorithms identify the global optimum, and deterministic methods improve the results.

4. Multi-Objective Optimization in Power Systems

OPF is a set of optimization problems in power systems engineering. An optimization problem having many objective functions is referred to as multi-objective optimization. Unlike one objective with a single solution, multi-objective optimization (MOO) issues have a group or set of solutions that reflect trade-offs between objectives [78]. Subject to both operational and physical limitations, a MOOPF problem aims to concurrently optimize many competing objectives in power systems, as explained in Section 3.2. Multi-objective optimization techniques are intended to generate these trade-offs [114]. Resolving these compromises is essential because it provides the information and resources necessary for designers and operators to understand and weigh all their possibilities [46,78]. The following is a typical mathematical expression for a multi-objective optimization problem:

$$Min\backslash Max\ f_m(x) \tag{1}$$

Subject to

$$x_l \leq x \leq x_u$$
$$g(x) \leq 0$$
$$h(x) = 0$$

where x is an independent variable vector, $f_m(x)$ is a vector of objective functions, x_l and x_u are vectors of lower and upper bounds, respectively, and $h(x)$ and $g(x)$ are vectors of equality and inequality constraints. For every aim in the objective function vector, there are two alternative outcomes: minimization and maximization.

A complex MOO problem that considers the interests of multiple parties is the design, operation, and planning of a power system. These stakeholders, which include investors, network operators, end users, and regulators, each have unique goals that periodically clash. It is necessary to bring together several opposing goals, even within the same participating party. Consider the government's concurrent focus on economic and environmental challenges. Investors seek solutions that increase investment earnings while lowering construction expenses. Operators aim to achieve a balance between lowering operating expenses and preserving network stability. Power system optimization basically involves negotiating a complicated environment of many objectives and trade-offs in order to meet the needs and expectations of various stakeholders [81,82].

It is important to employ a concept other than optimal in order to solve a multi-objective optimization problem. Pareto-optimality is the most often used concept of optimality in multi-objective optimization [3,14,41,78,115,116]. The solution is considered non-dominated, Pareto optimal, Pareto efficient, or non-inferior if it is impossible to increase the value of any of the objective functions without lowering some of the other objective values. When the concept of Pareto optimality is applied, Figure 7 shows that solutions 3 and 4 "dominate" both solutions 7 and solutions 8 and 9, while solutions 8 and 9 are "dominated" by solution 7. All of the solutions in the entire set P that are not being dominated by any other solution comprise the set of non-dominated solutions [78]. Without further subjective preference information, there could be (perhaps infinite) numbers of Pareto optimal solutions that are all thought to be equally good [116]. The Pareto front of objectives is known as the Pareto front. Multi-objective optimization can therefore be said to have two true purposes [78]: (1) to find a set of solutions that are as close to the Pareto-optimal front as possible, and (2) to find a set of replies that are as diverse as possible. The following paragraphs examine and evaluate a number of important studies that have applied MOO to power system issues.

4.1. Categories of Multi-Objective Optimization Algorithm

MOO techniques can be divided into three major categories according to the manner preferences are expressed. Methods with preferences that have been expressed earlier, methods without preferences, and methods with preferences that have been presented later fall into these categories. A priori articulation provides the optimization approach with the prior knowledge about the preference or priority of different objective functions. An optimal solution is selected from the Pareto front, which is first acquired at a posterior articulation [116]. In addition to these three categories, MOO problems are also commonly solved using multi-objective evolutionary algorithms (MOEAs) [115–119]. Evolutionary algorithms (EAs) can also be applied to many types of challenges and search domains.

Additionally, data-driven methods like neural networks and reinforcement learning are being utilized to address MOO problems in power systems as a result of advancements in machine learning. These techniques reveal complex relationships between selection criteria and objectives, giving decision-makers valuable data. As a result, each of these five groups is briefly described in Figure 8 along with a few examples.

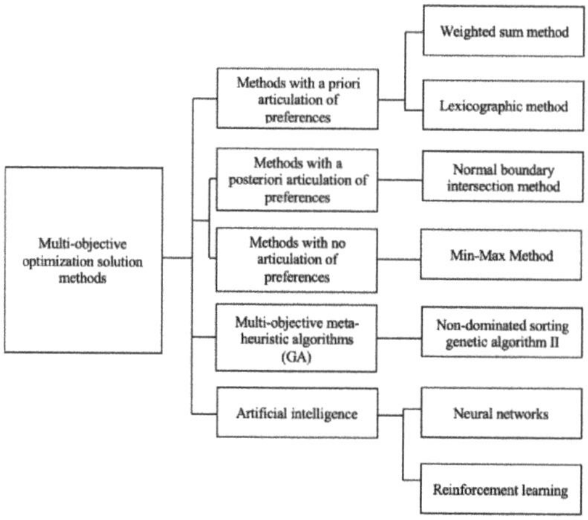

Figure 8. Categories of Multi-Objective Optimization Algorithm.

Since the methods listed in the three categories have different drawbacks, evolutionary algorithms (EAs) and AI-based algorithms are an excellent choice for solving multi-objective optimization issues [41].

4.2. Literature Review

MOO problems with hybrid and RES integration in power systems are addressed in [33–38], considering variabilities and uncertainties. In the first paper, a novel MOO technique that uses the Gravitational Search Algorithm (GSA) to lower CO_2 emissions, increase the usage of renewable energy sources, improve power dependability, and lower prices is introduced. The system's economic resilience is demonstrated by a sensitivity analysis to the carbon tax. In terms of solution diversity and quality, the GSA performs better than conventional techniques. The ideal configuration decreased environmental impact by 14.2% and increased the share of renewable energy by 18.4%. Similarly, in the second study, MOO is used to minimize power supply losses and cut costs. To determine which algorithm best balances cost and performance, seven algorithms are examined (Giant Trevally Optimizer or GTO, Gazelle Optimization Algorithm or GOA, Honey Badger Algorithm or HBA, Manta Ray Foraging Optimization or MRFO, Pelican Optimization Algorithm or POA, Sea Horse Optimizer or SHO, and Synergistic Swarm Optimization Algorithm or SSOA). Three scenarios (balanced supply, energy scarcity, and energy surplus) are used to test them. The third study suggests a framework for the MOO to determine the ideal placement and scale for distributed renewable generating in power networks. Uncertainties like demand variations, equipment malfunctions, and resource availability are taken into consideration. An OPF model based on Monte Carlo (MCS-OPF) simulates network performance and assesses the total cost of the system. A novel optimization technique that takes into account social, technical, economic, and environmental aspects is presented in the fourth study. It optimizes CO_2 emissions, human development index or HDI, loss of power supply probability or LPSP, and levelized cost of energy or LCOE all at once. The Pareto front is generated and simulated using the NSGA-II and MOPSO algorithms. In the fifth study an MO problem centered on network loss minimization and voltage profile augmentation was developed. MATLAB-2015 has been used to write the Newton–Raphson approach for load flow and the black hole algorithm. Finally, the applicability of the New Improved Differential Evolution (NIDE) method to the MOO-based Reactive Power Planning (RPP) problem is discussed in the sixth study.

In [40], Pareto effective solutions to the multi-objective reconfiguration problem are found using a multi-objective Tabu Search technique. A test has been carried out on an IEEE system to show how the multi-objective method works and how effective its use is.

Thyristor-controlled series compensators (TCSCs) are used in the study conducted in [42] to enhance power system performance by lowering power losses, increasing transmission capacity, and stabilizing the voltage profile. The MOOPF problem is solved using the adaptive parallel seeker optimization algorithm (APSOA). By determining the ideal size and position, the technique also reduces the cost of TCSC installation.

The OPF problem in [44] is successfully resolved by a multi-objective particle swarm optimization (MOPSO) method, which produces high-quality Pareto solutions in a single run. Similarly to this, other multi-objective techniques such as variable constants particle swarm optimization (VCPSO), genetic algorithm (GA), and particle swarm optimization (PSO) are also used in [47] to optimize the size and placement of distributed generators (DGs) with the goal of lowering power losses and improving voltage profiles. VCPSO is the most effective of these techniques. Additionally, the successful integration of renewable energy sources (RESs) into distribution networks is simulated using heuristic techniques including Ant Lion Optimization (ALO), Gray Wolf Optimization (GWO), Whale Optimization Algorithm (WOA), and PSO [73]. These methods decrease computing times and improve efficiency and convergence.

A two-step MOOPF solution technique has been suggested in order to preserve the economy, ecology, and security elements while the power system is operating [45]. In step 1, the knee point-driven evolutionary algorithm (KnEA) for the MOOPF problem may be introduced in order to find the Pareto-optimal solutions. In step 2, decision makers are given option supports through an integrated decision analysis technique that combines the Fuzzy C-Means (FCM) clustering approach and grey relational projection (GRP).

For the MOOPF problem addressed in [46], a novel MO Modified Imperialist Competitive Algorithm (MOMICA) is employed, accounting for the effects of fuel cost, voltage deviation, active power losses, and pollution. The industry-standard IEEE 30-bus power systems are used to evaluate the performance of a novel MOMICA approach.

Because RESs are unpredictable and irregular, integrating them into OPF becomes much more complex. To tackle this issue, the study in [48] presents two multi-objective algorithms centered on non-dominated sorting: the Non-Dominated Sorting Genetic Algorithm (NSGA-II) and its updated variant, the Adaptive Crossover Non-Dominated Sorting Differential Evolution (ACNSDE). These algorithms utilize a state-of-the-art constraint management technique called Superiority of Feasible Solutions (SF). In scenarios involving stochastic wind and solar energy, the proposed methods may effectively achieve the objectives of multi-objective OPF optimization, according to the actual results from several test cases. They are also capable of creating balanced, competitive solutions.

The multi-objective optimal reactive power dispatch (MORPD) problem, which aims to minimize active power loss and voltage deviation, has been addressed with a two-step approach. Classification-Based Pre-Selection (CPS) and Pareto Domination-Based Multi-Objective Evolutionary Algorithm (CPS/MOEA) are two MOO algorithms used in the initial step of this method to obtain Pareto optimum solutions (POSs) with uniformly distributed attributes. To further enhance these answers and reflect the preferences of the decision-maker, the Fuzzy C-Means Algorithm (FCM) and the Grey Relation Projection

Method (GRP) are coupled in the second stage. This combination approach appropriately addresses and solves the MORPD model [115]. Similarly, MOOPF is investigated in [117–119] using the MOEA/D based on decomposition. This technique allows one execution approach to produce a set of non-dominated results, or Pareto solutions. An innovative hybrid MOEA is then used to solve the MOOPF problem, particularly when combining RESs like solar and wind energy. This hybrid MOEA guarantees a range of workable options and enhances the selection process by fusing decomposition with the sum of normalized objectives.

Using a weighted sum approach, the Multi-Objective Cuckoo Search Algorithm (MOCSA) is created and used to determine the optimal network reconfiguration while guaranteeing that the voltage profile aligns with the goal of reducing power loss [120]. The Whale Optimization Algorithm (WOA) is used in another study [121] to address MOO, which includes lowering bus voltage variation (VD) and real power loss in grid-connected micro electrical systems with non-firm tiny power plants. These techniques were evaluated and compared with PSO, GA, and Artificial Bee Colony (ABC) using IEEE 6 and 14 bus systems.

In [122], cost, Voltage Stability Index (VSI), and loss objectives are examined using an updated PSO and the MOOPF via Pareto optimum approach. The research investigation also explains the key concepts of Ant colony optimization (ACO), PSO, and hybrid swarm optimization. The results of this proposed method provide the best compromise outcome with the quickest execution time when compared to PSO. The stochastic search optimization technique and fuzzy multi-objective optimal power flow (FMOPF) are used to address the OPF problem [123]. The proposed method minimizes the fuzzy satisfaction function of the objective function, which comprises active power loss, the total system cost, and voltage magnitude deviation, using PSO. The simulated results showed that the PSO approach might theoretically and successfully identify the optimal solution for OPF when compared to existing approaches and the proposed FMOPF. GA is used to solve the OPF problem in [124–128]. The developed algorithm will be checked using Matpower, which uses the interior point method to solve OPF.

In order to solve optimization problems with one or more objectives, as well as objectives like loss, generation cost, and severity value, two novel optimization techniques are proposed in [129]: the Hybrid Fruit Fly-based ABC (HFABC) approach and the Non-dominated Sorting Hybrid Fruit Fly-based ABC (NSHFABC) approach.

The recently proposed Multi-Objective Search Group Algorithm (MOSGA) [130], which leverages the benefits of the first search group algorithm, provides a powerful solution to the MOOPF problem. The use of fast non-dominated sorting, crowding distance calculations, and retaining select algorithms enables the acquisition of a non-dominated set in a single computing run. Similarly, in [131], the standard IEEE 30 bus is modified to accommodate RESs, and the MOOPF problem is resolved by the multi-objective pathfinder algorithm (MOPFA), which uses an elect-dominated collection and congestion.

A Harris Hawks Optimization (HHO) strategy is used in [132] to address single and multi-objective OPF difficulties in order to reduce the production emissions producers. The results are compared to those of several AI techniques, such as the Salp Swarm Algorithm (SSA), the WOA, the Glow Worm Optimization (GWO), and the Moth Flame (MF).

In [133], a new approach to the OPF problem is introduced, which utilizes the data-driven stacked extreme learning machine (SELM) framework. Because of its rapid training capabilities, SELM eliminates the need for the laborious parameter tweaking process typically associated with deep learning algorithms. However, it becomes challenging to directly apply SELM to OPF due to the intricate relationship between OPF solutions and the system's operating status. A data-driven OPF regression architecture that separates

OPF model features into three stages is created in order to address the issue. This reduces the possibility of learning bias in addition to making learning simpler. Additionally, it is demonstrated that this approach can be readily adapted to handle different test systems with only slight adjustments to a few hyperparameters. A deep reinforcement learning (DRL) approach is proposed in [134] to dynamically search for the OPF of power systems with a large adoption of RESs. This method utilizes power systems' spatial–temporal (ST) graphical data. The OPF problem is formulated as a MOO problem that considers production cost, transmission loss, and voltage variation, and the optimal solution is found using deep deterministic policy gradient (DDPG). Furthermore, the underlying temporal interactions and linkages among nodes within power systems are taken into consideration in the development of a multi-grained attention-based spatial-temporal graph convolution network (MG-ASTGCN). The purpose of this network is to extract ST graphical correlations and characteristics in order to provide a comprehensive understanding of the graphical dynamics of power systems. This knowledge is finally incorporated into the DRL algorithm's sequential Deep Deterministic Policy Gradient (DDPG) structure. This combination increases the ability to effectively meet the OPF challenge.

In [135], the research proposes the Hybrid Flying Squirrel Search Algorithm (HFSSA). The OPF is solved using the Squirrel Search method, a method inspired by the flying squirrel's innate hunting style. To boost its effectiveness, a mathematical crossover process is added. Even though several optimization methods have been proposed to solve OPF problems, optimal efficiency is still necessary. The Slime Mould Algorithm (SMA), first presented in [136], was inspired by the way the slime mould oscillation mode behaves in nature. The proposed method is commended for its clarity, ease of use, and ability to move forward to the ideal solution while preventing local optima from stagnating.

In order to maximize reactive power in power systems while improving voltage security, a method known as Improved Multi-Objective Particle Swarm Optimization (IMOPSO) has been developed in [137,138]. By adding an Adapted Binary Crossover (ABX) to fine-tune the particles' new positions and a diversity maintenance method based on Crowding Distance (CD) computations, the standard MOPSO is enhanced. In [139–141], Artificial Bee Colony (ABC) has been employed to solve the mixed-integer nonlinear Optimal Reactive Power Dispatch (ORPD) problem, which entails adjusting both discrete and continuous control variables.

In [142], a Constrained Dynamic Multitasking Multi-Objective Optimization (CDMTMO) is designed to solve the MOOPF issue. It employs three concurrent populations to solve the main constrained problem, a constraint-relaxed variant, and an unconstrained-to-constrained transition. To facilitate knowledge transfer and boost the quality of the solutions, it integrates a pre-selection technique, an improved dual ranking, and an improved ε-constrained method. This paper [143], tackles the drawbacks of conventional centralized economic dispatch techniques, including their slow calculation and lack of privacy, in response to the complexity of large-scale multi-area interconnected power systems (LMIPSs). A Distributed Multi-Objective Grey Wolf Optimizer (DMOGWO) is suggested as a solution to these problems, enabling the autonomous optimization of each area's sub-problem with little boundary information sharing. DMOGWO is shown to perform better than centralized approaches by lowering goal values, protecting data privacy, and improving overall optimization performance in case studies on IEEE 39-bus and 118-bus systems. The study in [144] suggests a Modified Pigeon-Inspired Optimization (MPIO) algorithm to solve non-differentiable OPF problems with competing objectives. Even with valve-point loading effects, the method efficiently optimizes goals such as active power loss, emissions, and fuel cost by combining the Penalty Function Method (PFM) and then improving it with a Constraint-Objective Sorting Rule (COSR).

In [145,146], the significance of probabilistic assessment in systems with high wind turbine (WT) penetration to improve power system performance and manage increasing renewable integration is highlighted. Using a MOPSO algorithm, it suggests an optimal allocation strategy for Interline Power Flow Controllers (IPFCs) with the goals of reducing active power losses, raising the Power Flow Index (PFI), and taking IPFC installation costs into account. Strong performance on the IEEE 30-bus test system is demonstrated by the method, which takes into account uncertainties in loads and wind speeds and uses a k-means-based data clustering method (DCM) for probabilistic evaluation.

The research study conducted in [147] aims to maximize reliability and performance while minimizing costs in series-parallel energy systems, especially those that use gas and solar generators. It presents a hybrid meta-heuristic algorithm, known as Bat Algorithm with Generalized Flight (BAG) that is applied to multi-objective redundancy design in power systems, which integrates the Ushakov method using the Universal Moment Generating Function (UMGF) for reliability evaluation and combines the Bat Algorithm (BA) and Generalized Evolutionary Walk Algorithm (GEWA). The integration of distributed renewables, electric vehicles, and storage systems presents operational issues for active distribution networks (ADNs) during the green energy transition [148]. The study addresses this by presenting a multi-objective optimization technique based on Analytical Target Cascading (ATC) that coordinates demand response (DR) across station areas and manages voltage and power flow using a Dynamic Optimal Power Flow (DOPF) model with Second-Order Conic Relaxation (SOCR). In [149], a self-adaptive algorithm inspired by nature called HHO was used for MOOPF. It performed exceptionally well in terms of convergence and managing several competing goals.

In [150], Information Gap Decision Theory (IGDT) is used to manage uncertainties in a multi-objective framework that strikes a balance between system flexibility and economic efficiency. The Normalized Normal Constraint (NNC) approach is used and verified on the IEEE 33-bus system in various circumstances to reconcile competing goals and produce evenly distributed Pareto solutions. In [151,152], studies introduced an Improved Strength Pareto Evolutionary method 2 (ISPEA2) which is an effective multi-objective evolutionary method for balancing several stability objectives in power system operation. Similarly, in [153], to guarantee Pareto optimality, a MOO strategy utilizing Extended Lexicographic Goal Programming was created and adjusted with the goal of reducing operating expenses, emissions, and asset deterioration. In [154,155], MOPSO is used in microgrids to distribute energy resources optimally while minimizing costs and environmental effects. Similarly, in [156], a hybrid technique called Binary Particle Swarm Optimization—Shuffled Frog Leaping Algorithm (BPSO-SFLA) is used to locate and size DGs optimally in order to minimize losses and enhance voltage stability. The complicated combinatorial problem of network reconfiguration and DSTATCOM placement in distribution systems is solved in [157], by modified ACO. The results demonstrate the importance of this hybrid method for utility operators in resource-constrained contexts, as it combined DSTATCOM deployment with network reconfiguration to cut losses by 83.57% and increase DSTATCOM efficacy by 50.71%.

In [158], the best Time Series Aggregation (TSA) techniques for Multi-Energy System (MES) design were chosen using a two-step MOO framework that minimizes both the total annual cost and the probability of load loss. A potent hybrid meta-heuristic method known as Hybrid Wavelet Mutation-based Shuffled Frog Leaping method and Particle Swarm Optimization (HWM^{2}SFLA-PSO) was created in [159], to manage the MOOPF complexity, particularly with the addition of FACTS devices like TCSC and UPFC. Similarly, in [160–162], first a Weighted Teaching-Learning-Based Optimization (WTLBO) algorithm which is an enhanced version of TLBO that uses weighted aggregation was used to solve

OPF problems with higher accuracy and multi-objective handling. Secondly, the nature-inspired technique known as Biogeography-Based Optimization (BBO) was used to solve limited, non-linear, multi-objective OPF problems. Thirdly, an improved BBO variant called Quasi-Oppositional Biogeography-Based Optimization (QO-BBO) uses opposition-based learning to boost global search and convergence for OPF problems. In [163], for effective MOOPF optimization, a hybrid evolutionary algorithm called Multi-Objective Coyote Optimization Algorithm with Meta-Lamarckian Learning (MOCOA-ML) that combines adaptive local search, external archives, and elite sorting was used.

In order to improve voltage security through a combined preventive-corrective control strategy that includes load shedding, generation rescheduling, and optimal FACTS device deployment, the study in [164] suggested a Multi-Objective Differential Evolution (MODE) method. Similarly, in [165], a Fuzzy Adaptive Hybrid PSO-Differential Evolution (FAHSPSO-DE), which is a hybrid metaheuristic algorithm that effectively solves complicated, MOOPF problems by fusing fuzzy logic with self-adaptive PSO and DE was used. As developed in [166], the hybrid Data Envelopment Analysis and Electromagnetism-like Algorithm (DEA-EMA) is a reliable worldwide optimization technique for multi-objective hydropower scheduling. The research conducted in [167], employed an ISAO-BiTCN-BiGRU-SA-IPBLS and Two-Stage Robust Optimization approach which is a hybrid framework that combines robust optimization for MOO power system balancing, deep learning for interval prediction, and intelligent swarm algorithm optimization. In [168], tri-objective demand side management (DSM) scheduling issues in smart grids are resolved using the evolutionary technique known as Multi-Objective Wind Driven Optimization (MOWDO), which draws inspiration from wind movement.

In [169,170], a modular optimization framework called Multi-Objective Optimization with Decomposition Strategy makes it possible to analyze energy systems in-depth and scalable ways in order to reduce costs and emissions. Then, for steady and highly accurate electrical power system forecasting, the Multi-Objective Dragonfly Algorithm (MODA) is used to fine-tune the Elman Neural Network. In [171], a dimension learning approach has been added to the Improved Archimedes Optimization Algorithm (IAOA) to improve performance in OPF applications, particularly in scenarios including grid integration and emission reduction. With multi-objective ε-constraint handling, the Flow Direction Algorithm efficiently resolved OPF with renewable uncertainty and integrates FACTS in [172].

An Improved Analytic Hierarchy Process (AHP) with Fuzzy Chance-Constrained Programming for managing uncertainty and maximizing several goals in renewable-integrated power systems has been developed in [173]. By optimizing thermal limit settings in [174], the Multi-Objective Genetic Algorithm (MOGA) can increase power transfer capacity and decrease system oscillations. The problem of choosing affordable transmission investments for small-scale power systems, particularly in areas with a high frequency of load shedding, is examined in [175]. In expansion planning, a multi-objective optimization framework is used to balance the costs of investment, operations, and load shedding. Soft Open Points (SOPs) and energy storage systems (ESS) are becoming vital instruments for controlling power flow and voltage as distribution networks develop into interactive systems with transmission networks and customers. In order to enhance load balancing and economic performance, [176] suggested a MOO technique that configures SOP and ESS deployments utilizing grid structure features and voltage sensitivity analysis. For OPF in hybrid renewable-integrated power systems, the Equilibrium Optimizer (EO) metaheuristic algorithm is employed in research [177], in both single- and multi-objective versions. In order to solve MOOPF, the Multi-Objective Search Group Algorithm (MOSGA) which is a hybrid metaheuristic that improves the search group algorithm by including diversity-preserving techniques and Pareto-based sorting has been used in paper [130]. For multimodal multi-objective optimization problems (MMOPs), DRSC-MOAGDE is a mix of Dynamic Reference Spaces-based Clustering (DRSC) and Multi-Objective Adaptive Differential Evolution (MOAGDE) that maximizes Pareto front diversity and solution accuracy developed in [178]. To reduce power loss and voltage imbalance, a MOO model is used in [179] and solved using the weighted sum approach. This model produces better results in LED lighting systems across case studies of 15-bus and 33-bus.

A multi-objective optimal scheduling model for grid-connected microgrids (MGs) that uses probabilistic constraints to account for the uncertainty of renewable generation while integrating several dispersed energy sources was developed in [180]. Using Sample Average Approximation (SAA), the model is reconstructed as a multi-objective mixed-integer linear programming (MILP) problem with the goals of reducing operating expenses and increasing customer satisfaction. To guarantee optimal and adaptable ORPD across several test networks, inheritance-based NSGA-II (i-NSGA-II) in conjunction with roulette wheel selection has been used in [181], as part of a day-ahead and real-time adjustment method. In [182,183], because of the nonlinearity of the problem, the most effective solutions that balance emissions and cost were chosen using the MOPSO method, a fuzzy-based decision mechanism, and non-dominated sorting. In order to manage power flow in systems that include thermal, wind, solar, and small-hydro sources while taking renewable energy unpredictability into consideration, [184] proposes a hybrid OPF model. Multi-Objective Thermal Exchange Optimization (MOTEO), which draws inspiration from Newton's Law of Cooling, is used to solve the model. Non-dominated sorting and crowding distance methods are added for solution diversity.

A MOGA has been developed in [185–193], a parallel ε-variable multi-objective genetic algorithm (Pev-MOGA) effectively solves the probabilistic optimum power flow (POPF) problem, producing precise optimal solutions across IEEE 30, 57, and 118-bus systems under various renewable and electric vehicle (EV) integration scenarios. In order to integrate renewable energy sources and solve the OPF problem a Modified JAYA (MJAYA) algorithm was created [194]. In order to lower emissions and improve economic efficiency in power systems, the study developed in [195,196] presents a Hybrid Dynamic Economic Emission Dispatch (HDEED) model that combines thermal, solar, and wind energy sources. To efficiently address the non-convex and high-dimensional HDEED issue, a new upgraded Moth–Flame Optimization method with a position disturbance updating strategy (MFO_PDU) has been created. Framework for knowledge-driven optimization was conducted in [197]; it combines multi-objective optimization procedures with data mining approaches.

In order to reduce generating costs, pollution, power losses, and voltage variations, [198] addressed the MOOPF problem in power systems integrated with wind farms. An improved constraint-handling technique was added to a novel decomposition-based MO horse herd optimization algorithm (MOHHO) to preserve the viability of the solution. In order to balance economic and environmental considerations, a multi-objective optimization model (MOOM) was developed in [199] to optimize wind power accommodation and total purchasing cost at the same time. A hybrid particle swarm optimization and gravity search algorithm (HPSO-GSA) was used to solve the problem. The best solution from the Pareto front was then chosen using a fuzzy satisfaction function. In order to solve the stochastic MOOPF problem in transmission networks under uncertainty from wind, solar PV, and plug-in electric vehicles (PEVs), the research conducted in [200] introduced the Enhanced Wombat Optimization Algorithm (EWOA). Papers [201,202] have investigated how hybrid systems improve energy conversion in renewable energy installations, especially those that use graphene. In order to address the OPF problem while taking into account thermal generation combined with unreliable wind energy sources, the Grasshopper Optimization Algorithm (GOA) was used.

With the goal of lowering expenses and emissions while enhancing dependability of the use of renewable energy, the study conducted in [203] tackles the best multi-objective design of Hybrid Renewable Energy Systems (HRES) for both isolated-island and grid-connected modes. A unified MOO approach was presented in [204–208] to coordinate sub-grid activities in large-scale power systems with unequal distribution of renewable energy. Then, based on the physical topologies and operational characteristics of wind turbines and photovoltaic (PV) units, a comprehensive reactive power optimization model was created. A stochastic optimization model that accounts for operational and financial variable uncertainty was developed in order to evaluate the economic feasibility of a hybrid energy system that combines wind, photovoltaic (PV) generating, and battery storage.

Pareto Envelope-based Selection Algorithm (PESA), a MOO technique, was used in [209] to identify the best configurations that balance technical, environmental, and economic objectives. Similarly, in order to tackle the OPF problem, [210] introduced a Hybrid Multi-Objective Artificial Physical Optimization (HMOAPO) algorithm, which solves the uncertainties in wind energy generation. Animal Migration Optimization (AMO) and Artificial Physical Optimization (APO) are combined in the HMOAPO to improve convergence and do away with the requirement for external control parameters. The Multi-objective Snow Ablation Optimizer (MOSAO) is presented in [211] as a solution to complicated OPF problems in power systems that integrate FACTS devices with renewable energy.

5. Results, Challenges and Future Directions

Optimization problems in power systems can be approached in a number of techniques. There are 41 papers under assessment, which are grouped according to their applications, techniques, and formulation of the problem that necessitates the choice of objective functions. The aggregated findings are shown in Tables 3–5 correspondingly.

Table 3. Applications of multi-objective optimization in power systems.

Year	Electrical Network Reconfiguration	Economic Dispatch/Optimal Power Flow	Power Distribution Planning	Operational Planning with RESs Integration
2010		[161]		
2011		[44]		
2012		[162]		
2013				
2014		[46]		
2015				[48]
2016		[123]		[20]
2017				
2018		[45,122]		
2019	[33]	[35]		
2020		[115,117,127,144,145]	[125]	
2021	[120]	[124]	[147]	[22,84,134]
2022	[48]	[123,129–132,136,143]	[129]	
2023	[47]	[135,137,160]		[21]
2024		[163]		
2025				[18,19]

Table 4. Algorithms developed for multi-objective optimization in Power Systems.

Approach (Method)	References
GOA, GTO, HBA, MRFO, POA, SHO, SSOA	[19]
MCS-OPF	[20]
BHA, DE, NIDE	[22,31]
Tabu Search	[33]
APSOA	[35]
MOPSO, IMOPSO, PSO, VCPSO, GA, GWO, ALO, WOA, FMOPF, DMOGWO, BPSO-SFLA, MOCOA-ML	[44,47,84,122,123,137,143,156,163]
MO-CSA, ABC, ACO, MPIO-PFM	[120,121,144]
KnEA, FCM, GRP	[45]
MOMICA	[46]
NSGA, NSGA-II, ACNSDE, CPF, NSGSA	[18,21,48,125]
CPSMOEA, MOEA/D, BA-GEWA(BAG)-UMGF	[115,117,118,147]
GAOPF, NLP-OPF	[124]
HFABC, NSHFABC, BBO, QO-BBO	[129,161,162]
MOSGA	[130]
MOPFA	[131]
HHO	[132]
SELM, DRL, DDPG, MG-ASTGCN, WTLBO	[133,134,160]
HFSSA	[135]
SMA	[136]

Table 5. Formulation of the MOOPF problem: number of objective functions.

Number of Objective Functions	References
2	[19,20,31,33,44,47,84,115,120,121,124,137,143]
3	[22,122,123,125,129,130,132–135,147,156,161–163]
4	[18,21,35,45,46,48,117,118,131,144]
5	[136]
6	[160]

MOO is becoming more and more popular in power systems, as shown in Table 3. Applications were restricted to basic operations like reactive and economic power dispatch between 2011 and 2015. Interest quickly increased between 2016 and 2020, extending to topics like integrating renewable energy sources and reducing emissions. Since 2021, MOO has been used more frequently to address more general issues such as demand response, distributed generation, and system planning, which reflects a move towards more intricate and varied power system demands. Key research gaps are revealed by the examination of multi-objective optimization (MOO) applications in power systems. These gaps include a lack of attention to reliability, sustainability, and social or environmental impacts, as well as a lack of investigation beyond conventional goals like cost and loss minimization. The majority of research is still limited to benchmark test systems, lacking scalability to large, complicated grids and real-world validation. Furthermore, the promise of hybrid approaches that combine deterministic, stochastic, and AI-based optimization is still underutilized, and uncertainty resulting from the integration of renewable energy sources is frequently simplified or disregarded. More thorough, intelligent, and uncertainty-aware optimization approaches that are applicable to current dynamic power systems are obviously needed.

With a focus on nature-inspired metaheuristics like GA, PSO, and more recent bio-inspired techniques like GWO and HHO, Table 4 demonstrates the diverse array of optimization algorithms used to solve multi-objective problems in power systems. It also illustrates the variety of approaches that have been investigated, such as physics-based, evolutionary, swarm intelligence, approaches-based AI and hybrid approaches. The long list of references and algorithms demonstrates a consistent research effort to modify and enhance optimization methods for the intricate problems of contemporary power systems.

According to Table 5, the majority of MOOPF research focuses on issues that have three objectives, like losses, voltage and cost or emissions. However, a need for more thorough optimization is reflected in the growing interest in three-objective formulations. There is a shift towards addressing the complicated and contradictory objectives in power system planning and operation, as seen by the lower but significant amount of research that examine four or five objectives.

The increasing complexity of the grid presents a number of challenges for optimization in power systems. Intermittency, forecasting errors, and the need to instantly balance competing technological, financial, and environmental goals are all brought about by the extensive integration of variable RESs. The nonlinear, large-scale, and frequently stochastic character of these challenges results in significant computational demands, and operational data security, availability, and quality continue to be crucial issues. Furthermore, as digitalization increases, cybersecurity threats are introduced into optimization processes, making resilience and secure operation major objectives.

In order to satisfy the demands of intricate, renewable-rich grids, future trends in power system optimization will concentrate on creating faster, more resilient, and more adaptable methods. In addition to AI-driven solutions like reinforcement learning, deep learning, and transfer learning for real-time and predictive decision-making, promising approaches include hybrid frameworks that blend intelligent and classical methods for improved accuracy and convergence speed. Stochastic and resilient formulations will better manage renewable variability and uncertainty, while distributed and multi-agent optimization will allow scaled control of decentralized resources.

The complexity of an optimization problem increases as the number of objective functions increases. This increase in complexity is tied to the increase in the search space and computing time requirements. Additional objectives, such as voltage stability and losses, increase trade-offs and hinder convergence, whereas two-objective problems, such as cost–emission, are comparatively straightforward. While evolutionary and swarm-based algorithms like NSGA-II and MOPSO can handle larger dimensions with increased computational work, classical approaches struggle with more than two objectives. In general, additional objectives increase the diversity of solutions and the flexibility of decisions, but they also necessitate more sophisticated algorithms and lengthier optimization durations.

The uncertainty of renewable energy generation is modelled using a collection of probability density functions (PDFs), with a different function used for each renewable resource [4,91]. When dealing with renewable resources, the probability distribution is often chosen based on the resource's physical attributes and validated by fitting it to historical data. Wind speed is typically represented by the Weibull distribution, and solar irradiation by the Beta distribution [68–72]. Wind energy uncertainty: the Weibull distribution is the most widely used and mathematically supported distribution for modelling the PDF of wind speed (v) at a certain place. Solar Energy uncertainty: the Beta distribution is widely used to simulate the uncertainty in solar irradiance (G), because its values are essentially constrained (between zero and a maximum corresponding to clear sky circumstances) [73–76].

Data preprocessing ensures data quality and consistency in MOOPF based on machine learning and deep learning [4,105–108]. It entails normalizing or standardizing inputs (such as voltage, demand, and generation), completing missing values, and developing relevant features. The input (state space) for DRL is the power system's operating states, whereas the action space is made up of control actions (such as generator outputs and tap adjustments). Typically, the training scenarios are conducted using simulated or historical datasets that reflect different grid situations, like faults, load swings, and renewable uncertainty. An agent interacts with a virtual grid in DRL, which is modelled as a Markov Decision Process [108–111]. Through feedback and repeated trials, the agent learns the most effective control rules. Overfitting is a major problem since models that were trained on ideal or constrained data may not function well in real-world scenarios. Techniques including cross-validation, dropout, early halting, and data augmentation are used to decrease it. Model generalization and reliability in deep learning models are enhanced by methods like testing across unseen grid designs and exploration strategies [107–113].

6. Conclusions

The present paper provided an overview of the existing optimization techniques and their applications, with a focus on multi-objective optimization in power systems. Multi-objective optimization of power systems is an important and developing area of research. As the energy industry grows and gives efficiency and sustainability more and more consideration, the need for multi-objective optimization will only increase. Many opposing objectives from different stakeholders are necessarily included in the planning, construction, and operation of power systems. From network stability and environmental sustainability to economic effectiveness, governments, investors, and operators all have different priorities and objectives. The literature review highlighted the important research initiatives in the field and demonstrated a range of tactics and methods. Numerous optimization techniques have been developed and applied by researchers to address the multi-objective challenges in power systems. The development of algorithms that employ artificial intelligence to solve the multi-objective optimization problem in power systems is the focus of current research and emerging trends as technology advances.

Author Contributions: Conceptualization, B.T.N.; methodology, L.M. and M.W.K.M.; investigation, B.T.N.; resources, B.T.N., L.M. and M.W.K.M.; writing—original draft preparation, B.T.N.; writing—review and editing, B.T.N., L.M. and M.W.K.M.; visualization, L.M. and M.W.K.M.; supervision, L.M. and M.W.K.M.; project administration, L.M. All authors have read and agreed to the published version of the manuscript.

Funding: This research received no external funding.

Institutional Review Board Statement: Not applicable.

Informed Consent Statement: Not applicable.

Data Availability Statement: No new data were created or analyzed in this study.

Conflicts of Interest: The authors declare no conflicts of interest.

Abbreviations

The following abbreviations are used in this manuscript:

ABC	Artificial Bee Colony
ABX	Adapted Binary Crossover
ACNSDE	Adaptive Crossover Non-Dominated Sorting Differential Evolution
ACO	Ant Colony Optimization
ADNs	Active Distribution Networks
AHP	Analytic Hierarchy Process
AI	Artificial Intelligence
ALO	Ant Lion Optimization

ANNs	Artificial Neural Networks
APSOA	Adaptive Parallel Seeker Optimization Algorithm
ATC	Analytical Target Cascading
BAG	Bat Algorithm with Generalized Flight
BBO	Biogeography-Based Optimization
BPSO-SFLA	Binary Particle Swarm Optimization–Shuffled Frog Leaping Algorithm
CD	Crowding Distance
CDMTMO	Constrained Dynamic Multitasking Multi-Objective Optimization
CFD/CFI	Constraint Feasibility Degree/Index
COSR	Constraint-Objective Sorting Rule
CPS	Classification-Based Pre-Selection
DCM	Data Clustering Method
DDPG	Deep Deterministic Policy Gradient
DEA-EMA	Data Envelopment Analysis and Electromagnetism-like Algorithm
DGs	Distributed Generators
DMOGWO	Distributed Multi-Objective Grey Wolf Optimiser
DOPF	Dynamic Optimal Power Flow
DR	Demand Response
DRL	Deep Reinforcement Learning
EAs	Evolutionary Algorithms
EO	Equilibrium Optimiser
ESSs	energy storage systems
EWOA	Enhanced Wombat optimization Algorithm
FAHSPSO-DE	Fuzzy Adaptive Hybrid Particle Swarm Optimization-Differential Evolution
FCM	Fuzzy C-Means
FMOPF	Fuzzy Multi-Objective Optimal Power Flow
GA	Genetic Algorithms
GEWA	Generalized Evolutionary Walk Algorithm
GOA	Gazelle Optimization Algorithm
GOA	Grasshopper optimization Algorithm
GRP	Grey Relational Projection
GSA	Gravitational Search Algorithm
GTO	Giant Trevally Optimizer
GW	Gigawatt
GWO	Glow Warm Optimization
GWO	Gray Wolf Optimization
HBA	Honey Badger Algorithm
HDEED	Hybrid Dynamic Economic Emission Dispatch
HDI	Human Development Index
HFABC	Hybrid Fruit fly-based Artificial Bee Colony
HFSSA	Hybrid Flying Squirrel Search Algorithm
HHO	Harris Hawks Optimization
HRES	Hybrid Renewable Energy Systems
HWMSFLA-PSO	Hybrid Wavelet Mutation-based Shuffled Frog Leaping method and Particle Swarm Optimization
IAOA	Improved Archimedes optimization Algorithm
IEEE	Institute of Electrical and Electronics Engineers
IGDT	Information Gap Decision Theory
IMOPSO	Improved Multi-Objective Particle Swarm Optimization
IP	Integer Programming
IPFCs	Interline Power Flow Controllers
IRENA	International Renewable Energy Agency
ISPEA2	Improved Strength Pareto Evolutionary method 2
KnEA	Knee Point-Driven Evolutionary Algorithm

LCOE	Levelized Cost of Energy
LMIPSs	large-scale multi-area interconnected power systems
LP	Linear Programming
LPSP	Loss of Power Supply Probability
MCS-OPF	Monte Carlo simulation–Optimal Power Flow
MES	Multi-Energy System
MF	Moth Flame
MFO_PDU	Moth-Flame Optimization Method with a Position Disturbance Updating
MG-ASTGCN	Multi-Grained Attention-Based Spatial-Temporal Graph Convolution Network
MGs	microgrids
MIP	Mixed-Integer Programming
MJAYA	Modified JAYA
MOADE	Multi-Objective Adaptive Differential Evolution
MOCOA-ML	Multi-Objective Coyote optimization Algorithm with Meta-Lamarckian Learning
MOCSA	Multi-Objective Cuckoo Search Algorithm
MODA	Multi-Objective Dragonfly Algorithm
MODE	Multi-Objective Differential Evolution
MOEA	Multi-Objective Evolutionary Algorithm
MOEA/D	Multi-Objective Evolutionary Algorithm based on Decomposition
MOHHO	Multi-Objective Horse Herd Optimization Algorithm
MOMICA	Multi-Objective Modified Imperialist Competitive Algorithm
MOO	Multi-Objective Optimization
MOOPF	Muti-Objective Optimal Power Flow
MOPFA	Multi-Objective Pathfinder Algorithm
MOPSO	Multi-Objective Particle Swarm Optimization
MORPD	Multi-Objective Optimal Reactive Power Dispatch
MOSAO	Multi-objective Snow Ablation Optimiser
MOSGA	Multi-Objective Search Group Algorithm
MOTEO	Multi-Objective Thermal Exchange optimization
MOWDO	Multi-Objective Wind Driven optimization
MPIO	Modified Pigeon-Inspired Optimization
MRFO	Manta Ray Foraging Optimization
NIDE	New Improved Differential Evolution
NLP	Nonlinear Programming
NNC	Normalized Normal Constraint
NSGA-II	Non-Dominated Sorting Genetic Algorithm
NSHFABC	Non-Dominated Sorting Hybrid Fruit Fly-Based Artificial Bee Colony
OPF	Optimal Power Flow
PESA	Pareto Envelope-based Selection Algorithm
PFI	Power Flow Index
PFM	Penalty Function Method
POA	Pelican Optimization Algorithm
POPF	Probabilistic Optimum Power Flow
POSs	Pareto optimum solutions
PSO	Particle Swarm Optimization
PV	Photovoltaic
QO-BBO	Quasi-Oppositional Biogeography-Based Optimization
QP	Quadratic programming
RESs	Renewable Energy Sources
SAA	Sample Average Approximation
SELM	Stacked Extreme Learning Machine
SHO	Sea Horse Optimizer
SMA	Slime Mould Algorithm
SOCR	Second-Order Conic Relaxation

SOPs	Soft Open Points
SSA	Salp Swarm Algorithm
SSOA	Synergistic Swarm Optimization Algorithm
ST	Spatial-Temporal
TCSCs	Thyristor-Controlled Series Compensators
TSA	Time Series Aggregation
TW	Terawatt
UMGF	Universal Moment Generating Function
VCPSO	variable constants particle swarm optimization
VD	Voltage Deviation
VSI	Voltage Stability Index
WOA	Whale Optimization Algorithm
WT	Wind Turbine
WTLBO	Weighted Teaching-Learning-Based Optimization

References

1. Bollen, M.; Hassan, F. *Introduction. Integration of Distributed Generation in the Power System*; Hanzo, L., Abhari, R., Eds.; IEEE press on power engineering; John Wiley & Sons: Hoboken, NJ, USA, 2011; pp. 1–5.
2. Grainger, J.J.; Stevenson, W.D. *Power Systems Analysis*; Stephen, W., Ed.; Electrical and computer engineering; McGraw-Hill: New York, NY, USA, 1994; pp. 329–376.
3. Valle, Y.D.; Venayagamoorthy, G.K.; Mohagheghi, S.; Hernandez, J.C.; Harley, R.G. Particle Swarm Optimization: Basic Concepts, Variants and Applications in Power Systems. *IEEE Trans. Evol. Comp.* **2008**, *12*, 171–195. [CrossRef]
4. Liang, J.; Venayagamoorthy, G.K.; Harley, R.G. Wide-Area Measurement Based Dynamic Stochastic Optimal Power Flow Control for Smart Grids with High Variability and Uncertainty. *IEEE Trans. Smart Grid* **2012**, *3*, 59–69. [CrossRef]
5. Alamo, D.H.; Medina, R.N.; Ruano, S.D.; García, S.S.; Moustris, K.P.; Kavadias, K.K.; Zafirakis, D.; Tzanes, G.; Zafeiraki, E.; Spyropoulos, G.; et al. An Advanced Forecasting System for the Optimum Energy Management of Island Microgrids. *Energy Procedia* **2019**, *159*, 111–116. [CrossRef]
6. Wei, M. Multi-Objective Optimisation of Highly Distributed Power System Management. Doctorate Thesis, University of Edinburgh, Scotland, UK, 2020.
7. Yan, C.; Wang, F.; Pan, Y.; Shan, K.; Kosonen, R. A multi-timescale cold storage system within energy flexible buildings for power balance management of smart grids. *Renew. Energy* **2020**, *161*, 626–634. [CrossRef]
8. Premkumar, M.; Jangir, P.; Sowmya, R.; Elavarasan, R.M. Many-Objective Gradient-Based Optimizer to Solve Optimal Power Flow Problems: Analysis and Validations. *Eng. Appl. Artif. Intell.* **2021**, *106*, 104479. [CrossRef]
9. Scheibe, C.; Kuri, A.; Feng, Y.; Zhao, L.; Xiong, X.; La Seta, P.; Liang, X.P.; Knödtel, J.; Holzinger, P.; Reichenbach, M.; et al. Interfacing Real-Time and Offline Power System Simulation Tools Using UDP or FPGA Systems. *Electr. Power Syst. Res.* **2022**, *212*, 108490. [CrossRef]
10. Cui, Y.; Geng, Z.; Zhu, Q.; Han, Y. Review: Multi-Objective Optimization Methods and Application in Energy Saving. *Energy* **2017**, *125*, 681–704. [CrossRef]
11. Vallés, M.; Reneses, J.; Frías, P.; Mateo, C. Economic Benefits of Integrating Active Demand in Distribution Network Planning: A Spanish Case Study. *Electr. Power Syst. Res.* **2016**, *136*, 331–340. [CrossRef]
12. Karmellos, M.; Mavrotas, G. Multi-Objective Optimization and Comparison Framework for the Design of Distributed Energy Systems. *Energy Convers. Manag.* **2019**, *180*, 473–495. [CrossRef]
13. Li, B.; Zhang, J. A Review on the Integration of Probabilistic Solar Forecasting in Power Systems. *Sol. Energy* **2020**, *210*, 68–86. [CrossRef]
14. Fadaee, M.; Radzi, M.A.M. Multi-Objective Optimization of a Stand-Alone Hybrid Renewable Energy System by Using Evolutionary Algorithms: A Review. *Renew. Sustain. Energy Rev.* **2012**, *16*, 3364–3369. [CrossRef]
15. Liu, H.; Li, Y.; Duan, Z.; Chen, C. A Review on Multi-Objective Optimization Framework in Wind Energy Forecasting Techniques and Applications. *Energy Convers. Manag.* **2020**, *224*, 113324. [CrossRef]
16. Barakat, S.; Osman, A.I.; Tag-Eldin, E.; Telba, A.A.; Abdel Mageed, H.M.; Samy, M.M. Achieving Green Mobility: Multi-Objective Optimization for Sustainable Electric Vehicle Charging. *Energy Strategy Rev.* **2024**, *53*, 101351. [CrossRef]
17. Khan, T.; Ullah, Z.; Agyekum, E.B.; Hasanien, H.M.; Yu, M. Multi-objective optimization of combined heat and power system integrated with multi-energy storage systems for rural communities. *J. Energy Storage* **2024**, *99*, 113433. [CrossRef]
18. Mahmoudi, S.M.; Maleki, A.; Ochbelagh, D.R. Multi-objective optimization of hybrid energy systems using gravitational search algorithm. *Nat. Sci. Rep.* **2025**, *15*, 2550. [CrossRef] [PubMed]

19. Shaier, A.A.; Elymany, M.M.; Enany, M.A.; Elsonbaty, N.A. Multi-objective optimization and algorithmic evaluation for EMS in a HRES integrating PV, wind, and backup storage. *Nat. Sci. Rep.* **2025**, *15*, 1147. [CrossRef]
20. Mena, R.; Hennebel, M.; Li, Y.F.; Zio, E. A multi-objective optimization framework for risk-controlled integration of renewable generation into electric power systems. *Energy* **2016**, *106*, 712–727. [CrossRef]
21. Cheraghi, R.; Jahangir, M.H. Multi-objective optimization of a hybrid renewable energy system supplying a residential building using NSGA-II and MOPSO algorithms. *Energy Convers. Manag.* **2023**, *294*, 117515. [CrossRef]
22. Mundra, P.; Arya, A.; Gawre, S.K. A Multi-Objective Optimization Based Optimal Reactive Power Reward for Voltage Stability Improvement in Uncertain Power System. *J. Electr. Eng. Technol.* **2021**. [CrossRef]
23. Huang, Z.; Fang, B.; Deng, J. Multi-Objective Optimization Strategy for Distribution Network Considering V2G-Enabled Electric Vehicles in Building Integrated Energy System. *Prot. Control. Mod. Power Syst.* **2020**, *5*, 7. [CrossRef]
24. Zhang, T.; Li, W.; Wang, R. Surrogated-Assisted Multimodal Multi-Objective Optimization for Hybrid Renewable Energy System *Complex Intell. Syst.* **2023**, *9*, 4075–4087. [CrossRef]
25. Li, J.; Zhao, H. Multi-Objective Optimization and Performance Assessments of an Integrated Energy System Based on Fuel, Wind and Solar Energies. *Entropy* **2021**, *23*, 431. [CrossRef]
26. Deng, H.; Xu, Y. Distributed Alternating Direction Method of Multipliers for Multi-Objective Optimization. *Adv. Pure Math.* **2022**, *12*, 249–259. [CrossRef]
27. Dong, Z.; Liu, J.; Lv, F.; Jing, W. Multi-Objective Optimization Evaluation Index System of Power System Resilience Considering Economy. In Proceedings of the CMAAE 2021: 2021 International Conference on Mechanical, Aerospace and Automotive Engineering, Changsha, China, 3–5 December 2021; pp. 20–27.
28. Anoune, K.; Bouya, M.; Astito, A.; Abdellah, A. Ben Sizing Methods and Optimization Techniques for PV-Wind Based Hybrid Renewable Energy System: A Review. *Renew. Sustain. Energy Rev.* **2018**, *93*, 652–673. [CrossRef]
29. Ge, X.; Ahmed, F.W.; Rezvani, A.; Aljojo, N.; Samad, S.; Foong, L.K. Implementation of a Novel Hybrid BAT-Fuzzy Controller Based MPPT for Grid-Connected PV-Battery System. *Control Eng. Pract.* **2020**, *98*. [CrossRef]
30. He, P.; Fang, Q.; Jin, H.; Ji, Y.; Gong, Z.; Dong, J. Coordinated Design of PSS and STATCOM-POD Based on the GA-PSO Algorithm to Improve the Stability of Wind-PV-Thermal-Bundled Power System. *Int. J. Electr. Power Energy Syst.* **2022**, *141*, 108208. [CrossRef]
31. Vadivelu, K.R.; Marutheeswar, G.V. Multi Objective Optimization Based optimal Reactive Power Planning Using Improved Differential Evolution Incorporating FACTS. *Int. J. Electr. Eng. Inform.* **2015**, *7*, 630. [CrossRef]
32. Chen, W.; Ren, H.; Zhou, W. Review of multi-objective optimization in long-term energy system models. *Glob. Energy Interconnect.* **2023**, *6*, 645–666. [CrossRef]
33. García-Martínez, E.; Espinosa-Juárez, S.; Pérez-Rojas, C. A Multi-Objective Optimal Reconfiguration of Electrical Networks to Improve Power Quality Aspects. In Proceedings of the IEEE International Conference on Computational Science and Computational Intelligence (CSCI), Las Vegas, NV, USA, 5–7 December 2019; pp. 1–5.
34. Grond, M.O.W.; Luong, N.H.; Morren, J.; Slootweg, J.G. Multi-objective optimization techniques and applications in electric power systems. In Proceedings of the IEEE 47th International Universities Power Engineering Conference (UPEC), London, UK, 4–7 September 2012; pp. 1–6.
35. Shafik, M.B.; Chen, H.; Rashed, G.I.; El-Sehiemy, R.A. Adaptive Multi Objective Parallel Seeker Optimization Algorithm for Incorporating TCSC Devices into Optimal Power Flow Framework. *IEEE Access* **2019**, *7*, 36934–36947. [CrossRef]
36. Bourennani, F. Leadership-Based Multi-Objective Optimization with Applications in Energy Systems. Doctorate Thesis, University of Ontario Institute of Technology, Oshawa, ON, Canada, 2013.
37. Nallolla, C.A.; Vijayapriya, P.; Chittathuru, D.; Padmanaban, S. Multi-Objective Optimization Algorithms for a Hybrid AC/DC Microgrid Using RES: A Comprehensive Review. *Electronics* **2023**, *12*, 1062. [CrossRef]
38. Ge, L.; Li, Y.; Li, Y.; Yan, J.; Sun, Y. Smart Distribution Network Situation Awareness for High-Quality Operation and Maintenance: A Brief Review. *Energies* **2022**, *15*, 828. [CrossRef]
39. He, H.; Wu, K. Research on Multi-Objective Optimization of Energy Power System Under Low Carbon Constraints. *J. Phys. Conf. Ser.* **2023**, *2442*, 012022. [CrossRef]
40. Alzahrani, A.; Hafeez, G.; Ali, S.; Murawwat, S.; Khan, M.I.; Rehman, K.; Abed, A.M. Multi-Objective Energy Optimization with Load and Distributed Energy Source Scheduling in the Smart Power Grid. *Sustainability* **2023**, *15*, 9970. [CrossRef]
41. Rahnamafard, Y. Multi-Objective Optimization Application in Power Systems. Master's Thesis, Memorial University of Newfoundland, St. John's, NL, Canada, 2019.
42. Mishra, S. Multi-Objective Optimization Methods for Various Power System Problems. *J. Microcontroll. Eng. Appl.* **2022**, *9*, 35–39. [CrossRef]
43. McGranaghan, M.F.; Dugan, R.C.; Beaty, H.W. *Electrical Power Systems Quality*; McGraw-Hill: New York, NY, USA, 1996.

44. Zaro, F.R.; Abido, M.A. Multi-Objective Particle Swarm Optimization for Optimal Power Flow in a Deregulated Environment of Power Systems. In Proceedings of the IEEE 11th International Conference on Intelligent Systems Design and Applications, Cordoba, Spain, 22–24 November 2011; pp. 1–6.
45. Yahui, L.; Yang, L. Two-Step Many-Objective Optimal Power Flow Based on Knee Point-Driven Evolutionary Algorithm. *Energy Econ. Environ. Ind. Prod. Process.* **2018**, *6*, 250.
46. Ghasemi, M.; Ghavidel, S.; Ghanbarian, M.M.; Gharibzadeh, M.; Vahed, A.A. Multi-objective optimal power flow considering the cost, emission, voltage deviation and power losses using multi-objective modified imperialist competitive algorithm. *Energy* **2014**, *78*, 276–289. [CrossRef]
47. Alajmi, B.N.; AlHajri, M.F.; Ahmed, N.A.; Abdelsalam, I.; Marei, M.I. Multi-objective Optimization of Optimal Placement and Sizing of Distributed Generators in Distribution Networks. *IEEJ Trans. Electr. Electron. Eng.* **2023**, *18*, 817–833. [CrossRef]
48. Li, S.; Gong, W.; Wan, L.; Gu, Q. Multi-objective optimal power flow with stochastic wind and solar power. *Appl. Soft Comput.* **2022**, *114*, 108045. [CrossRef]
49. Ayalew, F.; Hussen, S.; Pasam, G.K. Optimization techniques in Power System: Review. *Int. J. Eng. Appl. Sci. Technol.* **2019**, *3*, 8–16.
50. Bush, B.; Chen, Y.; Ofori-Boateng, D.; Gel, Y.R. Topological Machine Learning Methods for Power System Responses to Contingencies: Preprint. Available online: https://docs.nrel.gov/docs/fy21osti/77899.pdf (accessed on 9 November 2025).
51. Yaldız, A.; Gökçek, T.; Ateş, Y.; Erdinç, O. Overview and Advancement of Power System Topology Addressing Pre- and Post-Event Strategies under Abnormal Operating Conditions. *Sustain. Energy Grids Netw.* **2024**, *40*, 101562. [CrossRef]
52. El Berkaoui, A.; Bahsine, S.; Oukennou, A.; Nouh, F.A.; Rzine, B. Distribution Network Topology Planning and Optimization: A Brief Review. In Proceedings of the E3S Web of Conferences; EDP Sciences, Surakarta City, Indonesia, 27–28 September 2023; Volume 469. [CrossRef]
53. Hines, P.; Blumsack, S.; Sanchez, E.C.; Barrows, C. The Topological and Electrical Structure of Power Grids. In Proceedings of the Proceedings of the Annual Hawaii International Conference on System Sciences, Kauai, HI, USA, 5–8 January 2010.
54. Mokryani, G. Distribution Network Types and Configurations. In *Future Distribution Networks*; AIP Publishing: Melville, NY, USA, 2022; pp. 1–18. [CrossRef]
55. Wang, C.; An, J.; Mu, G. Power System Network Topology Identification Based on Knowledge Graph and Graph Neural Network. *Front. Energy Res.* **2021**, *8*, 613331. [CrossRef]
56. GE, H.; XU, B.; CHEN, W.; ZHANG, X.; BI, Y. Topology Identification of Low Voltage Distribution Network Based on Current Injection Method. *Arch. Electr. Eng.* **2021**, *70*, 297–306. [CrossRef]
57. Luan, W.; Xu, D.; Liu, B.; Jiang, W.; Feng, L.; Liu, W. Improved Topology Identification for Distribution Network with Relatively Balanced Power Supplies. *IET Energy Syst. Integr.* **2024**, *6*, 162–173. [CrossRef]
58. Cavraro, G.; Kekatos, V.; Zhang, L.; Giannakis, G.B. Learning Power Grid Topologies. In *Advanced Data Analytics for Power Systems*; Cambridge University Press: Cambridge, UK, 2021.
59. Zhu, J.; Member, S.; Hwang, A. Sadjadpour, Real Time Congestion Monitoring and Management of Power Systems. In Proceedings of the 2005 IEEE/PES Transmission & Distribution Conference & Exposition: Asia and Pacific, Dalian, China, 15–18 August 2005.
60. Nyingu, B.T.; Masike, L.; Mbukani, M.W.K. Optimal Sizing of Residential Photovoltaic (PV)—Battery Power System in an Off-grid Configuration. In Proceedings of the IEEE PES/IAS PowerAfrica, Johannesburg, South Africa, 7–10 October 2024.
61. Bre, F.; Fachinotti, V.D. A Computational Multi-Objective Optimization Method to Improve Energy Efficiency and Thermal Comfort in Dwellings. *Energy Build.* **2017**, *154*, 283–294. [CrossRef]
62. Kuroda, K.; Magori, H.; Ichimura, T.; Yokoyama, R. A Hybrid Multi-Objective Optimization Method Considering Optimization Problems in Power Distribution Systems. *J. Mod. Power Syst. Clean Energy* **2015**, *3*, 41–50. [CrossRef]
63. Finke, J.; Bertsch, V. Implementing a Highly Adaptable Method for the Multi-Objective Optimization of Energy Systems. 2022. Available online: https://mpra.ub.uni-muenchen.de/115504/ (accessed on 9 November 2025).
64. Subramanyan, K.; Diwekar, U.M.; Goyal, A. Multi-Objective Optimization for Hybrid Fuel Cells Power System under Uncertainty. *J. Power Sources* **2004**, *132*, 99–112. [CrossRef]
65. Crespo-Sánchez, G.; Pérez-Abril, I. Multi-Objective Reconfiguration of the Distribution Systems by Using NSGA-II and Local Improvement. *Dyna* **2023**, *90*, 89–96. [CrossRef]
66. Pathe, S.; Bertsch, V. Multi-Objective Energy System Modeling of the Rhenish Mining Area Minimizing Costs and Environmental Impacts. In Proceedings of the International Conference on Applied Energy, Bangkok, Thailand, 29 November–5 December 2021.
67. Pindoriya, N.M.; Singh, S.N.; Lee, K.Y. A Comprehensive Survey on Multi-objective Evolutionary Optimization in Power System Applications. In Proceedings of the IEEE Power and Energy Society General Meeting, Minneapolis, MN, USA, 25–29 July 2010.
68. Muralitharan, K.; Sakthivel, R.; Shi, Y. Multi-objective Optimization Technique for Demand Side Management with Load Balancing Approach in Smart Grid. *Neurocomputing* **2016**, *177*, 110–119. [CrossRef]
69. Kheiri, F. A Review on Optimization Methods Applied in Energy-Efficient Building Geometry and Envelope Design. *Renew. Sustain. Energy Rev.* **2018**, *92*, 897–920. [CrossRef]

70. Elkholy, A.M.; Panfilov, D.I.; ELGebaly, A.E. Comparative Analysis of FACT Devices for Optimal Improvement of Power Quality in Unbalanced Distribution Systems. *Sci. Rep.* **2025**, *15*, 2672. [CrossRef] [PubMed]
71. Farhat, M.; Kamel, S.; Abdelaziz, A.Y. Modified Tasmanian Devil Optimization for Solving Single and Multi-Objective Optimal Power Flow in Conventional and Advanced Power Systems. *Cluster Comput.* **2025**, *28*, 105. [CrossRef]
72. Güven, A.F.; Yörükeren, N.; Mengi, O.Ö. Multi-Objective Optimization and Sustainable Design: A Performance Comparison of Metaheuristic Algorithms Used for on-Grid and off-Grid Hybrid Energy Systems. *Neural Comput. Appl.* **2024**, *36*, 7559–7594. [CrossRef]
73. Risi, B.G.; Riganti-Fulginei, F.; Laudani, A. Modern Techniques for the Optimal Power Flow Problem: State of the Art. *Energies* **2022**, *15*, 6387. [CrossRef]
74. Siddaiah, R.; Saini, R.P. A Review on Planning, Configurations, Modeling and Optimization Techniques of Hybrid Renewable Energy Systems for off Grid Applications. *Renew. Sustain. Energy Rev.* **2016**, *58*, 376–396. [CrossRef]
75. Rajput, S.K.; Dheer, D.K. Forecasting Power-Factor Reductions in Rooftop PV-Integrated Industrial Power Systems: Mathematical Modelling and Experimental Validation. *Sustain. Energy Grids Netw.* **2023**, *33*, 100974. [CrossRef]
76. Sharafi, M.; ElMekkawy, T.Y. Stochastic Optimization of Hybrid Renewable Energy Systems Using Sampling Average Method. *Renew. Sustain. Energy Rev.* **2015**, *52*, 1668–1679. [CrossRef]
77. Yang, J.; Su, C. Robust Optimization of Microgrid Based on Renewable Distributed Power Generation and Load Demand Uncertainty. *Energy* **2021**, *223*, 120043. [CrossRef]
78. Rivas-Dávalos, F.; Moreno-Goytia, E.; Gutiérrez-Alacaraz, G.; Tovar-Hernández, J. Evolutionary Multi-Objective Optimization in Power Systems: State-of-the-Art. In Proceedings of the IEEE Lausanne Power Tech, Lausanne, Switzerland, 1–5 July 2007; Volume 451.
79. Géron, A. *Hands-On Machine Learning with Scikit-Learn, Keras, and TensorFlow*, 2nd ed.; O'Reilly Media: Sebastopol, CA, USA, 2019.
80. Bansal, R.C. Optimization Methods for Electric Power Systems: An Overview. *Int. J. Emerg. Electr. Power Syst.* **2005**, *2*, 1–23. [CrossRef]
81. Frank, S.; Rebennack, S. An introduction to optimal power flow: Theory, formulation, and examples. *IIE Trans. Oper. Eng. Anal.* **2016**, *48*, 1172–1197. [CrossRef]
82. Zhu, J. *Optimization of Power System Operation*; John Wiley & Sons: Hoboken, NJ, USA, 2015.
83. Mangasarian, O.L. A Newton Method for Linear Programming. *J. Optim. Theory Appl.* **2004**, *121*, 1–18. [CrossRef]
84. Özlü, I.A.; Baimakhanov, O.; Saukhimov, A.; Ceylan, O. A Heuristic Methods-Based Power Distribution System Optimization Toolbox. *Algorithms Plan. Oper. Power Syst.* **2021**, *15*, 14. [CrossRef]
85. Gavrilas, M. Heuristic and metaheuristic optimization techniques with application to power systems. In Proceedings of the 12th WSEAS International Conference on Mathem Methods And Comput Techniques in Electrical Engineer, Timișoara, Romania, 21–23 October 2010; pp. 1–10.
86. Shaheen, A.M.; Spea, S.R.; Farrag, S.M.; Abido, M.A. A review of meta-heuristic algorithms for reactive power planning problem. *Ain Shams Eng. J.* **2018**, *9*, 215–231. [CrossRef]
87. Eriksson, E.L.V.; Gray, E.M.A. Optimization of Renewable Hybrid Energy Systems—A Multi-Objective Approach. *Renew. Energy* **2019**, *133*, 971–999. [CrossRef]
88. Dang, J.; Zhang, S.; Wang, Y.; Yan, Y.; Jia, R.; Liu, G. Multi-Objective Power Supply Restoration in Distribution Networks Based on Graph Calculation and Information Collected by Multi-Source Sensors. *Sensors* **2025**, *25*, 768. [CrossRef]
89. Liang, R.H.; Wu, C.Y.; Chen, Y.T.; Tseng, W.T. Multi-Objective Dynamic Optimal Power Flow Using Improved Artificial Bee Colony Algorithm Based on Pareto Optimization. *Int. Trans. Electr. Energy Syst.* **2016**, *26*, 692–712. [CrossRef]
90. Jamal, R.; Zhang, J.; Men, B.; Khan, N.H.; Ebeed, M.; Kamel, S. Solution to the Deterministic and Stochastic Optimal Reactive Power Dispatch by Integration of Solar, Wind-Hydro Powers Using Modified Artificial Hummingbird Algorithm. *Energy Rep.* **2023**, *9*, 4157–4173. [CrossRef]
91. Bauer, R.; Mühlpfordt, T.; Ludwig, N.; Hagenmeyer, V. Analytical Uncertainty Propagation for Multi-Period Stochastic Optimal Power Flow. *Sustain. Energy Grids Netw.* **2023**, *33*, 100969. [CrossRef]
92. Fathy, A.; Yousri, D.; Abdelaziz, A.Y.; Ramadan, H.S. Robust Approach Based Chimp Optimization Algorithm for Minimizing Power Loss of Electrical Distribution Networks via Allocating Distributed Generators. *Sustain. Energy Technol. Assess.* **2021**, *47*, 101359. [CrossRef]
93. Sulaiman, M.H.; Mustaffa, Z. Solving Optimal Power Flow Problem with Stochastic Wind–Solar–Small Hydro Power Using Barnacles Mating Optimizer. *Control Eng. Pract.* **2021**, *106*, 104672. [CrossRef]
94. Biswas, P.P.; Suganthan, P.N.; Mallipeddi, R.; Amaratunga, G.A.J. Optimal Power Flow Solutions Using Differential Evolution Algorithm Integrated with Effective Constraint Handling Techniques. *Eng. Appl. Artif. Intell.* **2018**, *68*, 81–100. [CrossRef]
95. Grangereau, M.; van Ackooij, W.; Gaubert, S. Multi-Stage Stochastic Alternating Current Optimal Power Flow with Storage: Bounding the Relaxation Gap. *Electr. Power Syst. Res.* **2022**, *206*, 107774. [CrossRef]

96. Li, S.; Gong, W.; Wang, L.; Yan, X.; Hu, C. Optimal Power Flow by Means of Improved Adaptive Differential Evolution. *Energy* **2020**, *198*, 117314. [CrossRef]
97. Grover-Silva, E.; Heleno, M.; Mashayekh, S.; Cardoso, G.; Girard, R.; Kariniotakis, G. A Stochastic Optimal Power Flow for Scheduling Flexible Resources in Microgrids Operation. *Appl. Energy* **2018**, *229*, 201–208. [CrossRef]
98. Grover-Silva, E.; Girard, R.; Kariniotakis, G. Optimal Sizing and Placement of Distribution Grid Connected Battery Systems through an SOCP Optimal Power Flow Algorithm. *Appl. Energy* **2018**, *219*, 385–393. [CrossRef]
99. Lai, L.L.; Ma, J.T.; Yokoyama, R.; Zhao, M. Improved Genetic Algorithms for Optimal Power Flow under Both Normal and Contingent Operation States. *Int. J. Electr. Power Energy Syst.* **1997**, *19*, 287–292. [CrossRef]
100. Abaci, K.; Yamacli, V. Differential Search Algorithm for Solving Multi-Objective Optimal Power Flow Problem. *Int. J. Electr. Power Energy Syst.* **2016**, *79*, 1–10. [CrossRef]
101. Costa, A.L.; Costa, A.S. Energy and Ancillary Service Dispatch through Dynamic Optimal Power Flow. *Electr. Power Syst. Res.* **2007**, *77*, 1047–1055. [CrossRef]
102. Adhikari, A.; Jurado, F.; Naetiladdanon, S.; Sangswang, A.; Kamel, S.; Ebeed, M. Stochastic Optimal Power Flow Analysis of Power System with Renewable Energy Sources Using Adaptive Lightning Attachment Procedure Optimizer. *Int. J. Electr. Power Energy Syst.* **2023**, *153*, 109314. [CrossRef]
103. Surender Reddy, S.; Srinivasa Rathnam, C. Optimal Power Flow Using Glowworm Swarm Optimization. *Int. J. Electr. Power Energy Syst.* **2016**, *80*, 128–139. [CrossRef]
104. Kumar, S.; Chaturvedi, D.K. Optimal Power Flow Solution Using Fuzzy Evolutionary and Swarm Optimization. *Int. J. Electr. Power Energy Syst.* **2013**, *47*, 416–423. [CrossRef]
105. Ali, S.S.; Choi, B.J. State-of-the-Art Artificial Intelligence Techniques for Distributed Smart Grids: A Review. *Electronics* **2020**, *9*, 1030. [CrossRef]
106. Li, Y. Advanced Intelligent Optimization Algorithms for Multi-Objective Optimal Power Flow in Future Power Systems: A Review. *arXiv* **2024**, arXiv:2404.09203. [CrossRef]
107. Lissa, P.; Deane, C.; Schukat, M.; Seri, F.; Keane, M.; Barrett, E. Deep Reinforcement Learning for Home Energy Management System Control. *Energy AI* **2021**, *3*, 100043. [CrossRef]
108. Sun, B.; Song, M.; Li, A.; Zou, N.; Pan, P.; Lu, X.; Yang, Q.; Zhang, H.; Kong, X. Multi-Objective Solution of Optimal Power Flow Based on TD3 Deep Reinforcement Learning Algorithm. *Sustain. Energy Grids Netw.* **2023**, *34*, 101054. [CrossRef]
109. Al Khafaf, N.; Wang, J.; Jalili, M.; Sokolowski, P. A Deep Learning Approach for Detecting Distributed Generation in Residential Customers. *Sustain. Energy Grids Netw.* **2023**, *33*, 100966. [CrossRef]
110. Rocha, H.R.O.; Honorato, I.H.; Fiorotti, R.; Celeste, W.C.; Silvestre, L.J.; Silva, J.A.L. An Artificial Intelligence Based Scheduling Algorithm for Demand-Side Energy Management in Smart Homes. *Appl. Energy* **2021**, *282*, 116145. [CrossRef]
111. Huang, N.; Wang, S.; Wang, R.; Cai, G.; Liu, Y.; Dai, Q. Gated Spatial-Temporal Graph Neural Network Based Short-Term Load Forecasting for Wide-Area Multiple Buses. *Int. J. Electr. Power Energy Syst.* **2023**, *145*, 108651. [CrossRef]
112. Jackson, D.; Belakaria, S.; Cao, Y.; Doppa, J.R.; Lu, X. Machine Learning Enabled Design Automation and Multi-Objective Optimization for Electric Transportation Power Systems. *IEEE Trans. Transp. Electrif.* **2022**, *8*, 1467–1481. [CrossRef]
113. Judge, M.A.; Franzitta, V.; Curto, D.; Guercio, A.; Cirrincione, G.; Khattak, H.A. A Comprehensive Review of Artificial Intelligence Approaches for Smart Grid Integration and Optimization. *Energy Convers. Manag. X* **2024**, *24*, 100724. [CrossRef]
114. Abraham, A.; Jain, L.; Goldberg, R. *Evolutionary Multi-objective Optimization: Theoretical Advances and Applications*; Springer: Berlin/Heidelberg, Germany, 2005.
115. Zhang, M.; Li, Y. Multi-Objective Optimal Reactive Power Dispatch of Power Systems by Combining Classification- Based Multi-Objective Evolutionary Algorithm and Integrated Decision Making. *IEEE Access Artif. Intell. Technol. Electr. Power Syst.* **2020**, *8*, 38198–38209. [CrossRef]
116. Hussain, A.; Kim, H.M. Evaluation of Multi-Objective Optimization Techniques for Resilience Enhancement of Electric Vehicles. *Electronics* **2021**, *10*, 3030. [CrossRef]
117. Biswas, P.P.; Suganthan, P.N.; Mallipeddi, R.; Amaratunga, G.A.J. Multi-objective optimal power flow solutions using a constraint handling technique of evolutionary algorithms. *Soft Comput. Fusion. Found. Methodol. Appl.* **2020**, *24*, 2999–3023. [CrossRef]
118. Avvari, R.K.; Kumar, D.M.V. Multi-Objective Optimal Power Flow including Wind and Solar Generation Uncertainty Using New Hybrid Evolutionary Algorithm with Efficient Constraint Handling Method. *Int. Trans. Electr. Energy Syst.* **2022**, *2022*, 7091937. [CrossRef]
119. Zhang, B.; Che, A. An Enhanced Decomposition-Based Multi-Objective Evolutionary Algorithm with Neighborhood Search for Multi-Resource Constrained Job Shop Scheduling Problem. *Swarm Evol. Comput.* **2025**, *93*, 101834. [CrossRef]
120. Zainal, M.I.; Yasin, Z.M.; Zakaria, Z. Optimizing Voltage Profile and Loss Minimization using Cuckoo Search Algorithm. In Proceedings of the 11th IEEE Symposium on Computer Applications & Industrial Electronics (ISCAIE), Penang, Malaysia, 3–4 April 2021; pp. 1–7.

121. Ang, S.; Leeton, U.; Kulworawanichpong, T.; Chayakulkeeree, K. Multi-Objective Real Power Loss and Voltage Deviation Minimization for Grid Connected Micro Power System Using Whale Optimization Algorithm. *Int. Energy J.* **2018**, *18*, 297–310.
122. Rajalashmi, K.; Prabha, S.U. Hybrid Swarm Algorithm for Multiobjective Optimal Power Flow Problem. *Circuits Syst.* **2016**, *7* 3589–3603. [CrossRef]
123. Muangkhiew, P.; Chayakulkheeree, K. Multi-Objective Optimal Power Flow Using Fuzzy Satisfactory Stochastic Optimization. *Int. Energy J.* **2022**, *22*, 281–290.
124. Prioste, F.B. Optimal Power Flow Using Genetic Algorithm. *Soc. Bras. Inteligência Comput.* **2021**, *SC2021*, 1–6.
125. Arouna, O.; Imano, A.M.; Maurel, A.G.; Antoine, V.; Mitterand, D.; François-Xavier, F.; Ramanou, B.; Herman, T. Multi-objective Optimization of the Voltage Static Stability Margin of a Distribution Network by Genetic Algorithms. *Am. J. Eng. Res. (AJER)* **2020**, *9*, 155–165. Available online: https://www.ajer.org/papers/certificates/vol9(4)/AJER-17.pdf (accessed on 9 November 2025).
126. Deb, K.; Pratap, A.; Agarwal, S.; Meyarivan, T. A Fast and Elitist Multi-Objective Genetic Algorithm: NSGA-II. *IEEE Trans. Evol. Comput.* **2002**, *6*, 182–197. [CrossRef]
127. Konak, A.; Coit, D.W.; Smith, A.E. Multi-Objective Optimization Using Genetic Algorithms: A Tutorial. *Reliab. Eng. Syst. Saf.* **2006**, *91*, 992–1007. [CrossRef]
128. Naderi, E.; Narimani, H.; Pourakbari-Kasmaei, M.; Cerna, F.V.; Marzband, M.; Lehtonen, M. State-of-the-Art of Optimal Active and Reactive Power Flow: A Comprehensive Review from Various Standpoints. *Processes* **2021**, *9*, 1319. [CrossRef]
129. Mallala, B.; Papana, V.P.; Sangu, R.; Palle, K.; Chinthalacheruvu, V.K.R. Multi-Objective Optimal Power Flow Solution Using a Non-Dominated Sorting Hybrid Fruit Fly-Based Artificial Bee Colony. *J. Energ.* **2022**, *15*, 4063. [CrossRef]
130. Huy, T.H.B.; Kim, D.; Vo, D.N. Multi-objective Optimal Power Flow Using Multi-Objective Search Group Algorithm. *IEEE Access* **2022**, *10*, 77837–77856. [CrossRef]
131. Li, N.; Zhou, G.; Zhou, Y.; Deng, W.; Luo, Q. Multi-objective pathfinder algorithm for multi-objective optimal power flow problem with random renewable energy sources: Wind, photovoltaic and tidal. *Sci. Rep.* **2023**, *13*, 10647. [CrossRef]
132. Islam, M.Z.; Wahab, N.I.A.; Veerasamy, V.; Hizam, H.; Mailah, N.F.; Guerrero, J.M.; Nasir, M.N.M. A Harris Hawks Optimization Based Single- and Multi-Objective Optimal Power Flow Considering Environmental Emission. *Sustainability* **2020**, *12*, 5248. [CrossRef]
133. Lei, X.; Yang, Z.; Yu, J.; Zhao, J.; Gao, Q.; Yu, H. Data-driven Optimal Power Flow: A Physics-Informed Machine Learning Approach. *IEEE Trans. Power Syst.* **2021**, *36*, 346–354. [CrossRef]
134. Li, J.; Zhang, R.; Wang, H.; Liu, Z.; Lai, H.; Zhang, Y. Deep Reinforcement Learning for Optimal Power Flow with Renewables Using Spatial-Temporal Graph Information. *J. Latex Cl. Files* **2021**, *14*, 1–11.
135. Balasubbareddy, M.; Dwivedi, D.; Prasad, P.V. Optimal power flow solution using HFSS Algorithm. *J. Electr. Electron. Eng. Res.* **2023**, *12*, 1–11. [CrossRef]
136. Al-Kaabi, M.; Dumbrava, V.; Eremia, M. A Slime Mould Algorithm Programming for Solving Single and Multi-Objective Optimal Power Flow Problems with Pareto Front Approach: A Case Study of the Iraqi Super Grid High Voltage. *Energies* **2022**, *15*, 1–33. [CrossRef]
137. Hilawie, A.; Shewarega, F. Improved Multi Objective Particle Swarm Optimization Based Reactive Power Optimization for Ensuring Voltage Security of Power Systems. *Eng. Res. Express* **2023**, *4*, 045062. [CrossRef]
138. Yalcinoz, T.; Rudion, K. Multi-Objective Environmental-Economic Load Dispatch Considering Generator Constraints and Wind Power Using Improved Multi-Objective Particle Swarm Optimization. *Adv. Electr. Comput. Eng.* **2020**, *20*, 3–10. [CrossRef]
139. Ettappan, M.; Vimala, V.; Ramesh, S.; Kesavan, V.T. Optimal Reactive Power Dispatch for Real Power Loss Minimization and Voltage Stability Enhancement Using Artificial Bee Colony Algorithm. *Microprocess. Microsyst.* **2020**, *76*, 103085. [CrossRef]
140. Prajapati, B.S.; Srivastava, L. Multi-objective reactive power optimization using Artificial Bee Colony Algorithm. *Int. J. Eng. Innov. Technol. (IJEIT)* **2012**, *2*, 126–131.
141. Rezaei Adaryani, M.; Karami, A. Artificial Bee Colony Algorithm for Solving Multi-Objective Optimal Power Flow Problem. *Int. J. Electr. Power Energy Syst.* **2013**, *53*, 219–230. [CrossRef]
142. Zhu, J.; Yu, X.; Wang, F.; Mao, Y. Multi-Objective Optimal Power Flow Problem Using Constrained Dynamic Multitasking Multi-Objective Optimization Algorithm. *Swarm Evol. Comput.* **2025**, *93*, 101850. [CrossRef]
143. Yin, L.; Sun, Z. Distributed Multi-Objective Grey Wolf Optimizer for Distributed Multi-Objective Economic Dispatch of Multi-Area Interconnected Power Systems. *Appl. Soft Comput.* **2022**, *117*, 108345. [CrossRef]
144. Chen, G.; Qian, J.; Zhang, Z.; Li, S. Application of Modified Pigeon-Inspired Optimization Algorithm and Constraint-Objective Sorting Rule on Multi-Objective Optimal Power Flow Problem. *Appl. Soft Comput. J.* **2020**, *92*, 106321. [CrossRef]
145. Rezaeian-Marjani, S.; Ebrahimi, H.; Tousi, B. Probabilistic Multi-Objective Optimization Method for Interline Power Flow Controller (IPFC) Allocation in Power Systems. *IET Gener. Transm. Distrib.* **2022**, *16*, 4951–4962. [CrossRef]
146. Praveen, J.; Rao, B.S. Multi-Objective Optimization for Optimal Power Flow with IPFC using PSO. In Proceedings of the 3rd International Conference on Electrical Energy Systems (ICEES), Chennai, India, 17–19 March 2016.

147. Guerraiche, K.; Dekhici, L.; Chatelet, E.; Zeblah, A. Multi-Objective Electrical Power System Design Optimization Using a Modified Bat Algorithm. *Energies* **2021**, *14*, 3956. [CrossRef]
148. Zhao, Y.; Xue, Y.; Zhang, R.; Yin, J.; Yang, Y.; Chen, Y. Multi-Objective Optimization Operation of Multi-Agent Active Distribution Network Based on Analytical Target Cascading Method. *Energies* **2024**, *17*, 5022. [CrossRef]
149. Alsokhiry, F. Leveraging Harris Hawks Optimization for Enhanced Multi-Objective Optimal Power Flow in Complex Power Systems. *Energies* **2025**, *18*, 18. [CrossRef]
150. Hashemi, S.M.; Arasteh, H.; Shafiekhani, M.; Kia, M.; Guerrero, J.M. Multi-Objective Operation of Microgrids Based on Electrical and Thermal Flexibility Metrics Using the NNC and IGDT Methods. *Int. J. Electr. Power Energy Syst.* **2023**, *144*, 108617. [CrossRef]
151. HASHEMI, S.I.N.A.; LESANI, H.; AGHAMOHAMMADI, M.R. An Integrated Approach for Incorporation of Voltage and Transient Stabilities into Optimal Power Flow Study. *Electr. Power Syst. Res.* **2022**, *206*, 107784. [CrossRef]
152. Kharrich, M.; Mohammed, O.H.; Alshammari, N.; Akherraz, M. Multi-Objective Optimization and the Effect of the Economic Factors on the Design of the Microgrid Hybrid System. *Sustain. Cities Soc.* **2021**, *65*, 102646. [CrossRef]
153. Choobineh, M.; Mohagheghi, S. A Multi-Objective Optimization Framework for Energy and Asset Management in an Industrial Microgrid. *J. Clean. Prod.* **2016**, *139*, 1326–1338. [CrossRef]
154. Aghajani, G.; Ghadimi, N. Multi-Objective Energy Management in a Micro-Grid. *Energy Rep.* **2018**, *4*, 218–225. [CrossRef]
155. Reina, J.; Ortiz, R.; Lopez-Santiago, D.M. Multi-Objective Optimization of Multi-Energy Systems Planning in Remote Zones: The Bahía Málaga Colombian Case. *DYNA* **2023**, *90*, 56–65. [CrossRef]
156. Hassan, A.S.; Sun, Y.; Wang, Z. Multi-Objective for Optimal Placement and Sizing DG Units in Reducing Loss of Power and Enhancing Voltage Profile Using BPSO-SFLA. *Energy Rep.* **2020**, *6*, 1581–1589. [CrossRef]
157. Oloulade, A.; Imano, A.M.; Fifatin, X.; Vianou, A.; Tamadaho, H.; Badarou, R. Multi-Objective Optimization of the Safe Operation of the Electrical Distribution System by Placing D-FACTS and Network Reconfiguration. *J. Power Energy Eng.* **2019**, *7*, 94–113. [CrossRef]
158. Vaithiyanathan, V.; Mani, V.; Govindasamy, S.; Selvaraj, J. A Multi-Objective Time–Series Optimization for Optimum Planning Design of Integrative Power System with the Effects of Multi-Dimensional Sources of Uncertainty. *Electr. Power Compon. Syst.* **2024**, *52*, 891–904. [CrossRef]
159. Naderi, E.; Mirzaei, L.; Trimble, J.P.; Cantrell, D.A. Multi-Objective Optimal Power Flow Incorporating Flexible Alternating Current Transmission Systems: Application of a Wavelet-Oriented Evolutionary Algorithm. *Electr. Power Compon. Syst.* **2024**, *52*, 766–795. [CrossRef]
160. Ermiş, S. Multi-Objective Optimal Power Flow Using a Modified Weighted Teaching-Learning Based Optimization Algorithm. *Electr. Power Compon. Syst.* **2023**, *51*, 2536–2556. [CrossRef]
161. Roy, P.K.; Ghoshal, S.P.; Thakur, S.S. Multi-Objective Optimal Power Flow Using Biogeography-Based Optimization. *Electr. Power Compon. Syst.* **2010**, *38*, 1406–1426. [CrossRef]
162. Roy, P.K.; Mandal, D. Quasi-Oppositional Biogeography-Based Optimization for Multi-Objective Optimal Power Flow. *Electr. Power Compon. Syst.* **2011**, *40*, 236–256. [CrossRef]
163. Zhu, J.H.; Wang, J.S.; Zhang, X.Y.; Wang, Y.C.; Song, H.M.; Zheng, Y.; Liu, X. Multi-Objective Coyote Optimization Algorithm Based on Hybrid Elite Framework and Meta-Lamarckian Learning Strategy for Optimal Power Flow Problem. *Artif. Intell. Rev.* **2024**, *57*, 117. [CrossRef]
164. Roselyn, J.P.; Devaraj, D. Adaptive Multi Objective Differential Evolution with Fuzzy Decision Making in Preventive and Corrective Control Approaches for Voltage Security Enhancement. *J. Franklin Inst.* **2018**, *355*, 4553–4582. [CrossRef]
165. Naderi, E.; Pourakbari-Kasmaei, M.; Cerna, F.V.; Lehtonen, M. A Novel Hybrid Self-Adaptive Heuristic Algorithm to Handle Single- and Multi-Objective Optimal Power Flow Problems. *Int. J. Electr. Power Energy Syst.* **2021**, *125*, 106492. [CrossRef]
166. Jiekang, W.; Zhuangzhi, G.; Fan, W. Short-Term Multi-Objective Optimization Scheduling for Cascaded Hydroelectric Plants with Dynamic Generation Flow Limit Based on EMA and DEA. *Int. J. Electr. Power Energy Syst.* **2014**, *57*, 189–197. [CrossRef]
167. Li, J.; Wen, M.; Zhou, Z.; Wen, B.; Yu, Z.; Liang, H.; Zhang, X.; Qin, Y.; Xu, C.; Huang, H. Multi-Objective Optimization Method for Power Supply and Demand Balance in New Power Systems. *Int. J. Electr. Power Energy Syst.* **2024**, *161*, 110204. [CrossRef]
168. Ali, S.; Ullah, K.; Hafeez, G.; Khan, I.; Albogamy, F.R.; Haider, S.I. Solving Day-Ahead Scheduling Problem with Multi-Objective Energy Optimization for Demand Side Management in Smart Grid. *Eng. Sci. Technol. Int. J.* **2022**, *36*, 101135. [CrossRef]
169. Falke, T.; Krengel, S.; Meinerzhagen, A.K.; Schnettler, A. Multi-Objective Optimization and Simulation Model for the Design of Distributed Energy Systems. *Appl. Energy* **2016**, *184*, 1508–1516. [CrossRef]
170. Wang, J.; Yang, W.; Du, P.; Li, Y. Research and Application of a Hybrid Forecasting Framework Based on Multi-Objective Optimization for Electrical Power System. *Energy* **2018**, *148*, 59–78. [CrossRef]
171. Akdag, O. A Improved Archimedes Optimization Algorithm for Multi/Single-Objective Optimal Power Flow. *Electr. Power Syst. Res.* **2022**, *206*, 107796. [CrossRef]

172. Premkumar, M.; Hashim, T.J.T.; Ravichandran, S.; Sin, T.C.; Chandran, R.; Alsoud, A.R.; Jangir, P. Optimal Operation and Control of Hybrid Power Systems with Stochastic Renewables and FACTS Devices: An Intelligent Multi-Objective Optimization Approach. *Alex. Eng. J.* **2024**, *93*, 90–113. [CrossRef]
173. Chen, Y.; Chen, C.; Ma, J.; Qiu, W.; Liu, S.; Lin, Z.; Qian, M.; Zhu, L.; Zhao, D. Multi-Objective Optimization Strategy of Multi-Sources Power System Operation Based on Fuzzy Chance Constraint Programming and Improved Analytic Hierarchy Process. *Energy Rep.* **2021**, *7*, 268–274. [CrossRef]
174. Abubakar, A.; Mohammad, M.B. Multi-Objective Genetic Algorithm Optimization of Thermal Limit Parameters for Low Frequency Oscillation Control in Power Systems. *Int. J. Res. Innov. Appl. Sci.* **2024**, *9*, 536–540. [CrossRef]
175. Nwachukwu, T.; Ranade, S.; Rawn, B. Exploring Multi-Objective Transmission Planning for Investment-Constrained Power Systems. In Proceedings of the IEEE PowerAfrica Conference, Venue, Virtual, 25–28 August 2020.
176. Wang, Z.; Zhang, Z.; Luo, F.; Qiu, X.; Zhang, X.; Duan, J. Optimal Configuration of Soft Open Point and Energy Storage Based on Snowflake-Shaped Grid Characteristics and Sensitivity Analysis. *Appl. Sci.* **2024**, *14*, 503. [CrossRef]
177. Pandya, S.B.; Ravichandran, S.; Manoharan, P.; Jangir, P.; Alhelou, H.H. Multi-Objective Optimization Framework for Optimal Power Flow Problem of Hybrid Power Systems Considering Security Constraints. *IEEE Access* **2022**, *10*, 103509–103528. [CrossRef]
178. Akbel, M.; Kahraman, H.T.; Duman, S.; Temel, S. A Clustering-Based Archive Handling Method and Multi-Objective Optimization of the Optimal Power Flow Problem. *Appl. Intell.* **2024**, *54*, 11603–11648. [CrossRef]
179. Chew, B.S.H.; Xu, Y.; Wu, Q. Voltage Balancing for Bipolar DC Distribution Grids: A Power Flow Based Binary Integer Multi-Objective Optimization Approach. *IEEE Trans. Power Syst.* **2019**, *34*, 28–39. [CrossRef]
180. Chen, H.; Gao, L.; Zhang, Z. Multi-Objective Optimal Scheduling of a Microgrid with Uncertainties of Renewable Power Generation Considering User Satisfaction. *Int. J. Electr. Power Energy Syst.* **2021**, *131*, 107142. [CrossRef]
181. Liu, Y.; Ćetenović, D.; Li, H.; Gryazina, E.; Terzija, V. An Optimized Multi-Objective Reactive Power Dispatch Strategy Based on Improved Genetic Algorithm for Wind Power Integrated Systems. *Int. J. Electr. Power Energy Syst.* **2022**, *136*, 107764. [CrossRef]
182. Aghajani, G.R.; Shayanfar, H.A.; Shayeghi, H. Presenting a Multi-Objective Generation Scheduling Model for Pricing Demand Response Rate in Micro-Grid Energy Management. *Energy Convers. Manag.* **2015**, *106*, 308–321. [CrossRef]
183. Ghiasi, M. Detailed Study, Multi-Objective Optimization, and Design of an AC-DC Smart Microgrid with Hybrid Renewable Energy Resources. *Energy* **2019**, *169*, 496–507. [CrossRef]
184. Agrawal, S.; Pandya, S.; Jangir, P.; Kalita, K.; Chakraborty, S. A Multi-Objective Thermal Exchange Optimization Model for Solving Optimal Power Flow Problems in Hybrid Power Systems. *Decis. Anal. J.* **2023**, *8*, 100299. [CrossRef]
185. Morshed, M.J.; Ben Hmida, J.; Fekih, A. A Probabilistic Multi-Objective Approach for Power Flow Optimization in Hybrid Wind-PV-PEV Systems. *Appl. Energy* **2018**, *211*, 1136–1149. [CrossRef]
186. Roberts, J.J.; Marotta Cassula, A.; Silveira, J.L.; da Costa Bortoni, E.; Mendiburu, A.Z. Robust Multi-Objective Optimization of a Renewable Based Hybrid Power System. *Appl. Energy* **2018**, *223*, 52–68. [CrossRef]
187. Wang, R.; Xiong, J.; He, M.; Gao, L.; Wang, L. Multi-Objective Optimal Design of Hybrid Renewable Energy System under Multiple Scenarios. *Renew. Energy* **2020**, *151*, 226–237. [CrossRef]
188. Wang, R.; Li, G.; Ming, M.; Wu, G.; Wang, L. An Efficient Multi-Objective Model and Algorithm for Sizing a Stand-Alone Hybrid Renewable Energy System. *Energy* **2017**, *141*, 2288–2299. [CrossRef]
189. Sarshar, J.; Moosapour, S.S.; Joorabian, M. Multi-Objective Energy Management of a Micro-Grid Considering Uncertainty in Wind Power Forecasting. *Energy* **2017**, *139*, 680–693. [CrossRef]
190. Mayer, M.J.; Szilágyi, A.; Gróf, G. Environmental and Economic Multi-Objective Optimization of a Household Level Hybrid Renewable Energy System by Genetic Algorithm. *Appl. Energy* **2020**, *269*, 115058. [CrossRef]
191. Liu, Z.F.; Li, L.L.; Liu, Y.W.; Liu, J.Q.; Li, H.Y.; Shen, Q. Dynamic Economic Emission Dispatch Considering Renewable Energy Generation: A Novel Multi-Objective Optimization Approach. *Energy* **2021**, *235*, 121407. [CrossRef]
192. Elattar, E.E.; ElSayed, S.K. Modified JAYA Algorithm for Optimal Power Flow Incorporating Renewable Energy Sources Considering the Cost, Emission, Power Loss and Voltage Profile Improvement. *Energy* **2019**, *178*, 598–609. [CrossRef]
193. Alzahrani, A.; Rahman, M.U.; Hafeez, G.; Rukh, G.; Ali, S.; Murawwat, S.; Iftikhar, F.; Haider, S.I.; Khan, M.I.; Abed, A.M. A Strategy for Multi-Objective Energy Optimization in Smart Grid Considering Renewable Energy and Batteries Energy Storage System. *IEEE Access* **2023**, *11*, 33872–33886. [CrossRef]
194. Ascione, F.; Bianco, N.; De Masi, R.F.; De Stasio, C.; Mauro, G.M.; Vanoli, G.P. Multi-Objective Optimization of the Renewable Energy Mix for a Building. *Appl. Therm. Eng.* **2016**, *101*, 612–621. [CrossRef]
195. Bandaru, S.; Ng, A.H.C.; Deb, K. Data Mining Methods for Knowledge Discovery in Multi-Objective Optimization: Part A—Survey. *Expert. Syst. Appl.* **2017**, *70*, 139–159. [CrossRef]
196. Ida Evangeline, S.; Rathika, P. Wind Farm Incorporated Optimal Power Flow Solutions through Multi-Objective Horse Herd Optimization with a Novel Constraint Handling Technique. *Expert. Syst. Appl.* **2022**, *194*, 116544. [CrossRef]
197. Liu, Y.; Hao, L.; Xing, Z.; Jiang, Z.; Xu, J. Multi-Objective Coordinated Optimization of Power System with Wind Power Accommodation. *Energy Rep.* **2022**, *8*, 188–195. [CrossRef]

198. Nagarajan, K.; Rajagopalan, A.; Bajaj, M.; Raju, V.; Blazek, V. Enhanced Wombat Optimization Algorithm for Multi-Objective Optimal Power Flow in Renewable Energy and Electric Vehicle Integrated Systems. *Results Eng.* **2025**, *25*, 103671. [CrossRef]
199. Mandal, B.; Roy, P.K. A Probabilistic Multi-Objective Approach for Power Flow Optimization in Hybrid Wind-Based Power Systems Using Grasshopper Optimization Algorithm. *Int. J. Swarm Intell. Res.* **2020**, *11*, 61–86. [CrossRef]
200. Bisht, Y.S.; Poornima, E.; Aysola, S.C.; Sood, S.; Balassem, Z.A.; Kumar, S.; Cajla, P.; Khandelwal, U. Hybrid Renewable Energy System Design Using Multi-Objective Optimization. *E3S Web Conf.* **2024**, *581*, 01036. [CrossRef]
201. Ming, M.; Wang, R.; Zha, Y.; Zhang, T. Multi-Objective Optimization of Hybrid Renewable Energy System Using an Enhanced Multi-Objective Evolutionary Algorithm. *Energies* **2017**, *10*, 674. [CrossRef]
202. Zhao, L.; Meng, X.; Yang, L.; Wei, J. Unified Multi-Objective Optimization for Regional Power Systems with Unequal Distribution of Renewable Energy Generation and Load. *Eng. Rep.* **2023**, *5*, 12768. [CrossRef]
203. Xing, Q.; Cheng, M.; Liu, S.; Xiang, Q.; Xie, H.; Chen, T. Multi-Objective Optimization and Dispatch of Distributed Energy Resources for Renewable Power Utilization Considering Time-of-Use Tariff. *Front. Energy Res.* **2021**, *9*, 647199. [CrossRef]
204. Liu, B.; Peng, Z.; Liao, S.; Liu, T.; Lu, J. A multi-objective optimization model for the coordinated operation of hydropower and renewable energy. *Front. Energy Res.* **2023**, *11*, 1193415. [CrossRef]
205. Ma, X.; Liang, C.; Dong, X.; Li, Y. Multi-objective reactive power optimization strategy of power system considering large-scale renewable integration. *Front. Energy Res.* **2023**, *11*, 1213154. [CrossRef]
206. Sadeghi, S.; Ameri, M. Multi-objective Optimization of PV-SOFC-GT-Electrolyser Hybrid System. *J. Ren. Energy Env.* **2015**, *2*, 47–58.
207. Nagaleshmi, P. Solution for optimal power flow problem in wind energy system using hybrid multi objective artificial physical optimization algorithm. *Intern. J. Power Electron. Drive Syst.* **2019**, *10*, 486–503. [CrossRef]
208. Barbosa, A.M.; Rotella Junior, P.; Peruchi, R.S.; Rocha, L.C.S.; Pires, A.L.G.; Janda, K. Stochastic multi-objective optimization of hybrid distributed power generation with battery storage systems. *Energy Sources Part B Econ. Plan. Policy* **2025**, *20*, 2504487. [CrossRef]
209. Ndjependa, P.R.; Boum, A.T.; Essiane, S.N. A novel approach of a dynamic multi objective optimization of a power distribution system. *J. Electr. Syst. Infor. Techn.* **2021**, *8*, 17. [CrossRef]
210. Pandya, S.B.; Kalita, K.; Čep, R.; Jangir, P.; Chohan, J.S.; Abualigah, L. Multi-objective Snow Ablation Optimization Algorithm: An Elementary Vision for Security-Constrained Optimal Power Flow Problem Incorporating Wind Energy Source with FACTS Devices. *Int. J. Comput. Intell. Syst.* **2024**, *17*, 33. [CrossRef]
211. Seyam, S.; Al-Hamed, K.H.M.; Qureshy, A.M.M.I.; Dincer, I.; Agelin-Chaab, M.; Rahnamayan, S. Multi-objective Optimization of Hydrogen Production in Hybrid Renewable Energy Systems. In Proceedings of the 2019 IEEE Congress on Evolutionary Computation (CEC), Wellington, New Zealand, 10–13 June 2019; Volume 8790299. [CrossRef]

energies

MDPI

Article

Hierarchical Topology Knowledge Extraction for Five-Prevention Wiring Diagrams in Substations

Hui You [1,2], Dong Yang [3], Tian Wu [1,2,*], Qing He [4], Wenyu Zhu [3], Xiang Ren [3] and Jia Liu [1,2]

[1] College of Electrical Engineering and New Energy, China Three Gorges University, Yichang 443002, China
[2] Hubei Provincial Engineering Technology Research Center for Power Transmission Line, China Three Gorges University, Yichang 443002, China
[3] Xiangyang Power Supply Company State Grid Hubei Electric Power Co., Xiangyang 441000, China
[4] Electric Power Science Research Institute of State Grid Hubei Electric Power Co., Ltd., Wuhan 430077, China
* Correspondence: wutian_08@163.com

Abstract

Five prevention is an important technical means to prevent maloperations in substations, and knowledge extraction from wiring diagrams is the key to intelligent "five prevention logic verification". To address the error accumulation caused by multimodal object matching in traditional methods, this paper proposes a hierarchical recognition-based approach for topological knowledge extraction. This method establishes a multi-level recognition framework utilizing image tiling, decomposing the wiring diagram recognition task into three hierarchical levels from top to bottom: connection modes, bay types, and switching devices. A depth-first strategy is employed to establish parent–child node relationships, forming an initial topological structure. Based on the recognition results, the proposed approach performs regularized parsing and leverages a bay topology knowledge base to achieve automated matching of inter-device topological relationships. To enhance recognition accuracy, the model incorporates a Swin Transformer block to strengthen global feature perception and adds an ultra-small target detection layer to improve small-object recognition. The experimental results demonstrate that all recognition layers achieve mAP@0.5 exceeding 90%, with an overall precision of 93.9% and a recall rate of 91.7%, outperforming traditional matching algorithms and meeting the requirements for wiring diagram topology knowledge extraction.

Keywords: substation; wiring diagram; deep learning; object detection

1. Introduction

Substations serve as pivotal hubs in power systems, and their safe operation relies on five-prevention logic libraries constructed based on the topological relationships of switching devices [1]. The "Five-Prevention" is a core safety criterion widely adopted in China's power system to prevent maloperations in substations, which is essentially consistent with the safety interlocking philosophy advocated by Western standards. Its specific connotations include five key prohibitions: (1) preventing incorrect opening/closing of circuit breakers; (2) preventing incorrect opening/closing of disconnectors under live conditions; (3) preventing live connection of grounded equipment; (4) preventing grounding of live equipment; (5) preventing entry into live intervals. These requirements align with the core objectives of "Interlocking Logic" and "Safety Interlocks" defined by IEEE and IEC standards—both aim to eliminate hazardous maloperations through predefined logical constraints, physical interlocks, or electrical interlock mechanisms, thereby safeguarding the safe operation of substation equipment and personnel. As grid scales expand, the number of wiring diagrams proliferates with frequent version iterations [2]. Current digitization efforts merely achieve image archiving of diagrams, whereas practical applications still require manual interpretation, resulting in low efficiency and dependence on expertise. This renders traditional manual rule library compilation methods inadequate for meeting complex grid demands [3–6]. Consequently, to ensure grid operational safety and achieve intelligent "five-prevention logic verification," the extraction of topological logic from wiring diagrams is critically important.

With advancements in digital intelligence technologies, drawing digitization is evolving from image archiving towards autonomous information extraction systems that eliminate manual interpretation [7–12]. In this context, artificial intelligence technologies are being widely applied to the intelligent recognition and analysis of engineering drawings [13]. Through image and text detection, engineering drawings can undergo knowledge extraction and be converted into structured information. However, wiring diagram detection presents unique challenges compared to traditional image recognition:

1. The diversity of electrical components and significant variations in image dimensions the recognition process.
2. Wiring diagrams exhibit complex topological relationships that are difficult to represent mathematically.

For the former challenge, various solutions have been proposed, such as hybrid models based on Faster R-CNN [14], overlapping sliding window approaches using YOLOv4 [15], and hierarchical recognition techniques employing dual-layer architectures [16], which effectively alleviate multi-scale target recognition difficulties. For the latter, triple recognition frameworks that separately identify images, text, and connection lines have been primarily adopted to extract topological relationships [17,18]. Although these methods perform well in individual tasks, when multimodal tasks are combined, errors are not only amplified owing to inter-task influences but are also exacerbated through matching algorithms. In particular, in topological relationship matching, current approaches employing node traversal methods, such as VF2, QuickSI, TurboIso, and other subgraph matching methods [19], cannot match the detection accuracy and fail to adequately resolve the technical bottlenecks. Therefore, effectively integrating multimodal recognition tasks while ensuring high accuracy and accurately representing wiring diagram topological relationships remains a key challenge that requires resolution.

To address these technical challenges, this paper proposes a hierarchical recognition-based substation wiring diagram detection method, implementing the following improvements to the tripe recognition framework:

1. Construct a multi-level recognition system integrated with image tiling, which decomposes the complex wiring diagram recognition task into serial hierarchical subtasks (connection mode, bay type, switching device) to fundamentally circumvent algorithmic errors caused by multimodal matching—laying a reliable foundation for accurate topological relationship extraction.
2. Propose an improved YOLOv8-derived model named Type-YOLOv8 for bay recognition—incorporating the Swin Transformer module to strengthen global feature perception and adding an ultra-small target detection layer, which effectively improves the recognition capability of small objects and similar-type bays, thereby boosting the core link accuracy of the hierarchical framework.
3. Develop a rule-based regularized parsing module combined with a bay topology knowledge base, which realizes automatic inference of inter-device topological relationships and rationality verification of recognition results through equipment

https://doi.org/10.3390/en19020546

numbering matching—supporting the intelligent conversion of wiring diagrams into structured topological knowledge.

2. Wiring Diagram Detection Framework

The core challenge of topological knowledge extraction from substation wiring diagrams is the reconstruction of topological relationships. Traditional methods attempt to solve this problem by separately recognizing primitives, texts, and connecting lines and then matching them; however, they face a fundamental dilemma: under the multimodal matching framework, errors in any link are sharply amplified by the matching algorithm, leading to poor overall results. Therefore, to address the difficulty of topological relationship matching in wiring diagram detection, this paper proposes a hierarchical-recognition-based topological knowledge extraction method for substation five-prevention wiring diagrams. The research design, including key components such as research questions, sampling frame, and analysis pipeline, is summarized in Table 1 to ensure auditability, and the specific technical flowchart from raw data to evaluation is shown in Figure 1.

Table 1. Design at a glance.

Component	Details
Research Questions (RQs)	RQ1: How to avoid multi-modal matching error accumulation in substation wiring diagram topological knowledge extraction? RQ2: How to enhance small-target recognition and global feature perception for bay type detection? RQ3: How to realize accurate topological relationship reconstruction via hierarchical recognition?
Unit of Analysis	Substation five-prevention wiring diagrams; hierarchical recognition units (connection modes, bay types, switching devices); topological relationships between switching devices.
Sampling Frame	The data used in this experiment are derived from substation wiring diagrams of a company, totaling 167 images, including 136 images of 110 kV substation wiring diagrams and 31 images of 220 kV substation wiring diagrams, with an average resolution of 1700.59 × 919.34 pixels.
Inclusion/Exclusion Rules	Inclusion: (1) RGB-format wiring diagrams with complete electrical components; (2) 110 kV/220 kV five-prevention wiring diagrams; (3) diagrams with clear device number annotations. Exclusion: (1) Blurred or incomplete diagrams (e.g., missing key components); (2) non-five-prevention wiring diagrams (e.g., purely architectural drawings); (3) diagrams with non-standard device numbering.
Analysis Pipeline	1. Raw data annotation → 2. Triple image tiling (connection mode → bay type → switching device) → 3. Model training (YOLOv8 for connection mode/switching devices; Type-YOLOv8 for bay types) → 4. Depth-first strategy for initial topological structure → 5. Regularized parsing + topology knowledge base matching → 6. Performance evaluation (P/R/mAP@0.5) + comparative analysis.

https://doi.org/10.3390/en19020546

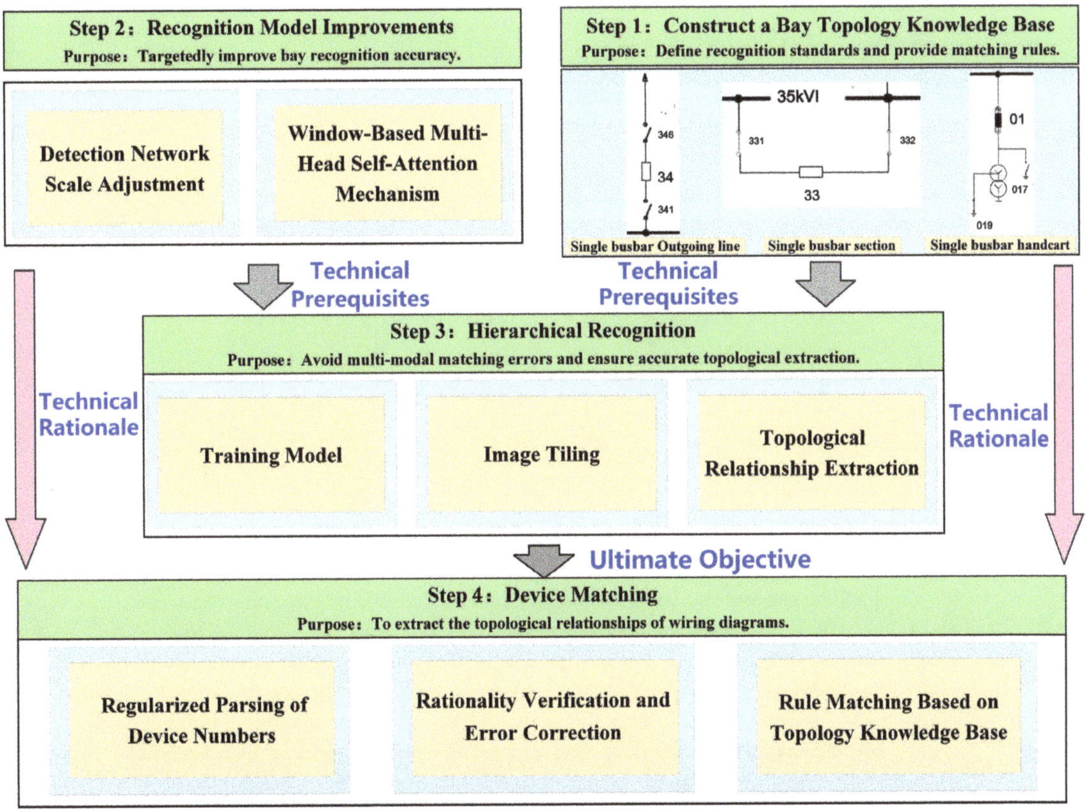

Figure 1. Technical flowchart.

First, a multi-level recognition strategy based on image tiling is adopted, decomposing the complete wiring diagram recognition task into three serial hierarchical levels from top to bottom: connection mode recognition, bay type recognition, and switching device recognition. Second, parent–child node relationships between levels are established through a depth-first strategy, merging the device recognition results into the corresponding bay units and bay units into the respective connection modes, forming a preliminary topological structure. Finally, rule-based regularized parsing modules are constructed by combining standard connection templates from bay topology knowledge bases to automatically match and populate identified specific device entities into corresponding template roles, achieving precise reconstruction of complete topological relationships and ultimately generating comprehensive wiring diagram topological knowledge.

2.1. Hierarchical Recognition

To address the low accuracy of connection line recognition and matching in wiring diagram knowledge extraction, this paper adopts a hierarchical recognition framework that decomposes tasks through image tiling, integrating image, text, and connection line triple tasks into a top-down holistic recognition of wiring diagrams. This approach circumvents topological matching in multimodal recognition tasks and accomplishes topological relationship extraction from the wiring diagrams, as shown in Figure 2.

https://doi.org/10.3390/en19020546

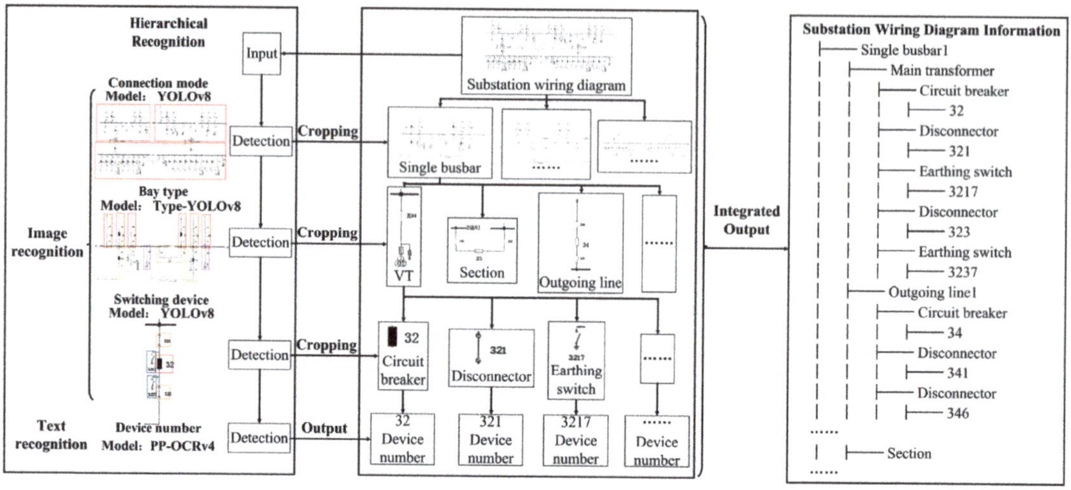

Figure 2. Wiring diagram detection framework based on hierarchical recognition.

2.1.1. Image Tiling

Image tiling is a common preprocessing method used to narrow the processing scope and enhance the accuracy of small target detection [20]. However, unlike natural images, wiring diagrams are essentially knowledge graphs that follow specific electrical rules. Their tiling strategy must ensure visual integrity and comply with the electrical semantic boundaries. As demonstrated in the literature [16], ensuring that the divided regions contain only one set of busbars achieves excellent small target recognition results. Building upon this, this paper employs triple image tiling, progressively refining recognition tasks into four hierarchical levels: connection mode, bay type, switching device, and device number, thereby realizing hierarchical recognition.

The specific process of triple image tiling is as follows:

1. The first tiling identifies and locates connection modes using the YOLOv8 model, then completes cropping according to their semantic boundaries to obtain independent connection mode subgraphs;
2. The second tiling further identifies and crops regions corresponding to bay types based on the connection mode subgraphs. Considering the significance and recognition difficulty of bay type, a specifically optimized model named Type-YOLOv8 (derived from the base YOLOv8) is utilized for this level, with detailed improvements elaborated in Section 2.2;
3. The third tiling focuses on switching devices in the bay-level subgraphs, using the YOLOv8 model to identify their distribution range and complete the final cropping. After completing the image recognition of switching devices through the third tiling, the text recognition model PaddlePaddle Optical Character Recognition v4 (PP-OCRv4) is employed to extract device numbers, forming a complete hierarchical recognition process.

To ensure the semantic accuracy and annotation consistency of tiling, this study constructs a standard library covering mainstream connection modes and bay types by sorting out relevant technical data, clarifying the typical range characteristics and corresponding names of various objects, which serves as the core basis for manual annotation.

Bay recognition serves as the core of the hierarchical framework. The key rationale is twofold: first, the topological relationship of a single bay is uniquely determined by its type; second, the topological relationships between different bays are relatively indepen-

 https://doi.org/10.3390/en19020546

dent. Based on these characteristics, we can construct a bay topology knowledge base and combine it with a subsequent regularized parsing module to realize the topological reconstruction of wiring diagrams—thus replacing the traditional connection line recognition and matching process.

Connection mode recognition and switching device recognition play auxiliary roles for bay recognition: the former enables wiring diagram tiling based on the topological characteristics of the main electrical wiring, reducing the complexity of bay type recognition and determining the busbar connections corresponding to each bay; the latter completes device identification and number extraction based on bay type recognition results, providing specific device entities for the topological templates of corresponding bay types.

While the dual-layer chunking approach proposed in [16] addresses basic scale variations in substation diagrams, this paper further optimizes the boundary definition between connection modes and bay types through a hierarchical splitting strategy. By prioritizing the preservation of electrical logic during image segmentation, this paper achieves higher structural integrity for complex symbols compared to the more generalized tiling used in [16].

2.1.2. Topological Relationship Extraction

Building on the horizontal task decomposition and execution of triple image tiling in Section 2.1.1, this section focuses on the vertical integration of all hierarchical levels, realizing the core feature of unifying image, text, and connection line triple recognition tasks into a holistic process.

The hierarchical recognition framework achieves vertical integration through a top-down topological relationship extraction logic, as shown in Figure 2. Instead of treating image recognition, text recognition, and connection line recognition as parallel and isolated tasks, the framework reconstructs them into a serially connected, strongly interdependent system: image recognition (completed via triple tiling) lays the foundation by identifying connection modes, bay types, and switching devices; text recognition is demoted to a targeted post-processing step, with its input strictly constrained to the switching device regions identified in the third tiling to ensure extraction accuracy of device numbers; connection line recognition is completely replaced by the combination of bay type recognition and a pre-constructed bay topology knowledge base. This integration transforms the traditional "bottom-up jigsaw puzzle" of topological extraction into a "top-down template filling" process—identifying bay types directly provides standard logical connection templates, and subsequent steps only need to populate the identified specific device entities and numbers into corresponding template roles to synthesize complete topological relationships.

To ensure the smooth vertical connection of each hierarchical level, a depth-first strategy is adopted: starting from the first image to be recognized at the current level, the process immediately proceeds to the next level after completion until the bottom-level text recognition tasks are finished, before returning to process the remaining tasks at the upper levels. This traversal logic not only ensures the sequential execution of recognition tasks but also naturally establishes the parent–child node connection (indicating that a device belongs to a specific bay)—since each device is identified within the subimage of a corresponding bay, no additional matching algorithms are required. In this vertically integrated structure, local features and nodes adapt to local observation variations, while higher-level nodes maintain the overall spatial arrangement of local components, endowing the framework with excellent generalization capability and making the high-precision holistic recognition of wiring diagrams feasible and practical.

https://doi.org/10.3390/en19020546

The entire traversal and recognition process is systematically elaborated in Algorithm 1. Specifically, leveraging the parent–child node connection relationships inherently established by this depth-first strategy, the recognition results at each level are processed and converted into a standardized format after detection:

$$T_c = \{N_i, C_n, N_p\} \tag{1}$$

where the T_c field identifies the type of recognition result, the N_i field assigns unique numbers to each recognition result, the C_n field records the specific recognition content, and the N_p field points to the number of upper-level recognition results.

After recognition, the results from various levels form a directed network capable of completely expressing the topological relationships between the upper and lower levels, as illustrated in Figure 3. As can be seen, there are 5 T_c layers: the first layer corresponds to the substation of the wiring diagram, which stores the corresponding recognition results during multi-diagram continuous recognition; layers 2 to 4 (Connection mode, Bay type, and Switching device) are identified and obtained by the image recognition part of hierarchical recognition; the last layer is the Device number, which is obtained by text recognition at the final stage of hierarchical recognition. It can also be observed that since the switching device and device number are in one-to-one correspondence, the N_i and N_p fields of this layer are completely consistent.

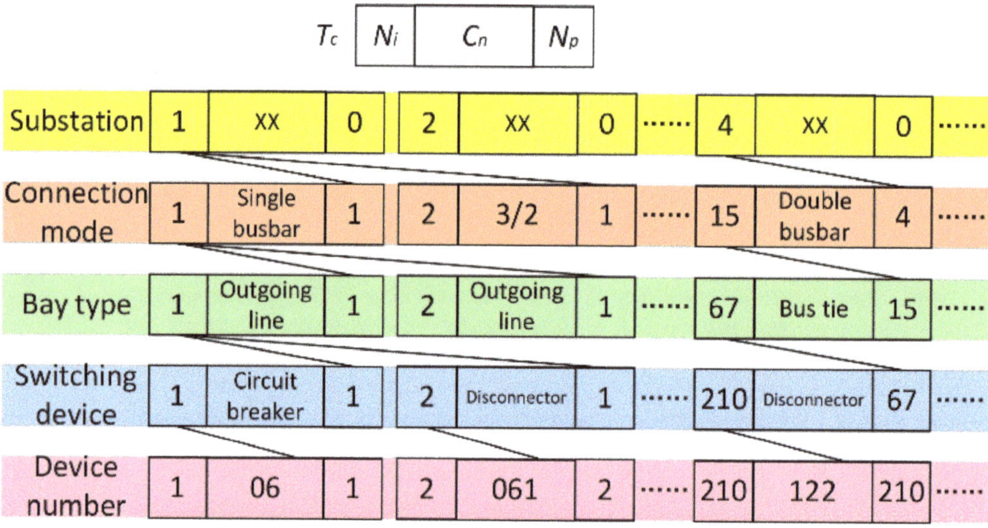

Figure 3. Structured information of the wiring diagram.

Although the tree-structured classification in [21] established a preliminary hierarchical framework for substation diagrams, this paper significantly extends this logic into a more comprehensive four-level recognition architecture. By implementing a depth-first strategy across connection, bay, device, and text layers, this paper ensures a much higher degree of functional completeness and topological integrity than the foundational method in [21].

https://doi.org/10.3390/en19020546

Algorithm 1. Hierarchical Recognition

Input:
I: Substation wiring diagram image (RGB format)
Output:
R: Equipment information table, where each record is $T_c = \{N_i, C_n, N_p\}$
begin

```
// Step 1: Load models
// - YOLOv8: For connection mode and switching device recognition
// - Type-YOLOv8: Improved YOLOv8 for bay type recognition
// - PP-OCRv4: For text recognition of device numbers
// Step 2: Initialization
ID_counter = 0    // Counter for unique node IDs
R = []    // Equipment information table
Q = [(I, "Connection Mode", "ROOT")] // Processing queue
// Step 3: Processing based on depth-first strategy
while Q is not empty:
// Extract the first task from the queue head
(current_img, current_layer, parent_id) = Q.pop(0)
// If it's the device number layer, process directly and skip to next loop
if current_layer == "Device Number":
// Recognize device number text using OCR
text = PP_OCRv4(current_img)
// Generate unique node ID
node_id = f"NODE_{ID_counter}"
ID_counter += 1
// Record to result table
R.append({"T_c": "Device Number", "N_i": node_id, "C_n": text, "N_p": parent_id})
// No next layer for device number layer; no new tasks enqueued
continue    // Skip to the next loop
// Select model and next layer for the first three layers
if current_layer == "Connection Mode":
model = YOLOv8_Detect
next_layer = "Bay Type"
layer_type = "Connection Mode"
elif current_layer == "Bay Type":
model = Type_YOLOv8_Detect
next_layer = "Switching Device"
layer_type = "Bay Type"
elif current_layer == "Switching Device":
model = YOLOv8_Detect
next_layer = "Device Number"
layer_type = "Switching Device"
// Detect objects in current layer using the corresponding model
bboxes, labels = model(current_img, corresponding_classes)
// Iterate over all detected objects
for bbox, label in zip(bboxes, labels):
// Generate unique node ID
node_id = f"NODE_{ID_counter}"
```


https://doi.org/10.3390/en19020546

Algorithm 1. *Cont.*

```
ID_counter += 1
  // Record to result table
R.append({"T_c": layer_type, "N_i": node_id, "C_n": label, "N_p": parent_id})
  // Crop subgraph and enqueue
sub_img = Crop(current_img, bbox)
Q.insert(0, (sub_img, next_layer, node_id))
  // Step 4: Output results
return equipment information table R
end
```

2.2. Recognition Model Improvements

The YOLO series of algorithms perform excellently in terms of speed, accuracy, and practicality, and have become widely used network models in the field of image recognition, with YOLOv8 being one of the most mature versions. The YOLOv8 network structure includes a backbone network responsible for feature extraction, neck network responsible for multi-scale feature fusion, and head network responsible for the final detection and classification tasks.

The bay type recognition is the core part of the recognition framework, which also performs the connecting line recognition in the original triple recognition framework. There are many types of errors, with small differences, and they have a significant impact on the final recognition result. Therefore, targeted adjustments to the recognition model are required according to the actual situation to improve recognition accuracy. As shown in Figure 4, compared with the original model, Type-YOLOv8 adds detection layers and detection heads and integrates the Swin Transformer module into the backbone network to enhance the model's global feature perception ability and improve the recognition ability of small targets.

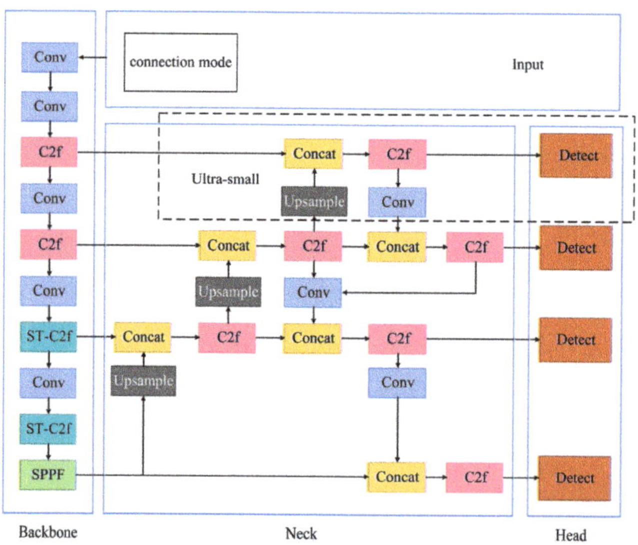

Figure 4. Type-YOLOv8 network model.

 https://doi.org/10.3390/en19020546

2.2.1. Detection Network Scale Adjustment

YOLOv8 adopts a multi-layer detection strategy, including three types of target detection heads—large, medium, and small—along with their corresponding detection layers. However, in multilevel tasks, this general design diminishes the detection performance. To study the impact, this paper analyzes the size of 167 collected wiring diagrams with an average resolution of 1700.59 × 919.34, and the results are shown in Table 2. Through image detection, statistical analysis of the size of images at all levels found that the single area of switching devices, such as circuit breakers, isolating switches, and earthing switches, is only 0.053% of the overall wiring diagram, but the quantity accounts for more than 70% of all components. The average size of the bay types was 112.16 × 286.25 pixels, and non-switching devices, as important features distinguishing different bays, accounted for an extremely low proportion, which led to difficulties in feature extraction during model training and difficulty in convergence.

Table 2. Statistical table of electrical elements.

Type	Average Number per Image	Average Pixel Size
Circuit Breaker	39	14 × 29
Disconnector	42	15 × 40
Earthing Switch	32	12 × 30
Arrow	22	10 × 16
Busbar	6	593 × 15
Voltage Transformer	6	39 × 57
Capacitor	4	26 × 41
Station Service Transformer	2	29 × 61
Main Transformer	2	78 × 87

Based on this finding, this paper optimizes the network structure by adjusting the backbone network, neck network, and detection head. As shown in Figure 4, for the Type-YOLOv8 model, an ultra-small target detection layer and a detection head specifically for small targets [22] were added based on the YOLO framework. The added detection head can detect more detailed information through higher-resolution feature maps and shallow feature fusion, enabling accurate distinctions between targets with small differences.

Compared to the study in [22] which primarily focuses on global scale variations, our analysis further elucidates the specific mechanism of the P6 layer in disambiguating visually similar electrical components, thereby providing deeper insights into the synergistic relationship between high-resolution feature fusion and topological consistency in industrial diagrams.

2.2.2. Window-Based Multi-Head Self-Attention Mechanism

To enhance the precision of bay type identification, this paper designs an ST-C2f module to substitute the original C2f module [23] in the advanced stage of the backbone network, integrating it into YOLOv8′s core architecture, with its structural configuration illustrated in Figure 5. While fully preserving the residual connections and channel fusion logic of the original module, it deeply embeds Swin Transformer to form a collaborative feature extraction mode of "local feature extraction + global topology perception."

https://doi.org/10.3390/en19020546

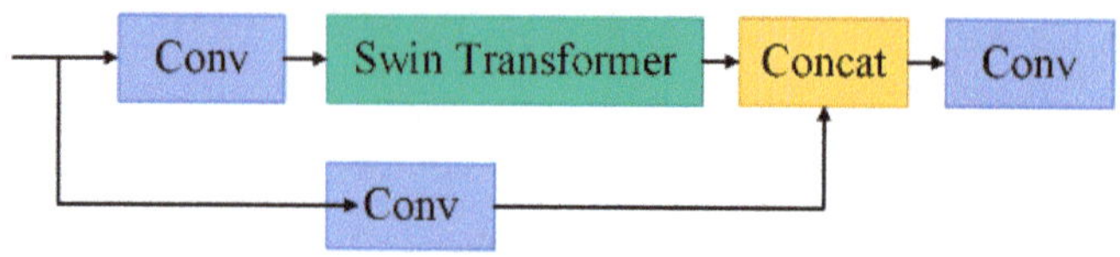

Figure 5. Network structure of ST-C2f modules.

The integration of Swin Transformer (ST) with the YOLO series has emerged as a mainstream optimization approach for object detection in complex scenes. However, the specific fusion strategies and implementation details vary significantly across studies: Reference [24] applies ST to the Head layer to enhance fine-grained classification, Reference [25] embeds ST in the Neck layer to assist multi-scale feature association, Reference [26] replaces residual modules in YOLOv5 with ST Blocks instead of C2f modules, and Reference [23] replaces only one C2f module with a focus on lightweight design. None of these approaches, however, are tailored to the specific characteristics of substation wiring diagrams. In contrast, this study strategically replaces two core C2f modules at the advanced stage of the Backbone—a critical juncture for feature extraction. This design continuously strengthens global topology perception and local detail capture capabilities, making it better suited for identifying similar intervals and ultra-small targets in substation wiring diagrams.

Swin Transformer [27] is a vision Transformer [28] architecture based on Window-based Multi-head Self-Attention (W-MSA), whose core idea involves dividing input images into non-overlapping small windows, performing local self-attention calculations within each window, while achieving global information interaction through cross-window connections, thereby maintaining global feature perception capability while reducing computational complexity.

As shown in Figure 6, MSA incurs high computational complexity, whereas W-MSA significantly reduces the computational burden by partitioning feature maps into non-overlapping local windows and independently calculating self-attention within each window. However, W-MSA is confined to window interiors and lacks global information interaction. To address this, the Swin Transformer adopts SW-MSA, which shifts windows from W-MSA by M/2 pixels to the right and downward from the upper-left corner, respectively, achieving information interaction between different windows and thus maintaining global information, as shown in Figure 7a. Additionally, the segmented windows are reassembled without changing the computational load, as shown in Figure 7b.

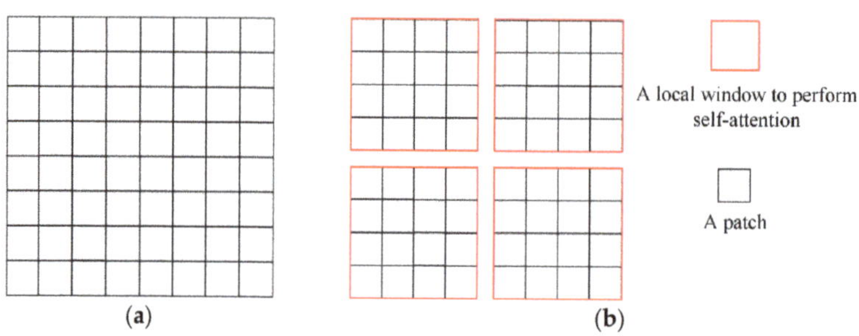

Figure 6. Window segmentation between MSA (**a**) and W-MSA (**b**).

https://doi.org/10.3390/en19020546

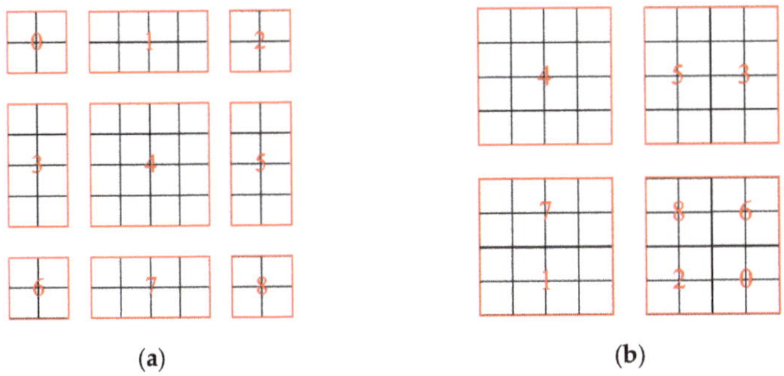

Figure 7. SW-MSA window segmentation. (**a**) Window shifting scheme of SW-MSA for information interaction between windows; (**b**) Segmented window reassembly scheme of SW-MSA showing; The numbers (0–8) act as unique indices for image patches, tracking their positions before and after shifting to visualize the patch reorganization process.

The detailed architecture of the Swin Transformer module is illustrated in Figure 8. Within each Swin Transformer module, W-MSA and SW-MSA are alternately employed, enabling the model to capture both local features and maintain global contextual information. Each module additionally incorporates Layer Normalization (LN) and Multi-Layer Perceptron (MLP) components for feature normalization and non-linear transformation, thereby further enhancing the model's representational capacity [29].

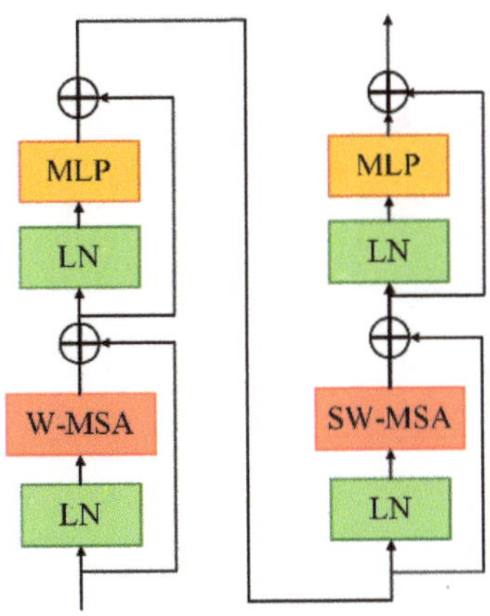

Figure 8. Network structure of Swin Transformer.

2.3. Device Matching Based on Regularization and Knowledge Base

The multilevel recognition strategy associates the recognition results between different levels through the depth-first strategy and parent–child nodes to obtain the initial topological information of the wiring diagram. However, compared with the relatively independent topological relationships between different bays, the specific topological relationships between devices cannot be fully expressed only through a hierarchical structure. To this end, this paper proposes a topological relationship matching method based on regularized number parsing and bay topology knowledge base constraints. This method realizes the automatic alignment of switching devices and template nodes through regularized parsing of the identified device numbers, combined with the standard connection modes defined in the bay topology knowledge base, and generates topological relationships that conform to electrical rules on this basis.

https://doi.org/10.3390/en19020546

2.3.1. Regularized Parsing of Device Numbers

In substation wiring diagrams, device numbers are the core carriers of device identity and functional attributes, and their naming system strictly follows specific technical specifications. This standardization makes the rule-based regularization method an ideal approach for extracting accurate semantic information from unstructured text. This module aims to convert the original, noisy text information output by Optical Character Recognition (OCR) into pure, structured semantic knowledge that can be directly reasoned by computers.

Firstly, unified regularization preprocessing is performed on the original input, including full-width to half-width conversion, case standardization, correction of common misrecognized characters, and removal of invalid symbols, to ensure the high unity of the input text in the character set and format. Subsequently, the semantic rule extraction stage based on regular expressions is entered. This paper pre-constructs several sets of regular expression rule bases covering the target plant and station numbering system using a set of predefined regular expression pairs, which can be matched in order of priority or selected manually. The processed numbers are parsed into structured triples through predefined regular expression patterns: {Ei, Et, El}, where Ei represents the device number, Et represents the device type, and El represents the device's location. Through this process, the device number is upgraded from a surface identifier to a deep semantic entity containing type and location information, providing a direct logical basis for subsequent topological matching.

2.3.2. Rule Matching Based on Topology Knowledge Base

The same bay information group obtained through the regularization parsing module is template-matched based on the bay topology knowledge base. The system can automatically infer the topological relationships between the switching devices and determine their actual positions in the bay connection template, as shown in Figure 9. For conventional bays, topological knowledge extraction can be completed directly using structured triples. For complex bays (such as various main transformers), a multi-bay collaborative analysis strategy is required. When the information of a single bay is insufficient to determine the complete topological relationship, the system will temporarily store the relevant devices in the pending area and perform comprehensive reasoning after obtaining complete information.

Due to the possible error transmission caused by the top-down depth-first strategy, its impact is even greater than that of the matching algorithm. Therefore, this process also serves as a post-processing link for the wiring diagram recognition, as shown in Figure 9. While matching topological relationships, the rationality of the recognition results is judged using hierarchical information combined with rules. According to the error ratio, if it is lower than 0.2 (the setting basis and experimental verification of this threshold are detailed in Appendix A), the erroneous devices are automatically corrected; if it is higher than 0.2, manual intervention is triggered, and the correction results are recorded.

Regarding the matching of devices and connection lines, Reference [21] utilizes a "serial" check logic primarily based on image-level geometric feature matching and region growth. In contrast, this paper implements a more robust four-level recognition architecture integrated with a depth-first strategy. By explicitly nesting electrical components with their regularized semantic identifiers, this paper ensures higher topological integrity and logical certainty, effectively resolving the complex primary wiring scenarios that remain challenging for feature-based matching methods like those in [30].

https://doi.org/10.3390/en19020546

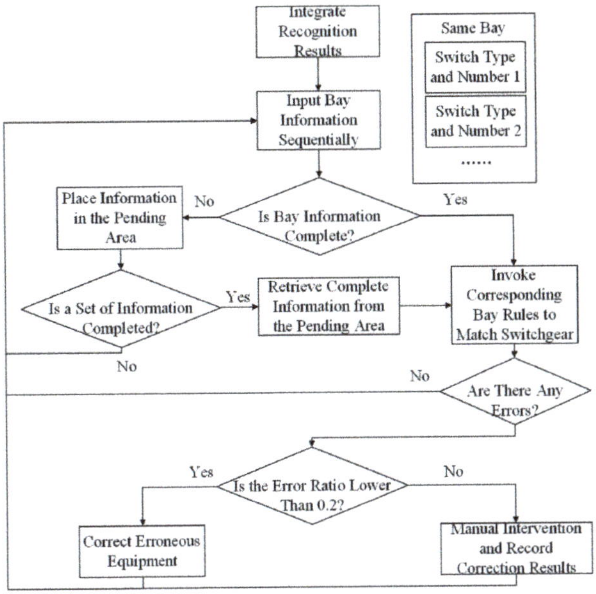

Figure 9. Topology Matching of Switching Device.

3. Experimental Results and Analysis

3.1. Dataset Processing and Training

The data used in this experiment are derived from substation wiring diagrams of a company, totaling 167 images, including 136 images of 110 kV substation wiring diagrams and 31 images of 220 kV substation wiring diagrams, with an average resolution of 1700.59 × 919.34 pixels. Specifically, the wiring modes involved are: (1) single-bus wiring, (2) double-bus wiring, (3) 3/2 circuit wiring, and (4) bridge-type wiring; the switching devices include: (1) circuit breakers, (2) disconnectors, (3) handcart switches, and (4) earthing switches. The dataset was annotated via LabelImg following the company's standards. Among them, the bay type dataset is shown in Figure 10.

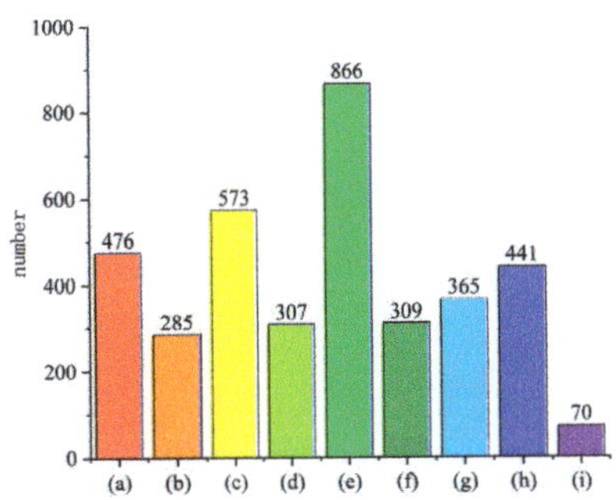

Figure 10. Distribution of bay types in the dataset. (a) voltage transformer bay, (b) transformer bay, (c) capacitor bay, (d) outgoing line bay, (e) handcart outgoing line bay, (f) section bay, (g) station transformer bay, (h) double-bus bay, and (i) 3/2 line bay.

For hierarchical model training, sub-datasets are generated through upper-level recognition and cropping: 167 images for connection mode recognition, 326 cropped images for bay type recognition, and 1000 screened images for switching device recognition. Training

https://doi.org/10.3390/en19020546

iterations are set to 100 epochs for connection modes and switching devices, and 200 epochs for bay types.

To ensure reproducibility and avoid data leakage, each hierarchical dataset was independently partitioned into training (60%), validation (30%), and test (10%) sets using a fixed random seed (369), as illustrated in Figure 11. A 'random partition + manual balance' strategy was adopted to align key category distributions. All test sets remained unseen during model training. Details regarding data and variable descriptions, the specific partitioning of the dataset, and the method's adaptability to practical deployment are provided in Appendix B.

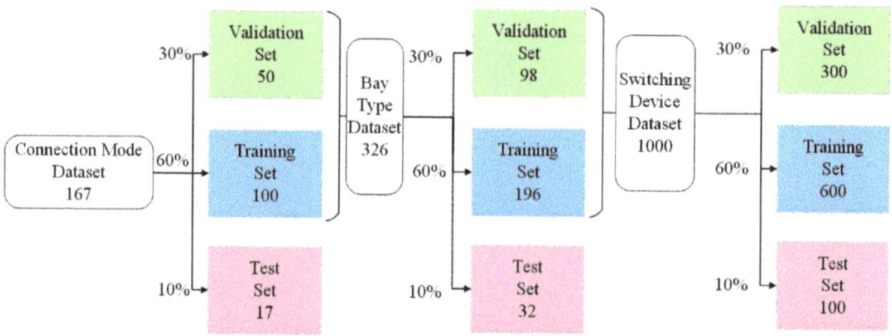

Figure 11. Schematic of Hierarchical Dataset Train/Val/Test Split.

3.2. Experimental Hardware and Parameter Settings

The code running environment and hyperparameters of the algorithm used in this experiment are shown in Table 3

Table 3. Experimental hardware configuration table.

Item	Strategy
CPU	Intel Core i5-12600KF
GPU	NVIDIA GeForce RTX 4060 Ti 16 GB
Operate system	Windows 11
Python	3.9.19
CUDA	12.1
Batch size	8
Optimizer	Adamw

3.3. Performance Evaluation Indicators

In the fields of deep learning and image processing, the evaluation of model performance is crucial. Therefore, precision (P), recall (R), average precision (AP), and mean average precision (mAP) are used as evaluation indicators for the model's anchor box detection ability. Among them, precision P and recall R are calculated as follows:

$$\mathrm{P} = \frac{TP}{TP + FP} \tag{2}$$

$$\mathrm{R} = \frac{TP}{TP + FN} \tag{3}$$

where TP represents the number of correctly classified positive samples; FP represents the number of misclassified negative samples; FN represents the number of misclassified positive samples.

https://doi.org/10.3390/en19020546

To calculate the model performance indicator mAP, first draw the P-R curve based on the recognition results of each category, obtain the AP value of each category through curve integration, and finally take the arithmetic mean of the AP values of all categories. The specific calculation formula is as follows:

$$\mathrm{AP} = \int_0^1 \mathrm{P(R)dR} \tag{4}$$

$$\mathrm{mAP} = \frac{\sum\limits_{k=1}^{n} \int_0^1 \mathrm{P(R)dR}}{n} \tag{5}$$

where n is the total number of annotated categories in the dataset.

To determine a reasonable error threshold for topological consistency checking, three indicators need to be analyzed: Correction Success Rate, defined as the proportion of successfully corrected topological relationships to total test cases; Natural Occurrence Probability, defined as the statistical proportion of each error scenario in the original dataset; and the Error Ratio (i.e., the error threshold), which is the proportion of erroneous devices to the total number of devices in a bay.

Additionally, to quantify the contribution of key components (e.g., the ST module and P6 detection layer) to model performance during ablation experiments, two supplementary indicators are introduced: Relative Drop Ratio, defined as the ratio of the drop in the core metric (mAP@0.5) on the test set after a component is disabled to the original value of the core metric, reflecting the relative importance of the component; and Absolute Drop (pp), defined as the direct drop in mAP@0.5 on the test set after a component is disabled, assisting in intuitively reflecting the component's absolute contribution (the unit "pp" denotes percentage points).

To ensure the consistency, accuracy, and readability of data presentation throughout the study, and to facilitate readers' quick understanding and comparison of key evaluation metrics, this table standardizes the unit definitions and decimal place retention rules for all core indicators involved in experiments. It includes core recognition and statistical metrics: Precision (P), Recall (R), Mean Average Precision (mAP), Relative Drop Ratio, Absolute Drop, Correction Success Rate, Natural Occurrence Probability, and Pearson Correlation Coefficient (r), clearly specifying the corresponding unit of each metric and the number of decimal places to be retained for unified expression, as shown in Table 4. Among them, Correction Success Rate and Natural Occurrence Probability are two key indicators analyzed to determine a reasonable error threshold for topological consistency checks, with detailed definitions provided in Appendix A. The Pearson Correlation Coefficient (r) is an indicator used to further evaluate the correlation between components, with detailed definitions provided in Appendix D.

Table 4. Specifications for Units and Decimal Place Retention of Core Indicators.

Recognition Tasks	Unit	Number of Decimal Places
Precision (P)	Percentage (%)	1
Recall (R)	Percentage (%)	1
Mean Average Precision (mAP)	Percentage (%)	1
Relative Drop Ratio	Percentage (%)	2
Absolute Drop	Percentage points (pp)	1
Correction Success Rate	Percentage (%)	1
Natural Occurrence Probability	Percentage (%)	1
Pearson Correlation Coefficient (r)	None	2

https://doi.org/10.3390/en19020546

3.4. Hierarchical Recognition Performance Verification Experiments

To verify the effect of the proposed hierarchical recognition in handling the size differences of wiring diagram targets, the test set is used to test the recognition effects of the connection mode, bay type, and switching device recognition models. The results are shown in Table 5. The connection mode and switching device recognition tasks perform excellently. The precision of connection mode recognition is 94.1%, the recall rate is 95.1%, and the mAP@0.5 is 95.7%; the precision of switching device recognition is 97.8%, the recall rate is 98.9%, and the mAP@0.5 is 98.9%. It is evident that the identification of connection configurations employs busbars as the criterion for discrimination, characterized by distinct features and straightforward recognition. For switching device identification, image tiling is utilized, which effectively eliminates substantial extraneous information from the recognition images and thereby reduces identification complexity. In contrast, the bay type recognition task has a precision of 91.3%, a recall rate of 87.7%, and a mAP@0.5 of 90.6%, which is lower than the other two models due to the high recognition difficulty. Detailed analysis of text recognition and overall recognition is provided in Appendix C.

Table 5. Image recognition results.

Recognition Tasks	P/%	R/%	mAP@0.5/%
Connection mode	94.1	95.1	95.7
Bay type	91.3	87.7	90.6
Switching device	97.8	98.9	98.9

3.5. Ablation Experiments

To investigate the impact of the ST module (i.e., the Swin Transformer module) and the P6 detection layer (focused on ultra-small target detection) in Type-YOLOv8 on recognition performance, a series of ablation experiments were conducted as shown in Table 6. A "√" indicates the adoption of the improved module. The comparative analysis of the experimental data is as follows:

1. After introducing the ST module, the model efficiently extracts global features and fuses local details with global contextual information, achieving comprehensive optimization of bay type recognition performance. Specifically, the precision increases by 1.8 percentage points to 87.8%, the recall rate rises from 83.4% to 84.9% (an increase of 1.5 percentage points), and the mAP@0.5 metric improves from 86.9% to 88.8% (an increase of 1.9 percentage points). This indicates that the ST module primarily enhances the model's ability to capture global topological correlations, thereby promoting the consistency of recognition results across complex bay scenarios.
2. The adoption of the P6 structure has a prominent impact on model performance. In terms of detection precision, it increases by 4.4 percentage points to 90.4%, which is the most significant improvement among single-module additions. The recall rate rises by 1.6 percentage points to 85.0% (from the baseline 83.4%), and the mAP@0.5 increases from 86.9% to 89.7% (an increase of 2.8 percentage points). These improvements confirm that the P6 structure effectively enhances the model's ability to detect small targets and distinguish similar bays.

https://doi.org/10.3390/en19020546

Table 6. Result of ablation experiments.

Group	ST	P6	P/%	R/%	mAP@0.5/%
1			86.0	83.4	86.9
2	√		87.8	84.9	88.8
3		√	90.4	85.0	89.7
4	√	√	91.3	87.7	90.6

Finally, Type-YOLOv8, which combines both components, exhibits the best comprehensive performance. Compared with the baseline (Group 1 without ST and P6), the model achieves a precision of 91.3% (an increase of 5.3 percentage points), a recall rate of 87.7% (an increase of 4.3 percentage points), and an mAP@0.5 of 90.6% (an increase of 3.7 percentage points). This synergistic effect demonstrates that the ST module's global feature perception and the P6 layer's small-target detection capability complement each other, leading to overall performance optimization.

To further quantify the contribution of key components to test-set performance, permutation importance analysis was conducted, and the detailed results are summarized in Table 7. The core logic is: on the trained Type-YOLOv8 model, each component is individually "disabled", and the drop in the core metric (mAP@0.5) on the test set is calculated—higher drop ratios indicate greater component importance.

Table 7. Permutation Importance Analysis Results.

Component	Full Model mAP@0.5/%	mAP@0.5 After Disabling/%	Absolute Drop/pp	Relative Drop Ratio/%	Importance Rank
ST Module	90.6	89.7	0.9	0.99	2
P6 Detection Layer	90.6	88.8	1.8	1.99	1

While Table 7 provides precise quantitative data, the differences in component importance are not intuitively perceptible. To address this, Figure 12 is plotted in the form of a bar chart, which visually presents the relative drop ratio of mAP@0.5 corresponding to each component. This visualization enables readers to quickly grasp the magnitude of contribution differences between the ST module and P6 detection layer, supplementing the quantitative results in the table with intuitive expression.

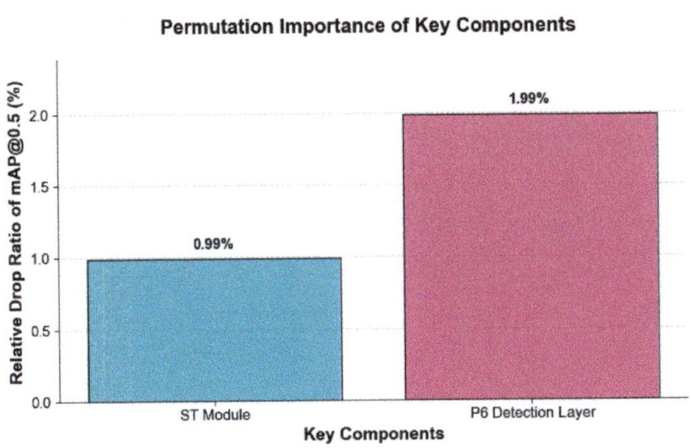

Figure 12. Permutation Importance of Key Components on Test Set.

https://doi.org/10.3390/en19020546

The ordinate represents the relative drop ratio of mAP@0.5 after component shielding, and the abscissa denotes the two key components. Higher bar heights indicate greater contribution to the model's generalization ability, which is consistent with the importance ranking in Table 7. Detailed verification of redundant contribution between the ST module and P6 detection layer, along with Pearson correlation coefficient (r) analysis, is provided in Appendix D.

3.6. *Comparative Experiments*

3.6.1. Type-YOLOv8 Model Comparative Analysis

In order to evaluate the performance of the Type-YOLOv8 model in the electrical component detection task for wiring diagrams, a comparative experiment was conducted with object detection networks such as Faster-R-CNN, SSD, YOLOv5x, YOLOv7x, and YOLOv8x under the same experimental conditions and dataset. To ensure fairness in comparison, the training epochs were uniformly set to 400 as some comparative models exhibit poor convergence; the 95% confidence intervals (95% CIs) for all models are derived from 5-fold cross-validation to guarantee statistical reliability. The results are shown in Table 8.

Table 8. Performance comparison of different object detection models.

Methods	P/% [95% CI]	R/% [95% CI]	mAP@0.5/% [95% CI]
Faster-R-CNN	77.2 [73.1, 81.3]	74.3 [70.6, 78.0]	77.4 [74.8, 80.0]
SSD	83.6 [80.7, 86.5]	76.3 [75.9, 76.6]	81.2 [80.2, 82.2]
YOLOv5x	84.9 [83.8, 86.0]	87.1 [86.7, 87.5]	88.4 [88.1, 88.7]
YOLOv7x	85.7 [83.4, 88.0]	85.2 [80.7, 89.7]	86.4 [84.9, 87.8]
YOLOv8x	86.0 [85.3, 86.7]	88.3 [87.2, 89.4]	90.2 [89.0, 91.3]
Type-YOLOv8	92.6 [90.9, 94.3]	90.9 [89.9, 91.9]	93.6 [91.8, 95.4]

All models were trained with 400 uniform epochs (fair comparison for poorly converging baselines), with YOLOv8x/Type-YOLOv8 metrics slightly higher than Table 5. For deployment, 200 epochs avoid overfitting.

As can be seen from the comparative experimental results in Table 8, the proposed Type-YOLOv8 model exhibits outstanding performance in the electrical component detection task for wiring diagrams, achieving significant leading advantages in core accuracy indicators compared with mainstream target detection networks.

In terms of the core evaluation metric mAP@0.5, Type-YOLOv8 reaches 93.6%, which is significantly higher than all comparative models. Specifically, it outperforms the traditional two-stage algorithm Faster-R-CNN by 20.2 percentage points, the one-stage classic model SSD by 12.4 percentage points, and the representative models of the YOLO series (YOLOv5x, YOLOv7x, YOLOv8x) by 5.2, 7.2, and 3.4 percentage points, respectively. This fully demonstrates that the targeted improvements of Type-YOLOv8—such as integrating the Swin Transformer module to enhance global feature perception and adding the P6 ultra-small target detection layer—effectively address the key challenges in wiring diagram component detection, such as complex topological relationships and small target dominance.

In terms of precision (P) and recall (R), Type-YOLOv8 also maintains a balanced and excellent performance. Its precision of 92.6% is the highest among all models, 6.6 percentage points higher than the baseline YOLOv8x, reflecting the model's strong ability to avoid false detections of similar components in wiring diagrams. Meanwhile, the recall rate of 90.9% is 2.6 percentage points higher than YOLOv8x, which is known for its high recall performance. This indicates that Type-YOLOv8 can effectively capture rare or small-sized electrical components without sacrificing precision, achieving a good balance between "detecting correctly" and "detecting completely".

 https://doi.org/10.3390/en19020546

A statistical check of the 95% confidence intervals across all core metrics further validates the superiority of Type-YOLOv8: there is no overlap between the 95% CIs of Type-YOLOv8 and those of the baseline YOLOv8x for precision, recall, and mAP@0.5. Detailed visualization of the metric stability of Type-YOLOv8 across 5-fold cross-validation, including the distribution and interquartile range (IQR) of core metrics, is provided in Appendix E, which further confirms the statistical rigor and reliability of the experimental results.

To provide a more intuitive comparison of model performance, the training data were consolidated to illustrate the relationship between mAP@0.5 and training epochs (using the highest mAP@0.5 values), as shown in Figure 13. From the training curves, it can be observed that the convergence speed of Type-YOLOv8 is second only to YOLOv8x, yet still surpasses that of YOLOv5x and YOLOv7x. Moreover, during the early to mid-training phase (after approximately 150 epochs), the performance of this model exceeds that of the baseline model YOLOv8x, achieving the highest accuracy among all models.

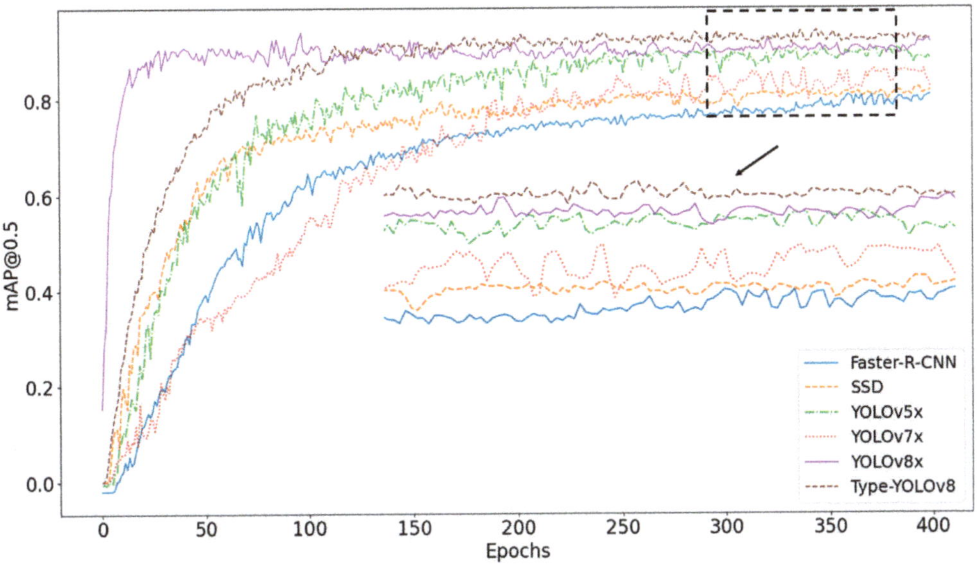

Figure 13. The training curve of mAP@0.5.

3.6.2. Hierarchical Topology Knowledge Extraction Method Comparative Analysis

To prove the superiority of this algorithm in extracting wiring diagram topology knowledge, it is compared with traditional methods. Due to the hierarchical recognition strategy, it is difficult to measure the overall performance with a single indicator. Therefore, a direct manual comparison scheme is adopted: the topological logic generated by different matching methods is manually compared with the actual topological information in the original wiring diagrams, so as to quantitatively evaluate the completeness and accuracy of topological knowledge extraction. To ensure the fairness of the comparison, all comparison methods adopt the same YOLOv8 and PP-OCRv4 models as this method, and the connecting line recognition adopts the Line Segment Detector (LSD) algorithm. The results are shown in Table 9.

https://doi.org/10.3390/en19020546

Table 9. Comparison of matching capability and performance.

Methods	P/%	R/%
Node traversal methods	61.3	76.2
VF2	82.7	72.8
QuickSI	81.5	83.5
TurboIso	86.7	88.3
Ours	93.9	91.7

Experimental results show that the recognition precision of this method reaches 93.9% and the recall rate reaches 91.7%. This result is not only significantly superior to the comparison methods in performance but also reflects the outstanding advantage of this method in the reconstruction of topological relationship completeness. The reason is that this method effectively avoids the problem of multi-modal error accumulation in the traditional triple recognition framework through hierarchical recognition: the recognition of connection modes, bay types, and devices is interrelated, ensuring the electrical semantic consistency of the recognition results. At the same time, a bay topology knowledge base is constructed, enabling topological relationships to be implicitly derived under template constraints, fundamentally avoiding errors caused by matching algorithms. Performance comparisons with other studies are presented in Appendix C.

4. Conclusions

Aiming at the technical problem of multi-modal matching error accumulation in the topological knowledge extraction of substation wiring diagrams, this paper proposes a hierarchical recognition-based topological knowledge extraction method. The main conclusions are as follows:

1. By constructing a multi-level recognition system and using image tiling to segment bay units, the algorithmic errors of multi-modal matching tasks are avoided. This method enables the three recognition layers to achieve excellent detection performance, with mAP@0.5 exceeding 90%, ensuring the accuracy of topological relationships.
2. The Swin Transformer module is introduced in the high-level stage of the backbone network of the bay recognition model to replace the original C2f module, and an ultra-small target detection layer is added. This allows the model to effectively improve the global feature perception ability without significantly increasing the computational complexity. The model's mAP@0.5 indicator reaches 90.6%, which is 7.7 percentage points higher than the basic YOLOv8x, while the model size only increases by 15.2 MB to 152.0 MB.
3. From the depth-first strategy to the rule matching based on the topology knowledge base, this method successfully realizes the accurate and complete knowledge extraction of wiring diagrams. Experimental verification shows that the overall recognition precision of this method on the test set reaches 93.9% and the recall rate is 91.7%, which is significantly superior to traditional matching methods such as node traversal and VF2.

Beyond computational performance improvements, the proposed method delivers tangible practical value for enhancing substation operation safety and operational efficiency: it automates the extraction of structured topological knowledge, eliminating labor-intensive manual wiring diagram interpretation and significantly reducing the compilation and iteration cycle of five-prevention logic libraries. The standardized output also reduces reliance on expert experience in daily maintenance and fault location, further optimizing operational efficiency while safeguarding substation safety.

https://doi.org/10.3390/en19020546

Despite the aforementioned advancements in accuracy, practical applicability, and technical innovation, this study has two main limitations: the limited scale and diversity of the dataset may lead to overfitting bias, restricting the model's generalization to rare substation wiring diagram types; meanwhile, the large model parameter size causes efficiency bias, requiring higher hardware support in practical deployment. In terms of validity scope, its conclusions apply to substation five-prevention logic verification scenarios, as the method focuses on extracting switching device information—which is key for five-prevention logic—rather than all wiring diagram details, thus not generalizing to full-element digitization tasks, such as wiring diagram archive management.

Future work will address these limitations by expanding dataset diversity to mitigate overfitting bias and enhance model adaptability, and adopting lightweight technologies, such as knowledge distillation, to optimize model efficiency for practical deployment.

Author Contributions: Conceptualization, H.Y. and D.Y.; methodology, H.Y.; software, H.Y.; validation, H.Y. and D.Y.; data curation, W.Z. and X.R.; writing—original draft preparation, H.Y.; writing—review and editing, H.Y., T.W., Q.H. and J.L.; visualization, H.Y.; supervision, T.W. and Q.H. All authors have read and agreed to the published version of the manuscript.

Funding: This research was funded by the National Natural Science Foundation of China, grant number 51807110.

Data Availability Statement: The data presented in this study are available on request from the corresponding author, as the substation wiring diagram dataset cannot be made publicly available directly—it contains proprietary grid infrastructure information that is subject to strict security protocols and regulatory compliance requirements in the power industry.

Conflicts of Interest: Authors Dong Yang, Wenyu Zhu and Xiang Ren were employed by the Xiangyang Power Supply Company State Grid Hubei Electric Power Co. Author Qing He was employed by the State Grid Hubei Electric Power Co., Ltd. Electric Power Science Research Institute. The remaining authors declare that the research was conducted in the absence of any commercial or financial relationships that could be construed as a potential conflict of interest.

Appendix A

To determine an appropriate error threshold for topological consistency checking, we conducted comparative experiments on the correction effect and occurrence probability of erroneous devices, with the results shown in Table A1.

Table A1. Erroneous Devices, Correction Success Rate and Occurrence Probability.

Erroneous Devices	Correction Success Rate	Natural Occurrence Probability
0	-	87%
1	100%	9%
2	95%	4%
≥3	≤60%	0%

Correction success rate is defined as the proportion of successfully corrected topological relationships to total test cases, natural occurrence probability refers to the statistical proportion of each error scenario in the original dataset, and cases with 3 or more erroneous devices do not exist in the dataset—their correction success rate is obtained by manually setting 50 groups of erroneous devices to verify the correction limit.

Experimental data indicate significant differences in correction effectiveness and natural occurrence probability corresponding to different numbers of erroneous devices within a single bay: when there is only 1 erroneous device, the rule-based regularized parsing module can achieve a 100% correction success rate through device number matching and logical constraints of the bay topology knowledge base. This scenario has a natural occurrence probability of 9% in the dataset, making it the most prominent error type in practical

https://doi.org/10.3390/en19020546

applications. When there are 2 erroneous devices, the correction success rate remains at a high level of 95%, but the natural occurrence probability is only 4%, which is a rare scenario in engineering practice. Cases with 3 or more erroneous devices have no natural occurrence records in the original dataset; their correction success rate (≤60%) is obtained by manually simulating 50 groups of error samples, primarily for verifying the model's correction limit. Such extreme scenarios have no substantial impact on practical applications.

Based on the above experimental data, the derivation process of the appropriate error threshold is as follows: first, combined with the distribution characteristics of error scenarios obtained from experimental statistics, it is determined that the threshold should prioritize covering high-frequency error scenarios, i.e., scenarios with at most 1 erroneous device within a single bay; second, considering engineering practical needs, the threshold setting should exclude low-probability scenarios with 2 or more erroneous devices from the scope of automatic correction, thus ensuring that such scenarios trigger necessary manual intervention; finally, based on the device quantity distribution characteristics of the bay topology knowledge base, the proportion intervals of two extreme scenarios are selected as the reference benchmarks—the lower limit of the proportion of a single error in the bay with the minimum number of devices, and the upper limit of the proportion of two errors in the bay with the maximum number of devices. With a moderate safety margin reserved, the 20% error threshold is finally determined as appropriate, with its core definition being covering scenarios with at most 1 erroneous device within a single bay.

Appendix B

Appendix B.1

To ensure transparency of data provenance and preprocessing details, Table A2 presents a comprehensive Data Sheet summarizing key information of the experimental dataset. It clarifies critical details such as data source, spatial-temporal scope, missing data handling, and outlier correction, aiming to enhance data traceability and experimental reproducibility in line with academic documentation standards.

Table A2. Data Sheet.

Item	Detailed Description
Data Source Identifier	Five-prevention wiring diagrams from a company (authorized for use)
Time Span (UTC)	No time-series data; single static collection (no special requirements for UTC time zone)
Spatial Scope	Covers selected 110 kV/220 kV substations of the aforementioned company
Missing Data Rate	0% (Images that are blurred or missing key components have been excluded through inclusion/exclusion rules, with 167 valid images retained finally)
Missing Data Imputation Rules	No data imputation; directly exclude images that do not meet inclusion rules (e.g., non-five-prevention wiring diagrams, non-standard device numbering, missing key components)
Outlier Handling	Correct incorrectly annotated images through manual secondary verification

Appendix B.2

To clarify the key variables involved in the experiment and ensure the rigor of data processing and model training, Table A3 presents a detailed Variables Table. It systematically summarizes the unit, transformation method of each core variable, and the corresponding train/test leakage prevention measures, which helps to improve the transparency of the experimental process and ensure the reproducibility of the results.

 https://doi.org/10.3390/en19020546

Table A3. Variables Table.

Variable Name	Unit	Variable Transformation	Train/Test Leakage
Image Resolution	Pixels	No scaling; retain original resolution (average 1700.59 × 919.34)	Uniform screening of resolution range before dataset division; no test set resolution information used for training set optimization, avoiding leakage
Device Bounding Box Coordinates	Pixels	Normalized to [0, 1] (YOLO training standard process)	Full annotation completed first, then random division into training/validation/test sets (6:3:1 ratio); training process only utilizes training set annotation data, no access to test set bounding box information
Device Type Label	Unitless	One-hot encoding (for model classification)	Unified label system formulated before full annotation; dataset divided independently, no test set label-related information involved in training
Detection Confidence	Percentage (%)	No transformation; directly output in [0, 100%]	Confidence threshold (0.8) determined only based on the validation set; no test set data used for threshold tuning
Device Number (Ei/Et/El)	Unitless	Regularization preprocessing → structured triple parsing	Parsing rules constructed based on public power industry standards; no test set number features used for optimizing parsing logic during training
Topological Relationship Matching Result	Unitless	Template matching based on bay topology knowledge base → structured output	Bay topology knowledge base templates built independently of the test set; no test set topological information introduced during model training

Appendix B.3

To verify the proposed method's adaptability to practical deployment and ensure the extracted topological knowledge conforms to engineering practice, this section elaborates on two core verification dimensions combined with real dataset characteristics and rule-based matching logic.

1. The experimental dataset consists of 110 kV/220 kV five-prevention wiring diagrams from in-service substations. Although future diagram iterations may involve layout optimization or auxiliary equipment additions, core functional components (circuit breakers, disconnectors, etc.) comply with industry-accepted engineering standards, featuring standardized visual, semantic, and functional attributes that remain unchanged. The model focuses on learning these stable core object features, ensuring reliable recognition performance for updated diagrams and long-term adaptability in practical deployment.
2. A bay topology knowledge base was constructed by sorting out industry specifications and design documents. This knowledge base defines standard connection logic and device numbering rules for typical wiring modes (e.g., double-bus wiring) and outgoing line bays, which are consistent with on-site device layout and operation norms. During the recognition process, the hierarchical framework accurately localizes bays and their internal switching devices in substation wiring diagrams, with extracted device numbers aligning with the rules in the knowledge base. Recognition results are automatically matched with corresponding templates via regularized parsing, realizing precise reconstruction of topological relationships. This rule-based matching logic ensures the extracted topological knowledge conforms to on-site engineering principles and meets the practical deployment requirements of intelligent five-prevention logic verification, as illustrated in Figures A1 and A2:

https://doi.org/10.3390/en19020546

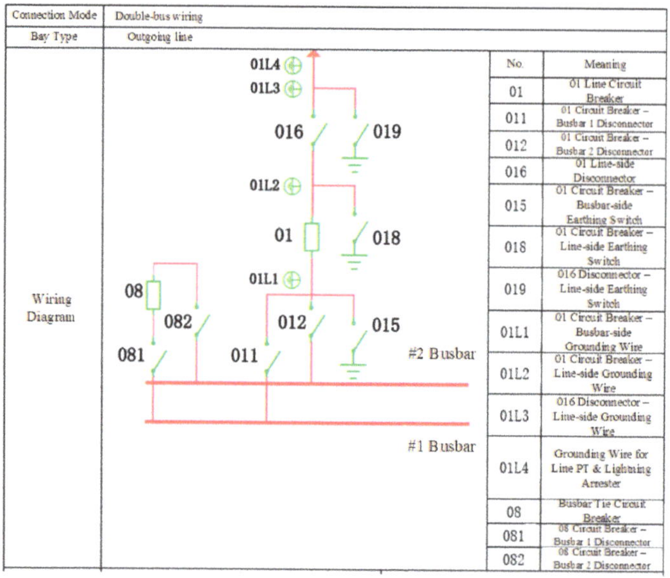

Figure A1. Partial Rule Base Example (Taking Double-Bus Wiring as a Typical Case). It presents the standard connection logic and device numbering rules for outgoing line bays, which are consistent with on-site device layout and operation norms, serving as a direct template for topological relationship matching.

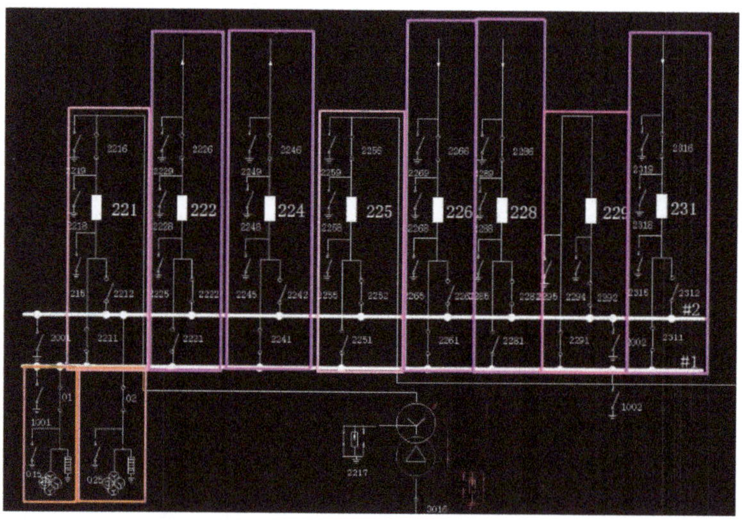

Figure A2. Bay Recognition Result Example. It demonstrates the accurate localization of bays and their internal switching devices in a substation wiring diagram, where the extracted device numbers align with the rules defined in the bay topology knowledge base. Real place names have been redacted for privacy protection.

Appendix C

Appendix C.1

To evaluate the performance of the PP-OCRv4 model, tests were conducted. The model comprises two components: text detection for locating recognition regions and

https://doi.org/10.3390/en19020546

text recognition for accurately extracting text information. Since the image recognition component of the Hierarchical Recognition framework has significantly narrowed down the detection scope, the text recognition results are excellent, as shown in Table A4. The text detection module can perfectly locate the switch numbers that need to be recognized. The slight deficit in the 95.6% precision of text recognition is mainly attributed to misrecognition of some low-pixel digits: e.g., the digit "0" is misrecognized as the letter "O", as illustrated in Figure A3. Since device numbers contain no letters, these errors can be corrected via regular replacement processing. Therefore, text recognition can basically fulfill the task requirements. The final recognition accuracy of the wiring diagrams directly adopts the results from the image recognition component.

Table A4. PP-OCRv4 Model Test Results.

Evaluation Metrics	Text Detection	Text Recognition
Precision (P/%)	99.9	95.6
Recall (R/%)	99.9	99.9

Figure A3. Recognition Errors.

Appendix C.2

Since the recognition component of the hierarchical recognition framework involves multiple levels and incorporates device matching, with chain dependency among the results, it is difficult to independently evaluate the standalone effectiveness of a single image recognition stage—a limitation also presents in the study of reference [16]. Therefore, this study conducts manual comparison and validation of the final topological knowledge extraction results using complete substation wiring diagrams, aiming to systematically assess the transmission effect of errors from higher-level recognition and the optimization effect of the post-processing procedure on the results, with the specific performance comparison shown in Table A5. It can be observed that errors from higher-level recognition stages do exert a notable negative impact on the final topological extraction performance (Comparison of switching device recognition accuracy 97.8% and recall rate 98.0%), while the proposed post-processing module yields a substantial improvement in the overall results.

Table A5. Wiring diagram topology knowledge extraction experiment.

Methods	P/%	R/%
hierarchical recognition	89.6	88.2
hierarchical recognition (with post-processing)	93.9	91.7

https://doi.org/10.3390/en19020546

Appendix C.3

A comparative analysis of the closest related studies was conducted across three dimensions: data source, method/model, and evaluation metric. The results are presented in Table A6. The connection line detection and matching algorithms of most studies have not been made public; meanwhile, text recognition models are relatively mature, making it difficult to distinguish their performance advantages. Therefore, this comparison focuses on image recognition performance. Our hierarchical recognition approach far outperforms all other related studies in image recognition performance. Its precision (93.9%) and recall (91.7%) are markedly superior to those of all comparative methods, demonstrating distinct advantages.

Table A6. Comparative experiment on topology knowledge extraction capability.

Reference	Data	Method	P/%	R/%
[13] Feng et al. (2025)	96	Improved Faster R-CNN	87.9	82.9
[14] Li et al. (2021)	93	Faster R-CNN	84.7	73.8
[15] Wang et al. (2023)	101	Overlapping sliding window + YOLOv4	86.3	79.7
[16] Cheng et al. (2022)	N/A	Dual-Layer Architecture + YOLOv5	85.4	87.6
[17] Zhang et al. (2024)	156	PP-YOLOE	87.5	84.0
Ours	167	Hierarchical Recognition	93.9	91.7

All data sources are main wiring diagrams of substations from power supply companies, and the data in the table refers to the quantity of images. The performance metrics were obtained through training on the dataset presented in this study.

Appendix D

To verify whether there is redundant contribution between the ST module and P6 detection layer, Pearson correlation coefficient (r) analysis was performed based on the mAP@0.5 improvement data of ablation experiments (main text Table 6). The Pearson correlation coefficient is a dimensionless statistical indicator that quantifies the strength and direction of linear correlation between two continuous variables, serving as a reliable tool to evaluate the interdependence of performance improvement effects between different components. Its value range is confined to $[-1, 1]$, where $|r| < 0.3$ indicates weak linear correlation, $0.3 \leq |r| < 0.7$ denotes moderate linear correlation, and $0.7 \leq |r| < 1$ represents strong linear correlation; $r = 1$ or $r = -1$ corresponds to perfect positive or negative linear correlation, respectively, while $r = 0$ implies no linear correlation. For the correlation analysis of the two components in this study, the variable set X was defined as the performance improvement amplitude of each individual component relative to the baseline YOLOv8x, and variable set Y as the interaction effect between the two components (calculated as the combined improvement amplitude minus the sum of individual improvement amplitudes). The Pearson correlation coefficient r was computed using the following formula:

$$r = \frac{n\sum XY - (\sum X)(\sum Y)}{\sqrt{[n\sum X^2 - (\sum X)^2][n\sum Y^2 - (\sum Y)^2]}} \tag{A1}$$

In the above formula, n denotes the number of components ($n = 2$, corresponding to the ST module and P6 detection layer), ΣXY represents the sum of the product of corresponding elements in X and Y, ΣX and ΣY are the sums of elements in X and Y, respectively, and ΣX^2 and ΣY^2 stand for the sums of the squares of elements in X and Y.

The calculation result yielded $r \approx 0.1$, which falls within the range of weak linear correlation ($|r| < 0.3$). This finding indicates that the performance improvement effects of the

https://doi.org/10.3390/en19020546

ST module and P6 detection layer are weakly correlated, implying no significant redundant contribution between the two components. The underlying reason lies in their distinct feature extraction mechanisms: the ST module enhances global feature perception, while the P6 detection layer optimizes small-target recognition. Such functional complementarity ensures that the combined application of the two components can synergistically improve the model's comprehensive performance, which is consistent with the optimal recognition results of Type-YOLOv8 observed in the ablation experiment.

Appendix E

To enhance the statistical rigor and reliability of our experimental results, we generated a visualization of the uncertainty of Type-YOLOv8's core metrics across 5-fold cross-validation (as shown in Figure A4), in response to the review comment on "statistical rigor & uncertainty". From the figure, it can be observed that the precision (P/%), recall (R/%), and mAP@0.5/% of Type-YOLOv8 exhibit minimal fluctuations across the 5 folds: all fold values strictly fall within the previously reported 95% confidence intervals. The narrow interquartile range (IQR) of each metric further reflects the high stability of the model in repeated experiments, confirming that Type-YOLOv8's superior performance is not accidental but statistically reliable.

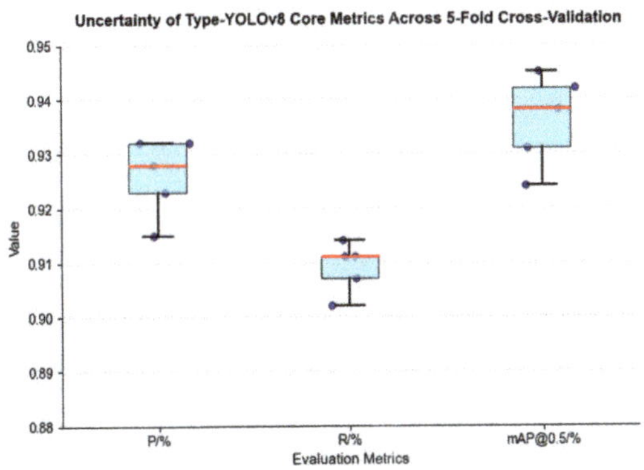

Figure A4. Uncertainty of Type-YOLOv8 Core Metrics Across 5-Fold Cross-Validation. The boxplots illustrate the distribution of each metric: the red central line denotes the median, the blue box represents the interquartile range (IQR), and the whiskers extend to 1.5 × IQR. The dark blue scatter points correspond to the original performance values of each fold in the 5-fold cross-validation.

References

1. Zhao, W.; Cui, A.; Fang, M.; Yang, L.; Chen, K.; Gong, X. State assessment of 110–220 kV intelligent substation based on multisensor fusion algorithm control and image vision. *Front. Energy Res.* **2023**, *10*, 1047359. [CrossRef]
2. Cheng, J.; Luo, Z.; Liao, H.; Tang, Y.; Sun, D.; Liu, S.; Chen, L. Verification Technology for Virtual Terminal Connection Based on Deep Learning and Attention Image Recognition. *Guangdong Electr. Power* **2024**, *37*, 73–79. Available online: https://www.cnki.net/KCMS/detail/detail.aspx?dbcode=CJFD&dbname=CJFDLAST2024&filename=GDDL202402009&uniplatform=OVERSEA&v=ykr5-j55S53ExRZSmYBLQI6UDOleyEnuYJv_GQRG1O5c8sB4yx0Ft5twiOT9v7sz (accessed on 13 January 2026).
3. Zhang, F.; Zhang, S.; Qiao, L.; Yao, K.; Han, W.; Wang, B. Research on intelligent verification technology of substation configuration files based on knowledge graph. *Electr. Meas. Instrum.* **2024**, *61*, 64–72. Available online: https://www.cnki.net/KCMS/detail/detail.aspx?dbcode=CJFD&dbname=CJFDLAST2024&filename=DCYQ202404010&uniplatform=OVERSEA&v=x00yOi7OX17HM8y8v_DXAJBCMuZxgFrqkqUt3I5eAwVLMoPF7gkpZYozUwx-gbPc (accessed on 13 January 2026).

https://doi.org/10.3390/en19020546

4. Sheng, H.; Ji, R.; Li, H.; Zhang, G.; Han, M. Research and application of mirror debugging technology for one key sequential control system based on an expert knowledge base. *Power Syst. Prot. Control* **2024**, *52*, 180–187. Available online: https://www.cnki.net/KCMS/detail/detail.aspx?dbcode=CJFD&dbname=CJFDLAST2024&filename=JDQW202403017&uniplatform=OVERSEA&v=BnISNiE6ii_QgAk0l_s1-QkvPP1jTDLL2DO24zSnzc-R3Fb0Z03sn--gqbz7vP03 (accessed on 13 January 2026).
5. Liu, Y.; Hu, Y.; Tai, N. Rule extraction method of operation and maintenance expert system for an intelligent substation based on the decision tree. *J. Electr. Power Sci. Technol.* **2019**, *34*, 123–128. Available online: https://www.cnki.net/KCMS/detail/detail.aspx?dbcode=CJFD&dbname=CJFDLAST2019&filename=CSDL201901017&uniplatform=OVERSEA&v=r4yiYz2w5Tbck3Cu5ElU8_lKiEc5_ckO8qR90Dz9naOVoMZxsx9dUaUEiwjaOI0f (accessed on 13 January 2026).
6. Zhang, H.; Zhang, S.; Liu, D.; Mu, Z.; Wang, G.; Shao, G.; Li, J. Design and application of a visualization check system for anti-misoperation blocking logic in a substation. *Power Syst. Prot. Control* **2021**, *49*, 181–187.
7. Cheng, L.; Yu, T.; Zhang, X.; Yin, L. Machine Learning for Energy and Electric Power Systems: State of the Art and Prospects. *Autom. Electr. Power Syst.* **2019**, *43*, 15–31. Available online: https://www.cnki.net/KCMS/detail/detail.aspx?dbcode=CJFD&dbname=CJFDLAST2021&filename=JDQW202112023&uniplatform=OVERSEA&v=RfrjQT_VlQl8Ty_3QqeKvYOYLRtxKuinvjEsw1IIChB8soPMcNPceLgVG9hgzW_w (accessed on 13 January 2026).
8. Moreno-García, C.F.; Elyan, E.; Jayne, C. New trends on digitisation of complex engineering drawings. *Neural Comput. Appl.* **2019**, *31*, 1695–1712. [CrossRef]
9. Ning, X.; Zhao, B.; Huang, B.; Zhu, M.; Zhang, Q.; Zhang, B. DrawingNet for Communication Tower Drawings Recognition. *IEEE Access* **2024**, *12*, 156378–156389. [CrossRef]
10. Elyan, E.; Jamieson, L.; Ali-Gombe, A. Deep learning for symbols detection and classification in engineering drawings. *Neural Netw.* **2020**, *129*, 91–102. [CrossRef]
11. Xu, X.; Xiao, G.; Sun, L.; Zhang, X.; Wu, P.; Zhang, Y.; Cheng, Z. Associative reasoning for engineering drawings using an interactive attention mechanism. *Autom. Constr.* **2025**, *170*, 105942. [CrossRef]
12. Sim, J.; Woo, H.; Kim, Y.; Kim, E.-T. Effective Detection of Materials in Construction Drawings using YOLOv4-based Small Object Detection Techniques. Digest of Technical Papers. In Proceedings of the IEEE International Conference on Consumer Electronics, Las Vegas, NV, USA, 7–9 January 2022. [CrossRef]
13. Feng, B.; Du, Y.; Jin, Y.; Zong, X.; Jin, H.; Liu, T.; Wang, C. Improved Faster R-CNN for substation electrical main wiring diagram element detection. *J. Harbin Inst. Sci. Technol.* **2025**, *30*, 39–47. [CrossRef]
14. Li, H.; Wang, S.; Geng, Y.; Wang, L.; Sun, W.; Miao, C. Wiring diagram detection and check based on deep learning and graph matching. *J. Beijing Univ. Aeronaut. Astronaut.* **2021**, *47*, 539–548.
15. Wang, Z.; Luo, Q.; Xiao, W.; Wang, Y.; Yu, T. Key Method of Wiring Diagram Recognition with Artificial Intelligence for Power Plant and Substation. *Power Syst. Autom.* **2023**, *47*, 115–124. Available online: https://www.cnki.net/KCMS/detail/detail.aspx?dbcode=CJFD&dbname=CJFDLAST2023&filename=DLXT202302013&uniplatform=OVERSEA&v=w-5wzqAE1sjHIRvYIGQ-bGERIL8A4LCDorMu5aRoOmpzf1oStfshBXM-b9gGtn3S (accessed on 13 January 2026).
16. Cheng, X.; Chu, X.; Deng, X.; Yang, K.; Tan, L.; Chen, Z.; Chao, W. Symbol detection method of electrical plant station wiring diagram symbols based on double layer-block detection network. *J. Southeast Univ. Nat. Sci. Ed.* **2022**, *52*, 1137–1144.
17. Zhang, Y.; Xu, D.; Cao, H.; Li, D.; Lyv, Y.; Zhang, X. Intelligent Recognition of Power Grid Station Wiring Diagrams Based on Multi-stage Collaboration. *Grid Technol.* **2024**, *48*, 4341–4350.
18. Mao, M.; Zhao, K.; Li, M.; Xu, H.; Yue, W.; Huang, K. Research on Substation Diagram Automatic Generation Based on Artificial Intelligence Algorithms. In Proceedings of the 2023 4th International Conference on Intelligent Computing and Human-Computer Interaction (ICHCI), IEEE, Guangzhou, China, 4–6 August 2023; pp. 219–225.
19. Kim, H.; Choi, Y.; Park, K.; Lin, X.; Hong, S.-H.; Han, W.-S. Fast subgraph query processing and subgraph matching via static and dynamic equivalences. *VLDB J.* **2023**, *32*, 343–368. [CrossRef]
20. Wen, W.; Luo, W.; Li, L.; Zhang, D.; Chen, W.; Wu, Z. Lane line damage detection algorithm based on YOLOv7 and image block. *Sens. Microsyst.* **2024**, *43*, 131–134+139.
21. Yang, D.; You, H.; Zhang, Y.; Ren, X.; Lu, B.; Jin, J.; Gu, T.; Jin, D. Identification of Primary Wiring Diagram in Substation Based on YOLOv5. In Proceedings of the 2024 IEEE 2nd International Conference on Power Science and Technology (ICPST), IEEE, Dali, China, 9–11 May 2024; pp. 603–609.
22. Chen, Q.; Li, L. Small Target Detection Algorithm Based on Improved YOLOv8n for Remote Sensing. *Laser Optoelectron. Prog.* **2025**, *62*, 368–379.
23. Huang, Z.; Fang, Q.; Guo, X. YOLOv8-TS traffic sign detection network integrating attention mechanism. *Mod. Electron. Tech.* **2025**, *48*, 179–186. [CrossRef]
24. Hui, Y.; Wang, J.; Li, B. STF-YOLO: A small target detection algorithm for UAV remote sensing images based on improved SwinTransformer and class weighted classification decoupling head. *Measurement* **2024**, *224*, 113936. [CrossRef]

https://doi.org/10.3390/en19020546

25. Wen, X.; Yao, Y.; Cai, Y.; Zhao, Z.; Chen, T.; Zeng, Z.; Tang, Z.; Gao, F. A lightweight st-yolo based model for detection of tea bud in unstructured natural environments. *IAENG Int. J. Appl. Math.* **2024**, *54*, 342–349.
26. Tian, J.; Tang, Z. Mine intelligent monitoring technology based on edge computing and ST-YOLO. *Coal Eng.* **2024**, *56*, 165–173.
27. Liu, Z.; Lin, Y.; Cao, Y.; Hu, H.; Wei, Y.; Zhang, Z.; Lin, S.; Guo, B. Swin transformer: Hierarchical vision transformer using shifted windows. In Proceedings of the IEEE/CVF International Conference on Computer Vision, Montreal, BC, Canada, 11–17 October 2021; pp. 10012–10022.
28. Vaswani, A.; Shazeer, N.; Parmar, N.; Uszkoreit, J.; Jones, L.; Gomez, A.N.; Kaiser, L.; Polosukhin, I. Attention is all you need. *Adv. Neural Inf. Process. Syst.* **2017**, *30*, 5999–6009.
29. Wang, X.; Bu, C.; Shi, Z. Face anti-spoofing based on improved Swin Transformer. *China Meas. Test* **2025**, *51*, 31–39.
30. Liu, H.; Yang, B.; Kang, F.; Li, Q.; Zhang, H. Intelligent recognition algorithm of connection relation of substation secondary wiring drawing based on D-LLE algorithm. *Discov. Appl. Sci.* **2025**, *7*, 34. [CrossRef]

https://doi.org/10.3390/en19020546

energies

MDPI

Article

Optimal Scheduling Strategies for Smart Homes Integrated with Grid-Connected Hybrid Renewable Energy Systems

Temitope Adefarati [1], Gulshan Sharma [1,*], Pitshou N. Bokoro [1] and Rajesh Kumar [2,3]

1 Department of Electrical and Electronic Engineering Technology, University of Johannesburg, Johannesburg 2006, South Africa; temitope.adefarati@gmail.com (T.A.); pitshoub@uj.ac.za (P.N.B.)
2 Department of Human Anatomy and Physiology, Faculty of Health Sciences, University of Johannesburg, Johannesburg 2094, South Africa; rkumar@uj.ac.za
3 Department of Electrical Engineering, Malaviya National Institute of Technology, Jaipur 302017, India
* Correspondence: gulshans@uj.ac.za

Abstract

The increasing demand for sustainable energy in residential buildings and public concerns on greenhouse gas (GHG) emissions has driven the integration of smart homes with hybrid renewable energy systems (HRESs). This research proposes an optimal scheduling strategy for home energy consumption in a grid-connected HRES that comprises a grid, wind turbines, photovoltaics and battery storage systems. The objective of the study is to reduce the net energy cost, scheduling inconvenience cost (SIC), GHG cost and battery degradation cost. An ant colony optimization algorithm is utilized in the MATLAB environment, with load profiles and meteorological data of Upington, South Africa, obtained from NASA and a residential consumption dataset to accomplish the objectives of the study. The outcomes of the study show that case study 3 is the most feasible configuration based on a net energy revenue cost of \$9.8382, GHG cost of \$0.0627, battery degradation cost of \$0.461 and SIC of \$0.66. Simulation results demonstrate that energy purchased from the grid has been reduced by 98% and 48% relative to case studies 1 and 2. The results of the study can assist households to improve the sustainability and resilience of the power system in residential environments where the grid supply is unstable and electricity costs are high.

Keywords: battery storage system; greenhouse gas emissions; hybrid renewable energy system; photovoltaic; scheduling inconvenience cost; wind turbines

1. Introduction

The global energy crisis is one of the critical challenges of the twenty-first century that affects economic stability, standard of living and environmental sustainability. This crisis has increased electricity tariffs, caused pressures on economies and renewed global commitment to energy diversification and autonomy [1]. The global power demand growth has been attributed to urbanization, economic development, technological advancement, population growth and industrial revolution [2]. According to the International Energy Agency (IEA) report of 2024, fossil fuels accounted for 80% of the global energy demand despite the adoption of cleaner and sustainable energy alternatives by many countries [3]. Over-reliance on fossil fuels has posed critical threats such as depletion of non-renewable energy reserves, proliferation of GHG emissions and aggravation of global warming [4]. This has forced many countries to transform their centralized energy systems into decentralized renewable systems with localized smart grids to reduce dependence on fossil fuels and associated hazardous effects. The IEA report of 2024 also shows that over 600 million Africans do not have access to an affordable and reliable power supply due to load shedding, frequent power outages, aging infrastructure, underdeveloped utility grids and limited power generation capacity [5]. This has led to economic losses, the reduction of job creation, industrialization constraints, education disruption and the interruption of healthcare delivery in African countries [6,7]. The global power system is currently going through a significant transformation in response to the urgent need to improve the security of power supply, reduce climate change and increase access to affordable electricity [8]. The transition is based on the international benchmarks to fast-track global deployment of renewable energy sources (RESs), improve the sustainability of the power system and achieve net-zero carbon emissions [9–11].

The sudden increase in power consumption is reflected in all sectors of the economy by creating supply challenges and increased energy prices [12]. The global power demand grew by 2.2% in 2024 based on deeper structural trends and short-term factors. This shows that energy demand grew at a faster rate in 2024 than the annual average of 1.3% recorded between 2013 and 2023 [2]. The global electricity demand has been projected to grow by 30% in 2030 as power consumption increases in different sectors of the economy based on the annual growth of 3.3% from 2023 to 2030 [13]. According to the global status report of 2025, industry accounted for 34% of global power consumption, followed by buildings (31%), transport (31%), agriculture (2.5%) and other energy uses (1.5%) [14]. This shows that the residential building plays a vital role in the energy market since it consumes three-quarters of the global energy generated from different sources. The breakdown of GHG emissions from the energy sector consists of electricity and heat (29.7%), transportation (13.7%), manufacturing and construction (12.7%) and buildings (6.6%) [15]. This report indicates that residential sector is a significant contributor to climate change. Carbon footprint emissions and energy demand from the construction and buildings account for almost a fifth of global GHG emissions [16]. The residential building alone accounts for nearly 30–40% of the global energy consumption, which makes it a key area for energy efficiency improvements and RES integration [17]. The environmental concerns, coupled with climate change, fossil fuel depletion, the urgent need for sustainable development and public health challenges have intensified the transition of fossil fuels to RESs [18]. The residential sector constitutes a significant portion of global electricity consumption, and improving household energy efficiency has emerged as a significant approach for the reduction of energy demand and GHG emissions [19]. Smart homes equipped with RESs and scheduling of appliances have been acknowledged as promising solutions that can be utilized to reduce electricity bills and improve user comfort [20].

The rapid increase in global power consumption, depletion of fossil fuels and mitigation of climate change has necessitated the application of sustainable energy systems to satisfy load demand [21]. Renewable energy sources have been globally accepted as potential alternative solutions to conventional fossil-based generation units because they are clean, affordable, sustainable and environmentally friendly [22]. An HRES that consists of multiple sources is a promising solution to overcome the intermittency and variability challenges of using a single source. The integration of multiple sources in HRESs can be used to increase energy availability, enhance efficiency and reduce over-dependence on the utility grid [23]. The stochastic characteristics of wind and solar resources present several challenges in maintaining a reliable and continuous power supply at the load points [24]. The improper management of the power system can cause a deficit of power supply and over-reliance on the utility grid during low-generation hours and wastage of excess renewable energy during high-generation periods [25]. These challenges can be overcome by using an optimization technique that coordinates household appliances,

https://doi.org/10.3390/en19051174

renewable generation, BSS and grid interaction and optimizes charging and discharging cycles of battery systems. The scheduling of home appliances and integration of renewable energy in the conventional power system can be used to achieve cost savings, improve the efficiency and resilience of the power system and minimize the net energy cost, reliance on the utility grid SIC and carbon footprint [26]. The benefits of HRESs in smart homes cannot be fully realized without scheduling of household appliances and effective energy flow in the power system. Therefore, it is imperative to coordinate energy flow within the power system to avert unnecessary stress on the battery system and utility grid, increased GHG emissions and reduced user comfort. The convergence of RESs and smart home technologies offers several significant benefits that can be utilized for the sustainability of HRESs. The effectiveness of RESs and smart home technologies depends on the optimization techniques applied to control home appliances, photovoltaics (PVs), wind turbines (WT), battery storage systems (BSSs) and utility grids [27]. Ant colony optimization (ACO) is applied to achieve the objective of the study due to its flexibility, adaptability, easy hybridization and robustness [28]. ACO is a powerful tool that can be used for complex optimization problems in energy management, routing and scheduling systems [29]. Therefore, appliance scheduling is applied in this study to harness the full potential of smart homes integrated with grid-connected HRESs and ensure that energy is efficiently managed to improve the economic feasibility and sustainability of the proposed power system.

Many research works have been carried out on the optimization of smart homes integrated with grid-connected HRESs. Deng et al. [30] presented model predictive control (MPC) for smart homes with PV, electric vehicle (EV) and battery systems to mitigate forecast uncertainty and improve cost savings while satisfying real-time computation constraints. Luna et al. [31] proposed MPC for energy demand management of smart houses based on optimal scheduling of appliances, variation of battery state of charge and market signals. Fan and Zhou [32] applied the harmony search method for techno-economic analysis, optimization of total annual cost and reliability of a residential-based HRES that consists of PVs, WTs, BSSs and a diesel generator (DG). Meanwhile, Gunmi et al. [33] proposed a methodology that jointly considered optimal sizing of PV and battery systems designed for a residential standalone microgrid (RSMG) and scheduling of loads under techno-economic constraints. The proposed scheme is incorporated into forecasting, economic dispatch and sizing decisions to minimize the lifecycle cost of an RSMG. Ibrahim et al. [34] presented an energy management strategy to reduce CO_2 emission, cost of energy (COE) and net present cost (NPC) and increase the renewable fraction of WTs, PVs, BSSs and DGs in HRESs. Liu et al. [35] proposed an improved dung beetle optimization algorithm that used step size as a convergence factor. The main objective of the study was achieved by reducing the lifecycle cost and COE and obtaining optimal sizing of PV, WT and BSS units. Nassar et al. [36] presented a grid-connected HRES to reduce energy shortages and scheduling strategies for deficit mitigation. The study laid more emphasis on the adaptive scheduling of load demand for unstable grid access in regions with protracted power deficit challenges. Molu et al. [37] applied HOMER Pro to design a grid-connected PV/DG HRES for a community in Douala, Cameroon. The authors focused on tariff sensitivity, dispatch scheduling, reliability and economic feasibility of HRESs in sub-Saharan Africa. Similarly, Shaban et al. [38] applied new mixed-integer quadratic programming for optimization of the energy cost and self-consumption of domestic PV systems in Egypt. The effectiveness of the proposed model was confirmed based on the minimum cost of energy obtained from various categories of Egyptian households. The literature review of other previous works is presented in Table 1.

https://doi.org/10.3390/en19051174

Table 1. Summary of literature review based on the existing techniques.

Configuration of the System	Utility Grid	PV	WT	BSS	Hydro	DG	EV	Techniques	Performance Indicators	Gaps
Grid-connected HRES [39]	✓	✓	✓	✓	×	×	×	HOMER software	NPC and levelized cost of energy (LCOE)	Did not include battery degradation
Grid-connected HRES [40]	✓	✓	✓	✓	×	✓	×	Multi-objective particle swarm optimization algorithms	LCOE and power supply reliability factor	Ignored user comfort and battery degradation cost
Grid-connected microgrid system [41]	✓	✓	✓	✓	×	✓	×	Quantum particle swarm optimization	Cost and emission	Did not include user comfort and battery degradation
Grid-connected HRES [42]	✓	✓	✓	✓	✓	×	×	MPC	Operating costs	Did not cover appliance scheduling
Standalone HRES [43]	×	✓	✓	✓	×	×	×	Particle swarm optimization and genetic algorithm (GA)	Total cost of the system and COE	Excluded user comfort and battery degradation
Grid-connected HRES [44]	✓	✓	✓	✓	×	×	×	HOMER	Net present value, internal rate of return, LCOE and payback period	Ignored comfort and battery degradation
Electric vehicle and utility grid system [45]	✓	×	×	×	×	×	✓	Hybrid GA–MPC approach	Battery life and ultra-capacitor utilization	Limited smart homes application
Grid-connected HRES [46]	✓	✓	×	×	×	×	×	Earth worm optimization algorithm and virulence optimization algorithm	Electricity bills, load factor and energy demand	Only tested with TOU tariffs and no integration with RESs
Grid-connected HRES [47]	✓	✓	✓	✓	×	×	×	Gravity search algorithm	Carbon emission and economic benefits	Limited scalability for real-time use
Islanded HRES [48]	×	✓	✓	✓	×	✓	×	GA, firefly algorithm and PSO	NPC, energy of cost and renewable energy fraction	Lack of field validation in real African homes

Based on the previous studies, significant progress has been made in the areas of home management systems by focusing on the optimization and economic analysis of HRESs. The research gaps found in the literature review are briefly summarized as follows: Most of the previous studies presented in the literature review are primarily focused on one or two objective functions without considering a multi-objective function that captures critical objectives such as GHG emissions reduction, net energy cost, SIC and battery degradation cost. It can be established from the above-mentioned literature review that the effects of battery degradation have not been fully addressed by considering degradation costs. This affects the economic performance of the system and leads to unrealistic scheduling strategies that shorten battery lifetime. It can be seen from previous studies that many scheduling models assume full flexibility of household loads and disregard scheduling inconvenience cost. This creates a gap between theoretical models and the real-time

https://doi.org/10.3390/en19051174

adoption of a smart home scheduling scheme. In addition, there is a limited study that addressed the challenges of developing countries such as unreliable grid supply, net energy cost, high cost of fossil fuels, over-reliance on utility grids and the need for affordable and sustainable energy solutions for each household. The trade-off between economic savings and GHG emissions is not fully analyzed in some studies. These research gaps strongly justify the novelty and contributions of the paper to the body of knowledge. This paper contributes a practical and sustainable scheme for smart homes integrated with grid-connected HRESs by addressing the above-mentioned research gaps.

The findings of the research can be used by academic researchers, international organizations, utility companies, policymakers and households to transit from fossil fuel-based power systems to clean and reliable power solutions. The outcomes of the study can be used to improve residential energy management, economic feasibility and environmental effect of smart homes within the context of the emerging power system. The originality of the current research work encompasses the following contributions to the existing body of knowledge and addresses the above-mentioned research gaps with novelty measures:

(i) Development of the models of a grid-connected HRES that consists of PVs, WTs and BSSs for smart home applications;
(ii) Formulation of an ACO-based multi-objective scheduling strategy to optimize GHG emissions, net energy cost, scheduling inconvenience cost and battery degradation cost;
(iii) Application of an ACO-based dispatch strategy for coordination of PVs, WTs, BSSs and utility grids to reduce energy purchased from the grid and improve energy sales;
(iv) Integration of battery degradation model into the scheduling of smart home system to improve the sustainability and cost effectiveness of the system;
(v) Development of scheduling inconvenience cost that can be used to measure satisfaction of consumers and integration of SIC into the multi-objective function for practical application;
(vi) Presentation of a multi-objective function that balances economic, environmental and comfort-related goals of a grid-connected HRES;
(vii) Contextual application of grid-connected HRESs in one of the developing countries where management of smart home energy systems is critical owing to load shedding and high electricity tariffs.

The rest of the paper is structured as follows: The mathematical model of each component of HRESs is presented in Section 2. Problem formulation of the objective function and associated constraints is presented in Section 3. Specifications for each component of the HRESs used in the study are presented in Section 4. The results and discussion are presented in Section 5. Finally, the study's conclusion is presented in Section 6.

2. Smart Home Energy Management System

A smart home energy management system (SHEMS) is an intelligent control system that is designed to coordinate energy generation, storage and energy demand within residential buildings [49]. It integrates RESs, battery storage systems, smart appliances and the utility grid by using a control system. The energy flow of the system is monitored using smart meters and optimization algorithms to schedule energy usage based on electricity tariffs, user preferences and abundant wind and solar resources. The primary objectives of SHEMSs are to minimize net energy cost, maximize renewable energy utilization, reduce GHG emissions, improve user satisfaction, improve energy efficiency and sustainability in residential buildings [50]. The operation of a SHEMS that integrates RESs, a BSS and the utility grid to achieve efficient energy utilization in a smart home is shown in Figure 1. The appliances of SHEMSs are categorized into non-shiftable and shiftable loads based on

https://doi.org/10.3390/en19051174

their operational flexibility [51]. The electrical power from the wind turbines, PV system and utility grid is designed to satisfy household power demand, while surplus PV and WT energy generation can be injected into the grid or used to charge BSSs.

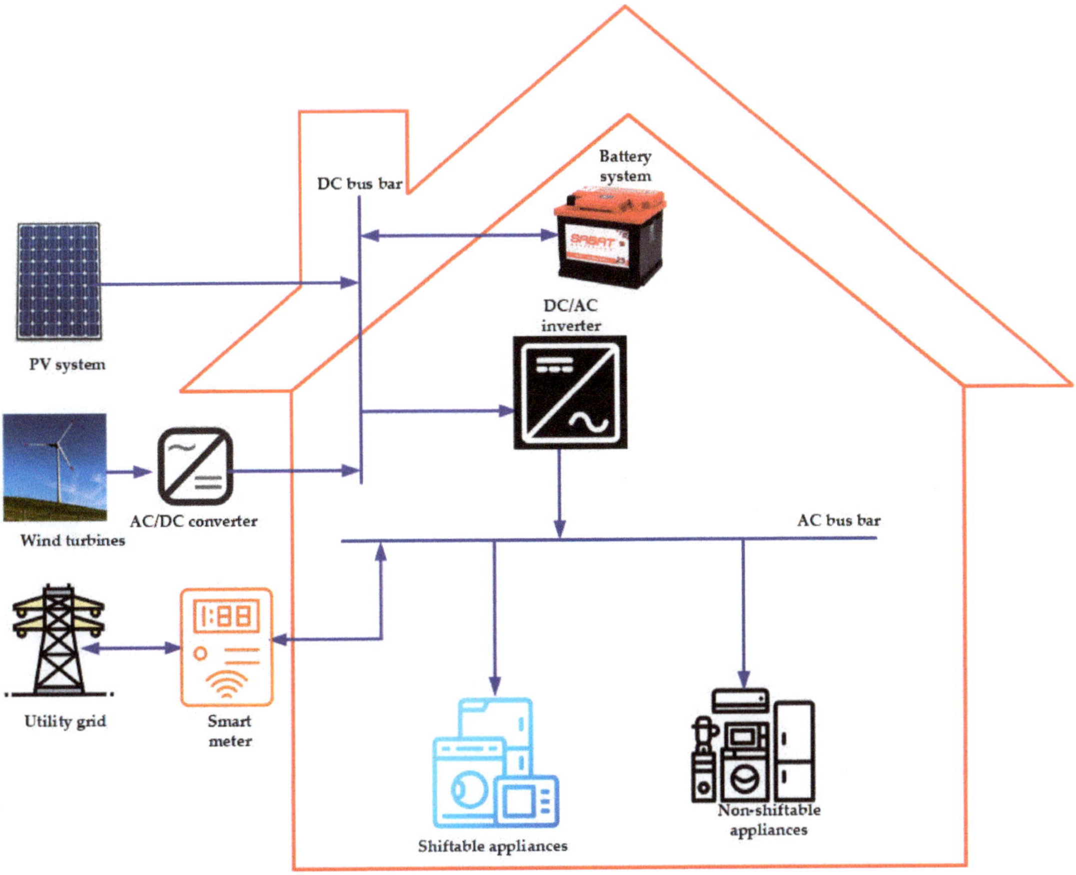

Figure 1. Schematic diagram of a smart home energy management system.

2.1. Hybrid Renewable Energy System

An HRES is an integrated energy system that combines two or more RESs, non-renewable backup sources and a BSS to supply reliable and sustainable electricity to the residential loads, as shown in Figure 2 [52]. Hybridization of numerous RESs such as PVs, WTs, BSSs and grid solar can be used to increase the reliability of power supply, improve efficiency and reduce over-reliance on fossil fuels [43]. The strength of one energy source can be used to compensate for the weakness of other sources of energy. HRESs are designed to provide cost-effective and sustainable electricity by overcoming the limitations of individual renewable energy sources, utilizing complementary characteristics of different sources, minimizing intermittent characteristics of solar and wind resources, optimizing energy utilization and increasing resilience of the system [53]. The components of HRESs are briefly explained as follows:

https://doi.org/10.3390/en19051174

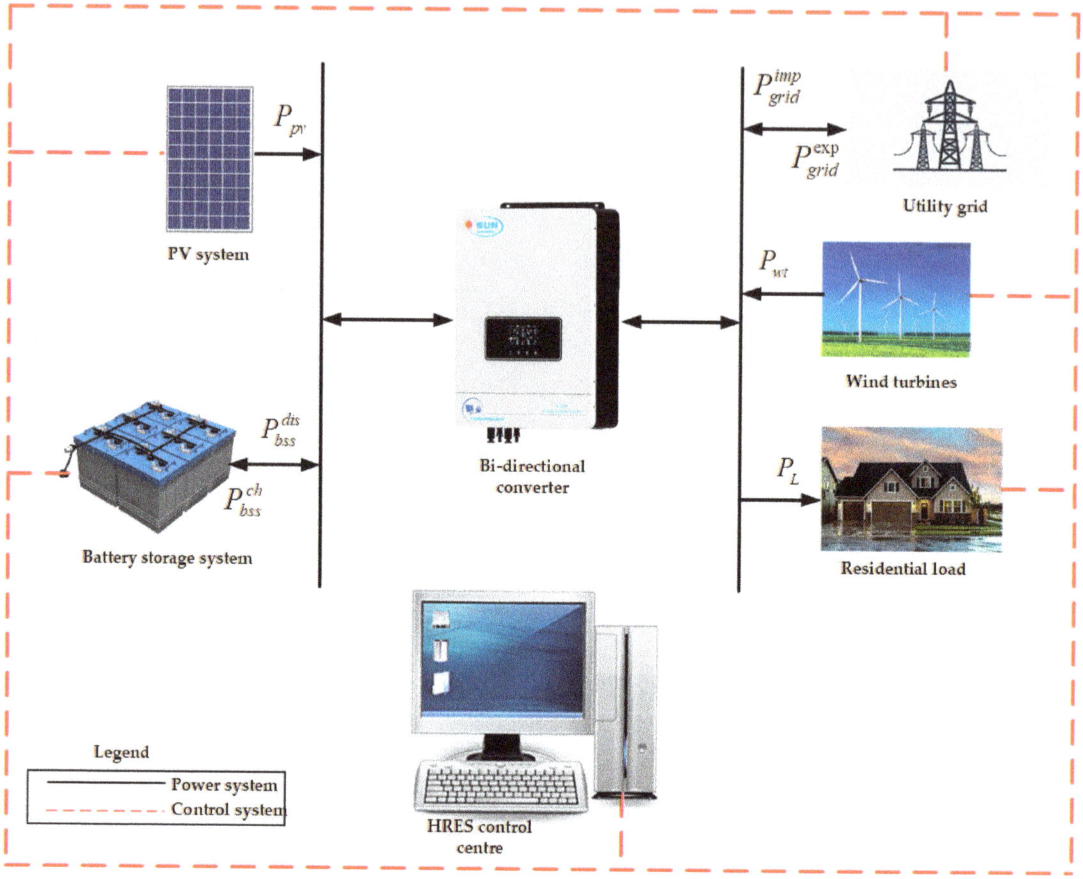

Figure 2. Typical diagram of a grid-connected HRES for a residential building.

2.1.1. Photovoltaic System

A photovoltaic system is a renewable energy technology that utilizes the photovoltaic effect of semiconductor materials to convert solar radiation into electrical energy [54]. The installed capacity of PV systems varies in size from residential rooftop power supply to utility-scale solar farms that supply electricity to the utility grid [55]. PV systems are one of the widely used clean energy solutions for commercial and industrial energy applications, rural electrification, solar-powered water pumping and street lighting due to their technical and economic benefits. The power output of the PV system is expressed in Equation (1) as [56]:

$$P_{pv} = G \times A \times \eta(T) \tag{1}$$

where A is the module surface area (m^2), G is the solar irradiance on the module surface (W/m^2), and η (T) is the module efficiency at operating cell temperature T_{cell}.

2.1.2. Wind Turbines

A wind turbine is a renewable energy generation technology that utilizes rotor blades and a generator to convert the kinetic energy extracted from wind speed into electrical energy [57]. Wind turbines are extensively used for both onshore and offshore applications to generate clean and affordable energy based on the unique design characteristics and

https://doi.org/10.3390/en19051174

economic considerations of each location [58]. The electrical power output of wind turbines is expressed in Equation (2) as:

$$P_{wt} = \frac{1}{2}\rho A v^3 C_p(\lambda,\beta)\eta_{sys} \quad (2)$$

where ρ is the air density (kg/m^3), A is the rotor swept area (m^2), v is the wind speed at hub height (m/s), $C_p(\lambda,\beta)$ is the power coefficient, λ is the function of the tip speed ratio, β is the pitch, and η_{sys} is the balance of plant/system efficiency (generator, gearbox and electrical losses).

2.1.3. Battery Storage System

Battery storage systems are electrochemical technologies that store electrical energy in chemical form and discharge it as electricity when required. A BSS is a technology that serves as a critical component in power systems by providing energy balancing, peak shaving and frequency regulation. It supports the regulation of power flow under varying conditions and backup supply [59]. The state of charge (SOC) of the BSS is presented in Equation (3) as:

$$SOC(t) = SOC(t-1) + \frac{P_{bss}^{ch}(t) \times \eta_{ch} \times \Delta t}{E_{bss}} - \frac{P_{bss}^{dis}(t)}{\eta_{dis}} \times \frac{\Delta t}{E_{bss}} \quad (3)$$

where $P_{bss}^{ch}(t)$ is the battery discharge power (kW), $P_{bss}^{dis}(t)$ is the battery charge power (kW), η_{ch} is the charge efficiency of the BSS, η_{dis} is the discharge efficiency of the BSS, E_{bss} is the nominal capacity of the BSS, and Δt is the time step (h).

2.1.4. Utility Grid

The utility grid is a centralized electrical network that supplies power to consumers and acts as a backup source and an energy balance source for HRESs [34]. The application of a utility grid in HRESs can be utilized to increase economic efficiency and the sustainability of power supply to the load points [60]. The utility grid power exchange is presented in Equation (4).

$$P_{grid}^{imp}(t) - P_{grid}^{exp}(t) = P_{Load}(t) + P_{bss}^{ch}(t) - \left(P_{pv}(t) + P_{wt}(t) + P_{bss}^{dis}(t)\right) \quad (4)$$

Here, $P_{grid}^{imp}(t)$ is the power imported from the grid (kW), $P_{grid}^{exp}(t)$ is the power exported to the grid (kW), $P_{Load}(t)$ is the load demand, $P_{pv}(t)$ is the power generated by PV system (kW), and $P_{wt}(t)$ is the power generated by wind turbines (kW).

2.2. Electricity Tariffs

An electricity tariff is a pricing structure set by utility companies to determine the amount of money that consumers pay for their electricity usage [61]. The cost of production and distribution, type of customers, location, government policies and subsidies are some of the variables that affect electricity tariffs [62]. The Eskom Time-of-Use (TOU) tariff based on the low demand season and high demand is shown in Figure 3 [63]. The grid-tied TOU tariff based on Eskom Homeflex is presented in Equation (5) as [64]:

$$p^{imp}(t) = \begin{cases} p_o = 0.14\,\$/\text{kWh}\ if\ t \in [0,6] \cup [22,24] \\ p_s = 0.17\,\$/\text{kWh}\ if\ t \in [6,7] \cup [10,18] \cup [20,22] \\ p_p = 0.25\,\$/\text{kWh}\ if\ t \in [7,10] \cup [18,20] \end{cases} \quad (5)$$

where p_o, p_s and p_p are the pricing models for off-peak, standard and peak periods.

https://doi.org/10.3390/en19051174

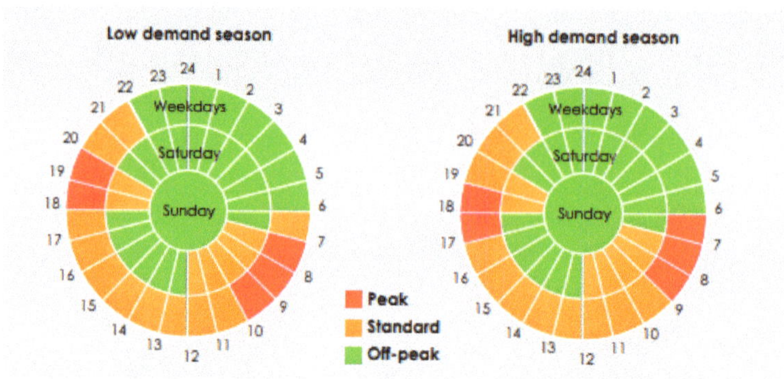

Figure 3. South Africa's schedule of standard prices for ESKOM tariffs.

The small-scale embedded generation (SSEG) rate is the feed-in tariff introduced by Eskom to pay customers who generate their own electricity from RESs and export surplus power back to the utility grid [65]. The SSEG feed-in tariff based on Eskom Gen-offset Homeflex is presented in Equation (6) [64]:

$$p^{\exp}(t) = \begin{cases} p_o = 0.087\,\$/\text{kWh } if\, t \in [0,6] \cup [22,24] \\ p_s = 0.12\,\$/\text{kWh } if\, t \in [6,7] \cup [10,18] \cup [20,22] \\ p_p = 0.19\,\$/\text{kWh } if\, t \in [7,10] \cup [18,20] \end{cases} \tag{6}$$

3. Objective Function of the Study

The primary objective of the research is to reduce net energy cost, scheduling inconvenience cost, GHG cost and battery degradation cost based on optimal utilization of RESs and scheduling of home appliances. The objective of the study is achieved through the optimal usage of the power supply by wind turbines, battery systems, PV systems and utility grids. The objective function of the study is presented in Equation (6) as:

$$\min_x J = \left(\sum_{i=1}^{n} E_{H,i}^{T}(t) + \delta_{sic,i} \sum_{i=1}^{n} SIC_{,i}(t) + \sum_{i=1}^{n} GHG_{,i}(t) + \sum_{i=1}^{n} B_{\text{deg},i}(t) \right) \tag{7}$$

where $E_{H,i}^{T}(t)$ is the net energy cost, $SIC_{,i}(t)$ is the scheduling inconvenience cost, $GHG_{,i}(t)$ is the cost of GHG emissions based on the value of power purchased from the grid, $\delta_{sic,i}$ is a decision variable of SIC, and $B_{\text{deg},i}(t)$ is the battery degradation cost.

The first component of the objective function is the net energy cost that depicts the difference between the monetary value of energy purchased from the grid and energy injected into the grid. It is presented in Equation (7) as:

$$E_{H,i}^{T}(t) = \left(\sum_{i=1}^{n} (P_{grid,i}^{imp}(t) \times \pi_{t,i}^{buy}) - \sum_{i=1}^{n} (P_{grid,i}^{\exp}(t) \times \pi_{t,i}^{sell}) \right) \tag{8}$$

where $\pi_{t,i}^{buy}$ is the TOU import tariff (\$/kWh), and $\pi_{t,i}^{sell}$ is the TOU export tariff (\$/kWh).

The second component of the objective function is the scheduling inconvenience cost that depicts the financial cost that is associated with user dissatisfaction when the operations of household appliances are shifted from the scheduled time of the user to the preferred time [66]. Scheduling inconvenience cost is introduced in this paper to capture the trade-off between economic optimization and occupant comfort of a residential building that is integrated with appliance scheduling. It plays a proactive role in bridging this gap by accounting for occupant comfort and lifestyle preference. Consumers can shift their

 https://doi.org/10.3390/en19051174

appliances operation from peak periods to off-peak periods to harness the benefits of lower electricity prices. The SIC for each appliance can be estimated by using the inconvenient time deviation and discomfort cost rate.

$$SIC_i = \sum_{t=1}^{T} \left(\alpha_i(t) \times \left|T_{s,i}(t) - T_{p,i}(t)\right|\right) \tag{9}$$

Here, α_i is the discomfort cost rate (\$/h), $T_{s,i}(t)$ is the scheduled start time, $T_{p,i}(t)$ is the preferred start time for appliance I, and T is the total scheduling period.

The total SIC can be expressed by summing the SIC values across all appliances. The total scheduling inconvenience cost is expressed as:

$$SIC_{total} = \sum_{I=1}^{n} SIC_i \tag{10}$$

$\delta_{sic,i}$ is a decision variable of SIC that is set to 1 or 0, as expressed in Equation (10).

$$\delta_{sic,i} = \begin{cases} 1 & Application\ of\ applinace\ scheduling \\ 0 & Otherwise \end{cases} \tag{11}$$

The third component of the objective function is the GHG cost that consists of CO_2, SO_2 and NO_x emissions based on the power purchased from the utility grid. It is expressed in Equation (11) as:

$$GHG_{,i}(t) = \begin{pmatrix} \sum_{i=1}^{n} P_{grid,i}^{imp}(t) \times EFCO_{2,i}(t) \times E_{grid}^{CO_2}(t) + \\ \sum_{i=1}^{n} P_{grid,i}^{imp}(t) \times EFNO_{x,i}(t) \times E_{grid}^{NO_x}(t) + \\ \sum_{i=1}^{n} P_{grid,i}^{imp}(t) \times EFSO_{2,i}(t) \times E_{grid}^{SO_2}(t) \end{pmatrix} \tag{12}$$

where $EFCO_{2,i}(t)$, $EFNO_{x,i}(t)$ and $EFSO_{2,i}(t)$ are emission factors of carbon dioxide, nitrogen oxide and sulfur dioxide based on energy purchased from the utility grid, while $E_{grid}^{CO_2}(t)$, $E_{grid}^{SO_2}(t)$ and $E_{grid}^{NO_x}(t)$ are emission externality factors of CO_2, SO_2 and NO_x emissions.

The fourth component of the objective function is battery degradation cost, which shows a gradual deterioration of the capability of the battery system due to charge and discharge of energy over time [67]. Battery degradation cost is expressed in Equation (12) as:

$$B_{deg,i}(t) = \sum_{i=1}^{n} C_{deg}\left(\eta_{ch} \times P_{bss}^{ch}(t)\Delta t + \frac{P_{bss}^{dis}(t)\Delta t}{\eta_{dis}}\right) \tag{13}$$

where C_{deg} is the cycle cost per kWh throughput of the battery system (\$/kWh).

The battery energy price is presented in Equation (13) as:

$$C_{deg}(t) = \frac{C_{bss}^{cap}}{2 \times E_{bss}^{usable} \times N_{cycle}} \tag{14}$$

where C_{bss}^{cap} depicts the capital cost of the battery system (\$), E_{bss}^{usable} is the usable energy of the BSS (kWh), and N_{cycle} is the life cycle of the BSS.

https://doi.org/10.3390/en19051174

The usable energy of the battery system is presented in Equation (14) as:

$$E_{bss}^{usable} = E_{bss}^{n}\left(SOC^{\max}(t) - SOC^{\min}(t)\right) \tag{15}$$

where E_{bss}^{n} is the nominal capacity of the BSS (kWh), $SOC^{\max}(t)$ is the maximum SOC of the BSS, and $SOC^{\min}(t)$ is the minimum SOC of the BSS.

3.1. Constraints of the Power System

The objective function of the study that is presented in Equation (6) is subject to the following constraints:

3.1.1. Power Balance Limits

The power balance of the proposed HRES is expressed in Equation (15) as:

$$\begin{pmatrix} \sum\limits_{i=1}^{n} P_{grid,i}^{imp}(t) + \sum\limits_{i=1}^{n} P_{pv,i}(t) + \\ \sum\limits_{i=1}^{n} P_{wt,i}(t) + \sum\limits_{i=1}^{n} P_{bss,i}^{dis}(t) \end{pmatrix} = \begin{pmatrix} \sum\limits_{i=1}^{n} P_{grid,i}^{\exp}(t) + \sum\limits_{i=1}^{n} P_{bss,i}^{ch}(t) + \\ \sum\limits_{i=1}^{n} P_{L,i}(t) \end{pmatrix} \tag{16}$$

3.1.2. Generating Limits

The generation capacity of PVs, WTGs, BSSs and utility grids should operate within the minimum and maximum limits to be efficient and produce power according to their capacities. The generating limitations of each component of the proposed HRES are presented in Equation (16) as:

$$\begin{cases} P_{grid,i}^{imp,\min}(t) \le P_{grid,i}^{imp}(t) \le P_{grid,i}^{imp,\max}(t) \\ P_{grid,i}^{\exp,\min}(t) \le P_{grid,i}^{\exp}(t) \le P_{grid,i}^{\exp,\max}(t) \\ P_{pv,i}^{\min}(t) \le P_{pv,i}(t) \le P_{pv,i}^{\max}(t) \\ P_{wt,i}^{\min}(t) \le P_{wt,i}(t) \le P_{wt,i}^{\max}(t) \\ P_{bss,i}^{ch,\min}(t) \le P_{bss,i}^{ch}(t) \le P_{bss,i}^{ch,\max}(t) \\ P_{bss,i}^{dis,\min}(t) \le P_{bss,i}^{dis}(t) \le P_{bss,i}^{dis,\max}(t) \end{cases} \tag{17}$$

3.1.3. State of Charge of the Battery System Limits

The capacity of the battery system used in the proposed smart home HRES operates within the minimum and maximum limits based on the technical specifications of the manufacturers. The SOC of the BSS operates within lower and upper limits, as expressed in Equations (17) and (18):

$$SOC^{\min} \le SOC(t) \le SOC^{\max} \tag{18}$$

$$SOC^{\min} \le SOC(0) + \eta_c \sum_{i=1}^{n} P_{bss,i}^{ch}(t) - \frac{1}{\eta_{dis}} \sum_{i=1}^{n} P_{bss,i}^{dis}(t) \le SOC^{\max} \tag{19}$$

3.2. Selected Location for the Study

Upington is geographically situated in the Northern Cape province of South Africa with a latitude of −28.44776°, a longitude of 21.25612° and a coverage area of about 580.8 km^2. The town currently boasts a population of 91,107 people and a population density of 156.9/km^2 [68]. Upington is located on the Northern banks of the Orange River,

https://doi.org/10.3390/en19051174

with an elevation of 835 m. Solar irradiance of Upington is among the top in South Africa, with an estimated global horizontal irradiance of 2600–2800 kWh/m^2-yr [69]. The wind speed is not the highest in South Africa, but it is suitable to spine wind turbines based on the technical specifications of the manufacturers. The capacity of wind generation can complement solar generation in the evening and winter season. The proposed HRES is designed for a smart home integrated with the scheduling of household appliances in Upington since the electricity tariff has been increased by 4.1% in the 2025/2026 financial year. The proposed HRES components are chosen in accordance with the energy requirements of the selected residential building, such as shiftable loads and non-shiftable loads. Optimal scheduling strategies are applied in the study to reduce unnecessary stress on the utility grid and optimize energy consumption. RESs are utilized in this research work to increase access to electricity in Upington and boost economic activities, education and healthcare delivery services, which are heavily affected by load shedding.

3.3. *Ant Colony Optimization Algorithm*

ACO is a population-based metaheuristic optimization technique inspired by the foraging behavior of ant colonies. Marco Dorigo developed the algorithm in the early 1990s to search for an optimal path in a graph based on the exploitation of food resources by ants. It is motivated by the foraging behavior of ant colonies in which individual ants find the shortest path between a food source and their nest. These trails guide subsequent ants in a probabilistic manner towards optimum routes. This observation is the basis of utilizing the ACO algorithm to search for optimal solutions to a given optimization problem. The applications of the ACO algorithm in the power system span across optimal scheduling of smart grid systems, optimization of microgrid systems or hybrid energy systems, load scheduling of smart homes, energy management of electric vehicles, optimal power flow, multi-objective optimization of smart grid and microgrid systems, optimal sizing of renewable energy resources and energy storage management. The ACO algorithm comprises eight principal steps that form the optimization loop, as presented in Figure 4. The following steps are implemented to achieve the objectives of the study: input system data, initialize ACO parameters, pheromone initialization, ant solution construction, constraint enforcement, objective function calculation, local and global best update, pheromone update, check termination and print the optimal schedule. The ant colony optimization algorithm is applied in this study owing to its proficiency to solve complex, discrete and non-linear problems that are associated with home appliance scheduling. The optimization of home appliance operation, renewable energy sources, battery system dispatch and utility grid interaction is a complex decision that traditional techniques cannot efficiently solve. ACO has a very strong global search capability, ability to prevent premature convergence and production of high-quality solutions under dynamic load demands and variability of solar and wind resources. It also supports the optimization of multi-objective functions like net energy cost, GHG cost, battery degradation and SIC. The capabilities of ACO such as scalability, robustness against renewable energy uncertainty and computational efficiency have made it an ideal choice for optimizing grid-connected HRES operation.

https://doi.org/10.3390/en19051174

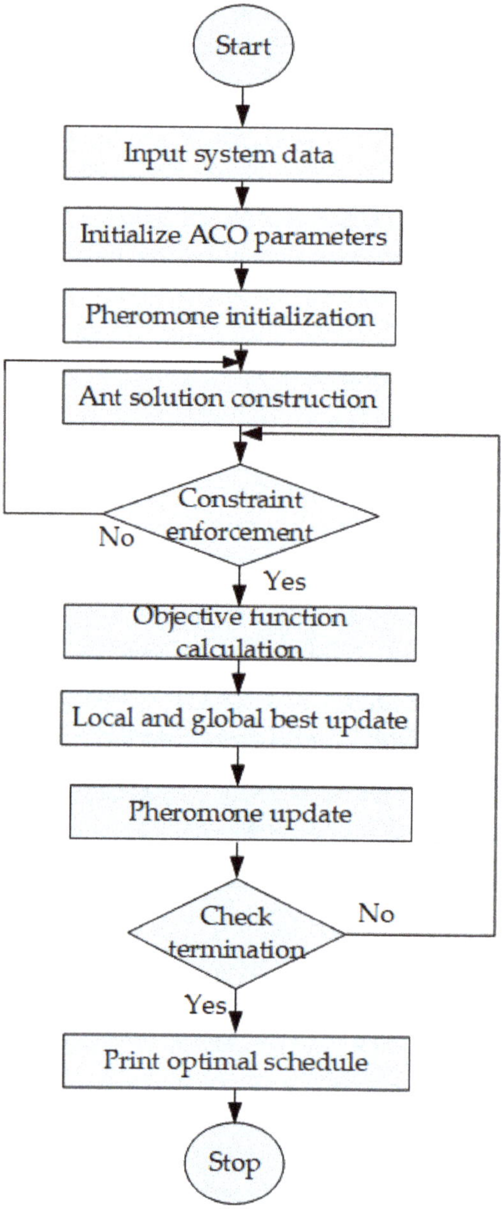

Figure 4. Flowchart of the ACO algorithm based on the optimal scheduling of smart home HRESs.

4. Technical and Economic Specifications of Hybrid Renewable Energy System

The technical specifications and economic details of the components of the proposed HRES are presented in this section. The proposed techniques are applied in the MATLAB environment by utilizing MATLAB software version R2025a in HP Laptop 14-ep0026ni 14′, Intel (R) Core i5-1334U, 4.6 GHz CPU and installed RAM of 16 GB. The technical and economic assessment of the proposed HRES is implemented by using the technical specifications and cost parameters of the components presented in Table 2. The key performance

 https://doi.org/10.3390/en19051174

indicators (KPIs) of the study can be evaluated by using the technical specifications and cost parameters of the proposed HRES. The above-mentioned KPIs are used to select the optimal results based on the optimization technique applied in the study. The performance of the HRES is evaluated by considering a typical load profile of a consumer in Upington, Northern Cape Province, South Africa. The home appliances based on their operating hours and rated power are presented in Table 3.

Table 2. Technical and economic data of the proposed HRES [70–73].

Description	PV System	Wind Turbines	Battery System	Converter
Installed capacity	10 kW	10 kW	6.22 kWh	15 kW
Nominal rating	500 W	2000 W	260 Ah	5 kW
Efficiency	20.7%	45%	80%	97.6%
Lifetime	25 yr	25 yr	5 yr	10 yr
Operational temperature	−40~+85 °C	−40–50 °C	−0 ~ +55 °C	−25–60 °C
Model	TSM-DEG18MC.20(II)	GH-2KW	CP48200	SUN-5k-SG-01LPI
Other technical parameters	Short-circuit current (ISC) = 12.13 A, open-circuit voltage (VOC) = 51.5 V, maximum power current = 11.53 A, maximum power voltage = 43.4 V, module dimensions = 2187 × 1102 × 35 mm, temperature coefficient of P_{max} = −0.35%/°C, temperature coefficient of VOC = −0.25%/°C and temperature coefficient of ISC = 0.04%/°C	Start wind speed = 3 m/s, rated wind speed = 8 m/s, working wind speed = 3–25 m/s, safety wind speed = 40 m/s and blade rotor diameter = 3.2 m	Nominal volage = 12 V, nominal capacity = 3.11 kWh, maximum capacity = 260 Ah, capacity ratio = 0.563, roundtrip efficiency = 80%, maximum charge current = 43 A and cost of battery = $220/unit	Output voltage = 220/230/240 V, output frequency = 50/60 Hz, AC output rated current = 21.7 A and maximum AC current = 25 A

The technical and economic specifications of the components are utilized to assess the feasibility and operational performance of the power system. Technical specifications of the components, as presented in Table 2, are used in the study as input parameters to evaluate the physical feasibility and operational performance of the power system. The economic specifications are utilized in the study to achieve financial viability and sustainability of the proposed power system. The optimal operation of grid-connected HRESs is based on coordination of technical and economic specifications of each component. The technical specifications of the components are selected from the datasheet of original equipment manufacturer. The residential loads that consist of shiftable and non-shiftable home appliances are considered in this study. The home appliances based on their operating hours and rated power are presented in Table 3. The operating hours of each appliance are selected to reflect energy usage characteristics of a residential building. The rated capacity of home appliances is the nominal power consumption during normal operation periods. It can be used for modeling of residential energy, optimization of HRESs and home appliance scheduling. The rated values of the selected appliances are based on manufacturer specifications to achieve realistic load representation.

https://doi.org/10.3390/en19051174

Table 3. Classification and scheduling parameters of home appliances.

Appliance	Rated Power (kW)	Shiftable	Operating Hours (h/Day)
Washing Machine	2.20	1	2
Dishwasher	1.80	1	2
Clothes Dryer	3.00	1	1
Vacuum Cleaner	1.20	1	1
Iron	2.00	1	1
Water Heater	3.00	1	2.5
Blender	0.30	1	0.5
Bread Toaster	0.80	1	0.3
Refrigerator	0.30	0	24
Freezer	0.25	0	24
Desktop Computer	0.30	0	4
Laptop	0.08	0	5
Printer	0.10	0	0.5
Electric Oven	2.50	0	2
Microwave Oven	1.60	0	1
Air Conditioner	1.50	1	6
Fan	0.07	1	8
TV + Decoder	0.07	0	5
Light	0.12	0	5
Phone Charger	0.02	1	3
Standby Devices	0.02	0	24

5. Results and Discussion

The impacts of RESs and appliance scheduling on a grid-connected HRES are assessed in this study by using some KPIs. This section presents the results of the three case studies and evaluates the performance of optimal scheduling strategies in a grid-connected HRES for smart home applications. The following three operational scenarios are considered in the study:

- Case study 1: Grid-only without appliance scheduling;
- Case study 2: Grid-connected HRES without appliance scheduling;
- Case study 3: Grid-connected HRES with optimal appliance scheduling.

The simulation results of each case study based on the associated KPIs are presented as follows:

5.1. Case Study 1: Grid-Only Supply Without Appliance Scheduling

The residential building that operates by using the utility grid alone to meet the load demand is presented in case study 1. The appliances of the residential building on an hourly basis under a grid standalone system to highlight their load characteristics are presented in Figure 5. The home appliances in this case study are divided into both shiftable loads and non-shiftable loads to identify opportunities for RES integration and application of home appliance scheduling in later case studies. It can be seen from Figure 5 that shiftable loads contribute a significant part of the total load demand from 7.00 to 10.00 and 12.00 to 19.00 h of the day, while non-shiftable loads contribute more uniformly throughout the day.

https://doi.org/10.3390/en19051174

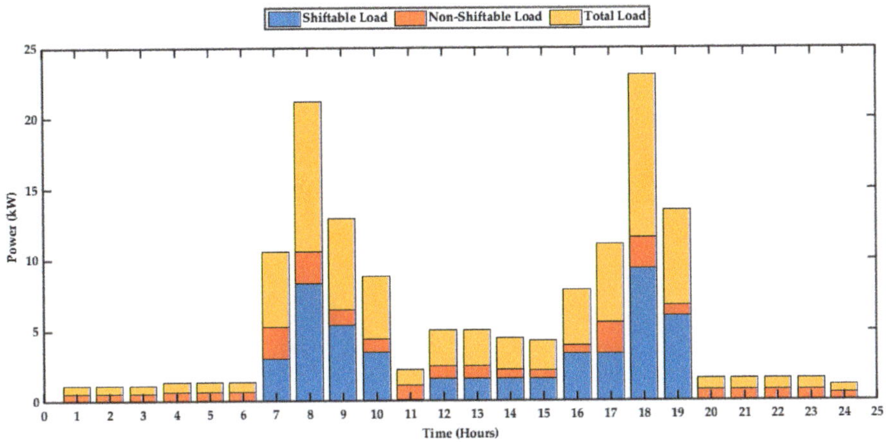

Figure 5. Total load demand, shiftable load and non-shiftable load on hourly basis for case study 1.

The characteristics of shiftable and non-shiftable loads are further illustrated in Figure 6. Shiftable loads dominate consumption during the morning and evening peak period, with load demands of about 3–10 kW, while non-shiftable loads remain relatively constant around 0.5–3 kW throughout the 24 h. The flexibility of the residential load demands can be established based on the distribution of shiftable and non-shiftable load demands. The overall performance of the proposed HRES can be improved by rescheduling the operation of shiftable appliances to off-peak hours. The low contribution of non-shiftable loads to total load demand indicates that more efforts should be focused on shiftable appliances to reduce energy purchase from the grid, net energy cost and GHG cost.

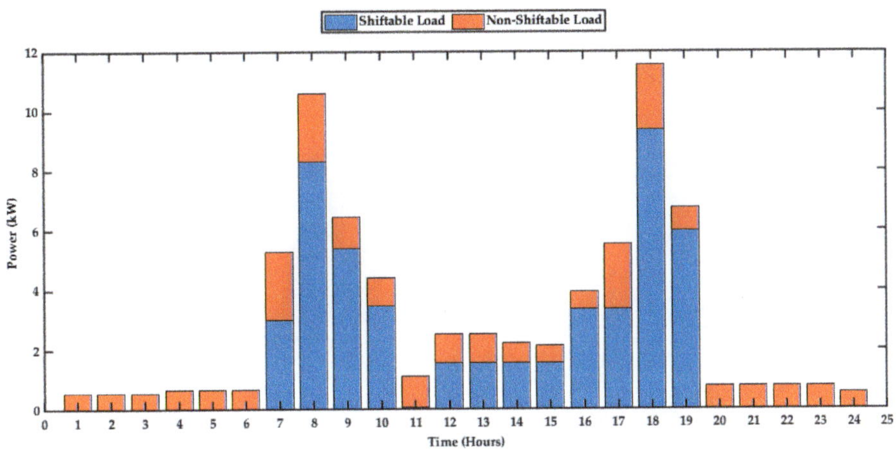

Figure 6. Shiftable load and non-shiftable load on hourly basis for case study 1.

The shiftable load profile based on individual appliances and hourly operation patterns is presented in Figure 7. The most energy-intensive shiftable appliances such as washing machines, dishwashers and water heaters are frequently utilized in the morning (08:00–10:00) and evening (16:00–19:00) periods. Other appliances, such as vacuum cleaners, irons, blenders, bread toasters, fans and phone chargers have shorter and less frequent operational cycles. The use of shiftable loads during peak periods demonstrates

https://doi.org/10.3390/en19051174

that appliance scheduling can improve the performance of the proposed grid-connected HRES.

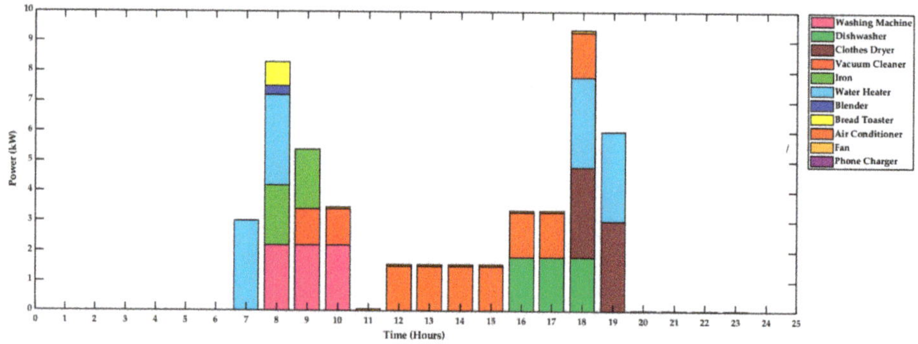

Figure 7. Individual shiftable loads on hourly basis for case study 1.

The non-shiftable appliances, such as such as lighting, refrigeration and freezers, operate continuously or frequently on an hourly basis, as depicted in Figure 8. The power consumption of non-shiftable appliances is nearly constant throughout the 24 h horizon, typically between 0.5 and 3 kW. The non-shiftable loads have become an integral part of the base load of the household energy demand, since these loads cannot be rescheduled without affecting user safety. Therefore, non-shiftable loads are treated as fixed load demands while focusing on optimizing the key components of the objective function.

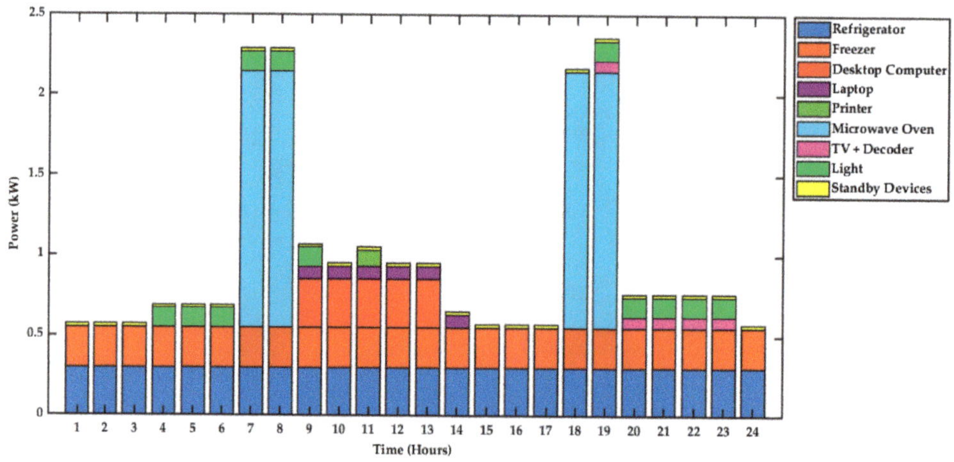

Figure 8. Individual non-shiftable loads on hourly basis for case study 1.

In this case study, the load demand is purchased from the utility grid without the utilization of PVs, WTs and BSSs and scheduling of household appliances. The hourly variation of residential load demand and power purchased from the grid over 24 h is presented in Figure 9a,b. Figure 9a shows that peak periods occur early in the morning (06:00–09:00) and later in the evening (17:00–20:00). These peak periods reflect the consumption pattern of residential consumers based on their appliance usage during times when occupants prepare for daily activities or return home from work. It can be established from Figure 9b that the pattern of power demand from the grid is the same as the load demand pattern, since the household depends on the utility grid only to meet its daily power demand without contribution from RESs and BSSs and scheduling of home appliances.

 https://doi.org/10.3390/en19051174

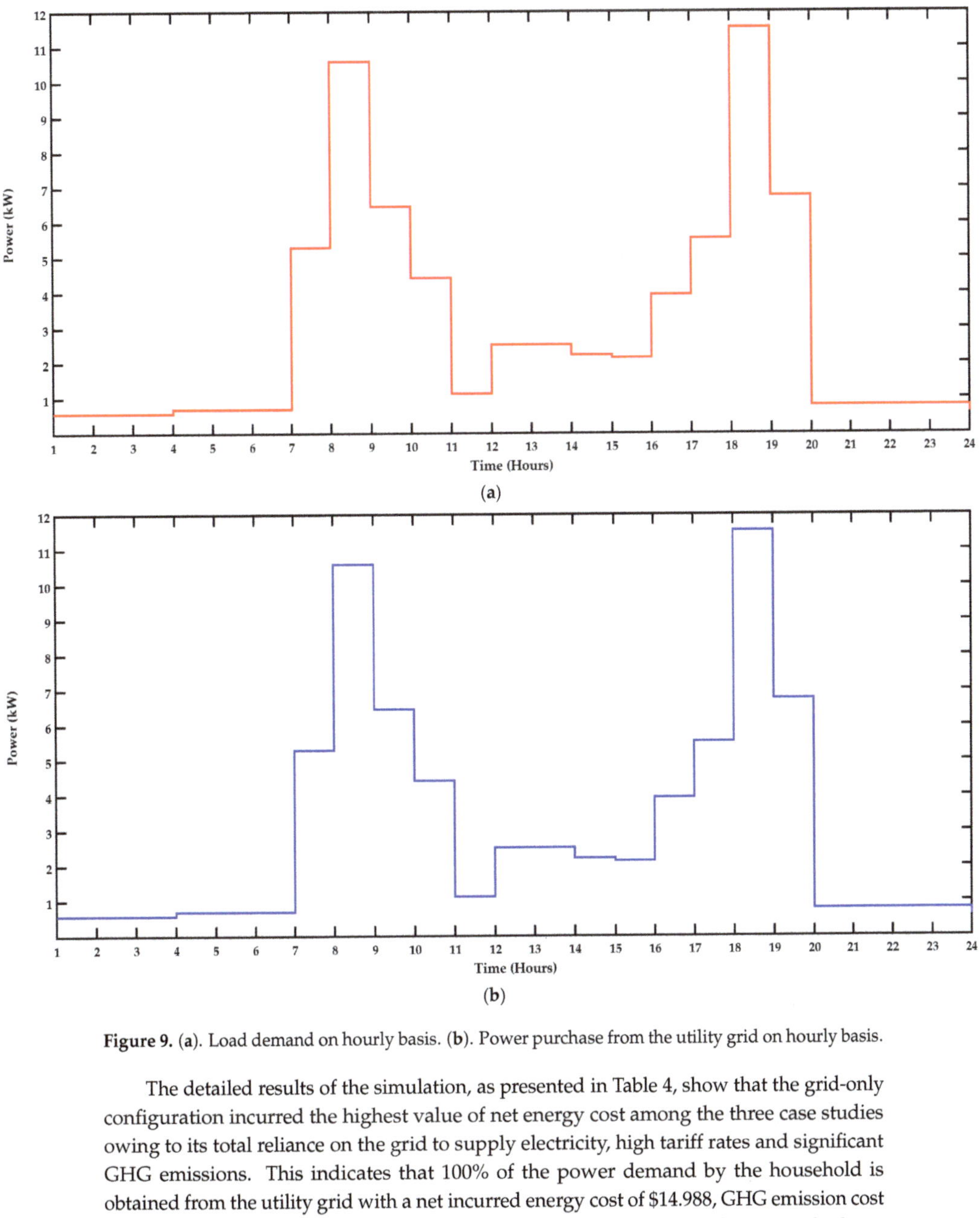

Figure 9. (**a**). Load demand on hourly basis. (**b**). Power purchase from the utility grid on hourly basis.

The detailed results of the simulation, as presented in Table 4, show that the grid-only configuration incurred the highest value of net energy cost among the three case studies owing to its total reliance on the grid to supply electricity, high tariff rates and significant GHG emissions. This indicates that 100% of the power demand by the household is obtained from the utility grid with a net incurred energy cost of \$14.988, GHG emission cost of \$2.693 and energy purchased of 75.138 kWh. The optimization results show a high net incurred energy cost and environmental impact of using the grid standalone configuration to satisfy load demand owing to the absence of load scheduling or renewable energy integration. This demonstrates that the uncoordinated operation of household appliances during peak tariff periods can cause economic inefficiency and increase unnecessary stress on the utility grid. The simulation results obtained in case study 1 demonstrate that the cost of energy purchased from the utility grid has become a significant component that

https://doi.org/10.3390/en19051174

determines the values of net incurred energy cost in the absence of renewable energy generation and appliance scheduling.

Table 4. Summary of the results obtained from the three case studies.

Description	Case Study 1	Case Study 2	Case Study 3
CO_2 (kg)	70.780	2.956	1.6487
SO_2 (kg)	0.522	0.022	0.0121
NO_x (kg)	0.317	0.013	0.0074
CO_2 ($)	2.123	0.089	0.0495
SO_2 ($)	0.475	0.0198	0.011
Nox ($)	0.095	0.004	0.002
Energy purchased (kWh)	75.138	3.138	1.750
Energy sold (kWh)	-	69.176	69.3
Energy purchased ($)	14.988	0.470	0.245
Energy sold ($)	-	7.908	10.083
Net energy cost (kWh)	-	−66.038	−67.55
Net energy cost ($)	14.988	−7.438	−9.838
GHG cost ($)	2.693	0.113	0.063
SIC ($)	-	-	0.66
Cost of battery degradation ($)	-	0.470	0.461
ACO finished; best cost ($)	17.681	−6.869	−8.654

The GHG cost of $2.693 obtained in this case study is based on intensive application of coal-based thermal plants in South Africa for electricity generation. The GHG-related costs show that CO_2, SO_2 and NO_x contribute $2.123, $0.475 and $0.095 to the total emission cost of $2.693. Specifically, CO_2 emissions accounted for the largest percentage of the total GHG costs (78.8%), while SO_2 and NO_x contributed 17.6% and 3.5%, as shown in Figure 10. These results have reflected the typical emission profile of thermal-based generation plants. The values of CO_2, SO_2 and NO_x emissions obtained in this case study are 70.780 kg, 0.522 kg and 0.317 kg based on the contribution of each pollutant, emission factors and the amount of power purchased from the grid. The high values of GHG costs and net energy cost obtained in this case study indicate that over-reliance on the utility grid to satisfy the load demand of households is not economically and environmentally sustainable. The results show that the cost of energy purchased from the utility grid dominates the total cost while GHG emissions contribute significantly to environmental costs. It is obvious from the results obtained from case study 1 that over-reliance on the utility grid can cause higher net energy cost and GHG emissions. This case study can be used as the baseline scenario to compare the technical, economic and environmental benefits of RESs and BSS integration in case studies 2 and 3. The results clearly demonstrate the necessity of using RESs and appliance scheduling to achieve cost reduction and sustainability of power supply. Hence, the outcomes of this case study can be utilized as a benchmark for assessing the benefits of distributed energy generation and scheduling of home appliances strategy in subsequent case studies.

https://doi.org/10.3390/en19051174

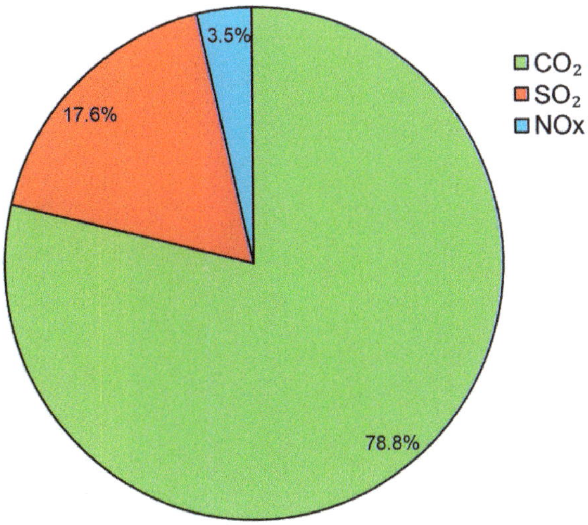

Figure 10. Breakdown of GHG costs by using the utility grid alone without scheduling of home appliances.

5.2. Case Study 2: Grid-Connected HRES Without Appliance Scheduling

In this case study, the residential energy system is integrated into a grid-connected HRES to utilize generated renewable energy and reduce reliance on the utility grid. The present configuration allows the exchange of energy between the utility grid and distributed energy generation units without scheduling of home appliances. This shows that home appliances operate according to their normal usage patterns shown in Figures 5–8. The power distribution profiles of the proposed HRES, which consists of load demand, power generated from PVs and wind turbines, as well as power purchase from the grid, power sold to the grid, battery discharge power and battery charge power, are presented in Figure 11a. The load demand of this case study is similar to case study 1 since there is no scheduling of home appliances. The power generation from the PV system contributed a considerable amount to the system between 9:00 and 16:00, while the contribution of the wind turbines to the entire power system varied intermittently throughout the day. The system is designed to charge BSSs during periods of surplus power from PVs and wind turbines and discharge during periods of deficit power from renewable energy sources. The relationship between the discharge power, charge power and SOC of the BSS throughout the day is presented in Figure 11b. The SOC of the BSS operates between the acceptable minimum and maximum limits to extend the lifespan of the BSS. The value of the battery degradation cost of \$0.47 that is obtained in this case study is relatively low. This confirms that the battery operates with the marginal value of the battery degradation cost under unscheduled operation and ensures that the health status of the battery is maintained based on the energy management strategy that was used in the study.

https://doi.org/10.3390/en19051174

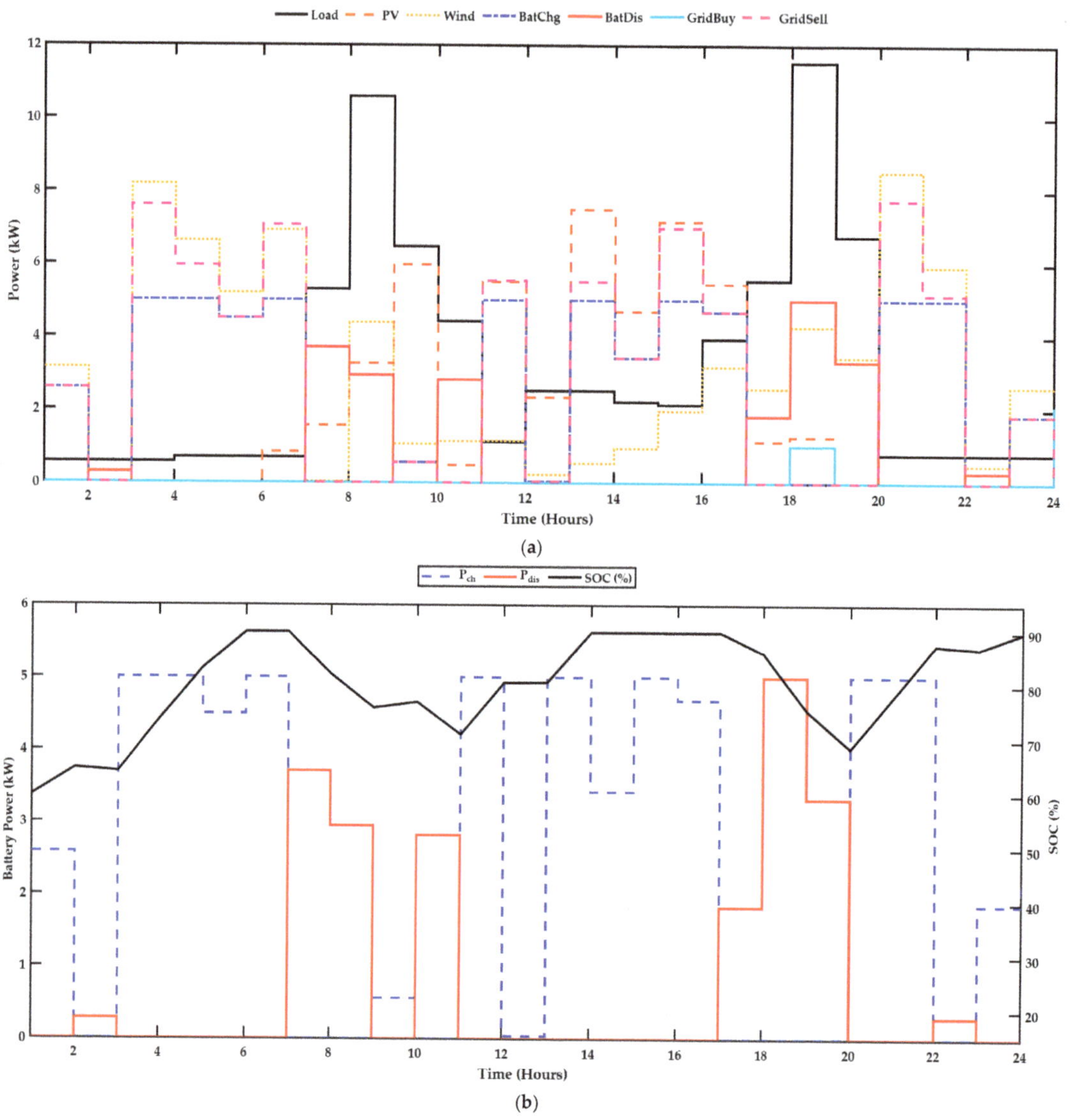

Figure 11. (**a**). Power profile of the grid-connected HRES for case study 2. (**b**). Charge and discharge power and state of charge of the battery system for case study 2.

The net energy revenue cost of $7.438 obtained in this case study confirmed the competence of the ACO technique to effectively optimize HRESs with grid interactions. This is the value of net revenue earned by the household when the amount of energy injected into the grid is more than the amount of energy purchased from the grid. The net energy revenue cost of $7.438 demonstrates a significant financial benefit that the household has derived from using the proposed HRES owing to the renewable energy generation potential of PVs and wind turbines and revenue obtained from selling excess energy to the utility grid. The summary of the results presented in Table 4 shows that 3.138 kWh of energy was purchased from the utility during low renewable energy generation hours, while 69.176 kWh of energy was injected into the utility grid when energy from PVs,

https://doi.org/10.3390/en19051174

WTs and BSSs exceeded local load demand. The amount of energy purchased from the utility grid has reduced by 96% relative to case study 1. This demonstrates that the system effectively utilized RESs to meet the local power demand. The excess energy from PVs and WTs contributed to the reduction of over-reliance utility grid and net energy cost as well the generation of economic credits.

The value of GHG cost has reduced from \$2.693 in case study 1 to \$0.113 in case study 2 because RESs and BSSs are used in the existing power system. This indicates a strong positive environmental impact of using RESs in the proposed HRES. The breakdown of emission costs obtained in this case study shows that CO_2, SO_2 and NO_x contribute \$2.956, \$0.021 and \$0.013 to the GHG cost of \$0.113. It can be seen in Figure 12 that CO_2 contributed 78.9% of the total GHG cost, followed by SO_2 (17.6%) and NO_x (3.5%). CO_2 emissions accounted for the largest percentage of the total GHG emissions with 2.956 kg, while SO_2 and NO_x contributed 0.022 kg and 0.013 kg. This shows that CO_2 emissions account for the majority of the environmental impact. The values of CO_2, SO_2 and NO_x costs obtained in this case study have reduced by approximately 96% when compared with case study 1. The significant reduction of CO_2, SO_2 and NO_x costs is attributed to the dominance of green energy technologies that displaced power obtained from the fossil fuel-based utility grid. The reduction of the amount of GHG emissions corresponds to a considerable reduction of GHG costs compared to the utility grid-only configuration, since most of the energy is sourced from clean renewable resources. Therefore, GHG emissions and associated costs are minimized. The significant reduction in the net energy cost, energy purchased from the grid and emission metrics recorded in this case study confirms the environmental and economic superiority of grid-connected HRESs over a grid-only configuration. The combined operation of PV and WT units significantly improved cost savings and reduced the carbon footprint in the absence of appliance scheduling. The system is not only satisfied local demand but also improved revenue through grid energy sales, reduced GHG emissions and improved the sustainability of the power system through the prospect of renewable energy generation. The scheduling of home appliances is introduced in case study 3 to coincide with high renewable energy generation or off-peak periods. It is anticipated that this will increase system efficiency and further maximize renewable self-consumption.

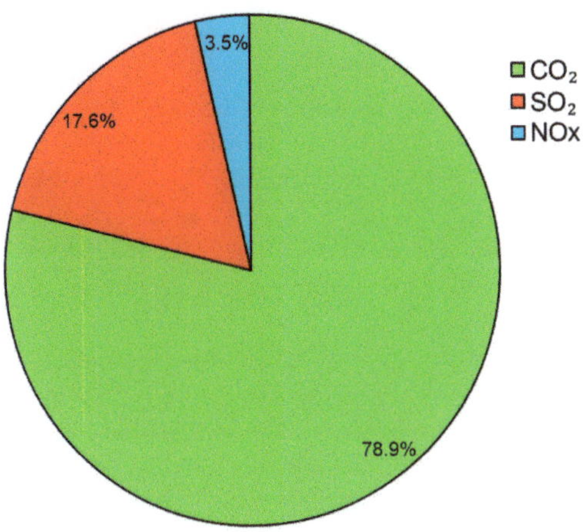

Figure 12. Breakdown of GHG costs by using HRESs without scheduling of home appliances.

https://doi.org/10.3390/en19051174

5.3. Case Study 3: Grid-Connected HRES with Optimal Appliance Scheduling

The HRES that consists of PVs, WTs, a BSS and a utility grid is considered in this case study with the scheduling of home appliances. The time-based appliance scheduling was introduced in this case study to shift shiftable loads to periods of higher renewable energy generation or off-peak periods when the electricity tariffs are low. The total load demand of the household is divided into shiftable and non-shiftable loads after rescheduling of home appliances, as presented in Figure 13. The figure shows that energy consumption is distributed across the 24 h horizon to align with renewable energy generation or low electricity tariffs. The shiftable loads of this case study are shifted towards high renewable generation or low tariff periods, especially early in the morning (3:00–6:00) and late in the evening (16:00–23:00) to achieve the objectives of the study.

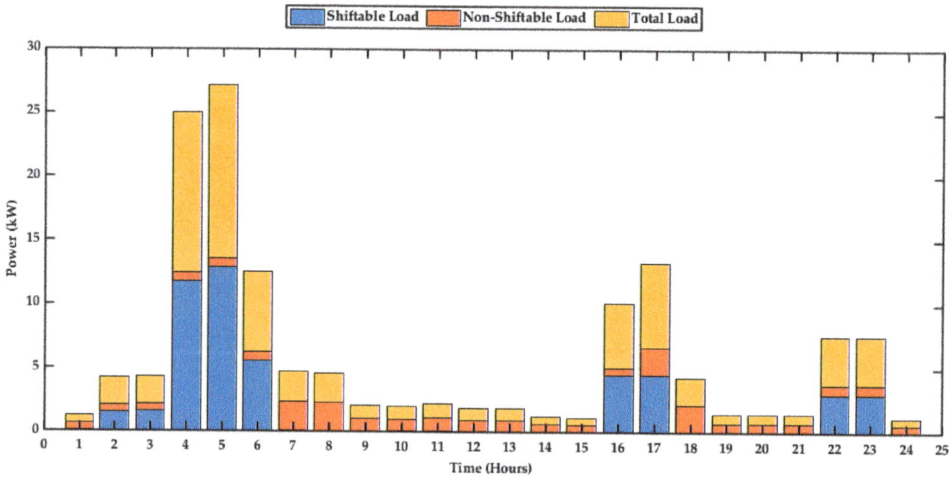

Figure 13. Total load demand, shiftable load and non-shiftable load on an hourly basis for case study 3.

The hourly variation of shiftable and non-shiftable loads after the implementation of appliance scheduling in the grid-connected HRES is presented in Figure 14. The figure illustrates the contributions of shiftable and non-shiftable appliances to the total load demand profile across a 24 h horizon. The shiftable loads dominate the total load demand in the early morning and later in the evening, while the non-shiftable loads remain steady throughout the day with a lower magnitude. This behavior demonstrates how appliance scheduling provides flexibility in modifying the load profile to increase the performance of the system. The introduction of load scheduling can be used to enhance the efficiency of HRESs, reduce energy purchase from the utility grid and improve the coordination of household energy demand and hybrid energy supply.

The operational pattern of individual shiftable appliances after the implementation of optimal scheduling in the grid-connected HRES is presented in Figure 15. The figure shows that energy-intensive appliances such as the washing machine, water heater, clothes dryer and air conditioner are scheduled to operate during off-peak periods of 0:00–6:00 and 22:00–24:00 when tariffs are low or during high renewable generation. The scheduling of shiftable loads can be used to reduce scheduling inconvenience costs and GHG costs and ensure that load demand aligns with renewable energy generation and low-tariff hours. This has established the role of scheduling mechanisms in achieving the objectives of smart home energy systems.

https://doi.org/10.3390/en19051174

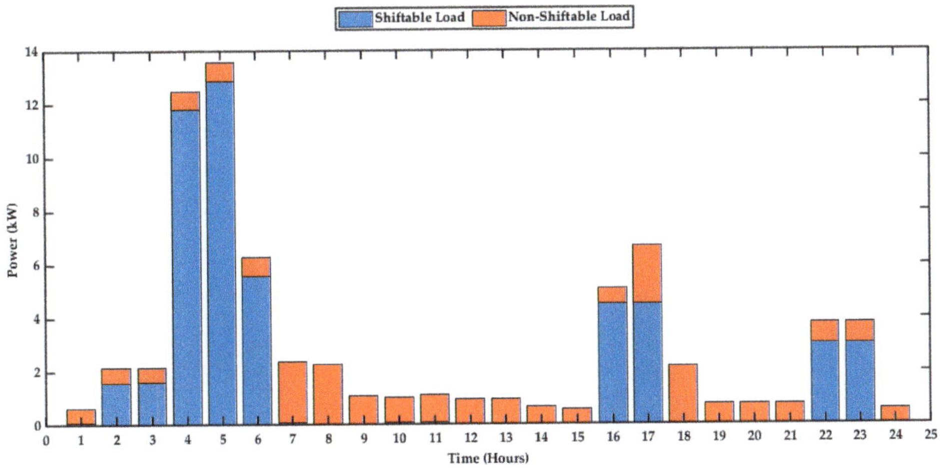

Figure 14. Shiftable load and non-shiftable load on an hourly basis for case study 3.

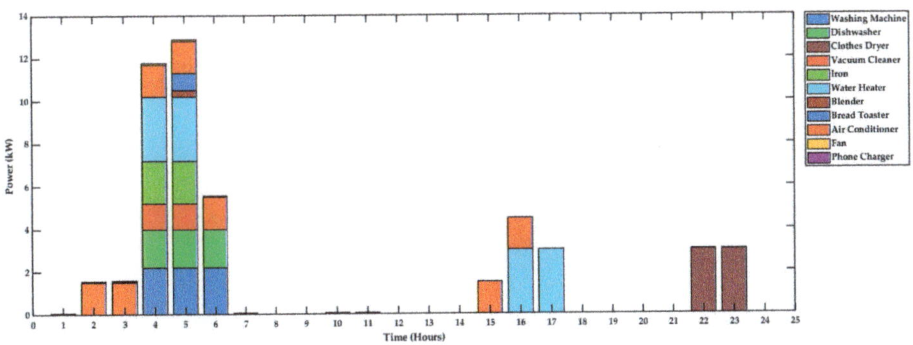

Figure 15. Individual shiftable loads on an hourly basis for case study 3.

The power demand of individual non-shiftable loads within the grid-connected HRES is presented in Figure 16. These non-shiftable loads must operate continuously or at fixed times to maintain essential services. They cannot be rescheduled without affecting normal household functionality or user comfort. It can be seen in the figure that non-shiftable loads maintain a baseline energy demand throughout the day, with significant increases during early morning (6:00–9:00) and evening hours (18:00–20:00). Shiftable and non-shiftable loads play complementary roles in achieving an optimal energy management strategy within smart residential systems.

The ACO technique was used in this case study to coordinate the operation of household devices, renewable generation and energy obtained from the grid and battery system. The power flows between the components of the proposed HRES, such as the WT, PV system, BSS and utility grid, under the scheduling of appliance operation is presented in Figure 17a. The figure shows that the PV system supplied a large percentage of the load demand during the daytime. The excess power from the PV system is utilized to charge the battery system or exported to the grid. A WT is utilized in the system to support the weakness of the PVs at night and early in the morning when solar radiation is low. The HRES is designed in such a way that grid power purchase only occurs in a situation when the power outputs of the PVs and WT and battery discharge are not sufficient to satisfy the load requirements. The pattern of power exchange among the components of the HRES

https://doi.org/10.3390/en19051174

demonstrates how appliance scheduling allows the system to operate in a coordinated manner. The SOC of the BSS, coupled with its charge and discharge power, is presented in Figure 17b. The introduction of home appliance scheduling in this case study has made the charging and discharging patterns of the BSS more dynamic than case study 2. The battery system is charged when the power outputs of renewable energy sources are more than the load demand and discharged during low renewable energy periods. The control cycling of the battery system has reduced over-dependency on the utility grid. The battery degradation cost of \$0.461 obtained in this case study indicates effective utilization of the battery system and moderate cycling. The efficient use of the BSS in this case study has improved the performance of the HRES and minimized the battery degradation cost relative to case study 2.

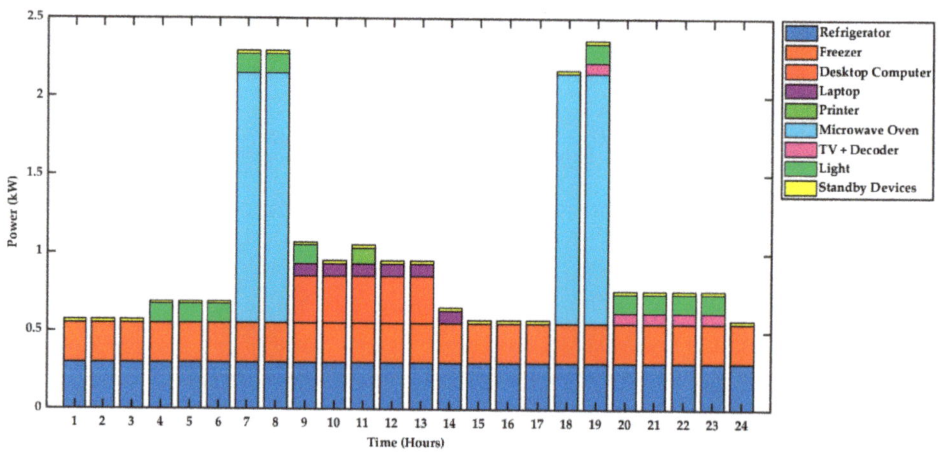

Figure 16. Individual non-shiftable loads on an hourly basis for case study 3.

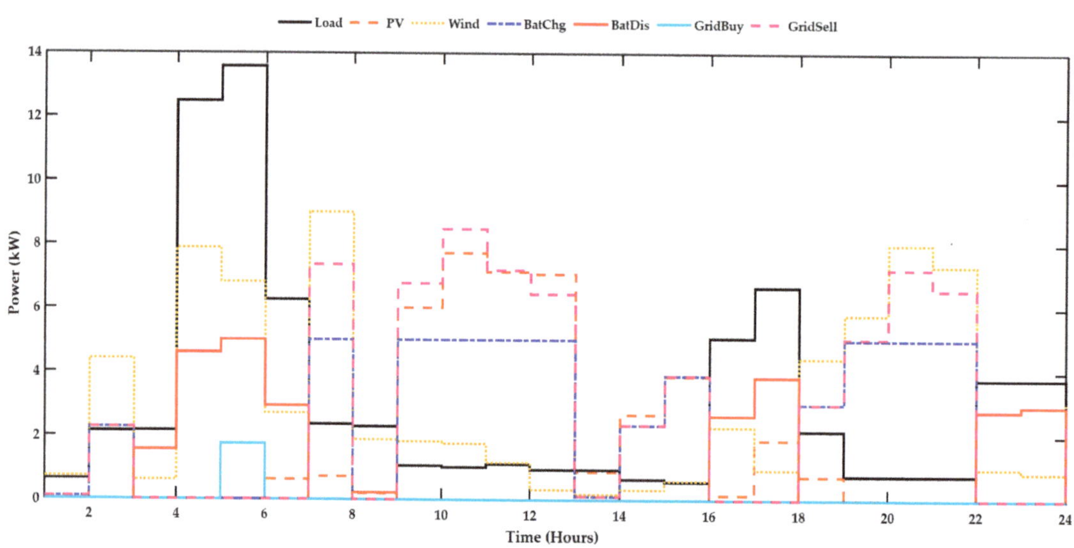

(a)

Figure 17. *Cont.*

https://doi.org/10.3390/en19051174

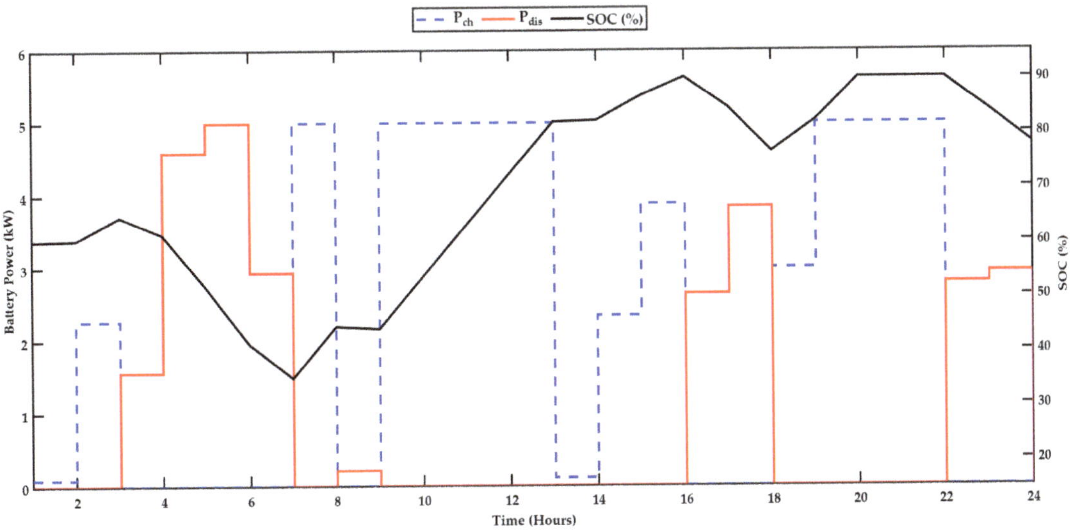

(b)

Figure 17. (**a**). Power profile of the grid-connected HRES for case study 3. (**b**). Charge and discharge power and state of charge of the battery system for case study 3.

The net energy revenue cost of \$9.838 obtained in this case study has signified a significant net financial benefit caused by excess energy generation from the WT and PV units and the amount of energy injected into the utility grid. The values of total energy purchased from the grid and energy injected into the grid are 1.750 kWh and 69.3 kWh. This illustrates a significant export of energy resulting from surplus energy generation from photovoltaics and wind turbines. The amount of energy purchased from the utility grid has reduced by 98% and 44% when compared to case studies 1 and 2. Conversely, the monetary value of energy injected into the grid also increased by 28% when compared to case study 2. This shows that case study 3 has not only reduced reliance on the utility grid but also increased generated revenue from the sale of electricity. The value of SIC obtained in this case study is \$ 0.66 with negligible user discomfort while achieving significant cost reduction. The SICs of individual appliances are presented in Figure 18 based on the application of appliance scheduling. The comparative performance of the three case studies as presented in Table 4 show that the integration of RESs and appliance scheduling caused reductions in the net energy cost, SIC, battery degradation cost and GHG cost.

The GHG cost of \$0.063 obtained in this case study is due to the environmental benefit of integrating the scheduling of home appliance strategies into the operation of HRESs. The costs of CO_2, SO_2 and NO_x emissions obtained in this case study are \$0.05, \$0.011 and \$0.002. It can be seen in Figure 19 that CO_2 contributed 79.1% of the total GHG cost, followed by SO_2 (17.7%) and NO_x (3.2%). The value of GHG cost has reduced by 97% and 32% when compared to case studies 1 and 2. This case study recorded the lowest value of GHG emissions with CO_2 of 1.649 kg, SO_2 of 0.012 kg and NO_x of 0.007 kg. The values of CO_2 emissions have been reduced by 98% and 44% when compared to case studies 1 and 2. Similar trends are observed for SO_2 and NO_x to indicate that load scheduling aligns energy consumption more closely with renewable availability to reduce power purchased fossil-based utility grid. The application of appliance scheduling in this case study has considerably reduced utility grid dependency, environmental impacts, net energy cost, degradation cost of battery system and SIC. The outcomes of case study 3 show that a grid-connected HRES with appliance scheduling is more economically and environmentally

https://doi.org/10.3390/en19051174

feasible than case studies 1 and 2. The significant amount of energy that was injected into the utility grid and low GHG emissions demonstrate the environmental and technical feasibility of integrating RESs into the grid. The outcomes of the study show that case study 3 is the best configuration based on the superior performance of the system with the integration of renewable energy and appliance scheduling strategy.

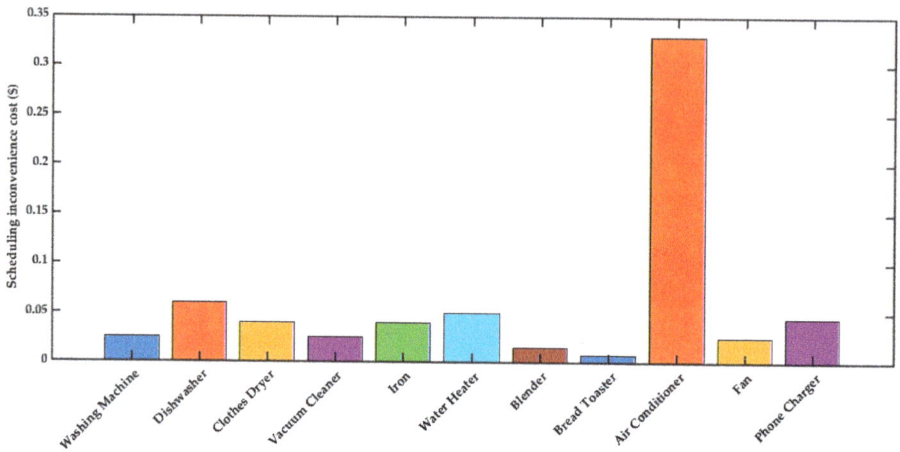

Figure 18. Scheduling inconvenience costs of individual appliances.

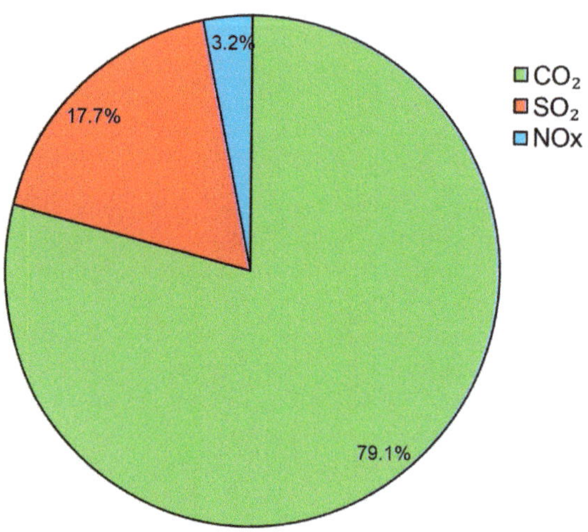

Figure 19. Breakdown of GHG costs by using HRES with the scheduling of home appliances.

5.4. Comparative Performance of the Three Case Studies

The comparative performance of the three case studies is summarized in this section to demonstrate the effectiveness of appliance scheduling and RESs in improving the overall performance of the power system. The results of case studies 1 to 3 demonstrate that the integration of RESs and the application appliance scheduling strategy significantly improved the economic and environmental performances of the power system. Case study 1 has the highest GHG cost of $2.693 and net incurred energy cost of $14.988 to demonstrate 100% dependency on the utility grid and fossil-based sources. The application of RESs in case study 2 has achieved a significant reduction in the values of GHG cost, net

https://doi.org/10.3390/en19051174

energy revenue cost and battery degradation cost to \$0.113, \$7.438 and \$0.47. This signifies improved net cost savings and GHG cost reduction of 149% and 96% relative to case study 1 through renewable integration and partial grid interaction. The minimum values of GHG cost of \$0.0627 and battery degradation cost of \$0.461 are achieved in case study 3 with the implementation of a grid-connected HRES and appliance scheduling. The net energy revenue cost of \$9.8382 with a small scheduling inconvenience cost of \$0.66 to quantify user discomfort is owing to the introduction of appliance scheduling in case study 3. This demonstrates that the values of net energy cost and GHG cost have been reduced by 165% and 97% relative to case study 1. The outcomes of the study show that the application of a scheduling strategy in the HRES significantly improved energy efficiency and cost effectiveness while achieving considerable GHG emission and SIC reduction.

The inherent trade-offs among economic, environmental, technical and scheduling inconvenience costs of the proposed grid-connected HRES are presented in this subsection. A radar diagram that illustrates the trade-offs among energy purchased, energy sold, GHG cost, net energy cost, battery degradation cost and scheduling inconvenience cost among the three case studies is presented in Figure 20. The figure provides a holistic visualization of the competing objectives and deeper representation of trade-offs among the three case studies. Case study 1, which operates without appliance scheduling and an HRES, has the highest value of energy purchase from the grid, GHG cost and net energy cost. This demonstrates that utility grid-only operation cannot be used to achieve cost-effective and environmentally sustainable energy management. The outcomes of case study 2, as reflected in Figure 20, show a significant reduction in energy purchased, energy sold, net energy cost and GHG cost through the integration of PVs, WTs and BSSs. It is obvious from the results of case study 2 that there is a clear trade-off between economic, technical and environmental benefits. The full benefits of local renewable energy sources cannot be fully harnessed in case study 2 due to the absence of appliance scheduling. The best overall technical, economic, environmental performance indicators are achieved in case study 3 with minimum net energy cost, energy purchase, energy sold, GHG cost, battery degradation cost and scheduling inconvenience cost. The improved performance of case study 3 reflects the mutual collaboration between load shifting and user comfort.

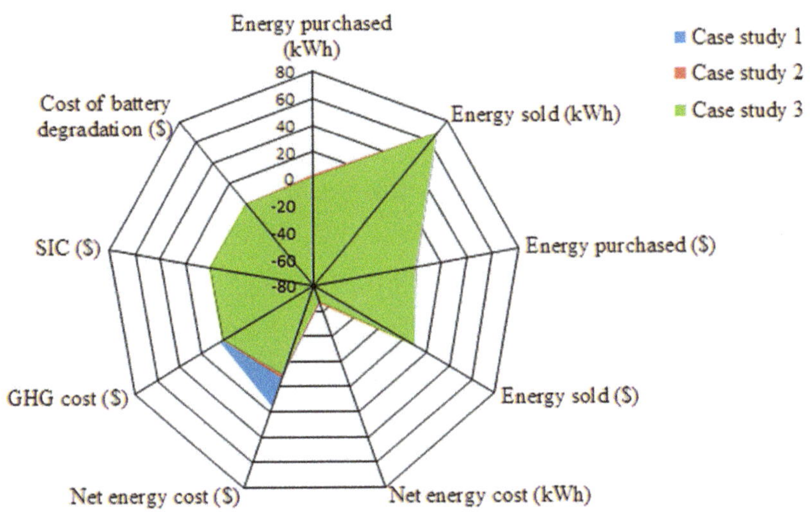

Figure 20. Radar diagram of economic, environmental, technical and comfort trade-offs of the proposed grid-connected HRES.

https://doi.org/10.3390/en19051174

6. Conclusions

The technical, economic and environmental effectiveness of using RESs and appliance scheduling to improve the performance of residential power systems is presented in this study using an ACO algorithm and three case studies. Simulation results reveal that case study 1 has the highest GHG emission cost of $2.693, energy purchased of 75.138 kWh and net incurred energy cost of $14.988. The application of RESs in case study 2 led to a reduction in GHG emission cost (96%) and net energy cost (149%) relative to case study 1. The values of GHG emission cost of $0.113 and net revenue energy cost of $7.438 obtained in case study 2 are further optimized in case study 3 by using an appliance scheduling mechanism. The best performance is achieved in case study 3 where the values of GHG emission cost and net revenue energy cost have been improved by 165% and 98% relative to case study 1. The findings of the study show that appliance scheduling and RES integration can be used to reduce grid dependency, improve environmental performance and improve the overall performance of grid-connected HRESs. This work can be extended by focusing on the real-time implementation of blockchain mechanisms and dynamic electricity pricing.

Author Contributions: Conceptualization, T.A. and G.S.; methodology, P.N.B. and R.K.; investigation, T.A.; resources, T.A. and G.S.; writing—original draft preparation, T.A.; writing—review and editing, G.S. and P.N.B.; visualization, R.K.; supervision, G.S. and P.N.B.; project administration, R.K. All authors have read and agreed to the published version of the manuscript.

Funding: This research received no external funding.

Institutional Review Board Statement: Not applicable.

Informed Consent Statement: Not applicable.

Data Availability Statement: The original contributions presented in the study are included in the article; further inquiries can be directed to the authors.

Conflicts of Interest: The authors declare no conflicts of interest.

Abbreviations

The following abbreviations are used in this manuscript:

A	**PV Module Surface Area**
ACO	**Ant Colony Optimization**
BSS	Battery Storage System
COE	Cost of Energy
DG	**Diesel Generator**
EV	Electric Vehicle
G	**Solar Irradiance**
GHG	**Greenhouse Gas**
HRES	Hybrid Renewable Energy System
IEA	International Energy Agency
LCOE	Levelized Cost of Energy
MPC	Model Predictive Control
NPC	Net Present Cost
PV	Photovoltaic
RESs	**Renewable Energy Sources**
RSMG	Residential Standalone Microgrid
SHEMS	Smart Home Energy Management System
SIC	Scheduling Inconvenience Cost

https://doi.org/10.3390/en19051174

SOC	State of Charge
SSEG	Small-Scale Embedded Generation
TOU	Time of Use
WTs	**Wind Turbines**

References

1. Farghali, M.; Mohamed, I.M.A.; Chen, Z.; Chen, L.; Ihara, I.; Yap, P.; Rooney, D.W. Strategies to save energy in the context of the energy crisis: A review. *Environ. Chem. Lett.* **2024**, *21*, 2003–2039. [CrossRef]
2. Global Energy Review 2025: Global Trends. Available online: https://www.iea.org/reports/global-energy-review-2025/global-trends (accessed on 20 October 2025).
3. Pathways for the Energy Mix. Available online: https://www.iea.org/reports/world-energy-outlook-2024/pathways-for-the-energy-mix?utm (accessed on 16 November 2025).
4. Bajoria, A.; Kanpariya, J.; Bera, A. Greenhouse gases and global warming. In *Advances and Technology Development in Greenhouse Gases: Emission, Capture and Conversion*; Elsevier Inc.: Amsterdam, The Netherlands, 2025; pp. 121–135.
5. Financing Electricity Access in Africa. Available online: https://www.iea.org/reports/financing-electricity-access-in-africa (accessed on 22 October 2025).
6. Avordeh, T.K.; Salifu, A.; Quaidoo, C.; Opare-Boateng, R. Impact of power outages: Unveiling their influence on micro, small, and medium-sized enterprises and poverty in Sub-Saharan Africa-an in-depth literature review. *Heliyon* **2024**, *10*, 33782. [CrossRef]
7. Mossisa, A.T.; Han, A.T. Transitioning to renewable electric energy in rapidly urbanizing Sub-Saharan Africa: Challenges and opportunities. *Energy Strategy Rev.* **2025**, *61*, 101842. [CrossRef]
8. Transition to Renewables Calls for New Approach to Energy Security. Available online: https://www.irena.org/News/pressreleases/2024/Apr/Transition-to-Renewables-Calls-for-New-Approach-to-Energy-Security?utm_source (accessed on 12 November 2025).
9. The UAE Consensus Foreword. Available online: https://www.cop28.com/en/the-uae-consensus-foreword?utm_source (accessed on 25 November 2025).
10. The United Nations Inter-Agency Mechanism on Energy Issues. Available online: https://www.un.org/en/energy/page/sdg-7-overview?utm_source (accessed on 13 October 2025).
11. The Paris Agreement. Available online: https://unfccc.int/process-and-meetings/the-paris-agreement (accessed on 8 October 2025).
12. Gajdzik, B.; Wolniak, R.; Nagaj, R.; Žuromskaitė-Nagaj, B.; Grebski, W.W. The influence of the global energy crisis on energy efficiency: A comprehensive analysis. *Energies* **2024**, *17*, 947. [CrossRef]
13. Global Electricity Review 2025. Available online: https://energychangemakers.com/wp-content/uploads/2025/04/Report-Global-Electricity-Review-2025.pdf?utm_source (accessed on 11 October 2025).
14. Renewables 2025 Global Status Report. Available online: https://www.ren21.net/gsr-2025/ (accessed on 18 November 2025).
15. Where Do Emissions Come From? 4 Charts Explain Greenhouse Gas Emissions by Sector. Available online: https://www.wri.org/insights/4-charts-explain-greenhouse-gas-emissions-countries-and-sectors (accessed on 12 October 2025).
16. González-Torres, M.; Pérez-Lombard, L.; Coronel, J.F.; Maestre, I.R.; Paolo, B. Activity and efficiency trends for the residential sector across countries. *Energy Build.* **2022**, *273*, 112428. [CrossRef]
17. Ghiasi, M.; Ghiasi, V.; Siano, P. Renewable energy integration into industrial and residential buildings: A study across urban, rural and coastal areas. *IET RPG* **2025**, *19*, e70108. [CrossRef]
18. Emezirinwune, M.U.; Adejumobi, I.A.; Adebisi, O.I.; Akinboro, F.G. Synergizing hybrid renewable energy systems and sustainable agriculture for rural development in Nigeria. *E-Prime—Adv. Electr. Eng. Electron. Energy* **2024**, *7*, 100492. [CrossRef]
19. Ma, Z.; Awan, M.B.; Lu, M.; Li, S.; Aziz, M.S.; Zhou, X.; Du, H.; Sha, X.; Li, Y. An overview of emerging and sustainable technologies for increased energy efficiency and carbon emission mitigation in buildings. *Buildings* **2023**, *13*, 2658. [CrossRef]
20. Juyal, V.D.; Kakran, S. Smart home energy management and active power loss analysis of a residential community. *J. Build. Eng.* **2024**, *91*, 109548. [CrossRef]
21. Awan, T.I.; Afsheen, S.; Mushtaq, A. Carbon-free energy—Free energy supply. In *Influence of Noble Metal Nanoparticles in Sustainable Energy Technologies*; Springer: Cham, Switzerland, 2025; pp. 19–47. [CrossRef]
22. Chang, L.; Li, Z.; Tian, X.; Su, J.; Chang, X.; Xue, Y.; Li, Z.; Jin, X.; Wang, P.; Sun, H. A two-stage distributionally robust low-carbon operation method for antarctic unmanned observation station integrating virtual energy storage and hydrogen waste heat recovery. *Appl. Energy* **2025**, *400*, 126578. [CrossRef]
23. Ali, E.S.; Elkholy, M.H.; Senjyu, T.; Abd Elazim, S.M.; Hassan, E.S.; Alaas, Z.; Lotfy, M.E. A flexible multi-agent system for managing demand and variability in hybrid energy systems for rural communities. *Sci. Rep.* **2025**, *15*, 16255. [CrossRef]
24. Manjula, A.; Niraimathi, R.; Rajarajeswari, M.; Devi, S.C. Grid integration of renewable energy sources: Challenges and solutions. In *Green Machine Learning and Big Data for Smart Grids*; Elsevier Inc.: Amsterdam, The Netherlands, 2025; pp. 263–286. [CrossRef]

https://doi.org/10.3390/en19051174

25. Shi, D.; Cui, Y.; Shen, X.; Gao, Z.; Ma, X.; Li, X.; Fang, Y.; Wang, S.; Fang, S. A review of the combined effects of environmental and operational factors on lithium-ion battery performance: Temperature, vibration, and charging/discharging cycles. *RSC Adv.* **2025**, *15*, 13272–13283. [CrossRef] [PubMed]
26. Dragomir, O.E.; Dragomir, F. Application of scheduling techniques for load-shifting in smart homes with renewable-energy-sources integration. *Buildings* **2023**, *13*, 134. [CrossRef]
27. Han, B.; Zahraoui, Y.; Mubin, M.; Mekhilef, S.; Seyedmahmoudian, M.; Stojcevski, A. Home energy management systems: A review of the concept, architecture, and scheduling strategies. *IEEE Access* **2023**, *11*, 19999–20025. [CrossRef]
28. Ibrahim, A.O.; Elfadel, E.M.E.; Hashem, I.A.T.; Syed, H.J.; Ismail, M.A.; Osman, A.H.; Ahmed, A. The artificial bee colony algorithm: A comprehensive survey of variants, modifications, applications, developments, and opportunities. *Arch. Computat. Methods Eng.* **2025**, *32*, 3499–3533. [CrossRef]
29. Islam, R.; Kabir, S.; Shufian, A.; Rabbi, M.S.; Akteruzzaman, M. Optimizing renewable energy management and demand response with ant colony optimization: A pathway to enhanced grid stability and efficiency. In Proceedings of the IEEE Texas Power and Energy Conference (TPEC), College Station, TX, USA, 10–11 February 2025. [CrossRef]
30. Deng, X.; Li, J.; Bao, H.; Zhao, Z.; Su, X.; Huang, Y. Efficient Energy Management for Smart Homes with Electric Vehicles Using Scenario-Based Model Predictive Control. *Sustainability* **2025**, *17*, 7678. [CrossRef]
31. de Oliveira Luna, J.D.F.; Naspolini, A.; dos Reis, G.N.G.; da Costa Mendes, P.R.; Normey-Rico, J.E. A novel joint energy and demand management system for smart houses based on model predictive control, hybrid storage system and quality of experience concepts. *Appl. Energy* **2024**, *369*, 123466. [CrossRef]
32. Fan, J.; Zhou, X. Optimization of a hybrid solar/wind/storage system with bio-generator for a household by emerging metaheuristic optimization algorithm. *J. Energy Storage* **2023**, *73*, 108967. [CrossRef]
33. Gunmi, M.A.; Hu, F.; Abu-Ghunmi, D.; Abu-Ghunmi, L. A smart home energy management system methodology for techno-economic optimal sizing of standalone renewable-storage power systems under uncertainties. *J. Energy Storage* **2024**, *85*, 111072. [CrossRef]
34. Ibrahim, M.M. Energy management strategies of hybrid renewable energy systems: A review. *Wind Eng.* **2024**, *48*, 133–161. [CrossRef]
35. Liu, X.; Wang, J.; Zhang, S.; Guan, X.; Gao, Y. Optimization scheduling of off-grid hybrid renewable energy systems based on dung beetle optimizer with convergence factor and mathematical spiral. *Renew. Energy* **2024**, *237*, 121874. [CrossRef]
36. Nassar, Y.F.; El-Khozondar, H.J.; Fakher, M.A. The role of hybrid renewable energy systems in covering power shortages in public electricity grid: An economic, environmental and technical optimization analysis. *J. Energy Storage* **2025**, *108*, 115224. [CrossRef]
37. Molu, R.J.J.; Naoussi, S.R.D.; Bajaj, M.; Wira, P.; Mbasso, W.F.; Das, B.K.; Tuka, M.B.; Singh, A.R. A techno-economic perspective on efficient hybrid renewable energy solutions in Douala, Cameroon's grid-connected systems. *Sci. Rep.* **2024**, *14*, 13590. [CrossRef]
38. Shaban, A.; Salhen, M.; Shalaby, M.A.; Abdelmaguid, T.F. Optimal household appliances scheduling for smart energy management considering inclining block rate tariff and net-metering system. *Comput. Ind. Eng.* **2024**, *190*, 110073. [CrossRef]
39. Oueslati, H.; Mabrouk, S.B. Techno-economic analysis of an on-grid PV/Wind/Battery hybrid power system used for electrifying building. *Energy Sources Part A Recovery Util. Environ. Eff.* **2023**, *45*, 9880–9893. [CrossRef]
40. Vaka, S.S.K.R.; Matam, S.K. Optimal sizing of hybrid renewable energy systems for reliability enhancement and cost minimization using multiobjective technique in microgrids. *Energy Storage* **2023**, *5*, 419. [CrossRef]
41. Paul, K.; Jyothi, B.; Kumar, R.S.; Singh, A.R.; Bajaj, M.; Hemanth Kumar, B.; Zaitsev, I. Optimizing sustainable energy management in grid connected microgrids using quantum particle swarm optimization for cost and emission reduction. *Sci. Rep.* **2025**, *15*, 5843. [CrossRef] [PubMed]
42. Lim, S.; Lee, J.; Lee, S. Model Predictive control-based energy management system for cooperative optimization of grid-connected microgrids. *Energies* **2025**, *18*, 1696. [CrossRef]
43. Adefarati, T.; Potgieter, S.; Sharma, G.; Bansal, R.C.; Onaolapo, A.K.; Borisade, S.G.; Oloye, A.O. Optimization of Renewable Energy based Hybrid Energy System using Evolutionary Computational Techniques. *Smart Grid Sustain. Energy* **2025**, *10*, 15. [CrossRef]
44. Li, R.; Jin, X.; Yang, P.; Sun, X.; Zhu, G.; Zheng, Y.; Zheng, M.; Wang, L.; Zhu, M.; Qi, Y.; et al. Techno-economic analysis of a wind-photovoltaic-electrolysis-battery hybrid energy system for power and hydrogen generation. *Energy Convers. Manag.* **2023**, *281*, 116854. [CrossRef]
45. Ma, B.; Li, P.H. Optimal flexible power allocation energy management strategy for hybrid energy storage system with genetic algorithm based model predictive control. *Energy* **2025**, *324*, 135958. [CrossRef]
46. Jasim, A.M.; Jasim, B.H.; Flah, A.; Bolshev, V.; Mihet-Popa, L. A new optimized demand management system for smart grid-based residential buildings adopting renewable and storage energies. *Energy Rep.* **2023**, *9*, 4018–4035. [CrossRef]
47. Shafiei, K.; Seifi, A.; Hagh, M.T. A novel multi-objective optimization approach for resilience enhancement considering integrated energy systems with renewable energy, energy storage, energy sharing, and demand-side management. *J. Energy Storage* **2025**, *115*, 115966. [CrossRef]

 https://doi.org/10.3390/en19051174

48. Güven, A.F.; Yörükeren, N.; Tag-Eldin, E.; Samy, M.M. Multi-objective optimization of an islanded green energy system utilizing sophisticated hybrid metaheuristic approach. *IEEE Access* **2023**, *11*, 103044–103068. [CrossRef]
49. Ameur, A.; Berrada, A.; Emrani, A. Intelligent energy management system for smart home with grid-connected hybrid photovoltaic/gravity energy storage system. *J. Energy Storage* **2023**, *72*, 108525. [CrossRef]
50. Adefarati, T.; Sharma, G.; Bokoro, P.N.; Kumar, R. Advancing renewable-dominant power systems through internet of things and artificial intelligence: A comprehensive review. *Energies* **2025**, *18*, 5243. [CrossRef]
51. Ghosh, A.; Goswami, A.K.; Basu, A.; Bose, M.; Basu, T.K. An IoT-based smart building energy management using DSM strategies. In Proceedings of the 3rd International Conference on Power Electronics and IoT Applications in Renewable Energy and Its Control (PARC), Mathura, India, 23–24 February 2024.
52. Bamisile, O.; Cai, D.; Adun, H.; Dagbasi, M.; Ukwuoma, C.C.; Huang, Q.; Johnson, N.; Bamisile, O. Towards renewables development: Review of optimization techniques for energy storage and hybrid renewable energy systems. *Heliyon* **2024**, *10*, 37482. [CrossRef]
53. Agajie, T.F.; Ibrahim, F.S.; Amoussou, I.; Agajie, E.F.; Paddy, E.Y.; Awoke, Y.A.; Nsanyuy, W.B.; Bajaj, M. Comparative techno-economic analysis of grid-connected solar PV-battery and PV-fuel cell systems for educational institutions sustainable academic laboratories. *Discov. Sustain.* **2025**, *6*, 674. [CrossRef]
54. Dada, M.; Popoola, P. Recent advances in solar photovoltaic materials and systems for energy storage applications: A review. *Beni Suef Univ. J. Basic Appl. Sci.* **2023**, *12*, 66. [CrossRef]
55. Wang, Y.; Lee, S.; Li, C.; Umair, M.; Yakhyaeva, I. Techno-economic evaluation of solar photovoltaic power production in China for sustainable development and the environment. *Environ. Dev. Sustain.* **2024**, 1–30. [CrossRef]
56. Bawonda, F.I.; Adefarati, T. Evaluation of solar energy potential in six geopolitical regions of Nigeria using analytical and simulation techniques. *Energy Convers. Manag.* **2023**, *290*, 117193. [CrossRef]
57. Barbosa, N.B.; Nunes, D.D.G.; Santos, A.A.B.; Machado, B.A.S. Technological advances on fault diagnosis in wind turbines: A patent analysis. *Appl. Sci.* **2023**, *13*, 1721. [CrossRef]
58. Tumse, S.; Bilgili, M.; Yildirim, A.; Sahin, B. Comparative analysis of global onshore and offshore wind energy characteristics and potentials. *Sustainability* **2024**, *16*, 6614. [CrossRef]
59. Sahoo, S.; Timmann, P. Energy storage technologies for modern power systems: A detailed analysis of functionalities, potentials, and impacts. *IEEE Access* **2023**, *11*, 49689–49729. [CrossRef]
60. Wang, Y.; He, X.; Liu, Q.; Razmjooy, S. Economic and technical analysis of an HRES (Hybrid Renewable Energy System) comprising wind, PV, and fuel cells using an improved subtraction-average-based optimizer. *Heliyon* **2024**, *10*, e32712, Retraction in *Heliyon* **2026**, *12*, e44550. [CrossRef] [PubMed]
61. Baiden, J.K. The Electricity Tariff and Utility Performance: Evidence from Ghana, Uganda, and Namibia Electricity Market. In *Energy Regulation in Africa: Dynamics, Challenges, and Opportunities*; Springer: Cham, Switzerland, 2024; pp. 235–253. [CrossRef]
62. Liu, J.; Hu, H.; Yu, S.S.; Trinh, H. Electricity pricing and its role in modern smart energy system design: A review. *Designs* **2023**, *7*, 76. [CrossRef]
63. Resource Efficiency and Cleaner Production. Available online: https://www.industrialefficiency.co.za/wp-content/uploads/2020/09/How-to-Read-Your-Electricity-guide-Book-2.pdf (accessed on 10 October 2025).
64. Residential Electricity Tariffs. Available online: https://mes.midstream.co.za/ViewDocumentAsPdf.aspx?dId=db8769c8-da9a-4683-89ae-b0d98f1d45fb&fn=1.+Residential+Tariffs+%281+April+2025+-+31+March+2026%29.pdf&utm_source (accessed on 3 October 2025).
65. Jaglin, S. Urban electric hybridization: Exploring the politics of a just transition in the Western Cape (South Africa). *J. Urban Technol.* **2023**, *30*, 11–33. [CrossRef]
66. Ramachandra, N.; Natarajan, R. State-of-the-art and real-time implementation of an IoT-based home energy management system for a cluster of dwellings. *Heliyon* **2024**, *10*, 35887. [CrossRef]
67. Li, R.; Kirkaldy, N.D.; Oehler, F.F.; Marinescu, M.; Offer, G.J.; O'Kane, S.E. The importance of degradation mode analysis in parameterising lifetime prediction models of lithium-ion battery degradation. *Nat. Commun.* **2025**, *16*, 2776. [CrossRef] [PubMed]
68. Upington Population. Available online: https://worldpopulationreview.com/cities/south-africa/upington (accessed on 21 October 2025).
69. Modern, Growing, Successful Province. Available online: http://www.northern-cape.gov.za/index.php/component/content/article?id=78 (accessed on 21 October 2025).
70. Bifacial Dual Glass Monocrystalline Module. Available online: https://solarbay.com.mx/FC/TRINA_495.pdf (accessed on 3 October 2025).
71. 2KW Wind Turbine Generator Complete Hybrid off and On-Grid System. Available online: https://www.permanent-magnetalternator.com/sale-36571638-2kw-wind-turbine-generator-complete-hybrid-off-and-on-grid-system.html (accessed on 2 October 2025).

https://doi.org/10.3390/en19051174

72. 5 kW Deye Hybrid Inverter. Available online: https://www.solarwaysuppliers.co.za/wp-content/uploads/2014/01/5kW-Deye-Sunsynk-Hybrid-PV-Inverter-Datasheet.pdf (accessed on 3 October 2025).
73. Innovative Battery Solutions. Available online: https://discoverbattery.com/products/tubular-batteries (accessed on 22 October 2025).

 https://doi.org/10.3390/en19051174

MDPI AG
Grosspeteranlage 5
4052 Basel
Switzerland
Tel.: +41 61 683 77 34

Energies Editorial Office
E-mail: energies@mdpi.com
www.mdpi.com/journal/energies

www.ingramcontent.com/pod-product-compliance
Lightning Source LLC
Chambersburg PA
CBHW061809210926
51850CB00006B/657
* 9 7 8 3 7 2 5 8 7 6 3 7 2 *